42nd Edition

the ARMY Officer's Guide

by
Lawrence P. Crocker
Lieutenant Colonel, U.S. Army, Retired

Stackpole Books

The Library of Congress Cataloged the thirty-ninth issue of this work as follows:

The Army officer's guide, 39th–   ed.
    [Harrisburg, Pa.] Stackpole Books [c1977–

    b.&w. ill. 24 cm.

    Continues: The Officer's guide
    Key title: The Army officer's guide, ISSN 0148–6799

    1. United States. Army—Officer's handbooks.
U133.A6O3   355'.00973   77–641374
ISBN 0–8117–2133–7   MARC–S
Library of Congress   77

42nd Edition

Contents

Foreword

The Army Officer's Guide is now in its sixth decade of service to the Army's officers. During all that time, it has been considered a trustworthy first place of reference by more than one million officers. The publisher and the author are confident that this 42nd revised edition continues to merit the trust of the Army's officers, knowing that this edition continues to provide sound advice and guidance to the officers and officers-to-be of today's Army, without sacrificing in any way the usefulness, maturity and professionalism of its predecessor editions.

The Army Officer's Guide is not an official publication of the US Army. However, it is produced by persons who are associated with and dedicated to the Army. Each edition is carefully checked against changes in the regulations and changes in the thinking of those who are responsible for the regulations to assure that the material presented is accurate and as up-to-date as possible. This edition is no exception. It provides the latest available information on matters of importance to all of the Army's officers: pay and allowances, professional development, the effects of the Defense Officer Personnel Management Act (DOPMA) on an Army career, uniforms, promotions and more. The chapters describing the branches of the Army also have been revised for this edition.

The annual revisions to *The Army Officer's Guide* are a continuing year-round effort. In addition to the changes to the regulations, ideas for discussion come from service journals. Readers often submit comments and suggestions regarding the book, which are always welcome. During the last few years, special efforts have been devoted to include matters of interest to the Army's warrant officers and to change the book as necessary so that it applies to female as well as to male officers. As a result, we are confident that this 42nd edition contains information that is of value and interest to all of the Army's officers. Officers of MILPERCEN, FORSCOM, TRADOC, the branch service schools, and the Office of The Surgeon General have provided advice and assistance in the preparation of appropriate portions of this edition. Their help is gratefully acknowledged.

A major objective of the book always has been to provide sound advice to junior officers and those young men and women who are contemplating an Army career. Part One of the book covers such matters as the officer's code, military courtesy, customs of the service, and the social aspects of Army life in an attempt to remove any mystery and any hesitancy to adopt the Army as a way of life. Parts Two and Three provide information on career development, schools, pay, uniform regulations, promotions and other matters of major interest to every officer. Part Four deals with the Army itself—how it is organized and what it does, with a brief description of each of the branches. The Appendix provides advice regarding how to approach some of the myriad of extra duties that confront officers, particularly junior officers. While the emphasis of the book is the junior officer, it also provides a convenient reference for more experienced officers who want to stay abreast of changes in the regulations and other matters that affect them personally, as well as members of their organizations.

The objective of the successive authors and publishers of *The Army Officer's Guide* always has been to assure that each edition was of maximum usefulness to the Army officers of that day. It remains the objective of this 42nd edition. The author and the publisher take pride in presenting this 42nd edition of *The Army Officer's Guide* for the consideration of the Army officer corps.

Preface

Address by General of the Army DOUGLAS MacARTHUR

General Westmoreland, General Groves, distinguished guests, and gentlemen of the Corps.*

As I was leaving the hotel this morning, a doorman asked me, "Where are you bound for, General?" and when I replied, "West Point," he remarked, "Beautiful place, have you ever been there before?"

No human being could fail to be deeply moved by such a tribute as this. [Thayer Award] Coming from a profession I have served so long, and a people I have loved so well, it fills me with an emotion I cannot express. But this award is not intended primarily to honor a personality, but to symbolize a great moral code—the code of conduct and chivalry of those who guard this beloved land of culture and ancient descent. That is the meaning of this medallion. For all eyes and for all time, it is an expression of the ethics of the American soldier. That I should be integrated in this way with so noble an ideal arouses a sense of pride and yet of humility which will be with me always.

Duty—Honor—Country. Those three hallowed words reverently dictate what you ought to be, what you can be, what you will be. They are your rallying points: to build courage when courage seems to fail; to regain faith when there seems to be little cause for faith; to create hope when hope becomes forlorn. Unhappily, I possess neither that eloquence of diction, that poetry of imagination, nor that brilliance of metaphor to tell you all that they mean. The unbelievers will say they are but words, but a slogan, but a flamboyant phrase. Every pedant, every demagogue, every cynic, every hypocrite, every troublemaker, and, I am

---

*To the Members of the Association of Graduates. U.S.M.A., The Corps of Cadets and Distinguished Guests upon his acceptance of THE SYLVANUS THAYER AWARD, United States Military Academy, West Point, New York, 12 May 1962. Published by permission of General MacArthur.

(Photo by U.S. Army)

General of the Army Douglas MacArthur

26 January 1880—5 April 1964

sorry to say, some others of an entirely different character, will try to down-grade them even to the extent of mockery and ridicule. But here are some of the things they do. They build your basic character, they mold you for your future roles as the custodians of the nation's defense, they make you strong enough to know when you are weak, and brave enough to face yourself when you are afraid. They teach you to be proud and unbending in honest failure, but humble and gentle in success; not to substitute words for actions, nor to seek the path of comfort, but to face the stress and spur of difficulty and challenge; to learn to stand up in the storm but to have compassion on those who fall; to master yourself before you seek to master others; to have a heart that is clean, a goal that is high; to learn to laugh yet never forget how to weep; to reach into the future yet never neglect the past; to be serious yet never to take yourself too seriously; to be modest so that you will remember the simplicity of true greatness, the open mind of true wisdom, the meekness of true strength. They give you a temper of the will, a quality of the imagination, a vigor of the emotions, a freshness of the deep springs of life, a temperamental predominance of courage over timidity, an appetite for adventure over love of ease. They create in your heart the sense of wonder, the unfailing hope of what next, and the joy and inspiration of life. They teach you in this way to be an officer and a gentleman.

And what sort of soldiers are those you are to lead? Are they reliable, are they brave, are they capable of victory? Their story is known to all of you; it is the story of the American man-at-arms. My estimate of him was formed on the battlefield many, many years ago, and has never changed. I regarded him then as I regard him now—as one of the world's noblest figures, not only as one of the finest military characters but also as one of the most stainless. His name and fame are the birthright of every American citizen. In his youth and strength, his love and loyalty he gave—all that mortality can give. He needs no eulogy from me or from any other man. He has written his own history and written it in red on his enemy's breast. But when I think of his patience under adversity, of his, courage under fire, and of his modesty in victory, I am filled with an emotion of admiration I cannot put into words. He belongs to history as furnishing one of the greatest examples of successful patriotism; he belongs to posterity as the instructor of future generations in the principles of liberty and freedom; he belongs to the present, to us, by his virtues and by his achievements. In twenty campaigns, on a hundred battlefields, around a thousand campfires, I have witnessed that enduring fortitude, that patriotic self-abnegation, and that invincible determination which have carved his statue in the hearts of his people. From one end of the world to the other he has drained deep the chalice of courage.

As I listened to those songs of the glee club, in memory's eye I could see those staggering columns of the First World War, bending under soggy packs, on many a weary march from dripping dusk to drizzling dawn, slogging ankle-deep through the mire of shell-shocked roads, to form grimly for the attack, blue-lipped, covered with sludge and mud, chilled by the wind and rain; driving home to their objective, and, for many, to the judgment seat of God. I do not know the dignity of their birth but I do know the glory of their death. They died unquestioning, uncomplaining, with faith in their hearts and on their lips the hope that we would go on to victory. Always for them—Duty—Honor—Country; always their blood and sweat and tears as we sought the way and the light and the truth.

And twenty years after, on the other side of the globe, again the filth of murky foxholes, the stench of ghostly trenches, the slime of dripping dugouts; those boiling suns of relentless heat, those torrential rains of devastating storms; the loneliness and utter desolation of jungle trails, the bitterness of long separation from those they loved and cherished, the deadly pestilence of tropical disease, the horror of stricken areas of war; their resolute and determined defense, their swift and sure attack, their indomitable purpose, their complete and decisive victory—always victory. Always through the bloody haze of their last reverberating shot, the vision of gaunt, ghastly men reverently following your password of Duty—Honor—Country.

The code which those words perpetuate embraces the highest moral laws and will stand the test of any ethics or philosophies ever promulgated for the uplift of mankind. Its requirements are for the things that are right, and its restraints are from the things that are wrong. The soldier, above all other men, is required to practice the greatest act of religious training—sacrifice. In battle and in the face of danger and death, he discloses those divine attributes which his Maker gave when He created man in His own image. No physical courage and no brute instinct can take the place of the Divine help which alone can sustain him. However horrible the incidents of war may be, the soldier who is called upon to offer and to give his life for his country, is the noblest development of mankind.

You now face a new world—a world of change. The thrust into outer space of the satellite, spheres, and missiles marked the beginning of another epoch in the long story of mankind—the chapter of the space age. In the five or more billions of years the scientists tell us it has taken to form the earth, in the three or more billion years of development of the human race, there has never been a greater, a more abrupt or staggering evolution. We deal now not with things of this world alone, but with the illimitable distances and as yet unfathomed mysteries of the universe. We are reaching out for a new and boundless frontier. We speak in strange terms: of harnessing the cosmic energy; of making winds and tides work for us; of creating unheard synthetic materials to supplement or even replace our old standard basics; of purifying sea water for our drink; of mining ocean floors for new fields of wealth and food; of disease preventatives to expand life into the hundred of years; of controlling the weather for a more equitable distribution of heat and cold, of rain and shine; of space ships to the moon; of the primary target in war, no longer limited to the armed forces of an enemy, but instead to include his civil populations; of ultimate conflict between a united human race and the sinister forces of some other planetary galaxy; of such dreams and fantasies as to make life the most exciting of all time.

And through all this welter of change and development, your mission remains fixed, determined, inviolable—it is to win our wars. Everything else in your professional career is but corollary to this vital dedication. All other public purposes, all other public projects, all other public needs, great or small, will find others for their accomplishment; but you are the ones who are trained to fight; yours is the profession of arms—the will to win, the sure knowledge that in war there is no substitute for victory; that If you lose, the nation will be destroyed; that the very obsession of your public service must be Duty—Honor—Country. Others will debate the controversial issues, national and international, which divide men's minds; but serene, calm, aloof, you stand as the nation's war-guardian, as its lifeguard from the raging tides of international conflict, as its gladiator in the arena of battle. For a century and a half you have defended, guarded, and protected its hallowed traditions of liberty and freedom, of right and justice. Let civilian voices argue the merits or demerits of our processes of government; whether our strength is being sapped by deficit financing, indulged in too long, by federal paternalism grown too mighty, by power groups grown too arrogant, by politics grown too corrupt, by crime grown too rampant, by morals grown too low, by taxes grown too high, by extremists grown too violent; whether our personal liberties are as thorough and complete as they should be. These great national problems are not for your professional participation or military solution. Your guidepost stands out like a ten-fold beacon in the night: Duty—Honor—Country.

You are the leaven which binds together the entire fabric of our national system of defense. From your ranks come the great captains who hold the nation's destiny in their hands the moment the war tocsin sounds. The Long Gray Line has never failed us. Were you to do so, a million ghosts in olive drab, in brown khaki, in blue and gray, would rise from their white crosses thundering those magic words, Duty—Honor—Country.

This does not mean that you are war mongers. On the contrary, the soldier, above all other people, prays for peace, for he must suffer and bear the deepest wounds and scars of war. But always in our ears ring the ominous words of Plato, that wisest of all philosophers, "Only the dead have seen the end of war."

The shadows are lengthening for me. The twilight is here. My days of old have vanished tone and tint; they have gone glimmering through the dreams of things that were. Their memory is one of wondrous beauty, watered by tears, and coaxed and caressed by the smiles of yesterday. I listen vainly for the witching melody of faint bugles blowing reveille, of far drums beating the long roll. In my dreams I hear again the crash of guns, the rattle of musketry, the strange, mournful mutter of the battlefield.

But in the evening of my memory, always I come back to West Point. Always there echoes and re-echoes Duty—Honor—Country.

Today marks my final roll call with you, but I want you to know that when I cross the river my last conscious thoughts will be of The Corps, and The Corps, and The Corps.

I bid you farewell.

1
The Code of the Army Officer

The code of the Army officer is the beacon which guides his or her course of action. Each officer applies this code as a first essential step in the performance of official responsibilities. Officers follow its principles in their relations with other people, military or civilian, on duty or off duty. It is a part of the development of officers throughout their careers, and is one of the standards by which they are compared or evaluated. It establishes the Army way of life which most officers find rewarding.

SIGNIFICANCE OF THE CODE

Is this code important? Other honored professions have their own codes and precepts. Honorable people in humble or high station in life, or around the world among members of the great religions, follow their own respected standards of ethics. While these are personal standards, for the most part, they nevertheless contribute to the security of a nation or even to the course of history. The extreme importance of the code of the Army officer stems from its significance to the United States. These responsibilities, shared equally with officers of the Navy, the Marine Corps, and the Air Force, involve the security of our nation, the protection of our people, plus the support of our nation's policies in its chosen courses of action in its relations with other countries. These missions, which the officer and all members of the armed forces are obligated to accept, may lead him or her to the distant places of the world and, if combat is encountered, may involve the life or death of subordinates as well as the success or the failure of the nation's mission. The duty may include placing the officer's own life on the line, for in combat all share the certain hazards.

1

These are reasons our armed forces are maintained, and why the code of the Army officer has such vast significance.

When and if our nation's civil leaders decide that war has been forced upon us, as at Pearl Harbor, or decide that the nation's obligations lead into combat short of declaration of war, as in Vietnam, it is the officer who provides the military leadership to restore the peace. In our republic—our democracy, if you prefer—the confidence of all of our people in the integrity and the professional capabilities of members of the corps of commissioned officers is a matter of supreme importance. Weigh this truth carefully. Without high confidence in the nation's military leaders, our citizens would be reluctant to serve in the armed forces, or to entrust their sons, their daughters or other citizens to the military service of their own country. Further, if this confidence were to become lacking, the President, his advisors, and members of Congress would be hesitant to adopt courses of action which might generate the need for force, no matter how essential such action might be to the nation's basic interests. These are reasons which make the code of the Army officer of such extreme importance to all of our citizens during this century of ferment and conflict.

What is the origin of this code of such national importance? Historically, there can be no truer foundation for the code of the Army officer than the example set by General Washington, with his own high standard of personal honor, of discipline, of personal sacrifice, of leadership, of complete devotion to his mission. Other great men in our history, whose names are household words of respect and trust, have embraced this code while adding to its strength. Men like General Washington, Generals Grant and Lee, General of the Armies Pershing, Generals of the Army Marshall, Eisenhower, MacArthur, Bradley, with their more recent counterparts—Generals Wheeler, Westmoreland, Abrams. There has been an infinite number of persons in junior as well as senior position, noncommissioned officers and soldiers as well as officers, who have helped to build and to sustain the code. Include always those legions who have won the Medal of Honor, the Distinguished Service Cross, and other awards of valor, the Distinguished Service Medal, the Legion of Merit, and other awards of achievement. Our code was developed and followed throughout our Army's history, and is supported by members of our great Army of today in the proudest tradition of our military service.

Members of the United States Corps of Cadets at West Point, past and present, are imbued with Duty, Honor, Country throughout their education and their training to become offficers. They carry these priceless symbols into their years of service throughout the Army. Proud histories of Regular and National Guard units prove their own essential contributions. Although formed in our century, members of the Army Reserve have enriched our history in World War I, World War II, the Korea War, and more recently with our Army in Vietnam. The building of the code, and the support of the code, is service wide, and has endured as long as our history.

Official documents enforce and solidify the code. Hence, it is part traditional and unwritten, part official and written.

The Officer's Commission or Warrant. The officer's commission or warrant is an excellent place to start consideration of the written code of the Army officer.

Think deeply about the phrasing of these documents. These are not mere ceremonial words. They mean exactly what they say, and never doubt nor question it.

The Oath of Office. Like the officer's commission or warrant, the officer's oath of office means precisely what it says.

THE
PRESIDENT
OF
THE UNITED STATES OF AMERICA

To all who shall see these presents, greeting:

Know Ye, that reposing special trust and confidence in the patriotism, valor, fidelity and abilities of JOHN FRANCIS DOE *, I do confirm this appointment as* SECOND LIEUTENANT, REGULAR ARMY *in the*

Army of the United States

to RANK *as such from the* THIRTIETH *day of* MAY *, nineteen hundred and* SEVENTY-SIX *. This Officer will therefore carefully and diligently discharge the duties of the office to which appointed by doing and performing all manner of things thereunto belonging.*

And I do strictly charge and require those Officers and other personnel of lesser rank to render such obedience as is due an officer of this grade and position. And this Officer is to observe and follow such orders and directions, from time to time, as may be given by me, or the future President of the United States of America, or other Superior Officers acting in accordance with the laws of the United States of America.

This commission is to continue in force during the pleasure of the President of the United States of America, for the time being, under the provisions of those Public Laws relating to Officers of the **Armed Forces of the United States of America** *and the component thereof in which this appointment is made.*

Done at the City of Washington, this THIRTY-FIRST *day of* JULY *in the year of our Lord one thousand nine hundred and* SEVENTY-SIX.

By the President:

Paul T. Smith
Major General
The Adjutant General

Martin R. Hoffman
Secretary of the Army

THE OFFICER'S COMMISSION

THE
ARMY
OF
THE UNITED STATES OF AMERICA

To all who shall see these presents, greeting:
Know Ye, that reposing special trust and confidence in the patriotism, valor, fidelity and abilities of _____,

the Secretary of the Army has appointed _____ a

in the Army of the United States

to rank as such from the _____ day of _____
nineteen hundred and _____. This Warrant Officer will therefore
carefully and diligently discharge the duties of the office to which appointed
by doing and performing all manner of things thereunto belonging. And all
subordinate personnel of lesser rank are strictly charged and required to
render such obedience as is due a Warrant Officer of this grade and position.
And this Warrant Officer is to observe and follow such orders and directions,
from time to time, as may be given by Superior Officers and Warrant Officers
acting in accordance with the laws of the United States of America.
Done at the City of Washington, this _____ day of _____
in the year of our Lord one thousand and nine hundred and _____, and of the
Independence of the United States of America the one hundred and _____.

Paul E Smith
Major General
The Adjutant General

WARRANT OFFICER WARRANT.

OATH OF OFFICE - MILITARY PERSONNEL

For use of this form, see AR 135-100, the proponent agency is the U.S. Army Reserve Components Personnel and Administration Center.

INDICATE THE APPOINTMENT FOR WHICH OATH IS BEING EXECUTED BY PLACING AN "X" IN APPROPRIATE BOX. REGULAR ARMY COMMISSIONED OFFICERS WILL ALSO SPECIFY THE BRANCH OF APPOINTMENT WHEN APPOINTED IN A SPECIAL BRANCH.

(See Instructions Below)

COMMISSIONED OFFICERS	WARRANT OFFICERS
X REGULAR ARMY _____AGC_____ *(Branch, when so appointed)*	☐ REGULAR ARMY
☐ ARMY OF THE UNITED STATES, WITHOUT COMPONENT	☐ ARMY OF THE UNITED STATES, WITHOUT COMPONENT
☐ RESERVE COMMISSIONED OFFICER	☐ RESERVE WARRANT OFFICER

I, ___JOHN FRANCIS DOE___   ___XXX-XX-XXXX___
(First Name - Middle Name - Last name)   *(Social Security Account Number)*
having been appointed an officer in the Army of the United States, as indicated above in the grade of ___2LT___

do solemnly swear *(or affirm)* that I will support and defend the Constitution of the United States against all enemies, foreign and domestic, that I will bear true faith and allegiance to the same; that I take this obligation freely, without any mental reservation or purpose of evasion; and that I will well and faithfully discharge the duties of the office upon which I am about to enter;

SO HELP ME GOD.

/s/ John Francis Doe
(Signature - full name as shown above)

SWORN TO AND SUBSCRIBED BEFORE ME AT Military District of Washington, USA, Washington, D. C.

THIS___31st___ DAY OF ___July___ , 19 76

___CPT, RA___   /s/ Thomas Roe
(Grade, component, or office of official administering oath)   *(Signature)*

INSTRUCTIONS

This form will be executed upon acceptance of appointment as an officer in the Army of the United States as indicated at top of form. Immediately upon receipt of notice of appointment, the appointee will, in case of acceptance of the appointment, return to the agency from which received, the oath of office *(on this form)* properly filled in, subscribed and attested. In case of non-acceptance, the notice of appointment will be returned to the agency from which received, *(by letter)* indicating the fact of non-acceptance.

FOR THE EXECUTION OF THE OATH OF OFFICE

1. Whenever any person is elected or appointed to an office of honor or trust under the Government of the United States, he is required before entering upon the duties of his office, to take and subscribe the oath prescribed by Section 1757, Revised Statutes, *(5 U.S.C. 16, M.L. 1949, Section 118).*

2. 10 U.S.C. 3394 eliminates the necessity of executing oath on promotion of officers.

3. The oath of office may be taken before any commissioned officer of any component of any Armed Force, whether or not on active duty *(10 U.S.C. 1031)*, or before any warrant officer serving on active duty as an adjutant, assistant adjutant, acting adjutant, or personnel adjutant in any of the Armed Forces *(See UCMJ, Article 136; 10 U.S.C. 936)*. A warrant officer administering the oath of office will show his title in the block to the left of his signature.

4. Oath of office may also be taken before any civil officer who is authorized by the laws of the United States or by the local municipal law to administer oaths, and if so administered by a civil official, the oath must bear the official seal of the person administering the oath, or if a seal is not used by the official, the official's capacity to administer oaths must be certified to under seal by a clerk of court or other proper local official.

DA FORM 71 1 AUG 59   PREVIOUS EDITIONS OF THIS FORM ARE OBSOLETE.   #U.S. GPO: 1973—540-840/8245

THE OATH OF OFFICE.

Similar forms for the commission and the oath of office are used for officers of the National Guard of the United States, the Army Reserve, or the Army of the United States. Regardless of component, officers bear the same obligation and responsibility.

The Uniform Code of Military Justice; Ethical Codes; Code of Conduct.

Specific codes establish standards and impose requirements on military personnel.

The Uniform Code of Military Justice imposes many restrictions upon members of the armed forces, far beyond those which pertain to the ordinary citizen. There are also published official Codes of Ethical Conduct, with procedures to enforce them. The Code of Conduct establishes standards for military personnel in combat and for prisoners held by an enemy.

These various codes are part of the background of the origin of the code of the Army officer, with reasons for its importance to the nation. The Army does not stand alone because the Navy, the Marines, the Air Force likewise have codes of similar strength and meaning. Collectively, they establish an ideal of national service, a way of life, essential for the nation's perpetual security as the final rampart of defense of our people and our Constitution.

Faith. The military code is a standard of action with much depth. It is a firm belief that the preservation of our nation is decidedly worthwhile. It is unswerving confidence in the loyalty of our people and their sons and daughters who wear their country's uniform. It is a solid conviction that the courses followed by our government are sound and just to all people everywhere. It is faith.

We shall adopt as expressing the code a statement made by Abraham Lincoln in his Cooper Union Address, 27 February 1860. *"Let us have faith that right makes might; and in that faith let us to the end, dare to do our duty as we understand it."*

FOUNDATION OF THE CODE

It is an honor to serve in the armed forces of the United States. It is a duty of our citizens to serve in the armed forces, as volunteers or in accordance with our nation's laws, and to perform the military missions which this service may require. If the day should come when a large portion of our citizens regard this service as less than an honor, and less than an obligation of citizenship, our proud nation has begun the descent to lie beside other peoples who were unable or unwilling to fight for their principles or for the retention of their freedoms.

The very foundation of the officers' code, the basic principle, is that all members of the Army accept and do their best to act upon, all orders and missions directed to them by the President, within his authority under the constitution. In practice, this means accepting also all orders and missions assigned by others lawfully appointed to positions of authority over the Army members. Our national leaders, and our thoughtful citizens, all take for granted —as they have a right to do—that each officer and each soldier will do his or her full part in the national mission assigned, accepting with courage the sacrifices and the hazards this service to our Nation involves.

In recent years, strident voices of a vocal minority of our citizens have expressed very strong opposition to national policies. The verbal barrages have been aimed specifically at the military forces and the so-called military-industrial complex. This vocal opposition reached a crescendo during the early 1970's and led to our withdrawal from Vietnam and abandonment of the people of that country. The active protestors have included, among others, elected officials of our government, a surprising number of educators and students, members of the clergy, plus the rather open advocacy of opposition to the national policies by some columnists, news broadcasters, and other citizens. Their motives must remain concealed in their own minds, whether idealistic, pacifistic, based upon their analysis of facts or opinions which they accept, or subversive. This is not a new phenomenon in our Nation, although it may have attained a broader base than during any period since the Civil War. It is a matter to be dealt with by the Nation's civil leadership.

There is an anomaly here which is rarely acknowledged; it deserves attention. As a citizen, the officer or soldier has the same right to weigh the factors leading to a decision and important action by the President, as any individual who has spoken or acted violently in opposition. Indeed, the Service member may conclude that a policy established by the President is entirely wrong. Now we reach a point of singular importance within the officer's code, and in such sharp contrast to the open opposition of some public officials and citizens as to justify thought and emphasis: *All officers of the armed forces, and all soldiers too, are bound by their Oath to do their utmost to achieve the prompt and successful completion of the mission assigned, even at the risk of their lives when necessity requires, and without regard to their personal views as to the correctness of the national policy or the wisdom of the orders under which they act.** The elected civil leaders of our nation decide these matters of high policy in international relations which may restore the peace, or result in war, or in combat short of formal declaration of war. *Once national policy has been decided by the constitutional civil leaders of our national government, the officer and the soldier must support it as their orders require. And this support must be with all their skill and all their determination, never divulging that they have doubts or that they have ever had doubts as to its wisdom.* Further, this obligation is identical for all members of the military services, without regard to their source of appointment, such as Regular or Reserve component, volunteer, or draftee.

This is the keystone of the code of the Army officer. He or she is an officer of the Executive Branch of our national government. The officer's appointment depends upon taking the Oath of Office. His or her retention anticipates and requires continual compliance with that oath. In the final analysis, the officer's readiness and willingness to lead United States troops in campaign or battle, or other mission, anywhere in the world the President may direct, against any kind of threat or enemy, foreign or domestic, is the true measure of the worth of the officer to our government which entrusted him or her with its commission. The essentiality of the principle cannot be refuted. In these days, with our military forces deployed around the world and with our national policies and our armed forces under attack at home, the principle needs understanding. It is an important element in the preservation of our government and the security of our people. For all the years which lie ahead, the Army and its sister services will continue to accept and to carry out this basic principle of the officer's code. *"My country. May it always be right, but my country right or wrong."*— Stephen Decatur.

Candor Required in the Military Leader's Recommendations. It is a normal experience of Army officers of all grades and degrees of experience to be asked by their commanders, or chiefs, for their opinion or recommendation. Such missions are the daily experience of staff officers for it is always the commander who makes the decision.

The duty reaches its zenith in the recommendations made by the Chief of Staff and senior members of the Army Staff, and the commanders of Joint and Specified Commands, in their relations with the Secretary of the Army, the

---

**Still, experienced military leaders know that officers and soldiers fight more courageously and sacrifice more willingly when they hold a deep conviction as to the worthwhileness and the justice of the cause for which they fight.*

Secretary of Defense, the President, as well as the Committees of the Congress as they consider legislation governing the armed forces. How far should they go in advancing their considered views? What is their duty if their views should be challenged? What is their duty if decision goes contrary to their convictions and their recommendations?

Here is a guide. In his first meeting with the Army Staff, General Matthew B. Ridgway, former Chief of Staff of the Army, had this to say about this vital subject:

"The point I wish to make here, and to repeat it for emphasis, is that the professional military man has three primary responsibilities:

"*First,* to give his honest, fearless, objective, professional military opinion of what he needs to do the job the Nation gives him.

"*Second,* if what he is given is less than the minimum he regards as essential, to give his superiors an honest, fearless, objective opinion of the consequences.

"*Third,* and finally, he has the duty whatever the final decision, to do the utmost with whatever is furnished."

It has never been said better.

WAR AND PEACE

It is essential that the officer understand a clear code as between statesman and soldier, regarding war and peace.

The instigator of war chooses military force as a means of achieving national objectives. The victim of the onslaught seeks by armed resistance to prevent its own destruction. Once war has started each nation seeks by use of force to impose its will upon the other. "Self-Defense is Nature's oldest law."—John Dryden. In our government, decision to resort to war is made by the President and the Congress.

Prior to war, the work of the statesman is to formulate foreign policy, subject to approval of the chief of state. The statesman's task includes all manner of problems intended to maintain friendly international relations. He or she strives to solve international problems while they are small, realizing that many of our world's biggest problems might have been solved at the time of their initial and perhaps small beginning. "Speak softly but carry a Big Stick," was the wise policy pronounced by the first Roosevelt. That is to say, a firm policy must be backed up by military capability or it is mere bluff—transparent bluff at that. History contains many examples of the failure of statesmen to resolve differences, and of minor problems which ballooned into big ones. In some of these instances, "settlement" became the difficult and costly task of the military. Clearly in this era of civilization the soldier and statesman must work together. The soldier must give professionally sound, accurate, fearless, objective information exactly as he or she sees it. Upon that solid foundation, when military capability is a consideration, the statesman may then proceed within his or her own sphere of responsibility to formulate sound policy.

A change has occurred in the traditional concept of the keeping of peace and the waging of war. It needs the spotlight. In this era, the soldier fights alongside the statesman to maintain the peace. Recall the swift gathering of forces to confront the placing of Russian missiles on Cuban bases; or a few years earlier the dramatic occupation of Lebanon to save that small nation; or, in 1948, the Berlin airlift. Consider our situation in Asia during the 1960's and early 1970's. The truth is here for all to see, who look, and think! Recurring events have placed the American soldier and the American officer at the side of the statesman to keep the peace and stem the attempted surges of aggressor nations. Now we must work and fight, and some must die, without formal declaration of war; and a case can be made that these deaths may occur without the understanding and national acclaim that our citizens extend to the soldier dead in a conventional war. This is the world we live in today.

Increased communications capability in the Space Age including those provided by satellites have altered the concepts of command and control. The President and other national command authorities, like the civilian Secretary of Defense, may control the level of warfare by selective release of authority to military commanders. Such control of escalation on a day-by-day basis allows for political negotiations between military actions. When negotiations fail, the military are required to act. But such actions must be consistent with the authority released by our political leaders. Civilian dominance of security policy and decisions is a principle of our Constitution and a doctrine of our republican government.

> *"The single most important factor in developing the strength required to meet aggression is the attitude and will of our citizens. While the intensity of world tension may ebb and flow, we must be prepared—from a position of strength and sincerity—for a long campaign to achieve our quest of a lasting peace. We must have the will to win—to overcome the doubts, the fears and, on the part of many, the complacency, and a lack of willingness to sacrifice. We must understand that we are not entitled to easy, automatic, and perpetual freedom."*
>
> General G. H. Decker, Chief of Staff, 1960–1962

INTEGRITY, THE ESSENTIAL INGREDIENT

The essential attribute of the Army and its members is integrity. It is the personal honor of the individual; it is the selfless devotion to duty which produces performance integrity in the discharge of individual missions; and it is the integrity of the Army as a whole in providing its share of the security of the nation in war or in peace.

The Army officer has a public vocation as an official of the government. Members of the officer's unit are sworn to obey his or her lawful orders and, in so doing, perform their own public duty. In time of war, the decisions the officer makes, and the orders he or she issues, may be matters of victory or defeat, life or death. The people of our country place their trust in Army officers, and officers of the sister services, so they may sleep peacefully at night, and so they may pursue their chosen vocations with minimum attention to military matters. The United States could not entrust its security to officers about whose integrity there is the slightest doubt.

There is a reward which accrues to the corps of officers, and to the individual officer, because of the wide acceptance of their integrity. Officers hold the trust of most government officials. Their statements of fact are accepted, and their opinions are respected as sincere. Communities extend to officers many privileges unavailable to the general public because of the high standing of officers and their spouses. There is the important fact of acceptance by honorable members of other vocations, *because he or she is an officer and presumed honorable.* It endures until the officer proves to be unworthy. These valued customs are a priceless heritage bequeathed to officers of today by their brother officers of the past. It is the reward of sustained integrity. Officers of the present era must preserve the code for officers of the future, if the nation is to remain secure in their charge. Integrity generates trust.

THE BASIC CODE

The basic standard of individual and group performance of military responsibilities is expressed by the code of the United States Corps of Cadets which is Duty, Honor, Country. This concept, which underlies all that is done in the field of character building of cadets at West Point, is equally the standard of the Army officer. This is the platform on which personal conduct and performance of duty is based.

Duty. In the Army, the performance of duty to the best of one's ability is a first requirement. Missions must be accomplished up to standard and on time. Always to be remembered in thinking of duty in the Army: It includes willingness to fight, to enter areas of great personal danger, to accept the hazards of battle death. There is little tolerance of slipshod work or half-way measures. Perform each duty as if your whole reputation depended upon its successful completion.

Most orders are of the mission type which state the job to be done but leave to the officer the selection of method. As an officer you will be expected to select methods which will accomplish the desired results, at the time required, with due regard for costs.

See work that needs doing and without transgressing into the responsibilities of others, do it. Within your own sphere of responsibility do not wait to be told.

Stand on your own feet. Your seniors are interested in your past only in so far as it may indicate future capacity. They want to know how well you perform your duty today, so that they may estimate what you will do tomorrow. The reputation which counts most is the one you earn today.

A philosophy of Abraham Lincoln, stated during the lowest ebb of his administration, has direct bearing upon the performance of duty, as he saw it when the going was toughest: *"If I tried to read, much less answer all the criticisms made of me and all the attacks leveled against me, this office would have to be closed for all other business—I do the best I know how, the very best I can—I mean to keep on doing this, down to the very end."*

Honor. Honor is the hallmark of officerlike conduct. It is the outgrowth of character. It means a person who has the knowledge to determine right from wrong, and the courage to adhere unswervingly to the right. It means that an officer's written or spoken word may be accepted without question. Facts will be identified as facts, and opinions for what they are. Actions will be made on considerations of the good of the unit, the Army, the Nation. They are all included in personal integrity.

The meaning of honor, in the sense used herein, includes the narrower term "ethics." As a part of honor in service of country, the officer is expected to lead the decent life. An officer does not lie, cheat, steal, or violate moral codes. An officer must never stoop to the petty chicaneries of wrongful acts "not specifically illegal," nor shady acts of any sort not mentioned specifically in departmental regulations. That is, he or she does not chisel. The officer is expected to rise and live above the frailties of other people in less exacting professions.

Do all officers follow this exacting code at all times, under all conditions? Of course not. Utopia has not arrived. But it can be said without chance of successful contradiction that the great bulk of officers do so as a matter of course. Those who do not live by its standards earn first the scorn of their associates, and if the offenses are more than trivial, they stand a fine chance of trial for conduct unbecoming an officer and gentleman or lady.

The code requires all officers to live and conduct all their activities so that they may look all persons squarely in the eye knowing that they are honorable individuals associating themselves with other honorable individuals.

Country. The profession of arms in which the officer is appointed a leader is a public, not a private, vocation. The American people maintain military forces for the preservation of their security and the sovereignty of the United States. They have the right to expect the highest standards of personal and official conduct from their officers. The responsibilities of the officer embrace all the people, and his or her oath of office, shown earlier in this chapter, prescribes the protection of the Constitution.

The Army officer holds a commission or warrant by choice. Each officer is a volunteer. He or she accepted a commission or warrant, and with it all its hazards and responsibilities as well as its rights and privileges. Each officer is a patriotic citizen who places country above self. Patriotism has this definition: "The willingness to sacrifice and endure discipline for the welfare of the community." From the occasionally maligned Thomas Paine: *"Those who expect to reap the blessings of freedom, must, like men, undergo the fatigue of supporting it."*

The Army officer and others who serve the United States willingly are patriots. Any citizen of our country may be a patriot. Here is a simple definition worthy of thought: *A patriot is one who exerts himself to promote the well-being of his country; one who maintains his country's freedom and rights.* Note in the definition the word "exerts." A patriot is one who does something, or stands ready to do something, for his or her country's freedom or rights. The test of patriotism lies in the basic beliefs of each individual. Our nation will thrive and remain secure as long as the number of patriots are in the vast majority, and while that patriotism remains as an honored and honorable state.

An occasional citizen, even persons of passing importance, scoff at the patriot as a short-sighted person of a passing era. Theirs is the philosophy of Samuel Johnson, 1709–1784, who originated the statement, "Patriotism is the last refuge of a scoundrel." Even then, even now, there are individuals who belittle the patriot and acclaim the greater importance of their own selfish goals or preferences, above those of our nation and its government. Patriotism is part of the code of the Army, its sister services, and their members who serve as volunteers or serve willingly, exerting themselves in the interests of the security of the nation.

It is not always true that the general public appreciates the value of its patriots in military service. When the threat of war recedes, there are real tests of fortitude by those who wear the uniform. Such reactions are not limited to our own country and are as old as armies. One of Marlborough's veterans, writing two and a half centuries ago, saw the same phenomenon and had this to say about it:

> *"God and the soldier, we adore*
> *In time of danger, not before;*
> *The danger passed and all things righted,*
> *God is forgotten, and the soldier slighted."*

The Standard Identical for All. The degree in which observance of the code is expected is the same for all officers, without regard to grade, or branch, or sex, or component, or length of service. Perhaps the meaning may be illustrated by comparison with the observance of the rules of a game, such as golf; the player whose score is rarely below 100 should be as careful to avoid improving the lie of the ball in the rough as the champion.

Now let us temper this principle with reason. Officers of short service require instruction in what is right and what is wrong as to many military requirements, just as they must be instructed in military techniques. Some deviations will be regarded as a subject for instruction or mild rebuke. For example, it is a custom that an officer provide first for the needs of his or her soldiers, before devoting time to personal needs; the officer who fails to do so may expect to be reminded of his or her duties. On the other hand, an offense involving character or honor, or deliberate fraud, will be regarded equally serious if committed by a newly appointed junior as the oldest and most experienced senior.

It is true that in matters of honor the standard is the same for all. But never to be forgotten is another great truth: The impetus for honor and honorable actions must come from the top. The officer and the senior officer must set the example.

THE MILITARY TRADITIONS

There are traditions of military service which have guided its members throughout all the years of our national existence.

Tradition of Public Service. As an Army officer, you are a public servant. You go where you are ordered and perform the tasks which your duty requires. In peace you prepare yourself and your subordinates for the requirements of war. During war you lead American troops in battle against the nation's enemies. But it is not the officer nor the Army who decides when a state of war exists; that responsibility is borne by The Congress and The President. But the peace having been forfeited, it is the duty of the officer to assist in restoring the state of peace. It may cost the officer's life and sometimes this occurs at an age at which members of other professions have retired to the garden and the front porch. The military life is devoted to the public service, and the officer is a public servant.

Tradition of Achieving the Mission. Accomplishment of mission is recognized as the primary requirement of the military leader and indeed of all members of the service. The "Army way" of undertaking a mission is to display enthusiasm, boldness, aggressiveness in getting any job done.

This means big things must be done, if properly ordered or required by the mission assigned. In battle, the attack objectives must be taken, and the defense objectives held. Training programs must be carried out effectively so that all are prepared for their tasks. Administrative and logistical responsibilities must be completed at the required high standards.

It means doing the little things correctly, too, as a matter of normal routine. The officer or soldier must be at the station directed at the time required and must wear the prescribed uniform with pride in the proper manner. It means following a directed course of action, and extending cooperation to adjoining units as may be required by the situation.

Whether the task is tremendous in its scope and importance, or a routine requirement, the military person is expected as a matter of course to undertake it as required and complete it up to standard, and on time. In these tasks he or she must accept the hazards of the vocation, and the frequent hardships of service. This is the important military tradition that the mission must be accomplished.

Tradition of Leadership. The officer is trained to lead. From your earliest days as an officer the tradition will be ground into you. You will become accustomed to receive and execute missions. This will require you to plan work, assign missions to others, and then to see that their work is done skillfully and in cooperation with others. As you grow older your training and experience will broaden and increase your capacities; this is generally accompanied by greater responsibilities. Thus the tradition of leadership deepens. Just as you are trained to lead others, you will be trained to be led by others. For no military person can rise so high, or attain so great a position, that he or she is not responsible to another. Military leadership requires ability to develop teamwork and at the same time to be a part of the team.

Tradition of Loyalty. Loyalty is demanded of the Army officer. It extends throughout the chain of command to the President, the Commander-in-Chief. It extends to your subordinates to include the newest private. And it extends to your peers. It must be a true loyalty and there is an essential reason for it. Members of the corps of officers have the common mission of protecting the nation and our people, which requires the coordinated best efforts of each individual. Even the suspicion of disloyalty would destroy the usefulness of any officer for no one would trust him or her or give the officer responsibility. It must include the chief whom you may dislike; your peers with whom in a sense you are in competition; and each of your subordinates. Think about it deeply. Once trust is forfeited it may never be regained. The loyalty of officers to the nation, to the Commander-in-Chief, to their seniors, their juniors, their peers, has been traditional in the Army since its very beginning.

The Tradition that an Officer's Word is His or Her Bond. An officer's statement of fact, opinion, or recommendation must conform fully with his or her belief. You must take adequate care that when you make a statement as to facts that you can provide the evidence to support it. If you render an opinion or make a recommendation, you must have given sufficient thought to the subject to enable you to reach a reasoned conclusion. All this must be true whether the statements are oral, in writing, or your initials extending a concurrence, or identifying initials on fact sheets, or retained copies of reports and correspondence. The added statement, "I certify" must not be interpreted as meaning "something extra" as to truth. Your word is your bond.

Tradition of Discipline. In order to develop discipline within its organization, the leader must set the example of discipline. Since the unit you command is only a part of a larger organization, or of the Army, you must execute objectives or missions which reach you as orders from your own superior officers. The United States Army is a disciplined army. And no army which is undisciplined is worth a nickel of the taxpayer's dollar. An undisciplined army would be worse than useless for it would constitute a public menace in itself. The tradition of discipline is as deeply ingrained into the mind and heart of the successful officer as the tradition of leadership.

Tradition of Readiness. One of the most striking qualities required of the Army officer is that he or she be in a position of readiness to meet whatever tasks arise, including sudden leadership in campaign and combat. In the broad sense this means that in the event of surprise action by a new enemy that the officer take troops into the field to fight effectively. There are countless other such examples in warfare. Unless the nation can rely upon its military leaders to shift their thoughts and actions from a state of peace to the immediate requirements of war our people are being deceived.

The principle applies with equal force to the routines of duty and the smaller things. You must be ready for an unexpected change of station, or duty assignment. You must be prepared to accept and execute effectively new requirements of your mission. The tradition of readiness includes flexibility of mind and mental processes; a willingness to reach out for new ideas; an ever-broadening capacity to undertake and do new things.

Your leadership capability and command efficiency are measured by your unit's readiness. Such readiness includes personnel, equipment and unit training to which must be added morale and discipline which are evidenced when the real test—combat—comes.

Tradition of Taking Good Care of Soldiers. A former Chief of Staff, General Maxwell Taylor, said, "Second only to accomplishing his mission, the officer's duty is to improve the moral, physical, and intellectual quality of his men . . . The Army is the service which, by the nature of its requirements, attaches the greatest importance to human values. It recognizes man as the basic element of military strength . . . It creates for them an environment of decent, clean living, intolerant of vice, dissipation, or flabbiness."

The officer who has the best record for accomplishment of battle missions with lowest sick and casualty rates is likely to be one who has cared best for his or her soldiers.

This means that members of a command must receive thorough training for their duties; have in their possession the individual and organization equipment and supplies according to their authorization and needs; receive as good quartering and mess facilities as is possible under the circumstances, and except under rigorous field conditions this standard should be no less than healthful and comfortable. They must have available splendid medical support under all conditions of service, including battle, and in any area wherever troops are dispatched in the world. It means many other things such as religious guidance and activities, athletic and recreation programs, advice and help on personal problems including legal counsel. It includes a sound discipline, with proper use of awards and punishment. It involves fairness and justice in all things including spreading the work load and hazards among all eligible individuals; complete absence of favoritism; promotions to be made on merit. All these things and more.

Tradition of Cooperation. Cooperation is the art of working with others to attain a common goal. This is a daily expectancy of service duties and it is traditional that cooperation be willing and wholehearted.

Neither a commander nor a staff officer, no matter how senior, can "go it alone." An officer must cooperate with others, and others must cooperate with him or her. In any staff or any command the problems for solution are very likely to involve two or more staff agencies, or a reconciliation of views between the unit commanders who execute a plan and those who plan it. It takes coordination and cooperation to accomplish a mission. The officer who neglects to cooperate with others invites failure.

Tradition of Being a Lady or Gentleman. It is a part of the code and traditional that officers are expected to be ladies or gentlemen. This must be manifest in their moral standards, their conduct, appearance, manners and mannerisms as well as the professional standards they establish in the performance of duty.

It must be displayed in the things they avoid doing. They avoid vulgarity. They do not drink to excess. They do not avoid the payment of just bills or tender bad checks.

The general good of the officer corps demands that all individuals display the qualities of ladies or gentlemen. Great prestige attaches to officers because as a group they have been generally accepted as such. They are accepted to membership in civilian clubs and associations often because of their commission. Their credit rating is high. Their word is accepted in and out of service. Their opinions bear weight. As a group they have the confidence and trust of the people. The officers themselves must guard and cherish this standing, and they must realize that the unfit among them reflect upon and damage the standing of all.

Tradition of Avoiding Matters of Politics. It is traditional that the Army member avoids partisan politics. This is particularly important for the Regular officer. The career officer serves in support of national policies without regard to the political party in power, and with equal zeal in their effective performance. The oath of office requires each officer to serve the elected leaders of the nation, without regard to their political party, and without regard to the officer's own political beliefs or affiliations.

It could not be otherwise and must never be otherwise. The armed forces are the final bulwark for the preservation of the constitution and the security of the nation. We could not tolerate "Republican officers" and "Democrat officers," with a vast switch of positions with each change of party in national power. Loyalties go to the nation and to its form of government.

RELATIONSHIP AMONG OFFICERS

There is a very special relationship among officers which must be understood as a part of the Code. They are appointed into the service for the same general purposes, and therefore have much in common. There is trust between them because they are officers and have subscribed to the officer's oath. An understanding of the status of the officer, and the relationship or responsiblity of one officer to all others of the corps, are matters of primary importance. We shall examine these matters.

Officer Defined. In the United States Army there are commissioned officers and warrant officers. Together, they constitute the corps of officers.

The term officer has this dictionary definition: "A person lawfully invested with military rank and authority by virtue of a commission issued him by or in the name of the sovereign or chief magistrate of a country". In our Army, commissioned officers are appointed by the President, or in the name of the President, with the approval of the Senate. Warrant officers who rank next below commissioned officers are appointed by warrant by the Secretary of the Army.

Your Brother/Sister Officers. The officers of the Army are a cross-section of the American public, drawn from all states and sections in representative numbers, and from all classes of the social order. A large percentage are graduates either of the Military Academy at West Point, or of the colleges and universities of the nation. Periodic attendance at service schools, postgraduate studies at great universities for some, extensive travel, and the nature of the duties performed, further increase their educational background. As a group, they are subject to the same ambitions, the same variations in viewpoint, even to the same human frailties as the people whom they serve. Drawn from the whole nation by a selective process they are fairly (no more and no less) representative of that larger group of citizens which furnishes the leaders in business, professional, and public life. The common denominator which binds this heterogeneous group together is interest in the welfare of the nation and in the National Defense.

The corps of officers is strengthened by the bonds of comradeship. It is the desire of all that a new officer succeed, and to aid in attaining that objective for others, many will go to great lengths. It will be taken for granted, when an officer joins an organization, that, commensurate with his or her experience, the officer knows the job, and has every intention of doing it well. If the officer fails it is likely to be his or her own fault. Competition exists in the Army as in all life, but it is the healthy striving for professional standing and the good will of associates, not alone for bread and meat. One officer's preferment can hardly be gained at the expense of another since the opportunity to compete is open to all. In the main, the best officers flow to the best assignments and there is room for all. The code of Duty well performed, of Honor, and of Country above self is the unspoken guide with which there is no compromise. It is a high standard. The unworthy eliminate themselves. For those who habitually meet the Code, the good will, professional recognition, and associations which ripen into friendships accrue to officers of all ranks and of all ages.

RELATIONS BETWEEN OFFICERS OF DIFFERENT APPOINTMENT SOURCES

The Army's officers are appointed from several sources—The USMA, the ROTC, the OCS, civil life, and many are Reserve component officers undertaking a second or third tour of active service. Newly appointed officers with short active service may be apprehensive as to a "cleavage" between these different groups. This is a good place to set the facts straight. There are some old wives' tales and straw men to knock down. Examples: the rumored estrangement between the Regular officer and officers of the Reserve components; the graduate of West Point from other Regular officers; the ROTC graduate from other officers, especially those with lesser academic credit; the holders of a doctorate or master's degree from those of lesser degrees; the graduate of the OCS who feels he or she is an outsider because of coming up from the enlisted ranks (some of our best leaders came over this road). The sooner these sources of appointment are forgotten, the better. Their importance is a myth. Indeed, if there are officers who feel "superior" or "inferior," because of their source of appointment, they are likely to be persons of meager stature and unworthy of much notice.

If such points of view ever existed, which is doubtful, the vast Army missions of wars, cold war, and other challenging missions around the world, have brought all officers into a closely-knit whole. If any reader has a lingering doubt, talk with officers of any category who have extensive combat or campaign experience. The vast majority couldn't care less about the source from which an officer was first appointed. What they do care about, and very firmly, is the extent of each officer's experience and capabilities, so they may judge with accuracy how well he or she may be expected to perform on a difficult mission today, or tomorrow, or next week. Once officers accept their commission and report for duty, they are received by fellow officers with full confidence that according to their grade and length of service they are qualified for their responsibilities and are determined to do them well. As time passes they advance or fail on the quality of their performance of duty.

The same principle applies, and must always apply, to the official and personal relationships between officers of the Army and the sister services. All are equally responsible to the commander-in-chief, and all are committed equally to the same mission—the nation's security.

THE UNITED STATES ARMY SOLDIER

The incoming enlisted soldier to the Active Army will represent a cross-section of American citizens, within a required age group, and less those found to be ineligible for service because of physical or other reasons. The great majority will be self-respecting, patriotic, decent good citizens willing to serve our country effectively and well. Their level of education is about the same as those who served during the wars and emergencies of previous years. Their understanding of national and international events will be deeper because of the vast increase in recent years of radio and television news coverage. Most will understand why the turmoil and the wars of our century have not faded into the millenium of peace, as all thoughtful people of all nations have hoped so ardently. In today's All-Volunteer Army, every soldier serves as a matter of choice, although the degree of individual motivaton may vary. The leader has no choice as to the individuals assigned to his or her jurisdiction for training, or for employment on important or hazardous unit missions. The leader's personal success will depend upon gaining the maximum possible performance of duty from each soldier.

The military leader must provide the example of national service, and the kind of leadership, which the great majority of our young people will follow willingly.

THE OFFICER'S RELATIONS WITH ENLISTED PERSONNEL

Every enlisted member wants to feel certain of getting a fair deal from his or her commander. Indeed, each officer wants to feel that he or she, too, will get a square deal from his or her commander and the Army itself. The Army has its faults. But there are mighty few large American organizations that do better, and none that try harder or have more dedicated professional leadership. The Army must discharge its world-wide missions, and at the same time act with the conviction that it is soldiers who do the Army's jobs, and that the motives to which soldiers respond best must be protected and observed. Some of the Army's ways and traditions are not always understood by either its critics or its members. This discussion seeks to clarify a few of the principles.

The relationship between a commander and his or her personnel must be developed to stand the strains of campaign and combat, as well as the less demanding conditions at posts and stations in the United States. There is no precise parallel with other vocations as to this total responsibility, against which to evaluate the need for unusually high standards of conduct, including abstentions. The relationship must include mutual trust and mutual respect. For our present purposes our subject is the off-duty, unofficial, and social relationships *on an individual basis* of officers and enlisted personnel.

In our Army, it is strong tradition that an officer does not gamble, nor borrow money, nor drink intoxicants, nor participate in ordinary social association with enlisted soldiers on an individual basis. Aggravated violations of the tradition may be handled under the Uniform Code of Military Justice. All are matters of simple common sense. Here is why. The officer must not have favored associates, or "buddies," chosen from enlisted personnel. To do so would first place in question and then weaken the vital belief in the officer's impartiality. Noncommissioned officers and soldiers want no favoritism whatever in the decisions of their seniors. In following the wise course, an officer may observe that one or more of the enlisted personnel may have an equal or greater educational background, or wealth, or civilian achievement, and several may exceed the officer's own length and variety of Army service. No matter. The officer is the responsible person, the one who leads and directs, with standards to uphold.

The officer need not sorrow as to these truths, nor be embarrassed by them. It is a natural preference that most enlisted soldiers prefer to associate socially or off-duty with their own military peers. Experienced noncommissioned officers, whose value in our Army is vast, are certain to support this point of view. There are some on-post and many off-post occasions attended by both officers and soldiers, such as athletic, civic, religious, fraternal, as well as social events. Good judgment should indicate the wise course to follow under all circumstances.

Even the suspicion of favoritism must be avoided. If an officer has social companions, obvious favorites, or "buddies," among his or her soldiers, and then sponsors one or more of them for promotion, a preferred assignment, or exemption from duty of special hardship or hazard, the officer destroys in the all-seeing eyes of others the essential standard of mutual trust and respect. Resentment by the less-favored will be prompt. The officer's usefulness declines. No officer and no soldier will choose to encourage the belief of personal inadequacy or untrustworthiness by his or her comrades. Indeed, determination to stand high in the judgments of comrades of all grades drives many good soldiers on to acts of great achievement and heroism. There must be no favoritism nor justified suspicion of favoritism. The officer cannot be a "jolly good fellow," nor "one of the boys." If he or she is popular in the minds of subordinates it is a by-product of leadership, human fairness, knowledge, wise decisions.

These are reasons for the Army traditions that an officer does not gamble, nor borrow money, nor drink intoxicants, nor engage in casual social relationships on an individual basis with enlisted members.*

In today's Army, where women make up an increasingly large percentage of both the officer corps and the enlisted ranks, this matter deserves even closer attention. Since we are all human, there are bound to be occasions when officers, be they male or female, are attracted to enlisted members of the opposite sex. No good can come from any relationship resulting from such attraction. Both the officer and the enlisted member would earn the scorn of their peers for establishing such a relationship, and the effectiveness of both members to the Army would be reduced. To any officer who may think of establishing a relationship with an enlisted member, we can offer only one word of advice: DON'T!

ACTION UPON OUTSIDE PRESSURES

The Army officer must expect to face requests or even demands from civilian sources which we call "pressures." Sought will be a change of an Army action regarding the conduct of its affairs. We are a democracy. Our people are interested in the national defense and in the citizens who are members of the armed forces. When a course of action taken by the Army is contrary to their

---

*For related discussions see Chapter 2, *Arrival at a New Station,* and its discussion, THE EARLY DUTY DAYS; Chapter 3, *The Officer Image,* with its EPILOGUE; and Chapter 16, *Responsibilities of Command,* and its main heading TAKING CARE OF YOUR MEN.

point of view, some are likely to object. Such objections may come from a newspaper editorial, a letter or petition, or a visit by an individual or group having a common purpose. Members of Congress provide many examples. The company commander, the commander of an Army post or of a major command, or a senior official of the Department of the Army may expect to receive many such applications. Needed is a personal code of action and a manner of proper procedure to apply when such occasions arise.

Dismiss at once from consideration the large number of mere requests for information. The Army is close to the people and many matters of its daily operations are of proper interest to citizens. Included are routine requests from members of Congress, or other officials, who ask for proper information which they wish to supply to a constituent. Be certain the disclosure is authorized and, if so, provide with promptness and courtesy the answer requested. It is routine.

But what of those pressures which seek reversal of an Army action or policy? Are they all selfish, wrong in intent, each to be denied? Not at all. Some may be very worthy objections and suggestions. They may be in the highest public interest. A company commander may receive a letter from a distraught parent about his soldier son. A post commander may receive a letter from an excited mayor. Required is a consideration of the matter as represented by the outside source, balanced against the facts as known by the Army. New and important facts may be introduced from the outside which were unknown when the action under examination was taken. Army actions are made with judgment but are not infallible. *Still, Army decisions, actions, policies, must not be changed lightly, or merely to accommodate an influential person, for to do so would invite endless confusion.* Even so, when the merits of the case are such as to indicate the justice of a change in a matter of some importance the proper action may be to make the change. Otherwise, deny it. Choose the course of the Army's best interest, and with which you can live as an officer worthy of trust.

Investigation of other such requests received from persons or groups, even individuals of importance, are quickly seen as unsound, selfish, and advanced for reasons other than those stated.

The apparent motive may be repugnant. Just determine the facts. Analyze the matter objectively. Remember that an Army action is not to be changed lightly. And take just and fair action. Objective action is necessary and a sound decision reached regardless of the motive behind the objection.

A final bit of psychology may be noted. If you decide to say "Yes" to a request, suggestion, even a demand, do so, and do it gracefully. If you decide to say "No," say it clearly, but say it. Never say "No but maybe—," or "No at this time—"; to give a qualified answer invites reopening at an early date with the whole gamut to run again. When the action is negative, avoid disclosing reasons for your action. Just say something like this: "After considering the facts in the situation which you have presented, I must conclude that the action you seek would be contrary to the public interest. Thank you for your interest in bringing it to my attention." Save your "reasons" for your commanding officer, if he or she should inquire about your action.

There is an exceptional situation which deserves illumination. Assume that a negative action has been taken on a subject of importance. Assume further that an appeal to higher military authority is made, urging reversal of the negative action taken. No junior should be reversed except in those rare instances of real importance where failure to do so would injure the national interest, or do a real injustice. Perhaps new facts are brought forth. Perhaps the situation was not fully known by the officer. Whatever the reason, assume that the senior officer decides it is necessary to reverse the action of a subordinate. How should it be done? *The officer must inform the junior of the imminent reversal, with reasons, before any other person learns of the action. Humiliation of the junior must be avoided. Perhaps it would be appropriate to extend opportunity for the junior to change his or her own stand, although the senior must stop short of urging or seeming to force a change of viewpoint. Extend opportunity for the junior to make the announcement of the reversal.* Such instances are uncommon. When reversal is considered to be necessary, the procedure must be done with judgment, lest great harm be perpetrated. The Army must be right and just, even when it is embarrassing to correct an error. Do it only when necessary as an act of justice; but do it right.

STANDARDS OF CONDUCT FOR ARMY MEMBERS

The Army has issued its own publication establishing standards of conduct, AR 600–50, based in part upon Executive Order 11222. These are basic rules, requirements, and prohibitions, which are applicable to all active duty officers and soldiers, and to retired personnel. This Army regulation is of such high importance, and so broad in its scope, that officers are urged to obtain a copy and place it in their personal libraries for reference.

CODE OF CONDUCT FOR MEMBERS OF THE UNITED STATES ARMED FORCES

The President issued an Executive Order in 1955 which establishes a Code of Conduct for members of the armed forces of the United States while in combat or captivity as a prisoner of war. See also AR 350–30, as amended. The order requires that specific training be given to all members liable to capture to better equip them to counter and withstand enemy efforts against them.

1. I am an American fighting man. I serve in the forces which guard my country and our way of life. I am prepared to give my life in their defense.

2. I will never surrender of my own free will. If in command I will never surrender my men while they still have the means to resist.

3. If I am captured I will continue to resist by all means available. I will make every effort to escape and aid others to escape. I will accept neither parole nor special favors from the enemy.

4. If I become a prisoner of war, I will keep faith with my fellow prisoners. I will give no information or take part in any action which might be harmful to my comrades. If I am senior, I will take command. If not I will obey the lawful orders of those appointed over me and will back them up in every way.

5. When questioned, should I become a prisoner of war, I am bound to give only name, rank, service number and date of birth. I will evade answering further questions to the utmost of my ability. I will make no oral or written statements disloyal to my country and its allies or harmful to their cause.

6. I will never forget that I am an American fighting man, responsible for my actions, and dedicated to the principles which made my country free. I will trust in my God and in the United States of America.

CADET PRAYER

It is fitting that this chapter, *The Code of the Army Officer,* end with the Cadet Prayer of the Corps of Cadets, United States Military Academy, for it states best the true code as to character and conduct which guides all men and women who are privileged to wear our country's uniform. The prayer:

O God, our Father, Thou Searcher of men's hearts, help us to draw near to Thee in sincerity and truth. May our religion be filled with gladness and may our worship of Thee be natural.

Strengthen and increase our admiration for honest dealing and clean thinking, and suffer not our hatred of hypocrisy and pretence ever to diminish. Encourage us in our endeavor to live above the common level of life. Make us to choose the harder right instead of the easier wrong, and never to be content with a half truth when the whole can be won. Endow us with courage that is born of loyalty to all that is noble and worthy, that scorns to compromise with vice and injustice and knows no fear when truth and right are in jeopardy. Guard us against flippancy and irreverence in the sacred things of life. Grant us new ties of friendship and new opportunities of service. Kindle our hearts in fellowship with those of a cheerful countenance, and soften our hearts with sympathy for those who sorrow and suffer. Help us to maintain the honor of the Corps untarnished and unsullied and to show forth in our lives the ideals of West Point in doing our duty to Thee and to our Country. All of which we ask in the name of the Great Friend and Master of men.— Amen.

2
Arrival at
a New Station

The Army officer must expect periodic change in station assignment and in duty assignment. The nature of the Army mission and Army service makes it inevitable. Each officer will attend one or several service school courses. Oversea service is by roster and rotation so there is a reasonable sharing of this duty. Some assignments have a standard or a maximum duration. Always the work of the Army must be done, and its mission is under continual change. For these reasons among others, officers should be prepared for unexpected change of station and duty assignment.

These periodic changes provide advantages to you as an officer. Your experience is broadened. Your acquaintances are multiplied. You will have the opportunity to see and to enjoy different sections of our country, as well as other nations on other continents. Each change extends an opportunity to make a new start and earn a better record.

If the occasion is reporting for duty at your first station, or your tenth, it is a new and interesting experience. It is part of the Army way of life. Make the most of it.

IMPORTANT TRUTHS FOR NEWCOMERS

The Army missions of these years support the nation's policy in a great many locations within the free world. These policies are established by our nation's civil leaders who have the sole responsibility for their correctness, and it is noteworthy that during each of the troublesome recent decades (including this one) they generally have had strong support from the great majority of our citizens. Your service is to support the national military program. Perform your duties so that you may have pride in serving your country well.

What May Officers Expect Upon Arrival at a New or a First Station? Officers may expect to be received with matter-of-fact courtesy and efficiency. The reception of individuals into a unit or station complement, whether newly appointed as an officer, warrant officer, noncommissioned officer or soldier, or an experienced oldtimer, is regarded as an important duty by commanders. It is carefully planned and required to be carried out with courtesy, understanding and efficiency. The unit commander will often appoint a sponsoring officer to write to you in advance and to assist you upon arrival. The commander knows the importance of your first impression.

The needs of newcomers are usually anticipated and prompt information provided. Uncertainties will be removed by prompt answer of questions. There will be no hazing nor embarrassments for the mere fact of your "newness." Newness is not a novelty in the Army of today. Enter with confidence and you will be made welcome, for your service is needed. If you should encounter an individual of the reception detail who is thoughtless and seems uninstructed, do not let the episode influence your conclusions about the Army or its programs. He or she will be the exception. Read your instructions carefully and complete them promptly. If there is something unclear, just inquire. People expect to help you, and they will help you. Perhaps they were the new ones a few weeks earlier. Later, when you are helping to receive newcomers, do your part to be helpful and understanding.

ASSIGNMENT AT THE FIRST STATION

This discussion aims at removing some of the perplexities encountered by newly appointed officers in reporting for duty at their first Army station. At the same time there is discussion of several matters of interest in the process of becoming established in the military environment. As will be made clear, it is neither complex nor difficult.

Action on the Tendered Appointment. As a newly appointed officer, you will receive from The Adjutant General a letter of notification and instructions, with your oath of office and other related papers. If you wish to accept the appointment you must complete the papers according to instructions, execute the oath of office (which should be read thoughtfully as it means exactly what it says), and return the completed papers.

Initial Assignment Expectancy. Although the emergency needs of the Army will be a factor for determining initial assignments of newly appointed officers, the following is the current expectancy and is included as a general guide.

Graduates of the United States Military Academy. The initial assignment of USMA graduates will be to their basic course of 9–12 weeks duration, followed by training in their basic entry specialty, prior to reporting to a unit. Or, depending upon quotas, physical fitness, and volunteering, they may first attend either the 9-week Ranger Course or the 3-week Airborne Course, or both. Ranger training is limited to combat arms, signal officers and officers going to Ranger units. There is no set sequence.

Graduates of the ROTC Program. ROTC graduates will attend a basic course of approximately 9–12 weeks upon entry on active duty followed by training in their basic entry specialty. They may volunteer for further training in courses like the Airborne course and flight training.

Distinguished Military Graduates. Distinguished military graduates who accept a regular commission are trained similar to USMA graduates. They have a priority for early attendance at their basic course.

Graduates of the OCS Program. OCS commissioned officers upon graduation attend the basic officer course of their commissioning branch followed by training in their basic entry specialty prior to reporting to their first duty station.

Doctors and Lawyers. Doctors and lawyers when called for active duty will usually receive training involving orientation, specialization, or bringing the officer up-to-date (refresher) depending upon their experience and professional background.

Army Aviation Training. Regular Army officers may apply for aviation training, but must have completed the basic officer course before entering flight school.

Exceptions to the troop duty assignment may be granted to Transportation Corps officers with Aviation Materiel Management as a basic entry specialty, and to Reserve officers who are graduates of the ROTC flight training program and who are needed to fill an immediate Army requirement.

Warrant Officers. Warrant officers, except Aviators and Physician's Assistants, normally are appointed directly from the enlisted ranks and proceed directly to their first assignment. Aviators are promoted to warrant officer upon successful completion of their flight training program at Fort Rucker, Alabama. Physician's Assistant warrant officers are promoted to that grade upon successful completion of their training at the Health Services Command at Fort Sam Houston, Texas.

Suggestions When the Initial Assignment is on Temporary Duty (TDY). Newly appointed officers may expect to be sent to attend a basic course, or other initial instruction, on temporary duty (TDY). Duration of this instruction is 9–12 weeks. See Chapter Eight, *Army Posts and Stations.*

Under normal conditions, sufficient time is allowed between delivery of orders for assignment and the date of reporting for duty to adjust personal affairs and prepare for Army service.

For TDY assignments there is a travel allowance for the officer. There is no provision for the travel of family members, nor are government quarters provided for a spouse who accompanies the officer at personal expense. Officers attending a basic course are usually assigned bachelor officers quarters (BOQ). A prescribed maximum weight of personal property may be shipped to the TDY station at Government expense. (Consult Chapter Twenty, *Travel Allowances.*)

Suggestions When the Assignment is Under Permanent Change of Station (PCS) Orders. Orders for permanent change of station may be the first orders received upon coming to active duty, or they may follow completion of the first TDY assignment.

Under orders for PCS the officer collects an allowance for personal travel; there is an allowance for the travel of specified family members including spouse and children; the shipment of household goods and personal property within a prescribed weight limit is at government expense.

Chapter Eight, *Army Posts and Stations,* will be very helpful. Many station commanders send to officers under orders to their command a booklet of information more complete than contained in this chapter. If this information is not received, or there are questions not answered in Chapter Eight, it is customary to write a letter to the station Adjutant and request the information desired. Include the number and date of your assignment order, and the date you are to report for duty. The letter should include the information the Adjutant will need to answer your questions, such as the age and sex and school status of your children should you ask about the school situation.

The Initial Purchase of Uniforms. Prior to reporting to your first duty station, you should procure at least a minimum supply of uniforms. (And at the same time abandon any idea you may have had of making a saving from the uniform allowance for other purposes.)

Information about the officer's uniform, including procurement, is contained in Chapter Twenty-one, *Uniforms of the Army.* The uniform allowance is stated in Chapter Nineteen, *Pay and Allowances.* Uniforms may be purchased at any Army post having a Clothing Sales Store or Post Exchange; as an officer under orders to active service, you will be permitted to purchase from these establishments by identifying yourself and showing a copy of your orders.

After reporting, and learning the expected conditions of service and duty, the total requirements may be added as found necessary.

However limited your initial supply of uniforms, see to it that what you wear is clean, neatly pressed, with insignia clean and placed accurately, shoes clean and neatly shined. Let care make up for the time being the shortages which you will soon correct.

How to Report for Duty. Orders assigning an officer to a station for duty include a date of reporting. You are complying with the order if you reach the station and report to the proper official prior to midnight of the date prescribed. But you should arrive during the hours of the ordinary business day, if at all practicable. Try to arrive before noon and as early as 0900 if you can. This will allow you to complete many important official and personal arrangements on the day of reporting. Try to report not later than 1600. If date of reporting lies within the discretion of the officer, he or she should avoid arrival at a new station on Saturday, Sunday, or an official holiday.

Should an officer report in uniform? Or is it acceptable practice to report in civilian clothing? Mindful of the usual long automobile drive, and the difficulty of unpacking to appear neat, freshly pressed, and with everything in top condition, the choice needs discussion. The correct garb is the uniform, clean, neat, well pressed, like the book says. *Suggestion:* Consider arriving in the area on the afternoon before you are due for reporting, stay at a convenient motor court, and make the necessary preparations. A good start is important. Reporting in civilian clothing is not unknown, in this day and age, but a good start is as important today as any time of the past.

Carry with you several copies of your orders. At least two copies will be needed for your travel pay voucher and other copies will be needed for administrative purposes at the new station. Ten should be sufficient. A copy should be placed in your personal records file.

Proceed to the post or station headquarters to report for duty.

In those cases where a large number of officers report within a short period, as at a training center, port of embarkation or other large troop concentration, the reception of arriving officers may be handled by a receiving committee. In such a case the formality of reporting consists only of presenting yourself at the proper office, which is usually indicated by signs, presenting your orders, signing the register, and receiving instructions. A member of this committee usually handles quartering and messing arrangements and provides, often in a mimeographed order, the information which the newcomer requires. At a later time a meeting may be held at which the commanding officer or a representative addresses the group for purposes of organization or orientation. When this procedure is followed be certain that you have received all of the instructions which should be in your possession and that you understand them thoroughly.

At other times the arrival of a single officer or a small group of officers is but an incident in the day's work, and no such elaborate machinery will be set up. Proceed to the post headquarters and the office of the adjutant. Remove your cap, knock, enter, and, if the adjutant is senior in grade to yourself, salute and report: "Sir, Lieutenant ──────── reports for duty"; at the same time extend a copy of your orders. If the adjutant is the junior in grade, as an Army custom it is proper to state: "I am Major ──────── reporting for duty." It is likely that the adjutant will welcome you to the garrison and give you the information you will need. He or she will arrange a time for you to call upon the commanding officer and arrange for you to meet your subordinate commander. The adjutant will tell you your quarters assignment or whom to see to obtain this information. It is probable that he or she will arrange for the delivery of your baggage to your quarters. Request a copy of the local garrison regulations, a map of the reservation, and any other information normally supplied to new arrivals. When you leave the adjutant there should be no doubt in your mind as to what you are to do initially and when and where you are to do it. Your first task, more than likely, will be to establish yourself in your quarters and prepare yourself for the duties to come.

Getting Established in Quarters. After reporting for duty, immediately get yourself established. If the assignment is for TDY, this may mean only the location of the BOQ and moving into your assigned room. If you arrive on PCS orders, and you have family members, getting established will involve the assignment and occupancy of government quarters, or the rental or purchase of other housing.

Most Army posts operate guest houses which are available for short periods to newly assigned personnel until they can find permanent housing. Rates are nominal. Space is usually reserved, when available, by application in advance of need to the Billeting Officer.

Subject to some limitation, like the unit going on maneuvers, the officer is normally given a reasonable period of time to arrange for personal affairs. (See *Proceed Time,* Chapter 23.) Your unit sponsor may have made some arrangements for you. In the case of reporting to a major post for a school or for further assignment to a unit, it is best that you arrive a few days earlier than required. A major post will have persons to assist you, like the Billeting Officer, and will have an Army Community Service Center, at which you can get a wealth of current information, an issue of cots, blankets, etc., to help your family, and many other kinds of assistance.

Collection of Travel and Transportation Allowances. Soon after arrival at the new station, you will wish to submit vouchers for collection of cash allowances such as those for your personal travel, family travel if such travel has been made, dislocation, per diem, or any other allowance, such as the uniform allowance, to which you may be entitled. Inquire of the personnel officer for the procedure and request assistance as needed. Copies of travel orders will be required.

Identification (ID) Card. The officer and family members are required to possess an identification (ID) card, and to show it upon request, in order to patronize the Post Exchange, the Sales Commissary, or the Post Motion Picture Theater. In addition, a special card is required for family members to obtain out-patient care or hospitalization at station medical facilities. The Personnel Officer will provide assistance in obtaining them.

Garrison Regulations. Make a careful study of the local garrison regulations. They usually contain much useful information on local conditions, facilities, and conveniences, as well as requirements which will assist you in making adjustments to the new environment. Comply with them fully.

The Post Exchange. A visit should be paid to the Post Exchange soon after arrival. It is a community store operated under the supervision of the commanding officer. At most stations the exchange consists of a general store, a tailor shop, shoe repair shop, cafeteria, and barber shop. It supplies other services for the benefit of the officers and enlisted personnel of the garrison. It is noteworthy that profits resulting from the operation of the exchange revert to the organization for expenditure as provided by regulations primarily for the benefit of the troops through the Central Welfare Fund.

Post Quartermaster and Post Transportation Officer. Both offices are important to the newly arrived officer. The Post Transportation Officer will assist you with problems associated with the movement of your personal and household property and any claims occasioned by loss or damage. The Post Quartermaster is concerned with sales of equipment, with commissary sales, with issues of supplies to troop units, storage of personal property, and a wide variety of other responsibilities.

Learn Your Way Around. Study a map of the post and locate the important buildings, roads, training areas, and recreational facilities.

Reporting Time for Starting to Work. Instructions from the adjutant or your immediate commander will indicate the time allowed you to become established.

THE EARLY DUTY DAYS

Arrival at a first station, and assignment to a unit with its responsibilities, provides an exceptional, interesting challenge. We shall examine it in detail to provide some light for guidance.

Start with this initial conviction of personal confidence: The Army selects its officers most carefully, and trains them so they will succeed. The education and the training programs at West Point, at Reserve Officer Training Corps units at our colleges and universities, at Officer Candidate Schools, at the branch service schools where most new officers go for initial active duty training, are all most carefully conducted. Although all newly appointed officers will have more to learn, a state which continues throughout the careers of all officers, each officer should start with confidence in his or her preparation.

Commanders of companies and battalions are fully aware of the problems encountered by newly appointed, incoming officers. They know the additional instruction each will require. Do understand that the success in command responsibility sought by your new commander, or chief, depends in part upon your own success. *Let this sink in—real deep:* Everyone gains when the incoming officer adjusts quickly and identifies with new associates as a trustworthy, capable addition to the command. Further, that all stand to lose if the newcomer should fail. It is fully understood that no officer could possibly "know everything" upon arrival. For this reason the newcomer will certainly receive detailed information, probably some material for study, and time to complete his or her preparation. The procedure is based upon infinite experience, free from mystery. Always—if you don't know—inquire; and don't hesitate to ask officers of your own rank and your subordinates.

The next essential step is up to the incoming officer, and no one can do much to help, except to provide the needed time and opportunity. At once, start getting acquainted with your people, whether officers, enlisted members or civilians. If you are to command the unit, start with the senior who will become your Number One Assistant. Learn his or her name and use it. Learn his or her background, special training, service experience, and aspirations. Invite his or her cooperation and his or her suggestions, which you will need. Never belittle yourself in doing these things, nor seem to boast, but explain your background, too, so he or she can judge wisely how best to advise you. Similarly, meet and talk with your other officers and noncommissioned officers, learn and *use* their names, and learn their service training and background. As time is available, talk with each soldier in the same manner. These interviews should be informal, objective, impersonal, but keep in your mind that you are inquiring, searching, learning, starting to build a new team with you as chief. A basic principle of leadership is to "know your personnel," and the step described is essential at the very start.

When you make your start on your new responsibilities, be very sure to understand the mission of today and tomorrow, next week, even next month. Your commander, or chief, will inform you. Go over the mission with your senior subordinate. You may find it wise to hold a discussion meeting with your noncommissioned officers, hearing their suggestions or special problems. This procedure starts the development of mutual understanding and teamwork, and is one good way of avoiding initial mistakes. It should not be long before you are prepared to say something like this, with confidence: "This is our job for tomorrow ——————. This is the way (and place and time) we will do it. Sergeant Jones, your mission is ——————. Sergeant Smith, you have the special mission of ——————." And so on with clarity, organization of work, teamwork. Finally, "Any questions? Make your own preparations and I will meet you here ready to go at 0700." Without cautious delay, take the baton of command in your own hand, and develop quickly the correct attributes of a leader.

Finally, and it is important, there is learning and adjusting to the "Army Way." It is a good way and need be neither confusing nor frustrating. Meet and become acquainted with your fellow officers in your quarters or theirs, at the open mess, at work, at battalion meetings, official or social. Although there may be some good natured jesting, there is no period of "hazing" nor of "probation." Each has been "new." They will take for granted that you know your job and that you are determined to do it well. They hope you will succeed, for your success will help them.*

All of the above guidance is essential. It works. In the past four decades, the Army has had on active duty far more than a million different officers, with

---

*An officer joining a unit in combat, or preparing to enter combat, may expect a thorough evaluation before assignment to command. When entering combat, the officer will be responsible for the lives of soldiers and for the unit's mission which can be essential to the entire command. Commanders will satisfy themselves of the newcomer's capabilities before entrusting the officer with a command responsibility.

combat in Europe, in Africa, in Asia, in the islands of the South and Mid Pacific, and missions vital to the nation throughout our world. The Army knows how to welcome and to prepare the new officer. If you have completed the training process, you can do the job. Never doubt it. Give it your best thought and your best effort. You will find help and guidance as it may be needed. But do make good. You are serving the nation.

OFFICIAL CALLS

The Adjutant or other qualified officer will inform the incoming officer of the local policy about official and social calls. Don't be apprehensive about them. They serve useful purposes in the military community because of swift changes of personnel.

Refer to Chapter 4, *Military Courtesy,* as to required calls. Refer also to Chapter 6, *The Social Side of Army Life,* for information about calling cards and social calls. Unless you have calling cards, delay their purchase until after reporting to learn the local custom.

ADJUSTMENT TO SERVICE LIFE

After the hurried experiences of reporting for duty, getting established, meeting new people, and starting to work for the early days of duty, there arrives a time to take stock. There are things to learn and things to do by the bachelor officer as well as the officer arriving with a family. The new Army spouse will share in these opportunities. It is a good time to review other chapters in this book: Chapter One, *The Code of the Army Officer;* Chapter Three, *The Officer Image;* and the established service standbys, Chapter Four, *Military Courtesy;* Chapter Five, *Customs of the Service;* and Chapter Six, *The Social Side of Army Life.*

There are basic differences between the life and experiences of the Army officer in contrast to the person of similar education and background in civilian employment. An officer does not hold an "office hour" job; your responsibilities will continue around the clock although on many assignments you will follow established hours. You are expected to observe and to uphold officer-like standards at all times. You do not shed your responsibilities at 5 PM, as you leave for the day; and you devote the hours to your duties which your responsibilities require.

Adjustment to Post Life. A sincere desire on your part to contribute your efforts and talents to appropriate post activities wherever they are desired or needed is a sound philosophy to adopt from the start. As a member of a garrison you will find your greatest pleasures in participation in the community, athletic and social events which are provided, as well as in the performance of your duties.

Early Membership in the Officers' Open Mess and Club. At most stations all officers are members of the Officers' Open Mess and Club, and in many instances membership for new arrivals is automatic. A modest monthly fee is charged. Early contact should be made at the office to learn of local facilities, membership policies, and costs. For further information refer to Chapter Five, *Customs of the Service.*

The "Good" Station and the "Poor" Station. Some Army stations are ideal. Some are less desirable than others from the standpoints of climate, locations near or away from cities, geography, size, and other matters. But within the meaning of this discussion, the descriptions "good" or "bad" are to be found in the mind of the individual.

Resolve to take each station in stride, getting the most from each in professional progress and personal satisfaction. You will soon develop the mixed emotions of experienced officers—always hating to leave a pleasant station but eager for the challenges and experiences of a new one.

Scorn the Habitual Critic. You will harm your personal standing in the eyes of worthy fellow officers by associating more than casually with the continual complainer and critic. Most organizations have one or more of this type. Such individuals are almost certainly of small capacity, mediocre record, and deserve the low esteem in which held. Correct them, if they work for you. Avoid them, if they don't.

Personal Records File. The day of arrival is not too soon to start a permanent file of personal papers and records. Start with Department of the Army orders covering your initial assignment. Add to it all official documents which pertain to you as an individual, receipts for property for which others hold you responsible, and similar papers. Notes may be added of important matters which may require later reference. Add to this file photographs of environmental things which you may find of interest in later years, not forgetting pictures and notes concerning other officers who have interested you particularly. Twenty years hence when the stirring events of today have retreated into the background, you will appreciate the opportunity of refreshing your memory on the numerous friendships and interesting events experienced during your career. Keep a record of the names, grades, and permanent addresses of your several commanding officers and the dates of your service with them. Such a file will serve many useful purposes.

JUNIOR OFFICER COUNCILS

Each Army installation and major unit may have a Junior Officer Council (JOC) representing the company-grade officers of the installation. The JOC's provide a means for the junior officers to communicate with the commander and the staff, provide the commanders with ready access to the views and problems of their junior officers, and provide an opportunity for all to benefit from improvement of local conditions and policies. Learn the name of and establish contact with your representative on the Junior Officer Council. He or she will be able to answer many questions you may have or obtain the answers, if necessary. Your active interest, and your participation if possible, will benefit both you and the Army.

REASSIGNMENT

Action Upon Receipt of Orders for Change of Station. The officer on duty confronted with reassignment must take prompt steps for relief from present responsibilities as well as arranging personal affairs prior to departure. A clean break must be made with all responsibilities.

There are few shortcomings more injurious to an officer's standing than leaving a residue of unfinished official business to annoy and confuse the officer's successor and his or her commander. Since an evaluation report will be prepared on your departure it is doubly important that you make arrangements for relief from current responsibilities completely and efficiently. Clearance must be obtained for all property and fund responsibilities. All unfinished transactions such as disposition of unserviceable or lost property, vouchers for fund expenditures, and the like, must be set forth clearly and fully, for responsibility will not be finally terminated until these matters are completed. Individual and organizational records which require action by the responsible officer must be brought up to date before departure, or face completion by mail after departure. A clear picture of the mission and responsibilities must be passed on to your successor so that he or she may start with essential information.

Personal bills and obligations must be satisfied and clearance from the post obtained. It is especially important that obligations to civilian merchants be paid before departure, or that, prior to that time, definite arrangements acceptable to the merchant be made for deferring payment.

Farewell calls should be made upon the next two senior commanders, upon other Army associates as is considered appropriate, and upon civilian friends who have extended their welcome. Drop around at the various offices where you have had frequent official transactions and say a pleasant farewell to all.

On the day of departure, check-out must be made with the organization to which assigned and with post headquarters.

3
The Officer Image

Oh wad some power the giftie gie us
To see oursel's as others see us!
It would frae mony a blunder free us,
And foolish notion.—Robert Burns.

This chapter is a thought-provoking stimulant for self-analysis. It has been developed as a study in human relations . . . "to see ourselves as others see us," and to weigh the importance of such impressions formed in the minds of others. Opportunities will abound to apply and to benefit by this concept in all assignments which pertain to an Army career.

The officer is an official of the Army, and hence of our government, and has authority sufficient for the discharge of assigned responsibilities. He or she receives a duty assignment and a mission, or series of missions, and is required to complete these tasks up to standard, on time, with the personnel and the equipment provided for his or her use. The officer's duty may be free from hazard, or may involve the gravest hazards from enemy action; it may be routine or of critical importance. It may involve technique, or tactics, or strategy; or the exercise of leadership or management with respect to other tasks. The accomplishment of mission—no matter what obstacles are encountered—is the dominant point to remember about an officer's responsibilities.

On most Army assignments, the officer has subordinates who are responsible for the execution of such of his or her responsibilities as he or she may delegate to them. In turn, the officer is responsible to a superior officer who is also his or her rating officer for the rendition of evaluation reports. There are still higher levels in the chain of command. The officer will also have associates, in the usual case, who have parallel missions to perform for the same chief, or commander, with whom the officer must act in smooth coordination and effective teamwork. The officer's responsibilities include those assigned by his or her immediate commander. There are also staff officers with whom smooth and effective official relations are essential. The conclusions or the impressions—the *image*— formed about an officer in the minds of these other human beings are important, and their shaping is the purpose of this discussion.

It is obvious that an officer's day involves many contacts with other people, on duty or off duty, personal or official, casual or of high importance. Each such contact may influence for better or worse the impression, or "image," the officer makes upon others. With the passage of time, and as the observations increase in variety and number, the image deepens and fills out in the minds of others. Each passing day has had its effect, and each new day presents its opportunity.

What is the image we should like to project? Some introspection here may prove quite rewarding. Before we consider means to communicate the image, let us (following the advice of the Apostle Paul) examine ourselves, and where we find a bit of rust or tarnish let us first diligently remove it.

What are the characteristics of this image we would portray in the minds of others? And how may these essential qualities be presented for observers to identify? To change the point of view in the quotation from Robert Burns, how can we be seen by others as we wish to be seen?

INTEGRITY

Personal integrity is the foundation upon which the standing of an officer rests in the minds of subordinates, associates, and superior officers. It is simple, basic, personal honesty. It is the hallmark of the honor code of The United States Corps of Cadets at West Point. See the General MacArthur's Preface to this book. In Chapter One, *The Code of the Army Officer,* integrity is shown as the essential ingredient of the Army code; it accounts for the sense of security taken for granted by our citizens whenever the Army is involved.

What is there about a person of integrity which identifies him or her to others? He or she possesses the self-discipline to see clearly the honorable course and to follow it; obtains and considers all the facts bearing upon a decision, or choice, and as a result his or her acts and orders are fair and just, as a matter of standard practice; and is objective and impartial, free from favoritism or bias, or desire for personal gain, in the line of duty. If such a person makes a mistake, he or she takes the rap for it. When credit is due others, they get it. When asked for an opinion, after gathering and evaluating the facts, that person says what he or she thinks, and means it. That person's word is good. His or her signature on a document is sufficient proof of personal belief in its correctness. Such a person of integrity proceeds in good conscience, in full retention of self-respect.

There is *performance integrity,* as well as personal integrity. It is the very best effort in achievement of mission within your capability. Your performance represents you and creates your personal duty image. In the Army, as in other vocations, some duties are more interesting, or more rewarding, or more pleasant or more hazardous than others. Whatever your preferences, be certain that the record you build is developed by performance. If you seek an image of excellence, you must perform all duties with excellence. In any case, you may as well understand that the Army insists upon standard results on all assignments.

Does this seem to be a goal unattainably or unnecessarily high? Or unrealistic? Think a while before cutting it back in importance. You are an official of government. You are a leader and you must achieve your mission through leadership of others in such a manner as to command their respect and their whole-hearted cooperation. You must "get results" and this means next week and next month, as well as today and tomorrow. Under predictable circumstances, you may be obliged to make decisions and direct actions which involve victory or defeat, life or death. As a member of the corps of officers, you may some day find you must make decisions which conceivably could determine the survival of the nation or even the freedom of our people. The personal and the performance integrity of each officer of the corps of officers is an asset beyond price in the life and security of our nation.

How can you convince others of your personal and performance integrity, in word and deed? In such matters, people cannot be deceived for long, if at all. How shall we go about establishing this favorable image?

Let us think for a moment of *good will,* an intangible having a very high dollar value in commerce and industry. Good will has been defined as "the sum of an infinite number of favorable impressions." A pertinent corollary: "The value of a product lies in the hidden ingredient, the *honor* and *integrity* of the manufacturer." Now we may return with clearer insight to the building of the favorable image. It is formed day by day, through innumerable contacts or observations, of large things and small ones, routines and emergencies, off duty and on duty; each one in some degree will influence the building of the image or impression formed about an officer. If on each occasion you are loyal, objective, fair, and unswerving in devotion to duty, the favorable image will grow. (And if, on some occasions you are a stinkeroo, the blemish will be retained.) An image is taking form.

Here is the image you seek. The subordinate might state it this way: "My captain is an honorable man. I trust and respect him." The commander this way: "This captain is a trustworthy and honorable man. I am glad to have him as an important subordinate." When this essential base of integrity is established, we may proceed to other components of the officer image.

Adherence to the Basic Code. There are other human traits and personal qualities which influence greatly the impressions formed about an officer. There must be a strong loyalty, with continual observance of the basic code. Special reference is made to Chapter One, *The Code of the Army Officer,* and to Chapter Fourteen, *Evaluation Reports.*

PROFESSIONAL COMPETENCE

The importance of integrity as a base or foundation for a proper image of an officer cannot be over-emphasized. But standing alone it is not enough. A structure must be built upon it.

The officer must know his or her job. The soldier has a right to expect an officer to be proficient in the military arts of his or her arm or service, and of the organization of which both are members. The soldier expects to receive effective instruction. The professional competence of an officer must be demonstrated in daily contacts with seniors and subordinates in the same manner and for the same reasons that the officer's integrity must be held under continual observation. The image of professional competence of an officer must be earned.

In our Army, the educational system and the professional development programs provide splendid opportunities throughout a long career. Successive, planned assignments are opportunities for increasing experience and capability. In each of our wars and emergencies, our system of officer selection, training, and development, has produced in abundance officers of all grades who provided the leadership which met and removed the perils to our nation. If proof is sought, there are two world wars, Korea, and Vietnam, to affirm it.

In this year, as in the past, and into the future as far as we may peer, each officer assuming the responsibilities of an assignment will desire to develop in the mind of each subordinate a favorable answer to the question: "Does my commanding officer know his or her job?" Your own commander, chief or boss, will also seek an answer to the same question.

How do you go about securing this favorable image of professional competence, of knowing your job? You must know your mission and the time set for its successful completion. You must know your personnel, their degree of training, their training shortcomings. You must know your equipment, its condition, and if there are shortages which can be replaced, you must get them. You must possess the priceless capability of identifying the right thing to do, and then decide the timing to commence as well as to complete the mission.

First, you must take your unit through the training process of individual and small unit training to bring them up to the standard required. Here they learn the fundamentals. You must be an effective teacher, or trainer, for no leader can effectively command until his or her subordinates are trained, disciplined, and ready to act in a determined, coordinated effort with others. "This is what we are to do," you tell them; "This is the way to do it," you show them; then direct them, "Now you do it," and under your guidance or the guidance of your assistants the soldiers undergoing instruction acquire their individual skills. Your image begins to form at the start of these instruction periods. You demonstrate your professional capability as you impart your knowledge in the training process.

Second, upon completion of the training cycle there may follow a period in readiness to respond promptly for whatever emergency action may be directed by our government; or there may be missions concerned with the national security; or there may follow prompt deployment in battle. There is the everpresent need to keep sharp and ready the ability of the unit to function effectively in combat. For this reason, as opportunity offers, there will be a return to training to refresh knowledge, or to correct weaknesses as they are disclosed, or to undertake new or more advanced training. You may be a leader, a commander, a teacher, an administrator, a staff officer, as your mission requires. Whatever your assignment, you must be competent in your field for your grade, extent of your training, with display of foresight, and with standards kept high, in whatever situation or mission you face. As observations multiply, and experience broadens, the image you will inspire in others becomes more pronounced.

Third, is caring for your personnel. It is a part of professional competence which also requires knowledge. A leader must care for subordinates to be successful. Never forget it. This factor is not a popularity contest where, for example, you know your soldiers like beer, so you arrange to expend unit funds to get them beer. Such superficialities have little application. *It means that you know your subordinates;* their abilities, training, integrity; their debts and their family situations; their health, their habits, their weaknesses; and, of course, what you may expect from each of them as to performance of duty. Knowing your subordinates, you are in an improved position to get from each his or her very best performance. You *must train your soldiers;* soldiers who are really trained will be far more successful in achievement of mission, and far less likely to be killed or wounded through the unwise acts of the inexperienced. *You must look after their personal welfare;* this includes many matters which may give concern to soldiers, or relieve their worries, or assist them in helping themselves. There is much good in the timely and proper provision of creature comforts, including on occasion the cold beer, and more essential items. These are things to do all day long, all week long, always.

Can any person "know everything" about the needs of his or her assignment? Of course not. You must learn as you go, recognize the new problem, and devise ways to meet it. You think, study, confer and plan, today and tonight, for the missions of tomorrow, or next week, or later. You must be ready with planned action for your responsibilities as they arise.

As illustration of the need to be prepared for entirely new conditions and missions, consider the mission assigned to General Harkins in Vietnam, in 1962, 1963, and the transfer of these responsibilities to General Westmoreland in 1964, and later to General Abrams. Decide for yourself whether in all our national history any leader, military or civilian, has received a more unique mission. United States forces were sent there to help—only to help—the people of Vietnam fight to retain their freedom. Our representatives could "advise" or they might "urge," but they could not "require" and they did not "command." The increase of our forces, and the acceptance of ground, air, and naval action in combat did not change the status of advisors to the South Vietnamese forces. Its reference here is to illustrate the need of the officer to be ready to meet the unexpected. In the ever-changing conditions of our world, this may indicate a common situation of the future. Who can foretell? The certainty is that other situations and conditions will arise, of importance to our nation and our allies, and that officers must be able—and willing—to handle with professional skill whatever threats may develop. Our national interests may require it. Have you thought of the military life to be dull, routine, uneventful? Without challenge? Look about you! See for yourself our forces in Europe; in the Far East; the Sixth Fleet and the Seventh Fleet, at sea; plus our atomic submarines; our vast power of the USAF; and our missiles in place and ready. Think hard about it, for our officers and their soldiers have our nation and our people to protect, and our national policies to support as the President—our Commander-in-Chief—may direct.

The responsible officer must identify the new opportunities and hazards, grow in professional capacity, and rise to the requirements of his or her mission. The assignment of an important military mission provides a fertile and rewarding field for all of one's wisdom, and all of one's foresight and courage. If the security of our nation, and our allies, seems important to you during these troubled years, look forward to your part in future history with anticipation and with determination. There are rewards as well as trials.

As time passes and these various cycles are completed, impressions about the professional competence of the officer form with clarity in the minds of all observers. Where the impression is favorable, the subordinate may state it this way: "My lieutenant (captain, colonel, general) is a reliable, well-trained officer. He knows his job." The superior officer might say: "This officer is well trained and has developed quickly into a valuable officer who knows his job." The associates with whom the officer works might say: "We are fortunate to have this officer beside us. He holds up his end of things." The citizens and soldiers of a friendly country receiving his aid might say: "With his help and guidance we can win. We are fortunate to have him."

The image of the officer has developed swiftly. He or she has been identified as a person of integrity and professional competence.

But there is more.

THE COURAGE TO ACT

You must prepare yourself to take action, often swift, sometimes hazardous, occasionally into the unknown. Your missions are infinite in variety. As a commander in combat, you may be required with your unit to defeat an enemy before the enemy can defeat you. Or to seize a hill, cross a river, hold a position against strong attack. Or to unload a ship, build a road, a bridge, or clear a harbor. There is a need also for "courage to act" on assignments other than command, in peace as well as in war. Peacetime decisions involve courage, guts, and in a controversial matter under development or discussion, to fight —with hard logic—for your own well considered point of view. The courage to act when action is needed is an essential requirement for an officer whatever the nature of the mission or assignment.

There are preliminaries to action, of course. They vary as to the time available for development of plan and deployment for execution of plan, from many months (as for the plans for the cross-channel invasion of Europe in World War II), to the instantaneous response to opportunity or emergency, (as the crossing of the Remagen bridge over the Rhine, or the swift support of small units under sudden attack in the forested jungles of parts of Vietnam). There must be a consideration of facts and the reaching of a decision—*what is to be done?* There must be planning—*where* and *how* will the action be taken, *when,* and *by whom?* Orders must issue to subordinate leaders so they will know their own missions, the timing, and the essential coordination with others.

These essential steps—deciding, planning, ordering—are preludes to action. They are essentials in the practice of command, or of "being in charge" in an administrative assignment. They are as necessary to the officer in the discharge of a mission as gasoline is to a motor car climbing a hill, or sunshine to growing corn. Opportunities to acquire these leadership skills are abundant. They are taught, logically and ably, at service schools and colleges, in maneuvers and training exercises. But without down-grading the importance of these institutions, their instruction is but a preliminary to the action which an Army officer must be prepared to accomplish.

In battle, and even in situations other than battle, there may be a vast difference between the requirements of the military leader in comparison with leaders in other fields. *In all decisions, the military leader must be right!* He or she must be right because there will be no second chance. The fact of being right may bring victory or success, instead of defeat and failure. Indeed, it may mean life, or death. It is an essential part of Army philosophy and training that the mission must be achieved. "Being right" must be a part of the Code of the Army Officer, which requires as a matter of course that you apply to vital responsibilities all of your knowledge and your training, and all your courage, to reach and direct a sound, workable solution at the instant needed.

We reach a quality, or a strength, which rises above character building and professional knowledge. Not all persons of fine physique, of splendid character, of excellent academic education, of thorough professional training, and patriotic motives, will make the best officers. Consider it carefully.

The officer who is a commander must be the one to order: "FOLLOW ME!" or "FIRE!" or "GO!" *He or she must have the courage to act at the very instant action is needed.* The commander will realize the hazards, the potential losses, and will measure the danger of defeat as well as the fruits of victory. There is no room here for a Charlie Brown or any other Timid Soul. Lost would be the brilliant thinker with faint heart who reaches a perfect decision tomorrow on a critical situation, or fleeting opportunity, demanding action today. These are the situations which separate the best officers from those not quite up to the highest standards.*

Now we may put in place the keystone of the conclusions which we have sought to develop in the inquisitive, searching, questioning minds of subordinates, associates, and superior officers who are also rating and reviewing officers. Without this final quality there may be defeat instead of victory, failure instead of success, despite an officer's integrity and professional competence. There must be *courage to act decisively* at the most favorable time, as well as in a sound manner. We reach the final conclusion which the officer should establish as his or her image: "When things need doing, this officer gets them *done right*—and fast!"

THE NATIONAL IMAGE OF THE OFFICER CORPS

The consensus of our citizens as to the integrity and the professional competence of the corps of officers of the armed forces has a vast national importance. While it is our elected civil leaders who make the war-or-peace decisions, it is the officers of the armed forces who provide the military leadership required for such peace-preserving or peace-restoring missions. If trust and confidence in our officers were to be weakened, our civil leaders would face severe handicaps in taking courageous action which the best interests of our nation may require. Equally serious would be the reluctance of our citizens to serve, or to entrust their sons or daughters to the armed forces. The importance of universal trust in the integrity and the professional competence of our military leaders of all grades, and of all services, should be very clear to thoughtful people. These qualities involve the nation's security.

What is not so clear, however, is the manner in which this total image is acquired by most citizens. Individual opinions about all officers are likely to be formed from observation of a small number. No person could observe more than a tiny portion of the total number of officers. A reason for this truth is that officers are seen in uniform, which aids the generalization that this one lieutenant (captain or major, colonel or general) must have similarity to all others of his or her grades. Hence, each officer has a very important influence upon the beliefs developed about all officers in the minds of observers. The nation's trust in its military leaders is a priceless asset which all officers must protect.

Lest a reader gain the impression that all Army officers must achieve the standards and standing of a Marshall, Eisenhower, or MacArthur, or of any of the renowned leaders of today's great Army, be sure to understand that officers are not expected to become "supermen." But they are required to be individuals of integrity, of unquestioned loyalty to their country, of courage both mental and physical, and of high professional competence. Their acts and their achievements should help to create in the minds of all thoughtful observ-

---

*In military actions, choices may not be sharply defined. In our Army, there are two ever-present responsibilities of a commander which may seem, at times, to oppose one another:

First, the requirement for accomplishment of mission; second, the safety and preservation of the command.

Quoting General Wolfe before Quebec, in 1759: *"Next to valour, the best qualities in a military man are vigilance and caution."*

The truth must be understood. Prompt, decisive action—so strongly advocated—is never to be confused with ill-conceived, foolhardy action with needless sacrifice of lives. "Aggressiveness" which invites severe, avoidable losses, is not invited by the principle. Wisdom must accompany the swiftest action.

ers that they possess these attributes. This is the "image" of national importance, to which each officer contributes to a degree greater than he or she may realize.

LOOKING FORWARD

Why is the individual and corps image of officers so important? Because a sound image is essential for effective leadership. Good soldiers stay with good leaders, and satisfied soldiers re-enlist. Or they return to their civilian vocations with pride in their service. The nation's military missions require an abundance of dedicated, capable, trusted, respected officers, noncommissioned officers and other grades who can surely be relied upon to get the jobs done, wherever they occur, and however prolonged or difficult the task.

The Army places its greatest trust and its highest expectations upon the capabilities and the determination of its officers and enlisted personnel. They must have the most effective weapons and equipment, of course. There must be an adequate allowance of time for training and for development of teamwork. When this stage of readiness has been attained, and missions have been assigned in combat or in support of combat objectives, it is the officer who is the leader. In time of combat, missions involve real hazard, for the enemy is as determined to avoid defeat as we are determined to inflict it. Soldiers fight best when they are led best. They will risk most when they have confidence in the integrity, the professional skill, and the wisdom of the orders of their officers. These intangibles are included in the image formed day by day in the minds of noncommissioned officers and soldiers as they observe their officers, and in the minds of junior officers as they observe their seniors. Be sure this truth is understood. Then strive to earn an "image" of which you may be proud. Battles are won, and peace restored, by officers, noncommissioned officers and soldiers, working together in the attainment of national objectives. The need for a wholesome national image of the corps of officers should be clear.

As we look into the 1980s, and the years which extend beyond, it is wise to glance again upon Robert Burns and evaluate ourselves according to his ageless wisdom—*to see ourselves as others see us.* Weapons will change through these coming years, and techniques will be modified as swiftly as increased knowledge will require. The officers of these coming years must keep pace. They must continue to provide military leadership for the nation's security and the completion of its military missions. The actions which win the approval of soldiers, and the motivations which encourage them to give their finest service, will remain unchanged. The officer who aspires highly will observe the importance of the simple virtues of integrity, of loyalty, of knowing his or her job, and demonstrating the courage to act. Whether you are in your first or your twentieth assignment, you must give your best. Your image will form progressively as the result of what you are and what you do. There can never be decrease in the importance of these truths.

This chapter has been developed to assist thoughtful officers to prepare themselves to stand with pride and confidence beside thousands of their fellow officers of the Army and the sister services, from all components and all origins of initial appointment, in dedicated national service. They are to be found in abundant numbers. As long as our nation possesses them, it is secure. They are citizens of character. Persons who know their jobs. Dependable individuals. They are men and women of action with courage to act swiftly and wisely when action is required. Their image will be lasting and it will be good. It is for such people of the present and the future for whom this chapter has been written. They are the ones who count.

EPILOGUE

Any man's world-view becomes more generous and imagi-
native and liberated when he succeeds, if only for the time
being, in seeing through the eyes of others.—Irwin Edman

AS A SENIOR NCO SEES IT*

I feel a tinge of regret that I am not young enough to be sitting out there as one of you. You have so many years of challenge and adventure to look forward to. So many of these years are behind me.

Soon you will meet your platoon sergeants, your first sergeants, your sergeants major, your other noncommissioned officers and your troops. What do we expect from you as officers, commanders, leaders?

We expect of you unassailable personal integrity and the highest of morals. We expect you to maintain the highest state of personal appearance. We expect you to be fair—to be consistent—to have dignity, but not aloofness—to have compassion and understanding—to treat each soldier as an individual, with individual problems.

And we expect you to have courage—the courage of your convictions—the courage to stand up and be counted—to defend your men when they have followed your orders, even when your orders were in error—to assume the blame when you are wrong.

We expect you to stick out your chin and say, "This man is worthy of promotion, and I want him promoted." And we expect you to have even greater courage and say, "This man is not qualified and he will be promoted over my dead body!" Gentlemen, I implore you do not promote a man because he is a nice guy, because he has a wife and five kids, because he has money problems, because he has a bar bill. If he is not capable of performing the duties of his grade, do not do him and us the injustice of advancing him in grade. When he leaves you, or you leave him, he becomes someone else's problem!

Gentlemen, we expect you to have courage in the face of danger. Many of you will soon be in Vietnam where there are no safe rear echelons. During your tour, opportunities will arise for you to display personal courage and leadership. Opportunities could arise from which you may emerge as heroes. A hero is an individual who is faced with an undesirable situation and employs whatever means at his disposal to make the situation tenable or to nullify or negate it.

Do not display recklessness and expose yourself and your men to unnecessary risks that will reduce their normal chance of survival. This will only shake their confidence in your judgment.

Now gentlemen, you know what we expect from you. What can you expect from us?

From a few of us, you can expect antagonism, a "Prove yourself" attitude.

From a few of us who had the opportunity to be officers, and didn't have the guts and motivation to accept the challenge, you can expect resentment.

---

*An address by Sergeant Major John G. Stepanek, U. S. Army Transportation School, Fort Eustis, Virginia. Credit is extended to ARMY DIGEST, August 1967.

Other discussions which relate in some degree to the subject are in Chapter 1, *The Code of the Army Officer*, in its THE OFFICER'S RELATIONS WITH ENLISTED PERSONNEL; Chapter 2, *Arrival at a New Station*, under its main heading, THE EARLY DUTY DAYS; Chapter 16, *Responsibilities of Command*, in the discussion TAKING CARE OF YOUR SOLDIERS; Chapter 18, *New Duty Assignment*, with special reference to MAKING THE BEST POSSIBLE FIRST IMPRESSION.

From a few of us old timers, you can expect tolerance.

But from most of us you can expect loyalty to your position, devotion to our cause, admiration for your honest effort—courage to match your courage, guts to match your guts—endurance to match your endurance—motivation to match your motivation—esprit to match your esprit—a desire for achievement to match your desire for achievement.

You can expect a love of God, a love of country, and a love of duty to match your love of God, your love of country, and your love of duty.

We won't mind the heat if you sweat with us. We won't mind the cold if you shiver with us. And when our cigarettes are gone, we won't mind quitting smoking after your cigarettes are gone.

And if the mission requires, we will storm the very gates of hell, right behind you!

Gentlemen, you don't accept us; we were here first. We accept you, and when we do, you'll know. We won't beat drums, or carry you off the drill field on our shoulders. But, maybe at a company party, we'll raise a canteen cup of beer and say, "Lieutenant, you're O.K." Just like that.

Remember one thing. Very few noncommissioned officers were awarded stripes without showing somebody something, sometime, somewhere. If your platoon sergeant is mediocre, if he is slow to assume responsibility, if he shies away from you, maybe sometime not too long ago someone refused to trust him, someone failed to support his decisions, someone shot him down when he was right. Internal wounds heal slowly; internal scars fade more slowly.

Your orders appointing you as officers in the United States Army appointed you to command. No orders, no letters, no insignia of rank can appoint you as leaders. Leadership is an intangible thing; leaders are made, they are not born. Leadership is developed within yourselves.

You do not wear leadership on your sleeves, on your shoulders, on your caps or on your calling cards. Be you lieutenants or generals, we're the guys you've got to convince and we'll meet you more than halfway.

You are leaders in an Army in which we have served for so many years, and you will help us defend the country we have loved for so many years.

I wish you happiness, luck and success in the exciting and challenging years that lie ahead.

May God bless you all!

4
Military Courtesy

Life is not so short but that there is always time enough for courtesy.—Ralph Waldo Emerson.

Courtesy is essential in human relationships. It stimulates harmonious association of individuals, smooths the conduct of affairs, and adds a welcome note to all manner of human contacts, civilian as well as military. It pertains to wholesome relationships between juniors and seniors, seniors and juniors, between young and old—with all persons. The importance of favorable impressions of others is discussed in Chapter Three, *The Officer Image.* Courtesy includes as an essential element a full and proper appreciation of the rights of others. Military courtesy includes special acts and ceremonial procedures which are prescribed in official regulations.

Our subject is far more inclusive than the newcomer or the poorly informed person considers to be the case. It includes the respects paid to the National Flag and the National Anthem; the courtesies appropriate for a soldier or a junior officer to extend to a fellow officer or a senior officer, as well as the answering courtesies paid as a matter of course by the senior; the honors extended to high military or civilian dignitaries; and finally, the honors and respectful procedures extended to the military dead. There are many things to learn about military courtesy, and by learning replace the embarrassments of ignorance with the confidence of knowledge.

The official sources from which the subjects discussed in the chapter are extracted are the following documents:

FM 22–5
AR 600–25

AR 840–10
DA Pam 600–5.

The courtesies enjoyed within the service include as a matter of course all those common acts of civility, good breeding, and thoughtfulness which are observed by ladies and gentlemen of the American scene. There are related subjects discussed in this volume of special interest to the officer and the officer's family. Reference is made to Chapter Five, *Customs of the Service;* Chapter Six, *The Social Side of Army Life;* and to add depth to understanding give thoughtful consideration to Chapter One, *The Code of the Army Officer.* When those chapters have been understood, you should see more clearly that there is nothing wrong with being military or with military courtesy; you will understand that the prescribed courtesies are a part of the ceremonial procedures which contribute color and dignity to our lives; that they are a part of the discipline needed for the attack to succeed and the defense to hold; and a part of the comradeship which binds together service members of all grades and ages who share the common responsibility of the nation's security.

An officer is expected to be a lady or a gentleman, and ladies and gentlemen have been defined as persons who are never intentionally rude.

THE CORRECT USE OF TITLES

Each member of the Army has a military grade, private to General of the Army, and this grade becomes his or her military title by force of regulation and custom. In official documents a member's grade, or title, always accompanies his or her name. In conversation it is also used, and below are listed several illustrations. Through custom and usage, military titles are used between civilians and the military just as custom has established the usage of "Doctor," or "Professor," or "Governor."

A person who has attained a military title carries it permanently, if so choosing, including into retirement, unless demoted to a lower grade, or military status is terminated.

Titles of Commissioned Officers. Lieutenants are addressed officially as "Lieutenant." The adjectives "First" and "Second" are not used except in written communications.

Other officers are addressed or referred to by their titles. In conversation and in nonofficial correspondence, (other than in the address itself) brigadier generals, major generals, and lieutenant generals are usually referred to and addressed as "General." Lieutenant colonels, under the same conditions, are addressed as "Colonel."

Senior officers frequently address juniors as "Smith" or "Jones," but this does not give the junior the privilege of addressing the senior in any way other than by the senior's proper title.*

"Ma'am" may be used in addressing a female officer under circumstances when the use of "sir" would be appropriate in the case of a male officer.

All chaplains are officially addressed as "Chaplain" regardless of their military grade or professional title.

Warrant Officers. The Warrant Officer formally ranks below Second Lieutenant and above Cadet. He or she is extended the same privileges and respect as a commissioned officer and differs only in that there are certain regulated restrictions on command functions. The Warrant Officer is the Army's top-grade specialist and is addressed as "Mister" or "Miss," as appropriate. Under less formal situations, warrant officers are often addressed as "Chief."

For a timely comment on the inappropriate use of first names see Chapter Fourteen, Evaluation Reports, "Personal Characteristics Which Influence Careers."

Titles of Cadets. Cadets of the United States Military Academy are addressed as "Cadet" officially and in written communications. Under less formal situations, they are addressed as "Mister" or "Miss."

Noncommissioned Officers and Specialists. Sergeants Major are addressed as "Sergeant Major." A First Sergeant is addressed as "First Sergeant." Other sergeants, regardless of grade, are addressed simply as "Sergeant," while a Corporal is addressed as "Corporal." All specialists are addressed as "Specialist." Officers generally address privates as "Jones" or "Smith." The full titles of the enlisted members are used in official communications.

Use of Titles by Retired Personnel. Individuals retired from the armed services not on active duty are authorized to use their titles socially, and in connection with commercial enterprises, subject to prescribed limitations. Official signatures will include the designated retired status after the grade, thus: "USA Retired" will be used by members on the U.S. Army Retired List (Regulars); "AUS Retired" will be used by those borne on the Army of the United States List, and non-regulars on the Temporary Disability Retired List. (DA Pam 600–5, *Retired Army Personnel Handbook.*)

THE SEVERAL MILITARY SALUTES

History of the Military Salute. Men of arms have used some form of the military salute as an exchange of greeting since the earliest times. It has been preserved and its use continued in all modern armies which inherit their military traditions from the Age of Chivalry. The method of rendering the salute has varied through the ages, as it still varies in form between the armies of today. Whatever the form it has taken, it has always pertained to military personnel, and its use definitely restricted to those in good standing.

In the Age of Chivalry the knights were all mounted and wore steel armor which covered the body completely, including the head and face. When two friendly knights met it was the custom for each to raise the visor and expose his face to the view of the other. This was always done with the right hand, the left being used to hold the reins. It was a significant gesture of friendship and confidence, since it exposed the features and also removed the right hand— the sword hand—from the vicinity of the weapon. Also, in ancient times the freemen (soldiers) of Europe were allowed to carry arms; when two freemen met, each would raise his right hand to show that he held no weapons in it and that the meeting was a friendly one. Slaves were not allowed to carry arms, and they passed freemen without the exchange of a greeting. In the Middle Ages gentlemen often went about clothed in heavy capes under which swords were carried; upon meeting a friend, the cloak was thrown back by raising the right arm, thus disclosing that the right hand was not on the sword hilt. The civilian counterpart of the salute is manifested in various ways such as raising the hand when greeting a friend, tipping the hat when meeting a lady, and using a sign of recognition between lodge members. This sign is always one of greeting between friends and is given willingly. The military salute is given in the same manner—that of pride in giving recognition to a comrade in the honorable profession of arms. The knightly gesture of raising the hand to the visor came to be recognized as the proper greeting between soldiers, and was continued even after modern firearms had made steel armor a thing of the past. The military salute is today, as it seems always to have been, a unique form of exchange of greeting between military personnel.

The Different Forms of the Salute. There are several forms in which the prescribed salutes are rendered. The officer normally uses the hand salute; however, when under arms he or she uses the salute prescribed for the weapon with which armed. Under certain circumstances, when in civilian clothes, the member salutes by placing the right hand over the heart (see illustration); if a male officer is wearing a headdress, he salutes by first removing the headdress and holding it in his right hand such that the hand is over the heart while the headdress is over the left shoulder.

In this chapter, unless stated otherwise, the hand salute is intended.

When to Use the Hand Salute and the Salute with Arms (AR 600–25). All Army personnel in uniform are required to salute at all times when they meet and recognize persons entitled to the salute, except in public conveyances such as trains and buses or in public places such as theaters, or when a salute would be manifestly inappropriate or impractical.

Salutes will be exchanged between officers (commissioned and warrant) and between officers (commissioned and warrant) and enlisted personnel. Salutes will be exchanged with personnel of the United States Army, the Navy, the Air Force, the Marine Corps, and the Coast Guard entitled to the salute. It is customary to salute officers of friendly foreign nations when recognized as such. Civilians may be saluted by persons in uniform when appropriate, but the uniform hat or cap will not be raised as a form of salutation.

Military personnel under arms will render the salute prescribed for the weapon with which they are armed, whether or not that weapon ordinarily is prescribed as part of their equipment.

If the exchange of salutes is otherwise appropriate, it is customary, although optional, for military members in civilian clothing to exchange salutes upon recognition. Civilian personnel, including civilian guards, do not render the hand salute to military personnel or to other civilian personnel.

Except in formation, when a salute is prescribed the individual either faces toward the person or colors saluted or turns the head so as to observe the person or colors saluted.

Covered or uncovered, salutes are exchanged in the same manner.

If running, a person comes to a walk before saluting.

The smartness with which the officer or soldier gives the salute is held to indicate the degree of pride the member has in his or her military responsibilities. A careless or half-hearted salute is discourteous.

Methods of Saluting Used by Officers. The hand salute is the usual method. While in most instances it is rendered while standing or marching at attention, it may be rendered while seated, *e.g.,* an officer seated at a desk who acknowledges the salute of an officer or soldier who is making a report.

The salute by placing the right hand over the heart is used under three conditions. At a military funeral all personnel dressed in civilian clothes use this form of salute in rendering courtesies to the deceased. Male members of the services in civilian clothes and *uncovered* (without headdress) and female members in civilian clothes, *uncovered* or *covered* (with headress), salute this way during *The National Anthem, To the Color,* or *Hail to the Chief.* While in the same dress, this salute is used in paying homage to the national flag or color. Males in civilian clothing who are *covered* stand at attention, holding the hand over the heart with the headdress held in the right hand over the left shoulder as a courtesy to the National Anthem or to the national flag or color.

| Exchanging salutes when in civilian clothes with or without headdress. | Saluting the flag or national anthem when in civilian clothes without headdress. | Saluting the flag or national anthem when in civilian clothes with headdress. |

FORMS OF THE SALUTE, WHEN IN CIVILIAN CLOTHES.

Execution of the Hand Salute. Do you *really* wish to salute correctly; to demonstrate to others that you are an officer; to show that this sign of recognition and greeting between military members means something to you? You may read the technical details below, but set about it in this manner. Before the instant arrives to render the salute, stand or walk erectly with head up, chin up, and pull in on the stomach muscles. Look squarely and frankly at the person to be saluted. If you are returning the salute of a soldier, execute the movements of the salute in the cadence of marching, *ONE, TWO.* If you are saluting a superior officer, execute the first movement and HOLD the position until the salute is acknowledged, and then complete your salute by dropping the hand smartly to your side. Do these things correctly and you will derive many rewards. Your soldiers will be quick to notice it, and vie with you in efforts to outdo their officer—a particularly healthy reaction. Thus you may set the example which may then be extended to other matters.

To execute the hand salute correctly, raise the right hand smartly until the tip of the forefinger touches the lower part of the headdress or forehead above and slightly to the right of the right eye, thumb and fingers extended and joined, palm to the left, upper arm horizontal, forearm inclined at 45°, hand and wrist straight; at the same time turn the head toward the person saluted. To complete the salute, drop the arm to its normal position by the side in one motion, at the same time turning the head and eyes to the front.

The enlisted member or junior officer executes the first movement, holds the position until it is returned, and then executes the second movement.

Accompanying the hand salute with an appropriate greeting, such as "Good Morning, Sir," and its reply "Good Morning, Sergeant," is encouraged.

The salute is rendered within saluting distance, which is defined as the distance within which recognition is easy. It usually does not exceed thirty paces. The salute is begun when about six paces from the person or color saluted or, in case the approach is outside that distance, six paces from the point of nearest approach.

Some of the more frequently observed errors in saluting are these: Failing to hold the position of the salute until it is returned by the officer saluted; failure to look at the person or color saluted; failure to assume the position of attention while saluting; failure to have the thumb and fingers extended and joined, a protruding thumb being especially objectionable; a bent wrist (the hand and wrist should be in the same plane); failure to have the upper arm horizontal. Gross errors include saluting with a cigarette in the right hand or in the mouth or saluting with the left hand in a pocket or returning a salute in a casual or perfunctory manner.

Uncovering. Officers and enlisted personnel under arms as a general rule do not uncover except when:

Seated as a member of or in attendance on a court or board. (Sentinels over prisoners do not uncover.)

Entering places of divine worship.

Indoors when not on duty and it is desired to remain informal.

In attendance at an official reception.

Interpretations of "Indoors" and "Outdoors." The term "outdoors" includes such buildings as drill halls, gymnasiums, and other roofed inclosures used for drill or exercise of troops. Theater marquees, covered walks, and other shelters open to the sides where a hat may be worn are also considered outdoors.

When the word "indoors" is used, it is construed to mean offices, hallways, mess halls, kitchens, orderly rooms, amusement rooms, bathrooms, libraries, dwellings, or other places of abode.

Meaning of the Term "Under Arms." The expression "under arms" will be understood to mean with arms in hand or having attached to the person a hand arm or the equipment pertaining directly to the arm, such as cartridge belt, pistol holster, or automatic rifle belt.

Cannon Salute. In addition to the salutes rendered by individuals, the regulations (AR 600–25) prescribe the occasions and the procedures for rendering cannon salutes.

A salute with cannon (towed, self-propelled, or tank mounted) will be fired with a commissioned officer present and directing the firing. Salutes will not be fired between retreat and reveille, on Sundays, or on national holidays (excluding Memorial and Independence Days) unless, in the discretion of the officer directing the honors, international courtesy or the occasion requires the exception. They will be rendered at the first available opportunity thereafter, if still appropriate. The interval between rounds is normally three seconds.

The salute to the Union consists of firing one gun for each State. It is fired at 1200 hours, Independence Day, at all Army installations provided with necessary equipment.

The national salute consists of 21 guns. It is fired at 1200 hours on Memorial Day. The national flag, displayed at half-staff from reveille until noon on this day, is then hoisted to the top of the staff and so remains until retreat. In conjunction with the playing of appropriate music, this is a tribute to honored dead.

Cannon salutes are rendered on the occasion of the death and funeral of the President and the Vice President of the United States, and other high civil and military dignitaries, as prescribed in AR 600–25.

The number of guns and the accompanying honors to be rendered to high dignitaries are shown in a chart later in this chapter.

The flag of the United States, national color or national standard, is always displayed at the time of firing a salute except when firing a salute to the Union on the day of the funeral of a President, Ex-President, or President-Elect. On these occasions, the salute will be fired at 5-second intervals immediately following lowering of the flag at retreat. Personnel will not salute.

COURTESIES RENDERED BY JUNIORS TO SENIORS

Application of Saluting Rules. The general rules for exchange of salutes are stated in an earlier paragraph.

Covered or uncovered, salutes are exchanged in the same manner.

The salute is rendered but once if the senior remains in the immediate vicinity and no conversation takes place.

A group of enlisted personnel or officers within the confines of military posts, camps, or stations, and not in formation, on the approach of a more senior officer, is called to attention by the first person noticing the senior officer; if in formation, by the one in charge. If out of doors and not in formation, they all salute; in formation, the salute is rendered by the person in charge. If indoors, not under arms, they uncover.

Drivers of vehicles salute only when the vehicle is halted. Gate guards salute recognized officers in all vehicles. Salutes otherwise are not required by or to personnel in vehicles. Members in civilian attire need not exchange salutes. Also, military headgear need not be worn while in other than official vehicles.

Organization and detachment commanders (commissioned and noncommissioned) salute officers of higher grades by bringing the organization to attention before saluting, except when in the field.

At the pay table, each enlisted member, as his or her name is called, answers "Here" in a loud clear tone, steps up to the table, salutes the paymaster, and signs the military pay voucher. The individual counts the money or verifies the amount of the check, but does not touch it until the paymaster has finished. The soldier then picks it up, counts it, and leaves the room. The paymaster does not return the salute of the soldier as he or she is too much occupied with paymaster duties.

In making reports at formations, the person making the report salutes first regardless of rank. An example of this is the case of a battalion commander rendering a report to the adjutant at a ceremony.

Members of the Army are urged to be meticulous in rendering salutes to and in returning salutes from fellow Army members and personnel of the sister services. Such soldierly attitudes enhance the feeling of respect which all should feel toward comrades in arms. *The salute must never be given in a casual or perfunctory manner.*

When NOT to Salute. Salutes are NOT rendered by individuals in the following cases:

An enlisted member in ranks and not at attention comes to attention when addressed by an officer.

Details (and individuals) at work do not salute. The officer or noncommissioned officer in charge, if not actively engaged at the time, salutes or acknowledges salutes for the entire detail.

When actively engaged in games such as baseball, tennis, or golf, one does not salute.

While crossing a thoroughfare, not on a military reservation, when traffic requires undivided attention.

In churches, theaters, or places of public assemblage, or in a public conveyance, salutes are not exchanged.

When carrying articles with both hands, or when otherwise so occupied as to make saluting impractical.

When on the march in combat, or under simulated combat conditions.

No salute is rendered to persons by a member of the guard who is engaged in the performance of a specific duty, the proper execution of which would prevent saluting.

A sentinel armed with a pistol does not salute after challenging. He or she stands at *Raise pistol* until the challenged party has passed.

The driver of a vehicle in motion is not required to salute.

Indoors, salutes are not exchanged except when reporting to a senior.

Reporting to a Superior Officer in His or Her Office. When reporting to a superior officer in his or her office, the junior (unless under arms) removes any headdress, knocks, and enters when told to do so. Upon entering, the junior marches up to within about two paces of the officer's desk, halts, salutes, and reports in this manner, for example: "Sir, Private Jones reports to Captain Smith" or "Sir, Lieutenant Brown reports to the Battalion Commander." After the report, conversation is carried on in the first or second person. When the business is completed, the junior salutes, executes about face, and withdraws. A junior uncovers (unless under arms) on entering a room where a senior officer is present.

Courtesies Exchanged When an Officer Addresses a Soldier. In general, when a conversation takes place between an officer and a soldier the following procedure is correct: Salutes are exchanged; the conversation is completed; salutes are again exchanged. *Exceptions:* An enlisted person in ranks comes to attention and does not salute. Indoors, salutes are not exchanged except when reporting to an officer.

Procedure When an Officer Enters a Messroom or Mess Tent. When an officer enters the messroom or mess tent, enlisted personnel seated at meals remain seated at ease and continue eating unless the officer directs otherwise. An individual addressed by the officer ceases eating and sits at attention until completion of the conversation. In an officers mess, although other courtesies are observed through custom, the formalities prescribed for enlisted men and women are not in effect.

Procedure When an Officer Enters a Squad Room or Tent. In a squad room or tent, individuals rise, uncover (if unarmed), and stand at attention when an officer enters. If more than one person is present, the first to perceive the officer calls, "Attention."* In officer's quarters, such courtesies are not observed.

Entering Automobiles and Small Boats. Military persons enter automobiles and small boats in inverse order of rank; that is, the senior enters an automobile or boat last and leaves first. Juniors, although entering the automobile first, take their appropriate seat in the car. The senior is always on the right.

---

*On suitable occasions the officer commands "Rest" or "At Ease" when expecting to remain in the room and does not desire them to remain at Attention.

OFFICIAL CALLS

Official calls are those prescribed by AR 600–25. They are in contrast to social calls, which are discussed in Chapter Six *The Social Side of Army Life*. We quote the official regulation:

GENERAL. The exchange of visits of courtesy is the primary basis for the establishment of those social contacts among officers of the Army essential to the development of that mutual understanding, respect, confidence, and teamwork which together with professional competence and physical ability insures adequate military leadership at all echelons. The present size and complexity of the Army may preclude the exchange of courtesy calls in accordance with traditional concepts. However, the established customs of the service in this respect should be adhered to by all concerned to the extent practicable. Failure to follow these customs of official and polite society may be prejudicial to the best interests of the service. Commanders will adhere as closely as possible to the principles outlined in this regulation but may exercise individual discretion as to the extent to which these principles can be observed in a given situation. Individual officers will obtain guidance as to the commander's wishes from the organization or installation adjutant, the commander's aide, or the executive officer of their agency, as applicable.

Visits of courtesy will be paid promptly and should be of approximately 15 minutes' duration. They should be made at a time presumably convenient to the officer being visited.

Visits of courtesy other than those made by departing officers should be returned in person within 10 days except in the following instances:

In cases where the numbers are so great that this is not possible, a general officer occupying the position of a major general or higher may designate a staff officer to return the courtesy visit of an officer below general officer grade.

In case of sickness or other unavoidable circumstances, such visits may be omitted. In such cases the officer should send his visiting card and a brief note expressing his regrets and the cause of his failure to pay the visit.

Calls may be returned by senior officers through a mass social function.

Courtesy visits are not required in connection with short absence on leave or temporary duty away from a home station.

MEANING OF TERMS. The terms "commander" and "commanding officer" as used in this regulation include chiefs of staff sections, installation commanders, division commanders, and heads of branches, offices, and agencies of comparable size.

VISITING CARDS. Visiting cards are used during calls as an individual optional courtesy. The grade of rank indicated on visiting cards will be the grade of rank in which the officer is serving and the service designated as United States Army. The visiting cards of chaplains will not designate grade of rank. Indication of branch is optional and component will not be shown. Size and type are optional; however, the most commonly accepted size is $3\frac{1}{4}$ by $1\frac{1}{2}$ inches, with shaded Roman engraving.

BY NEWLY ARRIVED OFFICERS. A newly arrived officer who will remain at an installation for over 24 hours will pay a visit of courtesy to his immediate superior and that officer's immediate superior. For example, a lieutenant assigned to an infantry battalion would call upon his company commander and his battalion commander. If the arriving officer is of higher rank than the ranking commander of the installation, the latter will pay the first visit. Official calls should be made at the offices of those called upon, within 48 hours after the officer's arrival. Courtesy visits to commanders will be repeated at their quarters as soon as practicable after arrival, at proper calling hours; the newly arrived officer's spouse should accompany him, unless, by reason of duty assignment, distances to be traveled make such visit impractical. Officers should inquire of the adjutant of the organization or installation, or the executive officer, as to normal calling hours.

BY DEPARTING OFFICERS. Officers who are about to depart permanently from an installation or unit will inquire of the adjutant thereof as to the visits of courtesy which should be made.

TO NEWLY ARRIVED OFFICERS. Each officer assigned or attached for duty to a company or battery; battalion, group, or comparable headquarters; division of a staff section of a corps, army or comparable headquarters; or branch of a staff section of a higher headquarters, except the commanders referred to above will pay a welcoming courtesy visit to each officer who has more recently arrived under permanent assignment to duty in the same organizational element.

ON NEW YEAR'S DAY. It is customary for all officers of a unit, organization or installation to call upon the commanding officer on New Year's Day. Usually the commander will designate a convenient hour and place for receiving such visits.

COURTESIES TO THE NATIONAL FLAG AND NATIONAL ANTHEM

The Flag of the United States. There are four names in use for the flag of the United States: *flag, color, standard, ensign.*

The *national color,* carried by dismounted units, measures 3' hoist by 4' fly and is trimmed on three sides with golden yellow fringe 2½ inches in width. The *standard,* identical to the *color,* is the name traditionally used by mounted, motorized, or mechanized units. The *ensign* is the naval term for the national flag (or flag indicating nationality) of any size flown from ships, small boats, and airships. When we speak of "flags" we do not mean colors, standards, or ensigns.

There are four common sizes of our national flag. The *garrison flag* is displayed on holidays and special occasions. It is 20 feet by 38 feet. The *post flag,* 10 feet by 19 feet, is for general use. The *storm flag,* 5 feet by 9 feet 6 inches is displayed during stormy weather. The *grave decorating flag* is 7 inches hoist by 11 inches fly.

Organization Colors. Regiments and separate battalions, whose organization is fixed by Tables of Organization, are authorized organization colors symbolic of their branch and past history. Such units are "color bearing organizations". The size is the same as the *national color.* The word "color", when used alone, means the national color; the term "colors" means the national color and the organization or individual color.

Individual Colors. Individual colors, 4 feet 4 inches hoist by 5 feet 6 inches fly, are authorized the President, Vice President, cabinet members and their assistants, the Chairman of the Joint Chiefs of Staff, the Chief of Staff and the Vice Chief of Staff, United States Army.

Pledge to the Flag. According to Congressional Resolution, 22 December 1942, the following pledge of allegiance should be rendered while standing, with the right hand over the heart:

> I pledge allegiance to the flag of the United States of America and to the republic for which it stands, one nation under God, indivisible, with liberty and justice for all.

Reveille and Retreat. The daily ceremonies of reveille and retreat constitute a dignified homage to the national flag at the beginning of the day, when it is raised, and at the end of the day, when it is lowered. Installation commanders direct the time of sounding reveille and retreat.

At every installation garrisoned by troops other than caretaking detachments, the flag will be hoisted at the sound of the first note of reveille. At the last note of retreat, a gun will be fired if the ceremony is on a military reservation, at which time the band or field music will play the National Anthem or sound "To The Color" and the flag will start to be lowered. The lowering of the flag will be regulated so as to be completed at the last note of the music. The same respect will be observed by all military personnel whether the National Anthem is played or "To The Color" is sounded.

The Flag at Half-Staff. The national flag is displayed at half-staff on Memorial Day as a salute to the honored dead, and upon the death and funeral of military personnel and high civilian dignitaries (AR 600–25).

When the flag is displayed at half-staff it is first hoisted to the top of the staff and then lowered to the half-staff position. Before lowering the flag it is again raised to the top of the staff. For an unguyed flagstaff of one piece, the middle point of the hoist of the flag should be midway between the top of the staff and the foot thereof.

Memorial Day. On Memorial Day (the last Monday in May) the national flag will be displayed at half-staff from reveille until noon at all Army installations. Immediately before noon the band will play an appropriate air, and at 1200 hours the national salute of 21 guns will be fired at all installations provided with the necessary equipment for firing salutes. At the conclusion of the salute, the flag will be hoisted to the top of the staff and will remain so until retreat. When hoisted to the top of the staff, the flag will be saluted by playing appropriate patriotic music by a band or a bugler or from a recording, depending upon availability. In this manner, tribute is rendered the honored dead.

Independence Day. On Independence Day (4 July), a 50-gun salute to the Union commemorative of the Declaration of Independence will be fired at 1200 hours at all Army installations provided with the necessary equipment for firing salutes.

When Independence Day occurs on a Sunday, the salute will be fired the following day.

Flag Day. Flag Day is celebrated on the 14th of June, upon proclamation by the President which calls upon officials of the Government to display the flag on all Government buildings and which urges the people to observe the day as the adoption on June 14, 1777, by the Continental Congress, of the Stars and Stripes as the official flag of the United States of America.

Salute to the President's Flag. When the President of the United States, aboard any vessel or craft flying the President's Flag, passes an Army installation which is equipped to fire salutes, the installation commander will cause the national salute to be fired. (See exceptions stated earlier under the discussion of Cannon Salutes which would exclude firing this particular salute between retreat and reveille.)

Salute to Passing Colors. When passing or being passed by the uncased national color, military personnel render honors by executing a salute appropriate to their dress and formation as indicated previously. If indoors and not in formation, personnel assume the position of attention, but do not salute. If the colors are cased, honors are not required.

Reception of an Officer on Board a Naval Vessel. The salutes to be exchanged upon boarding a naval vessel and leaving a naval vessel are prescribed in the following paragraph of United States Navy Regulations, to which all members of the Army visiting a naval vessel will conform (AR 600–25):

2108. Salutes to the National Ensign.

1. Each person in the naval service, upon coming on board a ship of the Navy, shall salute the national ensign if it is flying. He shall stop on reaching the upper platform of the accommodation ladder, or the shipboard end of the brow, face the national ensign, and render the salute, after which he shall salute the officer of the deck. On leaving the ship, he shall render the salutes in inverse order. The officer of the deck shall return both salutes in each case.

2. When passing by or passing the national ensign being carried, uncased in

a military formation, all persons in the naval service shall salute. Persons in vehicles or boats shall follow the procedure prescribed for such persons during colors.

3. The salutes prescribed in this article shall also be rendered to foreign national ensigns and aboard foreign men-of-war.

For further information as to Navy courtesies and customs see *Navy Customs Army Officers Should Know,* Chapter Five.

Courtesies to the National Anthem. *Outdoors.* Whenever and wherever the National Anthem, To the Color, or Hail to the Chief is played—

At the first note all dismounted personnel in uniform and not in formation, within saluting distance of the flag, will face the flag, or the music if the flag is not in view, salute, and maintain the salute until the last note of the music is sounded. Men not in uniform will remove the headdress with the right hand and hold it at the left shoulder with the hand over the heart. If no headdress is involved, stand at attention holding the right hand over the heart. Men in athletic uniform should stand at attention, removing headdress if any. Women not in uniform should salute by placing the right hand over the heart.

Vehicles in motion will be brought to a halt. Persons riding in a passenger car or on a motorcycle will dismount and salute. Occupants of other types of military vehicles and busses remain seated at attention in the vehicle, the individual in charge of each vehicle dismounting and rendering the hand salute. Tank and armored car commanders salute from the vehicle.

The above marks of respect are shown the national anthem of any friendly country when it is played at official occasions.

Indoors. When the National Anthem is played indoors, officers and enlisted personnel stand at attention and face the music, or the flag if one is present. They do not salute unless under arms.

Reveille. At reveille the procedures outlined above will be followed.

The method and personnel required for raising and lowering the flag on a flagstaff are prescribed in *FM 26–5, Interior Guard Duty.*

Dipping the Flag or Colors. The flag of the United States, national color, and national standard are never dipped by way of salute or compliment except by naval vessels. The organizational color or standard will be dipped in salute in all military ceremonies while the United States National Anthem, To the Color, or a foreign national anthem is being played, and when rendering honors to the organizational commander, an individual of higher grade to include foreign dignitaries of higher grade, but in no other case.

The United States Army Flag is considered to be an organizational color and as such is also dipped while the United States National Anthem, *To the Color,* or a foreign national anthem is being played, and when rendering honors to the Chief of Staff of the United States Army, his direct representative, or individual of higher grade to include a foreign dignitary of equivalent or higher grade, but in no other case.

The authorized unit color salutes in all military ceremonies while the National Anthem or *To the Color* is being played and when rendering honors to the organizational commander or an individual of higher rank, but in no other case.

Display and Use of the Flag. International usage forbids the display of the flag of one nation above another nation's in time of peace. When the flags of two or more nations are to be displayed, they should be flown from separate staffs, or from separate halyards, of equal size and on the same level.

The national flag, when not flown from a staff or mast, should always be hung flat, whether indoors or out. It should not be festooned over doorways or arches, nor tied in a bowknot, nor fashioned into a rosette. When used on a rostrum, it should be displayed above and behind the speaker's desk. It should never be used to cover the speaker's desk nor to drape over the front of the platform. For this latter purpose, as well as for decoration in general, bunting of the national colors should be used and the colors should be arranged with the blue above, the white in the middle, and the red below. Under no circumstances should the flag be draped over chairs or benches, nor should any object or emblem of any kind be placed above or upon it, nor should it be hung where it can be easily contaminated or soiled. When carried with other flags the national flag should always be on the right (as color bearers are facing) or in front. The flag of the United States of America should be at the center and at the highest point of the group when a number of flags of States or localities or pennants of societies are grouped and displayed from staffs.

When flown at a military post, or when carried by troops, the national flag is never dipped by way of salute or compliment. The authorized unit color is dipped as a salute when the reviewing officer has the rank of a general officer. This is done by lowering the pike (as the staff of a color is called) to the front so that it makes an angle of about 45 degrees with the ground. The national flag is used to cover the casket at the military funeral of present or former members of the military service. It is placed lengthwise on the casket with the union at the head and over the left shoulder of the deceased. The flag is not lowered into the grave and is not allowed to touch the ground.

The display and use of the flag by civilians or civilian groups is contained in Public Law 829—77th Congress as amended by Public Law 344—94th Congress.

DISPLAY OF UNITED NATIONS FLAG

There are no United States laws or policies adopted by the United Nations which cause conflict in the display of the United States Flag in conjunction with the United Nations Flag.

When the two flags are displayed together the United States flag is on the right, best identified as "the marching right." This is in accordance with United States law. The United Nations flag code states it can be on either side of a national flag without being subordinate to that flag. Both flags should be of the same size and displayed at the same height.

It should be noted that the United Nations flag may be displayed at military installations of the United States or carried by United States troops only on very specific occasions such as the visit of high dignitaries of the United Nations, when the United Nations or high dignitaries thereof are to be honored, or as authorized by the President (AR 840–10).

PERSONAL SALUTES AND HONORS TO DISTINGUISHED MILITARY AND CIVIL OFFICIALS

Certain military and civil officials in high position, including foreign officials, are accorded personal honors consisting of cannon salutes, ruffles and flourishes played by field music, and the National Anthem of our country or of the foreign country, the General's March, or march played by the band. These honors are extended upon presentation of the escort and as part of the parade

Entitlement to Honors—Grade, title, or office	Number of Guns		Ruffles and Flourishes	Music*
	Arrival	Departure		
President	21	21	4	National anthem or "Hail to the Chief," as appropriate.
Ex-President or President-elect	21	21	4	National anthem.
Sovereign or Chief of State of a foreign country or member of a reigning royal family	21	21	4	National anthem of foreign country.
Vice President	19	. .	4	"Hail Columbia"
Speaker of the House of Representatives	19	. .	4	March.
American or foreign ambassador, or high commissioner while in country to which accredited	19	. .	4	National anthem of United States or official's country.
Premier or prime minister	19	. .	4	National anthem of United States or official's country.
Secretary of Defense	19	19	4	March.
Cabinet member, President protempore of Senate, governor of a State, or Chief Justice of the United States	19	. .	4	Do.
Deputy Secretary of Defense	19	19	4	Do.
Secretary of the Army	19	19	4	Do.
Secretary of the Navy or Air Force	19	19	4	Do.
Director of Defense Research and Engineering	19	19	4	March.
Chairman, Joint Chiefs of Staff	19	19	4	General's or Admiral's march, as appropriate.
Chief of Staff, United States Army; Chief of Naval Operations; Chief of Staff, United States Air Force; or Commandant of the Marine Corps	19	19	4	Do.
General of the Army, Fleet Admiral, or General of the Air Force	19	19	4	Do.
Assistant Secretaries of Defense and General Counsel of the Department of Defense	17	17	4	March.
General or admiral	17	17	4	General's or Admiral's march, as appropriate.
Governor of a Territory or foreign possession within the limits of his jurisdiction	17	. .	4	March.
Chairman of a Committee of Congress	17	. .	4	Do.
Under Secretary of the Army	17	17	4	Do.
Under Secretary of the Navy or Air Force	17	17	4	Do.
Assistant Secretaries of the Army.	17	17	4	Do.
Assistant Secretaries of the Navy or Air Force	17	17	4	Do.
American envoys or ministers and foreign envoys or ministers accredited to the United States	15	. .	3	March.
Lieutenant general or vice admiral	15	. .	3	General's or Admiral's march.
Major general or rear admiral (upper half)	13	. .	2	Do.
American ministers resident and ministers resident accredited to the United States	13	. .	2	March.
American charges d'affaires and charges d'affaires accredited to the United States	11	. .	1	Do.
Brigadier general or rear admiral (lower half)	11	. .	1	General's or Admiral's march.
Consuls general accredited to the United States	11	. .	. .	March.

*The music indicated in the table will follow the ruffles and flourishes without pause. Unless otherwise directed, civilian officials of the Department of Defense and military departments receive the 32-bar medley in the trio of "The Stars and Stripes Forever."

Foreign military persons holding positions equivalent to those of Department of Defense and military department officials, both military and civilian listed above, will be rendered the honors to which the equivalent United States official is entitled, regardless of actual military rank. All other military persons will receive the honors due their actual rank or its United States Army equivalent.

A designated representative of an official entitled to honors will be afforded honors based on the representative's rank. (AR 600–25.)

HOW TO DISPLAY THE FLAG.

1. When displayed over the middle of the street, the flag should be suspended vertically with the union to the north in an east and west street, or to the east in a north and south street.

2. When displayed with another flag from crossed staffs, the US flag should be on the right (the flag's own right) and its staff should be in front of the staff of the other flag.

3. When flown at half-mast, the flag should be hoisted to the peak, then lowered to the half-mast position; but before lowering the flag for the day it should again be raised to the peak.

4. When the flags of states or cities or pennants of societies are flown on the same halyard with the US flag, the latter should always be at the peak.

5. When the flag is suspended over a sidewalk from a rope extending from house to pole at the edge of the sidewalk, the flag should be hoisted out from the building, toward the pole, union first.

6. When the flag is displayed from a staff projecting horizontally or at any angle from the window sill, balcony, or front of a building, the union of the flag should go to peak of the staff (unless the flag is to be displayed at half-mast).

7. When the flag is used to cover a casket, it should be so placed that the union is at the head and over the left shoulder. The flag should not be lowered into the grave or allowed to touch the ground.

8. When the flag is displayed other than by being flown from a staff, it should be displayed flat whether indoors or out. When displayed either horizontally or vertically against a wall, the union should be uppermost and to the flag's own right, that is, to the observer's left. When displayed in a window it should be displayed in the same way, that is, with the union or blue field to the left of the observer in the street.

9. When carried in a procession with another flag or flags, the US flag should be either on the marching right, or when there is a line of other flags, in front of the center of that line.

10. When a number of flags of states or cities or pennants of societies are grouped and displayed from staffs with our National flag, the latter should be at the center or at the highest point of the group.

11. When the flags of two or more nations are displayed they should be flown from separate staffs of the same height and the flags should be of approximately equal size. International usage forbids the display of the flag of one nation above that of another nation in time of peace.

or review of troops. The chart (AR 600–25) on page 51 states the specific honors of all persons who may be accorded such honors. A military escort is supplied during their rendition.

Ruffles and Flourishes. Ruffles are played on drums, flourishes on bugles. They are sounded together, once for each star of the general officer being honored and according to the following table of honors for other dignitaries. Ruffles and flourishes are followed by music as prescribed in the table.

Action of the Person Receiving the Honors. It is the usual custom for the person receiving the honors to inspect the escort. The appropriate time to do this is at the conclusion of the honors rendered by the escort upon his or her reception.

During the playing of the ruffles and flourishes and music, as indicated in the chart, the person honored and those accompanying him, if members of the armed forces, salute at the first note of the ruffles and flourishes and remain at the salute until the last note of the music. Persons in civilian clothes salute by uncovering.

Action of Persons Witnessing the Honors. Members of the armed forces who witness the salutes and honors render the hand salute, conforming to the action of the official party. Individuals in civilian clothing uncover.

PRECEDENCE OF MILITARY ORGANIZATIONS IN FORMATION

Whenever two or more organizations of different components of the armed forces appear in the same formation, they take precedence among themselves in order as listed below. This means from right to left in line, the senior organization on the right; and from head to tail of a column, the senior organization at the head (AR 600–25).

Cadets, United States Military Academy
Midshipmen, United States Naval Academy
Cadets, United States Air Force Academy
Cadets, United States Coast Guard Academy
United States Army
United States Marine Corps
United States Navy
United States Air Force
United States Coast Guard
Army National Guard of the United States

Army Reserve
Marine Corps Reserve
Naval Reserve
Air National Guard of the United States
Air Force Reserve
Coast Guard Reserve
Other Reserve training organizations of
the Army, Marine Corps, Navy, Air
Force and Coast Guard in that order,
respectively

During any period when the United States Coast Guard operates as a part of the United States Navy the cadets U. S. Coast Guard Academy, the U. S. Coast Guard, and the Coast Guard Reserve will take precedence, respectively, next after the midshipmen, U. S. Naval Academy, the U. S. Navy, and the Naval Reserve.

MILITARY FUNERALS

Officers should be thoroughly familiar with the prescribed courtesies to the military dead.* This involves a knowledge of the ceremonies incident to the conduct of a military funeral including correct procedure on the following occasions:
Officer in charge of a funeral.
Honorary pallbearer.
Command of a funeral escort.
Attendance as a mourner.
Essential references: AR 600—25, FM 22—5.

Courtesies at a Military Funeral. At a military funeral, all persons in the military service in uniform attending in their individual capacity will face the

---

*For burial rights of military personnel see Chapter Seven, *Financial Planning.*

casket and execute the hand salute at any time when the casket is being moved, while the casket is being lowered into the grave, during the firing of the volley, and while taps are being sounded. Honorary pallbearers in uniform will conform to these instructions when not in motion. Male personnel in civilian clothes, in the above cases and during the service at the grave will stand at "attention," uncovered, and hold the headdress over the left breast, or if no headdress is worn the right hand will be held over the heart. Female personnel in civilian clothes will hold the right hand over the heart. During religious graveside service, all personnel will bow their heads at the words, "Let us pray." All personnel except the active pallbearers will follow the example of the officiating chaplain. If he uncovers, they will uncover; if he remains covered, they will remain covered. When the officiating chaplain wears a biretta (clerical headpiece) during the graveside service all personnel as indicated above will uncover. When the officiating chaplain wears a yarmulke (skull cap, Jewish) all personnel will remain covered.

The active pallbearers will remain covered and will not salute while carrying the casket and while holding the flag over the casket during the service at the grave.

Female military personnel will remain covered during military funerals.

Badge of Military Mourning. The badge of military mourning is a straight band of black crepe or plain black cloth four inches wide, worn around the left sleeve of the outer garment above the elbow. But no badge of military mourning is worn with the uniform, except when prescribed by the commanding officer for funerals, or when specially ordered by the Department of the Army. As family mourning, officers are authorized to wear the sleeve band described above while at the funeral, or enroute thereto or therefrom. (AR 670–5.)

Elements of Military Funeral Ceremony. The military funeral ceremony that has been developed to demonstrate the nation's recognition of the debt it owes to the services and sacrifices of soldiers is based on a few simple customs and traditions. The casket of the soldier is covered with the American Flag. It is usually transported to the cemetery on a caisson.* It is carried from the caisson to the grave by six military body bearers. In addition to the body bearers, honorary pallbearers are usually designated who march to the cemetery alongside the caisson. At the cemetery, the casket is placed over the grave and the body bearers hold the flag-pall waist high over the casket. After the committal service is read by the chaplain, a firing party fires three volleys. A bugler stationed at the head of the grave sounds *Taps* over the casket and the military funeral is completed. The body bearers then fold the flag and it is presented to the next of kin. These basic elements are the foundation of all military funerals, whether last rites are being conducted over a private's casket or final honors are being paid at the grave of a general.

Honorary Pallbearers. The honorary pallbearers arrive at the chapel before the hearse arrives. They take positions in front of the entrance to the chapel in two facing ranks, as indicated in the accompanying illustration.

Upon arrival of the hearse and when the body bearers remove the casket from the hearse, honorary pallbearers execute the hand salute.

When the casket is carried between the two ranks that they have formed,

---

*Since caissons are no longer used in the Army, the vehicle carrying the casket is generally a civilian hearse or sometimes a light, open Army truck or an ambulance adapted for the purpose. This will be understood wherever the word "caisson" is employed in this description.

they come to the order, execute the appropriate facing movement, fall in behind the casket, and enter the chapel, the senior preceding the junior and marching to the right.

In the chapel, they take places in the front pews to the left of the chapel as indicated in the illustration.

After the chapel service, the honorary pallbearers precede the casket in column of twos as the two active pallbearers push the church truck to the chapel entrance. The honorary pallbearers again form an aisle from the chapel entrance to the caisson or hearse and uncover or salute as prescribed. When the casket has been placed on the caisson or in the hearse, they enter their conveyances or march. When marching, the honorary pallbearers form columns of files on each side of the caisson or hearse, the leading member of each column opposite the front wheels of the caisson or hearse.

When the entrance to the burial lot is reached, the honorary pallbearers take positions on either side of the entrance. As the body bearers lift the casket from the caisson, the honorary pallbearers execute the hand salute.

When the casket has been carried past them, they come to the order and fall in behind the casket, marching to the grave site in correct precedence of rank, senior to the right and to the front.

At the grave site they stand in line behind the chaplain at the head of the grave; the senior stands to the right and the junior to the left. They execute the hand salute during the firing of volleys, the sounding of *Taps,* and the lowering of the casket into the grave.

After the ceremony is over they march off in two files behind the colors.

Family. The family arrives at the chapel before the casket is received and is seated in pews in right front of the chapel.

When chapel service is over, family members follow the casket down the aisle until they reach the vestibule of the chapel, where they wait until the casket is carried outside and secured to the caisson.

When the procession is ready to form, members of the family take their places in the procession immediately behind the body bearers.

When the procession arrives at the graveside, the members of the family wait until the band, escort, and colors have taken their positions at the grave, and the casket is carried between the double rows of honorary pallbearers.

The members of the family take their positions at the side of the grave opposite earth mound side for the funeral service.

When the graveside ceremony is finished, a member of the family receives the interment flag from the Chaplain, cemetery representative, the officer in charge of the funeral, or the individual military escort.*

The family then leaves the cemetery.

Significance of Military Funeral. The ceremonial customs that comprise the elements of all military funerals are rooted in ancient military usage. In many cases, these traditions are based on expedients used long ago on the battlefield in time of war. The use of a caisson as a hearse, for example, was an obvious combat improvisation. In a similar manner, the custom of covering the casket with a flag probably originated on the battlefield where caskets were not available and the flag, wrapped around the dead serviceman, served as a makeshift pall in which he could be buried. Later, these customs assumed a deeper

---

*Upon this ending of the service it has become customary for close friends to express regrets to the bereaved at the graveside.

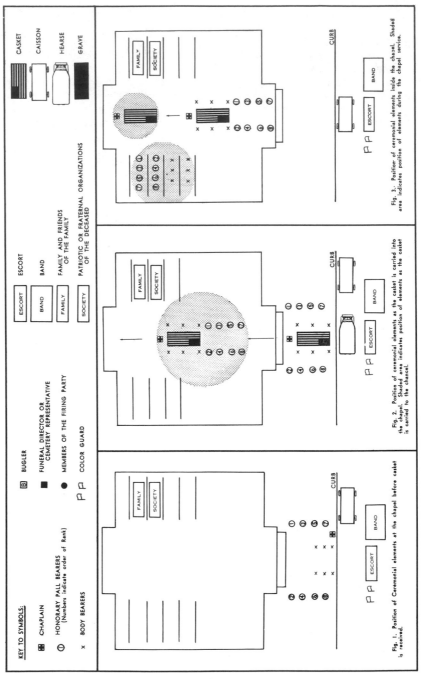

KEY TO SYMBOLS:

⊞ CHAPLAIN

⊖ HONORARY PALL BEARERS
(Numbers indicate order of Rank)

× BODY BEARERS

🅱 BUGLER

■ FUNERAL DIRECTOR OR
CEMETERY REPRESENTATIVE

● MEMBERS OF THE FIRING PARTY

⊓⊓ COLOR GUARD

ESCORT

BAND

FAMILY AND FRIENDS
OF THE FAMILY

PATRIOTIC OR FRATERNAL ORGANIZATIONS
OF THE DECEASED

CASKET

CAISSON

HEARSE

GRAVE

Fig. 1. Position of Ceremonial elements at the chapel before casket is received.

Fig. 2. Position of ceremonial elements as the casket is carried into the chapel. Shaded area indicates position of elements as the casket is carried to the chancel.

Fig. 3. Position of ceremonial elements inside the chapel. Shaded area indicates position of elements during the chapel service.

MILITARY FUNERALS, ARMY.

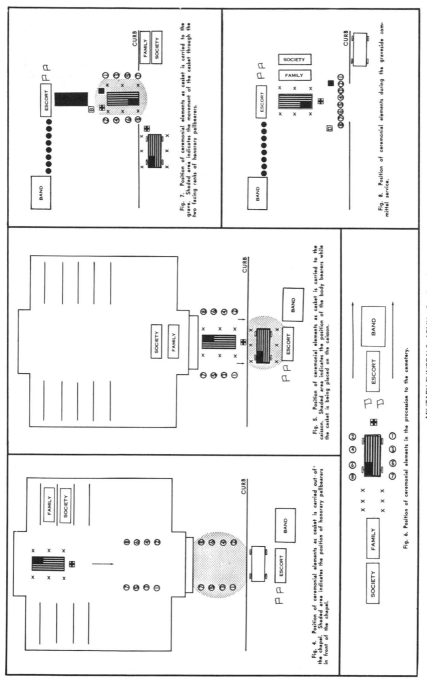

Fig. 7. Position of ceremonial elements as casket is carried to the grave. Shaded area indicates the movement of the casket through the two facing ranks of honorary pallbearers.

Fig. 8. Position of ceremonial elements during the graveside committal service.

Fig. 5. Position of ceremonial elements as casket is carried to the caisson. Shaded area indicates the position of the body bearers while the casket is being placed on the caisson.

Fig. 6. Position of ceremonial elements in the procession to the cemetery.

Fig. 4. Position of ceremonial elements as casket is carried out of the chapel. Shaded area indicates the position of honorary pallbearers in front of the chapel.

MILITARY FUNERALS, ARMY—Continued.

significance than that of mere expediency. The fact that an American Flag is used to cover the casket, for example, now symbolizes the fact that the soldier served in the Armed Forces of the United States and that this country assumes the responsibility of burying the soldier as a solemn and sacred obligation.

Finally, the sounding of *Taps* over the grave has an obvious origin in military custom. Since *Taps* is the last bugle call the soldier hears at night, it is particularly appropriate that it be played over his grave to mark the beginning of his last, long sleep and to express hope and confidence in an ultimate reveille to come.

5

Customs of
the Service

Nothing is stronger than custom.—OVID.

A custom is an established usage. Customs include positive actions
—things to do—and taboos—things to avoid doing. Like life itself,
the customs which mankind observes are subject to a constant but
slow process of change. Many practices which were habitual a
generation or two ago have passed through a period of declining
observance, and then into the limbo. New customs arise to sup-
plant the old. The resurrection of those which have become out-
moded would first be thought amusing, then peculiar. Others live
on and on without apparent change. Humans are eager to rely upon
established practice, upon precedent or custom, to an astounding
degree. The realization that the action they are taking coincides
with that which has been followed by others in similar circumstances bolsters their confidence, thus encouraging them to adhere to their course. Customs change with need; during a war
period this process is greatly accelerated. But, whether old or new,
the influence of custom is profound. It is Man's attempt to apply
to the solution of his immediate problems the lessons of the past.
It is itself a custom. Army customs conform to the Code of the
Army Officer, as they also conform to the established rules of
military courtesy.*

Army Customs and Their Importance. As long as harmonious
human relations continue to be important, which will be a very long
time indeed, the observance of useful, gracious, thoughtful cus-

*Commended for interesting reading is *Military Customs and Traditions*, Major Mark M. Boatner III, David McKay
Company, Inc., New York.

toms will be important in the lives of the Army's officers and their families. The established customs have come into general use by evolution and represent the preferences of officers and their spouses. The community of interests of officers on the same assignments, or at the same locations, with the singleness of purpose of the national security, provides opportunity as well as need for the recognition of customs. Customs enrich our life of national service. The newcomers are made welcome, given prompt opportunity to become known and to know others, to feel welcome and to "belong." There are ceremonial ways which add to the color of military life. There are things to do, and to avoid doing. Those who are departing receive a pleasant farewell. The sum of these customs adds appreciably to the interests, the pleasures, and the graciousness of Army life.

Life in the Army can be colorful, interesting, rich with friends and experiences. The customs and the courtesies help to establish these patterns. The commanding officer, or officer in charge of an activity, who overlooks an opportunity for building cameraderie is injuring his or her own cause and image. Leadership in observing worthy customs will help. Such observance smooths the way for harmonious official and personal relationships. They are the lubricants for developing teamwork and service pride. Have you questioned these views? If so, some earnest thinking is suggested. Army customs change with times and circumstances, but they have been developing through the years. They have stood the tests of many difficult periods, and they have not been tossed into limbo.

Did you know that the costs of many official or semi-official social occasions, or social get-togethers, are borne by your general or colonel, major, or captain? Only when foreign dignitaries are present, and then only in small amounts, is there an official allowance. These costs have been accepted by many senior commanders, when within their means, as a part of their responsibility. They know the importance of officers and wives or husbands meeting and becoming acquainted with one another, with their general and colonel; and for all to know and recognize Mrs. General and Mrs. Colonel. It is a step in developing pride in military service, of stimulating acquaintances and interests, as well as generating smooth and understanding official as well as community relationships.

This analysis should invite conclusions as to the potential rewards and pleasures of service life. There is the welcome extended to all—come out, become known, know others! Participate in the activities of your military community. Contribute your talents for worthwhile activities. Be more than a typed name on the official rolls. The glory of the Army is its fine people and the rewarding associations which may flow in abundance from its work and its life. It is a good life. A wholesome, interesting, rewarding life, if you learn its ways and grasp the opportunities extended. It can never be more to you than you, yourself, make it.

This chapter has been included in order to explain and to help perpetuate customs which have enriched many, many lives for many, many years. Your effort will soon be rewarded with enjoyable experiences and new friendships formed, all strengthening the purposeful service which the mission requires.

Many customs originating in antiquity are observed in our Army.* They are forms of military pageantry most of which are followed in one way or another

---

*The student of military customs of antiquity and of the older armies will find enlightening "Military Customs," Edwards and Kipling, Aldershot, Gale and Polden Ltd., Aldershot, Hampshire, England, 1961. Its purchase for station libraries is recommended.

in many armies. While most professional military people are convinced that their life has greater interest and stimulation than other vocations it is a fact that it has its drab aspects. These old customs add color, pageantry and ceremony to daily life and deserve careful perpetuation. For the most part they consist of acts honoring the nation's flag, or the military dead, or pay respects to comrades in arms. Each heightens the concept of purposeful men and women serving their country in an honorable profession.

The Salute. An interesting history of the military salute, one of the most ancient and universal military customs, is contained in Chapter Four, *Military Courtesy.*

The Evening Gun. The evening gun, fired at the time of the Retreat ceremony, signifies the end of the normal military day at which time in our service the flag is lowered. It is an extremely old custom of armies with one legend indicating that in the beginning the gun was fired at evening to drive away evil spirits. Whatever the facts may be as to its true origin it is particularly appropriate to signal the arrival of retreat throughout a military reservation so that it is heard beyond the range of bugle calls. In any event its precedent extends over centuries.

The Retreat Ceremony. The Retreat ceremony honors the Nation's flag at the end of day. In our service it is known to have been in use during the American Revolution at which time it was sounded with drums. The Retreat parade in which a ceremonial parade is combined with the Retreat ceremony including the sounding of the evening gun is one of the most inspiring Army ceremonies. It is entirely good for all members of a garrison out of doors at the time to pause for a moment in salute to the Nation's flag and the National anthem.

The "Sound Off" and The Three Cheers. During a ceremonial parade the Adjutant commands, "SOUND OFF." The band, in place, plays the *Sound Off* of three chords. It then moves forward, and changing direction while playing a stirring march, troops the line or marches past the troops in formation, then returns to its post. Upon halting it again sounds "the Three Cheers."

This custom is believed by some students to have originated at the time of the Crusades. The legend appears to have substance. At that time when detachments were sent away on those far-away campaigns it was the custom to assemble the garrison in formation with the departing troops in the place of honor on the right. The band of the period marched past troops being honored much as is now done during Sound Off. Three cheers for their departing comrades were then given by the troops remaining behind. The simple notes of the three cheers as they are used today could very well have this symbolic meaning. In any event it is a pretty legend with logic as to its authenticity.

The Three Volleys Over Graves. A special ceremonial at graveside honoring a military deceased is an ancient custom in itself the details of which are fully explained and pictured in Chapter Four, *Military Courtesy.*

After the committal service is read by the chaplain, a firing party fires three volleys with rifles which ceremony is followed by a bugler sounding *Taps* from a position at the head of the casket over the grave. This completes the military funeral.

The use of this custom by military people is said by students to have been in use during the 17th century. In concept it traces to the Romans who honored their dead by casting earth three times upon the grave, calling the name of the dead, and saying "Farewell" three times. It is also likened to the intent of saying an honorable farewell by the Three Cheers as used during the Crusades, discussed above.

The Raising of the Right Hand in Taking Oath. From the earliest days the taking of an oath as to the truth of statements or testimony has been a solemn and serious matter accompanied by ceremony. In essence it has always meant that the taker of the oath called upon his God to bear witness that the truth would be told. Ancient men bared their heads and raised their arms in appeal to their deity as a symbol of truth and honesty. A cynic might surmise that an ancient judge required the act as a means of increasing the probity of the testimony he was obliged to hear. Certainly this custom is as old as mankind, adding dignity and ceremony to a serious occasion.

The White Flag of Truce. The white flag of truce is a practice so old that its origin is unknown. A logical origin occurs through action in the middle ages by the Roman Catholic Church in connection with private wars in Europe. There were agreements between the church and warring barons whereby hostilities were suspended on certain days of religious significance including Sundays. *"La paix et la treve de Dieu"*—the peace and truce of God. Pope Urban II, in 1095, proclaimed the practice to be observed throughout Christendom. Thus may well have come the use of a simple white cloth as a means of obtaining quick cessation of fighting.

The Wearing of Decorations. The rewarding of individuals who have performed acts of military valor is very old in armies of history. An interesting sketch of the development is contained in Chapter Twenty-two, *Decorations, Service Medals and Badges.*

The Wearing of Unit Badges or Emblems. This custom originated as to our service during the American Civil War. An account of the occasion for its adoption may be found in a footnote, Chapter Twenty-one, *Uniforms of the Army.*

THE STRONGEST TRADITION: COMRADESHIP

The comradeship of military associates is the strongest and most enduring of Army customs. It is a reserved status. It is enjoyed by comrades in arms who have served together in some vast experience, such as a great campaign, where individual as well as group pride has developed. Age and grade are submerged here. It is an abiding trust and confidence in one's fellows which may develop swiftly in the hard crucibles of military service.

Men and women who are true comrades in arms have faith that when the chips are down each may depend fully upon his or her fellows. Ordinary soldiers will often choose the course of great hazard in the accomplishment of mission in preference to revealing themselves as weak in the eyes of their comrades. It is the ultimate in a feeling of belonging: "This is MY company. I am a member here. These are good soldiers. I trust them and they trust me."

It is a powerful tradition. Here is the hidden ingredient which binds those who serve the nation with pride and competence as dependable associates, comrades in arms.

The "Stand-To!". A special form of unit officer comradeship which has been developing and spreading in recent years is the "Stand-To." Expect to hear the directive, "All officers Stand-To at 1730." This means to join the unit officers at their local club for a beer and conversation. Usually held on Fridays, the growing custom calls for light-hearted jesting about the events of the week, or airing a minor gripe, and blowing off a little steam. It may also be a time to slip in a judicious request for a pass or even to inquire about taking a leave. The point to understand is the totally informal atmosphere in which the commander and the unit officers—and occasionally their spouses—stand together celebrating the week's passing with that good feeling of mission accomplished.

Battalion Parties and "Command Performances." Battalion parties and Command Performance parties are also becoming a periodic custom, especially in areas where officers and their families live off-post. Their purpose is to increase and strengthen acquaintances, and to weld the interest of all members in their unit. They are held on the occasion of arrivals, departures, promotions, or just for the fun of it. Don't miss them even if you prefer the entertainment elsewhere or, if you are a bachelor, you have the bachelor's suspicion that your betrothal is being plotted. These occasions serve many purposes of building unit cohesiveness and esprit. "Command Performances" are similar to battalion parties, but there is a clear inference to be drawn that your presence is expected. If they cost more than your current resources permit, or you have sufficient reason to be elsewhere, tell your commander and request permission to be absent. He or she will accept your statement as reasonable and will not assume you to be anti-social, unfriendly, or unresponsive to the commander's implied desires. But it is better to attend and help make the affair successful. Put on a happy face—and go!

Special Use of the Salute. The 15th Infantry of the 3d Infantry Division—The Marne Division—now stationed in Germany, follows a saluting custom which illustrates its history, its motto, and its spirit. A trim soldier in crisp fatigues crosses the path of his battalion commander and salutes smartly. "Can Do, Sir." The commander returns the salute and replies, "Can Do!"* "Can Do" is the motto of the regiment, born in its China service.

This is a fine example of the display of pride in a unit, its service to the nation, its current mission, and its motto.

An Old Custom of Formal Dining Renewed. The following is extracted and updated from the *Army Information Digest,* November 1965, "Dining-In Preserves an Old Tradition," as practiced at the John F. Kennedy Center for Military Assistance, Fort Bragg, N.C. News of the adoption of this colorful occasion by other organizations and units will be welcomed.

> The regimental mess has passed into oblivion and "dining-in"—that formal gathering of a unit's officers for an evening of dining and comradeship—has all but disappeared with the officer's saber and the tri-corner hat. But at the Kennedy Center for Military Assistance, Fort Bragg, North Carolina, the tradition has been preserved as officers gather periodically for a ceremonial evening held by the center headquarters staff and major units.
>
> Origin of the custom probably arose in the British Army where the dinner is still held regularly, and is indeed prescribed in Queen's Regulations. There, traditions have been established within the various regiments—in India one used to break the wine glasses after toasting the sovereign; two regiments drink the royal toast seated because they are descended from marine units where members bumped their heads on deck beams if they stood up; another passes around a champagne-filled solid silver bedroom piece captured from the personal baggage of Joseph Bonaparte at the Battle of Victoria in 1813.
>
> While such colorful customs never were established in the U.S. Army, European customs were generally followed, and before World War I small posts had devel-

---

*Credit to *Army Information Digest,* October 1965.

oped their own unbending rules of formal dining that called for formal dress, with no one allowed to be seated before arrival of the commanding officer. In the U.S. Army a more informal after-dinner smoker also became customary. This second phase was signaled when the commanding officer "removed the cloth" when served with his coffee.

Dining-in at the Center is a dignified, formal occasion. The evening begins with about one-half hour of informal conversation and refreshments. The colors are presented to the roll of drums by a color guard of Kennedy Center sergeants. A series of toasts are then presented—by the host officer to the United States of America, by the junior officer present to the President of the United States. Further toasts are offered to the U.S. Army and to the host unit. If foreign guests are present, toasts are offered to the chief of state of the guest's country. The colors are then posted.

The meal usually consists of four or five courses but as many as seven are sometimes served. Normally, there are no speeches.—*Information Office, Fort Bragg, North Carolina.*

RANK HAS ITS PRIVILEGES (RHIP)

General. Rank does indeed have its privileges, but there are important points for all officers to consider. Although certain courtesies, customs, and privileges are traditional and, indeed, historical, they were established and are honored for impersonal reasons. It is difficult to remember this at any age and rank; it is a little easier to understand as one gets more experience. Some privileges may be difficult to rationalize as being a matter solely of rank. For instance, getting quarters on a post involves rank, date of arrival, the number of quarters for your grade, the size of your family, and even the physical condition of members of your family. The lieutenant may not like the influence of rank on quarters assignment but the same can be said for the sergeant as he or she views the lieutenant's opportunities.

A second point to reflect on is that rank has no influence on many military matters. Enemy artillery shells do not seek out the captains alone; in combat all are vulnerable. To a well trained sniper, rank may be a special distinction resulting in a dubious privilege. The thousands of officers of all ranks who have been in replacement systems would have great difficulty in identifying any privileges granted because of their rank since all were equally and impartially processed with no special treatment according to rank.

A third point to consider is that privileges are dividends and rewards for faithful service, achievements, and for having more responsibility than those of lower rank. All of us are human and require recognition beyond salaries. If officers believe their achievements are recognized and their service appreciated by the evidence of such intangibles, as the privileges of rank, the Army is going to gain and retain better officers. These intangibles cannot be weighed or counted but they do greatly affect one's attitude, devotion and, ultimately, one's capability.

It is useful to observe that all society is organized and all organizations have a structure of ranks. This structure of ranks with resulting degrees of privilege is obviously not unique to the Services. Churches, colleges, corporations, government organizations, and many other professional groupings observe rank, status, and privileges. The junior officer does not have to apologize for entitled privileges to the noncommissioned officer nor accept the more senior officer's privileges with bitterness and rancor. Such privileges are an entitlement, occasioned by rank, which each officer receives and which each officer observes without compromise of any personal principles.

The Privilege of Being First to Choose. Whenever a choice is to be made, such as selection of billets or quarters or electing means of transportation, or numerous other examples, the option of selection follows rank, the senior first. This is in contrast to the way of first come first served, and devil take the hind most.

"I Wish" and "I Desire." When the commanding officer states, "I wish," or "I desire" rather than, "I order that you do so-and-so," this wish or desire has all the force of a direct order.

The Place of Honor. The place of honor is on the right. Accordingly, when a junior walks, rides, or sits with a senior, the junior takes position abreast and to the left of the senior. The deference which a young officer should pay to his or her elders pertains to this relationship. The junior should walk in step with the senior, step back and allow the senior to be the first to enter a door, and render similar acts of consideration and courtesy.

Use of the Word "Sir." The word "Sir" is used in military conversation by the junior officer in addressing a senior, and by all soldiers in addressing officers. It precedes a report and a query; it follows the answer of a question. For example: "Sir, do you wish to see Sergeant Brown?" "Sir, I report as Old Officer of the Day." "Private Brown, Sir." "Thank you, Sir."

Departing Before the Commanding Officer. Officers should remain at a reception or social gathering until the commanding officer has departed.

New Year's Call on the Commanding Officer. It is Army tradition that officers make a formal call upon the Commanding Officer during the afternoon of New Year's Day. Spouses usually attend when the event is held at the Commander's quarters, or at the Open Mess as a reception. The pressures of the current Army mission, the desires of the Commanding Officer, and local or major unit custom bear upon the holding of the event as well as the way it is done.

As a general guide, when the Commanding Officer elects to hold the event, timely information is provided as to the time and place, and the uniform to be worn. The uniform may be Army Dress, Army Blue, Army White, Army Green, with medals if the Commander wishes, and if the event is in the form of a party, Branch blazers may be authorized. At very large stations, the event may be held at the Officers' Open Mess as a reception with a receiving line; it may include a dance with light refreshments. If the senior commander does not hold the event, commanders of component units such as the brigade or battalion, may choose to do so. Official funds are not provided to defray the costs. Officers invited who are present and whose duties of the day permit are expected to attend. In any case, think of it as a pleasant, ceremonial formal or semi-formal social function, adding color to the military scene, starting the New Year in a spirit of general comradeship.

How to Obtain Appointment with the Commanding Officer. It is the custom to ask the adjutant, the executive, or an aide, as may be appropriate, for an appointment with the commander or other senior officer. There is no special formality about it. Just inquire, "May I see the commanding officer?" Often it will be appropriate to state the reason. Take your minor administrative problems to an appropriate staff officer of your own headquarters and avoid consuming the time of your commanding officer. Save your personal requests to him or her for a major matter which others cannot resolve in your behalf, or resolve as well.

Permission of the First Sergeant. It is the custom that enlisted personnel secure permission from the first sergeant before speaking to the company commander. It is essential to discipline that each soldier knows that he or she has the right to appeal direct to the captain for redress of wrongs.

The Open-door Policy. The soldier's right to speak to the company commander is echoed by each commander at a higher level. It is the "open-door" policy which permits each person in the Army, regardless of rank, to appeal to the next higher commander. Indeed, this right is checked and enforced by The Inspector General. It is not uncommon for a private soldier to talk to the battalion commander, since many administrative matters are performed by the battalion staff. The officer needs to expect this and not be arbitrary about barring his or her door to soldiers. Usually, if there is disagreement between a soldier and an officer, or a soldier believes he or she has a real grievance the soldier has the right to speak to the next senior commander and to have the matter resolved.

Payment for Personal Services. In the past, some soldiers in addition to their regular duties could also work, if willing to do so, as personal servants to officers and their families. In the Army the custom has always been that such work was entirely voluntary, with the officer compensating the soldier for his work. Historically, these men were known as "orderlies" or "strikers." Some soldiers desired such jobs to supplement their service pay, just as some soldiers of this period take off duty jobs, called "moonlighting". By custom and official restrictions the use of soldiers as servants of officers and their families in garrison assignments has terminated except for some senior officers and for special reasons in each case. However, for units in the field, in training or combat, an officer may be assigned a soldier orderly for personal services so the officer can devote maximum time to the responsibilities of command. Many times it is the driver of the vehicle assigned to the officer who performs such personal services.

Whenever officers utilize soldiers for personal services, always with the soldier's consent, compensation at some established or otherwise stipulated rate is required.

THE NEWCOMER SHALL BE WELL RECEIVED

Reception of a Newly Joined Officer. It is a custom that newly joined officers shall be cordially received and many acts of courtesy extended to the officer and his or her family to make their arrival more pleasant and convenient. It is taken for granted that a newly joined officer knows his or her professional duties, and has every intention of performing them ably.

Whenever conditions permit such niceties, the adjutant sends a letter of welcome to an officer under orders to join, with information on local conditions which may be important or interesting for the officer to know before arrival. The adjutant will inquire as to the date and hour of arrival, whether traveling by automobile or train, and the number of persons accompanying the newcomer. If the arrival is by train or plane an officer with transportation is at the station or airport to meet the new arrival.

Most stations and most units welcome incoming families through the sponsor system under which a designated military member and his or her family on the scene act as hosts and advisers to the new arrivals. Many officers believe that this one custom has been responsible for making more enduring friendships than any other. Certainly the warm welcome and thoughtful courtesies extended to newly arrived members of a unit goes a long way to gain the good start.

The adjutant usually introduces the newly joined officer to the commanding officer, and at the first assembly to the other officers of the unit. The adjutant should also inform the newcomer as to local regulations and customs which will be needed at once. A copy of the garrison regulations and a map of the post are especially useful to the stranger.

The officer and adult members of the family are usually accorded the courtesy of being in the receiving line at the first appropriate function after their arrival, discussed as an illustration in the chapter introduction. As newcomers, they may also be welcomed at a Battalion Party, or even a Command Performance, as described above. If you are the "Newcomers," make the most of the opportunity to meet and start acquaintanceships; if you are the "Oldtimers," do your full share of making the occasion useful and pleasant.

Receiving Officers of Sister Services. The officers of the host service accord a high degree of cordiality and hospitality to visiting officers from other services. This may include provisions for quarters, invitation to use an officers mess, extension of club privileges, social invitation, care to introduce the visitor to appropriate officers, and the like. But it includes above all else the hand of fellowship and comradeship to a brother or sister officer to stimulate a feeling of being welcomed among friends.

Military Weddings. Military weddings follow the same procedures as any other except for additional customs which add to their color and tone. Consult your chaplain for details and arrangements which will be suitable in making wedding plans.

At military weddings all officers should wear an appropriate dress uniform. Medals to which the individual is entitled may be worn with propriety, or merely the ribbons, whichever is preferred, and badges, too.

Frequently the national and unit colors are crossed just above and behind the position of the chaplain.

The members of the bridal party line up on opposite sides of the aisle. The groomsmen stand respectfully at attention as the bridal couple pass.

The saber? In all likelihood enough sabers to form the ceremonial arch of older days cannot be found. Perhaps if one is found it may be used for the first cut of the wedding cake as a polite bow to old tradition.

Reception of a Bride. Under conditions of today, bride and groom are usually placed in the receiving line at an appropriate social function and introduced to the officers and their spouses of the organization in that way. A special function may be held to welcome several brides at one time, if the command is large. The commander, or the commander's wife, may hold a personal reception to welcome a bride or bride and groom. Customs vary with conditions, and with regard to official missions and times.

Birth of a Child. When a child is born to the family of an officer the unit commander sends a personal letter of congratulation to the parents on behalf of the organization.

The adjutant may use the "baby cup" fund or the wives of the unit officers may purchase a silver cup from their club funds with engraving like "From the Officers and Wives of the 2d Battalion, 9th Infantry, Germany, 1967." The unit commander sends a letter of congratulations to an enlisted man and his wife, or to the enlisted woman and her husband; in some units enlisted personnel, particularly NCO's, observe the same tradition as to the "baby cup."

Upon request of parents it is usual that the organization color is made available for christenings so that the child may receive the ceremony under the colors of the member's organization. For the ceremony of baptism both the national and organization color may be made available.

Presentation of Recruits to Colors. In many commands there is a ceremony held in which recruits are presented to the colors. The form varies but the purpose is to show the recruits that they are accepted and welcomed into the organization. The ceremony is held semi-annually, or according to local arrangements.

CUSTOMS IN CONNECTION WITH SICKNESS AND DEATH

Visiting the Sick. An officer who is sick in hospital is visited by the officers of the unit in such numbers as may be permitted by the surgeon. An officer or soldier of the officer's unit visits the sick officer daily in order that his or her comfort or desires may receive attention.

An officer's spouse who is sick in hospital receives flowers sent in the name of the officers of the unit and their wives or husbands.

Death of an Officer or Family Member. When an officer dies an officer is immediately designated by the commanding officer to render every possible assistance to the bereaved family. A similar courtesy may be tendered, if desired, in the case of a death of a member of an officer's family.

A letter of condolence is written by the unit commander on behalf of the brigade, regiment, group or similar unit. Flowers are sent in the name of the officers of the unit and their spouses.

Death of an Enlisted Person. When an enlisted person dies a letter of condolence is written to the nearest relative by the immediate commander of the deceased soldier.

Flowers sent in the name of the members of the decedent's unit accompany the body.

The funeral is attended by all officers and soldiers of the deceased soldier's unit, his or her battalion commander, the band, and other members of the unit who so desire and whose duties permit.

SUPPORT OF POST AND ORGANIZATION ACTIVITIES

General. An officer will be expected to support the activities of the unit, such as a brigade or battalion, to which he or she may be assigned, as well as the activities of the entire garrison. The unit to which you are assigned consists of a closely knit group around which are entwined official duties, and athletic, social, and cultural activities for the benefit of all. You are a member of an official family. Your assignment must mean more than the place where your required and official duties are performed, important as they may be. You will be expected to support and assist, at least by your presence, many events which form a part of military life. A proper interest and pride in all activities of your unit and garrison are factors in stimulating morale. Each officer should be a good military citizen, sharing with other good citizens responsibility for the unofficial life and activities of the garrison.

The Officers' Club and Mess. The "Open Mess," or officers' club and mess, is the nucleus around which revolves much of the off-duty social and recreational life of officers and their spouses. At a large station there may be branches to serve the needs of separate organizations, or of distant areas, and there are also at all stations similar establishments for noncommissioned officers. The open mess is an integral part of the Army establishment, subject to the control of the station commander. Its activities are conducted in accordance with AR 230–60 and its funds are controlled and audited under AR 230–7.

Membership is voluntary and has three classifications:

Active. Such members may vote and hold office. The right of active membership is extended to all officers and warrant officers of all services on duty at the installation.

Associate. Such members neither vote nor hold office but may enjoy all its services and facilities. It is extended to officers and warrant officers at the installation who are on temporary duty, detached service, attached unassigned, or in a transient status.

Honorary. Extends the same privileges as the associate membership, usually on a non-dues paying basis.

Attendance at Unit and Organization Parties Sponsored by Enlisted Members. It is customary for officers and their spouses, when invited, to attend special social events sponsored by enlisted members of a unit or organization. Conditions vary so widely throughout the Service that no general customs as to details of attendance can be identified. The best source of guidance is the commanding officer.

These principles would have general agreement. Officers, or officers and their spouses, would be invited only on special occasions. When invited, officers attend in their official capacity as officers to assist in enhancing pride of service, morale and esprit. In conduct they will be mindful of the normal social amenities, and be guided by the example set by the senior officer present. If the unit or organization is authorized to serve intoxicants, it is accepted practice for the officer to drink in marked moderation; the non-drinker should ask for a coke, without excuse. Excessive drinking, exhibitionist dancing, and other ungentlemanly or unladylike behavior would harm the purpose of attendance and be frowned upon. At an appropriate time and after the customary amenities, officers depart with or immediately after the senior officer attending, leaving the party for the enjoyment of its enlisted members.

Attendance at Athletic Events Is Desirable. As a matter of policy to demonstrate an interest in organization affairs, as well as for personal enjoyment, officers should attend athletic events in which their teams participate.

Ceremonies at Holiday Dinners. On Thanksgiving, Christmas, and New Year's Day many organizations have a tradition that the officers will visit the companies during the meal or prior to the serving of the meal. The method varies rather widely. As an example only, the brigade, battalion or similar commander, his or her staff and field officers visit each mess hall just prior to the serving of the dinner. Officers of the company, their families, and families of married enlisted men of the company dine with the companies on these holidays.

Christmas Tree Entertainment. At Christmas an entertainment with a tree and presents for all children of the organization may be arranged by the Recreation Services Officer. The band may be present and appropriate ceremonies conducted. Funds for the purpose are raised by subscription and borne by welfare funds from such as those derived from Post Exchange profits.

At many stations members of the garrison join in singing carols after retreat or in the early evening. The band, orchestra, or chapel choir leads the group, and carols are sung outside the hospital, before the quarters of the commanding officer, and at several places about the post.

Farewell Tendered a Departing Officer. Prior to the departure of an officer from his or her organization or station on change of assignment, a reception, or other suitable function, is usually given in honor of the departing officer and family. Often one of the unit social functions is used for the purpose. The pressure of war usually prohibits this nicety.

TABOOS

Uniform Must Not Be Defamed. The officers' uniform and official or social position must not be defamed. Conduct which is unbecoming an officer is punishable under Article 133, Uniform Code of Military Justice. The confidence of the nation in the integrity and high standards of conduct of the officers of the Army is an asset which no individual may be permitted to lower.

Never Slink Under Cover to Avoid Retreat. As a good military person, always be proud and willing to pay homage and respect to the National Flag and the National Anthem. Now and then thoughtless people in uniform are observed ducking inside a building or under other cover just to avoid a Retreat ceremony and the moment of respect which it includes. Or do they merely convict themselves of ignorance as to the purpose of the ceremony and their own actions as it proceeds? See chapter Four for honors paid at retreat. Never slink away from an opportunity to pay respect to our flag and our anthem.

Wives, husbands and children of Army families will wish to stand at attention and face the colors, too, if the ceremony is explained to them.

Proffer No Excuses. Never volunteer excuses or explain a shortcoming unless an explanation is required. The Army demands results. More damage than good is done by proffering unsought excuses.

Abstentions by Officers, Relations with Enlisted Members. It is strong Army tradition that an officer does not associate with enlisted soldiers as individuals in ordinary social affairs, nor gamble, nor borrow money, nor drink intoxicants with them. See the discussion in Chapter 1. *The Code of the Army Officer,* under the main heading, THE OFFICER'S RELATIONS WITH ENLISTED PERSONNEL. Refer also to the several discussions, above, under SUPPORT OF POST AND ORGANIZATION ACTIVITIES.

Use of Third Person by Officers in Poor Taste. It is in poor taste for officers to use the third person in conversation with their seniors. For example, do not say, "Sir, does the colonel desire . . .?" Instead, say "Sir, is it your desire . . .?" Most senior officers frown upon the use of the third person under any condition as it is regarded as a form of address implying servility.

Servility is Scorned. Servility, "bootlicking," and deliberate courting of favor are beneath the standard of conduct expected of officers, and any who openly practice such things earn the scorn of their associates.

Avoid Praising Your Commander to His or Her Face. Paying compliments directly to your commander or chief is in poor taste. However genuine may be your high regard for your chief, to so express it partakes of apple polishing or flattery and thus is capable of misinterpretation.

If you particularly admire your boss you can show it by extending the standard military courtesies—and meticulously carrying out his or her policies and doing all in your power to make the organization more effective.

With respect to subordinates, on the other hand, recognition of good work on their part is an inherent part of the exercise of command; do not hesitate to commend a subordinate whose actions are praiseworthy.

"Old Man" to Be Spoken With Care. The commanding officer acquires the accolade, "The Old Man," by virtue of his position and without regard whatever to his age. When the term is used it is more often in affection and admiration than otherwise. However, it is never used in the presence of the commanding officer, and if used would be considered disrespectful.

Avoid "Going Over an Officer's Head." The jumping of an echelon of command is called "going over an officer's head." For example, a company commander making a request of the brigade commander concerning a matter which should first have been presented to the commander of his or her battalion. The act is contrary to military procedure and decidedly disrespectful.

Harsh Remarks Are to Be Avoided. The conveying of gossip, slander, harsh criticism, and fault finding are unofficerlike practices. In casual conversation it is wiser to follow this guide: "All the brothers are valiant, and all the sisters virtuous."

Avoid Vulgarity and Profanity. Foul and vulgar language larded with profanity is repulsive to most self-respecting men and women. Its use by officers is reprehensible. The need for the wartime officer to be a "lady" or "gentleman" in the country club, college campus, or drawing room sense of the word may be open to question. True leaders who know their jobs is the real need. However the traditional term is defined it would exclude foulness, repulsiveness, and vulgarity if respect is to be obtained and no officer, whether lady or gentleman or not, can lead others unless at the least he or she holds their respect.

Never Lean on a Senior Officer's Desk. Avoid leaning or lolling against a senior officer's desk. It is resented by most officers and is unmilitary. Stand erect unless invited to be seated. Don't lean!

Never Keep Anyone Waiting. Report at once when notified to do so. Never keep any one waiting unnecessarily. On the drill field when called by a senior officer, go on the double.

Avoid Having People Guess Your Name. Do not assume that an officer whom you have not seen nor heard from for a considerable period will know your name when a contact is renewed. Tell him or her at once who you are, and then renew the acquaintance. If this act of courtesy is unnecessary it will be received only as an act of thoughtfulness, while if it happens to be necessary it will save embarrassment. At official receptions always announce your name to the aide.

Carrying an Umbrella in Uniform. There is a longstanding Army taboo against a male officer in uniform carrying an umbrella. It is both authorized and proper for women in the Army to do so when not in formation.

Smoking Is Objectionable at Times. Unless invited to do so, officers do not smoke in the office of the commanding officer. Many commanding officers prefer that officers refrain from smoking during an official visit or inspection. At West Point smoking by spectators during ceremonies is considered objectionable, and the custom has spread through the Army generally.

Noncommissioned Officers Not to Work on Fatigue. A custom which is said to be as old as the Army is that which exempts noncommissioned officers from performing manual labor while in charge of a fatigue detail or while on fatigue. In recent years this custom has not always been observed.

THE ARMY'S BUGLE CALLS

Bugle calls by phonograph recordings, colorless and scarcely recognized, serve as reminders of past eras when the calls of the bugler regulated the military day, and served as an essential means of communication in battle. Remaining is "Taps," the last sound of the bugle, as a soldier is laid to rest.

Historically, the "beats" of the drum and the "calls" of the bugle go far into past centuries. The calls in current use date back to the very beginning of our Army and reflect the influence of the British and French armies. It is noteworthy that before the Civil War, each branch had its own calls, with the Infantry using the beats of the drum. But this created confusion when several units were involved in battle. In 1867, General Emory Upton prepared a document embodying changes made necessary by the Civil War, and requested Major Truman Seymour (later General) to prepare a new system of calls for all arms and branches of the Army. They have been continued in use. The history of a few selected calls follows.

First Call. Similar to the French Cavalry call, "Le Garde a Vous."

Reveille. Same as the French call, this dates from the Crusades. (The armies of the Crusaders were amazed and frightened at the military music of the Saracens, and their instruments were captured and copied. Thereafter, the European armies used music to greater advantage in both battle and ceremony.)

Assembly. The old cavalry assembly call, in use from about 1835, was replaced in 1867 by the present more martial-sounding call.

Mess Call. Similar to the French call "Le Rappel."

Retreat. French cavalry call dating from the Crusades.

To the Color. The old cavalry call "To The Standard," in use from about 1835, was replaced in 1867 by the present more military-sounding call.

Tattoo. Originated during the Thirty Years War, and called the *Zapfenstreich*. At 9:00 P.M., when the call was sounded, all bungs (Zapfen) had to be replaced in their barrels, signifying the end of the nightly drinking bout. A chalk line (Streich) was then drawn across the bung by the guard so that it could not be opened without evidence of tampering. "Tap-to" thus became "Tattoo." (See "Taps.")

In the United States Army, "Tattoo" is the longest call, consisting of 28 measures, but is still far short of the elaborate ceremony used in the British and German services. The first section of eight measures is the same as the French call "Extinction des Feux," (Lights Out) and was at one time used for "Taps" in our army. This French call was composed for the Army of Napoleon, and was the Emperor's favorite. The last section of 20 measures of our "Tattoo" is taken from the British "First Post," and comes originally from an old Neapolitan Cavalry call, "Il Silencio."

Prior to the adoption of the present "Tattoo" in 1867, two other versions were in use, the first during 1835–1861, and the second during the Civil War.

Attention. Taken from the British call "Alarm," at which time the troops turn out under arms.

Church Call. Same as the French "Church Call," this was one of those retained in the revision of 1867, and was taken from the "Sonneries de Chasseurs d' Orleans," promulgated in 1845.

THE BUGLER, MOUNTED, POST CIVIL WAR PERIOD.

Taps. General Daniel Butterfield of the Army of the Potomac composed the call in July 1862, for use in his own brigade, supposedly to replace the three volleys fired at military funerals so the Confederates would not know a burial was taking place. Soon thereafter, it replaced "Tattoo" (at that time the French call "Lights Out") as the last call of the day. Its use became popular throughout the Union Army.

When Major Seymour prepared the present set of bugle calls in 1867, he apparently did not know of General Butterfield's version, since the music was not changed to its present notation until 1874, when it first appeared in the Infantry Drill Regulations.

Reference to the word "Taps" has been found as early as 1861, and is variously explained, one version being that it originally was soldier slang for "Tap-To," as "Tattoo" was first spelled, and "Tap-To" in the Infantry was sounded on a drum—thus "Taps." (See "Tattoo.")

The earliest official reference to the mandatory use of "Taps" at military funeral ceremonies is in the *U.S. Army Drill Regulations of 1891*. Its unofficial use as a finale to the firing salute had been customary since its inception in 1862. (In the British Army, "Last Post" has been sounded over soldier's graves after interment since 1885, being prescribed in Standing Orders since that year.)

Fire Call. Similar to certain British and French calls.

1st Sergeant's Call. This call is first mentioned in the "Martial Music of Camp Dupont," 1816, when it was a drum call sounded when the Adjutant wished to summon the First Sergeant. The present bugle call, used to notify all First Sergeants to report to the Adjutant or Sergeant Major, comes from the German Army.

NAVY CUSTOMS ARMY OFFICERS SHOULD KNOW

Courtesies. There are Navy customs applicable to shore duty and to the special situations of life aboard a naval vessel. The courtesies pertaining to a naval vessel are provided as of noteworthy interest to officers of the Army on any occasion when they visit or serve aboard a unit of our fleet.

On appropriate occasions when visiting naval vessels, officers of the armed services, except when in civilian clothes, are attended by sailors known as "side boys" when they come aboard and when they depart. This courtesy is also extended to commissioned officers of the armed services of foreign nations. Officers of the rank of lieutenant to major inclusive are given two side boys, from lieutenant colonel to colonel four side boys, from brigadier to major general six side boys, and lieutenant general and above eight side boys. Full guard and band are given to general officers and for a colonel, the guard of the day, but no music.

During the hours of darkness or low visibility an approaching boat is usually hailed "Boat ahoy?" which corresponds to the sentry's challenge, "Who is there?" Some of the answers are as follows:

Answer	Meaning: Senior in boat is:
"Aye aye"	Commissioned officer
"No no"	Warrant officer
"Hello"	Enlisted
"Enterprise"	CO of Enterprise
"Third Fleet"	Admiral Commanding Third Fleet

Similarly if the Commanding General of the 1st Infantry Division is embarked or the Commanding General of Fort Monroe, the answers would be "1st Infantry Division" or "Fort Monroe."

On arrival, at the order, "Tend the side" the side boys fall in fore and aft of the approach to the gangway, facing each other. The boatswain's mate-of-the-watch takes station forward of them and faces aft. When the boat comes alongside the boatswain's mate pipes and again when the visiting officer's head reaches the level of the deck. At this latter instant the side boys salute.

On departure, the ceremony is repeated in reverse; the bosn's mate begins to pipe and side boys to salute as soon as the departing officer steps toward the gangway between the side boys. As the boat casts off the bo's'ns mate pipes again (Shore boats and automobiles are not piped.)

You uncover when entering a space where men are at mess and in Sick Bay (Quarters) if sick men are present. You uncover in the wardroom at all times except when under arms and passing through. All hands except when under arms uncover in the captain's cabin and country.

You should not overtake a senior except in emergency. In the latter case slow, salute, and say, "By your leave, Sir". Admirals, Commanding Officers, and Chiefs of Staff when in uniform fly colors astern when embarked in boats. When officials visit they also display their personal flags (pennants for commanding officers) in the bow. Flag officers' barges are distinguished by the appropriate number of stars on each side of the barge's hull. Captains' gigs are distinguished by the name or abbreviation of their ships surcharged by an arrow.

Use of Navy Titles. In the Navy it is customary to address officers in the grade of lieutenant commander and below, *socially,* as "mister" or "miss," and officers in the grade of commander and above by their titles. *Officially,* officers in both staff and line are addressed by their ranks.

Title of Commanding Officer of a Ship. Any officer in command of a ship, regardless of size or class, while exercising command is addressed as "Captain."

Visiting. Where accommodation ladders are rigged on both sides, the starboard ladder is reserved for officers and the port ladder for enlisted men and women. At the discretion of the officer of the deck (OOD), either ladder may be made available to both officers and enlisted personnel. See Chapter 4 for a quotation of Navy Regulations on courtesy to the Ensign.

Seniors come on board ship first. When reaching the deck you face toward the colors (or aft if no colors are hoisted) and salute the colors (quarterdeck). Immediately thereafter you salute the OOD and request permission to come aboard. The usual form is, "Request permission to come aboard, Sir." The OOD is required to return both salutes.

On leaving the ship the inverse order is observed. You salute the OOD and request permission to leave the ship. The OOD will indicate when the boat is ready (if a boat is used). Each person, juniors first, salutes the OOD; then faces toward the colors (quarterdeck), salutes and debarks.

The OOD on board ship represents the captain and as such has unquestioned authority. Only the executive and commanding officer may order him or her relieved. The authority of the OOD extends to the accommodation ladders or gangways. The OOD has the right to order any approaching boat to "lie off" and keep clear until the boat can be safely received alongside.

The OOD normally conveys orders to the embarked troops via the troop commander but in emergencies may issue orders direct to you or any person on board.

The *bridge* is the "command post" of the ship when underway as the quarterdeck is at anchor. The officer-of-the-deck is in charge of the ship as the representative of the captain. Admittance to the bridge when underway should be at the captain's invitation or with his or her permission. You may usually obtain permission through the executive officer.

The *quarterdeck* is the seat of authority; as such it is respected. The starboard side of the quarterdeck is reserved for the captain (and admiral if a flagship). No person trespasses upon it except when necessary in the course of work or official business. All persons salute the quarterdeck when entering upon it. When pacing the deck with another officer the place of honor is outboard, and when reversing direction each turns towards the other. The port side of the quarterdeck is reserved for commissioned officers, and the crew has all the rest of the weather decks of the ship. However, every part of the deck (and the ship) is assigned to a particular division so that the crew has ample space. Not unnaturally every division considers it has a prior though unwritten right to its own part of the ship. For gatherings such as smokers and movies, all divisions have equal privileges at the scene of assemblage. Space and chairs are reserved for officers and for CPO's, where available, and mess benches are brought up for the enlisted personnel. The seniors have the place of honor. When the captain (and admiral) arrives those present are called to attention. The captain customarily gives "carry on" at once through the executive officer or master-at-arms.

Messes. If you take passage on board a naval vessel you will be assigned to one of several messes on board ship, the wardroom or junior officers' mess. In off-hours, particularly in the evenings, you can foregather there for cards, yarns or reading. Generally a percolator is available with hot coffee.

The executive officer is ex-officio the president of the wardroom mess. The wardroom officers are the division officers and the heads of departments. All officers await the arrival of the executive officer before being seated at lunch and dinner. If it is necessary for you to leave early ask the head at your table permission to be excused as you would at home. The seating arrangement in the messes is by order of seniority.

Calls. Passenger officers should call on the captain of the ship. If there are many of you, you should choose a calling committee and consult the executive officer as to a convenient time to call. The latter will make arrangements with the captain.

Ceremonies. Gun salutes in the Navy are the same as in the Army except that flag officers below the rank of fleet admiral or general of the Army, are, by Navy regulations, given a gun salute upon departure only.

Saluting. By custom, Navy personnel do not salute when uncovered, although it is customary for Navy officers to return the salute of Army and Air Force personnel whether covered or not. Aboard ship, seniors are saluted only during the first greeting in the morning. The Commanding Officer (or any flag or general officer) is saluted whenever met.

AIR FORCE CUSTOMS ARMY OFFICERS SHOULD KNOW

Courtesies*. The rules governing saluting, whether saluting other individuals or paying honor to the color or National Anthem, are the same for the Air Force as the Army. Because the most frequent contact between the Air Force and the other services will probably be as a result of riding in or operating military aircraft, a special section will be devoted to passengers in military aircraft.

Visiting. It is assumed that the majority of officers visiting an Air Force base are there in conjunction with air travel to or from the base. In addition to the base operations officer, who is the commander's staff officer with jurisdiction over all air traffic, the Airdrome Officer is charged with meeting all transient aircraft, determining the transportation requirements of transient personnel, and directing them to the various base facilities. General officers and admirals usually are met by the base commander, if practicable. RON (remain over night) messages may be transmitted through base operations.

Passengers from other services, who desire to remain overnight at an air force station should make the necessary arrangements with the airdrome officer, and not attach themselves to the pilot who will be busy with his or her own responsibilities. By the same token, passengers of other services who have had a special flight arranged for them should make every effort to see that the pilot and crew are offered the same accommodations that they themselves are using, unless that base has adequate transient accommodations.

Passenger vehicles are never allowed on the ramp or flight lines unless special arrangements have been made with the base operations officer; this permission will only be granted under the most unusual circumstances.

*See THE AIR FORCE OFFICER'S GUIDE, Stackpole Books, Harrisburg, Pa.

Travel in Military Aircraft. The assigned first pilot, or the airplane commander, is the final authority on the operation of any military aircraft. Passengers, regardless of rank, seniority, or service, are subject to the orders of the airplane commander, who is solely responsible for their adherence to regulations governing conduct in and around the aircraft. In the event it is impracticable for the airplane commander to leave his or her position, orders may be transmitted through the co-pilot, engineer, or crew chief, and have the same authority as if given personally by the pilot.

The order of boarding and alighting from military aircraft—excluding the crew—will vary somewhat with the nature of the mission. If a special flight is arranged for the transportation of very important persons (VIPs), official inspecting parties, or other high ranking officers of any service, the senior member will exit first, and the other members of the party will follow either in order of rank, or in order of seating, those nearest the hatch alighting first. The duties of the crew preclude their acting as arbiters in matters of precedence, and order of boarding and alighting will be decided among the members of the party.

In routine transportation flights, officers will normally be loaded in order of rank without regard for precedence, except that VIPs will be on-and-off-loaded first. In alighting, officers seated near the hatch generally debark first, and so on to those who are farthest away. In the event dependents are being carried, they together with their sponsor generally are loaded and unloaded after any VIP and before the officers.

Aircraft carrying general or flag officers will usually be marked with a detachable metal plate carrying stars appropriate to the highest rank aboard, and will be greeted on arrival by the Air Force base commander, if the destination is an Air Force base. Other aircraft are usually met by the airdrome officer, who is appointed for one day only, and acts as the base commander's representative.

Since aerial flights are somewhat dependent on weather, especially when carrying passengers, the decision of the pilot to fly or not to fly, or to alter the flight plan en route will not be questioned by the passengers of whatever rank or service. Regulations governing the use of safety belts, against smoking during take-off, landing, and fuel transfer, or in the vicinity of the aircraft on the ground, and in wearing parachutes are binding on all classes of passengers.

A FINAL WORD OF CAUTION

There is a tendency, sometimes, to confuse customs, traditions, and social obligations. *Customs of the Service* as have been treated in this chapter are those which are more universally observed throughout the Army.

Traditions, on the other hand, are considered much less formal than the recognized customs of the Service. There are many more traditions than could be covered here. Many are confined to a particular unit, organization, station, or branch of Service and one is most likely to become acquainted with them quickly upon reporting for a new assignment. Such traditions may "catch on" and become widespread because of the mobile nature of Army life, especially so for those which have a more positive influence on one's personal living.

There is a danger, however, in the expectancy that others will quickly accept a particular thing once you are again outside the area where it has been observed. For example: Many inquiries have been received as to why previous editions of The Officer's Guide offered no counsel about how an officer recognizes his or her promotion in relation to fellow officers and civilian co-workers, if any. Research into this question reveals that, officially, there is no *custom of the service* to provide guidance, nor is there any well-entrenched tradition anywhere. In such an instance as this, inasmuch as promotion is a personal thing, and as such has differing degrees of meaning at various times and places, the officer may choose to do something or nothing, the former on any scale that befits his or her mood, position, or pocketbook at the time.

Caution, therefore, lies in getting acquainted with local traditions and customs and being sure that you are not a party to unjustified criticism of anyone when there is no tangible understanding in the military community about what one does upon this occasion or that.

6

The Social Side
of Army Life

Officers and their families are members upon arrival at a station of the social and cultural life of the military community. This feeling of "oneness" or "belonging" is a natural outcome of the singleness of purpose of the military mission on which all are engaged. It is enhanced by the fact that the problems, the hopes and expectancies, and even the fears, within one military home are similar to those in other military homes. This community of interest is a noteworthy contrast to the experience of newcomers in the usual civilian community where neighbors may not know neighbors, and may live in quite different social worlds. The military community enjoys many advantages.

This chapter is provided as an extension of the preceeding chapter, *Customs of the Service.* Related also to our subject is Chapter Four *Military Courtesy.* The reader should understand that the subjects presented assist in creating an atmosphere and an environment which can provide a pleasant, gracious, and rewarding life. This is important for life in the armed services because of the unusual circumstances of the official missions which are assigned, the frequent change of station, and occasional difficulties in living conditions. More rewarding lives can be experienced by a sensible application of service courtesies, customs, and social expectancies.

Officers and their spouses support activities and follow social customs in about the same manner as people of education and position in other vocations. As they are drawn from all states and regions of our country, they tend to adopt activities which have been enjoyed elsewhere. Army families have the great advantage of being bound together with the common interest of the Army mission and association together in joint undertakings. For these reasons, community interests are likely to be extensive and participation quite general. Like social and civic life elsewhere, including church, fraternal, and similar activities, each individual receives in benefit and enjoyment about the same as he or she contributes.

Army Social Customs. Most social practices observed in Army circles today are the same as in the sister services, or in civil life. Indeed, a large portion of career officers are assigned to duties where they are obliged to live within a civilian community remote from a military station. During a span of years the officer will have the social experience of the Army station as well as the civilian community. The newcomer may proceed with confidence that the social practices which are in good taste and general observance in our civilian communities have similar application within the service community. It is true that there is a heritage of Army social customs, just as there are special customs observed within other closely knit groups of people. In what other walk of life will there be the arrival of families returning from Europe, from a number of stations in the Pacific, Alaska, or other distant lands? Or families departing for these assignments? These situations account for some of the differences. There are infrequent formal dinners and receptions which are held for necessary purposes, as the reception of a high official of our government or of a friendly foreign nation. Take them all in stride. This chapter has been prepared to be helpful. Army social life consists of pleasant human relationships, adding to the enjoyment of service associations, and should be approached with anticipation. At the end of the chapter is a selected bibliography of publications that are useful in describing the social side of Army life.

This is an officer's book, written especially for officers and their families. Because not discussed herein, let no person assume that on Army stations the unmarried or married enlisted soldier draws a blank in social or cultural activities, for such is very far from the case. There are noncommissioned officers' clubs, the service club with professional hostesses, libraries, hobby shops, a broad athletic program, and other activities sponsored generally by Recreation Services.

A Special Message for Newcomers. The newly arriving officer, or officer and family, will find a sincere welcome from the members of the military community. You can eliminate any feeling of "newness" immediately. Unlike civilian communities, where residents reside for years and years, the assignment of officers to a station or duty may continue for no more than three or four years at the most, and where it is a command assignment the tenure may be even less than two years. So as a matter of plain fact, all members of an Army garrison, from the most senior to the most junior, are "new" in the sense of prolonged length of residence.

No person entering an Army community for the first time need be disturbed about the customs or the social practices. In the first place, Army people are kindly and understanding of the special problems of the newcomer, and if given the opportunity will be pleasantly helpful. The social practices are substantially the same as found in any large group of well-educated, professional people. If one is accustomed to the social life of a country club, or a university campus, the activities at an officers club or open mess will be entirely similar. If you have apprehensions, lay them aside. Enter with confidence this new life which can offer many rewarding experiences and friendships. Let people know who you are and that you are pleased to be among them. Seek acquaintances with individuals of your special interests, or backgrounds, or activities. You need not be the life of the party, nor the best dressed person in attendance. Just be a pleasant person, among other pleasant people, and do as you would at a similar social function anywhere.

You will not be expected to do more than normal entertaining which initially would mean the return of obligations, in due time, and in a manner entirely appropriate to your means. A later paragraph discusses with logic the return of hospitality accepted. You may defer the purchase of calling cards, if you do not have them, until you learn the local custom. You should attend the dances and other social activities sponsored by the officers club or open mess, which the payment of dues entitles you to attend. There may be a modest charge for such an event, but club charges will not be large. Participate in dutch treat gatherings, informal picnics, swim parties, and such pleasant events as come your way. Later, as you learn your way around better, and have developed acquaintances you may even organize inexpensive share-the-cost gatherings. Who knows—you may soon be able to help off to a pleasant start some newcomer "newer" than yourself! But manage your personal financial affairs, capably and firmly. You know your pay and allowances, as well as the obligations which you have assumed. You may be relieved to learn that most young officers, single or married, also face the "shortage of dollars" problem. Face it and adjust to it. But do a swell official job for the Army, and then have such good times with pleasant associates as circumstances permit.

The Officers' Club and Mess. The officers' club and mess, known as the "Open Mess," is the center of social activities for officers and their families. Here there are facilities for regular dining, for holding private dinner parties, plus a program of dances, card parties, and other forms of group entertainment desired by the members. (See also Chapter Five for operation of the Open Mess.)

Officials of the club are elected by the members. Committees are appointed to organize and sponsor desired activities. Costs are defrayed by monthly dues and the profits from operation of club activities.

An officer with permanent station at a post having a club should become a member at once. To fail to do so will cause the officer and the adult members of his or her family to miss the very heart of post social activity.

Cultural Opportunities. The cultural opportunities which are available at an established military station equal or exceed those of civilian communities of like size. They provide opportunity for the enjoyment of acquired interests and the development of new ones.

Many such activities are given strong sponsorship by the Officers Wives' Clubs. A number of these clubs are affiliated with state associations. Here will be held on a periodic basis meetings of general interest with lecturers, concerts, and the like. In addition to the general meetings there may be groups with special interests in music, literature, the study of antiques, language study, and any other worthy purpose which the members desire.

Station libraries are well equipped in nearly all instances and the regular receipt of new books and magazines is a usual expectancy. Libraries are under direction of a professional librarian who may be relied upon to render assistance to serious groups or individuals.

Opportunities for Community Service. Military stations and adjoining civilian communities provide opportunities for community service in many worthy causes. Members of Army families may find rewarding activities which pertain to problems of the garrison or join with civilian organizations in work beneficial to the complete community.

There are a variety of social organizations found on every post to which one can volunteer. The Red Cross sponsors Grey Ladies and Nurses Aides. The United Services Organization (USO) has need for workers and hostesses. Chaplains (and off-post ministers) need teachers and helpers. Schools are supported by the Parent-Teachers Association. Scouting and sports activities, like Little League baseball, need the support of all parents.

There are also some special organizations. It is important to identify a few for example but no slight is intended for other like, but unmentioned, organizations:

Daughters, United States Army, DUSA. This is an organization of daughters, stepdaughters, adopted daughters or granddaughters of commissioned officers of the Regular Army. Members must have attained age sixteen. Twenty-six chapters carry out the ideals, customs, and traditions of the Service by sponsoring worthy causes and patriotic activities as determined by each local chapter. They also award college scholarships on a national basis to eligible daughters, stepdaughters, or adopted daughters of retired or deceased Regular Army officers according to need, merit, activities, and other qualifications.

The Junior Army Navy Guild Organization, JANGO. These guilds form a link between the Services and the community while promoting a feeling of family relationship and loyalty to the Services. JANGO is composed of wives and daughters of active or retired commissioned or warrant officers of the Armed Forces of the United States. They provide volunteer services to canteens and hospitals and they raise funds for scholarships and local charitable organizations. For information write to JANGO, Inc., Henderson Hall, Fort Myer, Arlington, Virginia 22211 (Tel. 979-1492).

Social and Recreational Opportunities for Young People. An Army station is a healthy and interesting environment for young people because of the many very active organizations which in most cases are to be found in thriving condition. There is the same need for social and recreational opportunities for boys and girls living on or near an Army post as in civilian communities.

Boy Scout, Little League, Girl Scout, Cub Scout, and Brownie troops are established at most Army stations where families are present. Many stations provide a Teen-Age Club for boys and girls of high school age where there are dances, picnics, and other forms of entertainment attractive to healthy and active young people.

The Chaplain sponsors religious activities for young people.

Needed always are adults who will serve as leaders in these splendid activities and those who do find the experience rewarding and interesting.

Building Social Good Will. The building of social good will is the development of respect and esteem of a person within a military group. In gist it is the sum of an infinite number of favorable impressions. Almost certainly it will have an effect upon an officer's career. In any event the giving of social offense must do harm. This discussion deals with its fundamentals.

Strive to be on good terms with all. A member of a military family will have likes and preferences in developing friendships and friendly associations just as any other person. Avoid cliques. Avoid open expressions of criticism or dislike which develop hard feelings. Do not always restrict your dinner guests, golfing companions, and other social associates to the same individuals. Mix them up. Broaden your acquaintance. By so doing you will reap the reward of building more friendships and finding more people of interest.

Upon receiving a social invitation express appreciation at being included. Accept at once if that is your wish. Decline at once if unable to accept and again extend a courteous word of appreciation. If there is uncertainty about being able to accept state the reason for uncertainty. It is better to accompany uncertainty with a declination so the hostess, if she wishes to do so, may invite others. If invited to accept or decline at a later time give the answer at the earliest possible moment. Do not keep the hostess dangling in uncertainty longer than necessary. Remember in expressing appreciation that it is the hostess or host who is extending the courtesy—not the guest by accepting.

Have a social calendar and write in occasion, date, and hour.

Arrival for a dinner engagement should be promptly at the hour stated by the hostess. There are problems of timing which apply with equal force to the simple home dinner and the formal dinner for a large gathering. It is rude to arrive late at a dinner unless the tardiness is indeed unavoidable; even then the hostess should be informed by telephone if at all possible. Prompt arrival is essential at other social events, such as a card party, or gathering for other specific purpose where the presence of all invited guests at a stated time is clearly desirable. Where the invitation is for a stated period, as "6—8," the situation and custom differs. The invited guests may arrive after 6, and depart before 8, but they do not customarily remain more than briefly after the hour stated because it may interfere with other plans of host and hostess.

PRACTICAL TIPS

The Right Clothes.

In these days of informality, selection of the proper clothes to wear on various occasions can be a problem. The first point to consider is whether the the occasion is essentially a military function or a private affair. For military functions, the proper uniform may be specified, thus settling the problem immediately. However, if the proper uniform is not stated, the following are suggested:

Parades and retreats	Service uniform
Official call or informal dinner	Service uniform, with coat
Formal dinner or official reception	Evening dress uniform or Mess uniform

For informal private dinners or cocktail parties, a business suit for males or a cocktail dress, simple dinner dress or dressy buiness suit for females should be adequate. Your host or hostess may thoughtfully suggest appropriate attire for the occasion. When in doubt, it is better to overdress than to underdress for the occasion, but if in real doubt, inquire. And remember that the appropriate attire for your spouse is just as important as it is for you.

If you are proceeding from a cocktail party to a more formal function, it is proper to wear to the cocktail party appropriate attire for the more formal affair.

The Right Words.

Introducing your wife to any man (except Chiefs of State and very high church dignitaries): "Mary, this is Colonel Brown."

Introducing one lady to another: "Mrs. Jones, may I present Mrs. Green," or "Mary, this is Mrs. Green."

Introducing one officer to another: "Major Smith, this is Captain Brown."

Introducing yourself to an officer senior to you: "Sir, may I introduce myself? I am Captain Jones." (Wait for the other to extend his hand.)
Introducing yourself to an officer of equal or lesser rank: "I'm Captain Jack Jones." (Extend your hand.)
Introducing children or teen-agers to adults: "Lieutenant Jones, this is Jane Smith."
Responding to an introduction: "How do you do, Colonel Green."
Thanking host and hostess on departing a social function: "Thank you for a delightful evening."
If you *must* leave a function noticeably early: "Mrs. (Hostess), I'm so sorry I must leave early." (Then give reason and make it good, and be sure it is good.)
Using titles with names—
        Major General Black: "General Black."
        Brigadier General White: "General White."
        Colonel Smith: "Colonel Smith."
        Lt. Colonel Jones: "Colonel Jones."
        First Lieutenant Brown: "Lieutenant Brown."
        Second Lieutenant Green: "Lieutenant Green."

At any social gathering guests should strive to make the occasion pleasant for all. Conversation is important. Visit with all or many of the other guests. It is better to be a good listener than a good talker. But a good listener needs to be adept at starting subjects of conversation. What are the mutual interests? Who are mutual but absent friends? Has the other guest just returned from an interesting trip? Think of a subject above the commonplace and start the conversation. Then listen. *Avoid controversial subjects.* Let host and hostess set the pace. Avoid being a wet blanket. Do not "take over" the party. Be agreeable. Don't be one of the few who are adept at how to make enemies and antagonize people. Use the opportunity of your host's hospitality to broaden your acquaintance and strengthen friendships.

Social gatherings of military people will include in most cases officers of a wide span of grade and age. Most senior officers enjoy association with younger officers and their wives or husbands. Make a point of saying a pleasant greeting and having at least a brief conversation with the senior officers present and their spouses. The older or senior guests will do their part in making the younger ones feel at ease. Make a special point of greeting your company, battalion, and higher unit commander and general officers of your station, and their wives or husbands. Meet them as social equals, for such is your status as an officer or officer's spouse. Be polite and respectful but never subservient.

Is there a guest of honor or house guest? If so, make special effort soon after arrival to be sociable with them by conversation which indicates your true interest in them and their visit.

How long to stay as a guest after a dinner or other evening invitation depends upon the program of the hostess. Unless a reason exists to the contrary, a good rule to observe is to depart no more than an hour after the service of dinner is completed. In these busy days within military circles, the custom is for early departure. When the commanding officer is present as a guest, especially at a formal event, he or she is first to depart and has the special obligation of departing at the appropriate time. For purposes of general illustration assuming dinner guests arriving at 8, goodnights are often appropriate by 10:30. At informal affairs of any kind another good guide post is to depart before host and hostess can possibly begin to wonder as to the departure intentions of their guest.

In making a departure, do not dawdle. There are few things more irritating than the guest who prepares to depart, then stands on and on in hall or doorway, narrating little nothings while hosts stand patiently by. Arise, express your pleasure for the occasion, obtain outer wraps, say your gracious farewells, and leave.

Social Calls. Social calling on other officers and their wives or husbands, at their quarters, is an established, useful Army custom. It welcomes newcomers, broadens acquaintanceships, makes pleasant farewells. In view of varying local conditions, inquire as to the desired policy from the immediate commander, adjutant, executive, or from the commanding officer. Follow the established local custom.

Welcoming Newcomers. A delightful feature of Army life is that the newcomer is made to feel a part of the military community from the time of arrival. Those who live nearby are most likely to seek opportunity for informal meetings promptly after arrival to extend a greeting, to proffer small aids especially as to information, and the like. It will be assumed that the newly arrived officer and spouse are worthy and respectable people who will constitute an addition to the garrison. This doesn't mean that they are embraced as long lost friends, or their privacy invaded. It means that there is an absence of "standoffishness." A formal call will be appropriate after the newcomers are settled. *Suggestion:* Read the chapter conclusion.

Who Should Receive Calls. Army custom governs calling so that only infrequently is there confusion about who should receive first calls. At many stations the adjutant will tell the newcomer the local custom.

AR 600–25, prescribes official calls; this regulation is quoted extensively in Chapter Four, *Military Courtesy.*

Officers of the command other than the commanders stated pay the first call upon newcomers, and the newcomers return these calls as soon as practicable.

At large posts a reception may be given including a receiving line where all have opportunity to meet newcomers to the organization or station. Often this is announced as constituting the first call and its return.

In time of war or emergency, social calls may be announced as optional to the individual. But if you take such an announcement as justification for making no calls at all, you do an injustice to your spouse. You will meet your brother and sister officers in the daily discharge of your duties. But your spouse does not have this opportunity and may encounter loneliness which is easily avoidable.

Dress for Calls. A good principle is that the callers honor the family receiving the call by reasonable dignity of attire. An officer in semidress uniform is correctly dressed under all circumstances. A lady may elect with propriety suitable street clothing, or a suit, with hat and gloves.

How To Make a Call. Calls are made appropriately on Sunday afternoon, the hours of 3 to 4 or 5 being appropriate, or in the evening from 8 to 9. At some stations the calling hours are announced for the convenience of officers.

The duration of these calls is about 15 minutes.

If it is a first call upon a newcomer it is a pleasant, brief, get-acquainted meeting. It is a good occasion to offer to supply helpful information, if it seems to be desired, especially about matters of special interest regarding post activities which are known by the callers.

Make no excuses about the short stay upon departure. Indeed, to stay longer may embarrass your hosts with other plans. Arise, express your gracious farewells, leave your cards, and depart.

Return of Calls. An officer who receives callers, or calling cards as stated below, must return the calls, just as an officer receiving a salute must return the salute. The return call should be made within 10 days although where numbers are large such promptness may be out of the question.

Parting or Going Away Calls. Upon receipt of change of station orders it is an Army custom to make parting or going away calls. By custom, they should be made upon the commanding officer and it would be proper for a lieutenant to call upon his or her company commander, battalion and regimental commander, at their quarters, as one illustration. They are made to the extent desired upon friends.

Calls Upon Friends in Hospital. Army people are solicitous of friends in hospital. When they are able to have callers close friends drop by for a brief visit. It is appropriate to leave a gift of a plant, flowers, a book.

Calling Cards. An old social custom in civil as well as military life is the use of calling cards when making formal social calls, to accompany gifts, for writing a brief message, and other purposes. These cards are not used as extensively these days as in the 1930s and earlier years. But they are still quite useful.

Their continued use by Army officers serves a special purpose. The fluid nature of military assignments involves a continuous change of the station residents. All families of a garrison are "new" in contrast to civilian communities. Therefore official and social calls have a unique importance. They help increase acquaintances, some of which ripen into friendships. The use of calling cards is helpful in the difficult problem of names. Like most customs, the use of social calling cards has lived because it serves a useful purpose.

The accompanying illustrations are correct in form. Cards may be obtained from service school book departments, large department stores, engravers, and many jewelers.

Officers do not use social calling cards in their official contacts. There is no military counterpart of the civilian business card.

Leave cards without comment by placing them in a convenient receptacle provided for the purpose, or upon a table. An officer leaves a card for each adult member of the family, maximum 3. An officer's wife leaves a card for each adult lady of the household, maximum 3, while an officer's husband similarly leaves a card for each adult male of the household, maximum 3.

It is correct to leave cards at the door when hosts are not at home. It is Army custom, if this is done, to identify yourself at a later appropriate time and say something gracious as, "Captain Jones and I were sorry you were away when we called." Such calls require return, under Army custom, just the same as callers actually received.

The use of the initial P.P.C. in lower left corner, in ink, may be used for parting or going away calls, such as farewells preceding a change of station. The initials mean *pour prendre congé*—to take leave.

Calling cards for social use should be engraved. The lettering should be simple and clear. Upon promotion it is possible to have the plate changed at reduced cost to save part of the expense of a new plate. Some engraving companies insist upon making complete new plates. Some do not.

Folded Cards (not calling cards). Folded cards are often used as a means of extending invitations. "Cocktails 5 to 7" with the date, written upon an officer's card, if single, or a joint card, if a married couple are hosts, is a common practice. A joint unfolded card is equally appropriate for the purpose. Folded cards which provide more space than the conventional calling card are also used for brief written notes.

Folded cards may be mailed in envelopes. The Post Office accepts no envelopes smaller than 3 inches by 4 inches.

Some Questions and Answers. What sizes and types of cards should be used for official calls? The same size of social calling cards normally in good taste for civilian use. The cards in the accompanying illustrations are substantially correct in size and shape.

HAROLD LOUIS NEATE

LIEUTENANT
UNITED STATES ARMY

CAPTAIN NOAH MATTHEW JACKSON
AIDE-DE-CAMP TO MAJOR GENERAL SECREST

UNITED STATES ARMY

LIEUTENANT COLONEL AND MRS. NATHAN MENZO NEELY

Edna Trude Shope

Colonel
United States Army

EXAMPLES OF CALLING CARDS.

Should the complete name be used or may the middle initial be used? Example John Joseph Sawbridge or John J. Sawbridge? Usually the complete name is used and is the best form; where the name is unduly long for use on a calling card it is acceptable to use the middle initial.

Which is correct for a wife? Examples: Mrs. John Joseph Sawbridge or Mrs. Virginia Mae Sawbridge? Mrs. John Joseph Sawbridge is correct; it is never correct for a wife to use the latter form on social calling cards.

Should the branch of service be used on the military card? Only "United States Army," "United States Navy," or "United States Air Force" should be used. It is no longer considered good form to use the Army basic branch on calling cards.

How does an officer indicate his or her grade and service? As shown on the several examples accompanying this discussion. Officers on active duty whether Regular, National Guard, or Reserve use identical forms.

When should the joint card be used? They may be used as leaving cards at formal calls. They are convenient for the issue of invitations, or to accompany gifts.

Introductions. Adeptness must be developed in the art of making introductions. Here are the simple guides. See also "Practical Tips," above.

Gentlemen are introduced or presented to ladies, not the reverse. This holds even though the gentleman may be very distinguished and the lady very young. *Exceptions:* The President of the United States, a royal personage, a church dignitary.

The most common way to make introductions, always in good taste, is to state the names in proper sequence, the lady, the senior, or more distinguished, or more elderly first. "General Smith—Captain Jones." "Miss Youthful—Colonel Adams." "Mrs. Elderly Lady—General Cole." Use a rising inflection for the first name pronounced. The more formal method: "General Smith, may I present Captain Jones?"

Acknowledgement of an introduction by saying "How do you do?" is always appropriate.

When men are introduced they shake hands, standing, without reaching across another person, if possible. They may say nothing, just look pleasant or smile, or say a courteous, "It is nice to meet you," or "How do you do?"

When women are introduced to each other, with one sitting, one standing, the seated one rises to greet her hostess, or a very distinguished lady, as an act of respect. This would apply, for example, to the wife of a very senior officer. In the usual case, the seated lady does not rise. The reply to an introduction may be a simple, "How do you do?"

When a man is introduced to a lady he does not offer his hand unless the lady proffers hers. It is correct for a lady to bow in acknowledgement of an introduction. In Europe, men are taught to take the initiative in hand shaking. A lady does not refuse a proffered hand.

A lady or man, introducing husband or wife to another, may say, "This is my husband," or "May I introduce my wife?"

At a social occasion, host and hostess should shake hands with guests in greeting, and upon their departure.

Memory of Names. Military people meet officially or socially such a large number of people that remembering names is a difficult problem. Still, it is a very important attribute. To remember at all you must first understand the name clearly. Therefore, at time of introduction, be sure to hear and understand the name correctly. Repeat it aloud to assure correctness and to aid your memory; your interest will please and flatter many. During the occasion strive to use the name in conversation, and fix the name to the face of the person. Be very careful in making introductions to state names correctly, and distinctly.

A cherished treasure is a notebook in which you record the names of people you should remember. List their complete names and middle initials. List names of husband and wife. For family friends list names of children and birthdays if known. After the passage of months or years such a record may be of much interest and assistance.

A Glance at Social Precedence and Protocol. An understanding of basic principles of social precedence and protocol is essential to officers as well as to officials of many other professional groups who have a recognized or official title. *Examples:* Educators; ministers and high church officials; elected or appointed officials of the national, state, or local government; foreign military, government, or professional dignitaries; others. Protocol in simple definition is "the code of international politeness."

Precedence becomes a factor for host and hostess to consider in deciding who sits where at a dinner, or in deciding places at a speaker's table, or positions in a receiving line, or other formal occasion. It is important at universities whenever the faculty is assembled formally as at a graduation ceremony. Legislators in state or national capitol must make use of it.

The place of honor is on the right or in the lead: *Examples:* The senior walks on the right of the junior. Juniors step aside for the senior to be first to enter a door. The senior is last to enter an automobile, but is first to leave, and the right rear seat is reserved for him or her. The senior returns the salute of the junior. An officer of lesser rank is presented to the senior. Age is a very decided consideration in social precedence, especially in a mixed group as to profession and vocation.

The form of address is a related subject. It is "Mr. President," "Mr. Chief Justice," "Mr. Secretary," or "Mr. Secretary of the Army." In Massachusetts and some other states the governor has the official right to the title "Excellency"; thus by custom in all or most states it is "His Excellency, the Governor," or "Excellency"; it can be "Governor Jones," but it is incorrect merely to use the address "Governor."

Formal Receptions and Receiving Lines. For understandable reasons, the formal reception is probably used more within military stations than by other professional groups. This is likely to be true because of the frequency of receiving official visits by military and civilian dignitaries. They are convenient for other special events such as a wedding reception, honoring a newly married bride and groom, or the introduction at a social occasion of a group of newly arrived officers and spouses.

Invitations to official receptions are accepted as first priority unless duty prevents.

An officer will wear the Army Blue, other blue or white dress uniform, or service semidress, as prescribed or as local custom makes appropriate. Spouses dress appropriately to the occasion. In the evening a formal evening dress would be customary. In the afternoon a semi-formal gown, currently called a "cocktail" dress in some localities, would be in good taste. But let this be emphasized: in these days of swift changes and high prices, a lady dressed neatly in a nice street dress would cause no lifted eyebrows at a social event on an Army post.

Strict protocol is observed at formal receptions. At an official function the host ranks first, then the hostess, and then the honorees. For example, the commanding officer of the unit holding the reception is on the right of the receiving line, his wife on his left; next is the ranking honored guest, with his lady on his left; other officers and their wives extending the line in the same manner. If civilians are members of the receiving line their place is indicated by the host in which he will be guided by his own good judgment.

It is customary upon arrival at a reception for the guests to go down a receiving line. An aide or protocol officer is often used to announce the names of the guests to the host. Except at the White House or a diplomatic reception, the lady precedes the gentleman through a receiving line. At the White House the gentleman precedes and is presented to the President of the United States, then the officer presents his wife to the President. Each person in a receiving line usually introduces the guests to the person next on his or her left. A simple, cordial greeting, using correct names, is in order.

The ladies remove gloves for gentle but firm handclasps; it is both awkward and rude to have cigarettes or drinks in your hands when you proceed through the reception line.

Some occasion, dinner, dance, cocktails, etc., will follow, after which make appropriate farewells to the hosts and the guests of honor.

Order of Seating and Service at Dinner. At a seated dinner with guests the lady of honor sits at the right of the host, the second lady on his left. The gentleman to be honored is seated on the right of the hostess and the second gentleman on her left.

Where the guests are all from military families the arrangement is a simple one for all officers have an official standing, one with another. Wives are seated in the same order as their husbands. In a mixed military and civilian group some thought must be given to a precedence list to avoid embarrassment. This is true especially when the guests include officials of government, university, church, or other high professional status. It is customary for experienced Army hostesses to accord the first positions to the senior officer present and his or her spouse, unless there is an overriding reason to do otherwise. If the matter seems to be especially important consult Mrs. Commanding Officer who is almost certain to be an experienced hostess and willing to advise. Then make up the lists, lay out the place cards if used, and go ahead with confidence, making no excuses whatever, and look to the goal which is a pleasant occasion for all. A skilled hostess having considered seniority and other protocol factors will arrange the seating so that compatible partners result—ones who can entertain each other with mutual sociability, stimulating conversation, and the special program of the evening such as dancing.

The correct order of service is as follows: The untouched dish with unused serving utensils is presented to the lady seated at the right of the host. The dish then passes around the table to the right, the hostess being served in turn, and the host last. A second untouched dish may be presented to the second lady as a mark of respect with service thereafter passing to the left. At a luncheon for ladies with a guest of honor seated at the right of the hostess, service is started with the guest of honor and proceeds as stated above. There is only one occasion when the hostess is served first: at a table when the hostess is the only lady present such as the entertainment of a group of bachelor officers by a captain and his wife.

For wine service the host pours a small amount into his own glass and tastes it. If he thinks it a worthy wine, service starts; as for food, the host's glass is last to be filled.

Seating Arrangement at a Speaker's Table. At a luncheon, dinner, or banquet where there is a head table or speaker's table, the same principles apply in determining the order of seating. The chairman or other individual presiding at the gathering sits in the center. The most distinguished gentleman, who is usually the speaker, sits at his right. The next most distinguished is on his left, and so on alternately across the head table. If ladies are seated at the table a lady speaker would be seated at the right of the presiding official. If not the speaker, then the most distinguished lady is seated on his left. Thereafter alternate ladies and gentlemen, which places the younger or more junior people at the extremities.

Return of Hospitality Accepted. It is a good and sensible rule that hospitality accepted should be returned. Those who accept all invitations which come their way and never return the hospitality, earn deservedly much ill will.

There is another good and sensible rule. No person or family should entertain socially beyond their means. In the service there is no occasion or precedent for "keeping up with the Jones's." Most officers are dependent upon service pay. They have nothing to gain by trying to maintain a social standard beyond their bank accounts and if they do so they will receive more disapproval than favor. Still, hospitality accepted must be returned.

The saving grace is that hospitality accepted need not be returned on the same standard, or even by the same means. Let us work with an example. Colonel Oldtimer is in command of a brigade and has with him Mrs. Oldtimer,

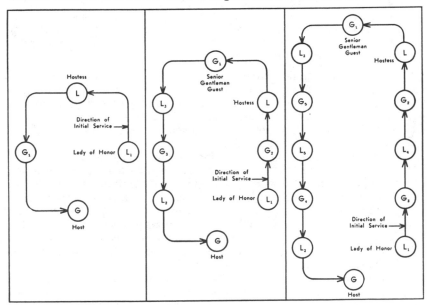

Fig. 1.
Seating, Dinner for Four.

Fig. 2.
Seating, Dinner for Eight.

Fig. 3.
Seating, Dinner for Twelve.

SEATING AND SERVING GUESTS AT DINNER.

a gracious lady who has a well equipped and fairly large home of which she is quite proud. Three new officers with their families join the command. Soon all three with their wives or husbands are invited to dinner. The Oldtimers go to some trouble to entertain them well, with their best china, linen, and silver, food and drinks. They have done this with no thought of "impressing" the newcomers, nor to emphasize their more senior position (and higher pay checks); they wish to show the newcomers that they are welcome and respected as valuable members of the organization. Also, being oldtimers, they have accumulated nice things which they enjoy using.

How may such hospitality be returned in good grace? By all manner of means. By a simple home dinner served by the hostess and aided by the host. By a buffet supper with an inexpensive and simple menu. By an outdoor picnic. By a dinner at the officers' club. Further to reduce expenses, two officers may go together as joint hosts and hostesses.

No excuses need be offered and to do so would express poor taste. All officers have gone over about the same financial hurdles. They know the costs of raising a family and the expenses of frequent changes of station. They have about the same unfavorable views of those who elect to live beyond their means. Don't do it.

Bachelor officers should follow the same course. While bachelors may not have quarters suitable for entertaining, there are a number of solutions. A dinner or cocktail party at the officers club, or a picnic, are examples.

Here is a social program which will meet the requirements and lie within the financial capabilities of nearly all officers. Belong to the officers' mess (club) and attend its social events. Sponsor or join Dutch treat dinners at these club events. Attend all official receptions because you are expected to attend them, if invited, and in general they establish no obligation. Accept invitations from your commanding officers, staff officers and close official associates, and from those other families whom you know and like, or whose friendship you wish to cultivate. With graciousness and politeness, decline the others.

The Art of Being a Good House-Guest. Much has been written about the art of being a good host. But all too little has been written about being a good house-guest, and it needs doing. Thoughtlessness or ignorance sometimes play havoc with cherished friendships. Thoughtfulness will cement and strengthen them. As in all other human relationships social manners are the result of a proper regard for the rights of others.

The host and hostess should be informed as nearly as practicable of the exact hour of planned arrival and departure. This will enable them to plan your visit and permit them to plan to resume their normal contacts and activities. Particularly annoying is the invited guest who accepts an invitation and states only that he will arrive during a day. The hostess is left in the dark. Will arrival be morning, afternoon or evening? Should she remain at home cancelling other things she has planned in order to be certain to receive the guest upon arrival? Shall she plan the evening meal for the guest's presence? Equally troublesome is the guest who neglects to announce a definite time as to departure. The hostess will wish to extend all possible consideration to the guest but upon departure will wish to resume the threads of other activities. She may wish to keep or cancel in advance a beauty shop appointment. Attend her bridge club. Complete necessary shopping. Uncertainty in these routine arrangements is displeasing. Of course the guest who arrives to stay 'for a few days' and fails to inform the hosts even as to the day of planned departure until descending with packed bags to say farewells passes entirely beyond the pale. One way to do it is a letter, telegram, or telephone call which might state: "Thanks for your kind invitation. We accept with pleasure. We plan to arrive at your home soon after four Friday afternoon and must start our return before nine on Monday morning." The houseguest who accepts a week-end or other invitation of more than short duration without making known these simple things which are usually left to the desires of the guest has taken a firm and certain step which often will deny him or her receiving further invitations. Having established these days and dates, bend heaven and earth to keep them.

A guest must adjust to the conditions of the household. A man guest should keep his things picked up and his room tidy. The bathroom should be left in the same condition as he found it. A lady guest should take complete care of her room and be similarly thoughtful of the bath. A lady guest in a servantless home should share in the household work to the extent that is welcome or acceptable. In this way hosts and guests have more uncrowded hours in which to enjoy one another and the hostess is spared excessive strains.

If plans have been made or suggested, the guest must show pleasure in sharing them. Adaptability is the pass-word.

Both host and hostess will require some time to be by themselves in order to take care of personal responsibilities. Make it easy for them to do so. Take a walk, write a letter, read a book. This will permit the hostess to go for her groceries, or visit the beauty parlor, and the host to discharge some small but essential responsibility.

An invitation by a guest to take the family of the host out to dinner is often a welcomed courtesy but it must not be pressed if once proffered and declined.

Prior to departure be certain no personal belongings are left behind for the host to package and mail. A remembrance to the hosts in the form of flowers, candy, a book, given either before or after departure, is generally most appreciated. A thank-you letter written a day or two after departure is a necessary but often overlooked courtesy.

The guest who fails to do these things and others which will suggest themselves will fall into the old saying, "making the hosts twice glad—glad when the guest arrives, and glad when the guest departs." Doing them may result in future invitations. The essence is regard for others.

MORAL STANDARDS

It is a natural curiosity for the newcomer to the military community to wonder about moral standards to be encountered. Will a person of high standards of morality and conduct be obliged to accept the repugnant from official or social associates? Will a person, man or woman, be helped or harmed by membership in the military garrison?

Officers and their spouses are drawn into the Army from our civilian population. For the most part they are men and women of better than average education and civilian background because of the definite requirements which must be satisfied to become an officer. They bring into the service the customs, standards, expectancies which are common in the communities in which they have lived. Now they enter a society which is concerned in a common cause. The officer is subject to military discipline and to the Code of Military Justice. He or she may be punished, even dismissed for "conduct unbecoming an officer." Transgressors from moral and conduct codes tend to eliminate themselves. In such a closely knit community it is natural that each person should wish to deserve the goodwill of associates, not their scorn. For these reasons it is a fact that the moral and conduct standards to be encountered in the military service are at least as high, and almost certainly, a little higher, than is to be encountered elsewhere.

Are all the brothers courageous, and all the sisters virtuous? Well, not quite all. Officers and their wives or husbands are people. Among them will be those whose frailties show. There will always be the few in any group who drink too much, or gamble too much. All of the problems of men and women have not been solved by the military.

We will attempt a word of advice: *Put your best foot forward and keep it there.* Think of the effect of your conduct upon others, newcomers and your juniors especially, with little thought or none to the effect of their conduct upon you. Your morals will continue to be what you make them.

PROBLEMS IN LIVING OFF POST

It must remain true that a very large portion of Army families seek off-post quarters for the inescapable reason that there are too few sets of family quarters to meet the need. Many officers will have a duty assignment within a post or station, but reside with their families in a civilian community. This condition presents problems which must be faced and solved as well as opportunities to be embraced.

The usual officer and family will wish to enjoy congenial relations with the residents of the new area. They may wish to participate in some community educational, religious, fraternal, or recreational facilities. Generally these facilities are made available to newcomers upon application, or upon an invitation extended. A little tact is called for. Make judicious inquiries. Remember that the good things enjoyed by a community were obtained by the vision and work of the residents, and paid for by taxes, dues or donated funds. It is likely that the residents will be entirely willing to share many of these things with the transient military family but they will do it more willingly when it is appreciated.

There are some negative considerations. If you think your own home town or city, or your last station, or your next one, are to be preferred to the present location—keep it carefully to yourself. If you think a particular merchant or landlord is overcharging, don't denounce all local merchants and landlords as cheats and gougers; just take your patronage elsewhere. Keep quiet about the more favorable prices at post exchange or commissary; local merchants cannot meet all of these prices. Avoid doing or saying the things which irritate and annoy. They may determine whether you receive the hand of fellowship, or the cold shoulder.

It is a wise course to meet and make yourself known to the businessmen and others with whom you will wish to have contacts. This means the banker, the grocer, the garage servicing your car, the minister of your church, perhaps the superintendent of schools. If you will need credit arrangements, make them in a businesslike manner. Establish yourself as a new and desirable member of the community.

You will have about the same privileges regarding facilities and activities on post as you would have if living in post quarters. That is to say, you will have full privileges of the officer's open mess, and post organizations and facilities of all sorts. Judicious choice must be made between the activities in town and those of the military station. The primary interest may properly lie on post. Divide your activities between post and town on the basis of convenience and use both.

As time passes associations may ripen into friendships and life itself be enriched by these local contacts.

ENCOURAGEMENT FOR THE SHORT-TIMER

The officer and spouse who are on a short active-duty tour want to profit by it, yet have a special problem of understanding and action. Both will wish to receive maximum enjoyment from their service experiences and to enrich their lives as may be possible from service associations and travel. But many short-timers sit back, assume they are neither especially wanted nor really welcome, and drift into the fringes and shadows of the military community. What a pity! This discussion is intended as a start into a more rewarding result.

Good advice to any service family, including especially those of short expectancy of service, is to participate fully in the various recreational and welfare activities of the military community. No one will care whether you are to become a "long-timer" or "short-timer." You are there today and that is all most people will wish to know about. Attend the official, social, athletic, and other events as time permits. Know your general, your colonel, major, captain, and their spouses, at the same time making sure as best you can that they know you. At social occasions be sure to introduce yourself to the senior officers, their spouses, and their guests; in departing, to the extent appropriate, express your farewells. You will soon become known. Accept membership on appropriate committees or activities which lie within your interests. Soon your reward will be a widened circle of acquaintances some of whom will become lasting friends. Point and reason will replace the mysteries of service customs. Indeed, you should find interest and appeal in a life which before might have seemed somewhat dull. The dullness resulted from your timid approach. You will get from the life about what you put into it.

ARMY DISTAFF HALL

The Army Distaff Hall provides a pleasant and congenial home for Army widows age 62 or older, and in addition the mother, daughter, sister or mother-in-law of a Regular Army officer, or of a Reserve officer with twenty years' active service. Eligible also are retired female officers.

It is a beautiful residence placed in beautiful grounds overlooking Rock Creek Park at 6200 Oregon Ave., N.W., Washington, D.C. It is a four-story multi-winged building designed with professional skill to meet the special needs of the residents. Army families are justified in taking pride in the achievement. A portion of the construction and equipment funds were raised by contributions from Army people, by funds raised at Army stations, as well as gifts from civilian sources.

Sustained financial support from individuals, and the important periodic contributions by Officers' Wives' Clubs, is needed for the financial progress of the Foundation and for the essential assistance of some residents of the Hall.

Inquiries are welcomed about eligibility, vacancies, or other matters of interest.

For information, write to the Army Distaff Foundation, at the address above.

CONCLUSION

The social side of Army life may now be understood as opportunity to participate actively in a wide variety of interesting and essential activities. Life will be interesting or dull, stimulating or empty—as *you* make it. There are dances, receptions, dinners, of course. There are activities of general appeal at the

Officers' Club or Open Mess. There are opportunities for athletics. But beyond the realm of the purely social and entertainment features are the many essential activities of life at an Army station, from assisting at work of the PTA or Red Cross, to acting as Den Mother of Cub Scouts, to coach of a team of the Little League, and many, many others. The garrison of an Army station, including off-post members as well as those who have quarters onpost, resembles any other American community, plus the added factor of the military mission which binds all together in common purpose.

A SELECTED BIBLIOGRAPHY

Useful books and magazines are available on social customs in general, and others with special reference to the military services. Post and station libraries are usually well equipped with these references. Each Army family should add selected ones to their home libraries.

Etiquette, Emily Post, Funk and Wagnalls Co.
Complete Book of Etiquette, Amy Vanderbilt, revised periodically. Doubleday.
The Army Wife, Nancy Shea, Harper Brothers.
The Complete Guide for the Serviceman's Wife, Land and others, Houghton Mifflin Co.
Service Etiquette, McCandless and others, U.S. Naval Institute, Annapolis, Md.

7

Financial Planning

A prudent officer will have a financial plan to assure personal security regardless of marital status. Bachelor officers should plan for security in later life and for the reasonable possibility of leaving the ranks of the unwed. Married officers face the greatest challenge for their plans must include security for their families. The foundation for an officer's financial planning is what the government provides in return for faithful and often hazardous service. Government benefits are a solid base. Objective, realistic foresight should identify the basic requirements of each person, while timely action will start the mission. As the years pass, the initial program will be adjusted as changing circumstances make necessary. The right start at the right time is important.*

The Army officer accepts definite hazards. Short tours of foreign service may require separation from the officer's family. Each of the last four decades has found our country involved in war or combat short of war, with intervening threats to the nation's security. Whatever may await our government and our citizens in the coming years, we must recognize that the hazard of war will continue until the nations and peoples of the world learn to live in peace with one another. Many officers of the Army of today have been in combat in the Korean War, or in Vietnam, or both. The prudent officer, planning for future possibilities, should include the possibility that part of his or her future active service may be in combat, or combat support. It is a harsh platitude to state that combat may result in death or disability, but it is true and it needs

---

*(Suggested supplemental reading: OFFICER'S MANUAL OF PERSONAL FINANCE AND INSURANCE—*Stackpole Books*. All about finance, insurance, investments, etc., for the officer's personal program.)

saying. An Army officer should identify as accurately as possible future responsibilities and goals, and decide what action is necessary to attain them.

This chapter is provided to help all officers in their financial planning for personal and family security. Other sources of study and reference are cited for detailed guidance. The chapter goal is to provide a concise, informative introduction to the subject. Thought and foresight are needed. Since the Army wife or husband may need to manage these affairs during the absence of the service member, many officers see the wisdom of sharing the entire process of deciding and acting in program development.

If the task or the responsibility seems heavy, be encouraged by the truth that most career officers find it possible to lead interesting, rewarding lives and at the same time provide for the uncertainties and potential requirements of their future years.

WARPROOF YOUR PERSONAL AFFAIRS

FINANCIAL SECURITY

Financial security is a continuous requirement while one is on active service and while one is retired. A security program thus provides both for emergencies and planned events. An Army husband and wife team must identify their family goals through retirement by planning, budgeting, saving, and otherwise providing for such events as college education, buying a home, paying a major dental bill, and going on a retirement tour. Even without the hazards of combat, parents must face with realism the untimely death of either husband or wife. Having foreseen their obligations and responsibilities, they must previously have taken the security actions that are reasonable, prudent, and adequate for their situation.

Even during cold war service, about 30 percent of the Army is overseas; consequently, an officer can expect an oversea assignment early in his or her career. Family separation usually results, sometimes for as long as the officer's complete tour. Hazardous duty, with conflict imminent, calls for the same security measures that combat does. An officer must do all the things which could be helpful to his or her spouse before departing so that the spouse can be a good manager of family affairs during their separation. To be discussed in more detail later are such matters as reviewing one's critical personal records, such as wills, and arranging for insurance coverage. Taking careful stock now and placing security affairs in order are joint actions of the husband-and-wife team in honest and sincere recognition of their mutual responsibilities.

The above motivation serves to introduce the need and to urge an officer to implement a planned security program and to review its adequacy and currency at such critical stages as going overseas, the imminent birth of a child, a promotion, retirement, and others. A partial review is in order each year when one computes income taxes. Such planning and reviewing calls for the following steps which will be detailed in subsequent sections:

Learn the elements of security planning;
Review your current family and financial status;
Choose your short- and long-range goals;
Identify your service benefits;
Establish a reasonable insurance program;
Supplement your estate with investments;
Be aware of the many assistance societies; and
Take care of vital personal administration.

FUNDAMENTALS OF SECURITY PLANNING

Security planning consists of evaluating your financial situation, comparing it to your requirements and goals, and deciding what must be done to have a program that meets today's needs while providing security for the future. "Estate analysis" is a similar term usually employed by insurance salesmen who are oriented on security through insurance programs. As used here, *security planning* involves one's total financial program to include salaries, property, savings, insurance program, governmental benefits, investments, and other monetary assets. It involves the integration of these finances into a formal plan. Finally, it takes into consideration today's and the immediate future's needs as well as those of the future. Overcommitment of your salary to security programs can deny yourself and your family the opportunities of building a living estate of wonderful, memorable, and educational recollections of vacations, entertainment, hobbies, and all those other events and circumstances that might not constitute absolute necessities. A term often encountered is "insurance poor" for one who buys too much insurance, but the term applies equally to other types of estate building. Thus, security planning is a management science to some extent yet it also could be classified as an art because of its intimate relation to personal philosophies.

Reference Material. There are many useful sources of information to assist you in estate planning, such as:

Officer's Manual of Personal Finance and Insurance, Stackpole Books, Harrisburg, Penna.

Estate Planning for Military Personnel, published by Dyke F. Meyer, C.L.U., Col., USAF ret., San Antonio, Tex.

AR 40–121, *Uniformed Services Health Benefit Programs.*

DA PAM 600–5, *Handbook on Retirement Services.*

DA PAM 608–2, *Your Personal Affairs.*

You do not need to obtain all these since some are special purpose while some duplicate information in the others. There are other references to include more current information in newspapers and magazines which you can study and save. With your broad understanding of what you are trying to do and your references available you are ready to begin your estate planning.

STATUS, GOALS, AND REQUIREMENTS

The next steps of security planning involve determining your financial situation, establishing your goals, and deciding on the actions required to meet these goals. The first two, status and goals, are to be discussed in this section along with the broad plan of action for establishing security. Detailed sections will then follow on how to implement the broad plan of action.

Your Financial Status. Your financial status is based upon your salary and any other income. To analyze your situation further it is necessary for you to consider your service benefits, insurance programs, savings, investments, social security credits, real estate equities, and any other assets. This is the point where you realize what you are worth financially should you live, be incapacitated, or die. It is generally useful to study and review other personal affairs records at this time along with your financial data.

Your Financial Goals. Next, you have to determine personal and family goals. Since this is an officer's guide, an officer's career is assumed to be the planning base. The first consideration of one's long-range career plans is definitely goal determination. The period or length of service is most influential on security planning. For example, officers who are involuntarily separated with more than five but less than 20 years of service are entitled to a separation payment equal to 10% of annual base pay times years of service, up to a maximum of $30,000. Officers having 20 years' service often retire to begin a second career with many service benefits accrued including a retirement pay of one half their base pay. Officers who are fulfilling an obligation for a few years or contemplate 20-year or 30-year retirement will each have different security programs. Whether or not to become a Regular Army officer and retirement at 20 years are discussed in other chapters. It is useful for security planning purposes, however, to illustrate that the monthly retired pay of a major retiring with 20 years' service is equal to that provided by an annuity worth over $150,000; that of a colonel with 30 years' service, the equivalent of income from an annuity worth over $250,000. So the first step is to determine your likely career program. Will you reach the rank of colonel or general? Conservative financial planning would be based on lieutenant colonel grade as indicated in the chapter on promotions.

Next comes your personal plans as to married life. One of the reasons marriage is often called a partnership is the financial relationship of the spouse. The spouse's attitudes, philosophies, financial responsibility, monetary assets, age, health, and other characteristics, all influence to some degree an officer's planning. Then there are the children. How many? College education? Establish in business? What is the influence of their personality, intelligence, hopes, educational plans, and other factors that affect the family's way of life and long-range program? These general and philosophical planning components serve to assist in the identification of financial goals and requirements so that subsequent planning to meet them can be realistic, practical, and more logically derived. Once an officer-spouse team has considered all these matters with objectivity, the decisions are made clearer and the courses of action are more readily discerned.

You may be assisted by considering your future lives as comprising a few main periods, and then estimate the conditions which are to be expected within each one, such as the following examples:

• The period of active duty which should continue until ——— (year) at the earliest, or until ——— (year) at the latest.

• The years in which children are growing up, receiving education, and becoming self-supporting, now foreseen until ——— (year).

• Family wishes for the period immediately following military retirement and reestablishment in a civilian community of their choice.

• The years between military retirement date and eligibility to receive social security old age payments in ———(year).

Also, consider the situation and requirements which would follow the death of either husband or wife during each of the above periods of family planning.

A wise start requires candid and searching answers to personal questions, such as those which follow.

The Spouse and Children To Be Protected. "What would happen if———
—?" The reasonable person recognizes that the duration of life is uncertain. He or she proceeds without undue morbidity or overemphasis to face facts. Proceed as you would in making a military estimate. Is your spouse qualified to be self-supporting if suddenly faced with the necessity to do so? Or would he or she need training to resume a former vocation or to undertake a new one? Consider your spouse's present age, health, potentials, wishes and inclinations. At what age should it be considered that he or she would be unable to provide

a part of the required income, or would not wish to do so? When there are children, at what year will each be prepared for life and be self-supporting? Are there physical or mental frailties to be considered and provided for? How much income per month will be needed, and for how many years, for the support and education of the children? Be realistic and inclusive. Later in your estimate you will balance potential outgo against potential income to see whether there is a gap to bridge. Right now, just determine the facts.

What Is Your Present Life Insurance Program? The family insurance program stands beside Family Net Worth as a sound foundation to family security.

It is true that military service establishes important benefits for family protection far above those of most vocations. But it is equally true that the hazards are greater, and the possibilities of estate accrual are more difficult. The termination of some benefits upon retirement, with the reduction or uncertainties of others, requires careful identification for each family situation. There are gaps to be filled in service benefits during the active career of the officer. There are more and wider ones to face upon retirement. Life insurance of the appropriate type, in carefully determined amount, is one proven way of providing at once for the potential needs of the future. There are other ways, of course. Identify the gaps, and fill them prudently.

Have You an Investment Program? Many military families have entered upon such a program with farsighted wisdom. They may have bought a home and are increasing their equity through rental. Others are buying securities such as government bonds, mutual funds, and common stock, or have opened an Individual Retirement Account.

Do You Have Reasonable Expectancy of an Inheritance? If so, include it as a possibility. But don't place extensive reliance upon it; old age, ill-health, many hazards, plus taxes, can reduce an estate. Just weigh the possibilities and go ahead.

To What Extent Do Present Military Survivor Benefits Meet the Total Needs? Basic information is contained in this chapter to be studied as a start in this investigation of potential resources. You will wish to make a detailed study of Departmental publications and consult experts about some phases of the subject.

You will see at once that for all officers the benefits are valuable. The officer on active duty and the officer's family are better protected than ever before. After military retirement there are important benefits but there are also potential gaps in protection which must be identified. Some previous benefits have been eliminated or curtailed. Study is needed to apply these laws to your situation and the requirements of your family.

What Sort of Program for the Future Can You and Your Spouse Afford Today? There are common sayings which illustrate an approach to answering the question. "Insurance poor" or "property poor" present one side of the matter, and "time for sowing" is the other. This chapter provides much information about future security, so let us seek for a moment to establish a balance. Each family has its own way of life, with its daily needs, and its own dreams of the future. It is true that a family's immediate and continuing happiness—such as children growing up with proper food, clothes, books, family outings, dinners at the club—is important, too. Prudence is needed for family security, of course, and its importance must not be minimized; but prudence is also required in avoiding overcommitting the family income for estate building. Once an officer–spouse team has considered all these matters with objectivity and realism, the best decisions are usually clear. For most families, expenditures of today can be controlled so that some part of income can be diverted to the family program of the future.

Should Your Family Have a Budget? Officers and their spouses usually manage their finances with either a formal budget or a working budget. With a formal budget, a detailed system of planned expenses and records serves to guide the expenditures for the various parts of the living and the security programs. In the working budget, the officer-spouse team establishes habits which cause them to accomplish the basic parts of their programs while not exceeding their income or depleting their cash reserve. A cash reserve is maintained in both cases for emergencies and for planned spending on major events (or things) in the near future. A two months' salary cash reserve is recommended. Savings beyond this should be invested if the other elements of the security program are met. An exception is the planned expense in the near future on an appliance, a trip, clothes for college, etc. Those who maintain a formal budget usually will do better at managing their finances but some people do not enjoy the detailed accounting that is required. Having a program, meeting it, and staying within one's income is also a practical way to security without detailed budgeting. The choice is yours.

Your Financial Plan. Having faced the basic questions of financial status and goals, estate planners say that now you are ready to make your basic financial plan. Here is what you must do:
- Establish a solvent financial situation;
- Build a cash reserve;
- Establish a sound insurance program;
- Invest your remaining income.

You, however, are an officer and cannot complete your security planning until you first consider the benefits of being in the service and a citizen of the United States.

BENEFITS ACQUIRED BY MILITARY SERVICE

There are many benefits acquired through military service. They are provided by the Government in recognition of the hazards of military service as well as to furnish a definite portion of the salary and financial security. These benefits are a complementary base for estate planning. They are enacted and made legal by detailed administrative regulations designed for the protection of the individual and the government. Unfortunately, such detailed implementation can result in confusion, misunderstanding, and oversight of important security matters. This section attempts to simplify and to make more clear your earned benefits; but you are also cautioned to study the regulations and the references and to seek the counsel of local appointed experts.

The benefits to be discussed are: Military Medical Care Program; Survivor Benefits Act; Social Security; Survivor Benefit Plan; Scholarships and Education Loans; Burial Rights and Benefits; and Veterans Benefits (G.I. Bill).

MILITARY MEDICAL CARE PROGRAM

A most detailed description of this program is found in AR 40–121, *Medical Service, Uniformed Services Health Benefits Program.* Should this be too legalistic or otherwise not understandable, you can obtain fact sheets and information directly from any of the Uniformed Services hospitals. Normally, a newly arriving officer will be apprised about which hospital to use and which civilian facilities are recommended. The Uniformed Services facilities include those of the Army, Navy, Air Force, and Coast Guard. In the absence of instructions, you should go to the administrator of the nearest such facility.

It is important to know your medical benefits and, for your and your family's security, to understand where security gaps could occur which must be covered by other measures. This section summarizes the more important provisions and shortcomings; however, the previously cited regulations provide the significant detail which must be consulted for individual cases not sufficiently explained herein.

In general, the officer, personally, will receive essentially complete medical care until retirement. After retirement, use of military medical facilities will be on a space-available basis. Now, after retirement you (and your dependents) may seek civilian outpatient service with reimbursement as later explained. At the age of 65, retirees and their dependents who become eligible for the Social Security Medicare Program will be eligible for space-available care in military facilities but no longer entitled to civilian hospitalization and outpatient care under the military medicare program. Before examining medical care provisions for an officer's dependents it is important that "dependents" be defined.

Who Is a Dependent? Dependent means any person who bears to a member or retired member of a uniformed service, or to a person who died while a member of a uniformed service, any of the following relationships:

1. The lawful wife.
2. The unremarried widow.
3. The lawful husband.
4. The unremarried widower.
5. An unmarried legitimate child, including an adopted child or stepchild, who either—
Has not passed his or her 21st birthday, regardless of whether or not the child is dependent on the active-duty or retired member; or
Has passed his or her 21st birthday but is incapable of self-support because of a mental or physical incapacity that existed before the 21st birthday and is, or was at the time of death of the active-duty or retired member, dependent on the member for over one-half of his or her support; or
Has not passed his or her 23d birthday and is enrolled in a full-time course of study in an institution of higher learning approved by the Secretary of Defense or the Secretary of Health and Human Services, as the case may be, and is, or was at the time of death of the active-duty or retired member, dependent on the member for over one-half of his or her support.
6. A parent or parent-in-law, who either—
Is dependent on the active-duty or retired member for over one-half of his or her support and is residing in a dwelling place provided or maintained by the member; or
Was at the time of death of the member dependent on him or her for over one-half of his or her support and was residing in a dwelling place provided or maintained by the member.

Important Administrative Features. When applying for any kind of medical care at a military or a civilian facility, military personnel active and retired and their dependents are required to provide evidence of their eligibility by means of the Uniform Services Identification and Privilege card (DD Form 2A or DD Form 1173). If a person uses, or allows another to use this card to obtain medical care to which he or she is not entitled, a fine of up to $10,000 and imprisonment for up to 5 years may result!

A new system called DEERS, for Defense Enrollment Eligibility System, is being initiated worldwide to eliminate fraudulent use of military health facilities.

The civilian physician or facility must be participating with the government in the military medicare program for your subsequent reimbursement. You can identify those who do participate by inquiry at the local Medical Bureau, American Medical Association, or an appropriate local governmental office.* Do so in advance, if it is possible. After receiving medical care, in particular emergency and costly care, be certain to save *all* receipts for doctor care, hospitalization, medicines, and related services. Costs, themselves, will be briefly explained in a later section.

Dependent Medicare Benefits. Most of the special benefits to which your dependents are entitled are described below. However, you are cautioned to check with your local medical facility, if for no other reason than to determine its capability to serve you and your family.

Election of Facilities. The following beneficiaries may elect to obtain authorized health benefits in Uniformed Services facilities or from civilian sources: retired members and their spouses and children, spouses and children of deceased members, and spouses and children of active-duty members who are residing apart from their sponsor. Spouses and children of active-duty members who are residing with their sponsor may elect to obtain authorized *outpatient* care and drugs from Uniformed Services or civilian facilities. They are, *however,* required to obtain *inpatient* care in Uniformed Service facilities when such facilities are within reasonable distance of their residence and capable of providing the needed care, except in an emergency, when the residing "apart" changes to residing "with", when already hospitalized or obtaining maternity care, or while on a trip away from the sponsor's household. (See p. 11, AR 40–121). DD Form 1251, *Nonavailability Statement—Dependents Medical Care Program,* will be furnished to spouses and children residing with their sponsors who must use civilian facilities. The non-availability statement *must* be obtained prior to use of civilian facilities for non-emergency care.

Costs. In military facilities, the per diem (day) charge is $6.30 for dependents for inpatient service with usually no charge for outpatient service; the law does permit charges if they are considered advisable. Officers pay a daily charge of $3.70.

In civilian facilities, for spouses and dependents of active duty personnel, the outpatient costs are $50 per year per person (but not to exceed $100 per family) and 20% of the remaining costs. For retirees and their dependents, the costs are $50 per year per person (but not to exceed $100 per family) and 25% of the remaining costs. The total bill for a family unit for twelve months must exceed $100 in both cases for reimbursement of the remaining part by the government.

Hospitalization costs in civilian facilities for retirees and their dependents and the dependents of deceased personnel are paid at a rate of 25% by the person with 75% reimbursement by the government. Dependents of active duty personnel pay either $25 or $6.30 per day, whichever is more.

For long term care of mentally retarded and physically handicapped spouses

---

*Civilian hospitals and physicians are best acquainted with this program under the name of CHAMPUS, which stands for "Civilian Health and Medical Program, Uniformed Services."

or children, a sliding scale of reimbursement is provided up to a total monthly bill of $350.

Cautions. The law has taken care of most of what were classified as security "gaps." The remaining gap for all types of dependents and retirees is that of outpatient dental care. Such dental care is only authorized overseas and in certain remote locations on a space-available basis. Dental care may be provided in relation to some other medical or surgical condition when a dependent is hospitalized.

Costs of routine physical examinations and immunizations at *civilian facilities* are not paid for by the government except when the dependents are preparing to go overseas. Note that these are given at military facilities with no charge. Costs of the care of new-born children and, later, their well-baby care at civilian facilities will not be paid for by the government. The same applies to eye examinations; however, again, all of these are available, usually by appointment, at military facilities. Drug and medicine costs provided in connection with outpatient care may be reimbursed only in the case of written prescriptions of a licensed physician or dentist. An exception is insulin; an inclusion is oral contraceptives. If you require any drugs or medicines over a long period, you should carefully consult with the regulations and authorities to save these costly expenses.

In general, the medical care programs for all service personnel and their dependents are now expanded to where no crucial security gaps other than dental care exist. As in all matters of government life, the regulations are complex to insure that the benefits are given to those who earn them.

SURVIVOR BENEFITS ACT

Topping the list of laws contributing to the security of a service family is the Survivors Dependency and Indemnity Compensation Act of 1974. Initially started as the Servicemens' and Veterans' Survivor Benefits Act of 1956, survivors are compensated for the loss of an officer or soldier whose death is attributable to military service. All *service connected deaths* which occur in peace or wartime and while in or out of the service qualify the eligible survivors for the Dependency and Indemnity Compensation (DIC). Retired officers' survivors may qualify also providing the Veterans Administration rules the death to have been from service connected causes. As amended in 1982, the Act now provides monthly payments to an unremarried widowed spouse ranging from $563 for the spouse of a W-1 and an O-1 to $1139 for the spouse of an O-10. Thus, the higher the pay grade of the deceased member, the higher the compensation payable to the member's survivors. Once established, however, the DIC rate is fixed. Rate increases are only by separate Congressional action. A serious security gap occurs as to retired officers whose deaths are not service-connected as to cause of death. (A small pension may be paid to the widow or widower, as discussed later, provided her or his income is below a stated minimum.) This gap must receive consideration in developing a total family security plan.

Compensations may be increased for widows and widowers with children under 18 by $48 for each child. Compensation is paid of an additional $206 in the case of a child over 18 who is incapable of self-support. An additional sum of $55 is awarded for each child between 18 and 23 who attends a VA approved school. All such compensations are income tax-free. The officer's surviving children will receive compensations should the spouse die. Dependent parents likewise qualify for compensations. Your finance officer or any

Veterans Administration office can assist you in computing the various possible compensations and pensions for your particular family situation.

Pay and Six-Months Death Gratuity. At the time of a service member's death there will be pay due for a month or a fractional part of a month. The spouse receives this arrears of pay upon claim to the nearest finance center, or by writing to the U.S. Army Finance and Accounting Center, Indianapolis, Indiana 46249.

In addition to the arrears in pay, a death gratuity is payable to the survivors of the service member who dies on active duty, active duty for training, or inactive duty training (weekly drills), and of a retired service member who dies of a service-connected disability within 120 days after separation from the Active List. The amount of this gratuity is six months basic pay, with a minimum payment of $800 and a maximum payment of $3000. To be remembered, as discussed elsewhere, is the lump sum payment of up to $255 paid to the surviving spouse of an officer who has qualified for Social Security payments.

These payments should be included in the determination of assets and benefits in an individual's estate security plan.

Pension for Dependents of Retired Personnel and Veterans Whose Deaths Were Not Service Connected. Rates stipulated by law and tied to the dependents' other income are payable (by the Veterans Administration) to dependents of veterans or retired personnel when retirement was for a reason other than physical disability or death occurred for a reason other than a service-connected cause. The spouse and children of the veteran or retired individual are the only eligibles.

The following payments are not considered "income" as to death pension payments:

Government life insurance proceeds and, in some cases, commercial life insurance proceeds.

The six months' death gratuity.

Donations from public or private relief or welfare organizations.

Payments of pension, compensation, and dependency compensation of the Veterans Administration.

Retired Serviceman's Family Protection Plan annuities.

Survivor Benefit Plan.

Lump sum Social Security death payments.

Payments to an individual under public or private retirement, annuity, endowment, or similar plans or programs equal to his or her contributions thereto.

Proceeds of a fire insurance policy.

Amounts equal to amounts paid by the survivors of a deceased veteran for his or her just debts, the expenses of the last illness, and burial expenses which are not reimbursed by the Veterans Administration.

Apply for the benefit, or for consideration of factors bearing upon it, at a convenient office of the Veterans Administration.

SOCIAL SECURITY

Military personnel accrue Social Security benefits for active duty service as an important element of their overall security program. Participation is mandatory. Under the Social Security program, your base pay is taxed at a prescribed rate which will increase periodically to a high of 7.65% for the year 1990 and after. The maximum taxable earnings will be increased automatically as average wage levels rise. At the same time, the benefits payable will also increase. The amount of the benefit received from Social Security will depend upon the Average Monthly Earnings (AME) and the number of years of credit that have been accrued. The benefit of most general interest is the monthly income which an officer and eligible members of the officer's family attain at age 65. (Reduced benefits may be selected for ages 62, 63, and 64, as well). The young officer will wonder of what benefit is the program before such ages. Payments are provided for disabled officers and for their spouses and children. Monthly income is provided for an officer's widow or widower with children under 18 years of age, or for children alone, or for a widow or widower at age 60, or for dependent parents. These important benefits, then, supplement other insurance-type security programs the young officer may establish.

In summary, Social Security is a mandatory governmental insurance program whose coverage and benefits are paid by you.

SURVIVOR BENEFIT PLAN (SBP)

The SBP, which replaced the older Retired Serviceman's Family Protection Plan (RSFPP), became effective in September 1972. It allows members of the uniformed services to elect to receive a reduced retirement pay in order to provide annuities for their survivors or for another person with an insurable interest in the service member. Under SBP, the Federal Government pays a substantial portion of the overall cost, which means that reductions in retired pay are considerably lower than was the case under RSFPP for the same coverage. The SBP is open to all future retirees, including members of the Reserve Forces. Current retirees have previously been afforded the opportunity to participate.

Under SBP, future retirees can elect to leave up to 55% of their retired pay to their selected annuitants. Participation in SBP is automatic for those still on active duty or for Reservists not yet entitled to retired pay. Prior to retirement, the member must fill out an election form, DD Form 1883, electing the full 55% coverage or a reduced coverage, or the member may decline to participate. The minimum base amount of retired pay upon which SBP is based is $300 per month unless the actual retired pay is less than this amount.

Costs for spouse-only coverage under SBP are 2.5% of the first $300 of the selected base amount, plus 10% of the remainder. Thus, a member entitled to $500 per month in retired pay, who desired to leave 55% ($275.00) to his or her spouse pays $27.50 per month ($7.50 for the first $300 and $20 for the last $200). Additional coverage for a child or children costs about $\frac{1}{2}$ of 1% of the base amount of retirement pay per month. In the above example, this additional coverage would cost the member approximately $2.50 per month.

There are a number of points about the SBP which deserve careful consideration. Most decisions made are irrevocable. However, deductions under the plan cease during any month in which there is no eligible beneficiary. Further, the coverage may be switched to a new spouse if the retiree remarries. An important advantage of SBP is that the amount of coverage is tied to the Consumer Price Index (CPI). Whenever retired pay is adjusted on the basis of the CPI, the amount selected by the retiree as an annuity base, the deduction from retired pay covering the adjusted base, and the annuity payable to selected beneficiaries will be adjusted accordingly. The plan thus provides for automatic cost of living adjustments. The plan also contains a provision that when the beneficiary becomes eligible for Social Security survivor benefits, the SBP payments will be permanently reduced by the amount to which the beneficiary is entitled from Social Security, based solely upon the member's military pay, up to a maximum of 40% of the SBP payment. This offset occurs even if the survivor is working and not receiving Social Security benefits. The plan also provides that if a retiree dies of a service-connected cause, as a result of which his or her survivors are entitled to DIC payments (see Survivor Benefits Act earlier in this chapter), the SBP payment will be reduced so that the total of the two payments —DIC and SBP—will be equal to the full amount otherwise payable under SBP. Thus, the total income to the survivors from SBP, DIC, and Social Security can equal or be slightly higher than the SBP income alone, depending upon the extent of the Social Security offset. On the other hand, since SBP, (as well as Social Security) is tied to the Consumer Price Index, the retired member also is assured that the spending power he or she has provided through SBP will remain relatively constant regardless of cost-of-living increases.

It is apparent that participation in SBP has definite advantages and, perhaps, disadvantages which call for study, obtaining advice, and care in deciding if coverage is desired and in selecting the amount. SBP is not necessarily a panacea for all military retirees, but it deserves careful consideration as a benefit accruing to you as a result of military service which is available for use in planning your estate.

SCHOLARSHIPS AND EDUCATION LOANS

College education costs of dependent children are of growing concern with the increased costs of tuition and board. In planning one's estate, settlement options of life insurance and educational endowment insurance are often selected or purchased as coverage. Some provide this security by purchasing bonds and participating in other savings and investment programs. Should this be insufficient, there are a number of scholarships that can be won through good grades and successful competition through examinations. A current listing of these is contained in DA Pam 352-2, "Educational Scholarships, Loans and Financial Aids." Many of the states have statutes and educational programs which provide scholarships and financial aid to dependents of disabled and deceased veterans. These are listed in the cited pamphlet.

The "Junior G.I. Bill" or "War Orphan's Educational Assistance Act of 1964" provides benefits to sons and daughters of service personnel who die or become disabled as a result of a wartime or extra-hazardous peacetime disease or injury. Up to $270 per month for 36 months may be received. One cannot predict one's disease or disabling injury but this benefit should be known to the service member.

The National Defense Education Acts of 1958 and 1965 provide low cost loans to college-age dependents of service personnel. This too cannot be specifically included in an estate plan but it is comforting to know it is there to assist peacetime veterans and their dependents.

The young married officer will be encouraged by some insurance salesmen to provide for college education of the children through insurance contracts. Such endowment insurance for education is expensive and may not be the best method for you. Competing with insurance for this purpose are the above programs, savings programs like government bonds, and long-range investment programs.

BURIAL RIGHTS AND BENEFITS

The government has provided burial and funeral allowances in the event of the death of active duty, retired, and honorably discharged officers. The allowances vary from complete for an active duty officer's death to the transportation of the remains of dependents who die overseas to place of interment. These allowances can amount to as much as $2,000 in these days and are a very important part of your security program. You must consider the eventuality of death in security planning as you do when considering insurance; you should acquaint your responsible dependents with desired and government arrangements. This, of course, calls for an awareness on your part of the details; this section provides the most significant details, DA Pamphlet 608–2 provides much more.

Burial Rights. It should be noted that the government respects its departed service member and desires that interment be proper and at as little expense to the member's survivors as possible. Thus, the government will take charge of most of the arrangements if the surviving kin so desire. The standards of the services provide every proper consideration; it is usually best to leave arrangements for preparation of the remains and burial to the military authorities at the place of death. When a member of the Army dies while on active duty, active duty for training or during inactive duty training, the government will provide for care of the remains and delivery to the place desired and will pay interment allowances, as required, including:

1. Services of preparation at the place of death (pickup, embalming and other preservation, casket and shipping case, and hearse service to the cemetery or shipping terminal) and funeral director's service.
2. Cremation and a suitable urn (if requested in writing).
3. A flag for the casket and a uniform for the deceased, if not available.
4. Transportation of remains with a military escort. (The widow, widower or a relative may accompany.)
5. An allowance for interment:
    $400 maximum, private or civilian cemetery, death not service-connected;
    $800 maximum, private or national cemetery, death service-connected;
    $250 maximum, when remains are consigned to a funeral director and are interred in a national or post cemetery; or
    $75 maximum, when Army authorities consign remains direct to the national or post cemetery officials.
(Such maximum costs are meant to defray the costs of the coach, flowers, vault, church services, obituary notices, car for the family, services of the funeral director, gravesite, opening and closing of the grave, and use of cemetery equipment.)

Retired and Honorably Discharged Officers. If you die after completing your service, the Veterans Administration will pay a $150 plot allowance if burial is not in a Federal cemetery, provided:

You were a veteran of wartime or recognized conflict service; or You were a peacetime veteran receiving compensation; or You were a veteran discharged or retired for disability incurred in line of duty; and Your discharge or release was under honorable conditions. The maximum allowance is $1,100 for death of service-connected causes.

Dependents. When a dependent dies while the member is on active duty (other than for training) transportation may be furnished for the remains at Army expense. Certain privileges related to national and post burial sites are authorized and discussed below.

Control of Cemeteries. The control of all national cemeteries except Arlington and those operated by the service academies and the Soldier's and Airmen's and the Naval Homes was transferred to the Veterans Administration by PL 93–43. Post cemeteries remain under control of the Army.

Burial in a National or Post Cemetery. The deceased active duty officer may be buried in any national cemetery in which grave space is available. The surviving spouse, minor children, and in certain instances, unmarried adult children, are also eligible for burial in the same cemetery. A total of not more than two adjoining gravesites is authorized. Burial at a post cemetery is subject to determination and approval of the post commanding officer and in keeping with Army regulations. At post cemeteries, immediate members of the family beyond those authorized at national cemeteries may be buried on post approval. Certain posts will accept gravesite reservations in writing for surviving spouses. Retired and honorably discharged service members are, likewise, entitled to burial in a national cemetery, if space is available. Detailed additional information on these matters may be secured from a Superintendent of a National Cemetery or from the Office of Support Services, DA, Washington, D.C. 20315. Local veterans organizations will also provide much assistance and information.

Honors and Headstones. Military honors will be provided by the Army when requested for interment at a national or post cemetery. At certain national and at civilian cemeteries, these honors are rendered by a local Reserve unit or a veterans' organization upon request. The chapter on *Military Courtesy* provides further detail on the ceremony.

Headstones and markers which are proper, appropriate, and otherwise suitable are provided in memory and honor of the service member at little or no cost. Such provision is made by the service, the Veterans Administration, and/or the State. No service member's grave will be unmarked because of lack of funds. At national and post cemeteries, this honor is virtually automatic with no action, other than consent, required by the kin.

In summary, your government is grateful and proud of your service; in the grim instance of death, it is desired that your burial be in keeping with your dedication. Consequently, most of the expenses of burial are paid by or shared in by the government as your deserved and earned benefit.

VETERANS BENEFITS

There are a number of important benefits provided by the government for veterans of service to their country during times of strife. These programs along with the foregoing survivors' benefits are administered primarily by the Veterans Administration with assistance from other federal agencies. Veterans of "Cold War" conflict or peacetime service are now included in certain veterans' acts. The "G.I. Bill," in particular, includes those on active duty and those who have served honorably in peacetime who may not have been in combat. The basic benefits are the G.I. Bill, the V.A. compensation, and the V.A. pension which assist active duty, discharged and disabled veterans and provide financial help to survivors.

G.I. Bill. Veterans of the conflict in Vietnam and those officers who have served not in conflict but on active duty between 31 January 1955 and 30 June 1976, are eligible for benefits under the law known as the G.I. Bill. This law provides a permanent system of education, home loans, job placement, job preference in federal employment, burial flag and medical care for veterans who have served more than 180 days. It provides education and home loan benefits for personnel who remain on active duty. The G.I. Bill terminated on 30 June 1976. Members entering military service after that date receive no benefits, although a member may establish an education account for later use under a contributory system whereby monthly contributions by the member are matched on a 2 to 1 basis by the government.*

The home loan under the Veterans Administration provides the opportunity of buying a home with low down payment. (FHA in-service home loans are also available to the active duty officer and should be investigated by the home buying officer).

---

*As this edition went to press, Congress was actively considering a new G.I. Bill to replace the existing contributory system.

V.A. Compensation. Should an officer be disabled in peacetime or in wartime while in service, the Veterans Administration will provide a supplementary compensation to that paid by the Survivor Benefits Act. Since you cannot forecast your disability or its degree of incapacitation, you cannot program any certain amount into your security plan. This information is provided, then, for you and your dependents in the unfortunate event of your being disabled. The percentage of disability is a legal assessment by the V.A. in consideration of your future capability to earn a living. The compensation goes to the officer and, if he or she dies, to his or her dependents. The amounts vary with the percentage and kind of disability, when the disability occurred, and the number of dependents.

Disabled service members with less than 8 years active duty may or may not receive service disability retirement or severance pay depending on the circumstances. They could receive the V.A. disability compensation. Officers who are involuntarily separated with more than five but less than 20 years of service are entitled to a separation payment equal to 10% of annual base pay times years of service, up to a maximum of $30,000. These matters should be clarified before you leave the hospital and are separated.

V.A. Pension. The Veterans Administration will provide a pension to the survivors of a veteran who died while in retirement from a cause that was neither associated with the physical disability causing him or her to retire or that was service-connected. This partially covers the security gap not accounted for in the service Survivor Benefits Act. The amounts vary according to the need as identified by the yearly income and number of children. Again, you cannot program this security element but you should be aware it exists.

INSURANCE PROGRAMS

All estate planners, be they insurance salesmen, investment brokers, or bankers, advise that the first step to security after having a sound financial base is to establish an insurance program. How much insurance should an officer buy? There are two solutions to the question. One is the "needs approach"; the other is to follow advice of insurance counselors and recommended literature. The "needs approach" calls for an analysis of how much the survivors will require should the breadwinner die. This includes living expenses, housing, and education of children, among many other things. The prudent officer also considers his or her spouse's capabilities to be employed. Remarriage is a difficult planning factor, to say the least. The bewildered officer will usually seek the advice of a reputable salesman or insurance estate planner and match that advice against that of the literature referenced at the beginning of this chapter.

The Army Mutual Aid Association and many others provide suggested life insurance programs for the career Army officer. One rule of thumb is:

Status	Minimum Amount of Insurance
Bachelor (male or female)	$15,000
Married	$30,000
Additional for each child	$10,000 to $15,000

The need for expert counsel becomes more apparent when one recognizes there are six basic types of life insurance: reducing term, level term, ordinary (whole) life, limited pay life (20- or 30-year pay), endowment, and annuity (retirement income) insurance. There is no less expensive way to provide for security; however, as more options are selected the costs increase. Other options are found within the basic kinds: war risk, aviation coverage, suicide, disability waivers, dividend options, double indemnity, settlements, endowments for education, surrender cash values and loan values. These should be carefully checked in your contract; at least you should understand for what you are paying. Many benefit and mutual associations offer packaged family insurance programs which provide coverage for the entire family at moderate rates. As in other financial programs, if you do not pay very much, you do not accrue much cash or loan value. In insurance programs you do have security, however, not provided by other investment-type programs.

Servicemen's Group Life Insurance (SGLI). This government sponsored insurance program provides up to $35,000 of life insurance coverage for active duty members and for drilling members of the National Guard and Reserve at a premium of $4.06 per month. It also is available to members of the Retired Reserve under age 60 at slightly increased rates, depending upon age. Upon separation from active duty, the coverage is continuable as low-cost term insurance for 5 years under the Veterans' Group Life Insurance (VGLI), after which you are guaranteed the right to convert to a permanent insurance program whatever the status of your health may be. Since this conversion to permanent insurance would be at rates applicable to your attained age, it could be expensive. The career officer should consider this as a bonus program and definitely not drop or forego other insurance coverage.

Survivor Benefit Plan (SBP). The SBP has been discussed in an earlier section as a qualified benefit. Actuarial studies indicate that the cost of coverage under SBP is significantly less than the cost for the same coverage by a commercial insurance company. Actual comparison, of course, is dependent upon the age of both the retiree and his or her spouse as well as the amount of coverage selected. Nonetheless, participation in SBP offers the military member a means of extending important protection for loved ones into the retirement years. Coverage by SBP should be considered in planning one's estate in conjunction with other insurance and investments. Each officer should seek counsel related to his or her personal situation.

Other Kinds of Insurance. In addition to life insurance, other kinds of insurance are necessary for security. These include fire insurance on a home, insurance against loss or theft of personal property, personal liability, and automobile insurance. Some later-referenced associations package these kinds of insurance at lower costs to service personnel; your consideration and study of their programs is in order. Each will provide literature, advice, and cost and coverage quotations for your particular situation. As in the case of life insurance, the study of referenced literature and seeking the advice of experienced officers and professional counselors can save you significant funds.

INVESTMENT PROGRAMS

By carefully budgeting his or her salary and after establishing the other discussed priority components of a financial estate, each Army officer can arrive at the opportunity for savings and investing. Actually, your retirement income is an annuity which the government is saving for you. The impact of retirement pay as an annuity was previously mentioned; another way to consider its value is to determine how much you would have to invest to receive retirement pay for a certain number of years. Assume you retire on a monthly retired pay of $1000 and you have a life expectancy of 25 years. During your retirement, you would collect $300,000 in retired pay, for which you would have had to invest $161,000 at a 5.5% interest rate. Should you live for 30 years after retirement, the amount that would have had to be invested at the same interest rate is nearly $175,000. Thus, retirement, like Social Security income, could be included in the percentages of funds considered invested. Further, both Social Security and retirement income provide relatively fixed purchasing power, as opposed to fixed income, since both now are adjusted according to the Consumer Price Index (CPI). You may not have realized that you (with government's assistance) began two investment programs upon entering the service.

An investment program may consist of fixed dollar investments and variable dollar investments. Fixed dollar investments are those which have a fixed value and return a certain yield, such as bonds and savings accounts. Variable dollar securities grow or decline in value at the risk of the investor. These would include common stocks and investment in real estate. There is increased risk in such purchases since there is no guarantee of eventual sale at a stipulated price. The purchase of carefully selected common stocks, or carefully chosen real estate, is made with the goal of increasing values, combined with dividend or rental return. Many investment advisory companies recommend a suitable mix between fixed dollar investments and variable dollar investments—highly rated bonds with highly rated common stocks, as examples.

There are mutual funds which have investments wholly in common stocks, wholly in bonds, with the major portion having a judicious mix of their own selections of each type of security.

Each service member also is entitled to establish an Independent Retirement Account (IRA) to which he or she can contribute up to $2,000 per year. The amount contributed each year can be deducted from annual income for tax purposes and the earnings in the IRA accumulate tax free. However, the funds in the IRA cannot be used until age 59½ without penalty. When used, the proceeds from the account are taxed as ordinary income.

How should an officer enter this interesting and potentially rewarding field? First, you should enter into investment planning as early in your career as possible. *The less you have to invest the more important your study and investigation.* There are good books on investment planning. There are good magazines devoted to business, finance, and investment. There are investment advisory services. There are investment counsellors. There are brokers who can provide study material, detailed information, and many will assist in financial planning. As an initial step, go to your local libraries. See what they have available for your reading and study. When you have some investment money —make your start.

ASSISTANCE FACILITIES AND ASSOCIATIONS

Servicemen and women have many assistance and advisory associations that will help them and their dependents in solving problems related to personal affairs and security. There are also many mutual insurance associations that provide all types of insurance at very reasonable rates while also assisting in associated administrative matters. Knowing about them can affect your security planning. They also can and will assist your dependents while you are away or should you die. You should determine your eligibility and study what each association can provide.

Army Community Service (ACS). The Army has consolidated a number of services to personnel and their families with the missions of providing information, assistance, and guidance in meeting personal and family problems beyond the scope of their own resources. The functions of Army Emergency Relief, Army Personnel Affairs, Survivors Assistance Officer, and Retired Affairs are integrated with ACS as local conditions permit. Information is provided on financial assistance, availability of housing, transportation, relocation, medical and dental care, legal assistance, orientation of new arrivals, care of handicapped children, recreation, and many other community matters. The theme is "Self-Help, Service, and Stability." It is particularly devoted to the assistance of dependents whose sponsors are away for whatever purpose. If you or your dependents have a problem, the ACS agency is the place to begin for information and assistance.

The Veterans Administration. The many services, rights, and benefits of veterans of peace and wartime are administered by officials of the Veterans Administration assisted by members of the American Legion and Veterans of Foreign Wars in many cases. Most cities and county seats have offices where you can get assistance.

The American Red Cross. There is a broad program of directed and voluntary aid to military personnel by officials and volunteers of the American National Red Cross. Their assistance in hospitals is well known. There will be a director at each post to assist in emergency notifications, investigations, provision of financial aid, child welfare, and other related matters of emergency.

Army Emergency Relief. Although primarily an association to give financial loans and grants to enlisted personnel, the Army Emergency Relief officer at every post can also assist an officer or the officer's family if the situation warrants. Each case is determined on merit and need, usually in association with American Red Cross officials and those of the ACS program.

Social Security Field Offices. The many complex rules and administrative matters of the Social Security program can be clarified at their field offices located in most cities. They will determine eligibility and assist in obtaining the many benefits that this increasing welfare program provides.

Army Distaff Hall. Army widows age 62 or older and the mother, daughter, sister or mother-in-law of a Regular Army commissioned or warrant officer, or of a Reserve officer with 20 years service are eligible to apply to reside at the Army Distaff Hall. Retired female officers also are eligible. Inquiries should be mailed to 6200 Oregon Avenue, N.W., Washington, D.C.

Army Mutual Aid Association. This mutual insurance association began in 1879. It offers low cost life insurance to Regular Army officers and warrant officers and those reserve officers and warrant officers in the indefinite category who have completed three years of continuous active service. The Association offices are at Fort Myer, Arlington, Virginia 22211. They provide gratuitous services for survivors in preparing pension and other claims on the government. They will also store your valuable papers in their vault. All officers are urged to investigate the Association programs.

The Armed Forces Relief and Benefit Association. This worthwhile mutual association has similar eligibility rules as that of the Army Mutual Aid Association and provides low cost group life insurance. It is at 1156 15th Street N.W. Washington D.C. 20005.

The Association of the U.S. Army. Officers who have joined the Association of the U.S. Army are eligible for group life insurance at very low cost. Generally no physical examinations are required and there are no exclusions. All risk protection and disability waiver of premium payments are included. You can get more information by writing AUSA Members Life Insurance Plan, 1529 18th Street N.W., Washington, D.C. 20036.

United Services Automobile Association. This association provides low cost automobile insurance for most active and retired officers. The policies are tailored to each officer's need and location. Dividends serve to lower the costs. The Association also provides homeowners, personal liability, boat-owners, household goods and personal effects, and life insurance. It offers two no-load mutual funds for investments. Officers are invited to write to USAA Building, 4119 Broadway, San Antonio, Texas 78215.

Armed Forces Cooperative Insurance. This association, formerly the Armed Forces Cooperative Insuring Association, offers very low cost insurance of personal and household effects in the case of fire, theft, and other like losses without regard to station or duty and at actual cost to members. Eligibility is like that for the Army Mutual Aid Association. Members do the promoting and most of the assessing. The association's promptness and payment of reasonable claims without argument are well known throughout the service. It also provides fire insurance on a house, personal liability, and can insure for theft and pilferage losses. Officers are urged to write to Armed Forces Cooperative Insurance, Fort Leavenworth, Kansas 66027, for complete information.

Other Associations. There are many other associations that insure and assist military personnel. Only a few of the best known and longest established societies have been mentioned. There are, in particular, a number of mutual life insurance associations that offer low cost protection. Their names are excluded in the interests of brevity but in such exclusion it should not be inferred that such associations are more expensive, untrustworthy, or unreliable. The ones recommended can save the officer considerable sums of money should he or she insure with them or like organizations. Your support of the mentioned societies is not suggested from other than the aspect of their proved assistance to officers throughout the past.

PERSONAL ADMINISTRATION RELATED TO SECURITY PROGRAMING

No security program review is complete without a study and inspection of one's personal administration. Such matters as records, state and federal taxes, estate and death taxes, wills, trusts, powers of attorney, and joint ownership of property will be discussed below. You should review these records each year (at income tax time, for instance) and, in particular, prior to going overseas with or without your spouse. All matters should be clearly explained to your spouse and the places where your records are stored clearly identified.

Records. The officer should know where all personal records are and their status. The important ones should be filed in a safe deposit box, a safe, or a fireproof vault (The Army Mutual Aid Association stores life insurance policies and wills, for example), or some other secure location. Photostatic or otherwise certified copies of the original may then be kept at home as your working file. A partial list of important records would be: birth certificates, marriage certificates, wills, powers of attorney, trusts, deeds, mortgages, active duty and retirement orders, automobile ownership certificate, life insurance policies, bonds and stocks, baptism and confirmation papers, and other valuables and valuable papers. Less important records could be filed at home with a personal file of military records. Such a file would include financial records, promotion records, personal property record, bank and savings account records, other kinds of insurance policies, etc.; the more important ones can and should be filed in a strong, relatively fireproof, portable box.

State and Federal Taxes. All officers must file a federal and (in most cases) a state income tax report each year and pay these taxes as required. Your finance officer withholds federal pay for this purpose and advises you of the amounts withheld each year by means of the W-2 form. Under provisions of the Soldiers' and Sailors' Civil Relief Act of 1940, you are excluded from paying state income and personal property taxes to a state where you temporarily reside because of military duty, provided you can prove to that state you are domiciled—legally reside—in another. You must pay federal income tax on your basic pay, dislocation allowances, and per diem pay in excess of needs, and all other sources of taxable income. All units and posts have personnel advisors who can assist you in most uncomplicated filing matters. Your spouse is not excluded from state income and property taxes, if he or she earns an income and possesses property in that state. It is wise to establish a legal residence in a single state and pay your taxes there accordingly; however, there are states which have no income taxes and some officers will establish a legal residence in them in the interests of lower overall taxes. Such establishment should be done carefully having in mind the future and not a saving of a few dollars through legal "loopholes." Since the career family moves often, this problem will recur. Facing it with honesty, foresight, and advice from experts is in order.

Estate and Death Taxes. The federal government may tax your estate in the event of your death if the adjusted gross estate is sufficiently large. State death taxes take the form of inheritance or an estate tax. Each state has a different system of such taxation; therefore, consult with a nearby legal officer. Your will (and estate) must be examined, appropriately implemented, and taxed by a state official. The process known as probation is accomplished prior to execution of the will or disbursement of the estate. Bank officers will record the contents of safe deposit boxes and may not allow the papers therein to be taken or assumed until after the probation. It is too complicated to compute your potential estate tax while you are alive. Changes to the federal tax laws made in 1981 established a Unified Estate and Gift Tax credit under which increasingly large estates can be transferred tax free. The amounts that can be exempted range from $225,000 in 1982 up to $600,000 in 1987. The matter of estate taxes is complicated, however, and the advice of a specialist in estate planning is recommended. Total income including insurance benefits is the basis in many states for the inheritance tax. The issue for you is one of awareness that such taxes do exist so that they can be considered and expected.

Wills. Without exception all references and counselors advise an Army officer to execute a will and to keep it current. Your spouse should also have a will. If you die without one, the state will, in effect, make one for you. Unfortunately, regardless of how little you have, the state cannot make such a will and distribute your estate as well as you could have done by a will. On a draft write what you believe you desire in a will, then go to the legal assistance officer for expert help.

There are many dos and don'ts for will making, a few of which follow: Don't do it by yourself; don't change it by pen and ink unless legally supervised; don't delay doing it; don't fail to re-examine it upon records review and especially when changing legal residence; don't specify amounts, in general use percentages; don't sign more than one copy; do choose an executor with business sense; and do keep the original signed copy in a secure place. Specify names and property or assets, only if you have to; many a family has had temporary and permanently strained relationships develop out of contests for estate assets. Use relations and terms like "to the children, share and share alike." The important advice is re-emphasized: make a will with legal help and keep it current!

Power of Attorney. A power of attorney is a legal instrument whereby one person may designate another person to act in his or her behalf in legal or personal matters. This authority may be granted by a husband to his wife or any other person of legal age and capacity. It can be made very general and unlimited in scope, or it can be restricted to specific functions, as desired by the grantor. Do not fail to understand that when a Power of Attorney is given to another person, that person has the legal right to act under it; and if the powers granted include the right to buy or sell, or give away the grantor's property, such acts are binding. *It has been called "the most potentially dangerous document that man has ever devised."* Therefore a prudent person will be very certain to entrust such powers only to an individual in whom he or she places complete trust and confidence.

The document has particular value to officers. Many officers provide their spouses with power of attorney. Thereafter, when the officer is performing extended travel, or is assigned overseas with the family remaining behind, essential business or legal matters may be performed without the officer's presence or signature.

The authority given in a power of attorney, unlike that of a will, becomes invalid upon death of the grantor.

By all means, consult a legal assistance officer, or attorney in the preparation of this document. Explain carefully the purpose in mind. It may be true that a restricted rather than a broad form may be best. Again, as with a will, there are variations between State laws. A special form must be used to authorize cashing of government checks. A power of attorney must be acknowledged before a notary public.

The use of a "form" to give to another these powers is discouraged. Consult a Legal Assistance Officer, or an attorney, and have it done correctly and thoughtfully.

Trusts. A trust is an agreement whereby an individual gives property to a trustee for the benefit of the beneficiary or beneficiaries. Individuals, trust companies, or banks act as trustees. Trusts are somewhat like powers of attorney and wills but are actually special legal contracts. By participating in life insurance contracts, home mortgages, and mutual funds management you are probably in a "trust" arrangement without knowing it. Trusts may be specified while you are alive, for retirement, as testaments for financial income to specified individuals after your death, as revocable, and as irrevocable. As contracts, they require legal and business advice and should be entered only with knowledge and care.

Joint Ownership by Husband and Wife. For many years, this Guide has presented a discussion advocating for husband and wife a joint bank account, joint ownership with right of survivorship of other property such as real estate, stocks and bonds, and the family automobile. In view of sudden orders for TDY, foreign service unaccompanied tours, and other temporary family separations, the method has definite advantages. The wife or husband staying behind to manage the family and its affairs has fewer strictures. On the death of one of the joint owners, the property passes immediately to the other. It is not subject to the cumbersome processes of the probate courts and there is the avoidance of potentially heavy legal fees. These are important advantages.

As the years have passed, experience has proven that the method has weaknesses. Some states do not recognize joint ownership with right of survivorship. Others are community property states in which wives are presumed to own half the estate accumulated by the husband during marriage. Difficulties arise when the joint owners are divorced or one becomes incompetent. In the absence of a will, difficult problems arise if the co-owners die in a common disaster. There are estate and inheritance taxes, federal as well as state, and if the estate becomes sizable joint ownership presents additional problems. There are gift taxes which may need to be paid in the transfer of title to a spouse. These are all matters for expert guidance including the special situation of the state in which assigned to Army duty.

Consult the Legal Assistance Officer. Or consult a civilian attorney. State all the facts with candor. Joint ownership is not condemned. Under the conditions of Army service and as to most officers, it may be the preferred method of ownership. Get legal advice so decision can be made with prudence and wisdom.

Personal and Property Record. Your complete security program can be detailed on a form and changed with each review if necessary. Many associations provide such forms and it is in your interest to secure them and to fill them in. You will find as the years go by that such a record requires several pages which can be conveniently bound in a folder or a notebook. Property records are similarly inclined to grow and can be included in your folder. The need to keep the file up-to-date, in a relatively secure location, and where your spouse can find and review it is obvious but worthy of noting.

SUMMARY

Security or estate planning calls for step-by-step analysis of one's situation, goals, and benefits, and supplementing these with savings, insurance, and investments. The plan must be reviewed and altered as each change in your personal and financial situation occurs but, in particular, prior to departure for overseas and combat. There is no simple plan or checklist for you to follow because of the numerous financial programs and the personal variables introduced by each officer and his or her dependents. This chapter, hopefully, has provided you with a base for such planning; by following its sections in order and checking off each point as it applies to you, you will be able to draw up your own plan. Then, by reading the references and seeking counsel, you will be able to assure yourself of security for you and your dependents.

Advice for the Widow or Widower. Although the primary purpose of this chapter is to enable officers and their spouses to understand their rights and benefits, and plan for all eventualities in their future lives together, it also contains a great store of information for those who have already become widows or widowers.

The Army Mutual Aid Association will provide upon request a booklet, "Notes for a New Widow." Like a similar one entitled "Help Your Widow While She's Still Your Wife!" provided by the Retired Officers Association, it has blanks to be filled in to constitute a summary of vital information and guidance for the new widow. The guidance is equally applicable to widowers. A thoughtful officer will, of course, keep the information up to date as financial plans and estates are altered.

The Army takes thoughtful, effective, and thorough care of the families of its deceased members. This extends to funeral arrangements and wise council as to the settlement of all residual affairs.

You will receive promptly Army Pamphlet No. 608–4, *For your Guidance,* which contains all or certainly most of the information which families of deceased service members will need. The Installation Retirement Services Offices, throughout CONUS, are available to provide information and assistance. The local ACS agency also can provide help. Veterans organizations are eager to help all service widows or widowers with the complexity of administration affairs. Contact all of these plus the Social Security field office, your banker, and all insurance companies. Finally, make all contracts and sign all papers with care and counsel. Your spouse would want you to grieve, but be sensible with your emotions when it comes to your and the family's security. All administrative matters of long-range importance can be settled within reasonable periods of time and do not require your immediate attention while you are in mourning. You are urged to read elsewhere in this guide about the social side of Army life for widows and widowers because the Army and its people desire you to retain your ties with the service and your friends.

"Forewarned, forearmed, to be prepared is half the victory."—Cervantes.

8

Army Posts and Stations

'Tis a good and safe rule to sojourn in many places, as if you meant to spend your life there; never omitting an opportunity to doing a kindness, or speaking a true word, or making a friend.—John Ruskin.

This chapter contains information of special interest to officers and their families about most Army posts and stations in the continental United States. It has been developed as a dependable "first place to look" after receipt of orders for change of station. The information was obtained through the generous cooperation of Post Commanders and their Information Officers. It purposely has been made general in nature, designed to provide only a brief introduction to a particular post or station.

Shortly after receipt of assignment orders, you may expect to receive from your new unit or your new post commander a welcoming letter containing detailed information about the post. Many station commanders send a descriptive pamphlet about their station to officers who receive assignment orders. If this information is not received, it is standard practice for an officer to write to the station adjutant and inquire about matters of pre-arrival interest. When writing, be sure to include information about your family status, to include numbers, ages, and sex of children so that the adjutant can furnish information specifically applicable to your needs. If the health of family members, or other reasons, require special treatment or facilities, it is proper also to inquire as to the availability of the needed services. Be assured that the Army values its members and their dependents, and each commander recognizes the importance of their morale, including the importance of first impressions. Each commander will be anxious that you are fully and accurately informed as to what you may expect at your new post. Any questions you may have will be answered as quickly and as completely as possible.

An assignment to a new post or station should be approached with the feeling that, "Here is a real opportunity" not readily available to other persons of our society. It provides the opportunity to see perhaps a new and different area of the country from any you have seen before, with the difference to be measured not only in terms of topography, scenery, climate or historic sites, but in terms of people and their customs. The new assignment will provide also the opportunity to meet new Army members, many of whom you may never meet again, but others who will become life-long friends with whom you will serve again on other future assignments. The total opportunity of a new assignment is limited only by your ability to learn, to understand, to meet others and to be met by them, to participate in the activities of the station, and to pursue actively the off-duty recreational activities which will be available. Your own attitude will be the major determinant in making the new assignment a rewarding and pleasant experience.

There is another facet to each new assignment which should not be overlooked. Referred to here is the post itself. It should be recognized that each post came into being as a result of a definite Army need. Examples are Fort Wadsworth (recently deactivated) and Fort Totten, which originally were Coast Artillery forts helping to protect the approaches to New York harbor from possible attack from the sea. Another example is Fort Riley, Kansas, which served as the base for the operations of Custer's 7th Cavalry Regiment during the days our western states were being settled. Or Fort Sheridan, Illinois, which was established in 1887 in order to have troops near the city of Chicago during the period of labor unrest in that area, of which the Haymarket Riot of 1886 was a part.

As the years have passed, Army needs have changed, resulting in changed or changing missions for the various posts and stations. Some, like Fort Totten and, more recently, Fort Sheridan, have become housekeeping and support facilities serving Army members and members of the Army's sister services stationed in the area, while others, like Fort Riley, still play an active role in the training and support of Army units, but with a mission changed considerably from that originally assigned.

Regardless of location and current mission, each Army post has a fascinating history. Study of the origins and historical activities of any post is both interesting and professionally rewarding. Such study does much to increase one's knowledge of the Army's heritage and serves as well as a fine base for more thorough knowledge and understanding of the local area. It is recommended as a subject of early priority upon assignment to a new post.

The typical, established Army post is a pleasant place to live. Where there are quarters for families, the activities will be substantially the same as in civilian communities. The ties of neighborliness and breadth of friendships are especially noteworthy because all are engaged in the common mission of the nation's security. The vast majority of Army members are young and active. The provision of extensive off-duty athletic, cultural, recreational, and social activities recognizes the needs and expectancies of young officers, noncommissioned officers, and soldiers, and their spouses and children. Opportunities for an interesting life are abundant for all individuals who participate actively in the life of the post.

There is a wide variation in the living and recreational facilities of Army stations. Some have been in use for decades and have been progressively developed so that the resulting environment is highly pleasing with excellent athletic, cultural, social, and recreational facilities. Others were built during World War II and are less extensively developed. The variation in number and adequacy of family quarters is wide; inadequate housing is considered by some officers to be the most serious objection to an Army career. This chapter does not seek to minimize it. But the Army's leaders have fought hard for action to improve it; there has been considerable construction and improvement in the situation during past years. The progress must continue until all of our truly "permanent" posts and stations are provided with adequate housing which is up to the standards of professional people in other walks of life. The complete environment must be a good place for Army officers, Army spouses, and Army children to live, with which we link the Army's noncommissioned officers and families, and our soldiers.

Attention is invited to Chapter Six, *The Social Side of Army Life,* and Chapter Nine, *Foreign Service.*

The facilities described below are common to Army posts.

Commissaries. Most stations are authorized a commissary where groceries and household supplies substantially as sold at civilian supermarkets may be purchased.

These outlets are a convenience for on-post families. The prices average less than those for commercial stores resulting in patronage by both on- and off-post families. An ID card is required for entrance and usually personal checks may be cashed for the value of the purchase.

Post Exchanges. Excellent post exchanges are provided at Army stations. The Army and Air Force Exchange Service (AAFES) prescribes the items and services which may be sold. Army members should know that the profits generated by exchanges are used for the support of athletic and recreational programs, including provisions for athletic fields and other facilities. Post exchanges add to the convenience as well as the economy of post life. An ID card is required for entrance and purchase of merchandise. Checks up to a usual limit of $100 may be cashed.

Motion Picture Theaters. All stations in CONUS and overseas are provided motion picture service, and many stations have excellent motion picture theaters. Through the cooperation of the motion picture industry, and the good work of the Army and Air Force Exchange Service, the best and most recently released films are shown. Like the post exchange, the profits are returned as dividends to be expended for athletic, recreational, and other programs for the general improvement of post life.

Athletic Facilities. Athletic programs and essential indoor and outdoor recreational facilities are provided at most stations. At permanent installations the facilities are outstanding. They include playing fields, bleachers and dressing rooms for baseball and football, swimming pools, bowling alleys, tennis courts, many of which are illuminated for night use; field houses for basketball and other indoor sports; and many posts have excellent golf courses. The climate and recreational potential of the region has a bearing on the activities of maximum popularity. The Army goal is to provide a normal, interesting off-duty life for its members.

Religious Activities. Most Army stations are provided with religious facilities and programs. The services of Chaplains of the Protestant, Catholic, and Jewish faiths are almost universally available to military members. Religious programs are conducted in much the same manner as in civilian communities. Chaplains are appreciated and valuable members of the unit or station.

Library Service. Nearly all stations have a good station library and in most instances the services of a professional librarian. New books, newspapers, and magazines are provided regularly. Individuals interested in study may receive important assistance from the librarian and the library facilities.

Officers' Open Messes. All permanent and semi-permanent Army stations, and many units, have an officers' Open Mess, or club, the facilities of which are available to officers and mature members of their families. Dues are charged which defray the operating expenses. The social life of club members centers about the programs and facilities of the Open Mess. Regular dining facilities are standard. Dances, social gatherings, athletic activities, are examples of recreational opportunities which are usually available. Officers joining a station or unit having an Open Mess should join it at once, as a matter of course.

Schools. All Army stations at which dependents are authorized, which includes all stations in the Continental United States, are provided as a matter of course with school facilities for children of Army members. In general, the attempt is made to provide on-post schools for children through the 6th grade, with the junior and senior high school students attending local schools near the post. There are exceptions, of course. Many posts have kindergarten facilities. In all cases where any distance is involved, bus transportation is provided free of charge. Parochial or other private schools are available near many posts and may be utilized if desired. Consult the local authorities.

Medical Facilities. Most large Army posts have a station hospital, while smaller posts may be equipped only with a clinic or dispensary, relying upon a nearby military hospital for more extensive medical services. In any case, splendid medical care is available to Army personnel and family members, including those residing in off-post housing. See Chapter 7, *Financial Planning*, for a complete description of medical care available and the procedures for obtaining this care.

Family Quarters. As mentioned earlier, the problem of providing adequate quarters for Army members and their families is a serious one. The actual housing situation varies not only from post-to-post, but also with time at any particular post, depending upon the numbers of arriving and departing personnel. A post with an adequate number of family quarters today could find itself woefully short of quarters tomorrow when a major new unit is assigned.

In general, it should be assumed that upon assignment to any post there will be a waiting period before on-post quarters may be obtained. This necessitates a rental or lease, or perhaps purchase of local housing in the nearby civilian community prior to moving on post. The actual waiting period may vary from a few days to many months, and in some cases, such as for most personnel assigned to the Washington, D.C., area, there is no post housing available regardless of waiting period. Take this in stride. It is a recognized disadvantage of Army life, but it should be viewed in total context along with the many advantages available to Army members.

In all cases, be realistic and businesslike in your approach to providing housing for your family. It ALWAYS is advisable to obtain the very latest quarters information from the Housing Officer at your new post. If this information is not received within a few weeks after you receive assignment orders to a post, be sure to write for it. While advice is always welcome from those who have previously been stationed at your new post, remember that their information regarding quarters availability almost surely is out of date. Get the correct, up-to-date information about both on-post and off-post housing from the post Housing Officer and then make your personal plans accordingly.

One note of caution: When arriving at a new post, be sure to check with the Housing Office prior to making any commitments for lease or purchase of off-post quarters. While policies vary, in most cases you must have the permission of the Housing Officer to reside off-post.

Most stations have guest houses or other temporary-type accommodations which may be utilized for short periods of time (5 to 10 days usually) while a family is making arrangements for permanent quarters. These facilities generally are limited in number and reservations are in order well in advance of intended use. Write the post Housing Officer.

Activities for Spouses and Children. Most Army stations have organizations such as the Officers' Wives' Club, Parent-Teacher Association, and youth activities of many kinds such as Boy Scouts, Girl Scouts, Teen Age Clubs, and others. Active participation in the undertakings of these organizations is encouraged. It is a way for the newcomer to become acquainted, and to add his or her talents to the life of the post.

ARMED FORCES HOSTESS ASSOCIATION

The Armed Forces Hostess Association, Room 1A–736, The Pentagon, Washington, D. C., 20310, provides a unique service for all newcomers in the Washington metropolitan area. Local files include information on animal care, camps, entertainment, furniture repair, schools, vacation, touring and other helpful items. Files are also maintained on all CONUS posts. Information on either your CONUS or Washington assignment will be provided on request.

ABERDEEN PROVING GROUND, MARYLAND 21005 AND 21010

Aberdeen Proving Ground, consisting of two post areas, is 25 miles northeast of Baltimore, on Chesapeake Bay, adjacent to Aberdeen, Maryland. It is reached via Interstate 95, U.S. 40, or via Bel Air U.S. 1.

Major Activities. Headquarters, U.S. Army Test and Evaluation Command; Army Ordnance Center and School; related research laboratories. All of these activities are located on the main post, ZIP 21005. At the sub-post, ZIP 21010, are located Edgewood Arsenal; Army Environmental Hygiene Agency; HQ 4th Battalion (NH) 1st Air Defense Artillery; Army Department of Biological Research.

Quarters. There are about 220 units of family housing for officers, about equally divided between the two post areas. Adequate numbers of BOQs are available. There are two guest houses. Nearby off-post housing is limited.

ARMED FORCES STAFF COLLEGE, VIRGINIA 23511

The Armed Forces Staff College is on Hampton Boulevard, 2 miles south of the Main Gate, Norfolk Naval Base, Virginia.

Family Quarters. Quarters are sufficient for most married officers and their families of the faculty, staff and officer students. BOQs are available. Off-post housing is available.

FORT BELVOIR, VIRGINIA 22060

Fort Belvoir is bisected by U.S. 1, 16 miles south of Washington, D.C.

Major Activities. U.S. Army Engineer Center; Engineer School; Defense Systems Management School; Davison Army Airfield; Computer Systems Command; Engineer Topographic Laboratories; DeWitt Army Hospital.

Quarters. There are nearly 500 sets of family quarters for married officers. BOQs are available for both permanent party and TDY personnel. Limited guest house facilities are provided. Off-post housing is available, but expensive.

FORT BENNING, GEORGIA 31905

Fort Benning is 9 miles south of Columbus, Georgia, on U.S. 27.

Major Activities. The U.S. Army Infantry Center; The U.S. Army Infantry School; 197th Infantry Brigade; Officer Candidate School; Infantry Board; U.S. Army Infantry Center Aviation Command; 36th Engineer Group; U.S. Army Infantry Museum; Martin Army Hospital.

Quarters. There are about 1000 sets of family quarters; rentals in Columbus are good with many types of apartments and houses, furnished and unfurnished. BOQs and temporary accommodations are available.

FORT BLISS, TEXAS 79916

Fort Bliss is 7 miles northeast of downtown El Paso, adjacent to Highway 54, and with an exit off I-10.

Major Activities. The U.S. Army Air Defense Center; Air Defense School; 11th Air Defense Artillery Group; U.S. Army Air Defense Board; 3rd Armored Cavalry Regiment; U.S. Army Nuclear Agency; U.S. Army Sergeants Major Academy. (See also William Beaumont Army Medical Center.)

Quarters. Nearly 1000 sets of family quarters are provided for officers. Ample BOQs are available, many with kitchens. Guest house facilities are available.

FORT BRAGG, NORTH CAROLINA 28307

Fort Bragg is 10 miles northwest of Fayetteville, adjacent to Highway 24.

Major Activities. Hq, XVIII Airborne Corps; Hq, XVIII Airborne Corps Artillery; 82d Airborne Division; John F. Kennedy Center for Military Assistance (Abn); U.S. Army Institute for Military Assistance; 5th Special Forces Group; 35th Signal Group; 16th MP Group; 1st Corps Support Command; Headquarters, First ROTC Region; Womack Army Hospital.

Quarters. Nearly 1000 sets of family quarters are available for married officers and the majority of officers with families live on post. BOQs and guest house facilities are provided.

FORT CAMPBELL, KENTUCKY 42223

Fort Campbell is on Highway 41A, 16 miles south of Hopkinsville, Kentucky 5 miles north of Clarksville, Tennessee.

Major Activities. 101st Airborne Division (Air Assault); Campbell Army Airfield.

Quarters. There are more than 900 sets of family quarters for officers. Several housing projects near Clarksville or Hopkinsville are available at reasonable rentals. Transient quarters are available on post. The post also has a modern motel-type guest house.

CARLISLE BARRACKS, PENNSYLVANIA 17013

Carlisle Barracks touches the eastern limit of Carlisle, on U.S. Highway 11, 18 miles west of Harrisburg. This ancient post was established in 1757.

Major Activities. US Army War College; Strategic Studies Institute; US Army Garrison; U.S. Army Communications Command, Operations Group; Omar N. Bradley Museum; Military History Research Collection; Dunham Army Hospital.

Family Quarters. Quarters are sufficient to house approximately 80 per cent of the staff, faculty, and students. BOQs are available. There is a Guest House for limited stays. Civilian housing in the immediate area of Carlisle Barracks is expensive and scarce. There are many convenient motels and hotels.

FORT CARSON, COLORADO 80913

Fort Carson is 4 miles south of the city limits of Colorado Springs. Between Colorado 115 and Interstate 25.

Major Activities. Headquarters, 4th Infantry Division (Mech.); 43rd Support Group.

Quarters. There are approximately 230 sets of family quarters available for officers. BOQs and guest house facilities are provided. Off-post housing is available in Colorado Springs and other nearby communities.

FORT DETRICK, MARYLAND 21701

Fort Detrick is located in Frederick, Maryland, approximately 45 miles from both Baltimore and Washington, D.C.

Major Activities. The garrison provides services and support for 17 tenant activities, including several research activities of the U.S. Army Health Services Command, a laboratory of the U.S. Department of Agriculture, and a cancer research center of the National Institutes of Health. The U.S. Army Health Services Command Historical Unit and Health Services Data Systems Agency are located here. Also at Fort Detrick are the USACC East Coast Telecommunications Center and the U.S. Army Communications Electronics Engineering Installation Agency—CONUS.

Quarters. Less than 60 sets of officer's quarters are available. BOQs also are limited. Adequate rental apartments in the surrounding community are in short supply and are rather expensive, although adequate hotel and motel accommodations are available locally.

FORT DEVENS, MASSACHUSETTS 01433

Fort Devens is 1 ½ miles from Ayer, on State Route 2, 40 miles northwest of Boston.

Major Activities. U.S. Army Security Agency Training Center and School; 10th Special Forces Group (Airborne); Headquarters, Army Readiness Region 1; U.S. Army Hospital.

Quarters. More than 400 sets of permanent family quarters are available and the majority of all assigned officers live on post. BOQs and guest house facilities are available. Off-post rentals are scarce and the prices are high.

FORT DIX, NEW JERSEY 08640

Fort Dix is located off Exit 7, New Jersey Turnpike, near Wrightstown, on State Highway 68, 17 miles south of Trenton. It is co-located with McGuire Air Force Base.

Major Activities. U.S. Army Training Center; Headquarters, Army Readiness Region II; U.S. Army Personnel Center; Walson Army Hospital.

Quarters. Approximately 430 sets of family quarters are provided for assigned officers. BOQs and a modern guest house are available.

FORT DRUM, NEW YORK 13610

Fort Drum is located about 9 miles east of Watertown, New York, off Exit 47, I-81, approximately 25 miles from the Canadian border and some 70 miles north of Syracuse, New York.

Major Activities. The U.S. Army Garrison supports the major training center of the northeastern U.S. for Reserve and National Guard forces; cold weather training site for active Army and Marines; Wheeler-Sac Army Airfield; New York and New Jersey Army National Guard Annual Training Equipment Pools.

Quarters. Nearly 100 sets of family quarters are available. Transient family quarters and BOQs are provided. Off-post rentals are scarce.

DUGWAY PROVING GROUND, UTAH 84022

Dugway Proving Ground is 74 miles southwest of Salt Lake City. It is reached via U.S. Highway 40 (Interstate 80) and unnumbered County road, or State Routes 36 and 199 from Tooele, Utah.

Major Activity. Desert Test Center, which plans, schedules, and conducts tests to assess the military value of chemical weapons and chemical-biological defense systems and other test weapons as assigned.

Quarters. There are quarters for all assigned officers with families with no waiting period. Limited transient quarters are available for temporary occupancy. BOQs are provided for single officers.

FORT EUSTIS, VIRGINIA 23604

Fort Eustis is on State Highway 105, between Williamsburg and Newport News, off I-64.

Major Activity. U.S. Army Transportation School; training Transportation units.

Quarters. Approximately 375 sets of family quarters are available. Off-post housing is available at reasonable rates. Transient family quarters and BOQs are provided.

FITZSIMONS ARMY MEDICAL CENTER, COLORADO 80240

Fitzsimons Army Medical Center is on U.S. Highway 40, 9 miles east of Denver, in the city of Aurora.

Major Activities. U.S. Army General Hospital; Office for Civilian Health and Medical Program for Uniformed Services; Medical Research and Nutrition Laboratory; Optical Maintenance and Medical Activity.

Quarters. Approximately 125 sets of family quarters are available, which is insufficient to accommodate the assigned officers. Off-post housing is available, but expensive. A guest house of limited capacity is available.

FORT GORDON, GEORGIA 30905

Fort Gordon is 9 miles south of Augusta, between U.S. Highways 1 and 78.

Major activities. U.S. Army/School Training Center; Signal School; Dwight D. Eisenhower Army Medical Center.

Quarters. Approximately 160 sets of family quarters are available for officers. Off-post housing is available in the moderate to high price range. BOQs and a modern guest house are available.

FORT HAMILTON COMMAND, NEW YORK 11252

Fort Hamilton is the headquarters of the Fort Hamilton Command which includes Fort Totten and Bellmore Direct/General Support Maintenance Activity, New York: Fort Hamilton is in the Bay Ridge section of Brooklyn, near the Verrazano-Narrows Bridge. Reach it from Exit 13, New Jersey Turnpike, via the Staten Island Expressway (Interstate 278) and the Verrazano Bridge. Take the exit for 92d St.-Bay Ridge, make two consecutive left turns, and follow Ft. Hamilton Parkway to the main gate.

Major Activities. 26th Army Band; Armed Forces Examining and Entrance Station. The station provides administrative and logistic support to activities in the New York area.

Quarters. Nearly 800 units of family housing are available at Fort Hamilton. The entire command has approximately 1340 sets of quarters for officer's families. BOQs and a guest house are available.

FORT BENJAMIN HARRISON, INDIANA 46216

Fort Benjamin Harrison is two blocks off State Highway 67 (Pendleton Pike) and just off I-465, 11 miles northeast of downtown Indianapolis.

Major Activities. U.S. Army Institute of Personnel and Resource Management; TRADOC Administration Center; U.S. Army Finance and Accounting Center; Finance School; Adjutant General School; Defense Information School; Enlisted Personnel Support Center; Enlisted Evaluation Center.

Quarters. The post has approximately 45 family housing units and 330 BOQ units. Guest facilities are very limited. Homes for sale or rent are available in nearby areas.

FORT A.P. HILL, VIRGINIA 22427

Fort A.P. Hill is three miles east of the small town of Bowling Green, about 36 miles north of Richmond and approximately 72 miles south of the Nation's capital. U.S. 301 intersects the post, with a large range complex on the south side of the highway and the post headquarters, training areas and campsites on the north side. State Route 2 bounds the post on the east and U.S. 17 forms the western boundary.

Major Activities. The post's mission is to support training of active Army and Reserve components as well as training and/or testing by the Navy, Marines, Air Force and other government agencies. A.P. Hill has 30 training areas and

13 campsites, 10 of which use tentage for troops in the field, primarily during the annual training period which usually runs from May to September.

Quarters. There are six inadequate family housing units on post plus a 10-space trailer court. Family quarters are available to A.P. Hill personnel at the Naval Surface Weapons Center at Dahlgren, 30 miles distant. Limited housing is available in Bowling Green; and more housing is available in Fredericksburg, 20 miles away.

FORT HOOD, TEXAS 76544

Fort Hood is in central Texas, 60 miles north of Austin and 65 miles southwest of Waco. It is adjacent to Killeen, on U.S. Highway 190.

Major Activities. The largest armored post in the free world, Ft. Hood is the home of Headquarters III Corps; 1st Cavalry Division; 2d Armored Division; 13th Support Brigade; and a number of separate signal, aviation, engineer, ASA, military police, and military intelligence battalions; MASSTER; Computer Support Command Support Group; Tactical Systems Development Group; Hood Army Airfield; Robert Gray Army Airfield; Darnall Army Hospital.

Quarters. Approximately 900 sets of family quarters are available for officers. Off-post housing is limited, but is becoming more adequate monthly. BOQs and a new 88 room guest house are available.

FORT SAM HOUSTON, TEXAS 78234

Fort Sam Houston is within the city limits of San Antonio, near Interstate Highway 35 and U.S. 81.

Major Activities. Headquarters Fifth U.S. Army; U.S. Army Health Services Command; Brooke Army Medical Center; Academy of Health Sciences; Headquarters, Army Readiness Region VII.

Quarters. Quarters for officers are available for about 35 percent of eligible officers; off-post rental apartments and houses are adequate. The Housing Office maintains listings and assists families in finding locations. Adequate motel, hotel, and trailer accommodations are available near the post.

FORT HUACHUCA, ARIZONA 85613

Fort Huachuca (Wah-CHOO-Kah) is in Cochise County, 70 miles southeast of Tucson, on State Highway 90, 28 miles south of Interstate Highway 10, at the Benson cut-off. The Main Gate is in Sierra Vista.

Major Activities. Headquarters, U.S. Army Communications Command; U.S. Army Electronic Proving Ground; U.S. Army Security Agency Test and Evaluations Center; U.S. Army Intelligence Center and School; Libby Army Airfield; Raymond W. Bliss Army Hospital.

Quarters. There are more than 600 permanent-type housing units for married officers. This generally is sufficient to accommodate the housing demand.

HUNTER ARMY AIRFIELD, GEORGIA 31409

Hunter Army Airfield is adjacent to Savannah, Georgia. Fort Stewart and Hunter Army Airfield operate as a single command although separated 40 miles.

Major Activities. 1st Battalion (Ranger), 75th Infantry. Support of Ranger training and National Guard and Reserves summer training.

Quarters. More than 250 sets of family quarters for officers are available on post. Guest house facilities and BOQs are provided. Rental housing is available in Savannah.

FORT HUNTER LIGGETT, CALIFORNIA 93941

Fort Hunter Liggett is a sub-post of Fort Ord.

FORT JACKSON, SOUTH CAROLINA 29207

Fort Jackson is 6 miles from downtown Columbia, between 1-20, U.S. 1 and U.S. 76.

Major Activities. U.S. Army Training Center; First U.S. Army Drill Sergeant School; Moncrief Army Hospital.

Quarters. Approximately 160 sets of adequate family quarters are available for officers. Off-post housing is available at reasonable rates. A high-rise BOQ provides modern quarters for 160 officers.

FORT KNOX, KENTUCKY 40121

Fort Knox is 35 miles south of Louisville, on U.S. Highway 31-W.

Major Activities. U.S. Army Training Center, Armor Center and School, Headquarters, Second ROTC Region; Headquarters, Army Readiness Region VI; U.S. Armor and Engineer Board. Ireland Army Hospital. At Fort Knox is the U.S. Gold Depository.

Quarters. Approximately 1600 family housing units are available for assignment to married officers. Guest house facilities and BOQs are provided. Nearby off-post housing is limited.

FORT LEAVENWORTH, KANSAS 66027

Fort Leavenworth is just north of the city of Leavenworth, Kansas, 35 miles northwest of Kansas City, Missouri.

Major Activities. U.S. Army Command and General Staff College; Combined Arms and Services Staff School; Combined Arms Center; Combined Arms Combat Developments Activity; Midwest Telecommunications Center; United States Disciplinary Barracks; the Armed Forces Insurance Exchange, formerly the Armed Forces Co-operative Insuring Association.

Quarters. Approximately 420 sets of family quarters (both adequate and inadequate) are available for permanently assigned officers and approximately 900 sets of family quarters (both adequate and inadequate) are reserved for Command and General Staff College students. Off-post housing is available at reasonable rates. Guest house facilities are available and BOQs are provided, but their use is not required for field grade officers.

FORT LEE, VIRGINIA 23801

Fort Lee is 3 miles east of Petersburg, on State Highway 36.

Major Activities. The U.S. Army Quartermaster Center, Quartermaster School; 1st Field Army Support Command; TRADOC Logistics Center; 20th Air Division; Computer Command Support Group; Combat Service Support Group and Kenner Army Hospital.

Quarters. Approximately 450 sets of family quarters are available for assigned officers. BOQs are provided. Off-post housing is not plentiful.

FORT LEWIS, WASHINGTON 98433

Fort Lewis is on Puget Sound, 50 miles south of Seattle, midway between Olympia and Tacoma, on Interstate Highway No. 5.

Major Activities. 9th Infantry Division and Strategic Army Forces Units; Headquarters, Fourth ROTC Region. Vancouver Barracks and Yakima Firing Center, are sub-posts. McChord Air Force Base and Madigan Army Medical Center are nearby.

Quarters. There are about 880 sets of officer's quarters at Fort Lewis. Madigan General Hospital has an additional 85 sets. Temporary lodging is available at the Fort Lewis Lodge. BOQs are provided for single officers. Excellent motel and hotel accommodations are available within a few miles. Off-post housing is available within reasonable distance of the post.

FORT MCCLELLAN, ALABAMA 36201

Fort McClellan is 3 miles north of Anniston, Alabama, on State Highway 21, near U.S. Highways 78 and 431.

Major Activities. U.S. Army Training Center; Military Police School; Chemical School; U.S. Army NCO Academy; Advanced Infantry Training Brigade; Noble Army Hospital.

Quarters. Approximately 100 sets of family housing units are available for married officers. BOQs and guest house facilities are provided. Adequate off-post rental housing is available.

FORT MCCOY, WISCONSIN 54656

Fort McCoy is located in west-central Wisconsin on State Highway 21, midway between the cities of Sparta and Tomah.

Major Activities. U.S. Army Garrison; USACC Detachment; Readiness Group (ARR V). The primary mission of Fort McCoy is to serve as a training center for Reserve and National Guard units.

Quarters. There are 16 sets of sub-standard family quarters and fair rental rates have been established. Assignment is on a voluntary basis. Off-post housing is adequate within short distances at average to high rates. Five completely furnished mobile homes are available for temporary rent by new arrivals. BOQ facilities are available.

FORT LESLEY J. MCNAIR, D.C. 20315

Fort McNair is on the Potomac River, a short distance from the National Capital, at 4th and P Sts., S.W.

Major Activities. Hq. Military District of Washington (MDW); National Defense University, including the National War College and the Industrial College of the Armed Forces; Inter-American Defense College; Company A, 1st Battalion (Reinf) 3d Infantry, "The Old Guard."

Quarters. The limited number of on-post quarters are reserved for key officers. Off-post housing is available. On-post accommodations for officers without families are sufficient.

FORT MCPHERSON, GEORGIA 30330

Fort McPherson is in Atlanta, on U.S. Highway 29 and State Highway 166.

Major Activity. Headquarters, U.S. Army Forces Command (FORSCOM).

Quarters. On-post family housing for officers is limited to about 75 sets of quarters. However, a Wherry-type housing unit is adjacent to the post where quarters usually are available. Off-post housing for rent or purchase is adequate. Temporary accommodations are provided.

FORT GEORGE G. MEADE, MARYLAND 20755

Fort Meade is centered in the triangle formed by Baltimore, Washington, and Annapolis, about 20 miles from each city. It is 2 miles south of the Baltimore-Washington Parkway, with the exit to the post at Route 175 at Jessup, or at Route 198 at Laurel.

Major Activities. Headquarters First U.S. Army; Headquarters, Army Readiness Region III; U.S. Army Intelligence Command; National Security Agency of the DoD; 35th Artillery Group; Kimbrough Army Hospital.

Quarters. Approximately 620 units of family housing are available for assigned married officers. BOQs and guest house facilities are provided.

MILITARY TRAFFIC MANAGEMENT COMMAND BROOKLYN, NEW YORK 11250

The Eastern Area, MTMC, has its headquarters at 58th St., and 1st Ave., Brooklyn, New York. The Military Ocean Terminal, Bayonne, is at Bayonne, N.J. 07002.

Major Activities. The EAMTMC has jurisdiction over terminal units and activities in the 34-State eastern and midwestern portion of the United States and overseas. The Military Ocean Terminal, Bayonne, processes for shipment Department of Defense sponsored cargo and equipment primarily with ocean-going vessels.

Quarters. For EAMTMC personnel, see Fort Hamilton. For Military Ocean Terminal, Bayonne, approximately 125 units of family housing are available. No BOQ facilities are available at Military Ocean Terminal, Bayonne. Off-post housing is available, but rather expensive.

FORT MONMOUTH, NEW JERSEY 07703

Fort Monmouth is between Red Bank and Eatontown on State Highway 35. When traveling north on the New Jersey Turnpike, exit at Interchange 8, take Route 33 to Freehold and 537 to Eatontown; traveling south, exit at 11, follow route 35 to the post. On the Garden State Parkway, exit at 105 and follow the signs.

Major Activities. U.S. Army Electronics Command; Communications Systems Agency; Satellite Communications Agency; TRI-TAC offices; Defense Language Institute; USMA Prep School; Chaplain School; Patterson Hospital.

Quarters. There are approximately 350 sets of quarters for officer's families. Off-post housing is available in nearby communities, but may be difficult to obtain during the summer vacation period. BOQs and guest house facilities are provided.

FORT MONROE, VIRGINIA 23351

Fort Monroe is at Old Point Comfort, Virginia, on the waters of Hampton Roads, Chesapeake Bay, and Mill Creek. It is reached via Interstate Highway 64 and U.S. Highways 60 and 258.

Major Activities. Headquarters, U.S. Army Training and Doctrine Command (TRADOC).

Quarters. Family quarters are inadequate in number. Off-post housing, while available, may be difficult to obtain during the summer season. BOQs are available. Guest house facilities are very limited, but the Hotel Chamberlin, on the post, offers special rates for personnel under official orders.

FORT MYER, VIRGINIA 22211

Fort Myer is in Arlington, just across the Memorial Bridge, adjacent to Arlington Cemetery. It is on U.S. Highway 50, Arlington Boulevard.

Major Activities. 1st Battalion (Reinf), 3d Infantry "The Old Guard"; The U.S. Army Band.

Quarters. On-post family housing is limited in quantity and is largely reserved for assignment to senior officers on the Department of the Army Staff. BOQs are limited and are considered sub-standard. Limited guest facilities are available. Off-post housing is abundant, but expensive.

OAKLAND ARMY BASE, CALIFORNIA 94626

Oakland Army Base is in West Oakland adjacent to the east approach to the San Francisco Bay Bridge.

Major Activities. Western Area, Military Traffic Management Command (WAMTMC) whose main activity is the movement of military cargo and passengers to overseas ports. The U.S. Army Personnel Center processes personnel proceeding to and from oversea stations.

Quarters. There are about 30 permanent housing units for officer's families at Oakland. Off-post government leased housing is available and off-post housing in general is plentiful. Limited space is available for visitors.

FORT ORD, CALIFORNIA 93941

Fort Ord is on Monterey Bay, on California State Highway No. 1.

Major Activities. Headquarters, 7th Infantry Division; U.S. Army Infantry Training Center; Army Combat Support Schools; U.S. Army Combat Developments Experimentation Command. Fort Hunter Liggett is a sub-post; the Presidio of Monterey is a sub-post for the West Coast Branch, Defense Language Institute, and Unit #3 of the Human Resources Research Organization.

Family Quarters. There are approximately 720 sets of officer's quarters. A limited number of guest units are available for officers and families in transit.

FORT PICKETT, VIRGINIA 23824

Fort Pickett is located on State Highway 40 and U.S. Highway 460, about two miles east of Blackstone, Virginia, and approximately 40 miles southwest of Petersburg, Virginia.

Major Activities. Training area for U.S. Army Reserve and National Guard units. Also utilized by active units from all branches of service. No units permanently stationed on post.

Quarters. On-post and off-post family housing is extremely limited both in quantity and quality. A post trailer park is available. All on-post housing, including BOQs, are considered sub-standard. Twelve guest cottages are available.

FORT POLK, LOUISIANA 71459

Fort Polk is in western central Louisiana, near Leesville, about 50 miles west of Alexandria. The post may best be reached via U.S. 171 which connects with I-20 at Shreveport, about 120 miles to the north, and with I-10 at Lake Charles, about 70 miles to the south.

Major Activities. Headquarters, 5th Infantry Division (Mechanized); U.S. Army Infantry Training Center; U.S. Army Hospital.

Quarters. Fort Polk has a critical housing shortage. On post there are only about 140 family housing units for officers and about 400 trailer spaces. The post housing office handles assignments of an additional 350 family units which are privately owned and located in New Llano, about 8 miles from the post. BOQs are available, consisting of 60 new units and some that have been renovated.

THE PRESIDIO OF MONTEREY, CALIFORNIA 93940

The Presidio of Monterey is in the city of Monterey. It is a sub-post of Fort Ord.

THE PRESIDIO OF SAN FRANCISCO, CALIFORNIA 94129

The Main Gate of the Presidio of San Francisco is at Lombard and Lyons Streets, 2 blocks west of U.S. Highway 101, near the south approach of the Golden Gate Bridge. State Highway No. 1 crosses the reservation and joins U.S. 101 near the Golden Gate Bridge Toll Plaza.

Major Activities. Headquarters Sixth U.S. Army; Letterman Army Medical Center; Headquarters, Army Readiness Region IX. Sub-posts are Fort Baker, Fort Barry, and Fort Cronkhite.

Quarters. There are approximately 490 sets of family quarters for officers and 60 BOQ facilities. Temporary accommodations are limited. Off-post rentals are available, but expensive.

FORT RILEY, KANSAS 66442

Fort Riley is 4 miles east of Junction City, Kansas, on State Highway 18; Interstate Highway 70 and U.S. 40 connect with Fort Riley.

Major Activities. 1st Infantry Division (MECH); Headquarters, Third ROTC Region; Marshall U.S. Army Airfield; Irwin Army Hospital; 138th Engineer Group (Construction); Fifth Army NCO Academy.

Quarters. More than 530 family housing units are provided for married officers. BOQs are available. There are two guest houses on post which provide temporary accommodations, and trailer courts are available in nearby communities.

FORT RITCHIE, MARYLAND 21719

Fort Ritchie is in northwest Maryland, 2 miles west of Blue Ridge Summit, Penna., near Cascade, off State Route 81.

Major Activity. U.S. Army Communications Command—Continental United States.

Quarters. On-post family quarters for officers number about 70. BOQs are provided as well as a new, modern guest house facility. Off-post housing is limited in nearby areas.

FORT RUCKER, ALABAMA 36362

Fort Rucker is northwest of Dothan, on State Highway 85.

Major Activities. The U.S. Army Aviation Center; Aviation School; U.S. Army Agency for Aviation Safety; Army Aeromedical Center; U.S. Army Aviation Test Board; Army Aviation Human Research Unit; Army Aviation Museum.

Quarters. There are approximately 675 sets of family quarters for officers. Student officers on PCS are eligible for these quarters. New, modern, motel-type BOQs will accommodate about 500 officers. Limited guest house facilities are available.

FORT SHERIDAN, ILLINOIS 60037

Fort Sheridan is 22 miles north of Chicago, on the shore of Lake Michigan. It is reached via Interstate 94 to the Highwood cutoff, thence to the post.

Major Activities. U.S. Army Recruiting Command; Headquarters, Army Readiness Region V; Administrative and logistical support center for Midwest defense installations.

Quarters. There are nearly 220 sets of officer's family quarters available. BOQs are provided. A guest house furnishes limited temporary accommodations.

FORT SILL, OKLAHOMA 73503

Fort Sill adjoins Lawton, Oklahoma, on the H. E. Bailey Turnpike, and U.S. Highways 62, 277, and 281.

Major Activities. U.S. Army Field Artillery Center; Field Artillery School; III Corps Arty; 1st AIT Brigade U.S. Army Training Center, Field Arty; Field Artillery Aviation Command; Reynolds U.S. Army Hospital; U.S. Army Field Artillery Board.

Quarters. Nearly 500 family housing units for officers are provided. Approximately one-fourth of these are reserved for student officers attending the Advanced Course. BOQs are plentiful. Off-post housing is available nearby in Lawton.

FORT STEWART, GEORGIA 31314

Fort Stewart is adjacent to Hinesville, Georgia, 40 miles southwest of Savannah. State routes 63, 67, 119, 129, and 144 pass through the reservation. (See also Hunter Army Airfield.)

Major Activities. Headquarters, 24th Infantry Division. The Fort is used in the summer for National Guard and Reserve training.

Quarters. More than 170 sets of family quarters and about 15 trailer sites are available on post for officers. Guest house facilities and BOQs are provided. Rental housing is limited in Hinesville and the surrounding area.

THE U.S. MILITARY ACADEMY, WEST POINT, NEW YORK 10996

West Point is on the west bank of the Hudson River, 12 miles south of Newburgh, on U.S. Route 9W. From New York City cross the George Washington Bridge, turn right into Palisades Parkway, proceed 50 miles to Bear Mountain Bridge to Bear Mountain Circle, thence north on U.S. 9W.

Major Activity. The United States Military Academy.

Quarters. There are about 900 sets of on-post quarters to accommodate officers desiring post housing. Off-post rentals are high. The Hotel Thayer, on the reservation, provides temporary accommodations at nominal rates. BOQs are available.

WALTER REED ARMY MEDICAL CENTER, WASHINGTON, D.C. 20012

Walter Reed is located at 16th St., N.W., near Silver Spring, Maryland. It is 2 miles south of Exit 23 of the Capital Beltway.

Major Activities. Walter Reed Army Medical Center; Walter Reed General Hospital; Walter Reed Institute of Research and U.S. Army Institute of Dental Research; Armed Forces Institute of Pathology; U.S. Army Medical Biochemical Research Laboratory; Walter Reed Army Institute of Nursing. At the Forest Glen Section are the Army Audiology and Speech Center and the Army Physical Disability Agency.

Quarters. There are several sets of quarters for key officers whose presence is needed on post. Apartments are plentiful in Washington and Maryland suburbs. Rentals range from moderate to expensive.

WILLIAM BEAUMONT ARMY MEDICAL CENTER, TEXAS 79920

This Army Medical Center is in El Paso, adjacent to Fort Bliss.

Major Activity. U.S. Army Medical Center with teaching, outpatient and specialized treatment facilities.

Quarters. There are approximately 70 sets of family quarters for married officers. Off-post housing is available in El Paso. Guest house facilities are provided.

FORT LEONARD WOOD, MISSOURI 65473

Fort Leonard Wood is 6 miles southeast of Waynesville, Missouri, 136 miles southwest of St. Louis on Interstate Highway 44 (U.S. Highway 66).

Major Activities. U.S. Army Training Center (Engineer).

Quarters. There are more than 600 family housing units for officers on post which generally are adequate to accommodate the married officers assigned to the post. Excellent BOQs are available and guest house facilities are provided.

TRAVEL AND RECREATION.

Military posts or facilities, either of the Army or its sister services, are located in each of the 50 states and around the world where there are concentrations of U. S. military personnel. As a general rule, each of these facilities has some provision to accomodate visitors, although the quality of the accommodations may vary from austere to modern, motel-like structures. In addition, many of the military bases operate recreation areas, either on the station or close to nearby attractions. As with the guest quarters on the bases, the facilities at the recreation areas vary widely. Some are equipped only for daytime use, while others have accomodations ranging from camp sites, to dormitory rooms, to individual cottages.

All of these temporary quarters and recreation areas have one thing in common. They are available for the use of any military personnel, active or retired, and their families. Proper identification is required. In some cases there are priorities for occupancy, and there generally are limits on how long the post guest facilities or recreation facilities may be used. However, by making proper inquiry and planning ahead, it is possible for a military family to travel around the country and to vacation in the mountains or at the seashore, and at many attractive spots in-between, all at prices substantially below the cost of commercial facilities. It is an important benefit that accrues to all military personnel.

A good source of information on temporary military lodging and "R&R" (see Chapter 23, *Authorized Absences*) is Military Living Publication. This company publishes a travel newsletter, the *R&R Report,* a Washington, D.C. area magazine, *Military Living,* and travel books. Two popular Military Living books are *Temporary Military Lodging Around the World,* and *Military Recreation Areas Around the World.* The *R&R Report* contains current information on temporary military lodging; space available travel on U.S. military aircraft; military recreation areas; and more. The $-Saver section of the *Report* provides information on discounts available to military I.D. Card holders in the civilian travel sector to include hotels, motels, transportation, food and entertainment. The *R&R Report* serves as a clearinghouse for information provided by military readers sharing their travel experiences around the world.

To receive information on any of these publications, send two first class stamps along with your request to: Military Living Publications, P.O. Box 4010, Arlington, Virginia 22204; or call (703) 521-2927 or 521-7703

9
Foreign Service

Where a man can live, there he can also live well—Marcus Aurelius.

This chapter is provided as a source of "first information" for Army families under orders for oversea assignment. It includes information extracted from official publications, gathered from the experiences of Army members who have provided suggestions, and supplied by oversea commands. There are informative official pamphlets on most oversea commands which are supplied to officers after they receive orders for change of station. The oversea commands also mail informative pamphlets which they have prepared for incoming personnel. These pamphlets are especially important since they include recent developments which may be of great interest.

The following travel documents are of special importance:

AR 55-46, *Travel of Dependents.*

PAM 608-1, *Dependent Travel Information.*

ARMED FORCES HOSTESS ASSOCIATION

An information service of unique value is provided by the Armed Forces Hostess Association, Room 1A736, The Pentagon, Washington, D.C. 20310. Telephone 202 OX7 3180.

This is a volunteer association of officers' wives from all Services who will provide you upon request considerable information on your overseas post, including climate, appliances, schools, clothes, travel, shipment of pets and other helpful tips. Be sure to give the exact location (APO if possible) and expected date of departure.

THE OPPORTUNITY AND THE RESPONSIBILITY

During the span of a normal Army career, an officer and his or her family may expect several overseas assignments. Today, with approximately one-third of the Army serving overseas, it is typical that an officer can expect to spend about one-third of his or her tours in overseas assignments. Tour duration will generally be three years or less.

Here is opportunity unlimited to observe and to learn the history, the culture, the language, the economics, the religions, and the ways of life of other nations. Army people, including Army children, enjoy a unique opportunity to broaden their knowledge of the people and problems of these nations.

The officer and the officer's family have many opportunities to enrich their interest and their understanding about the flood of events which shake our world.

Army officers and their families who have served the conventional oversea assignments have become travel-sophisticates, who know their way about our nation and our world, what to do, how to do it, and also what not to do, and why. Most will have taken advantage of their travel opportunities. They will have taken the pains to learn enough of the history and culture of the countries visited to be well informed. Some will have learned the language of the host nation. Most will have made lasting friendships, with memories to be cherished. These well-traveled, well-informed people are a national asset and they have earned a wider recognition as to this truth than has been extended. They have done well and deserve credit for it.

International Emergencies and Family Travel. There is one phase of family life in the services which had best be faced with candor and fact. Members of the Army must be sent into international trouble spots in order to discharge the nation's responsibilities. In addition, there are regions of the world where facilities for families are so scant, or so primitive, as to make the presence of Army families inadvisable. Assignment to these primitive or troubled areas is indeed a hardship, but the Army is careful to distribute such hardship tours to make family separations as few and as equitable as possible. But in a troubled world, with the vast responsibilities faced by our nation, the situation must be understood. Army families must look to the administration in control of our government, and to departmental officials, to keep family separations at a minimum.

FOREIGN SERVICE TOURS

The policies regarding foreign service for officers are stated in AR 614–30 and are summarized below.

The Broad Policy Selection. The paramount consideration in selecting an officer for service outside CONUS is the existence of a valid requirement coupled with the officer's military qualifications to perform the duties required. To the maximum extent practicable, oversea tours will be alternated between long and short tour areas and attempts will be made to achieve geographic and climatic variety. CONUS is the sustaining base for all oversea assignments, and officers can normally expect a minimum of 12 months in CONUS after completion of an oversea tour. However, the requirements of the Army dictate the length of a tour in CONUS prior to return overseas. The policy is that each officer will receive a proportionate share of foreign service. The oversea commands have the option to fill vacancies either with qualified individuals already in their commands or through requisition upon the Continental United States. As to an assignment in the Continental United States, some are of fixed duration from which an officer may not be released prior to its completion, even for an oversea assignment. So it goes. In principle, the officer of a grade and specialty with the least credit for oversea service will generally be the next to fill a requisition from an oversea command.

Officer Volunteers. Officers may volunteer for oversea assignment ahead of their normal expectancy for such duty. They may state a preference for a specific oversea command or for several commands in order of preference. Officers who volunteer are considered to be immediately available. However, officers serving in stabilized positions will not be voluntarily reassigned until they have completed their stabilized tours.

Temporary Deferment of Oversea Assignment. Where the oversea movement of an officer would cause serious hardship, it is possible to secure temporary deferment for compassionate reasons. Officers who find it necessary to seek deferment are advised to study Chap. 3, AR 614–30, before making request.

Length of Foreign Service Tour. Normal tours of foreign service for all Army personnel, exclusive of general officers and officers assigned to the Army Attaché system are shown in the table following. For purposes of departmental records, foreign service tours commence on the day an individual departs from an ocean or air terminal in the United States and terminate on the date of return to such a United States terminal. The day of return is counted as a day of foreign service.

Personnel who are accompanied or joined by their dependents will serve the tour prescribed for those "With Dependents" or 12 months after arrival of dependents, whichever is longer. The tour prescribed for "All Others" will be served by personnel who elect to serve overseas without their dependents; are serving in an area where movement of dependents is restricted; are not authorized movement of their dependents at government expense; or who do not have dependents. There are special rules and provisions for service members married to each other. See AR 614-30 for details. In specified European and South American countries, and others, bachelor officer and enlisted personnel, male and female, will serve the "With Dependents" tour.

Tours normally are uniform for personnel of all services at the same station. The service having primary interest (the most personnel) will develop, in coordination with the other affected services, a mutually satisfactory tour length applicable to all military personnel in the locality.

The standard tour may be reduced to not less than 12 months for personnel who have dependents entitled to be present at the oversea station, but who elect to serve unaccompanied.

There are provisions for reassignment between oversea commands without intervening tours in CONUS. The rules for computing tour lengths in this case are complex and can easily be misunderstood. The first delineation involves voluntary versus involuntary reassignment. Officers are advised to consult their personnel officers and AR 614-30 for details. An officer who is voluntarily reassigned will serve the complete prescribed tour in both areas. An officer who is involuntarily reassigned between oversea commands or between areas within an oversea command will serve a tour in the new command in accordance with the following:

1. Personnel serving without dependents ("all others" tour), reassigned

directly to a short tour area: Tour will be adjusted to give credit for that portion of the normal tour in the new area corresponding to the portion of the normal tour already served in the area from which reassigned. For example, an officer who completed one-third of some other tour would be credited with having served 4 months of the normal 12-month tour in Korea.

2. Personnel serving without dependents who are reassigned to a long tour area will serve the normal tour in the new area.

3. Personnel serving with dependents who are reassigned to a short tour area will serve the normal tour in the new area.

"Geographical Areas" and Tours. (The following information has been extracted from AR 614–30.) The intent of designating geographical areas is to provide the maximum geographic variety between successive oversea tours. For example, an individual whose last oversea tour was a short tour in Korea and who is now eligible for another oversea tour, should normally be reassigned to a long tour area other than the Far East and Pacific Area, consistent with requirements.

There are five geographic areas, defined generally and abbreviated as follows:

Africa and Middle East Area (AMEA)
European Area (EURA)
Far East and Pacific Area (FEPA)
North America and North Atlantic Area (NANA)
South America and Caribbean Area (SACA)

For a complete list of oversea tours, see AR 614–30, as amended. Areas with large numbers of Army people are stated below, with length of tour prescribed.

Length of Foreign and Oversea Duty Tours

United States Areas	Geographical Areas	Tours in months With dependents	All Others
Alaska:			
Anchorage Area including Elmendorf AFB and Fort Richardson	NANA	36	24
Big Delta Area including Fort Greely	NANA	24	18
Fairbanks Area including Eielson AFB and Fort Wainwright	NANA	30	18
Hawaii	FEPA	36	24
Puerto Rico	SACA	36	24

Other Countries	Geographical Areas	Tours in months With dependents	All Others
Belgium	EURA	36	24
France	EURA	36	24
Germany	EURA	36	24
Italy	EURA	36	24
Japan	FEPA	36	24
Korea	FEPA .... ST	24	12
Philippine Islands	FEPA	24	15
Ryukyus Islands	FEPA	30	18
Taiwan	FEPA .... ST	24	15
Thailand	FEPA .... ST	NA	12
(Bangkok not ST)		24	18
Turkey	AMEA	24	15
(Ankara, Incirlik, Izmir)			
(For other areas see AR)			
United Kingdom	EURA	36	24

ST—Short Tour   NA—Dependents not allowed

PREPARATION FOR OVERSEA TRAVEL

Seasonal Uniform Dates. The uniform to be worn on foreign assignments, with changeover dates from winter to summer and the reverse, if applicable, is prescribed in AR 670–6.

Action Before Departure. Official orders of the Department of the Army assigning an officer to an oversea command prescribe the timing, method of transportation, and other essential information about the journey. At the outset the officer should receive, or should have prepared, about 50 copies of his or her orders, needed on many occasions incident to the movement. For example, six copies are required with each shipment of personal property. Orders will also be required for pay, travel allowances, and other matters en route and after arrival.

Upon receipt of orders, an officer should immediately report to the personnel officer, finance officer, quartermaster, transportation officer, and surgeon, to obtain detailed instructions regarding the pending move and must be certain to understand these instructions and follow them to the letter. The officer must set his or her official and personal house in order so that no dangling, unfinished business will arise the last minute before departure or, worse, after departure. All personal bills or obligations must be paid, or definite arrangements made for future payment. See Chapter 7, *Financial Planning* on wills, insurance, and check-up suggestions for personal affairs.

Concurrent Travel of Families. Families may accompany the officer to an oversea station (concurrent travel), or they may be obliged to join the officer after a period of delay when it has been determined that there will be quarters available upon their arrival. The regulation of general information is AR 55–46, which should be consulted upon receipt of orders for oversea movement.

Shipment of Household Goods. The amount of household goods which may be shipped overseas on permanent change of station is stated in Chapter Twenty, *Travel Allowances.* Area restrictions or other temporary reductions in allowances may occur. Consult the transportation officer. In those oversea stations where furniture and equipment are supplied to a military family, the authorized allowances for shipment of personal belongings are sharply reduced.

With careful planning, and consideration of the advice you have received, you should be able to ship all of the necessities plus a few "nice to have" items within the weight limit prescribed. The special items may not be essential but may add to satisfaction with the new environment; these items could include a favorite painting, a choice piece of furniture, a popular family game, a few cherished books, or any of many other items which could add to family enjoyment.

Shipment of Automobile. In most oversea assignments the use of a privately owned automobile is essential. Consider at once the suitability of the car owned. Service for the car including spare parts is the thing to consider.

If shipment of a car is desired, the best advice you can possibly get is to consult the Transportation Officer at once. He or she will give you the detailed information which may assist in having your car arrive at the oversea destination in much less time than would be the case if one essential step is missed along the line. It is also recommended that you review AR 55–71, *Transportation of Personal Property and Related Services.*

See to it that your orders permit travel to the port in your own car, if such travel is your desire. Be sure to deliver the car at the port no later than the time prescribed. Further, since cars may be loaded in order of arrival, it may be wise to get there a day early. The same advice applies to shipment of a trailer. Have ready several copies of your travel orders, a Certificate of Title to the car, or a statement that the vehicle is free from any legal encumbrance which would preclude its shipment.

Ask your Transportation Officer about buying marine insurance, which generally is regarded as desirable but is not required.

It is not unusual that a car arrives overseas as much as a month behind the owner. Careful attention to the requirements which may permit it to be shipped on an earlier transport may save lots of walking.

Shipment of Pets. Officers who own pets need to ascertain definite information as to the regulations governing the shipment of pets to the oversea destination, and also the laws or regulations governing their re-entry into the United States upon termination of tour.

The shipment of pets must be planned with the same care as the travel of the rest of the family to avoid a family crisis. Pets must be vaccinated, placed in crates on some occasions, wear muzzles as required, be fed, exercised, and for some destinations they must be shipped separately.

Passports. Officers should ascertain at their home stations whether passports will be required either for themselves or for their families. AR 600–290 governs the procedures to obtain passports. See also par. 18, AR 55–46. Consult Chapter Twenty, *Travel Allowances.* If passports are required, take action early to obtain them, since considerable time is often required.

Mode of Travel. Authorization for travel of Army members and their families to, from, and between oversea commands by sea transportation ended in early 1973. From that date, sea travel is authorized only as an exception when the service member or the member's dependents, for medical reasons, cannot travel by air. Since World War II, use of sea transportation had been steadily declining in favor of the more rapid movement of personnel by air. By 1973, the lack of U.S. passenger liners, the extra cost of surface transportation and the extra time involved for changes of station by surface transport, all combined to eliminate further travel by this means. Still in the military vocabulary, however, are many terms left over from the days of sea transport, such as hand baggage, hold baggage, and port of embarkation. These terms generally are applied to air transport just as they were in the past to sea transport.

Hand Baggage and Hold Baggage. Hand baggage is that baggage accompanying the passenger on board the aircraft, either in the flight cabin or checked for stowage in the cargo compartment. For travel outside the continental United States, hand baggage normally is limited to 65 pounds per person.

Hold baggage is that additional baggage authorized to be shipped with the traveler, as contrasted to household goods which generally follow later. Hold baggage is limited to 600 pounds per person, and generally is packed and shipped prior to the date of departure so as to be available at the destination at about the time the traveler arrives.

Judicious use of the weight allowances for the hand and hold baggage enable the military family to have on hand at the oversea destination those clothes and other essentials they will need during the month or more they may have to wait before arrival of their household goods.

Action at Port of Embarkation (POE). The orders for oversea movement will prescribe the point of departure and the date and hour arrival at the POE is required.

Be certain to arrive on time. Report to the prescribed headquarters or to the office charged with processing transient personnel. Receive from them detailed instructions which will be complete and study them carefully. Quarters will be provided while awaiting departure, including quarters for families. It is considered more satisfactory to utilize quarters furnished than to choose to await departure at a hotel or the homes of friends. Sometimes you must go to a local hotel because the port facilities are crowded; if you arrive early enough in the day the chances for space assignment are increased. The more children and pets you have, the more time you must allow the port personnel to help you. While the government quarters furnished you may not be luxurious, they will certainly be comfortable, clean, and adequate for the short stay required. Terminal commanders take pride in these facilities as well as the smoothness of their operation; recreation facilities are provided; the officer and his or her family may be reached promptly for medical or other processing requirements; and costs to the traveler are low.

Travel Aboard Aircraft. The Military Airlift Command (MAC) provides extensive oversea transport service for personnel including family members, and freight, serving equally all military services. Except as may be authorized for medical reasons, all personnel movement now is by aircraft.

Family members normally are moved to and from oversea areas by the MAC. MAC now uses commercial airline terminals to handle passenger traffic that previously processed through McGuire AFB, New Jersey and Travis AFB, California.

Travel aboard airplanes of the MAC is substantially the same as aboard commercial airlines—in fact, MAC uses many aircraft chartered from the commercial airlines. Stewardesses are provided. Special diets for babies and young children must be taken aboard by the sponsor.

While MSTS transport may be involved with troop transport to areas of conflict, it can be expected that air transport will be more frequent. MAC has a proud tradition of service and will provide outstanding transportation to those who follow its advice and regulations. The officer and family who plan and think through their air travel and follow instructions will have a delightful, but short, travel experience and arrive overseas in the best condition.

TIPS FOR FAMILY TRAVEL

High standards of personal conduct, including that of the children, with due regard for the rights of others, is a necessity. While it is true that the journey by air is of much shorter duration than was the case when travel was by ship, it also is true that the quarters are more cramped. Thoughtfulness and consideration by all fellow travelers will do much to make the trip a pleasant experience for all.

A large, all-purpose bag or handbag will be handy for carrying aboard the aircraft the personal items that will be needed during the journey. Do not overlook a few books, toys, or small games that can help the children pass the hours.

You will be informed by or for the terminal commander as to the time your presence is required for processing prior to boarding the aircraft. For the long oversea flights, this normally is two hours prior to flight time, to enable complete processing of passengers and their baggage. Transportation from your temporary quarters to the terminal will be provided. It is necessary only that individuals be at the starting point on time, with hand baggage, official orders, passports (if required), immunization records, and any other pertinent papers, ready to board the aircraft.

After the short delay for check-in, which is necessary to assure that all personnel are present who are scheduled for that particular flight, and that they have the required official papers, as well as for processing baggage, you will board the aircraft. Families normally board first so that they may arrange seating by family groups, followed by any VIPs who may be on the flight, followed by other military members traveling alone.

As an aside to our readers who may be traveling without dependents, it is often the case that you will note at the air terminal a mother with perhaps several small children, proceeding overseas to join her husband. She will be encumbered with bags and more often than not the processing procedures will be strange to her. It is perfectly proper to offer your services to help her wrestle bags or children, or both, and to help make their journey a more pleasant one. Such a practice will pay rich dividends, not only in terms of the gratitude of the mother involved, but in terms of the day when your family may be traveling overseas to join you and a stranger offers a helping hand. Such acts of courtesy and thoughtfulness are in keeping with service customs and the officer's code.

Special For Families With Children. Each service family generally comes equipped with several children. Thus, it is quite possible for the number of children aboard an aircraft to exceed the number of other passengers. A journey overseas provides a unique test of the way parents have reared their children. Within a few hours in the air, all passengers will have ample opportunity to judge the results of your efforts in this regard.

No one expects children to be other than children, but sometimes even this can be fearsome when the quarters are cramped. Try to plan your trip to have on hand those items which will entertain and satisfy the needs of your children. Such forethought will go a long way toward earning for you, as for most other service families, the accolades of fellow passengers for a job well done.

Words of Caution. Except when there are unusual circumstances of health, the care of families including children at air terminals (POE's), on MAC aircraft, and at the port of debarkation overseas, will present no great problems to an officer's family if plans are well thought out in advance and instructions are carefully followed. The requirements are well understood, facilities are adequate, and if the officer follows carefully the standing operating procedures as to events, time and place, it will all proceed smoothly and pleasantly. Personnel operating the POE's and aircraft have been confronted by nearly all possible problems and generally have a solution ready to apply promptly and with good grace. But if there are unusual circumstances, such as medical supplies for a child, or special foods, or other unusual matters, the officer should make all necessary plans and arrangements in advance and in person.

Foresight at the home station before departure will pay rich dividends. What to take and what to leave behind, in storage, is an important matter. Considerations of the climate to be encountered will answer many questions. Within limitations of baggage and freight allowances, in case of doubt it is wiser to take questionable articles of personal property than to leave them behind. Fragile or valuable non-essentials are best left behind in storage; even under the assumption that packing and crating will be done perfectly, which is an overly generous assumption, these shipments are subject to much handling which involves considerable hazard of damage and pilferage. Do not relegate your "best things" to storage just because they are your best. Remember that you will probably be spending 10% or more of your service career at the oversea station and you will want to have and to use your best things there as well as at stations within the continental United States.

SATISFACTION OF FAMILY NEEDS IN OVERSEA COMMANDS

The Army is keenly concerned about physical facilities to serve the needs of its officers and enlisted personnel and their families overseas. It has been necessary to do so because provision for at least a reasonable minimum of the necessities of Army families is essential to the peace of mind of its members which in turn permits them to devote their full energies to their duties.

Grade school and high school facilities are provided in all established commands. Standards are closely supervised. Considering the intangible values to be derived from travel and life in an oversea land for a span of a few years, most parents consider that their children have benefited by the experience. In the unusual case where children's schools are not provided under military control, parents should inform themselves of facilities used by American citizens resident in the area, or ascertain the possibilities for instruction by mail with home tutoring. Unless there are very unusual circumstances indeed, there is no strong reason for Army families to be separated merely because of the school situation of their children because educational facilities for our children have been provided in a manner which is acceptable to most parents.

Post exchanges in most oversea commands are not so sharply restricted as to what can be sold as is the situation in the United States where civilian retail facilities are available. Although unusual needs must be anticipated, and arrangements made for their satisfaction, the ordinary wants and necessities, with some items of luxury, may be obtained from that source. It is wise to arrange with a U.S. merchant before departure so that special requirements can be shipped upon receipt of an order from you. All oversea exchanges have working arrangements with large U.S. mail order houses so that merchandise not stocked in the exchange may be obtained.

Officers' clubs and recreational facilities are provided at nearly all stations.

Movies are provided by the Army and Air Force Exchange Service on a standard comparable to that in the ZI, and the pictures shown are the latest produced by the industry.

Commissaries are provided at which the usual commissary items may be purchased as at posts in the United States.

LIFE IN OVERSEA COMMANDS

The information about living conditions in oversea areas where United States Army personnel are stationed, accompanied or joined by their families, is presented as a helpful "first reference" for officers receiving foreign service orders. The discussions have been extracted from official publications, with up-to-date references from the headquarters of our commands.

In all cases, official information is sent to officers receiving assignment orders to reach them as early as practicable.

ALASKA

The U.S. Army component of the Alaskan Command (ALCOM), has its headquarters at Fort Richardson, near Anchorage, with mail zip code number APO

98749 Seattle. Other Army installations are at Fort Wainwright (APO 98731 Seattle) near Fairbanks, and Fort Greely (APO 98733 Seattle), 106 miles south of Fairbanks. For administrative purposes, Alaska is considered an "oversea command."

An Army family whose sponsor receives orders to duty in Alaska may look forward with pleasureful anticipation to the experience. Quarters, schools for children, and shopping facilities are available, and recreational, cultural and sporting facilities and opportunities are abundant.

Excellent official documents about service in Alaska are supplied to officers soon after they receive their assignment orders. The pamphlets are current, well illustrated, informative. The following documents were consulted in choosing the extracts herein, as initial information of immediate interest to officers and their families:

DA Pam 608–9.
Welcome to United States Army, Alaska, Pam 360–1.

Concurrent Travel. Concurrent travel and on-post housing are automatic for colonels, lieutenant colonels, and CWO-4s. Other officers should request concurrent travel to Alaska, for which see AR 55–46. If approved, apply to the nearest Transportation Officer for shipment of household goods. A sponsor's program assists incoming officers and their families and direct communication with the sponsor is encouraged.

Shipment of Automobile. Privately owned automobiles, after authorization, are shipped from the port at government expense. Consult the Transportation Officer. Recommended is that cars be put in in the best possible mechanical condition, as cost of repairs and maintenance is high; and that cars be winterized to −40° in the Anchorage area, and −75° in the Fairbanks area. A recommended item is a trickle charger for batteries.

Travel by Alaska Highway. Travel via the Alaska Highway may be authorized provided certain conditions are met. Requests for permission for such travel should be sent to the Commanding General, ALCOM or through the CONUS Army area in which you reside. Consult your Finance Officer for authorized reimbursement for travel via the Alaska Highway.

Family Quarters. Government quarters are generally apartment-style, frame two-story, or single and duplex style with a full basement. Basements are concrete, warm and dry, with outlets for appliances. These quarters are at Fort Richardson, Fort Wainwright, and Fort Greely.

Each apartment is furnished to include dressers with mirrors, single beds with mattresses and pads, pillows, night-tables, coffee end tables, lamps, wastepaper baskets, bookcase, desk, living room rug, easy chairs, occasional chairs, kitchen step stool, kitchen table, electric range and refrigerator. Not furnished are such items as nursery furniture, bedding, draperies, linens, dining ware, kitchen utensils, pictures, curtain rods, freezers, washers, dryers, and electrical appliances.

Off-post housing of the 1- and 2-bedroom apartment type units are more readily available than larger units. Rental rates and utility costs are higher than in CONUS locations. There is an additional quarters allowance for individuals authorized to occupy off-post housing.

Clothing Suggestions. Quoting from the official publication: "It is not wise to overstock the family with heavy winter clothing, as most of it is little used.

Winter clothing may be purchased from local stores at slightly higher prices than normal, and from exchanges which supply practically any item normally available in CONUS. Mail order service is satisfactory and utilized extensively." There are national chain-type department stores in Anchorage and Fairbanks.

Quartermaster laundry and dry cleaning facilities are available.

Schools for Children. On-post schools provide adequate educational opportunity for children. At most posts there are schools for children from kindergarten level through the 8th grade. Smaller children, below the age of 6, may attend kindergarten at Forts Richardson, Wainwright, and Greely. The minimum age for entrance to Alaska schools is 6 years, and this age must be reached by the 1st of November of the school year. A birth certificate is required for grade one and evidence of promotion for all other grades.

On-base school facilities include:

Fort Richardson: Kindergarten through 9th grade.
Fort Wainwright: Kindergarten through 8th grade.
Fort Greely: Kindergarten through 8th grade.

Military dependents of Fort Wainwright (9th through 12th grades), Fort Greely (9th through 12th grades), and Fort Richardson (10th through 12th grades) attend schools in the local community with bus transportation furnished by civilian authorities.

Your Leisure. Posts in Alaska have much the same opportunities for recreation as those in CONUS.

Officers and Noncommissioned Officers Open Messes and Service Clubs are found at each post. Craft, Woodworking, and ceramics shops are provided. There are gun clubs, skeet clubs, drama and art clubs, and others.

Individual sports include swimming, golf, tennis, bowling, skiing, skating, sled dog racing, and on and on.

Sportsmen come to Alaska just to hunt and fish. It's an expensive outing for them. But not nearly so expensive for the service member, for you can hunt and fish to heart's content at small expense.

HAWAII

The State of Hawaii, Paradise of the Pacific, is "foreign service" only in the sense that it is outside the continental limits of the United States. Its climate resembles Southern California and Southern Florida. It is one of the few areas where local claims as to climate and scenery are justified by experience. See DA Pam 608–14.

The Army's stations are Fort Shafter, Tripler Army Medical Center, and Schofield Barracks.

Major Activities. Fort Shafter is the Headquarters, U.S. Army Western Command. Schofield Barracks is the home station of the 25th Infantry Division. Tripler Army Medical Center is a large hospital facility serving all military forces and their dependents on the islands.

Family Quarters. Station and civilian facilities are at least equal to their mainland counterparts.

Under normal conditions as to size of the Army strength, the number of family-type housing units is short of the number needed for married families. Studio and one-bedroom apartments are in good supply. Civilian housing for families of more than four members is scarce. Rents are high. The Armed

Services Community Housing Service, Fort DeRussy, on Waikiki, will assist in securing temporary as well as permanent type accommodations.

Temporary Lodging Allowance. Costs for temporary housing can be extremely high. There is a housing allowance, separate from the basic allowance for quarters, which may be obtained to defray excess housing costs pending assignment of government quarters or obtaining permanent civilian housing. See AR 37–104, and the Joint Travel Regulations for the amounts, which are variable. As a maximum, this allowance can last no more than 30 days. *Caution:* Within one working day after arrival, application for government quarters should be made to qualify for payment of *Temporary Lodging Allowance* and establish priority for obtaining government quarters based on date of departing CONUS.

Schools for Children. Adequate school facilities are available throughout the command. There are several outstanding private schools.

Automobile. A privately owned automobile is quite essential. Consult the Transportation Officer as to authorization for shipment.

Pets. Pets can be taken to Hawaii, and returned to the mainland. Dogs and cats must undergo mandatory quarantine in Hawaii for 120 days at the State Quarantine Station.

Recreation Facilities. Service in Hawaii provides for unusually varied and enjoyable recreation facilities. There are extensive facilities for team sports, golf, tennis, water sports of all kinds, with outstanding programs for participation. There are active organizations to sponsor interesting activities for young people, and officers' clubs and Open Messes function in Hawaii as elsewhere.

The Recreation Center, Fort DeRussy, in the heart of Waikiki, is especially cherished as a service benefit. Individuals and families can secure accommodations for a day or several days, and enjoy at small cost all the pleasures of the tourist paradise at Waikiki. DeRussy has a fine beach for swimming, picnic area, a good restaurant and club with entertainment. In addition, a post office, liquor store, post exchange with car rental, laundry, flower shop, and outdoor ice dispenser. A high-rise hotel, the *Hale Koa,* provides comfortable, modern temporary quarters. It can be contacted via a toll-free telephone number — (800) 367-6027.

On the Island of Hawaii is the Kilauea Military Camp, a recreation facility adjacent to the Hawaii National Park. Military families go there at minimum expense for a stay of several days duration. The camp is at an elevation of 4000 feet which provides a climate change—and a temporary need for warmer clothing than is worn on Oahu. Tours by bus are scheduled to points of beauty and interest. The accommodations are adequate and include a restaurant.

GERMANY AND BELGIUM

Service with the United States Army, Europe (USAREUR), provides an opportunity for service of importance to the nation and, in addition, an unusual opportunity for travel and acquiring an understanding of the people, the cultures, and the problems of the nations of Europe allied with the United States. See DA Pam 608–12 and USAREUR Pam 360–8.

Preparation for Travel to Germany. *Passports.* Family members require passports secured prior to departure from the United States. (See Chapter Twenty, *Travel Allowances.*)

Immunizations. Consult station surgeon upon receipt of orders.

Hand Baggage and Hold Baggage. Plan these choices most carefully. An earlier discussion in this chapter supplies details as to allowances. It is recommended that there be included in hold baggage: A small supply of bed linens, bath linens, and cooking utensils for use prior to the arrival of household goods.

Travel Conditions Enroute to Germany. Travel to Germany will be via aircraft of the Military Airlift Command (MAC) or in commercial aircraft chartered by MAC. The accommodations are equivalent to commercial tourist class. The prescribed uniform for travel is any type of Class A uniform.

Copies of Orders. Family members should have a minimum of 5 copies of travel authorization in their possession upon arrival in Germany.

Major Army Installations in Germany. The main Army installations in Germany are located in or near the following cities:

Augsburg	Kaiserslautern
Berlin	Kreuznach
Frankfurt	Munich
Fulda	Nurnberg
Giessen	Stuttgart
Hanau	Wurzburg
Heidelberg	

Climate in Germany. The climate is mild. German summers are delightful with warm days and cool nights. There are very few thunderstorms, but considerable gentle rain. Winters are less severe than in our northern and central states; they compare with those of Maryland or Virginia. There is some snow, but except in the mountains it does not remain long. In the mountainous areas winters are much colder, the snow deeper, and winter sports are popular.

Housing Situation. Family housing is available in limited quantities for assignment to eligible sponsors. The number of eligible sponsors at most stations exceeds available housing, creating waiting periods of 4 to 52 weeks. Colonels and above are authorized concurrent travel to Europe. All other officer grades are initially denied concurrent travel based on nonavailability of government quarters. It is possible, however, to obtain concurrent travel even though government quarters are not available if the sponsor can prove that suitable economy quarters are available.

Bachelor officers occupy rooms in BOQs constructed for this purpose, or they may be housed in hotels or small apartments. Necessary furniture and bed linen is supplied.

Family housing for officers is of two types. There are apartments of American design; and there are German houses or apartments. Quarters are classified into categories corresponding to the rank of the sponsor, and consideration is given to the size of the family.

Family housing procured by an individual on the local economy is difficult to obtain, expensive, and substandard as compared to housing in the United States. To assist officers in locating private rental quarters, installation billeting officers maintain a list of quarters available to US personnel. When a service family arrives in Germany, and must establish themselves in a rented house or apartment until military quarters are available, they should be prepared to bear heavy initial expenses.

Household Furnishings Supplied. Basic items of household furniture are provided dependent families assigned to Government-controlled quarters in Germany. For this reason the weight allowances in shipment or household property have been reduced. Consult Transportation Officer. Furniture is supplied for living room, dining room, kitchen, hall, bathroom, and each bedroom. The basic items, including baby beds, are adequate and acceptable. Your own fragile or expensive items are best stored in the United States. Germany is a good market for china and glassware, porcelain, paintings, leather goods.

Electrical Appliances. German alternating current is 50 cycles, instead of our 60. Consequently, synchronous electric motors operate at $\frac{5}{6}$ of normal speeds. Other types of motors may be damaged. Phonographs may be adjusted to the slower speed at slight cost. Clocks lose 10 minutes each hour. Washing machines should be equipped with 220 volt 50-cycle motors. Toasters, roasters, irons, and appliances with only a heating element operate satisfactorily with a 220 volt-110 volt transformer. At Exchanges operated by the AAFES in Germany electrical items may be purchased which avoid these difficulties of current difference. German stores sell all types of electrical appliances, but prices are higher than stateside.

Clothing. The officer will need the same uniforms as would be required for duty in the United States. Uniforms may be purchased in Germany.

Civilian clothing is authorized for wear by all military personnel in Germany. It may be purchased at Post Exchanges or at German stores. Many excellent tailors are to be found. English textiles can readily be obtained.

Dependents are advised to take with them a complete wardrobe. Evening clothing is worn on occasion by both men and women.

Also advised is establishment of a mail order account with a stateside department store. Mail order service is also utilized in Germany through Sears Roebuck and Montgomery Ward, where catalogs are available at the Post Exchange. Mailing costs, owing to the APO system, are low.

Civilian clothing for men, women and children is available at post exchanges.

The Currency Exchange Rate. For many years following World War II, American personnel in West Germany benefited from a very favorable exchange rate between the dollar and the deutschmark. The effect was that items purchased on the local economy were very inexpensive in terms of dollars. This no longer is the case. In recent years, the dollar has declined in value such that it is now worth only about half of what it was worth previously. Officers and their families have had to adjust their spending habits accordingly.

Army and Air Force Exchange Service (AAFES). The Army and Air Force Exchange Service operates a very extensive chain of stores of different types which provide a wide choice of merchandise at retail. Retail outlets are readily available, ranging from large department stores to convenience counters. The American officers and soldiers in Germany, their family members, and others authorized to use AAFES facilities have substantially the same retail facilities as they would enjoy at home, and in some types of merchandise the prices are lower.

The Privately Owned Automobile. An automobile for a family in Germany is a "must." It may be shipped from the United States for pickup at Bremerhaven, purchased in Europe through AAFES facilities, bought second hand from another American; or you may purchase one of the many excellent English or European cars. Most service people recommend against shipping an American car. Maintenance and repairs are very expensive. A foreign car may be imported to the U.S. for personal use without paying an import tax. The individual, however, must pay transportation charges.

In June, 1964, AAFES assumed the responsibility for operating all service stations in West Germany, except the station in West Berlin, which remained a Quartermaster responsibility. The AAFES service stations operated by the AAFES dispense both regular and premium gasoline. Gasoline may be purchased at German stations using gasoline coupons purchased from the AAFES.

The operator is required to have the official USAREUR Operator's License, and meet the requirements as to physical condition, knowledge, and driving ability. Vehicles must meet safety standards and be registered. No vehicle may be registered unless covered by recognized liability insurance and in this connection one of the several authorized companies is our own (mutual) *United Services Automobile Association.* The International Insurance Certificate ("Green Card") will be required if you plan to travel in countries other than West Germany. An International Driver's License may also be required.

Driving conditions in Germany provide the *Autobahn* which is comparable to our best highways, and secondary roads most of which are blacktop. Operators must learn the International Road signs. The AAFES operates repair shops, lubrication facilities, and arranges for spare parts. However, the AAFES cannot maintain a complete stock of repair parts for all cars and it makes no attempt to stock parts for cars more than 6 years old.

Elementary and Secondary Schools. Education in grades 1 through 12 is provided for eligible dependents. Students from outlying areas are transported daily or live in dormitories. Quality of instruction and accreditation meet the standards of the North Central Association of Colleges and Secondary Schools. There are approximately 5,000 carefully selected American teachers.

College-Level Education. Opportunities abound for officers stationed in West Germany to continue their personal and professional development. College-level courses are offered at Army Education Centers scattered throughout the USAREUR area. Courses are offered by 11 colleges and universities and include programs for certificates as well as associate, baccalaureate, and advanced degrees. There are opportunities to take vocational, academic and technical courses. In general, credit hours acquired may be applied to degrees to be received overseas or used as transfer credit to colleges and universities in the United States.

Medical and Dental Facilities. Medical facilities comparable to those available in the United States are available to military personnel and their dependents. Dental defects should be corrected before travel to Germany. However, dental care is provided. All dependents of USAREUR military personnel, including those dependents who are not command-sponsored, are entitled to free medical care. Civilian medical care reimbursable under CHAMPUS (see Chapter 7) is available for military dependents under certain circumstances.

Recreational Facilities. Service in Germany provides an especially interesting opportunity for travel and study of the historical heritage of European peoples. It provides the broadest sort of opportunity for planned recreational activities. In addition to the standard facilities to be found at stations at home, there are sports centers, leave and rest areas, and special tours. There are unusual opportunities for hunting, fishing, boating, mountaineering, and winter sports. World famous civilian resorts are available.

There are several outstanding resorts in Europe where the facilities are U.S. controlled (and paid for); the cost of vacations can be reduced by one half as a result at Garmisch, Berchtesgaden, Chiemsee, and others.

Belgium (SHAPE Hq., etc.) Much of the information concerning Germany applies to the headquarters, logistic, and communications installations in Belgium. At SHAPE Hq., Casteau, Belgium, there are a very few governmental-provided apartments occasioning a waiting list for these and others. Housing on the local economy is scarce with high rental fees. Facilities are equivalent to those in Germany; adequate medical, dental, PX, and commissary facilities are located in Casteau or nearby Chievres. The caution pertaining to electrical appliances in Germany is applicable in Belgium which also has 220 volt, 50-cycle electricity. There is an abundance of American products adapted for Belgium in local stores at slightly higher prices than stateside.

JAPAN

The majority of installations and troop units of the U.S. Army Japan are in the area west of Tokyo, convenient to both Yokohama and Tokyo. The living conditions and facilities are excellent. The climate resembles that of the Middle Atlantic coastal plain, generally similar to Washington, D.C. June and September are rainy; bring good raincoats. See DA Pam 608–10, and USARJ Pam 360–1.

Concurrent Travel. Except for officers in grades 0–6 and above, who are automatically authorized concurrent travel, approval of dependent travel at government expense is based on availability of government housing or approved private rental housing.

Family Quarters. Government quarters are on or near all Japan installations except Akizuki Ammo Depot. Single officers and officers unaccompanied by family members are housed in BOQs. Comfortable family quarters are located on Army reservations and include attractive single and multiple-unit houses with large play areas for children, chapels, theaters, clubs, and shopping centers. Officers are required to occupy government housing, except when not available for immediate assignment, in which case temporary occupancy of private rental quarters is authorized.

Government-occupied quarters are adequately furnished for family living. Not furnished and to be supplied by the individual officer are the following: kitchen equipment, utensils, china and glassware; sheets, blankets, and pillow cases. However, these articles are obtainable by issue during the first 60 days and the last 60 days of quarters occupancy to assist officers in establishing and ending residency in the command.

A washing machine and clothes dryer are furnished in all government quarters. Not furnished and needed is an ironing board. A vacuum cleaner, radio, and record player are enjoyed and there are television broadcasts, by the Armed Forces Radio and Television Service. Air conditioners are readily available, both new and used, and merit consideration, as the summers are hot and humid.

The electric current is 50 cycle, 120 volts. Most electrical appliances, except clocks, can be adjusted.

Personnel who do not own, or choose not to ship, household appliances will find most items available in the PX.

Schools for Children. In the Camp Zama area, there is on-post schooling for eligible children of military and civilian personnel from kindergarten through high school. Courses of study parallel those in the United States. Standard textbooks are used. The high school offers general and college preparatory courses and is fully accredited by the North American Association of Colleges and Secondary Schools. Nursery schools are also available on a tuition basis.

Private Automobiles. It is most convenient to have a car in Japan. Upon receipt of assignment orders, officers should consult the Transportation Officer regarding shipment requirements and guidance as to insurance and other matters. Because of strict emission and safety standards imposed by the Government of Japan, POV's manufactured after 31 March 1976 may not be shipped to Japan. Shipment of large POV's is discouraged as most roads are narrow by U.S. standards. Used Japanese cars are readily available and are usually relatively inexpensive. All privately owned vehicles must be registered with the Japanese Prefectural Government and with the Provost Marshal's Office. Insurance is mandatory in liability amounts of $5,000/$10,000/$5,000. The Japanese Compulsory Insurance Law requires car owners to purchase Japanese insurance in addition to liability coverage. Driving is on the left side of the road.

Individuals who have a State Driving License are eligible to receive a U.S. Forces Operator's Permit after passing a written test on local traffic laws and regulations.

Banking and Currency. U.S. dollars are the authorized currency for U.S. personnel in Japan. Local currency (yen) is available from on-post facilities for transactions off-post.

Military banking facilities furnish all regular banking services. Recommended is the retention of an account in a bank in the United States to negotiate Stateside transactions. There is also a federal credit union.

Pets. Pets must be shipped by commercial means at the owner's expense. Owners may leave pets in the U.S. until arriving in Japan and completing necessary paperwork, or they may have the pets accompany them.

Domestic Help. Domestic help is available. Relative costs depend on the yen-dollar exchange rate.

Passport. A passport is required for each dependent family member.

Civilian Clothing. Military personnel are authorized to wear civilian clothing after duty hours, and as regulations permit.

Recreation and Cultural Facilities. The U.S. Army Japan has provided well for the cultural and recreational facilities of all stations and bases. The activities include an extensive program of athletics and recreation. Outdoor facilities include lighted softball and baseball fields, volleyball and badminton courts, swimming pools, tennis courts, golf course and golf driving range. There is a Consolidated Club and an Officers' Wives Club. There are organized youth activities, theaters, USO, religious activities, arts and crafts facilities, and a Travel Bureau to facilitate trips in Japan and the Far East.

KOREA

In most of metropolitan Korea, especially those areas identified as dependent areas (Seoul, Taegu, Pusan, and Chinhae), living approaches a near-western style. The climate is four seasonal and similar to that of the eastern seaboard of the United States. DA Pamphlet 608–15, "Helpful Hints for Personnel Ordered to the Eighth US Army, Korea," contains information which most service members have found useful. A booklet published by the Public Affairs Office, United States Forces, Korea entitled "Korea, Your New Destination" is another excellent source of orientation for a tour in Korea.

Military Activities. The American servicemen and women serving in the Republic of Korea are collectively known as the United States Forces, Korea (USFK). The major U.S. Command in Korea is the Eighth United States Army (EUSA). The major subordinate commands include Combined Field Army (ROK·US), 2nd Infantry Division, 38th Air Defense Artillery Brigade, and the 19th Support Command. Other supporting elements include the 1st Signal Brigade, the 501st MI Group, JUSMAG-K, and the USA Support Group, JSA.

The United Nations Command (UNC) is responsible for maintaining the 1953 Armistice agreement which ended the Korean conflict.

The Combined Forces Command (CFC), established in 1978, symbolizes the joint commitment of ROK/US to maintain peace and security on the Korean peninsula. The organizational structure of the CFC is a combined ROK/US staff.

Housing. Government family quarters are limited and are available only to command-sponsored personnel on a "with dependents" tour. The five areas where dependents are authorized and where some government quarters exist are Seoul, Pusan, Taegu, Chinhae and Osan.

There are not enough family units to house all command-sponsored personnel and over 60 per cent live off post on the economy. Economy housing which meets the needs and desires of USFK personnel is scarce and expensive. A combination of urban renewal projects, new tax laws and increasing population has created a severe housing shortage. Rents of up to $500 per month and security deposits of up to $5,000 are not uncommon.

Personnel serving an unaccompanied tour who consider bringing their families to Korea do so at their own expense.

Education. There are 20 education centers serving U.S. personnel in Korea. The centers offer a variety of high school, college, vocational, military and advanced degree programs. For command sponsored dependents there is guaranteed tuition-free schooling provided by the Department of Defense.

Education centers located in areas of heavy troop concentration offer degree programs from the associate to the graduate level. Hands-on vocational/technical programs are offered through Central Texas College and Los Angeles Community College; undergraduate level courses are offered by the University of Maryland's world-wide campus; two master's degree programs are offered by both the University of Southern California and the University of Oklahoma.

DOD overseas school systems in Korea maintain schools which provide educational opportunities (kindergarten through grade 12) in sufficient numbers and types to provide quality education for eligible dependent children.

Non-command-sponsored dependent children of DOD personnel assigned to Taegu, Pusan and Chinhae may enroll in DOD Dependent Schools on a space available basis. Non-command-sponsored children arriving in the Seoul area are ineligible to attend the DOD Dependent Schools there because of overcrowded facilities. There are three private English-speaking schools available to non-command-sponsored dependents in the Seoul area. Annual tuition costs at these private schools range from $1,000 to $2,000.

Banking and Currency. The dollar is used as the currency in all U.S. military facilities. All USFK personnel and their dependents can use two types of financial institutions. Throughout the ROK many installations have branches of the military banking facility (Bank of America) and a federal credit union (San Diego Federal Credit Union). There are check cashing services available at PX's, military clubs and the Bank of America. The won is the Korean currency and must be utilized for transactions on the Korean economy.

Recreational and Cultural Activities. Numerous and assorted cultural and recreational facilities are available according to individual interests.

The Recreation Services Agency, Korea (RSAK) provides entertainment throughout the Republic of Korea. Some form of entertainment is offered at the remote sites as well as at the larger installations.

Both oriental entertainment and a variety of Western pastimes are offered. For the sportsman, basketball, golf, skiing, softball, swimming, bowling, fishing and soccer are available. Taekwondo and other martial arts are also available. For the more urbane, night clubs, theaters, concerts, opera, Korean folk dancing and "kisaeng" entertainment is available.

In the Seoul, Pusan and Taegu areas, RSAK offers a wide variety of Dependent Youth Activities. These activities include a year-round youth sports program.

The Korean Travel Bureau, USO and other private tour groups offer a diverse selection of tours.

10

The Sources of Army Officers

The Army provides broad opportunities to win appointment as an officer. The Regular Army, the Army National Guard, and the Army Reserve must have stable and constant sources of new officers to perform the Army mission of the present and future.

This chapter contains a summary discussion of the separate roads to a commission or warrant, with historical background.

SOURCES AND PREREQUISITES

Sources. The sources for training and selection of Army officers are as follows.

The United States Military Academy
The Reserve Officers Training Corps
The Officer Candidate School
Appointment from Civil Life
Combat Zone Appointments
Regular Army Appointments
Warrant Officers Appointments

Prerequisites. There are prerequisites to appointment which applicants must satisfy. They must be citizens, be within specified age brackets for the component and branch in which they seek appointment, of good physique as established by a thorough physical examination, and of high moral character. Relatively few are appointed who have not received an academic degree. Information about the complete requirements for appointment should be sought from the Personnel Officer of any Army post or station.

Numbers of Appointments. Approximately 900 2d Lieutenants are appointed annually from the U.S. Military Academy. The number is limited by the size of the Academy. The annual appointment of officers from the Reserve Officer's Training Corps varies according to the needs of the Army and the number of graduates available. Since the total number of officers potentially available to the Army each year from the Military Academy and from the ROTC is relatively constant and not subject to rapid change, the annual input of officers from the OCS program and by direct appointment is varied by the Army to meet its actual yearly needs. Warrant officers are appointed in numbers sufficient to satisfy the Army's requirements for these highly skilled specialists.

METHODS OF APPOINTMENT

Throughout our nation's history there have been different methods by which citizens have obtained appointment as Army officers, for the Regular Army, for wartime services, and for the Reserve components including especially the Army National Guard which has units antedating the American Revolution. In our democracy it is an absolute necessity that the nation's military officers be completely free from even a suspicion that any appointment was made on any basis other than individual merit in meeting established standards. Selection must be from the best qualified individuals. It is noteworthy that the system of officer selection, training, and appointment has the trust of the nation and of the members of the Army.

THE UNITED STATES MILITARY ACADEMY

The United States Military Academy, West Point, New York, since its establishment by the Congress in 1802, has provided well-educated, highly trained professional Army officers who have served the nation with distinction. Its famed Long Grey Line which includes the names of Generals Grant, Lee, Pershing, Bradley, MacArthur, and Eisenhower, to name a few where it would be better to name many, has fulfilled its mission through all emergencies, and all the wars which have confronted the nation since the founding of the Academy. The active Army of today has approximately 10,000 graduates.

Appointment to the Academy. A prospective candidate for West Point must first obtain a nomination from an authorized nominating source. Approximately 85 percent of the nominations available each year are from Members of Congress for residents of their States or Congressional Districts. Competitive examinations determine the appointments from several eligible groups.

Forty appointments at any time are available to the children of veterans either deceased or with 100 percent disability, of any recognized war or conflict including Vietnam. There are 170 appointments awarded annually on a competitive basis to enlisted men and women of the Regular Army and the Army's Reserve components. Sons and daughters of members of the Regular Components of the Army Forces, who are still in service, retired, or who died while serving, and of officers in the Reserve components who have served a minimum of 8 years and are still on active duty, are eligible to compete for 100 cadetships reserved annually for Presidential appointment. There is no limit on the number to be accepted from sons and daughters of recipients of the Medal of Honor, our nation's highest award for valor. There are 20 additional appointments provided annually to honor military schools (high school or junior college level); honor military schools are determined annually by DA or Navy inspectors.

Regardless of the categories which are mentioned above, all candidates must pass a medical and physical aptitude and academic examination.

West Point Preparatory School. Noteworthy is the Army's USMA Preparatory School at Fort Monmouth, New Jersey, where successful active-duty enlisted personnel who are applicants for West Point undergo intensive training and instruction. Instruction lasts from mid-August to the end of May.

USMA Course. The four-year course leads to a baccalaureate degree, with military training to orient cadets toward careers as officers of the Regular Army. The scope of the instruction includes the humanities, engineering, history, military training in all branches, physical development, and character building. AR 350-5, AR 350-56 and the USMA Catalog of Information provide detailed information; write to Director of Admissions, USMA. West Point, New York 10996.

RESERVE OFFICERS TRAINING CORPS

The Reserve Officers Training Corps (ROTC) was formally established by the National Defense Act of 1916. But the concept of military training in degree-granting institutions of higher learning had its origin at the American Literary, Scientific and Military Academy, in 1820, at Norwich, Vermont. It was founded by Captain Alden Partridge, a graduate of West Point, and its Superintendent prior to 1820. Subsequently, in 1834, its name was changed to Norwich University and it continues to provide graduates into military as well as civil leadership at its present location at Northfield, in the state of its origin. Virginia Military Institute, Lexington, Virginia, (Alma Mater of General of the Army George C. Marshall, WWII Army Chief of Staff) in 1839, and the Citadel, Charleston, South Carolina, in 1842, were the next degree-granting institutions to adopt the principle of the John Milton (1608–1674) *Tractate on Education: "I call therefore a complete and generous education that which fits a man to perform justly, skillfully and magnanimously all the offices, both private and public, of peace and war."*

President Lincoln saw the need for increased educational facilities, including a requirement for military training. Under his leadership the Morrill Act of 1862, known as the "Land Grant Act," provided for the establishment of state universities which encouraged the start of many of our great state universities of today.

Many officers of the World War I period received training in the military training programs of the Land Grant colleges and universities. During World War II more than 100,000 ROTC graduates were on active duty from the beginning of the emergency, and served in all grades. During the War in Korea more than 120,000 Reserve officers served on active duty, the vast majority from the ROTC. In the active Army of today, approximately one-fourth of the Army's general officers and over 40 percent of all its officers were appointed as officers from the ROTC.

The Junior Division, ROTC, provides military training in secondary schools. Included are some 650 public and private schools having a total enrollment of about 115,000, including about 35,000 female cadets.

The Senior Division, ROTC, offers military training at college level providing officers for the Army Reserve and the Regular Army. Enrollment varies from year to year, but is about 65,000 in nearly 300 colleges and universities and almost a dozen junior colleges. Female enrollment in the Senior ROTC comprises about 20% of the total.

Honor graduates from these courses may be appointed into the Regular Army, while the balance of the graduates are appointed into the Army Reserve, and may or may not be called to immediate active duty.

The Senior ROTC program includes 4- and 2-year programs. The 4-year program involves a 2-year basic course followed by a 2-year advanced course with a six-weeks summer training camp normally attended between the junior and senior years. The 2-year program was designed for students who were for some reason unable to enroll in the basic course. Transfer students from junior colleges which have no ROTC program are in this category. In lieu of the basic course, they must attend a six-weeks basic summer camp prior to taking the advanced course. The student receives monthly pay at basic summer camp plus travel pay.

Those enrolled in the advanced course receive $100 per month for subsistence. While at advanced summer camps, they receive one-half the base pay of a second lieutenant with less than 2 years service.

Upon graduation and initial entry on active duty, the officer receives a uniform allowance of $300.

High school graduates who enroll in the 4-year program may apply for a 4-year scholarship. Applicants for a 2-year scholarship apply during their second year of the basic course. Scholarship winners agree to accept a commission and to serve not less than 4 years on active duty. They must meet certain age requirements. They do receive $100 per month for the duration of the scholarship, plus tuition, textbooks and laboratory expenses.

OFFICER CANDIDATE SCHOOLS

Officer Candidate Schools are a tradition of the modern Army. They have produced well-trained officers to meet swiftly expanding Army requirements during World Wars I and II, the Korean War, and Vietnam. It is a program to meet emergencies.

The origin of the OCS is attributed to two voluntary camps, held during the summer of 1913, for undergraduate students age 17 or older. At Gettysburg, Pennsylvania, 159 young men from 63 universities and colleges, and at Monterey, California, 85 young men from 63 institutions of higher learning, received military training. Expenses for transportation, subsistence, and clothing were paid by the trainees. Subsequently, in 1915, under the inspiration of General Leonard Wood, a military camp of instruction for business leaders and professional men was held at Plattsburgh, New York. With the Declaration of War, May 6, 1917, there followed swiftly the establishment of several *First Officers' Training Camps,* and others which followed provided the bulk of officers for WWI.

The program was resumed in 1941 which resulted in the training and appointment from the warrant officers and enlisted men of the Army of more than a quarter million Army officers, exclusive of the similarly large program of the Army Air Corps. Many of these officers were subsequently appointed in the Regular Army.

AR 351-5 details the regulations for volunteering for OCS for enlisted personnel and warrant officers. Enlisted men and women are permitted to return to college for 24 months to obtain certain baccalaureate degrees with the Army's financial assistance after which they attend OCS. College graduates may enlist for the purpose of attending an OCS course, serving 2 years after appointment. They receive 8 weeks basic training prior to starting the OCS course. Length of the OC course is 14 weeks. This selective process and the program of training provide officers splendidly trained and ready for assignment as junior officers of their branch.

The Officer Candidate School is located at Fort Benning, Georgia. Both male and female candidates attend this school.

Following the OCS course, the new officers attend the Basic Officer Course at their branch service school. Selection of candidates is for the most part confined to those who are college graduates or who have had some college training. The number selected each year is established according to the Army's needs to augment the annual officer input from the ROTC and the Military Academy.

Warrant Officer Candidate Courses. Warrant officer candidate courses are conducted as needed by the Army to meet requirements for warrant officers. At present only two such courses are in operation, one at the Aviation School at Fort Rucker, Alabama, providing training for entry into the Aviation career field, and one at the Academy of Health Sciences at San Antonio, Texas, which provides training for entry into the Health Services career field.

OFFICERS APPOINTED FROM CIVIL LIFE

Officers may be appointed from civil life, without completing a special course of training in order to qualify for a commission. The Army has a continuing need for officers who have completed their professional or technical training. For example, physicians and surgeons may be commissioned directly from civil life, or they may be appointed after completion of ROTC training. Other examples are chaplains, lawyers, engineers, scientists, and others needed to meet Army requirements.

When the need is great, as in time of war or emergency, members of professions or vocations of civil life may be appointed in an appropriate grade, depending upon their achievements in their profession with a consideration also of their age and background.

The Army does, in practicality, recognize the civilian competition for these essential individuals and that they have devoted additional years towards attaining their education, specialization, and status. Consequently, special inducements are proffered to gain their initial service and, hopefully, to retain them on active duty.

Individuals who wish to obtain information about appointment as an officer in a profession or other specialty are advised to consult a personnel officer of a nearby Army post; or the Headquarters of the U.S. Army in the area of their residence.

REGULAR ARMY APPOINTMENTS

An appointment as an officer of the Regular Army may be achieved in several different ways. West Point is an important source but at its present size can supply only a portion of the total requirement. The ROTC provides approximately 40 percent of the number appointed each year through its Distinguished Military Graduate program. Graduates of the US Naval Academy and the US Air Force Academy may apply upon graduation for an Army appointment. Distinguished graduates from the U.S. Army Officer Candidate School may apply for regular appointments. Officers on active duty, and college graduates who, as students, did not have opportunity to participate in an ROTC program, are eligible to apply. In accordance with the Defense Officer Personnel Management Act of 1981 (DOPMA) each active duty officer must have accepted a Regular Army commission prior to the 11th year of service (see chapter eleven, *Regular Army Career,* and chapter fifteen, *Promotion.* The broad field of eligibility is noteworthy and in its implementation provides members of the corps of officers from representative backgrounds to add their talents to meet the Army's needs.

The requirements for appointment as a Regular Army officer are substantially the same for all applicants. He or she must be a loyal citizen of the United States, of good moral character, and be able to meet a high standard of physical fitness as determined by examination. With exceptions, as in the case of appointees from the professions, an applicant must be at least 21 and less than 27 years of age. In recent years there has been increasing stress upon possession of an academic degree. Individuals on active duty must have completed at least two years' study at an accredited college or university or its equivalent; and individuals who have not attended college may qualify by passing a two-year college equivalency evaluation or a qualifying score on the Educational Requirement Test.

APPOINTMENTS IN A COMBAT ZONE

In combat, warrant officers and soldiers who demonstrate a high potential in leadership deserve special recognition and utilization of their full capabilities. Battlefield (Direct) appointment of such individuals was authorized during WW II. Such appointees must be qualified in a combat arm, i.e., Infantry, Air Defense Artillery, Field Artillery, Armor, Corps of Engineers; in a combat support arm, i.e., Signal Corps, Military Police, Military Intelligence; or in the Transportation Corps.

WARRANT OFFICERS

Warrant officers are appointed by warrant by the Secretary of the Army to meet Army requirements for personnel with particular skills and knowledge. The Department of the Army projects vacancies and invites applications from interested personnel who desire to compete for an appointment. Selection for appointment is made on a best qualified basis by a selection board at Headquarters, Department of the Army. Eligible personnel include enlisted men and women from the active Army, the Reserve components, and other military services. Qualified civilians also may apply, as may commissioned officers provided their application is accompanied by a conditional resignation of commission.

Initial appointments are in the U.S. Army Reserve with concurrent call to active duty and an obligated service tour, normally three years. The regulations provide that at the end of the obligated service tour, individuals may apply either for appointment in the Regular Army or for a Voluntary Indefinite status. The applicable regulations are AR 135–100, AR 611–85, AR 611–112 and DA Pam 600–11.

There are distinctions between commissioned officers and warrant officers as regards command status (for which see AR 600–20) and certain other matters. In general, however, and as used in this book, the term officer includes both commissioned officers and warrant officers.

Warrant officers have the status and privileges of commissioned officers, as stated in Chapter 4, *Military Courtesy.*

11
Regular Army Career

"I am convinced that there is no more important vocation or profession than serving in the defense of the Nation—not just any nation, but a nation that is prepared to provide the dignity to man that God intended—our Nation. All the benefits that our citizens enjoy exist behind the defense barrier that is manned by the members of the military establishment. No greater honor can be given to any man than the privilege of serving the cause of freedom." General Harold K. Johnson, Fargo, N.D., 1967, Chief of Staff, United States Army, 4 July 1964–2 July 1968.

This chapter has been developed as an objective analysis of the current national importance of the professional military officer, with a candid discussion of the favorable and the unfavorable factors of the career. Its purpose is to assist the interested individual who is eligible for appointment to the Regular Army to make an informed analysis. The subject is of vast importance to our nation. The Army's officers and soldiers are serving on all continents, and in more than 70 foreign nations. Their specific duties are infinite in variety. The total mission of our military leaders is a part of the single objective to maintain the security of our country and our people, and, in accordance with policy determined by our nation's elected civil leaders, to help maintain the freedom of friendly nations who need and request our help. The realist understands that the price of peace is firmness with patience, judgment as to what is right and what is wrong, and a constant readiness for future trials which may beset the nation. Thoughtful citizens understand that until universal peace is obtained, which day must come, our nation with our allies must be ready to parry any threat or win any war which may be thrust upon us.

THE MILITARY PROFESSIONAL—THE "PRO"

It is the Regular, always the volunteer, who provides the professional foundation and the continuity upon which our military strength is based. To the Regulars of the nation's corps of officers must be added in the current decades the Reserve component officers who serve as volunteers, on long tours of active duty, who contribute their full share to the professional foundation of our Army. While the interest of members of the general public in their military services may fluctuate between wide extremes, as international relations are tensed or relaxed, national security requires at all times a sufficient number of professional military leaders who are men and women of integrity, competence and determination, prepared and willing to carry the highest responsibilities of military leadership under any conditions, anywhere. In view of the history of the past five decades, citizens should see with easy clarity the need for armed forces under competent leadership.

Throughout our nation's long history, the very core of military leadership has been the professional military officers. In this modern era they are products of varied educational and military background, as should be the case in our democratic America. There are graduates of West Point, or the ROTC; many enter from the Officer Candidate Schools, and others are appointed from civil life to meet Army needs in professional, scientific or technical fields. Whatever their background at the outset, if they remain as career officers, they continue to demonstrate a sense of mission to serve the national purpose coupled with a commitment—the "soldier's soul", as Professor Huntington, a penetrating writer on military subjects, has described it. It is a commitment that drives them just a little farther when the going is roughest—for that last fifteen minutes in battle when victory is often won, or lost forever; it is a personal sense of duty—a love of country—which maintains an unflagging standard of excellence on the job from day to day. These are the true professionals—the "Pros" —who are needed today to a degree which may not be fully understood.

In these harried days, much is made of dissent, a privilege granted under our precious Constitution. The reasons for sharp disagreement with national policy are varied. They may be expressions of idealism, or the reaching of different conclusions than government policy after careful consideration of the same set of basic facts. The reasons may also stem from ignorance, weakness, or concealed intent for subversion. Only the dissenter knows his or her own motive. Despite our troubled years, our citizens cling with undiminished determination to our great freedoms. Our proud nation may become stronger as it learns to accept or to cope with these vast turmoils of expression.

What must be clear to thoughtful citizens is the pressing need for maturity of judgment in reaching long-range decisions, followed by the courage of decisive action. Our United States has been thrust into a position of world leadership, a status *it did not seek*. International catastrophe might be inevitable if this responsibility is terminated. We must continue to reach for the Utopia of international peace and tranquility between nations, while we stand ready to thwart threats to our lands or people either from within or from without our national boundaries. The military professionals surely will continue to be the final rampart for the preservation of our form of government against change by force, as well as the security of our people from outside aggression or internal insurrection. They must provide a living reflection of the words, DUTY, HONOR, COUNTRY, in their broadest, most meaningful context. The life of our proud nation depends upon it.

The life of the Army officer is rewarding and stimulating for those individuals who are adapted by their convictions and their talents for its requirements. It is an exacting life with its own cherished code, special hazards, and rewards. Not all individuals may expect to find the life either attractive or agreeable, which is a reason for laying the facts on the line in this chapter. The person who wants a sheltered, safe, uneventful life, with work from nine to five, the five-day week, and other niceties of today, is unlikely to be adaptable to the vast variety of missions and worldwide places of assignment of the Army officer. But the future security of our nation requires that a sufficient number of our splendidly qualified young citizens elect this choice of career. For them, it will be a good life. There must be capable hands and minds all along the slender line from lieutenant to general. There is a clear need for young men and women to enter the corps of officers, and progress in grade and responsibility to meet with competence the unknown requirements of our nation in the years ahead.

THE PEOPLE WITH WHOM YOU LIVE AND WORK

In the enjoyment of any career the qualities of the people with whom you are associated are of high importance. Your success will be influenced by the manner in which they perform their duties. Among them you will find the personal friends who may enrich your life.*

Much of the work of officers is with soldiers who, for the most part, are young people in their formative years, of excellent physique, with those of lesser mentalities excluded. They have the enthusiasms, the ambitions, and interests of youth and there are few responsibilities equal in satisfaction to their training, development, and leadership. In these tasks you will be assisted by older soldiers who are the noncommissioned backbone of our Army and will become individuals you will respect and treasure.

Army officers are a carefully selected corps, talented, well educated. The larger portion are trained to lead, and to command troop units. Included also are physicians and dentists, lawyers, clergymen, engineers, scientists of many kinds and specialists in many fields of importance today.

During the past few decades, the Army has made a continuing, determined effort to assure that its Corps of Officers is exceptionally well educated. Educational opportunities, both in military schools and in civilian institutions, are detailed in Chapter 13, *Army Schools and Career Progress.*

Author's comment: In each revision of this volume, officers having special knowledge of our subjects, or unusual experience, are invited to review chapters or subjects and supply their candid comments. These objective reviews are invaluable. The letter which follows is the personal analysis made by an outstanding young officer as to his own choice of the Army as a career. It was not written for publication. But it is so illuminating and so human in its sincerity that it deserves to be read by men considering a service career. The writer is a young officer of the Corps of Engineers who holds the Degree of Master of Science in Engineering from a leading university and is a graduate of West Point.

"I find that this is a rather difficult subject to consider in a logical fashion. My problem, I suppose, is largely one of emotion. My reasons for entering the Military Academy were mostly selfish, in that I wanted a college education and I had heard that the Academy offered an excellent one, free of charge. The decision to enter is one I have not regretted.

"As to my reasons for staying in the Army, this is where emotion really enters the picture. In terms of the typical American attitude toward monetary matters, I think it would be hard to make a case for a Regular Army career, either in terms of pay and allowances or in terms of the so-called fringe benefits. For a trained engineer, the pay is probably less than I could demand in civilian life, even less by a considerable margin than I could expect to receive in Civil Service. On the other hand, my training has been entirely due to the generosity of the service, and for that I cannot help but feel a certain sense of obligation . . . not necessarily connected to a specified term of service.

"The real reason I stay in is that I LIKE the Army, or more specifically, perhaps I should say, the people who make up the Army. I am sure that in no other field could one find the high percentage of highly qualified, dedicated people as one can find in the Army. For me it is a pleasure to associate with them. Also I like the periodic changes of assignment and duty stations. It is a continual challenge to move in and learn about a new job, and then try to excel at the performance of whatever the duties may be. I recognize that there are drawbacks to this, too, particularly if a person is upset by newness or strangeness. As for me, I don't think I would be happy at a job where I could see that I would be doing about the same work at the same location into the foreseeable future.

"As for my sons, I would be most happy to see them enter West Point. . . ."

As a result of this emphasis on education, in the Regular Army of today more than 90 percent of the commissioned officers possess at least a Bachelor's degree. In addition, approximately 25 percent of all Regular Army commissioned officers also have advanced degrees—Masters, PhD's, or Professional. Fewer than 2 percent of all Regular Army commissioned officers have had less than two years of college.

The off-duty standards, interests, and activities of officers will be found to be about the same as other successful men and women of better-than-average educational and cultural background. It is a subject worthy of careful consideration in choosing a vocation.

THE APPEALS OF MILITARY DUTY AND ARMY LIFE

After you have evaluated the vocation as to its true worth, and considered the characteristics of your potential associates, it is logical to proceed to analyze the broad pattern of its duties and its life, remembering to consider years of peace as well as war or emergency. Will you find stimulating the tasks, missions, or responsibilities which you will be required to complete? Will you be interested by the travel involved in many changes of station as well as duty assignment, within the United States and in other lands? Will you enjoy and cherish the comradeship and friendship of the sort of people who adopt the military life as a vocation?

The person of action who likes to lead, to work with people, to get things done, to express personal views and stand firmly is quite likely to enjoy the military life. Or he or she may wish to develop in some military technique or professional specialty, such as medicine and surgery, the law, or as a chaplain. The scope of Army requirements is a band of great width. In the paragraphs which follow we attempt an analysis of some of these characteristics.

The Officer's Code of Duty and Conduct. This is a most important consideration. The officer lives under a strong and inspiring code which acts as a guide in the standards of official and personal acts. It assures the officer that he or she will be associated in worthwhile missions with other officers whose loyalty to the nation, personal trustworthiness, and honor are of the highest order. Here will be found the welding of common interests which results in military teamwork, in comradeship, and friendships with others of all ages and grades. It provides an environment which its members regard with pride and self-respect. It is the sort of life which many good men and women have loved and do love. Life under the code is good for the nation, and for most officers a rich and gratifying experience. See Chapter One, *The Code of the Army Officer.*

The Officer as a Leader. At the outset of your career you may expect opportunity to command, to train others, to guide and direct, to lead and set the example. As you progress in experience you will be taught more and more of leadership. It pertains to the leadership of tactical units, and to units in support; it applies also to tasks of management or administration other than in tactical units. You will be "in charge" of something for which you are responsible. You will have a mission. In the usual case other officers, or soldiers, or civilian employees will be assigned to assist you in the discharge of mission. You will be a manager. Initially, you will be a junior executive, progressing with experience to command or executive responsibilities of the greatest scope. This is the part of Army life which has the strongest appeal for many officers because they reach positions of responsibility requiring the use of leadership more swiftly than in other careers. Military leadership is never static, but is continually embracing new conditions. Consider the probable effects upon leadership of rockets and missiles, new more powerful weapons, air mobility of combat units, better communication and transportation. It is growth-leadership, not stand-still leadership. Furthermore, the ultimate expectancy as to scope of leadership is far greater than in other vocations. If opportunity to lead is the primary reason for electing the military life, you choose wisely. Responsibility and leadership will be your life.

CONSIDER THE SCOPE OF MILITARY LIFE

The single purpose of service in the Army or its sister services is the nation's security in this divided and troubled world. Although the life has this single purpose, the one certainty of the Army officer is that his or her duty assignments will have infinite variety, with location of place of duty throughout the United States and in many foreign lands.

As your training proceeds and your capabilities are recognized, you will encounter progressively the full force and flavor of missions of great variety. The work of the Army must be done and its missions achieved. Abroad there are our forces in Europe and Asia, working in close unison with our allies. There are also Military Aid and Assistance Groups, Military Missions, and our Army Attaches stationed wherever we have State Department representation. You must expect to live and serve, and execute ably the assigned mission, wherever you are needed.

Within the United States there is the structure for the total administration and development of the Active Army, the Reserve components, and the Reserve Officers Training Corps. There is the training of individuals and organizations at training centers, Army and civilian schools, and in tactical units such as those assigned to the U.S. Army Forces Command (FORSCOM). There is research and development into scientific and other fields to increase our security of the present and future. There is the logistical support of Army units and personnel everywhere, from guns and ammunition to their medical and hospital requirements. There is much more. The mission of the Army officer involves a great variety of individual assignments which will take him or her from one end of our country to the other.

But let us keep this great variety of mission and location in a reasonable perspective. It is true that there is the widest opportunity for an interesting, useful life, in almost worldwide locations. There is also routine. There is hum-drum. All is not top secret and all is not glamorous. It is a life of service with important rewards and many disappointments. As an officer, you may live and work under the highest standards of surroundings or facilities; it is equally true that you may expect to live and work under some conditions that are most difficult indeed. Over the years of a professional career, you may feel as you encounter them that there are too few of the former and too many of the latter. At the end, you may realize that your greatest achievements occurred where the going was hardest and roughest. It is necessary to see deeply into the expectancies in order to choose wisely.

The Chance to Grow in Capability and Knowledge. The Army officer is provided with unique opportunities to increase personal knowledge, and to expand personal capabilities. These good things develop from the consecutive assignments which increase in importance with experience. It is an intentional, planned program which is accomplished through the Army's extensive system of service schools and colleges, with the use of civilian institutions of learning. There is opportunity to complete necessary college level courses to qualify for an academic degree. And there are opportunities to attend a university to attain an advanced degree. The strongly emphasized career planning program of the Army provides guidance and control to the undertaking. The goal is to develop the individual officer so that each may reach his or her own level of maximum capacity. (See Chapter Twelve, *Career Development,* and Chapter Thirteen, *Army Schools and Career Progress.*) For those normal individuals who have the character, the zeal, and the inherent ability to absorb and apply knowledge, and to work effectively with their fellow men, it is opportunity unlimited.

Travel. Over any period of years the officer may expect to serve at several stations within the United States and in other countries. You will travel extensively. You may acquire considerable knowledge of London, Paris, Rome, and other capitals of Europe, as well as Tokyo and other great cities of the Far East. You will acquire a broad and thorough understanding of our own great country, and you will learn much of other lands and other people. Through this experience you will gain understanding of the cross currents of world opinion. Your interests will tend to become national and international, in contrast to local and restricted. Your acquaintanceships will expand to other individuals of many vocations who also have the larger concepts. It is a constant education.

This is a satisfying phase of military life of primary attractiveness to most officers. The individual who prefers the roots established by life in a single community, with sameness in the place of residence, the daily experiences and associates, is unlikely to enjoy the military life. It is a point of serious consideration. (See Chapter Eight, *Army Posts and Stations;* and Chapter Nine, *Foreign Service.*)

The Courtesies, the Customs, and the Off-duty Life. Military life includes the use of ceremonial procedures which give it dignity and charm. They consist of courtesies paid to the National anthem and the flag; between senior and junior; between officer and soldier; to the high civilian officials of government, or of friendly foreign governments; and to the military dead. (See Chapter Four, *Military Courtesy*). There are customs of the service as universally observed as the prescribed courtesies which add to the smoothness and enjoyment of official as well as unofficial and social contacts. They are procedures which are learned quickly and applied gracefully. They are quite similar to the protocol of the foreign service, or as applied to faculty members on a university campus, or other grouping of gentlemen and ladies where there is recognition of position. The only thing unique about the Army's customs and courtesies is that they have been established over many years and for that reason are less subject to change. (See Chapter Five, *Customs of the Service.*)

For those whose assignments are on military posts, particularly where there are quarters for family occupancy, the athletic, social, and cultural opportunities are often outstanding. This is especially true of the large, older stations where there is a considerable amount of permanent construction of quarters for families. The officers' club and mess is the focal point of social and off-duty activities for the officer and adult members of his or her family. This traditional institution of good fellowship provides about the same sort of service to its members as the faculty club at a university, or the country club or city club whose members are the professional and business leaders of a community. Officers' clubs operate by means of dues and profits from activities, without expense to the Government. It is a distinct advantage in the military community because of the opportunity for group activities, and the broadening of acquaint-anceships. (See Chapter Six, *The Social Side of Army Life.*)

CONSIDER THE TOTAL REMUNERATION

It is entirely fitting that an individual contemplating a career as an officer should consider with great thoroughness the complete situation as to service pay, allowances, special pay for which he or she may qualify, service rights and benefits, rights as to retirement, and the benefits after retirement including veterans' benefits which are provided by our government. *The Army officer must have the right to aspire and to achieve at least the same standard of living and security as do people of similar education and responsibility in other vocations, civil or government. Indeed, since the officer may be required to lay his or her life on the line in the performance of assigned duties—a hazard excluded from the usual expectancies of other fields of employment—a case can be made that he or she should receive special consideration.*

Military Pay—the "Cash Flow." Pay is a proper factor for an individual to consider in choice of career. There are others, of course, as discussed in this chapter. But the dollar-and-cents item is certainly to be considered in choosing a vocation specifically in determining one's own willingness to serve our government as an officer. You should be secure in the conclusion that throughout your years of active service you will be able to support your family, including the education of your children, at a standard of living which is acceptable. After retirement, you should be confident that you and your spouse will live in comfort and dignity. If you should pre-decease your spouse, before or after retirement, you should feel secure that his or her essential needs are assured. This is a broad view of "remuneration." Whatever the level of cash income, never to be forgotten is the continuing need for financial management, and for prudent, individual financial planning.

This discussion does not presume to argue that total armed service pay and total remuneration is either sufficient or insufficient for the responsibilities, the hazards, and other factors involved. The reader is referred to Chapter Nine-teen, *Pay and Allowances,* with special reference to the introductory state-ments about future increase prospects, and to Chapter Seven, *Financial Planning,* as to service and social security benefits available to the officer and his or her dependents. The aggregate should be carefully evaluated. Is the total sufficient, in comparison with other vocations? It is a determination to be made by each individual. In candor and helpful truth, however, it should be stated that career officers who have observed reasonably good financial management of their affairs, with reasonably far-sighted and prudent planning for their own futures, have been able to provide the financial obligations of parenthood, lead interesting lives, and then enjoy rewarding, financially secure, comfortable lives during their retirement years.*

Promotion. Subject to performance of duty in an efficient manner, with the continued observance of required standards of personal honor and conduct, advancement in rank and position is quite certain for the Regular officer. Under

---

*The motivation for choosing a service career has been above a dollars and cents evaluation. The nation has been most fortunate in the caliber of people who have been attracted to its service, and continued with it—through thick and thin. Officers of the stature of Generals Marshall, Eisenhower, MacArthur, Bradley, Taylor, Wheeler, Johnson, and Westmoreland, and thousands of other of their brother officers of all eras similarly motivated, have placed the nation's security and the privilege of its service as the reason for their choice of career. Their value to the nation is beyond price and there will always be a need—with ultimate appreciation—for more like them.

provisions for promotion currently in effect, the opportunity for promotion on a selective basis is favorable for the outstanding officer who works hard and achieves highly. Merit will take the officer upward.

The Regular officer who enters the service at the normal age of the early or mid twenties may anticipate a career of 30 years or to age 60. Most will retire in their fifties through the operation of laws. Promotion is selective and above the grade of captain or CW2 is on the "best qualified" basis. Essential is the retention of good health and the receipt of commendable evaluation reports and ratings. Many officers who continue on active duty will attain the grade of colonel, which is a very high grade indeed. A small portion of officers will become generals, to provide the topmost leadership in the Army. On a percentage basis it is clear that only a few will achieve the grade of general. The stars are there, however, for those of special aptitude or capability. Highly successful officers may be confident of attaining the grade of colonel before retirement, with a few in the grade of general. (See Chapter Fifteen, *Promotion.*)

Tenure of Position. The Regular officer has a very important degree of protection as to tenure of position. The Regular cannot be separated from active duty for such administrative reasons as "reduction in force," nor separated at all except in due process of applicable laws. If the officer's work is of acceptable standard, his or her conduct above serious reproach, and if he or she retains physical and mental health, the officer may expect with confidence to retain a commission with all its rights and benefits until retirement, and thereafter in retired status until death.

During the first three years after appointment the Regular Army officer is in probationary status and the appointment subject to administrative termination. Elimination may occur after the probationary period by approved findings of a Board of Officers because of low standards of duty performance, or for character or other weakness. Elimination may occur through failing twice to be selected for promotion to a new permanent grade. Conviction by general court-martial may involve dismissal. Physical disability acquired during the first 8 years' service results in severance pay, not retirement, but important VA rights accrue. Beyond service in the 8th year, retirement pay for physical disability depends upon degree of disability and length of service. (See Chapter Twenty-five, *Resignation and Elimination,* and Chapter Twenty-six, *Retirement.*)

Annual Leave With Pay. The Army provides 30 days' leave annually with pay, which may accumulate for 2 years. (See Chapter Twenty-three, *Authorized Absences.*)

Medical Care and Hospitalization. The officer is provided medical care and hospitalization without cost, except for a small subsistence charge when hospitalized.

Under the amendments to the Medicare Program for dependents discussed in Chapter Seven, *Financial Planning,* the situation as to medical care and hospitalization of family members has been broadened and strengthened. Spouses and children of service members are able to obtain very complete medical and hospital care, in service facilities or in civilian facilities, without regard to the military station of the military member of the family. Especially gratifying is the provision for major help for handicapped or mentally retarded children of service families.

Noteworthy is the extension of medical and hospital care in civilian facilities to retired officers and their family members. This added authorization deserves special consideration of all who consider Army career service.

The provisions for medical care and hospitalization for an officer and his or her family members, while in active service or in retired status, provide an important benefit to career service. (See also Chapter Seven, *Financial Planning.*)

Six Months' Pay as Death Gratuity. Upon the death of a military person on active duty, the beneficiary receives 6 months' pay, $3,000 maximum, tax exempt, as a gratuity.

Privileges of the Post Exchange and Commissary. The post exchange and the commissary are highly appreciated institutions with histories that reach deep into the past.

In addition to being convenient for on-post residents, they provide many items at savings to all who have the privilege to use them. Their associated facilities of laundry, dry cleaning, shoe repair, barber shop, bowling alleys, snack bars, delicatessen, gas station, etc., provide other opportunities to stretch one's dollars and still lead the good life. Commissaries derive no profits, whereas the small dividends from Post Exchange sales are given to welfare funds for athletics and recreation.

Retirement. The Regular Army officer has an important factor of security in the retirement laws for which reference is made to Chapter Twenty-six, *Retirement.* They provide for voluntary retirement upon completing 20 years of service, subject to departmental approval. There is retirement for physical disability for those who have completed 8 years of service. Forced retirement becomes operative upon attaining the statutory age limit. Low efficiency, character weakness, or failure twice to be selected for promotion may cause obligatory retirement. (See Chapter Fifteen, *Promotion;* and Chapter Twenty-five, *Resignation and Elimination.*)

Veterans' Benefits and Other Rights and Privileges. Any veteran including the Regular Army officer has many rights and privileges which are of great importance. The Veterans Administration is the agency of administration.

CONSIDER THE DISADVANTAGES

There are factors concerning the military service which many will consider disadvantages of serious importance. Some of them may be eliminated as time passes, for our officials are making real progress in improving the life and lot of service people of all grades. Some are inherent to the service itself and depend upon international conditions, the requirements and missions to be met, even the conduct of war. The disadvantages deserve evaluation.

The officer must be prepared to perform an officer's duty in war, in campaign, or battle. There are hardships and there are hazards. It is the reason the government granted the commission or warrant.

The Shortage of Family Housing at Posts and Stations. While real progress has been made in recent years in increasing the number of quarters available for assignment to officers at our posts and stations, the shortage continues. It varies between stations, as can be seen quickly by consulting Chapter Eight, *Army Posts and Stations.* The most enjoyable and the most economical life is obtained by occupying suitable quarters on the post of assignment. Great care is taken to assign the quarters which are available on a fair and equitable basis.

But at many stations there is a wait, and at others the number of officers assigned is so far above the number of sets available as to make residence off-post the expectancy. The situation improves each year as new funds are provided for quarters. But the shortage persists and must be faced.

Family Separation. The nature and place of duty assignments have caused some necessary separation of families. There have been wars, and combat short of formal war. The Army mission has required some officers and soldiers to be sent into regions so undeveloped or unhealthy that families cannot be accommodated. These regions are short-tour areas where duration is curtailed to less than 18 months; however, the duty is essential to the national security which officers and their spouses have accepted as an essential national service. The duration of tours unaccompanied by families is indicated for many areas in Chapter Nine, *Foreign Service.*

The American public and our elected officials know that family separation in peacetime is abnormal. It is Army policy established in AR 614–30 that family separations are directed only when there are no accommodations for family members, or the family's presence would have an adverse effect upon a unit's mission or combat capability. These are facts of life which the officer and his or her spouse must be prepared to face. The occasions are infrequent; such duties are distributed carefully so that individuals do not bear a disproportionate degree of separation. Still, when the international situation becomes tense and uncertain, potential zones of combat are not the place for families. It is a fact to be faced courageously.

Frequent Changes of Station. Station changes occur from causes integral with service opportunities or needs. In times of military quiet, when economy rules with a firmer hand, the officer may wish for more frequent station changes. Take this one in stride.

THE REACHING OF CONCLUSIONS

At the beginning of this chapter the purpose was stated of presenting a calm and objective discussion of the vocation of Regular Army Officer, with its advantages as well as its recognized disadvantages. Frequent references are made to other chapters of *The Army Officer's Guide* where detailed information on each important subject may be found. The purpose has been to present facts so that you, as an eligible young man or woman, can decide a little more accurately your own election as to military life.

The security of our great nation requires a sufficient number of able leaders of all grades and ages, from top to bottom, who are eager to serve their country wherever and however such service is needed; they will serve their country because they think the task is worthy, because they like the military life as well as their associations with others of like mind; and they will place their confidence in the appropriate officials of government as to pay and other benefits of future service. For the Government has the first interest here, and must be relied upon to treat fairly its defenders in uniform. If it should fail to do so, it will cease to attract and hold in willing career service the quality and numbers of individuals needed for the people's future security. Indeed, a person who has genuine fears as to the fairness of our government officials had best elect another career, for in one sense it is their powers and capacity to govern justly we stand ready to fight to preserve.

Needed by the Army are young men and women of good minds and education, of good physique to stand the rigors of service, who are willing to work, to study, and to learn, so as to be ready for greater responsibilities as they come.

The young officers of today who enter the Regular service will expect to reach the time of retirement during the 2000s which seems almost an infinity away. In this coming period they will undertake tasks not yet envisioned but which we may be certain will be challenging and interesting. When that final day comes it is almost a certainty that these officers will not be persons of wealth from savings from their salaries. But they will have lived lives of fairly adequate security including the amount of monthly pay. The officers will have endured some bruises and have suffered some hardships, for their lives will not have been easy ones. But overshadowing all these matters will be a pride of service in having completed successfully, at home and overseas, many interesting and important assignments. The officers will have helped make history, always more interesting than mere reading of the exploits of others. They will have developed valued comradeships and strong friendships, priceless beyond measure. The officers' interests will center in national and international affairs and their friends are likely to include many people of similar interests who may be civilian or military. The officers will be familiar and at home in most parts of the United States and in many oversea regions and nations because their duties will have taken them there. They will probably have a genuine love of the service, its responsibilities, its unique life, and its cherished associations. The officers might say, as many other officers are saying as they leave active service in these fascinating days, "If I could live it over, I would choose the Army again. For me it has been best." It is such men and women the nation will need in the challenging years which lie ahead, and it is only for such men and women who may become our future revered leaders, that this chapter has been written.*

> *"I'm glad I'm in the Army, not only for the people who are in it and for the breadth of experience which it offers, but because of the feeling I have of belonging to an outfit which really matters, one which has a mission of tremendous significance."*—General Maxwell D. Taylor, Chief of Staff, 1955–1959, Chairman, Joint Chiefs of Staff, 1962–1964, Ambassador to Vietnam, 1964–1965, and Special Assistant to the President of the United States, 1965–68.

---

*Readers are referred to an article in the February 1973 edition of *Army* by General Maxwell D. Taylor, *"Is an Army Career Still Worthwhile?"* It provides a most illuminating and thought-provoking discussion of the subject matter of this chapter.

12

Professional Development

Everything a person does is in some way preparation for future respon-sibilities. This is true whether one plans it that way or not, but forethought is likely to produce more fruitful results than is chance. General Bruce K. Holloway, then Vice Chief of Staff USAF, in an address to the Air Command and Staff College, 7 June 1968.

The Army provides for its officers of all grades exceptional oppor-tunities for development of their own potentials which may lead with relative certainty into rewarding assignments of importance to the Nation. The programs for professional development have been improved progressively by the best talent in this complex field. The officer who studies the total program as presented briefly in this chapter, and strives to take maximum advantage of his or her opportunity, is certain to benefit.

The prime purpose of this chapter is to assist you as a junior officer in the beginning and the early years of your service in advancing your own career progress. You must understand the role and functions of the Army, through its Officer Personnel Manage-ment Directorate, at the Military Personnel Center (MILPERCEN). It is essential that you understand the responsibility placed upon your immediate commander as to implementing the program for each officer within his or her jurisdiction. Most of all, you must understand what you are expected to do about your own career development, and how you go about it. With an understanding of these three areas of responsibility, of which your own is the base, you can proceed into your Army service with knowledge of how your career may be developed.

The official documents, DA PAM 600–3, *Commissioned Officer*

Professional Development and Utilization, or DA PAM 600–11, *Warrant Officer Professional Development,* should be obtained from the unit personnel officer, studied, believed, and pertinent material extracted for a personal library and reference file. Each warrant officer on extended active duty is furnished a copy of DA Pam 600–11.

There are differences in the professional development programs for commissioned officers and warrant officers, arising principally from differences in their utilization. The commissioned officer is expected to be a leader first, but with particular areas of expertise in which these leadership qualities may be employed. The warrant officer is expected to be highly skilled in a particular technical area or areas and to serve repetitive assignments in positions utilizing these skills. Thus, while the chapter as a whole is applicable to all officers, a section toward the end of the chapter provides details applicable specifically to warrant officers.

There are related subjects in this program of professional development. The *Army Officer's Guide* chapters named below relate directly to the subject and their study with professional development procedures is urged. These are matters of extreme importance in gaining total understanding of the surest and quickest way to achieve a successful, rewarding Army career.

Chapter 1. *The Code of the Army Officer.* This is your foundation.

Chapter 3. *The Officer Image.* You must win a good one.

Chapter 13. *Army Schools and Career Progress.* Opportunity is abundant.

Chapter 14. *Evaluation Reports.* Strive to deserve the best.

Chapter 15. *Promotion.* Above captain and CW2, it is for the "best qualified."

Chapter 25. *Resignation and Elimination.* There are ways out.

REACH FOR THE TOP

Responsibility for very large and very important enterprises, or missions, which require the highest levels of managerial as well as leadership skill, is the justified expectancy of a considerable portion of the Army's career officers. In our society, no other large professional group has such extensive opportunities to undertake tasks of maximum importance. Fortunately, the Army provides educational and training opportunities to prepare its officers for the nation's responsibilities which are entrusted to its military leaders.

When a person accepts a warrant or commission in the Army, or enters upon extended active service, he or she should develop a long-range plan to rise as high as possible, as quickly as possible. The officer's talents, achievements, and future capability will be under continual observation and evaluation. The Army provides infinite opportunities to perform missions of high importance in command and staff, the professions, and in managerial, scientific, technical, or administrative assignments.

Our Army is competitive. Realization of this simple fact is the key to understanding why there should be individual choice of goals with the essential resolution and sustained drive to achieve them. Above the junior grades, promotion is by selection. Students attending the senior service colleges and the Warrant Officer Senior Course are chosen from the best qualified. The more important assignments in command and staff, managerial and other major missions, are decided after thorough comparison. Selection by qualification is utilized far more than seniority, except for filling temporary vacancies.

This brief discussion is titled-*Reach for the Top.* It implies a single "top", such as aspiring to be the Army's Chief of Staff, which is misleading. The fact is, there are many "tops", which change as service lengthens and experience broadens.

Retained for last mention is the importance in our Army of the human element, and personal relations with others. Officers responsible for missions undertake them with other officers, noncommissioned officers, soldiers, civilians. The responsible officer will strive for teamwork. Teamwork with your own commander and staff; within your own headquarters staff agencies; and with your subordinate units or individuals. Favorable personality factors are essential. The good will of subordinates, seniors, associates, is a vital ingredient of any person's program for success. Choose your own goals. Qualify early for the prerequisite steps. Compete strongly, and very fairly, because any worthy mission will require the successful achievements of many individuals. Army life can prove to be very rewarding. It is competitive. Voltaire put it this way: "Cultivate your own garden".

OFFICER PERSONNEL MANAGEMENT SYSTEM (OPMS)

During World War II, but not really recognized until much later, the Army was caught up in a technological revolution which was at least as great, and perhaps greater, than that experienced by our country's business and industrial community. One has only to review the rapid development and use of the airplane during those years, or the great strides that have been made in communications, or the development and use of the computer to understand just how great these changes have been.

These changes have also impacted upon the Army's officer corps. With each new development, each advanced capability, the Army has needed officers who were specially trained and able to understand the new capabilities, and use them correctly and efficiently. This need has not been confined to the technical fields and advances in weaponry. There have been corollary requirements for improved logistics management, intelligence functions, communications as well. The warrant officers with their special skills have filled much of the need for specialists, as evidenced by the fact that about 14 percent of the active duty officers in today's Army are warrant officers.

However, there also was a need for commissioned officer specialists, and during the quarter century following World War II the Army encouraged qualified commissioned officers to participate in various specialist programs such as logistics, research and development, atomic energy, or aviation. During this period, officer assignments were controlled by the officer's basic branch, and each commissioned officer was expected to maintain proficiency in his basic branch. That is, the commissioned officer was expected to remain "branch qualified". This included serving tours of duty in the type assignments followed by other members of his branch, including serving the requisite tours in command of troops. As the years passed and the need for specialists expanded, it became increasingly apparent that a commissioned officer really could not be expected to be a specialist in one particular area of Army need while still maintaining complete branch proficiency. During tours spent in a specialty assignment, the individual commissioned officer tended to lose touch with what his branch was doing, while during tours with his branch to maintain proficiency in that area, he tended to lose touch with advances in his specialty area. The result was that many fine commissioned officers found themselves in positions where they not only were behind in their specialty, but also were not really equipped to perform all of the duties that may have been required of officers of their grade and branch.

In an effort to correct this problem, in 1970, under the direction of the Deputy Chief of Staff for Personnel, a study of the officer corps was undertaken. The study results indicated that in an era of decreasing size of the Army, a skill imbalance in the officer corps was developing. There were continually increasing needs for officer specialists of various types, and there were decreasing opportunities for commissioned officers to command the fewer Army units. At the same time, however, the promotion system still encouraged generalization and emphasized command duty. A need for change was indentified to both improve the professionalism and at the same time enhance the career satisfaction of the Army's officers. The result was a basic change in the way the Army managed its officer corps, through adoption of the Officer Personnel Management System (OPMS) in April, 1972. After a several year transition period, OPMS became fully implemented in 1975.

The Officer Personnel Management System is the total of all policies and procedures by which commissioned officers are procured, trained, assigned, developed, evaluated, promoted and separated from active duty. It is the Army's reaction to the rapidly changing technological environment with its attendant demands for increasing expertise; to changing attitudes toward specialization and job satisfaction among younger career officers; to the need to assure equitable opportunity for advancement among officers serving in diverse career fields and specialties; and lastly to the increased challenges of troop command, coupled with more limited command opportunities in a smaller Army.

The purpose of OPMS is to enhance the effectiveness and professionalism of the officer corps. Within limits of the Army's needs, it also provides the mechanism to take advantage of the wide diversity of aptitudes and interests of the individual officers. OPMS applies to all of the Army's officers except those in the Army Medical Department, the Judge Advocate General Corps, and the Chaplain Corps. Each of these branches has its own professional development program, with specialties comparable to those discussed in this chapter.

There are two primary missions of the Officer Personnel Management Directorate (OPMD) which is responsible for the implementation of OPMS:

- To access and designate officers in the numbers and with the right skills to satisfy Army requirements.
- To develop the professional capacities of officers through planned schooling and progressive assignments.

Interrelated with these missions are the three subsystems of OPMS. These include everything that is done from the time an officer is brought on active duty until he or she separates from the service. These subsystems are all interrelated and any change in one has a direct impact on the others.

- The first subsystem is strength management. Emphasis is placed on developing the right number of officers with the right skills.
- The next subsystem—Professional Development—provides for the development of professional attributes and capabilities of officers to meet the needs of the Army through planned assignments and schooling.
- The third subsystem is Evaluation, the objective of which is to identify those officers most qualified for advancement and assignment to positions of increased responsibility.

The interrelationship of the three subsystems is further enhanced by the Central Selection Process. This process impacts on the strength of the officer

OPMS

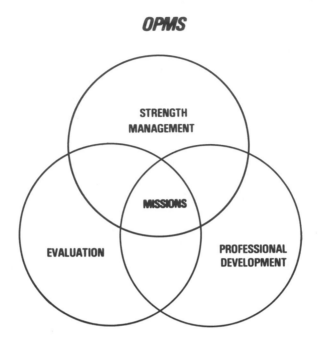

STRENGTH
MANAGEMENT

MISSIONS

EVALUATION

PROFESSIONAL
DEVELOPMENT

corps, professional development opportunities, and takes into account the commanders' evaluation of each officer's past performance. The Centralized Selection Process is used for the catagories shown here:
- Promotion
- Command and Staff College/Senior Service College
- Command (LTC-COL)
- Project Manager
- Selective Continuation
- Regular Army Integration

Dual Specialty Development. The heart of the Officer Personnel Management System for commissioned officers is dual specialty professional development. Each commissioned officer, upon entry on active duty, is assigned an initial entry, or accession, specialty. Then, by about the completion of the eighth year of service, each officer will also be assigned an additional specialty.

The term *specialty* needs a definition. As used by OPMS, a specialty is a particular grouping of duty positions which are distinct, supportive, and have a specific function, application or scope. The duty positions within a specialty require skills, knowledge and job requirements which are mutually supportive in the development of officer competence to perform in the specialty at the grade of colonel.

The considerations that go into the selection of the initial entry specialty designation include the Army's requirements, the new officer's education and experience, and the officer's stated preference. Later designation of the additional specialty is based on the same considerations plus the officer's demonstrated performance and potential. Some disciplines have a very high correlation with certain specialties, such as a civil engineer being assigned to the Engineer specialty, or an electronics engineer being assigned a Communications-Electronics specialty. On the other hand, a graduate in business administration may well wonder how he was assigned the Infantry specialty. The Army's needs are foremost, and nearly half of all Army company grade officers are needed in the combat arms branches. He may well find that the satisfactions of working with and commanding troops are what he has always desired. Many other officers have experienced that feeling. Besides, there will be ample time later for selection of an additional specialty, such as in the Finance or Comptroller fields, that might more closely suit initial desires.

Restrictions. There are restrictions on specialty assignments which should be understood. First, there are some specialties that are not available for assignment as initial entry specialties. These non-accession specialties are identified by asterisks in the accompanying listing of specialties. In essence, these non-accession specialties are in fields where there are no requirements for junior officers or where more senior, experienced officers are desired to fill the assignments. There also are important restrictions for female officers. By regulation, women may not be designated in Specialty 11 (Infantry) nor in Specialty 12 (Armor). Nor may a woman serve as Cannon Field Artillery Officer (13 E), Air Defense Artillery SHORAD Officer (14 B), Combat Engineer Officer (21 A), Unconventional Warfare Officer (48 E), or as an Aerial Scout. Women may hold a Specialty 15 (Aviation) designation, but may not pilot helicopters in the attack role. Further, female officers are subject to a combat exclusion policy which prohibits their assignment to battalion or squadron sized units, or smaller, of the infantry, armor, cannon field artillery, combat engineers, and low altitude air defense artillery. Finally, it should be noted that selection of a combat arms specialty as an additional specialty is precluded unless there is an accompanying branch transfer to the branch associated with that specialty. Otherwise, subject to the above restrictions, all of the basic entry specialties plus the non-accession specialties are available for selection as an additional specialty.

Relationship of Specialties and Branches. The branches of the Army are discussed in detail in Chapters 28 through 32. However, some discussion is needed as to the relationship among the branches and the specialties. Whereas a specialty is a grouping of duty positions, a branch is a grouping of officers. Branch officers are developed and utilized in various specialties. Note that certain specialties are closely related to certain branches, such as Specialty 11 (Infantry) with the Infantry branch or Specialty 13 (Field Artillery) with the Field Artillery branch. All basic entry specialties are affiliated with a particular branch. Other specialties, such as Specialty 43 (Community Activities Management) or Specialty 46 (Public Affairs) have no particular branch relationship, nor can they be designated as entry or accession specialties. Except for the restriction noted earlier on selection of a combat arms specialty as an additional specialty, in principle, officers from any branch could be assigned to any specialty.

PROFESSIONAL DEVELOPMENT PLANNING AT THE DEPARTMENT OF THE ARMY

The Officer Personnel Management System is administered by the Department of the Army through the U.S. Army Military Personnel Center (MILPERCEN), which functions under the Army Staff supervision of the Deputy

11 INFANTRY
12 ARMOR
13 FIELD ARTILLERY
14 AIR DEFENSE ARTILLERY
15 AVIATION
21 ENGINEER
*22 TOPOGRAPHIC ENGINEER
25 COMMUNICATIONS-ELECTRONICS
27 COMMUNICATIONS-ELECTRONICS
      ENGINEERING
#30 INTELLIGENCE MANAGEMENT
31 MILITARY POLICE
35 MILITARY INTELLIGENCE
36 COUNTERINTELLIGENCE—SIGNAL SECURITY
      AND HUMINT
37 SIGNAL INTELLIGENCE—ELECTRONIC WARFARE
#40 PERSONNEL MANAGEMENT
*41 PERSONNEL PROGRAMS MANAGEMENT
42 ADMINISTRATIVE AND PERSONNEL SYSTEMS
      MANAGEMENT
#43 COMMUNITY ACTIVITIES MANAGEMENT
44 FINANCE

*45 COMPTROLLER
*46 PUBLIC AFFAIRS
*48 FOREIGN AREA OFFICER
*49 OPERATIONS RESEARCH/SYSTEMS ANALYSIS
*51 MATERIAL ACQUISITION MANAGEMENT
*52 NUCLEAR WEAPONS
*53 AUTOMATED DATA SYSTEMS MANAGEMENT
*54 OPERATIONS, PLANS AND TRAINING
#70 LOGISTICS MANAGEMENT
71 AVIATION LOGISTICS
72 COMMUNICATIONS-ELECTRONICS MATERIEL
      MANAGEMENT
73 MISSILE MATERIEL MANAGEMENT
74 CHEMICAL
75 MUNITIONS MATERIEL MANAGEMENT
81 PETROLEUM MANAGEMENT
82 SUBSISTENCE MANAGEMENT
91 MAINTENANCE MANAGEMENT
92 MATERIEL/SERVICES MANAGEMENT
*95 TRANSPORTATION MANAGEMENT
*97 PROCUREMENT

*Cannot be designated a basic entry speciality
#Not assigned to individuals—position code only

COMMISSIONED OFFICER SPECIALTIES

Chief of Staff for Personnel. The interior organization of MILPERCEN includes an Officer Personnel Management Directorate (OPMD) and an Enlisted Personnel Management Directorate. An organization chart of the Officer Personnel Management Directorate accompanies this discussion.

The OPMD has eight divisions, five of which are directly concerned with officer development and assignments and three of which plus an Administrative Support Office that are in a general support role for the Directorate. The Directorate handles the monitoring and assignment of all of the Army's commissioned officers and warrant officers except for those officers assigned to the Army Medical Department, the Judge Advocate General Corps and the Chaplain Corps. Officers of these branches are controlled by their own branch.

The Combat Arms Division of OPMD has five branches and the Foreign Area Management Section. Four of these, the Infantry Branch, Armor Branch, Field Artillery Branch and Air Defense Artillery Branch, each monitor officers of all grades from lieutenant through lieutenant colonel who have basic entry specialties associated with that branch, and are thus assigned to that branch. The Aviation Branch monitors the development and assignment of all officers in the grades of lieutenant through lieutenant colonel who have a basic entry specialty in Aviation, regardless of the branch to which they may be assigned. Similarly, the Combat Support Arms Division monitors officers with basic entry specialties associated with the Combat Support Arms branches of that division, and the branches of the Combat Service Support Division monitor officers who have basic entry specialties associated with the combat service support areas. From the time an officer is selected for promotion to colonel, monitoring responsibility is passed to the Colonels Division which monitors the assignment of all colonels, regardless of basic entry specialty. The Warrant Officers Division is responsible for monitoring the development and assignment of all of the Army's warrant officers controlled by OMPD.

The Officer Personnel Management Directorate of MILPERCEN has two mis-

OFFICER PERSONNEL MANAGEMENT DIRECTORATE

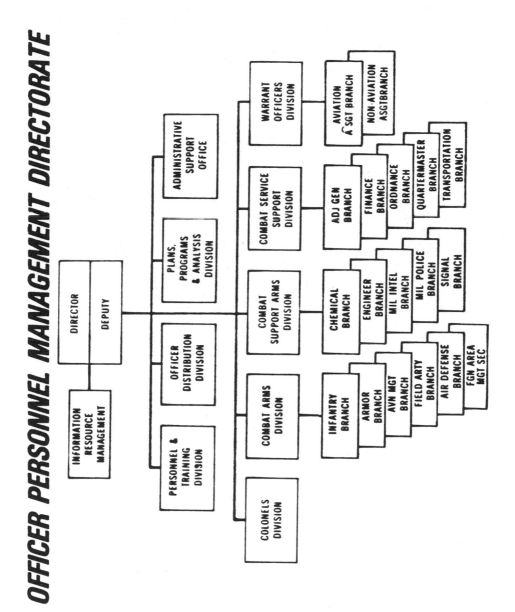

sions: It serves the Army as an organization which selects and distributes Army personnel to meet requirements in a situation which changes continually. It also serves the individual officer through the professional development program, which involves selection of individuals for attendance at service schools and colleges, for varied troop and staff duty in the continental United States and overseas, and for other special assignments. In the execution of these two missions, there is always an added factor which is considered—*the expressed desires of the individual.*

At times the two missions, with due regard for the expressed desires of the individual, will seem in conflict with one another. Some thought is needed. The world-wide missions and duties assigned to the Army must be performed, and this requires the assignment of qualified individuals in numbers sufficient to do the job. Despite conflicting requirements, and new missions requiring officers, the assignment officers of OPMD strive for a high degree of officer satisfaction by carefully weighing every consideration in making each assignment. The need for an equitable means of insuring that one group of officers is not exposed to undue hardship, in comparison with others, is a daily concern. In these troubled years, we must face the inescapable fact of occasional conflicts in Army requirements, career management planning, and officer desires. The work of the Army must be done. But the desires and needs of the individual are considered, if disclosed to the OPMD by statement of preference; and where circumstances permit, they are observed.

The records necessary for making these selections with wisdom include evaluation reports and Officer Assignment Preference Statements.

Capable people are assigned to perform these selective tasks and officers may feel complete confidence that assignment selections are made objectively, wholly on their merits, with the best interests of the individual and the Army thoroughly considered.

The Overall Career Plan. The overall career plan is based on 30 years which is the approximate maximum career expectancy of Regular officers.

Professional Development Patterns. Professional development patterns are representations of pathways or ladders that can be followed by officers in progressing from beginning levels to the highest positions of responsibility they are capable of assuming. The professional development pattern depicts the basic pattern for professional development applicable to all officers. Specific patterns show the application to each specialty.

DA Pamphlet 600-3, *Commissioned Officer Professional Development and Utilization,* contains professional development patterns for each specialty open to commissioned officers and DA Pam 600-11, *Warrant Officer Professional Development,* contains the patterns for each warrant officer MOS.

Although these patterns are designed especially for active duty officers, they apply, with modification, to officers not on active duty as well.

These patterns provide guidance in officer assignments. They show each officer the program appropriate in his or her case and indicate the type assignments to seek to advance personal progress. They are also a guide to field commanders and supervisors, as well as officers of the OPMD in Washington, in assignments of officers.

It is so easily overlooked in our interest in details, we shall look again at the *goal:* the purpose of the Army is the nation's security. If war should come, the Army's purpose is the restoration of peace with the defeat of our enemies. All our people of the armed forces, our weapons and our equipment, are provided by our government so that our citizens may practice in safety the arts of peace.

THE OFFICER'S RESPONSIBILITY FOR CAREER PROGRESS

The personnel managers from units and commands to the Department of the Army's Officer Personnel Management Directorate, Deputy Chief of Staff for Personnel, and the Chief of Staff really try to provide individual professional development and management. However, officers are responsible in large part for their own development and progress toward the "top."

The Officer's Initial Choice. At the very beginning of a service career the commissioned officer exercises individual choice, or preference, for a basic entry specialty, the designation of which determines also the branch assignment. It is an important decision. Unless the officer later transfers to another branch, which may be done, most subsequent assignments during the first eight years of service will pertain to that specialty; service school training will be at that branch service school; and the manager of that basic entry specialty, in conjunction with the professional development officer in OPMD, will monitor successive assignments, evaluate the officer's capabilities, and make many decisions or recommendation which determine the officer's assignments and progress.

By the end of the eighth year of service, an additional specialty will be assigned to each commissioned officer, based upon the officer's stated desires, any special training or qualifications possessed by the officer, the officer's demonstrated performance and potential, and the Army's needs. From that point through the major and lieutenant colonel grades, successive assignments will be monitored by the officer's basic entry specialty manager in conjunction with the additional specialty manager. The officer may expect assignments in either the basic entry specialty or the additional specialty, designed to develop and maintain his or her specialty skills. Colonels may expect utilization assignments in either specialty as dictated by Army requirements.

How does an officer determine at the start of a military life the sort of Army activities of his or her greatest interest or aptitudes? For many officers the choice is clear. When the individual has been trained as a physician, dentist, lawyer, clergyman, or engineer, he or she will enter the appropriate branch as indicated by the professional training. For others, the field of their college major may indicate the choice which may also be acceptable to the Army. In the fields of electronics and communication, there are the Signal specialties. In Ordnance there are many specialties in engineering and science. In transportation there are the Transportation specialties. In the field of finance and business administration there are the Finance and Quartermaster specialties. The field of one's college training may not suit the individual, as a career preference, nor fit the requirements of the Army as to utilization of the knowledge. But for the majority of individuals college training is an important factor in choosing the basic entry specialty and branch assignment.

Where do your innermost interests lie? What sort of work gives you the greatest thrill or satisfaction? What are your best attributes as to education? These are a number of the considerations which should guide you in initial planning of your military life. Does this illuminate the problem? Do you begin to see the influences you are expected to have upon your own career?

One of the greatest needs of the Army, and for many persons its most attractive opportunity, is the requirement for leaders to command its units. Do you enjoy working with people, and especially young people? Do you enjoy training them, organizing and inspiring them, leading them into interesting achievements? Or would you like to learn how? You will be welcome indeed, for leaders must be identified and trained to fill command assignments all along the slender line from lieutenant to general, from platoon to the field army. Infantry, Armor, Field Artillery or Air Defense Artillery may be your choice of specialty and branch. It is in this field of command that the Army may hold forth its greatest inducements because officers attain rewarding assignments earlier in their careers than in other vocations. In time of war, skilled military field leaders are the priceless ones; it is their names which are perpetuated in honor in our national history.

The Army needs the very best battalion and brigade commanders. While nearly every officer will have an opportunity during his or her early years to command a platoon and/or company level unit, only those officers who are selected by a DA Selection Board will be given commands of OPMS-designated battalions or brigades. The key elements of the selection procedure of officers to fill battalion and brigade level command positions are as follows:

Separate DA selection boards are convened for combat arms, combat support arms, and combat service support.

Selection boards designate officers best qualified for troop command and prepare a rank order list by command category.

Assignments are made by DA based on command position vacancies, an officer's standing on the selection board's rank order list, the qualifications desired by the field commander, and the officer's specialties and skill qualifications.

Later Choices Which Influence a Career. As an Army career lengthens, other options or opportunities arrive which may influence a career. New developments are introduced; international conditions change; all manner of changing conditions serve to provide new opportunities to consider, adopt, or reject. It is important to understand this condition, and it is essential that it be utilized. The one certainty of an Army career is change, and the alert officer must be ready for it.

The Officer's Opportunity to Attend Service Schools and the Service Colleges. Each officer has opportunity for attendance at courses conducted at service schools, and for selection to attend one or more courses at the service colleges.

During the first eight years' service all commissioned officers and most warrant officers attend their Basic and Advanced Courses. Applications to attend are not necessary. However, appropriate entry should be kept current on the *Officers Assignment Preference Statement,* discussed later. The earlier in the eligibility period these courses are completed the better; the knowledge gained will widen the officer's assignment eligibility and will also bring eligibility for selections which follow completion of the advanced course. During this period, qualifications for the additional specialty will be identified or developed. During the seventh through ninth years of service, each commissioned officer will also attend the Combined Arms and Services Staff School (CAS³), which is designed specifically to teach staff skills.

The higher schools, such as the Command and General Staff College and the Warrant Officer Senior Course, train officers of the Army, a small number of officers from the sister services, and officers of nations allied with the United States. Attendance of Army officers at these courses is selective and competitive, which means that the records of eligible officers are evaluated and compared. About half of the Army's career officers will attend one of these college courses. Let the selection odds be seen in true light, for selection to attend is a very important factor for later selection for high command or staff duty. The odds are not extreme. Half of those eligible on the basis of the prerequisites to attend these advanced courses will attend the Command and General Staff College; and about 30 percent of those eligible will attend a course at the Senior Service College level. About 10% of the warrant officers will attend the Warrant Officer Senior Course. The officer who makes the most of his or her opportunities, and does his or her best on all assignments, has an excellent chance for selection. Completion in the earliest practicable year of the stated assignments of the officer's professional development pattern enhances selection opportunities as the member will be considered during each year of eligibility.

Opportunity to Attend Civilian Colleges and Universities. The goal is for all commissioned officers of the future Army to hold academic degrees and all warrant officers to hold associate degrees. In recent years the percentage of Army officers holding academic degrees has risen sharply, which is also true for holders of advanced degrees. Part of this increase has resulted from the Army's programs to facilitate the earning of degrees by active duty officers.

General educational development of officers is conducted through off-duty academic instruction. As a supplement to the program, a Degree Completion Program is available. It is sound advice that officers who lack an appropriate degree seek this opportunity because an academic degree is of great importance to the Army officer. Individual application is necessary.

Officers are selected to attend civilian universities to seek important and useful education and a master's or even a doctor's degree for specialties where the Army has requirements. Such selections are highly competitive and are made only to fill vacanies validated by the Army Educational Requirements Board. Only about 400 commissioned officers and six warrant officers are sent to graduate school each year.

Clearly, the Army's professional development program has splendid opportunities for higher study through the service schools and colleges, and through civilian institutions including post graduate studies for advanced degrees. It adds importantly to the attractiveness of an Army career.

The Importance of the Officer's Evaluation Record. The officer who aspires for ultimate selection for the higher schools and colleges, and the more important assignments, must deserve and receive a commendable series of evaluation reports. These assignments are selective on the "best fitted" basis, which is the best system for the individual as well as the Army. This need not be a cause for alarm. Rating officers are required to prepare the reports objectively, thoughtfully, in accordance with the Army regulations for the subject. *It is not required that an officer be in the upper one percent, or ten or twenty percent. But it is necessary to have a sustained record of successful performance of duty with an accompanying favorable personal record of integrity and conduct. This is more important than "percentage" placement.* Perhaps it is made clearer by saying flatly that supermen are not required, and few exist. Do a good job and you will fare well.

Should an Officer Volunteer for Hazardous or Dangerous Duty? There is an old Army saying, now heard rarely, which has done much harm: "Keep your mouth shut, your nose clean, and volunteer for nothing." For the run-of-the-mill person without special ambition it may be a comforting philosophy. He or she is prepared to take whatever comes along, rocks with the punches, and may get nowhere. But there is another end of this same stick. Many splendid officers believe the most officer-like course is to perform all assigned missions to the highest standard, state their assignment wishes fully on the *Officer's Assignment Preference Statement,* and thereafter leave to the appropriate officials the decisions as to the next assignment. The latter policy is followed by most officers.

What, then, about volunteering or applying for special assignments? Take combat in Vietnam, as an example, or service in Korea during that war, or combat service in *any* war. The Chief of Staff, acting through the Army Staff and the commanding generals of major commands, will have procedures which control assignments. Certainly it is neither necessary nor expected that an individual volunteer. Still, many officers and many soldiers do volunteer for combat service, or service in a combat area, and many others apply to extend their period of service in such areas. Some thought about it is stimulating.

The actual reasons an individual volunteers for hazardous duty, such as combat, are very personal and may only be surmised. Some may feel very deeply about the rightness and the importance of the mission. Others may wish to extend service of maximum value to the Army and the nation. Some may believe that the experience to be gained will advance their careers as professional Army officers, and it is this latter point of view which is most susceptible to analysis. Let us consider it thoughtfully.

Our Army is an active, determined, combat-ready force, led by officers who in most instances have had extensive combat experience. Our government raises and supports its armed forces so they will surely be ready for combat, when and if our elected civil leaders decide the need has come. The Army trains its officers, noncommissioned officers, and soldiers for combat duty. It is a fact entirely justified that officers with combat experience, especially those of the combat arms who have been outstandingly successful as combat leaders, are in a more favorable position for subsequent preferred assignments and promotion than officers without this experience. It is the "center ring," the central arena, where most eyes are focused; and it is also the place where the success or the failure of the Army mission may be resolved. Therefore, to give high value to combat service during or after periods in which the Army has a combat mission is completely justified. Indeed, to fail to do so would be unfair. It must not be more than one of several factors considered for selection to fill important assignments, or promotion, but it merits added weight.

This discussion is neither to advocate nor to discourage volunteering for hazardous or other special duty. It is a personal choice, and the reasons are equally personal. It is included to stimulate thought about a subject which receives periodic consideration.

During the action in Vietnam, some 5,000 officers volunteered annually either for duty or to extend their tour there. In many instances they were assigned to serve in command or staff positions which should enhance their promotion status. For information on the length of tour and other details concerning volunteering, see Chapter 9, *Foreign Service.*

Importance of the Officer's Assignment Preference Statement and Other Individual Records. There are four official records of special importance to each officer. When changes occur the officer must be alert to have them promptly recorded. These records are:

The Officer's Assignment Preference Statement, DA Form 483.
Officer Master File (OMF).

Officer Record Brief (ORB).
The U. S. Army Register, Volume I, Regular Army Active List, and Volume II, Reserve Officers Active Duty List.

The Officer's Assignment Preference Statement, DA Form 483. This form enables an officer to state preferences for detail or assignment for personal

---

OFFICER ASSIGNMENT PREFERENCE STATEMENT
For use of this form, see AR 614-100; the proponent agency is MILPERCEN.

SEE INSTRUCTIONS ON REVERSE

DATA REQUIRED BY THE PRIVACY ACT

AUTHORITY: Section 301, Title 5 USC.

PRINCIPAL PURPOSE: To show the individual officer's preference for type of duty, location, training and other considerations which he/she desires to make known to the personnel manager.

ROUTINE USES: Form is used by the officer to indicate his desires to the military personnel manager; used by the personnel manager to correlate officer's preferences with the existing requirements at time of reassignment/rotation/retirement.

DISCLOSURE: Disclosure of personnel data is mandatory. Failure of service member to disclose appropriate data would be a violation of departmental regulations IAW Article 92, UCMJ.

1. LAST NAME - FIRST NAME - MIDDLE INITIAL | 2. GRADE | 3. SSN | 4. PRIM SPEC | 5. ALT SPEC

6. CURRENT DUTY ASSIGNMENT *(Job Title and Date Assigned)* | 7. DUTY SPEC | 8. DATE LAST PCS | 9. DEROS

10. UNIT OF ASSIGNMENT, DUTY ADDRESS AND AUTOVON TELEPHONE NUMBER

11. ASSIGNMENT PREFERENCE

a. ☐ CONTINENTAL U.S. | b. ☐ OVERSEAS ACCOMPANIED | c. ☐ OVERSEAS UNACCOMPANIED

☐ DUTY ASSIGNMENT | ☐ DUTY ASSIGNMENT | ☐ DUTY ASSIGNMENT
(1) (2) (3) for each

☐ MACOM/ACTIVITY/LOCATION | ☐ MACOM/ACTIVITY/COUNTRY | ☐ MACOM/ACTIVITY/COUNTRY
(1) (2) (3)

12. PROFESSIONAL DEVELOPMENT COMMENTS

13. PERSONAL DATA

a. DEPENDENTS | RELATIONSHIP | DOB | b. CURRENT RESIDENCE *(Address and Phone No.)*

(CHECK ONE) ☐ OWN ☐ RENT ☐ GOVERNMENT QUARTERS
c. POINT OF CONTACT DURING TRANSIENT STATUS *(Address and Phone No.)*

d. PERSONAL CONSIDERATIONS

DATE | SIGNATURE

DA FORM 1 NOV 75 **483** REPLACES DA FORM 483, 1 AUG 70 AND DA FORM 483-R(PAS), 26 SEP 75, WHICH ARE OBSOLETE.

OFFICER ASSIGNMENT PREFERENCE STATEMENT

career development, or special needs or preferences. The officer is required to submit the form periodically, and encouraged to forward one whenever his or her preferences for assignment are changed, or when important events have occurred which should be known by the manager of the officer's basic entry specialty, OPMD. See the illustration herein. The reverse of the form contains instructions.

Block 12, *Professional Development Comments,* and Block 13d, *Personal Considerations,* are there to invite each officer to state with candor the facts he or she wishes considered in deciding a future assignment. Specialty management officers do strive to meet the officer's wishes insofar as it is practicable for them to do so. But they are not mind readers. The officer must keep them informed and this is one way to do it.

When the assignment desired is unusual, or beyond the jurisdiction of field commanders, or the time factor indicates the need, write a letter through channels to your basic entry or career specialty manager, Officer Personnel Management Directorate, US Army Military Personnel Center, 200 Stovall Street, Alexandria, Virginia 22332, or telephone. Indeed, when a particular assignment is essential to your career progress your inquiry and applications are urged.

Officer Record Brief (ORB). The Officer Record Brief is produced automatically, upon demand, from the information stored in the Officer Master File, a computerized collection of data pertaining to each officer. The ORB contains all pertinent data on each officer necessary for the officer's consideration for assignments, school selection, promotion, and other decisions affecting his or her career. Maintaining up-to-date data on the ORB is thus of extreme importance and is the responsibility of the individual officer. You will have the opportunity annually to audit your ORB to assure that it is correct.

Officer Master File (OMF). The OMF is the computerized source of data from which the ORB is produced when desired. It is maintained up-to-date by the annual audits conducted by the officer concerned and by the data fed to the file by the unit personnel officer. Each officer should be sure that the OMF reflects important changes affecting his or her career such as service school courses completed, changes as to civilian education, credit for overseas tours, changes in numbers of dependents, and so forth.

The Army Register. One of the printed outputs from the *Officer Master File* appears in the U.S. Army Register, with special reference in this discussion to Volume 1, *Regular Army Active List, and Volume II, Reserve Officers Active List.* The information contained therein often is used, particularly by the receiving command, when an officer is being considered for a particular assignment. It is important that the data be accurate and up to date since selection for a choice assignment could well depend on what the Register shows. Each officer should check his or her entry in the Army Register as soon as it is received, and report at once any errors or omissions.

Officer Active Duty List. All commissioned officers on active duty are carried on the Active Duty List which lists officers by rank and date of rank.

THE COMMANDER'S RESPONSIBILITIES

An officer's immediate commanding officer, or chief, has important responsibilities for that officer's professional development. Higher commanders in the chain of command are also responsible. Indeed, the success of the program requires the effective completion of the commander's missions.

The commander should consult the specialty career pattern of the officer and check the progress made in completing essential assignments, in comparison with the officer's length of service. What has the officer completed and what are the lacks? A commander may be able to rotate an officer within the unit to provide the experience which is contemplated in the specialty career pattern. The commissioned officer may command a platoon or a company; and then be rotated to a position on the battalion staff. A battalion or a brigade has different types of units as to weapons or mission, and breadth of experience may be advanced by rotation through two or more of such assignments. If the needed duty is not available within a command, the commander may report the need to a higher commander with a recommendation. All this is extremely important if officers are to gain in minimum time the breadth of experience they need. However, let another part of this picture be considered. The efficiency and perhaps the combat readiness of the unit must be the first consideration. Rotation of officers can be accomplished and should be accomplished; but there must also be recognition of mission.

Commanders are instructors and in this capacity they use their experience to advise their subordinates. No military unit can ever be "commanded" in the true sense of the word until each member is instructed and proficient in individual duties. "This is what we are to do," the commander will direct; "this is the way we shall do it," and he or she announces specific missions for subordinate units and key individuals; then, at the proper time, "Let's Go." If officers or soldiers do something which is incorrect, or in a manner of reduced efficiency, tell them or show them how to do it right. The commander uses his or her greater experience to increase the knowledge of members of the command. Teaching may not always be understood as part of "professional development," or "career planning"—but it is.

A commander, or chief, who has officers under his or her command or jurisdiction, has the responsibility for rendering evaluation reports upon them. This is the most important series of reports which accumulate about each officer's achievements, personality traits, and value to the service. These records are consulted within the Department of the Army, evaluated, and from their study, officers are chosen for all assignments, including duties which are most sought by those working hard to reach maximum goals. The officer who prepares the evaluation report on another officer accepts a very important responsibility. The circumstances under which an officer may see personal evaluation reports are stated in this chapter in the discussion, *Finding Out How You Stand;* reference should also be made to Chapter Fourteen, *Evaluation Reports.*

The commander's counseling of officers for whom he or she will prepare evaluation reports is an especially important responsibility. Counseling may start on the first day an officer reports for duty, as the need to do so occurs, and continues as an important command responsibility throughout an officer's assignment. Effective counseling helps the officer to improve performance of duty and the progress of his or her career. Reference: *Professional Development Responsibilities,* DA Pam 600–3, *Commissioned Officer Professional Development and Utilization,* and DA Pam 600–11, *Warrant Officer Professional Development.*

The OER Support Form, DA Form 67-8-1 (see Chapter 14, Evaluation Reports) requires that, at the beginning of each rating period, the rating officer, who normally is the immediate commander or chief, discuss with the rated officer the duties and the performance objectives that he will be expected to accomplish during the rating period. These duties and responsibilities should also be reviewed with the rated officer as necessary during the rating period. Each of these discussion sessions should be used by the rating officer as an opportunity for counseling the rated officer.

What does "counseling" really mean? Just as the confidence of officers is enhanced and reinforced by recognition of their special capabilities, talents, strengths, they must be informed early in their careers of their weaknesses and their deficiencies, and positive means for improvement suggested. Subsequent consultation periods should be arranged in order that favorable results can be accomplished prior to the date an evaluation report must be prepared. In the great majority of instances where wise, objective counseling is done at the appropriate time, the results are bound to be favorable. Further, a priceless feeling of mutual trust and respect may follow a good job of counseling because officers aspire to succeed and appreciate guidance which will help them forward. The commander may benefit more than he or she could possibly have anticipated; by making the study of the officer, and the officer's work, aspirations, and career pattern, the commander is likely to discover individuals who have unused talents he or she had not identified. It works both ways. The worth of any military unit is the sum of the capabilities, the determination, and the developed teamwork of its subordinate units and all of its individual members.

FINDING OUT HOW YOU STAND

If you aspire to the maximum development of your capabilities in the shortest span of years, you need to find out from time to time exactly how you stand and you are encouraged to do so. This discussion is provided as a summary of well-known procedures, often considered separately, which are really a single, continuing need. In any case, here are definite steps for consideration.

It is essential that you study your own professional development pattern before consulting other officers. You should consider your present and past assignments, including school courses, and decide for yourself whether you are falling behind. When you have a pleasant assignment in a location you enjoy, a commander you admire, or a set of quarters especially pleasing, it is easy to succumb to the attempt to keep things as they are. This is one way to fall behind. Check your own development pattern and see. Another measure which should be verified before consulting others is that your expression of desires is stated fully and accurately on your *Officers Assignment Preference Statement,* which is on file with the Officer Personnel Management Directorate, in Washington.

The first source of information is from the immediate commanding officer, or chief, for he or she is the one charged with an important part of professional development, and is the one who prepares your evaluation reports on which so much depends. We shall make these assumptions: You have not been to Washington to see your evaluation report file nor have you visited your basic entry specialty manager. Further, time is running short within the first 8 years' service to gain staff (or command) experience and to attend the Advanced Course. Assume further that you have stated these desires on your preference statements. With this situation in mind, what may you do?

You may request an interview with your commanding officer for a personal discussion, and you may visit Washington to inspect your file of evaluation reports, followed by an interview with your basic entry specialty manager. If you choose to do so, you may authorize another officer to inspect the evaluation report file for you, and you may write to the Chief of your Division in OPMD to make inquiries as appropriate. A periodic visit is better. Now we proceed to some details.

Gaining the Commander's Conclusions and Advice. First, your rating officer, who normally is your commander or chief, is required to discuss with you, at the beginning of each evaluation report rating period, the duties you are to perform and the performance objectives you are to accomplish during the rating period. (See Chapter 14, Evaluation Reports.) This required counseling session, plus other discussions as may be appropriate during the rating period, provide an excellent opportunity for you to obtain your commander's advice. However, it does not follow that your commander will include in the discussions subjects that are of special interest to you. You must decide in advance what matters you would like to discuss with your commander and be prepared to guide the discussion to these matters if your commander does not.

Prior to each such session, review your professional development pattern to see how you stand; make notes of the items of particular interest about which you will seek your commander's advice. Decide before the discussion session the precise information you wish to learn; and then, during the discussion, be sure to bring up these subjects of special interest about which your commander can provide advice based upon his or her greater experience or knowledge. Such questions as the following might be appropriate: You are in your 6th year of service, and have no staff experience as depicted by your Professional Development Pattern. Inquire, what can be done to fill this gap? You have not attended the Advanced Course. Can the commander suggest action which will help secure the assignment? Mindful that evaluation reports are based upon performance of duty, and the image which is in continual formation by observation, it is appropriate to ask these pointed, personal questions: Can the commander suggest ways to improve your standard of work, which is a polite way of inquiring—"if you believe my work can be improved, please tell me specifically what to do about it?" Be sure you are prepared to hear the truth, for if you ask candid questions you are almost certain to receive candid answers— the only ones worthy of adoption. You may ask, "Can you suggest ways to improve my personal mannerisms to get better results?" There will be other questions, of course. Ask them, being sure from start to finish that your commander is certain to understand that you are seeking guidance in order to do a better job, and become a better officer. Never offer alibis nor become argumentative. Can such an inquiry do harm to an officer's standing? Will such questions offend the commander or rating officer? No, certainly not, if the questions are asked objectively, and if the answers are received without argument or objection. Indeed, most commanders welcome such discussions with their subordinates.

Examination of Evaluation Reports. As stated in Chapter Fourteen, *Evaluation Reports,* you are authorized to examine your evaluation reports, in Washington, or you may authorize another officer to do it for you. Official records are on file at the MILPERCEN in the Hoffman Building at 200 Stovall Street, Alexandria, Virginia, just off Interstate 95. Call Commercial 325-9618 or Autovon 221-9618 for an appointment to assure immediate availability since these are the records used by promotion and selection boards. Three days advance notice normally is required. The custodian will advise you of the strict rules and provide you a desk, privacy and writing materials. A microfiche copy of the official file will be provided to you. Also, you may request that the microfiche copy be mailed to you.

These are the principal records which are consulted in the Department of the Army in deciding each of the important personnel actions which make up your career. Valuable lessons as to strengths and weaknesses may be learned from their reading.

How often should you inspect your official file? Certainly you should do so before visiting your specialty manager, discussed below. When you are passing through Washington, and there are reports you have not seen, it is wise to stop at MILPERCEN for the short time necessary to see the reports and learn, for certain, how you stand.

Visits to OPMD. Officers are encouraged to visit their specialty managers at OPMD, and discuss with a counseling officer the evaluation of their records, their future assignments, and other matters of their interests. Forecasting the future of any individual is difficult and uncertain in any vocation. The Army provides this exceptional opportunity for such glimpses into the possible future for the excellent reason that it strives hard to help each officer attain maximum capability as early in the officer's career as his or her talents and hard work may justify. The purpose of the following discussion is to assist an officer to make a productive visit, and to decide when such visits should be made. The officer who knows the goal sought may learn by these visits whether he or she is following the right road, at the right speed, and the hurdles, if any, which must be cleared.

The various Divisons and Branches of OPMD are located in the Hoffman II Building, Alexandria, Va., which may be reached by official bus from the Pentagon Concourse. A special appointment is not required. A visit with a counselor, your specialty manager and/or your professional development officer, should be helpful and will certainly be informative.

The value of counseling by your specialty manager will depend somewhat upon your preliminary thinking. What information should you seek? You should ask "how you stand" as to evaluation ratings in comparison with officers of your grade and length of service. Are you in the middle categories with the majority of officers of your grade and length of service? Below the middle? Or are you one of the Army's "comers," in the running at the appropriate time for the C&GSC, the Armed Forces Staff College, one of the Senior Service Colleges, the W.O.S.C., postgraduate studies for a high academic degree, the most responsible assignments of command and staff? (Each as you near eligibility for such assignments.) Are you near promotion in either the primary or secondary zones? Are you likely to "make it"? Or are you vulnerable to non-selection? Are you approaching eligibility to attend one of the service colleges where students are selected on the best qualified basis? If so, what are your prospects? Are you becoming due for an oversea tour? If so, you may wish to inquire the probable timing. Is it likely to be a long tour or a short tour? These are questions of common, personal interest and are included as suggestions. If you ask precise questions, you may expect precise answers. Questions may be asked which the counseling officer cannot answer because he or she is not authorized to divulge the information sought, or because the information has not been determined. Counseling officers will go as far as they can, as to the information told to a visiting officer because candor and openness are essential. These visits can have an important influence on your entire career and should be made at appropriate times.

At what periods in your service should you visit your specialty manager for counseling? DA Pam 600–3 and DA Pam 600–11 recommend that visits be made at three-year intervals. Place this spacing against your own Professional Development Pattern, and see how it fits. You will wish to make these visits sufficiently in advance of the end of each career period so that time will remain to complete the obvious unfinished requirements. A visit each 3 years is an excellent general rule, to be advanced or retarded by individual reasoning.

WARRANT OFFICER PROFESSIONAL DEVELOPMENT

The warrant officer is initially appointed in a particular MOS, but this does not preclude subsequent reclassification as the Army's needs change. Such reclassification can be involuntary, as when the Army no longer has a valid requirement for warrant officers in a particular MOS. More often, reclassification is the result of voluntary action on the part of the individual to reduce a surplus in a particular MOS, to become cross-qualified in a related MOS, or to develop additional skills, all of which serve to keep in balance the available numbers of qualified officers to fill the stated Army requirements.

The career patterns for warrant officers are based on five principles of progression. These are referred to as phased development, vertical mobility, lateral mobility, skill progression, and development of managerial talent.

Phased Development. Career patterns are phased in terms of years of warrant officer service to represent a continuum of experience and knowledge ranging from the least to the most efficient.

Phase 1 comprises the first four years of warrant officer service. It provides a period for the individual to adapt to officer status, to complete initial or refresher training as required, to complete the initial period of obligated service, and to gain experience in a variety of entry level assignments.

Phase 2, from the 4th to 11th years of warrant officer service, is character-

0 SERVICES
  01 HEALTH CARE DELIVERY
  02 CLUB MANAGEMENT
  03 MUSIC
  04 FOOD SERVICE
  05 VETERINARY SERVICES
1 AVIATION OPERATIONS AND MAINTENANCE
  10 AVIATION OPERATIONS
  16 AVIATION MAINTENANCE
2 ELECTRONICS EQUIPMENT SYSTEMS OPERATION
  AND MAINTENANCE
  20 GENERAL ELECTRONICS MAINTENANCE
  21 FIELD ARTILLERY ELECTRONICS MAINTENANCE
  22 AIR DEFENSE ELECTRONICS MAINTENANCE
  25 STANDARDS AND TEST EQUIPMENT
    CALIBRATION AND REPAIR
  26 NUCLEAR WEAPONS
  27 LAND COMBAT SUPPORT MISSILE SYSTEM
    REPAIR
  28 COMMUNICATIONS-ELECTRONICS REPAIR
  29 TELECOMMUNICATIONS OPERATIONS AND
    MAINTENANCE
3 FACILITIES OPERATIONS AND MAINTENANCE
  31 UTILITIES OPERATION AND MAINTENANCE

4 PRECISION MAINTENANCE
  40 AIRDROP EQUIPMENT EMPLOYMENT &
    MAINTENANCE
  41 AMMUNITION
  42 ARMAMENT REPAIR
  44 METALWORKING
5 MARINE OPERATIONS & MAINTENANCE
  50 MARINE OPERATIONS
  51 MARINE MAINTENANCE
6 MECHANICAL MAINTENANCE
  62 ENGINEER EQUIPMENT REPAIR
  63 AUTOMOTIVE REPAIR
7 ADMINISTRATION
  71 PERSONNEL & OFFICE MANAGEMENT
  74 DATA PROCESSING
  76 SUPPLY
8 GRAPHICS
  81 DRAFTING & CARTOGRAPHY
  82 SURVEYING
  83 REPRODUCTION
  84 TERRAIN
9 INVESTIGATION, SECURITY AND INTELLIGENCE
  95 CRIMINAL INVESTIGATION
  96 MILITARY INTELLIGENCE
  97 GENERAL INTELLIGENCE
  98 SIGINT/ELECTRONIC WARFARE

WARRANT OFFICER CAREER FIELDS

ized by advanced course attendance, expanded skill training, and development of expertise in appropriate subspecialties of the officer's career field.

Phase 3, from the 11th year until termination of service, is the period during which the warrant officer will make the greatest contribution. All warrant officers entering this phase will be proven performers in their career fields. Selected individuals from this group may be assigned to positions requiring the greatest judgment, maturity, and independence of action; the very best officers will be selected to attend the Warrant Officer Senior Course.

Vertical Mobility. Assignment patterns are echeloned from lower to higher levels of command and as the officer gains experience, consideration is given to assignment at the higher levels. Availability of higher echelon assignments varies considerably depending upon the specialty area, however, and progressive assignment to higher echelons is not necessary as it is with commissioned officers.

Lateral Mobility. In many specialty areas, particularly the common support specialties, progression may be by lateral mobility, wherein the officer is assigned the same basic job, but in different arms or services. The officer thus becomes a combined arms technician, familar with the organization, missions, methods and interrelationships of the various arms and services. It is wise to avoid the tendency to "homestead" in repetitive assignments with the same branch.

Skill Progression. Acquisition of additional skills in the form of an advanced MOS, or qualification in a subspecialty are examples of skill progression when such are related to the officer's basic specialty area. Qualification in an additional MOS also is an example of skill progression. Skill progression broadens the assignment possibilities for the individual officer and enhances the Army's ability to obtain properly qualified warrant officers for its needs. Participation is by individual application to attend an MOS producing course or by application for direct award of the MOS based on occupational or educational experience.

Development of Managerial Talent. As each warrant officer progresses through the development phases, demands for his or her services as a "hands on" operator will decrease, while demands for his or her services as a technical administrator, staff advisor, and specialty administrator will increase. Development of managerial talent is thus an important part of the individual's development program. Both the advanced and the senior warrant officer career courses stress the development of managerial talent.

No discussion of warrant officer professional development would be complete without a consideration of the Regular Army program. Like commissioned officers, other-than-RA warrant officers may apply for RA status at any time, following completion of two years of active duty. Warrant officers are automatically considered for integration into the Regular Army upon completion of 15 years service, (and three years of warrant service on current tour) There are no provisions for other-than-RA warrant officers to remain in the Army beyond 20 years' service. It is very much to the career warrant officer's advantage to apply for Regular Army status as soon as possible, since the 9,000 RA spaces are parceled out by MOS and year group. The early applicant will stand a much better chance of gaining entry into the RA than will the officer who waits for automatic consideration, by which time many more RA spaces in his or her MOS and year group are likely to have been taken. Since every career warrant officer will want to be able at least to consider remaining in the Army beyond 20 years, Regular Army integration is essential.

THE FINAL POINT

In this discussion there has been frequent reference to selection of the "best qualified" officers for assignments of the highest importance. It is entirely true that there is competition for the choice positions. It is one of several reasons our nation has such a splendid Army today, and such a fine corps of officers. But this "competition" has some points about it which need understanding. *First,* there is no favoritism, or "influence" or "Pull"; an uninformed person may attempt such pressures but they will be negative as to results. For one important reason, these choices go through many hands for evaluation and recommendation, or for concurrence in a recommended choice. *Second,* the Army is fortunate in having a wealth of talent so that the selection of the "best qualified" is made from a number of officers who are "fully qualified." *Third,* the Army is large enough, and its mission broad enough, that positions requiring the highest talents are abundant and all officers may expect to be placed in assignments which utilize their full talents, always remembering the work of the Army must be done. *Finally,* each officer has a personal responsibility in the development of his or her career. This chapter has been written to help each officer understand the importance of this point.

13

Army Schools and Career Progress

The program for training and developing the Army's leaders is the very foundation of the nation's security. Missions and weapons change. Times and requirements change. Administrations change and bring new viewpoints. Officers must be replaced continually through termination of active duty, retirement, death, or other causes. The Army faces limitless tasks during peace, in war, or the gray in-between of the cold war. It is the Army's educational system which produces the leaders with the essentials of character, knowledge, and professional skill, as well as the essential capability for growth.

ARMY EDUCATIONAL OPPORTUNITIES

This chapter is provided to disclose the scope of the total program, and to provide information to help the individual officer choose his or her own goals for military or civil school or college training. It is an essential part of career development.

It is helpful to think of the Army military and civil school and college program as having three purposes: (1) Selection and training of highly qualified young men and women to become officers; (2) development of officers to proficiency in their initial entry and additional specialties; and (3) training and development of officers who have the highest potential for the most important responsibilities of command, staff, and special fields.

Suggestion is made that this chapter be considered with Chapter twelve, *Professional Development,* and Chapter fourteen, *Evaluation Reports.* Information about The United States Military Academy, The ROTC Program, and the Officer Candidate Schools, has been placed in Chapter Ten, *The Sources of Army Officers.*

THE ARMY SCHOOL SYSTEM

Army officers receive their initial entry specialty training, following appointment as officers, at the basic course. The Advanced Course is to be completed prior to completing 8 years' service. Thereafter, if selected as best qualified, they may attend one of the intermediate and senior level courses conducted at the Army's colleges, at the colleges conducted under the supervision of the Joint Chiefs of Staff, or at the Air Force, Navy, or Marine colleges.

It is a progressive system, resembling extended postgraduate education, to prepare the required number of officers for the assignments of peace or war of greatest importance to the Army and to the nation. These courses are interspersed with assignment to duty with troops, staff, administrative, instructor, specialist, and other responsibilities.

	PROFESSIONAL MILITARY EDUCATION	SPECIALTY EDUCATION		
30				
29				
28		Additional Specialty Training		
27				
26				
25				
24				
23	Army War College National War College		Civilian	
22	Industrial College of the Armed Forces	Cooperative	and	
21	Naval War College Air War College	Degree	Military	
20	Inter-American Defense College British Royal College of Defence	Programs	Non-	Resident Civilian Education
19	Canadian National Defence College AWC Corresponding Studies Course	and	Resident	Degree Completion
18		Electives	Courses	Programs
17				
16				Doctoral Study For Selected Officers
15	Army Command and General Staff College			
14	Armed Forces Staff College			
13	Navy Command and Staff College Marine Command and Staff College			Advanced
12	Air Force Command and Staff College School of the Americas			Degree
11	CGSC Non-Resident Course			Programs
10				
9	Combined Arms and Services Staff School			Top 5% Program for USMA and ROTC
8	(CAS³)	Electives and Degree Programs Arranged With Civilian Colleges and Universities		
7				4-10 year Consideration if Performance Competitive
6				
5				
4		Skill Training: Ranger, Aviation, Airborne, etc.		
3				
2		Accession Specialty Training		
1		Basic Course		

COMMISSIONED OFFICER PROFESSIONAL EDUCATION SYSTEM.

Type of Training	Primary Zone of Consideration	Selection Criteria
MILITARY SCHOOLING		
Entry level		
—Preappointment courses; Warrant Officer Candidate courses	1–2 years prior to appointment as WO	As needed
MOS-producing courses; orientation courses; equipment or job qualification courses	0–4 years of warrant officer service	As needed
Advanced level		
—Warrant Officer Advanced Courses (WOAC)	3–9 years of warrant officer service	Top half
Senior level		
—Warrant Officer Senior Course (WOSC)	7 years of warrant officer service to: 15 years of total AFS (if OTRA), or 25 years of total AFS (if RA)	Best qualified
Functional training		
—Any course leading to skill refinement, job proficiency, equipment update, or specialty development, including MOS-producing courses taken for cross-qualification or skill progression	Throughout career	As needed
CIVIL SCHOOLING		
Fully funded		
—Advanced Degree Program (ADP). Note that this program is employed only to qualify personnel to fill AERB-validated positions.	5 years service (3 years WO service) through 23 years AFS	Best qualified
—Warrant Officer Associate Degree Program (WOADP)	5 years service (3 years WO service) through 23 years AFS	Best qualified
Partially funded		
—Degree Completion Program (DCP); nicknamed "Bootstrap"	5 years service (3 years WO service) through 23 years AFS	Best qualified
—Cooperative Degree Program (CDP)	5 years service (3 years WO service) through 23 years AFS	Best qualified
—Tuition Assistance Program (TAP)	Throughout career	As needed
Order		
—Any training required for technical proficiency that is not available in the service school system, including training with industry, courses offered by other government agencies, or specialized instruction in civilian educational institutions.	Throughout career	As needed

WARRANT OFFICER PROFESSIONAL EDUCATION AVAILABILITY.

Warrant officer military education consists of entry, advanced, and senior level training plus functional training available in various Military Occupational Specialties (MOS) throughout the officer's career. With the exception of the Warrant Officers Senior Course, which is the same for all, warrant officer training is tailored to the individual MOS or career field, and varies widely as do the duties performed by the Warrant Officer Corps. DA Pam 600-11, *Warrant Officer Professional Development,* describes the various courses available in each of the warrant officer MOS.

Attention is invited to the diagram accompanying this discussion, *Commissioned Officer Professional Education System.*

Basic Course. This is a course to prepare newly appointed commissioned officers for their first duty assignments. The emphasis is on fundamentals required at company or battery level. It includes intial entry or accession specialty training.

Advanced Course. Most commissioned officers will have opportunity to attend their advanced course during their first 8 years' service. This instruction prepares them fully for assignments pertaining to the heavier responsibilities of command, to include company command. Completion of this course is a prerequisite for consideration for the Command and General Staff College.

Combined Arms and Services Staff School (CAS^3). A course of instruction specifically designed to teach staff skills. Commissioned officers selected for attendance will be in their 7th to 9th year of active federal commissioned service. The course duration is approximately 9 weeks. CAS^3 requires a non-resident instruction phase as a prerequisite for resident attendance.

Command and General Staff College. This instruction deals with command and staff responsibilities for large units of the combined arms and with many other vital matters of major commands and staffs. It is a prerequisite for consideration for attendance at a senior service college. Selected Army commissioned officers may attend the Air Command and Staff College, the Naval College of Command and Staff, the Marine Command and Staff College or the School of the Americas in lieu of attendance at the Army's Command and General Staff College.

Armed Forces Staff College. This is a joint service school with students chosen from each of the services. It prepares commissioned officers for staff and command duty in joint and combined operations. The Army has a quota of about 180 commissioned officers who receive a military educational level credit equal to the Command and General Staff Course.

Senior Service Colleges. The Army War College, The National War College, The Industrial College of the Armed Forces, The Naval War College, The Air War College, The Inter-American Defense College, The British Royal College of Defense Studies and The Canadian National Defense College are considered senior service colleges of the same military educational level. A total of approximately 300 commissioned officers are selected to attend these colleges each year. No Army commissioned officer may attend more than one of these colleges.

Schools of Other Military Services. In order to promote better inter-service understanding, to provide the Army viewpoint and insights, and to acquire skills and specialties not taught in Army schools, selected commissioned officers are sent to various schools of the Navy, the Marine Corps, and the Air Force.

Schools of Foreign Nations. Selected commissioned officers pursue courses of instruction at schools of foreign nations. The purpose of such attendance is to afford these officers the opportunity to broaden their knowledge and experience by close relationship with the language, techniques, and staff procedures of other armies. These assignments are voluntary, and in most cases are tied to a subsequent in-country assignment.

Schools of Federal Civilian Agencies. Commissioned officers are regularly trained in the schools maintained by many civilian agencies, such as the Department of State, the Department of Labor, the Treasury Department, and the U.S. Civil Service Commission. This training is conducted under the Interagency Training Programs.

The Army Civil School Program. The Army makes extensive use of civilian colleges and universities in its program of officer training. Civilian schools augment the courses provided at Army and armed forces schools and colleges.

The general educational development of officers is conducted through off-duty academic instruction. In addition, there is a Degree Completion Program under which officers may apply to attend a civilian educational institution on permissive temporary duty (TDY) for periods up to 20 weeks, or on PCS for periods of from 20 weeks to 18 months, to satisfy degree requirements. Selections are made by the career branches.

Where a definite military requirement exists in a civilian field, selected officers are sent to civilian universities to receive the needed training. In all cases this includes a course leading to a master's or doctor's degree, followed by assignment to utilize the knowledge for the benefit of the Army. Such courses may require two years. The expenses are borne by the Army.

Officers selected for this education are required to remain on active duty for three years for each year of schooling or fraction thereof, with a maximum obligation of four years.

Language Training. Army officers are performing assignments in more than 70 foreign countries. Language fluency is essential for the effective accomplishment of many of these missions, and will be helpful in all of them. Career officers are encouraged to attain and to maintain proficiency in at least one foreign language. This instruction may be obtained by extension courses, on-duty study, and other means. The Department of Defense provides very extensive language study courses at the Defense Language Institute, Presidio of Monterey, California.

On-the-Job Training. Saved until last, and most important of all educational opportunities is on-the-job training. Here the individual officer comes to grips with a specific mission, officers and enlisted personnel with whom to work, and a series of actual problems which must be solved in infinite variety and scope. This is the testing ground.

Completion of service school courses helps greatly, of course. But in many instances the requirements of an assignment have not been covered in a school course, or its responsibilities may attain heights beyond the scope of their instructional mission. Such tasks must be learned while performing the tasks, often with little or no opportunity to prepare at all. On the highest level, consider the self-training which General Eisenhower had to complete to enable him to do his job as Supreme Commander. Or the new responsibilities thrust upon him by assuming the task of organizing the Supreme Headquarters, Allied Powers Europe. A further example was the discharge by General MacArthur of his occupation tasks in Japan. Or the ways of accomplishing his mission which had to be developed by General Bradley as first Chairman of the Joint Chiefs of Staff.

But it is not alone in these assignments of tremendous responsibility that on-the-job training is applicable. It is valuable and common all down the scale of military responsibilities. The young officer will prepare today and tonight for the tasks of tomorrow and next week; will consult noncommissioned officers who may be expert in some activity in which aid is needed; and will read, and study, and think.

There is no educational opportunity more important than that of holding the responsibility, and bending heaven and earth to do it well. This is on-the-job training, the most important of all.

Summary. The Army's system of progressive education of its officers is very extensive and very thorough. With selective assignments interspersed with service college courses, the pathway to careers of important national service is well established. This is a competitive Army, in the proper meaning of the term. Selection to attend the service colleges, and the key assignments which flow to their graduates, is on the solid basis of the "best qualified." Opportunity is abundant, but it must be won. The Army has the finest corps of officers in its history. The program of military education through the branch service schools and the service colleges deserves a fair share of the credit for this national asset.

The information for this chapter has been extracted from the official sources listed below and from discussions with knowledgeable officers:

AR 351-1, *Individual Military Education and Training.*

AR 10-41, *United States Army Training and Doctrine Command.*

AR 350–101, *Joint Colleges.*

AR 621-1, *Training of Military Personnel at Civilian Institutions.*

AR 621-7, *Acceptance of Fellowships, Scholarships or Grants.*

DA Pam 600–3, *Commissioned Officer Professional Development and Utilization.*

DA Pam 600–11, *Warrant Officer Professional Development.*

THE US ARMY BRANCH SERVICE SCHOOLS

Each branch of the Army conducts its own service school to prepare officers for branch assignments. There are also other Army service schools which are attended by officers without regard to their branch assignments, such as the US Army Aviation School, Military Assistance School, and others. For information about the several courses conducted at each school, their duration and dates of beginning, consult a unit training officer who will have available the Army Formal Schools Catalog with its latest changes.

Name and Location

US Army Adjutant Generals School, Fort Benjamin Harrison, Ind.

US Army Air Defense School, Fort Bliss, Tex.

US Army Armor School, Fort Knox, Ky.

US Army Aviation School, Fort Rucker, Ala.

US Army Chaplain School, Fort Wadsworth, N.Y.

US Army Engineer School, Fort Belvoir, Va.

US Army Field Artillery School, Fort Sill, Okla.
US Army Finance School, Fort Benjamin Harrison, Ind.
US Army Infantry School, Fort Benning, Ga.
US Army Institute of Personnel and Resources Management, Fort Benjamin Harrison, Ind.
US Army Institute/JFK Center for Military Assistance, Fort Bragg, N.C.
US Army Intelligence School, Fort Huachuca, Ariz.
US Army Judge Advocate General's School, University of Virginia, Charlottesville, Va.
US Army Logistics Management Center, Fort Lee, Va.
US Army Medical Field Service School, Fort Sam Houston, Tex.
US Army Military Police School, Fort McClellan, Ala.
US Army Missile and Munitions School, Redstone Arsenal, Ala.
US Army Ordnance School, Aberdeen Proving Ground, Maryland.
US Army Primary Helicopter School, Fort Rucker, Ala.
US Army Quartermaster School, Fort Lee, Va.
US Army Signal School, Fort Gordon, Ga.
US Army Transportation School, Fort Eustis, Va.

Branch School Courses. The branch schools of the Army, such as the Infantry School, conduct commissioned officer basic courses and advanced courses. The *Officer Basic Course* is to prepare newly commissioned officers for their first duty assignments with emphasis on leadership and on the fundamentals, weapons, equipment, and techniques required at company/battery level. Basic courses last from 9 to 19 weeks with most of the officers being on temporary duty (TDY) and billeted in BOQ's.

The *Officer Advanced Course* is for career officers who will attend while in the grade of captain. This course is to prepare commissioned officers for command. Emphasis is primarily on command with understanding of command functions, branch responsibilities of command support, and development of managerial and specialist skills. Non-active duty Reserve officers attend an advanced course. Duration of these courses requires a permanent change of station (PCS) with a variety of billeting and on- and off-post housing situations.

Warrant Officer Advanced Course. Several Warrant Officer Advanced Courses (WOAC) are available which provide mid-career level training for warrant officers. The ultimate goal is to provide WOAC training for all specialties. The training is conducted by the service schools for all specialties that are functionally or occupationally related to the skills and doctrine for which the school is the proponent.

Warrant Officer Functional Training. Functional training to obtain specific knowledge for an assignment, to obtain transitional instruction in new equipment or techniques, and to expand one's skill progression is available by taking the functional courses at the Army's service schools, listed in DA Pam 351–4, *Formal Schools Catalog.*

Army Extension Courses. Army Extension Courses provide a progressive non-resident course of instruction for personnel of all components of the Army. Courses are available from branch training level through the U.S. Army Command and General Staff College level to that of U.S. Army War College where the education includes all Services. Reserve officers are able to gain point credits for retirement and to meet certain promotion requirements.

STAFF COLLEGES OF THE ARMY AND THE ARMED FORCES

Combined Arms and Services Staff School (CAS³). All commissioned officers can expect to attend a CAS³ course of about 9 weeks duration during their 7th through 9th years of active federal commissioned service. This course is specifically designed to teach staff skills at division/installation level.

Officers through lieutenant colonel with 8–11 years of active federal commissioned service are automatically considered for attendance at an intermediate service college designed to prepare them to assume command and staff positions at battalion and brigade level. In addition to the service and grade requirements, the other prerequisite for attendance includes credit for attendance at an officer advanced course.

The U.S. Army Command and General Staff College. The C&GSC, Fort Leavenworth, Kansas, conducts the following courses:

The Command and General Staff Officer Course
The Command and General Staff Officer Course (Reserve Component)
The Command and General Staff Officer Course (Nonresident)
The Command and General Staff Officer Refresher—Division Support Command
The Command and General Staff Officer Refresher—Combat Division
The Command and General Staff Officer Refresher—Separate BDE/ACR
Battalion Command Group Refresher Course
U.S. Army Reserve Instructor Orientation Course
Allied Officer Preparatory Course
Pre-Command Course (Phase III)

The purpose of the Command and General Staff Officer Course is to prepare selected commissioned officers for duty as battalion and brigade commanders and as principal general staff officers with the Army and at all levels of the defense establishment; to provide these officers with an understanding of the functions of the Army General Staff and of major Army, joint, and combined commands; and to develop their intellectual depth and analytical ability.

The Navy, the Marine Corps and the Air Force also operate colleges equivalent to the C&GSC. Several Army commissioned officers normally are selected to attend these colleges each year.

The Armed Forces Staff College. The Armed Forces Staff College under control of the National Defense University is located at Norfolk, Virginia. The Chief of Naval Operations is charged with the responsibility for the operation and maintenance of required facilities.

Its mission is to conduct a course of study in joint and combined operations, planning and operations, and in related aspects of national and international security. It prepares selected Army, Navy, and Air Force commissioned officers for duty in all echelons of joint and combined command.

There are two courses per year, each of five months' duration, beginning about the first week of January and the first week of August. Each class numbers about 270 officers, drawn from each of the three services.

Warrant Officer Senior Course. The Warrant Officer Senior Course is open to warrant officers of all specialties and all components. It is located at Fort Rucker, Alabama, where it is conducted in the Warrant Officer Career College that is co-located with the U.S. Army Aviation School, the Commandant of which has responsibility for conduct of this training mission. The course is slightly less than six months in length, and there are two classes each year, starting in January and July. It is a PCS course and students are encouraged to bring their families.

SENIOR SERVICE COLLEGES OF THE ARMY AND THE ARMED FORCES

The Army and its sister services operate five, co-equal senior service colleges (SSCs) designed to prepare commissioned officers for command and staff duties ranging up to the highest levels within our military establishment. Attendance at one of these SSCs is on a best qualified basis, although 50% of available seats are filled based upon the Army's needs for individuals in particular specialties. Only a portion of the Army's officers can expect to attend one of these SSCs, although all should aspire to do so, since credit for attendance is required for many high-level assignments and is given due consideration by promotion boards. It is from among graduates of the SSCs that the Army's top leaders are selected.

Three of the senior service colleges are the Army War College, the Naval War College, and the Air War College, under control of their respective services. The Joint Chiefs of Staff control the National War College and the Industrial College of the Armed Forces, both subordinate elements of the National Defense University. In addition, the British Royal College of Defence, the Canadian National Defence College, and the Inter-American Defense College are considered equivalent to an SSC. An Army commissioned officer may attend only one of these colleges.

Attendance at any of the eight SSC-level colleges is upon recommendation by a DA selection board and approval by the Secretary of the Army. To be eligible for attendance, an Army commissioned officer must have completed not more than 23 years of promotion list service as of October 1 of the year the course begins; must be in the grade of lieutenant colonel through colonel as of 1 August of year of schooling; must be a graduate of, or have credit for attendance at a service college of the command and general staff level; must not have attended, nor declined to attend, any of the eight SSC-level colleges.

The U.S. Army War College. The Army War College, Carlisle Barracks, Pennsylvania, is the senior college under Army control. It prepares selected senior commissioned officers for command and high-level staff duty with emphasis on Army doctrine and operations, and it advances interdepartmental and interservice understanding.

The length of the course is 42 weeks, one course annually, starting in September. Each class consists of Army, Navy and Air Force commissioned officers, plus a few civilians from various Federal departments.

The National Defense University. The National Defense University was created by the Department of Defense in 1975. The National War College and the Industrial College of the Armed Forces, co-located at Fort McNair, Washington, D.C., are subordinate elements of the NDU, each maintaining its own mission and unique identity. The mission of the NDU is to insure excellence in professional military education in the essential elements of national security and their interrelationships, to enhance the preparation of selected personnel of the Department of Defense, Department of State, and other governmental agencies for the exercise of senior policy, command and staff functions, the planning of national strategy, and the management of resources for national security. The mission is achieved primarily through the educational programs of the National War College and the Industrial College of the Armed Forces. The National

Defense University also controls the Armed Forces Staff College at Norfolk, Virginia.

The National War College. The National War College, a component of the National Defense University, is a unique military educational institution. The NWC mission is to conduct a senior-level course of study and associated research in national security policy, with emphasis on its formulation and future directions, in order to enhance the preparation of selected personnel of the Armed Forces, the Department of State, and other U.S. Government departments and agencies for the exercise of joint and combined high-level policy, command, and staff functions in the planning and implementation of national strategy.

One class is conducted each year, usually commencing in the latter half of August, and lasting about ten months. A class normally consists of 140 students, three-fourths military and one-fourth civilian. Students are selected for assignment to the National War College by their parent organization on the basis of superior past professional performance and outstanding future potential. They are colonels or lieutenant colonels or equivalent naval ranks or civilian grades.

The Industrial College of the Armed Forces. The Industrial College of the Armed Forces is an equally unique component of the National Defense University. It is the only senior service college dedicated to the study of management of resources for national security. ICAF's mission is to conduct senior-level courses of study and associated research in the management of resources in the interest of national security in order to enhance the preparation of selected military commissioned officers and senior career civilian officials for positions of high trust in the Federal Government.

A class normally consists of about 180 students: Army, Navy, Marine, Air Force, and various governmental departments and agencies. The student composition and class size vary from year to year depending on the personnel requirements of the individual services. As with the National War College, students are selected to attend the Industrial College of the Armed Forces by their parent organization based on superior performance and future potential to hold positions of increased responsibility and high trust in the Federal Government. They are colonels or lieutenant colonels or equivalent naval ranks or civilian grades.

OPPORTUNITIES FOR ACADEMIC EDUCATION

While the completion of courses at Army schools or schools under control of the Joint Chiefs of Staff constitute the main sources of officer training, there are other important opportunities which should be understood. Officers who desire to be considered for this training as it applies to specific programs should consult the appropriate regulations and apply. Assistance may be obtained from the Training or Personnel branches of any army or unit staff.

Degree Status, Commissioned Officers of the Active Army. As pointed out in Chapter 11, *Regular Army Career,* the Army has made a determined effort to assure that its officers are highly educated. In the case of the Regular Army, this policy has resulted in more than 90% of all Regular commissioned officers possessing at least a Bachelor's degree. Approximately 25% of all career commissioned officers also have master's degrees. The actual percentage figures may be less for the active Army since it consists also of officers receiving commissions through the Officer Candidate Schools or direct battlefield appointments who may not have had an opportunity to attend college. For those commissioned officers without degrees who remain on active duty, this is a situation which can be, and generally is, remedied.

The desired goal for commissioned officers is a bachelor's (baccalaureate) degree and for warrant officers the goal is an associate degree. Those officers who do not meet these goals are strongly urged to pursue on- and off-duty courses to supplement their education. Such educational activity along with enrollment in extension courses often occasions a favorable evaluation report comment concerning self-improvement, thereby influencing selection for promotion, desirable assignments, and attendance at service schools and colleges.

Courses at Colleges and Universities. The Army provides exceptional opportunities for higher education in civilian colleges and universities.

Commissioned officers appointed into the Regular Army in recent years have been selected primarily from individuals having academic degrees. There has also been a sharp increase in the number of commissioned officers holding advanced degrees, with a continuing program for commissioned officers to pursue courses leading to the higher degrees. This is accomplished under the Advanced Degree Program wherein officers on PCS status can pursue a graduate degree for up to two full years (although normally limited to 18 months) while on full pay and allowances and with tuition and an allowance for books paid by the Army.

An Associate Degree Program is available for warrant officers. This is a fully funded program with the officer on PCS assignment and drawing full pay and allowances with the Army paying school costs. A period of up to 18 months (although normally limited to 12 months) is authorized for the warrant officer to complete the requirements for an associate degree. A limited number of warrant officers may also be authorized baccalaureate or graduate level training fo fill a handful of positions validated by the Army Education Requirements Board.

The Degree Completion Program, commonly called "Bootstrap" provides an opportunity for officers to attend a civilian college or university to complete studies for a baccalaureate degree, with temporary duty up to 20 weeks, or on PCS for periods of from 20 weeks to 18 months (12 months for warrant officers). In some cases, part of the costs will be borne by the government through veterans educational assistance programs. The Army encourages officers who are near completion of a degree to complete their studies. Funding limitations and the requirements for assignment on required missions are limiting factors for the number who can participate in the program at one time.

Attendance at civilian colleges or universities to take studies to satisfy Army requirements, culminating in a master's or doctor's degree are assignments highly sought by officers of the highest professional standing and attainments. Assignments are on the best qualified basis.

Officers selected for this education are required to remain on active duty for three years for each year of schooling or fraction thereof, with a maximum obligation of four years. Normally, the officer is assigned directly to a utilization tour of duty applicable to this education.

Officers who are interested in any phase of the civil school program are urged to consult their unit personnel officer, their specialty officer in Washington, and are referred to DA Pam 600–3 *Commissioned Officer Professional Development and Utilization* or DA Pam 600–11, *Warrant Officer Professional Development,* and the Army Regulations cited below.

The general publication of reference, which includes administrative matters, is AR 621–1, *Training of Military Personnel at Civilian Institutions.*

Training with industry in industrial procedures and practices and advanced management training programs are available to Army officers. These courses are of short duration (one year) and are not degree producing.

Officers of the several corps of the Army Medical Service have exceptional opportunities for further professional training in Army schools as well as civilian professional medical schools. Reference: AR 350–219, *Professional Training of Army Medical Department Personnel.*

Unit or station personnel officers and training officers should be consulted as to opportunities available at any particular time.

Advanced Degrees, Top 5 Percent of West Point and ROTC Graduates. AR 621–1 provides that cadets from both West Point and the ROTC entering the Regular Army who graduate in the top 5% of their classes have priority over other civilian schooling applicants and will be able to attend graduate school during their fourth through tenth years of commissioned service. The graduate schooling is authorized only in those disciplines for which the Army has a valid requirement. A maximum period of two years is allowed to complete the requirements for the advanced degree.

Advanced Degrees, ROTC Graduates. Graduates of the ROTC entering the Regular Army may delay entry on active duty for up to two years in order to obtain an advanced degree (AR 145–1).

Scholarships, Fellowships and Grants. Regular Army officers and Reserve officers in a Voluntary Indefinite category are authorized to compete for certain scholarships, fellowships and grants. Regular officers must not have more than 19 years of promotion list service and Reserve officers not more than 15 years of Federal active service at the time of commencement of the education. The academic study or grant research tours normally will not exceed 24 consecutive months, although exceptions may be authorized. See AR 621–7 for details.

Advanced Degree Program for ROTC Instructor Duty. This program is designed to increase the overall academic qualifications of all commissioned officers assigned to ROTC instructor duty, by allowing the officers to pursue advanced degrees while serving as ROTC instructors. Officers with or without a master's degree may apply. Those already having a master's degree who are accepted into the program will be assigned a three-year stabilized tour as an instructor/student. Those who do not have a master's degree will be permitted to attend advanced civil schooling for up to 15 months to obtain their degree in a shortage specialty, following which they normally are assigned as an ROTC instructor for a two-year stabilized tour. All direct schooling costs are borne by the officer, although eligible officers may use VA benefits to help defray expenses. See AR 621–101 for details.

University of Maryland Oversea Program. The University of Maryland conducts a complete program of college courses in most oversea areas.

For information concerning the University of Maryland courses, consult your local education office or write to: University College, University of Maryland, College Park, Maryland, 20740.

Extension Courses Leading to College Credits. Officers are eligible to participate in the program of Extension Courses leading to college credits which is sponsored by the Armed Forces Information and Education Program.

Off-Campus Study Programs. Those officers fortunate to be near universities and colleges that have continuing education programs can attend off-duty courses. These courses, like extension courses, can be taken to receive credits towards degrees but, unlike extension courses, are taught by professors accredited by or from the college. The local service (Army, Navy, Air Force) education office can provide information. Tuition funds are available which partially defray education costs and which incur service obligations. The Veterans Administration also provides in-service schooling benefits. (See Chapter 7, *Financial Planning.*) A Veterans' Counsellor will assist you at most colleges.

MILITARY PERIODICALS

The following list of military magazines has been included to provide Army officers with the titles of the various periodicals of special interest and value to their military education.

Air Defense Magazine, (bi-m), U.S. Army Air Defense School, Ft. Bliss, Texas 79916

American Rifleman, (m), 1600 Rhode Island Avenue, N.W., Washington, D.C., 20036

Armor, (bi-m), 1145 19th Street, N.W., Washington, D.C., 20036

Army, (m), AUSA, 1529 18th Street, N.W., Washington, D.C., 20036

Army Administrator, U.S. Army Administration Center, Ft. Benjamin Harrison, Indiana 46216

Army Aviation, (m), 1 Crestwod Road, Westport, Conn., 06880

Army Logistician, (bi-m), U.S. Army Logistics Management Center, Fort Lee, Virginia 23801

Army Finance Journal, (bi-m), P.O. Box 793, Alexandria, Va. 22313

Army Reserve Magazine, (m) OCAR, DA, Washington, D.C., 20025

Army Times, (w), 2201 M Street, N.W., Washington, D.C., 20037

Artillery Trends (q), U.S. Army Artillery and Missile School, Fort Sill, Oklahoma, 73503

Infantry Magazine, (bi-m), Box 2005, Fort Benning, Georgia, 31905

Journal of the Armed Forces, (w), 1710 Connecticut Avenue, N.W., Washington, D.C., 20009

Military Affairs, (q), American Military Institute, P.O. Box 568, Benjamin Franklin Station, Washington, D.C., 20044

Military Chaplain, (q), 7758 Wisconsin Ave., N.W., Washington, D.C. 20014

Military Chaplain Review, (q), U.S. Army Chaplain Board, Ft. Wadsworth, Staten Island, N.Y. 10305

Military Engineer, (bi-m), 800 17th Street, N.W., Washington, D.C., 20006

Military Medicine, (m), 1500 Massachusetts Avenue, N.W., Washington, D.C., 20005

Military Police Journal, (m), P.O. Box 3385, Hill Station, Augusta Ga., 30904

Military Review, (m), Command and General Staff College, Ft. Leavenworth, Kansas, 66027

National Defense Transportation Journal, (bi-m), 1612 K Street, Northwest, Washington, D.C., 20006

National Guardsman, (m), 1 Massachusetts Avenue, N.W., Washington, D.C., 20001

Officer, (m) Reserve Officers Association, 1 Constitution Ave., N.E., Washington, D.C., 20001

Ordnance, (m), American Ordnance Asso., 815 17th Street, N.W., Washington, D.C., 20006

Post Exchange and Commissary, (m), 336 Gunderson Dr., Wheaton, Ill., 60187

Signal, (m), Armed Forces Communications and Electronics Assn., 1725 Eye Street, N.W., Washington, D.C., 20006

Soldiers, (m) Cameron Station, Alexandria, Virginia, 22314

The Army Communicator, (q), U.S. Army Signal School, Ft. Gordon, Georgia 30905

The Army Trainer, (q), U.S. Army Support Training Support Center, Ft. Eustis, Virginia 23604.

The Chaplain, (q), 122 Maryland Ave., N.W., Washington, D.C. 20002

14

Evaluation Reports

The system of evaluation ratings and periodic reports on the performance of duty of each officer of the Army is of the highest importance to the Army, as to its personnel administration, and to each officer as to his or her own career development. It is a program for increasing human effectiveness. It provides better careers for Army officers, and it produces higher standards throughout the corps of officers.*

All officers aspire to a favorable record, or series of evaluation ratings, and to reach their maximum capability as their experience increases. This chapter has been developed to explain the important parts of the system, and also to suggest ways to increase the probability of receiving good reports as well as avoiding bad ones.

The main subjects discussed in this chapter are the following—
The Evaluation Report and Career Planning.
Special Thoughts Regarding Warrant Officers.
Features of the Officer Evaluation Report, DA Form 67–8, 1979.
Helpful Words for Preparing Comments.
How to Please the Boss.
Avoiding Bad Reports.
Personal Characteristics Which Influence Careers.

---

*The Army pioneered the evaluating and rating of officers. The requirement for submitting an annual efficiency report (now, evaluation report) began early in this century, with less formal letter reports in earlier periods, as illustrated at chapter end with the 1813 example. A standard rating scale was used successfully during World War I. DA Form 67–8, effective from 15 September 1979, is a direct descendant of the "Form 67," adopted soon after World War I. The form reproduced in this chapter is the eighth major revision since World War II. Each edition of *The Officer's Guide,* starting with the 3rd Edition, 1939, contains copies of the successive forms with helpful information to readers of the period covered.

Evaluation Report Appeals.
Efficiency Report, 1813 Model.

The subject of evaluation ratings has such a strong, abiding, and determinative influence upon the career of each officer, starting at his or her first assignment, that it is a wise plan to study the related subjects which are discussed in the chapters listed below: Chapter One, *The Code of the Army Officer;* Three, *The Officer Image;* Eleven, *Regular Army Career;* Twelve, *Professional Development;* Thirteen, *Army Schools and Career Progress;* and Fifteen, *Promotion.*

This chapter seeks to explain important features of the report and the accompanying regulation. It contains additional information based on experience to help officers who wish to improve their own chances of getting good reports —and avoid bad ones.

It is emphasized that this chapter is not a substitute nor a condensation of AR 623–105. Consulted also in the preparation of the chapter: DA Pam 623–105, *The Officer Evaluation Reporting System, "In Brief",* DA Pam 600–3, *Commissioned Officer Professional Development and Utilization* and DA Pam 600–11, *Warrant Officer Professional Development.* For the preparation and submission of evaluation reports, see the official regulations, always.

THE EVALUATION REPORT AND CAREER PLANNING*

The most important periodic contribution to the officer's record is the official rating and description provided by the evaluation report. This report is used in all personnel actions at Headquarters, Department of the Army, including the following important matters for each officer:

Assignments.	Regular Army integration.
Promotions.	Elimination
Selections for schools.	Others.

Unless the officer's capabilities and deficiencies are reflected accurately in evaluation reports, intelligent assignment and evaluation cannot be accomplished. Each evaluation report must contain a comprehensive, objective appraisal of an officer's abilities and capabilities. Positive recommendations for the correction of weaknesses and deficiencies, together with results of counseling by the rating officials, serve to provide a basis for comparison of future reports concerning these deficiencies.

The evaluation report requires careful consideration and thorough preparation by the rating officer and senior rater who must prepare it. Evaluation reports that are lacking in completeness, accuracy and objectivity deprive commanders and personnel action agencies of any firm basis for evaluating progressive development and may injure the individual officer.

SPECIAL THOUGHTS REGARDING WARRANT OFFICERS

All members of the evaluation chain from the individual being rated up through the rater, the intermediate rater and the senior rater, should be aware that the warrant officer is, by definition, a skilled technician, as opposed to the commissioned officer who is broadly trained. The warrant officer should be assigned to, and evaluated in light of performance of those duties associated with that officer's field of specialization. Assignment of the warrant officer to

---

*This is the substance of DA Pam 600–3, *Commissioned Officer Professional Development and Utilization,* and DA Pam 600–11, *Warrant Officer Professional Development,* as they pertain to the importance of evaluation reports.

duties outside his or her technical field is a disservice both to the individual and to the Army. Preparation of an evaluation report heavily weighted by consideration of performance of duties outside the scope of the officer's area of expertise is a great disservice to the individual.

This is not to say, however, that the warrant officer is never assigned to duties other than those described by his or her MOS. Neither does it mean that the warrant officer is not evaluated in the same light as the commissioned officer as regards possession of those characteristics and personal traits expected of an Army officer. The officer's character and personal attributes such as integrity, loyalty, dedication, perseverance, and moral courage are weighted as heavily when evaluating the warrant officer as when preparing the report for a commissioned officer. However, care should be exercised in the assignment to, and the evaluation of performance in extra duties far afield from the warrant officer's area of specialization.

Concerned individuals are urged to study AR 623–105, *Officer Evaluation Reporting System,* and DA Pam 600–11, *Warrant Officer Professional Development,* for special consideration to be given to preparation of evaluation reports on warrant officers.

FEATURES OF THE OFFICER EVALUATION REPORT, DA FORM 67-8, 1979

The evaluation procedure now used by the Army first became effective on 15 September 1979. It builds upon the best features of its predecessors, but it represents a significant change from earlier evaluation forms and procedures. The aim of the new procedure is to dampen the inflated ratings that occurred with the earlier evaluation reports, provide improved performance counseling to the rated officer, increase communications within the chain of command, and provide a better evaluation of performance and potential. A major objective of the new procedure is to increase the role of senior officers in the evaluation process.

The changed procedures should be welcomed by all officers. It has been difficult to identify the best officers within a group of superior, highly rated individuals. Selections for the most important assignments of command, staff, and technology, for the senior service colleges, and for university training to attain a master or doctor degree, are on the basis of choosing the best-qualified. Promotion to CW3 and CW4 and to commissioned grades above captain is highly competitive and also on the basis of the best-qualified. Records which facilitate wise selections are clearly essential in the interests of the officers considered, and of the Army itself.

The new evaluation procedure uses three forms. DA Form 67-8 is the Officer Evaluation Report (OER) form. An OER is prepared on each officer in the Army at least annually, or more often as prescribed by the regulations *(AR 623-105).* The completed OER is forwarded to the Department of the Army where it becomes a permanent portion of the rated officer's personnel records. The new procedure also uses a Support Form, DA Form 67-8-1, which is designed to involve the rated officer in a meaningful way in the evaluation process and to improve counseling. The third form, DA Form 67-8-2, is designed for the use by Headquarters, Department of the Army. This form is titled Senior Rater Profile Report and is provided to maintain a rating history of senior rating officials.

The new procedure uses a rater and a senior rater for the evaluation of a rated officer. In those cases where there is an intermediate level of supervision between the rater and the senior rater, provision is made for an intermediate

OFFICER EVALUATION REPORT SUPPORT FORM
For use of this form, see AR 623-105; proponent agency is US Army Military Personnel Center.

Read Privacy Act Statement and Instructions on Reverse before Completing this form.

PART I — RATED OFFICER IDENTIFICATION

NAME OF RATED OFFICER *(Last, First, MI)*	GRADE	PRINCIPAL DUTY TITLE	ORGANIZATION

PART II — RATING CHAIN — YOUR RATING CHAIN FOR THE EVALUATION PERIOD IS:

	NAME	GRADE	POSITION
RATER			
INTERMEDIATE RATER			
SENIOR RATER			

RATED OFFICER'S SPECIALTIES/MOS _____   DUTY SSI/MOS _____

PART III — RATED OFFICER *(Complete a, b and c below for this rating period)*

a. STATE YOUR SIGNIFICANT DUTIES AND RESPONSIBILITIES

b. INDICATE YOUR MAJOR PERFORMANCE OBJECTIVES

c. LIST YOUR SIGNIFICANT CONTRIBUTIONS

_____
(Signature and Date)

DA FORM 1 SEP 79 **67 — 8 — 1**

OFFICER EVALUATION REPORT SUPPORT FORM DA FORM 67–8–1

rater in the evaluation process. The rater normally is the immediate supervisor of the rated officer. The senior rater must be senior to the rater and (if any) to the intermediate rater, must have a grade of at least major, and must be at least two grades higher than the rated officer if the rated officer is a warrant officer or a commissioned officer through the grade of major. For the rating of officers in the grades of lieutenant colonel and colonel, the senior rater should be two grades higher, but circumstances may arise where a senior rater only one grade higher may be authorized. Brigadier generals and major generals must have a senior rater who is at least senior in date of rank to the rated officer, the rater, and the intermediate rater (if any). Provisions are made for civilian raters and senior raters in the regulations. If the senior rater is a civilian, then the first Army officer in the chain of command above the senior rater will provide an additional review of the completed OER, using an addendum to the report.

Rated Officer. Under the new procedure, the rated officer has two formal requirements associated with the rating process (see the copy of the Support Form, DA Form 67-8-1, accompanying this discussion).

As a rated officer, you will receive a copy of the Support Form at the beginning of each rating period. Part I of the form will be filled out identifying you as the rated officer. Part II will be partially filled out, indicating the name and position of your rater and the position of your intermediate rater (if any) and your senior rater. Within 30 days, you must initiate discussion with your rater concerning your duty description and your major performance objectives. The results of this discussion are intended to serve as a guide for your performance, but they are not necessarily all-inclusive. You also are responsible for all that is normally expected of an officer of your grade and duty position. The discussion with your rater should enable you to complete Part III of the form in draft, representing an agreement between you and your rater as to your significant duties and responsibilities and your major performance objectives. You should review these duties and objectives periodically during the rating period, including further discussions with your rater if necessary or desired, to assure that they reflect any changes in missions or emphasis.

At the end of the rating period, you will receive another copy of the OER Support Form with Parts I and II completely filled out. At this time, you will be expected to fill out Part III of the form completely, indicating not only your agreed upon duties and major performance objectives, but also your significant accomplishments and contributions. At the same time, you will receive a copy of your evaluation report, DA Form 67-8, with appropriate information in Parts I and II filled out (see the copy of DA Form 67-8 accompanying this discussion). You will be responsible for verifying the correctness of the information pertaining to you and the correct designation of your rater, intermediate rater (if any), and senior rater. If this information is correct, you sign the form in Part II. You then send both forms to the rater.

Rater. The rater is required to counsel the rated officer within 30 days of the start of the rating period as to the rated officer's major duties and responsibilities and the performance objectives for the period. At the end of the rating period, the rater then evaluates the rated officer as to his or her performance of these duties and the rated officer's potential for promotion.

As a rater, you have considerable latitude in developing the rated officer's duties and objectives. You may develop them yourself, you may develop them during your discussion with the rated officer, or you may task the rated officer to develop them. Remember, however, that the Support Form is only a guide. The rated officer is still responsible for, and should be evaluated on all that is normally expected of an officer of that grade serving in that duty position. During the rating period, you should assure that the duty description and major performance objectives of the rated officer are kept current. This periodic review affords you an excellent opportunity to coach or counsel the rated officer, and to provide him or her with the benefit of your knowledge and experience.

At the end of the rating period, you will receive the completed Support Form and the partially completed OER from the rated officer. The information on the Support Form should enable you to write a more accurate and complete OER. You should review the Support Form and sign it on the back. If the information on the form is inadequate or inaccurate, it is appropriate to discuss this with the rated officer and to suggest changes. However, you may not require the rated officer to change the information on the Support Form. You then fill out Parts III, IV and V of the OER.

Take heed that the success of the officer evaluation system depends upon the complete and accurate use of the report and the regulations governing its preparation. You must understand that the success or failure of the evaluation system depends in part upon your ability to report accurately and objectively. You should also be mindful as the report is prepared that you are helping to make a selection of the future leaders of the Army. It is a heavy responsibility of leadership. You must apply the same painstaking care in the completion of reports rendered on subordinates as you would expect in the preparation of your own reports. The rated officer is to be evaluated fairly, as an individual, based upon current grade, experience, and military schooling, in comparison with officers of similar grade.

Note that Part V of the OER is to be used to comment on the specifics of the rated officer's performance. What did the officer do and how well did he or she do it? Gimmicks such as underlining or excessive capitalization are not permitted, and generalizations that are unsupported are of no value. This is the place to "Tell it like it is". The later section in this chapter, *Helpful Words For Preparing Comments,* may assist you in preparing more accurate narrative statements for Parts IV and V. When you have completed your evaluation of the rated officer, you forward both the Support Form and the OER to the senior rater (or to the intermediate rater, if any).

Intermediate Rater. In most cases, there will be no intermediate rater. For those instances where an intermediate rater is designated, the intermediate rater will use Part VI of the OER form to comment on the rated officer's performance and potential. If there is no intermediate rater, Part VI of the form is left blank.

Senior Rater. The senior rater is responsible for both the final rating chain review of the OER and for a critical evaluation of the rated officer's potential. Part VII of the OER is reserved for the use of the senior rater.

As senior rater, you are expected to provide an objective evaluation of the performance and potential of the rated officer, based upon your additional experience, a broad organizational perspective, and your focus on organizational requirements and actual performance results. You are required to compare the potential of the rated officer against a hypothetical average population of 100 officers of the same grade. Your evaluation should recognize that across the entire officer corps, there is a normal distribution in terms of quality and potential. It is highly unlikely that all or most of the officers for whom you act as senior rater are in the top few percent of the officer corps. Your evaluation should be accurate and fair, both to the rated officer and to the Army. As with the rater, you must "Tell it like it is."

You accomplish your evaluation by placing an X in the appropriate box in the column marked SR, and your comments in Block b. Your comments generally should address the potential of the rated officer, but they may also address performance, administrative review, or the evaluations of the rater and the

For use of this form, see AR 623-105; proponent
agency is US Army Military Personnel Center.

PART I – ADMINISTRATIVE DATA

a. LAST NAME · FIRST NAME · MIDDLE INITIAL	b. SSN	c. GRADE	d. DATE OF RANK	e. BR	f. DESIGNATED SPECIALTIES	g. PMOS (WO)	h. STA CODE
			Year Month Day				

i. UNIT, ORGANIZATION, STATION, ZIP CODE OR APO, MAJOR COMMAND	j. REASON FOR SUBMISSION	k. COMD CODE

l. PERIOD COVERED						m. NO. OF MONTHS	n. MILPO CODE	o. RATED OFFICER COPY (Check one and date)	p. FORWARDING ADDRESS
FROM			THRU					1. GIVEN TO OFFICER ___	
Year	Month	Day	Year	Month	Day			2. FORWARDED TO OFFICER ___	

q. EXPLANATION OF NONRATED PERIODS

PART II – AUTHENTICATION (Rated officer signature verifies PART I data and RATING OFFICIALS ONLY)

a. NAME OF RATER (Last, First, MI)	SSN	SIGNATURE	
GRADE, BRANCH, ORGANIZATION, DUTY ASSIGNMENT			DATE

b. NAME OF INTERMEDIATE RATER (Last, First, MI)	SSN	SIGNATURE	
GRADE, BRANCH, ORGANIZATION, DUTY ASSIGNMENT			DATE

c. NAME OF SENIOR RATER (Last, First, MI)	SSN	SIGNATURE	
GRADE, BRANCH, ORGANIZATION, DUTY ASSIGNMENT			DATE

d. SIGNATURE OF RATED OFFICER	DATE	e. DATE ENTERED ON DA FORM 2·1	f. RATED OFFICER MPO INITIALS	g. SR MPO INITIALS	h. NO. OF INCL

PART III – DUTY DESCRIPTION (Rater)

a. PRINCIPAL DUTY TITLE	b. SSI/MOS

c. REFER TO PART IIIa, DA FORM 67-8-1

PART IV – PERFORMANCE EVALUATION – PROFESSIONALISM (Rater)

a. PROFESSIONAL COMPETENCE (In Items 1 through 14 below, indicate the degree of agreement with the following statements as being descriptive of the rated officer. Any comments will be reflected in b below.)

		HIGH DEGREE		LOW DEGREE	
		1	2	3	4	5
1. Possesses capacity to acquire knowledge/grasp concepts	8. Displays sound judgment					
2. Demonstrates appropriate knowledge and expertise in assigned tasks	9. Seeks self-improvement					
3. Maintains appropriate level of physical fitness	10. Is adaptable to changing situations					
4. Motivates, challenges and develops subordinates	11. Sets and enforces high standards					
5. Performs under physical and mental stress	12. Possesses military bearing and appearance ,					
6. Encourages candor and frankness in subordinates	13. Supports EO/EEO					
7. Clear and concise in written communication	14. Clear and concise in oral communication					

b. PROFESSIONAL ETHICS (Comment on any area where the rated officer is particularly outstanding or needs improvement)

1. DEDICATION
2. RESPONSIBILITY
3. LOYALTY
4. DISCIPLINE
5. INTEGRITY
6. MORAL COURAGE
7. SELFLESSNESS
8. MORAL STAND-
   ARDS

DA FORM 67-8
1 SEP 79

REPLACES DA FORM 67-7, 1 JAN 73, WHICH IS OBSOLETE, 1 NOV 79.   US ARMY OFFICER EVALUATION REPORT

OFFICER EVALUATION REPORT, DA FORM 67-8 (FRONT).

intermediate rater (if any). You then return the Support Form to the rated officer and forward the completed OER to Headquarters, Department of the Army.

At Headquarters, DA, your evaluation of the rated officer will be combined with your ratings of other officers of similar grade to produce an updated profile of your rating tendency. This profile, for officers of that grade, will be entered in Part VII of the OER by DA, providing a graphic indication of how you rated this particular officer compared to all other officers of his or her grade that you have previously rated.

Your Senior Rater Profile, DA Form 67-8-2, will be produced annually by DA, based upon the cumulative total by grades of all of your senior rater evaluations. One copy of this Senior Rater Profile is retained by DA in your personnel records and one copy is forwarded to you. The form is designed to track your rating history and to make this information available both to you and to DA,

PERIOD COVERED

PART V – PERFORMANCE AND POTENTIAL EVALUATION *(Rater)*

a. RATED OFFICER'S NAME   SSN

RATED OFFICER IS ASSIGNED IN ONE OF HIS/HER DESIGNATED SPECIALTIES/MOS   ☐ YES   ☐ NO

b. PERFORMANCE DURING THIS RATING PERIOD. REFER TO PART III, DA FORM 67—8 AND PART III a, b, AND c, DA FORM 67—8—1

☐ ALWAYS EXCEEDED REQUIREMENTS   ☐ USUALLY EXCEEDED REQUIREMENTS   ☐ MET REQUIREMENTS   ☐ OFTEN FAILED REQUIREMENTS   ☐ USUALLY FAILED REQUIREMENTS

c. COMMENT ON SPECIFIC ASPECTS OF THE PERFORMANCE. REFER TO PART III, DA FORM 67—8 AND PART III a, b, AND c, DA FORM 67—8—1. DO NOT USE FOR COMMENTS ON POTENTIAL!

d. THIS OFFICER'S POTENTIAL FOR PROMOTION TO THE NEXT HIGHER GRADE IS

☐ PROMOTE AHEAD OF CONTEMPORARIES   ☐ PROMOTE WITH CONTEMPORARIES   ☐ DO NOT PROMOTE   ☐ OTHER *(Explain below)*

e. COMMENT ON POTENTIAL

PART VI – INTERMEDIATE RATER

a. COMMENTS

PART VII – SENIOR RATER

a. POTENTIAL EVALUATION *(See Chapter 1, AR 623-105)*   b. COMMENTS

SR   DA USE ONLY

HI

LO

A COMPLETED DA FORM 67-8-1 WAS RECEIVED WITH THIS REPORT AND CONSIDERED IN MY EVALUATION AND REVIEW   ☐ YES   ☐ NO *(Explain in b)*

OFFICER EVALUATION REPORT, DA FORM 67–8 (BACK).

where it may be used by various selection boards in their consideration of how you have performed your duty. Use of the Senior Rater Profile is intended to emphasize your responsibility to provide credible evaluative information to DA. This responsibility is considered to be one of your most important, since it affects the selection of the Army's future leaders and it has a critical impact on the way the Army accomplishes its missions.

HELPFUL WORDS FOR PREPARING COMMENTS

Form 67–8, 1979, has space for the rater, the intermediate rater and the senior rater to provide narrative comments on matters not specifically covered elsewhere or to amplify other parts of the report. It is expected that the narrative will be completed within the space provided. Careful wording is required to permit cogent but full evaluation of the officer, while avoiding less meaningful but lengthier narratives. It should be clear that brevity is an objective but more important are accuracy, objectivity, fairness, and amplification or explanation of other parts of the report.

As a help to rating officers, extensive lists of words with fine shades of meaning are included for reference in preparing these accurate and descriptive narratives.

Manner (Outward Qualities). This category is self explanatory.

civil	sincere	enthusiastic	congenial
polished	sprightly	serious	frank
active	modest	composed	alert
pleasant	polite	earnest	ardent
likeable	urbane	animated	grave
forthright	energetic	unassuming	tranquil
intelligent	affable	courteous	intent
warm	attractive	suave	vivacious
sedate	candid	forceful	retiring
calm	clever	sociable	courtly
diplomatic	unresponsive	listless	rough
dynamic	uncommunicative	insensitive	vociferous
gracious	impertinent	overbearing	selfish
magnetic	languid	rude	obstinate
outspoken	unemotional	blatant	ascetic
quick-witted	abrupt	self-centered	curt
fervent	callow	assertive	frigid
solemn	strident	austere	secretive
serene	egocentric	brusque	obtrusive
urgent	dogmatic	cold	lackadaisical
spirited	stern	reserved	harsh
shy	blunt	meddlesome	disdainful
positive	indifferent	spiritless	crude
severe	reticent	unfeeling	boisterous
bluff	officious	supercilious	egotistical

Presence (Outward Qualities). This is the unit mental impression that certain officers produce on others. Occasionally an officer will have a real and definite presence which can be summed up in one word, such as attractive. However, it must be recognized that this presence—so called—is often compounded of minor personality traits which make a definite and unit impression on the observer. In such cases often the better way of summing up the officer is to ascertain by analysis what these minor traits are and then list them.

On the other hand, an officer's presence may be characterized by some outstanding trait which everyone at first contact recognizes and thereafter, consciously or unconsciously, mentally affixes to the officer. In this respect, note the word "slovenly." Compare this word with the word "impressive." What causes an officer to give a slovenly impression could easily be listed but is not necessary. The word "slovenly" is sufficient. But what makes the officer impressive is often baffling and not easily ascertained without study, nor does the word carry a clear image to the reader. Therefore it may be necessary at times to analyze and list the qualities that make the individual impressive. However, proper selection of words under other headings will round out this picture.

dignified	stately	grand	impressive
commanding	noble	august	majestic
well-balanced	attractive	distinguished	magnificent
neat	trim	trig	immaculate
dapper	tidy	spruce	jaunty
well-mannered	well-bred	inspiring	magnetic
staid	sober	somber	severe
undignified	unbecoming	unseemly	indecorous
fastidious	dandyish	finical	foppish
careless	untidy	slipshod	slovenly
unimpressive	undistinguished	uninspiring	colorless
unattractive	repelling	disagreeable	odious
showy	pretentious	ostentatious	pompous
odd	eccentric	erratic	queer

Disposition (Outward qualities generally denoting possession of inward mental or emotional traits). An officer possessing one or more of these qualities may impress the rating officer favorably or unfavorably, but this is not to be taken as a sign that the officer is what he or she appears on the surface. Do not rate personality or character on these surface qualities alone. The rating officer should not make long mental jumps and conclude that an officer outwardly reflects inward qualities—though quite often this is true. For instance a cheerful, tactful person with a generous disposition may be all that he or she seems and yet in character be weak, cautious, and disloyal when pressure is put on. Again a person may have none of the finer inward qualities that certain outward qualities suggest, but is using them for a front—consciously or unconsciously. At the same time a morose, gloomy individual who has occasional periods of irritation may be steady, thoroughly loyal, with a high degree of moral courage, and absolutely trustworthy. Yet too often such an individual will not receive credit for his or her sterling worth.

tactful	courteous	considerate	attentive
liberal	generous	bountiful	magnanimous
friendly	sympathetic	cordial	genial
unselfish	kindly	cooperative	helpful
considerate	benign	thoughtful	sympathetic
agreeable	conciliatory	helpful	cooperative
kind	good-tempered	patient	forbearing
cheerful	happy	light-hearted	joyful
gay	merry	jovial	blithe
compliant	submissive	humble	meek
complaisant	good-natured	amiable	obliging
animated	spirited	vivacious	impulsive
sensitive	high-strung	mercurial	excitable
phlegmatic	indifferent	spiritless	insipid
bland	mild	placid	quiet
charitable	benevolent	lenient	indulgent
guileless	innocent	credulous	gullible
self-complacent	self-centered	conceited	vain
discontented	complaining	fault-finding	hypercritical
peevish	irritable	querulous	resentful
testy	touchy	cross	petulant
cranky	irascible	choleric	splenetic
moody	down-hearted	melancholic	pessimistic
gloomy	glum	morose	sullen
gruff	surly	crabbed	saturnine
proud	haughty	arrogant	imperious
fierce	truculent	ferocious	barbarous

Character (Inward traits, to be learned only after long and close association). A person's character is his or her most precious asset. Too much care cannot be taken in selecting the exact words to describe it. One can make a mistake in describing other personal attributes and the harm will not be so great, but no mistake can be tolerated here. Unless the rating officer knows the subordinate's character he or she should not attempt to use this word. One should confine oneself to the things one knows. These would certainly be manner, presence, disposition, mentality, and the like.

brave	courageous	valiant	dauntless
firm	unswerving	determined	resolute
strong	stout	stalwart	tenacious
stable	steady	dependable	trustworthy
constant	faithful	loyal	steadfast
aggressive	assertive	dominating	militant
upright	honest	scrupulous	honorable
unselfish	altruistic	self-sacrificing	self-less
praiseworthy	exemplary	magnanimous	noble
sincere	conscientious	earnest	zealous
cautious	circumspect	prudent	discreet
unbiased	open-minded	forbearing	tolerant
fair	unprejudiced	just	impartial
spontaneous	impulsive	instinctive	automatic
bold	venturesome	daring	audacious
plastic	pliant	pliable	adaptable
rash	reckless	foolhardy	temerarious
imperious	domineering	peremptory	imperative
positive	dogmatic	assertive	arbitrary
opinionated	stubborn	prejudiced	obstinate
biased	narrow-minded	intolerant	bigoted
indecisive	capricious	vacillating	weak
inattentive	careless	heedless	imprudent
impractical	idealistic	dreamer	visionary
narrow	egocentric	self-centered	selfish
irresolute	unsteady	timorous	timid
inconstant	fickle	evasive	unstable
limp	lax	flabby	flaccid
critical	captious	caviling	censorious
uneasy	restless	impatient	fidgety
superficial	shallow	simple	crass
time-serving	obsequious	subservient	menial
untrustworthy	disloyal	faithless	perfidious

loyal (to superiors; to subordinates): unquestioned, excellent, good, average, fair, indifferent, poor. (seeks, avoids, accepts): *responsibility.*

Mentality (Type of, and ability to use intellectual equipment).

imaginative	independent thinker	original thinker	creative
analytical	judicious	discerning	discriminating
bright	sparkling	brilliant	scintillating
shrewd	sagacious	perspicacious	astute
sensible	sane	sage	wise
keen	sharp	smart	acute
ingenious	brainy	intellectual	intelligent
piercing	penetrating	deep	profound
many-sided	well-rounded	balanced	versatile
logical	level-headed	long-headed	farsighted
careful	reliable	deliberate	mature
watchful	wideawake	alert	vigilant
apt	agile-minded	quick thinker	quick-witted
practical	sound	hard-headed	realistic
precise	exact	mathematical	unequivocal
humorous	witty	facetious	jocose
expedient	politic	adroit	clever
theoretical	academic	formalistic	impractical
medium	normal	average	ordinary
artful	cunning	calculating	knowing
cursory	superficial	shallow	careless
undistinguished	mediocre	second-rate	inferior
rigid-minded	inflexible	unimaginative	one-track mind
inept	insipid	banal	inane
sluggish	dull	obtuse	stupid
erratic	eccentric	abnormal	queer

Knowledge (By knowledge is meant the amount of subject matter an individual possesses, and not necessarily his or her ability to use it. Knowledge should not be mistaken for intelligence or wisdom).

well-informed	erudite	scholarly	learned
conversant	cultivated	enlightened	educated
talented	endowed	gifted	accomplished
well-grounded	well-read	well-versed	well-instructed
thorough	broad	deep	profound
skilled	proficient	adept	expert

articulate	literate	lettered	studious
didactic	formal	pedantic	bookish
credible	colorable	plausible	specious
unsophisticated	artless	naive	simple
dilettante	dabbler	smatterer	half-scholar
tyro	neophyte	beginner	amateur
inexperienced	immature	undeveloped	limited
untrained	unprepared	uninstructed	untaught
cursory	unwitting	superficial	shallow
unread	unscholarly	unversed	illiterate
uninformed	unlettered	unlearned	ignorant
dense	thick	crass	stupid

informed: (highly, well, moderately, poorly) on (world affairs, professional affairs, cultural matters,————).

Application (An emotional quality, the product of many factors, which manifests itself in the way the individual attacks and carries through his or her problem or duties).

zealous	enthusiastic	ardent	fervent
faithful	loyal	resolute	steadfast
persistent	tenacious	enduring	unremitting
attentive	persevering	diligent	devoted
industrious	painstaking	assiduous	sedulous
punctilious	careful	meticulous	scrupulous
vigorous	energetic	arduous	forceful
decided	determined	unwavering	steady
tireless	untiring	unwearying	constant
thorough	methodical	systematic	precise
quick	prompt	ready	apt
fast	rapid	swift	speedy
unhurried	ponderous	slow	sluggish
intermittent	fluctuating	wavering	vacillating
fitful	spasmodic	delaying	procrastinating
listless	lethargic	indolent	lazy
disinclined	reluctant	unwilling	averse
inattentive	indifferent	careless	slack
lax	negligent	neglectful	remiss

Results (Degree, kind, or type of results obtained).

outstanding	remarkable	extraordinary	superior
exemplary	inimitable	unequalled	unparalleled
valuable	decisive	invaluable	priceless
creditable	laudable	praiseworthy	commendable
sure	certain	positive	infallible
unfailing	invariable	indisputable	indubitable
prominent	signal	striking	conspicuous
undoubted	assured	unquestionable	unmistakable
apparent	evident	manifest	patent
plain	clear	distinct	obvious
dependable	reliable	trustworthy	meritorious
efficacious	effectual	effective	efficient
unusual	uncommon	noticeable	choice
first-class	excellent	splendid	admirable
advantageous	profitable	worthy	beneficial
firm	substantial	enduring	permanent
precise	correct	accurate	exact
favorable	competent	conclusive	successful
useful	dependable	presentable	adequate
good	moderate	satisfactory	acceptable
mediocre	average	ordinary	undistinguished
fair	questionable	passable	admissable
vague	ambiguous	equivocal	obscure
uncertain	questionable	doubtful	dubious
undependable	unreliable	untrustworthy	unsatisfactory
imperfect	unavailing	incompetent	inadequate
inaccurate	incorrect	faulty	unsound
second-rate	below par	valueless	futile
ineffective	ineffectual	inefficient	useless
bad	defective	worthless	execrable

HOW TO PLEASE THE "BOSS"

It is a fact that the military leader must be pleased with the work of an officer, and satisfied with that officer's personal standards of conduct, before signing an evaluation report containing numerous flattering entries.

There are some very human and common sense elements to be considered about earning good evaluation reports, as there are also in avoiding bad ones. We shall discuss some important ones. But first, let us be sure one fact is clearly understood: *The boss will be pleased only when there has been effective execution of duty throughout the period. Make no mistake about that.* Our subject has nothing whatever to do with laughing at poor jokes, dating an unattractive daughter, subservient actions, or unworthy efforts to avoid the results of poor work.

How the Junior Should Treat His or Her Senior. Much has been written about the way a senior officer should treat junior officers and soldiers. Now we seek to put the shoe on the other foot. Beyond the conventional prescribed actions and attitude, how should the junior officer treat a senior?

Treat your commander or chief, your boss, as a man or woman. At the same time do your own part of acting as an adult. You are both mature, trained officials of government. The junior officer is not a child standing in the presence of a stern parent, nor an ignorant tyro facing a person of unique skill. You are a capable officer of one grade, presumably, associated in a joint undertaking with a more experienced officer who holds a higher grade, or higher relative rank. In most cases a senior will be older in years. Treat your chief honorably and respectfully behind his or her back as well as face-to-face. Be business-like. Stand on your own feet.

Respect the authority of your commander. Understand his or her mission and responsibilities, for your own will be a fraction of the total. Your commander's success depends, in part, upon the results of your work. Teamwork means harmonious effort with all members of the organization—not just with the boss.

Keep your chief informed. Give him or her the information needed as to your own progress and give it straight, clear, on time. Don't conceal bad news, nor try to slip it past. Don't embellish the good news. Your chief needs essential facts for his or her own planning, and for coordination with other subordinates. There are few furies equal to that of a military leader who makes a wrong decision which was based with logic upon incorrect or misleading reports of a subordinate.

Apply standard military courtesies and customs of the service, neither overdrawn nor underdrawn. Know these things and apply them sensibly. Let the chief set the pace in the degree of formality or informality of routine, official contacts. Especially let this be the case as to outside-of-duty relationships. In these latter contacts a chief may call you "Bob," but be certain to address him or her as "Captain." Extending compliments to your chief is in poor taste, and will be so regarded. Don't do it! These are very important goals and this brief discussion of common sense matters of military courtesy deserve careful compliance.

Know your chief's military and personal background. Identify his or her human likes and dislikes. Commanders are human, to the same degree as subordinates. Be attuned, or responsive, to these characteristics of your chief, as you also avoid acts or mannerisms which serve no real purpose which you learn are upsetting to your "boss." An understanding of the person for whom you work is helpful in developing a proper teamwork.

Some commanders issue broad, mission-type orders and encourage subordinates to exercise considerable latitude as to method or procedure for execution. Others give detailed instructions which they wish followed meticulously. Do not take advantage of the one with unnecessary delay, or a bit of laziness;

and don't rebel at the latter because you prefer your chief to work with a looser rein. In fact, don't fight this problem at all. Learn what the chief wants, and conform to it.

Engrave in your mind: You are a part of your commander's team, not he or she of yours. You are the head of your own team, with your own subordinates. Develop your team wisely.

Bed Rock Qualities to Win Good Reports. This is an era during which officers strive to complete their studies for an academic degree, earn a higher degree, and especially to complete the courses at service schools and colleges for which they are eligible. These are very important goals and this brief discussion does not belittle them. But there are other essential factors, and in the zeal to earn degrees and attend service schools let them be remembered.

Commanders charged with heavy responsibilities are deeply interested in the capabilities of each officer within their command jurisdictions. They want to know the past record and the full background of each officer so they may make a reliable estimate today of how well each officer may be expected to produce results on the hard missions of tomorrow. This fact penetrates to the bed rock of a rating officer's evaluation of subordinates.

The commander will give great consideration to each officer's I CAN (confidence), and to the officer's I WILL (determination). The finest education and the highest achievements of training must be accompanied by an outstanding philosophy of I CAN and I WILL, lest the first named goals be diluted. Furthermore, the successful commander will strive to guide and to inspire subordinates of all grades so as to create confidence and determination in the minds and hearts of those who look to him or her for leadership.

These are factors to be considered by the officer who strives to win outstanding reports as well as by the officer who prepares them.

AVOIDING BAD REPORTS

It is not sufficient to strive through job performance to obtain good evaluation reports. You must also strive to avoid bad evaluation reports. About this latter we can be very precise. Officers may be accorded preferment on the intangibles of faith, confidence, and the like. But they are punished, eliminated, or held back in many cases by definite acts of transgression or shortcomings. Stated below is a summary of those shortcomings which can mar and injure a record otherwise filled with many examples of achievement. Therefore, a guide to the avoidance of bad evaluation reports is quite easy to prepare: Conduct yourself in such a manner as to avoid the likelihood of any of the following things appearing on your evaluation reports or in your other military records.

Shortcomings in Personal Conduct. These shortcomings can be identified and corrected.

Intemperance in the Use of Liquor. Excessive drinking, or the results thereof, probably has ruined the careers of more officers than any other single cause. Drinking to any degree of intoxication while on duty is punishable and can reflect severely upon an officer's record. Similar results can obtain as a result of excessive drinking when off-duty, particularly when your resultant behavior reflects on the service, or your intemperance lowers your following performance of duty. The single beer at noon can develop into a martini. Remember that it is far easier not to start a bad habit than to stop one, and that it is easier to avoid a bad episode than to undo one. Few commanders or seniors of any grade insist upon their officers being teetotalers with respect to this matter. Rather, they will expect that there will be about the same percentage of users and abstainers as in our general population. An officer who wishes to remain in the Army and enjoy a successful career, however, must avoid excesses in use of liquor and avoid permitting its immoderate use to reduce the effectiveness of his or her work or warrant criticism for personal conduct.

Financial Difficulties. Officers have the same sort of family and personal financial responsibilities and difficulties as other citizens. It is not to be expected that many officers will avoid debt at one time or another or many times in their lives. Debt is credit and a standard practice in our economy. Trouble arises when the officer assumes greater obligations than he or she can discharge within the time limit of the agreement to pay. When debts have not been paid when due, it is a frequent practice for merchants to write to the commander, or to The Adjutant General, and ask assistance in making the collection. The receipt of a number of such letters is very harmful to the reputation of an officer. It indicates a deficiency in conducting personal affairs and implies a weakness in ability to administer affairs of the Army.

Avoid financial difficulties! Live within your income—with some to spare, if possible. Maintain close scrutiny of your spouse's checkbook as well as your own and avoid writing checks on the assumption that, "The money will be in the bank by the time the check clears." Should you for some reason become submerged in debt, make an exact list of the indebtedness; go to your creditors and seek to arrange a plan of payment which is agreeable to them and within your means. If complaints are likely to be filed, go to your commanding officer and lay the cards on the table. He or she may be able to suggest to you a solution. At least your commander will know that your intentions are honorable.

The Army cannot permit its officers to acquire a general reputation of being poor credit risks for such a condition would reflect upon all who wear the uniform. Such action uncurbed in a few officers would harm the general credit standing of all. The officer in debt must have a definite understanding with creditors as to when and how much he or she can pay on overdue accounts. Having reached such an agreement the officer must meet these obligations or negotiate a new understanding. The worst action the officer can take is to permit the creditor to reach a conclusion that the debtor seeks to evade an honest and just debt. More than a few officers over a period of years are considered for elimination because they have failed to observe these simple practices.

Transgressions of Moral Codes. Such transgressions constitute another avenue to evaluation report difficulties. For the male officer, be honorable in your dealings with all women. Avoid association with known prostitutes; such association is crude and indicative of a lack of moral strength befitting an officer. Avoid also entanglements with other men's wives; treat all women as you would like your wife or your sister to be treated. The shadows of venereal disease, divorce, contempt of one's fellow officers, and disciplinary action overhang all immoral associations. A similar admonition is appropriate for female officers as relates to their associations. Rating officers generally will comment adversely upon officers who have openly and flagrantly violated the codes of conduct, or do so under conditions which bring discredit upon an organization or group of officers.

Closely akin to this situation is gross vulgarity or obscenity in any form. By definition, an officer is a gentleman or a lady and is expected to avoid the use of coarse, crude, or vulgar language. Habitual use of vulgarity indicates first that the person speaking is too lazy to search for the right descriptive word and second that the person speaking is no gentleman or lady. Avoid the use of vulgarity yourself and avoid continual association with vulgar persons. Neither can do your reputation nor your evaluation report any good.

Officers are expected to be gentlemen or ladies in their personal as well as their official conduct. Low evaluation ratings inevitably will follow transgression of moral codes.

Violations of Honor. An officer's word, signature, or initials of concurrence must be backed by facts, accuracy, honor. There must never be a doubt as to the truth of any statement which bears his or her authentication. The officer's oral or written word is his or her bond. If your statements either written or oral, contain opinions as well as facts, take care to identify the opinions for what they are.

The acceptance of an officer as an honorable individual by all who meet or know him or her is traditional in the Army. Thus it has always been and thus it must always be if the Army is to retain its status as a reliable instrument to implement national policy. It goes without further emphasis that acts of deliberate cheating, lying, or quibbling cannot be condoned. Violations of honor will be noted on the evaluation report or in other records.

Misconduct. Misconduct or misuse of official position are items which surely will affect both the evaluation report and the reputation of an officer; serious frauds, minor acts for personal gain, personal use of government property, abuse of privileges, rowdy or disorderly conduct, are examples of these weaknesses.

PERSONAL CHARACTERISTICS WHICH INFLUENCE CAREERS

Officers and soldiers of the great Army of today have the same human aspirations, likes and dislikes, strengths and frailties, as they had a decade or ten decades ago. All are responsive to human appeals, and some are prone to succumb to human temptations. Listed below are a number of human characteristics, or qualities, which are especially worthy of consideration. It is people who make the Army, and people who win its victories. Human relationships are important, always*.

Guidelines. *Be Strong on Principle.* This lets people know where you stand. It helps create a feeling of confidence among associates.

Be Cool-Headed. Learn the facts, establish the truth, then stand up and be heard. These are the individuals who are sought out for the preferred assignments.

Be Willing to Adjust. Without compromising mission or basic issues, there is the need to hear and consider the views of others or the interests of others. This often involves negotiation or adjustment in order to gain understanding and agreement.

Be Certain to Preserve Unity. Disrespect and distrust develop disunity, and disunity invites defeat. Recognize and treat with respect members of the sister services. Recognize as fact that other branches of the Army than your own are important and treat their members with the respect which is their due. Let there be an end to slanderous accusations of those who serve in forward areas directed against those in rear areas; all serve where ordered. The good officer builds unity.

---

*Chapter 3, *The Officer Image,* is commended for further study as to the importance to a career, and to evaluation reports, of the impressions formed in the minds of others.

Don't Be a Die-hard. Be not the last to identify a truth or adopt the new. While a military leader must often follow the hard right instead of the easy wrong, there can be avoidance of sheer bullheadedness. (A bullheaded person has been defined, we wish we knew by whom, as a person with very determined ideas, many of them unsound, to which he or she clings with more than usual tenacity.)

But Don't Be a Timid Soul. Don't fear to advance your considered views, or to take issue, or point out a fault, just for fear of causing annoyance. Don't go along with the crowd for fear of expressing a contrary view. Don't hold back to let another grasp the lead. The retiring person on the fringe of discussion, who may have the skill to reason to sound conclusions but lacks the fortitude to express or defend them, will have no influence on history or the outcome of battles.

Nor a Know-it-all. On a par of ineffectiveness with the timid soul is the know-it-all, or wise guy, who has a glib solution to all problems with or without knowledge of the subject or time for consideration. In a meeting this person is the one to advance an immediate solution without waiting to hear the facts bearing upon the problem. "Off with his head," before hearing the evidence. Or, if a platoon leader, such an individual may direct an unwise action because he or she failed to explain the task and listen to the suggestions of the NCOs. Neither the Timid Soul or the Wise Guy will have much if any influence on history. The former will supply nothing, either good or bad; but the latter may do much harm until his or her associates learn better. Aggressive advancement of hasty conclusions may sound plausible and be adopted only to develop the bugs at a later time.*

Seek the Loyalty of Subordinates. It is not enough to seek it, this loyalty; you must earn it. Fair treatment and the human touch will help. If there is something good to which your soldiers are entitled, and are not getting, go after it and get it. Stand up for your troops or for your employees. While you are not to conceal their transgressions, nor let offenses go unpunished, you can certainly identify and encourage their strengths. Be the first to get the full share of improved facilities for living, for work or recreation, if you can, and seek opportunities for your subordinates to advance their own goals. When the "boss" does these things his or her rewards may be abundant. And when he or she fails to do so the penalties may be severe. When subordinates have thoughtful reason to respect and trust their commander, or chief, the results can become important.

Associate with the "Comers." It is a good idea to identify the officers of an organization who stand high officially, have attained a promising record, and seem destined to go forward rapidly. They are the ones worth knowing. They should be the most interesting associates, too, because of their probable breadth of experience and knowledge. Have a wide acquaintance, of course, and seek to gain the good will, trust and respect of all. But identify yourself more closely with those whom you consider to be headed for big and interesting things.

Avoid the Political. Be somewhat guarded in your political comments. Offic-

---

*Attributed to General Freiherr von Hammerstein-Equord of the German Army of pre-World War I, is the following advice about officer classification. Officer's Guide is pleased to perpetuate it. "I divide my officers into four classes as follows: The clever, the industrious, the lazy, and the stupid. Each officer always possesses two of these qualities. Those who are clever and industrious I appoint to the General Staff. Use can under certain circumstances be made of those who are stupid and lazy. The man who is clever and lazy qualifies for the highest leadership posts. He has the requisite nerves and the mental clarity for difficult decisions. But whoever is stupid and industrious must be got rid of, for he is too dangerous."

ers are entitled to have as firm opinions on matters of politics and national policy as any citizen. They have the same right and duty to vote to record their convictions. But it is unwise for officers to become too plainspoken in approval or disapproval of either political party, or of the leading members of either party. Indeed, officers are prohibited from using disrespectful language about government officials, for which see Chapter Twenty-four, *Rights, Privileges and Restrictions.* Army officers serve in turn Democrat administrations and Republican administrations. Soldiers must be non-political and serve each with equal zeal. The higher the grade they achieve, the more important becomes this caution.

The "First Name" Problem. There has developed in the Army an excessive use of first names by seniors to juniors, officer to officer, even officer to soldier. The problem deserves consideration.

In the prescribed uses of military courtesy members of the service are addressed by their proper titles on all official occasions. On social occasions the practice would be governed by good taste. In athletic sports, or hunting or fishing trips, and activities wholly unconnected with official relationships it is merely two or more kindred spirits out for the enjoyment of a hobby. This paragraph pertains to the use of first names on official duty.

This is not to advocate the "Stuffed shirt" attitude, nor the martinet. It states a principle with which you can live. As leaders officers have stern duties involving discipline, reward and punishment, selections for promotion, selections for favored assignment or hazardous duty. *Officers must never play favorites nor by their actions permit the suspicion that they are doing so.* Officers simply cannot be on terms of personal familiarity today, and tomorrow, when duty requires that they admonish an individual, revert to the official title.

There is just one rule to follow on this first name business in official relationships: *Don't use it.*

Influence of the Officer's Spouse and Family. A spouse's attitude and conduct within the military or civilian community in which the officer performs his or her duties may have a profound bearing upon the member's effectiveness. If the spouse exerts a wholesome, normal, pleasant influence, he or she will meet the basic standard. There are some assignments involving extensive semi-official relations with others not in our own service where the role of the spouse is extremely important. A helpful reference is Chapter Six, *The Social Side of Army Life.* Objectionable incidents may nullify an officer's otherwise outstanding record.

Conclusion. We seek through the above illustrations of common traits of the good and bad variety to illustrate a principle. Military reputations are not built alone on schools attended, battles fought, or assignments held satisfactorily. There are important personal factors. As the officer builds a personal reputation he or she should be mindful of them.

EVALUATION REPORT APPEALS

An officer may discover upon reviewing the evaluation report file that some administrative error was made. In such a case, the officer may file an appeal in the form of a military letter, in duplicate, addressed to HQDA, (DAPC-POR-EA), Alexandria, Virginia 22332. This is MILPERCEN, located at 200 Stovall Street in Alexandria. If the appeal concerns the substance of the report, it must be accompanied by substantial evidence in support of the appeal. This substantial evidence can be in the form of documentary evidence from official sources and/or sworn statements by third parties who were in official positions which enabled them to observe directly the manner of performance of duties during the rated period by the officer concerned.

Appeals are screened by, and those based on a claim of administrative error are resolved by, MILPERCEN. Other appeals are forwarded through the officer's specialty manager to a Special Review Board. The Board determines if the claim has foundation and decides what corrective action, if any, is warranted. The Board may instruct MILPERCEN to leave the report in the officer's file or amend it or delete it as deemed appropriate. MILPERCEN will notify the officer of the decision on the appeal. All appeals should be submitted within five years of the "thru" date reflected on the DA Form 67–8 concerned.

AR 624–100 provides that an officer within a zone of consideration for promotion may write a letter to the selection board inviting attention to any matter of record in DA concerning himself or herself which the member feels important. Priorities for processing are established in accordance with paragraph 9-6, AR 623-105.

EFFICIENCY REPORT, 1813 MODEL

This 1813 example of an Army efficiency report is authentic. It was printed in *The Adjutant General's Bulletin, 1942,* and has been reproduced in many editions of *The Army Officer's Guide.* Although it is an amusing throwback to our early years, it separates the good ones from the bad ones, and the very good ones from the merely acceptable. This rating officer described his officers with accuracy, precision, candor. It is an example of accurate, colorful observation worthy of retention and consideration.

"Lower Seneca Town, August 15th, 1813.

Sir:

I forward a list of the officers of the —th Regt. of Infty. arranged agreeable to rank. Annexed thereto you will find all the observations I deem necessary to make.

Respectfully, I am, Sir,

Yo. Obt. Sevt.,

Lewis Cass"

—th Regt. Infantry

Alexander Brown—Lt. Col., Comdg.—A good natured man.
Clark Crowell—first Major—A good man, but no officer.
Jess B. Wordsworth—2nd Major—An excellent officer.
Captain Shaw—A man of whom all unite in speaking ill—A knave despised by all.
Captain Thomas Lord—Indifferent, but promises well.
Captain Rockwell—An officer of capacity, but imprudent and a man of violent passions.

Captain Dan I. Ware
Captain Parker   Strangers but little known in the regiment.

1st Lt. Jas. Kearns
1st Lt. Thomas Dearfoot   Merely good—nothing promising.

1st Lt. Wm. Herring
1st Lt. Danl. Land   Low, vulgar men, with the exception of Herring. From the
1st Lt. Jas. I. Bryan   meanest walks of life—possessing nothing of the char-
1st Lt. Robert McKewell   acter of officers and gentlemen.
1st Lt. Robert Cross—Willing enough—has much to learn—with small capacity.
2nd Lt. Nicholas Farmer—A good officer, but drinks hard and disgraces himself and the Service.
2nd Lt. Stewart Berry—An ignorant unoffending fellow.
2nd Lt. Darrow—Just joined the Regiment—of fine appearance.
2nd Lt. Pierce
2nd Lt. Thos. G. Slicer   Raised from the ranks, but all behave well and promise to
2nd Lt. Oliver Warren   make excellent officers.
2nd Lt. Royal Gore
2nd Lt. Means   All promoted from the ranks, low, vulgar men, without one
2nd Lt. Clew   qualification to recommend them—more fit to carry the
2nd Lt. McLear   hod than the epaulette.

2nd Lt. John G. Sheaffer
2nd Lt. Francis T. Whelan   Promoted from the ranks. Behave well and will make good
                                                  officers.

Ensign Behan—The very dregs of the earth. Unfit for anything under heaven. God only knows how the poor thing got an appointment.

Ensign John Breen
Ensign Byor   Promoted from the ranks—men of no manner and no promise.

Ensign North—From the ranks. A good young man who does well.

A fitting conclusion for this chapter, which succinctly states the case for striving to receive a series of commendable evaluation reports, is the following quotation from *The Rubaiyat* of Omar Khayyam.

> *The Moving Finger writes; and, having writ*
> *Moves on: nor all thy Piety nor Wit*
> *Shall lure it back to cancel half a Line,*
> *Nor all thy tears wash out a word of it.*
> —The Rubaiyat.

15
Promotion

The Army uses a very sound promotion system. Officers who meet the standards, and most do so, are justified in believing that their future promotions will be spaced to provide a rewarding career. At the same time, the work of the Army must be done, and its promotion system must and does provide the flow of trained and ready officers to move into higher and higher responsibilities. These future leaders must be identified, trained and finally provided with the degree of authority which each will need to discharge greater responsibility and authority. Training of good officers through schools and successive selected assignments is the justification for promotion so that good men and women will be ready when needed.

The Army promotion system for commissioned officers operates in accordance with the provisions of the Defense Officer Personnel Management Act (DOPMA), which became effective on 15 September 1981. DOPMA applies equally to all the military services and, for the first time, brings the promotion systems of all the services under a common set of guidelines. Henceforth, an Army officer can expect to be advanced at about the same rate as his or her counterpart in the Navy or the Air Force. DOPMA applies only to commissioned officers. Warrant officers are still promoted under the previous system of temporary and permanent grades.

For the Army, DOPMA establishes a single promotion system for all active duty commissioned officers, be they Regular or Reserve, and it eliminates any distinctions, real or perceived, that may have existed previously between male and female officers as regards promotion. All of the active Army's commissioned officers are treated equally under DOPMA.

The intent of DOPMA is to encourage a career commissioned officer corps of Regulars. Toward this goal, the DOPMA law increased the authorized size of the Army's corps of Regular officers to 63,000, and authorized the Army to establish an all-Regular commissioned officer force beyond the eleventh year of service.

This chapter explains the system of promotion as an aid to the officer who seeks the full attainment of the rewarding service which the Army provides its members. The chapter is based upon AR 624–100.

GOALS OF A SOUND PROMOTION SYSTEM

The system of selection for promotion in use by the Army is of the highest importance. Unless it causes the best officers to reach the positions of importance and highest responsibility, the mission of the Army as well as the security of the nation is endangered. Unless officers are satisfied that hard work and achievement will place them in line for promotion, and that a reasonable career expectancy as to promotion may be anticipated, they cannot be satisfied fully with their choice of vocation. The present system of promotion is considered to be an equitable program, fair to the government, and fair to individual officers. Only wartime promotion actions should change such a system; and then only to hasten decision through decentralization or to include other promotion authorizations made advisable by circumstances.

These are its goals:

To provide career incentives so as to draw men and women of high potential into the corps of officers of the Army.

To retain the officers of high potential, in willing, career-duration service, including those who possess special training for new or swiftly developing programs.

To advance to the higher grades during the peak years of their effectiveness the best qualified officers according to their achievement records.

To give promotion opportunity to officers of all branches and specialties.

To provide equality of promotion opportunity among officers of the Active Army.

To eliminate the ineffective officers, as they show themselves to be below standard, as early as such a determination may be justly made.

PROMOTION AND CAREER PLANNING

The Army's promotion system is an essential part of its broad program of career planning. A commendable series of evaluation reports is a prerequisite to promotion on the best-qualified basis, and is also a decisive factor in career planning. It is urged that officers study the promotion system, in this chapter and its official references, with Chapter Twelve, *Professional Development,* and Chapter Fourteen, *Evaluation Reports.*

A sound promotion system is recognized as an important motivating factor in choosing a career as an Army officer. Officers wish to be assured that if they earn good evaluation ratings, their periodic promotions will coincide with their increasing capabilities for heavier responsibilities. They wish to feel confident that they will reach field grade, and the senior field grades, at an age sufficiently young to constitute a true reward for their finest efforts. They wish to reach eligibility for selection to the grade of colonel, and to general officer, at an age which, if selected, will allow adequate length of service in those grades. The warrant officers aspire to reach their higher grades in the same manner and for the same reasons.

THE GRADE STRUCTURE OF THE ARMY

The grade structure of the Army is controlled by *The Defense Officer Personnel Management Act.* The table below lists the grade authorizations for various officer strengths of the Active Army.

When total officer strength is:	Colonel	This distribution is allowed as a maximum: Lt Colonel	Major
70,000	3,447	8,718	12,963
75,000	3,631	9,107	13,654
80,000	3,814	9,495	14,346
85,000	3,997	9,884	15,037
90,000	4,496	10,532	16,060

It should be noted that the officer strength varies in accordance with the overall strength of the active Army. When the total number of Army members is increased, as during World War II or the Korean War or the years in Southeast Asia, the number of officers on active duty must be increased to provide the necessary, excellent leadership to which our soldiers are both entitled and accustomed. Conversely, when the crisis is past and the total Army strength is reduced, the number of officers on active duty also is reduced.

The actual number of officers on active duty with the Army at any time approximates 10 per cent of the total Army active duty strength. Warrant officers on active duty comprise approximately 14 percent of the officer corps, depending upon the Army's needs for these highly skilled specialists.

Promotions Depend Upon Vacancies. When the authorized grade strengths are attained, future promotions depend upon vacancies. Vacancies occur from many causes including death, retirement, termination of active duty, resignation, and others. A promotion requires a corresponding vacancy.

PROMOTION PROCEDURES

There are a number of terms and concepts that need to be understood in order to understand the promotion system.

Promotion Selection Boards. The Army makes use of selection boards to recommend which officers should be promoted. Board members must be senior in grade to the officers they are to consider for promotion. Each member arrives at an independent conclusion as to the selection of each officer. The entire record of each officer considered is available for examination and is used in making individual determination. A majority vote is required from board members to select an officer for promotion.

After the boards have acted and submitted their recommendations, and after the recommendations have been approved, promotions are made as vacancies occur. Approval of selection board recommendations is by the President, although the Secretary of the Army normally approves promotions for grades through colonel; by the President for brigadier generals and major generals; and by the President, subject to confirmation by the Senate, for lieutenant generals and generals.

Promotion Consideration. Consideration for promotion is on a year group basis. That is, all officers with dates of rank in a given year group will be considered for promotion with that year group. The system is arranged such that all officers, regardless of year group size, have the same cumulative opportunity for promotion. Officers whose records are good, and without conduct or character blemish, may approach the time of selection with confidence; the probabilities for their selection are strong. However, attention is invited to the earlier table showing numbers of officers authorized at the various grade levels. There are only about two-thirds as many lieutenant colonels authorized as there are majors, and only slightly more than one-third as many colonels as there are lieutenant colonels. Selection for promotion to the higher grades is highly competitive with a smaller portion of eligible officers attaining promotion as the grade levels increase.

The groups of officers considered by a selection board for promotion come from three zones.

Primary Zone. That year group of officers who are under primary consideration for promotion by a particular selection board are in the primary zone. The majority of selection board recommendations are from this year group.

Secondary Zone. Officers in the year group following the year group under primary consideration are in the secondary zone of consideration. For colonel selection boards, two year groups comprise the secondary zone. An officer in the secondary zone who has an outstanding record has an opportunity to be selected for promotion ahead of his or her contemporaries. The maximum selection rate of secondary zone officers is established at 10 percent of the list for any grade. This rate may be raised to 15 percent by the Secretary of the Army. However, the current maximum below-the-zone, or secondary zone, selection rates are set at 5 percent for promotion to major and 10 percent for promotion to lieutenant colonel and colonel.

Previously Considered. Officers who were previously considered for promotion, but who were not selected, i.e. "passed over," have an opportunity to be selected on a subsequent promotion list. As can be seen from the charts following, the odds of a previously considered, but passed over, officer being subsequently selected for promotion, at least to the grades of major and lieutenant colonel, are quite good. A passover does not signal the end of an Army career. It does, however, signal to the officer concerned that he or she should take immediate and effective steps to improve the manner of performance such that the next selection board might look upon him or her more favorably.

Fully Qualified for Promotion. This term applies to officers considered by a promotion board as qualified professionally and morally, and capable of performing the duties and assuming the responsibilities of the next higher grade. This method of promotion is utilized for all officers being considered for promotion to captain, first lieutenant and CW 2. The several promotion lists are named in a separate paragraph, below.

Best Qualified for Promotion. Under this method the selection boards recommend officers whom they consider the best qualified of the fully qualified in the zone of consideration.

The promotion board bases its recommendations on an impartial consideration of all officers in the zone of consideration. The factors considered include, but are not limited to, ability, efficiency, seniority and age, together with those special instructions received in the Letter of Instructions to the board. The actions of the board are advisory in nature. That is, they recommend to the

President or to the Secretary of the Army. The composition of the board and the Letter of Instructions to the board may be changed until such time as the recommendations of the board have been finally approved.

The board recommendation categorizes the officers considered as follows:

Recommended—Those officers the board recommends for promotion, listed in order of seniority.

Not Recommended—Those officers not recommended for promotion. Reconsideration of this recommendation by the board is not subject to appeal except in cases where there was a material error in the records of an officer in the primary zone.

Selection Rates. The established selection rates for promotion to major, lieutenant colonel and colonel are shown on the following table:

	SELECTION RATES		
	MAJOR	*LT COLONEL*	*COLONEL*
Previously Considered	19%	13%	4%
Primary Zone	76%	64%	47%
Secondary Zone	5%	10%	10%
Cumulative Promotion Opportunity	80%	70%	50%

Each year group has the same cumulative opportunity for promotion, regardless of the size of the group. A large year group results in a large selection list, while a smaller year group results in a smaller selection list. Since the number of officers that can be promoted is dependent upon the vacancies that occur in the grade to which they are to be promoted, how fast a selection list is exhausted depends both upon the size of the list and the number of vacancies that occur. Note that while about 8 of 10 captains may anticipate promotion to major, only about 1 of 2 lieutenant colonels can expect promotion to colonel. It is a fact to be faced in planning your career. Not everyone can reach the top. However, if you do a fine job and acquire a series of commendable evaluation reports, with no major blemishes on your record, you should have little concern about promotions. They will come.

Selection for promotion to first lieutenant and captain is made on a fully qualified basis. All such officers who are deemed to be fully qualified will be promoted at the appropriate time. See the later section on *Promotion through Colonel.*

Promotion Lists. The Army Promotion Lists are 12 in number, and promotions are made separately from each of these lists. Each officer's promotion list number (PL) is shown in the personal data of each officer appearing in the Army Register which is published annually.

Separate promotion lists are maintained for:

Army   Medical Service Corps
Army Nurse Corps   Professors, USMA
Chaplains   Veterinary Corps
Dental Corps   Warrant Officers
Judge Advocate General Corps   Army Medical Specialist Corps
Medical Corps   General Officers Seniority List

The Army Promotion List includes all of the combat arms, combat support arms, and combat service support arms, except the Chaplain corps, the Judge Advocate General Corps and the six Corps of the Army Medical Department. Unless otherwise stated, the information throughout this chapter pertains to the Army Promotion List as modifications are provided in the other lists.

Transition to DOPMA. Prior to adoption of the DOPMA promotion procedures on 15 September 1981, the Army had used, since the end of World War II, a dual promotion system. Under this earlier system, officers on active duty held permanent grades in their component and temporary grades in the active Army. Thus, a Regular officer might have held a grade of major in the Regular Army (USA) while serving in the grade of lieutenant colonel in the active Army, the Army of the United States (AUS). Similarly, a Reserve officer might have held a commission as a colonel in the Reserves while serving on active duty in an AUS grade of lieutenant colonel. Under this earlier system, Reserve officers could and often did serve full careers in the active Army, just as their Regular Army counterparts. Active duty officers under this earlier system were subject to consideration for promotion for both the temporary grades they held in the Army of the United States and the permanent grades they held in their components.

Under DOPMA the dual promotion system has been abandoned and the Army has adopted an all-Regular force concept. Henceforth, by the eleventh year of service, all active duty officers must integrate into the Regular Army. DOPMA authorized an increase in Regular Army strength to 63,000 officers to accommodate the all-Regular force concept.

Those field grade and promotable captain Reserve officers who were on active duty at the time the DOPMA promotion system went into effect were offered the opportunity of integrating into the Regular Army, provided: they were U.S. Citizens; they could complete 20 years of active service by age 55; they were physically qualified; they had no adverse personnel action pending; and they were not in a promotion non-select status. The law allowed a two-year period to complete the transition into DOPMA. The Secretary of the Army was authorized to grandfather entitlements of the old system as necessary to provide for a smooth transition. Those affected officers who did not qualify for integration into the Regular Army or who elected not to integrate have been allowed to remain on active duty under certain conditions.

Under DOPMA, company grade Reserve officers on active duty will be encouraged to integrate into the Regular Army during their early years. Those who have not become Regular Army officers by the time they are selected for promotion to major, or by their eleventh year of service, will be required to integrate into the Regular Army at that time or be separated from the service without being promoted.

Under DOPMA, a single Active Duty List is maintained for all commissioned officers. Promotion consideration is by year group from this Active Duty List.

CAREER EXPECTATIONS

Under the provisions of DOPMA, it is possible to plan your career, depending upon the assumptions you make regarding your relative standing among other officers of your grade and service.

Promotion through Colonel. Under the single promotion system established by DOPMA, there are minimum time-in-grade requirements established for "due course" officers. A "due course" officer is one who is selected for promotion along with his or her contemporaries, neither at an advanced rate by virtue of being promoted from a secondary zone nor delayed for promotion by being passed over by one promotion board and then later selected for promotion from among the group of previously considered officers. These minimum time-in-grade requirements are shown in the following table. Exceptions are made to allow for early secondary zone promotions.

Promotion to	Minimum Time-In-Grade
First Lieutenant	18 months
Captain	Two years
Major	Three years
Lieutenant colonel	Three years
Colonel	Three years

As noted earlier, actual promotions are dependent upon vacancies since there are maximum numbers of officers authorized by law at each grade level. A promotion cannot occur without a corresponding vacancy. The time in service (TIS) promotion opportunity for officers is expected to be about as follows:

Promotion to	TIS	Cumulative Opportunity
First Lieutenant	18 months	Fully Qualified
Captain	3.5 years	Fully Qualified
Major	$10+1$ years	80%
Lieutenant colonel	$16+1$ years	70%
Colonel	$22+1$ years	50%

Maximum Career Expectation. A commissioned officer who enters the active Army today, either as a Regular Army officer or as a Reserve officer who later integrates into the Regular Army, and who achieves the grade of colonel, may expect to serve a full career of 30 years. If the top grade attained is lieutenant colonel, the maximum career expectancy is 28 years.

A major who twice fails to be selected for promotion to lieutenant colonel may be separated from the service. Based upon the expected promotion expectancy, this would occur at about the seventeenth year of service. However, DOPMA provides for selective continuation on active duty of some majors who fill specialty needs. If the major in question were to be selected for continuation, he or she could serve to a maximum of 24 years, at which time the officer would be eligible to retire in the grade of major.

Similarly, a captain who twice fails to be selected for promotion to major may be separated from the service. The second passover would be expected to occur at about the eleventh year of service. However, captains also can be selectively continued to fill Army specialty needs. A captain who is selectively continued can remain on active duty to a maximum of 20 years, and thereafter be eligible for retirement.

Lieutenants, captains, and majors who receive two passovers and who are not selected to be continued on active duty in grade (captains and majors only) must be separated from the active Army.

Separation Pay. Officers who are separated from the active Army involuntarily because of non-selection for promotion prior to completion of 20 years of service are not entitled to draw retired pay based on length of service. Nonetheless, these officers have performed valuable service to the Army. The DOPMA law contains provisions for such officers to receive a one-time separation payment equal to 10 percent of their latest annual base pay times their years of service, up to a maximum payment of $30,000. The separation payment rewards the officer for service to the nation and provides funds to tide the officer over until a new career is selected.

Promotion of General Officers. A single promotion system is established for promotion to the general officer grades as a continuation of the system used for lower ranking officers. Under the law, colonels and brigadier generals must serve at least one year in grade before they are eligible for promotion.

Promotion to brigadier general confers tenure for up to 30 years of service or five years in grade, whichever occurs later. Promotion to major general, lieutenant general or general confers tenure to 35 years of service or five years in grade, whichever occurs later. Promotion to lieutenant general and general is subject to confirmation by the Senate, as are the subsequent assignments and reassignments of these officers.

Under the law, the President may vacate or cancel a promotion to brigadier general before the officer has served 18 months in grade. The law also contains provisions for selective early retirement of brigadier generals and major generals who have reached the four-year time in grade point. The President also may extend the service of major generals, lieutenant generals, and generals beyond their mandatory retirement dates.

Promotion of Warrant Officers. Warrant officers are not included under the provisions of the new DOPMA law. Instead, they continue to be considered for promotion under the previous laws, which provide for both temporary and permanent grades. Warrant officers, WO1, who have demonstrated they are fully qualified, attain eligibility for temporary promotion to Chief Warrant Officer, CW2, on the day following completion of twenty-four months of duty as a WO1, or three years cumulative service as a Reserve officer. Selection for temporary promotion to CW3 and CW4 is on a best qualified basis. Non-Regular warrant officers who twice fail to be selected for promotion to CW3 or CW4 are relieved from active duty.

Regular Army warrant officers become eligible for promotion to CW2 after three years in grade as a WO1, and after six years in grade as a CW2 for promotion to CW3 and six years in grade as a CW3 for promotion to CW4.

Regular Army warrant officers who have at least 20 years of active federal service are retired not later than 60 days after they reach age 62. Those who have completed 30 years of active Federal service are retired on the last day of the month in which 30 years and 60 days of active Federal service is completed, except that retirement may be deferred until 60 days after reaching age 62 upon recommendation and with the consent of the officer.

POLICIES FOR PROMOTION SELECTION BOARD

It is essential that officers have confidence in the objectivity and impartiality of the system used by the Army for the selective promotion of officers, both in decentralized field promotions, and by the decisions reached by promotion boards in the Department of the Army. There is obvious need for general belief that it is done fairly, studiously, objectively, and that selections are made by officers senior to those being considered and who hence cannot benefit person-ally. These goals are attained by the Army.

Whenever lists are published, and individuals note the names omitted as well as those fortunate enough to have been selected, there is a natural wonder as to the good fortune of one and the misfortune of another. No informed person would deny the chance of human error because choices must be made follow-ing study and analysis of official records which were prepared by human beings in the discharge of their duties. Indeed, when we consider the extremely high quality of the corps of officers as to education and military training, dedication to the performance of their service, and the importance to the nation of a high proportion of current assignments, it should be understood that the borderline between those selected and those to be left in grade is often very slender. But officers who have performed duty as board members, and others who have observed them, know for sure that they are determined to make the choices accurately, wisely, and objectively in the interests of the Army and the individu-als considered.

The Letter of Instructions provides information which guides board members in the matters to be considered in their selections. The evaluation reports accumulated during an officer's service are the principal records, but there are other records which are also made available as appropriate to enable wise decisions to be reached. Officers who wish to develop detailed knowledge of the complete system are urged to study the complete regulation.

NAMES OMITTED FROM PROMOTION ANNOUNCEMENTS

There are severe disappointments endured by those officers who read the lists of those who are selected for promotion, and search in vain for their own names. It may extend from disappointment, through chagrin, with acute appre-hension about termination of military career. None the less, it is a necessary policy which provides for the nation the best possible corps of officers, and better careers for the officers who serve the expected standard length of service. There are very important human problems involved.

Missing Names, Secondary Zone of Consideration. Selections of officers from the secondary zone of consideration are on the order of 1 in 10, or 1 in 20 of those promoted from both zones. These few officers gain a considerable advantage over their contemporaries. Competition among those who have the very highest evaluation ratings is very keen and the selections are very close. The officers chosen will certainly have all the prerequisites of outstanding achievements, and a "something extra" which was convincing to members of the promotion board. Even so, there is widespread chagrin among those who were considered but not selected for swift promotion. Take this one in stride! Be the first to congratulate the fortunate ones. There are ample opportunities ahead.

Officers Categorized "Not Recommended". These officers receive an official passover. There may be a slender chance for their subsequent selection for promotion because elimination requires negative action by two promotion boards. Surely their chances for selection are not great, but neither are the odds insurmountable.

What to do? Perhaps the officer knows a great deal about his or her total record from visits to the specialty manager, from knowledge of personal evalu-ation reports, or from counseling sessions conducted by the rating officer. Whatever course the officer elects to follow, he or she must make the final choice between staying on active duty as long as the law permits, and thereby qualifying for separation pay (see the earlier discussion) if ultimately separated involuntarily as a result of a second passover, or to resign. Those officers who choose to strive for favorable future board action as to their promotion will receive fair and even kindly consideration, but they should realize that the odds are against them.

THOUGHTS FOR ALL OFFICERS

At times in the Army, one might hear that "they" (whoever "they" are) say that some individual was selected for promotion based upon political pull or because he or she was in special favor for some reason. Dispel this notion from your mind. Promotion boards are composed of human beings, all subject to human frailties, but each member of each promotion board is an honorable member of the Corps of Officers, and each is equally determined to do the best he or she can to assure selection of the most highly qualified individuals for advancement. Political pressures are without value in gaining special consideration for any individual by a promotion board; any in-service pressure that may be applied is equally sterile. Let there be no doubt, the Army's promotion system is impartial, thorough, and fair.

PROMOTION OF OFFICERS IN THE RESERVE COMPONENTS

The policies and procedures for promoting commissioned officers of the Reserve Components of the Army below the grade of brigadier general are published in AR 135–155.

USAR promotions of Army Reserve officers are effected by the area commander within whose geographical area the officer's records are maintained. There are three exceptions: (1) USAR officers on active duty, except for second lieutenants under the jurisdiction of the area commander for Reserve matters, will be considered for promotion at Headquarters, Department of the Army. (2) An Army Reserve second lieutenant on 6 months active duty for training (ACDUTRA) will be considered for promotion by the area commander under whom the officer is serving the ACDUTRA provided he or she is otherwise qualified. (3) Army National Guard of the United States (ARNGUS) promotions for all ARNGUS officers will be made at Headquarters, Department of the Army.

Let us look to the service rather than the reward.—Calvin Coolidge.

Few men have the natural strength to honor a friend's success without envy.— Aeschylus.

16

Responsibilities of Command

Command of an Army unit of any size is a rewarding and satisfying assignment. In the command of the platoon or company, even the battalion, the commander and other officers assigned have the rich experience of personal contact where they know their troops, and troops know their officers. Teamwork flows from working together, and with a healthy teamwork comes confidence in the personnel who form the unit. An officer assigned in any capacity to duty with troops is privileged, and should enter upon responsibilities with determination to succeed.

Duty with a troop unit involves a wide variety of different responsibilities. There is the mission, or a series of missions; the training of members of the command, or training of incoming replacements; supply, care, and maintenance of equipment; provision for a mess and its continual supervision; unit transport; unit administration; the overall requirement for good management; finally, all of the infinite variety of human problems in being responsible for men and women. The total requirement is leadership combined with professional competence.

All officers assigned to troop units need an understanding of Army command policy, and they need to know and apply sound methods of management. The service schools provide excellent instruction in the subjects an officer requires with a unit of his or her arm or service. But there is a distinct difference between a thorough "knowing about," in the academic sense, and the "knowing how," which is gained by on-the-job experience. The capability of knowing how is the goal to seek.

The subjects discussed in this chapter are common to Army units of each arm and service. They are included for the officer made responsible for one or more of these missions, often effective at once, who has the need for immediate reference information, suggestions, guidance. What is stated here represents the experience of many officers and is provided as sound counsel. The brief discussions are to help you make a confident start. You will need to study the official manuals, of course, just as you must learn at once the standing orders in effect for your unit. These discussions are important for reference by officers on troop duty, and the sooner experience is gained in these essential duties the better.

Army Command Policy	Leadership and A.W. 15
Management Principles	Taking Care of Your Soldiers
Training of Junior Leaders	Off-duty Activities
Food Service	Special Problems
Unit Readiness	Conclusion
Unit Administration	

Readers are referred to the Appendix for a brief discussion, with references to the pertinent regulations, of many of the more common additional duties to which officers may be assigned. It is a first place to look for the officer with a newly assigned additional duty who wants to start off on the right foot.

ARMY COMMAND POLICY (EXTRACTS AND DEFINITIONS)

Army Command Policy and Procedure, AR 600-20, is of such importance that officers are urged to add a copy to their personal library for reference in routine as well as emergency situations.

Right to Command. Command is exercised by virtue of office and the special assignment of members of the Armed Forces holding military rank who are eligible by law to exercise command.

Assignment and Command. Members of the Army are assigned to stations or commands where their services are required, and are there assigned to appropriate duties by the commanding officer.

Warrant Officers. Warrant officers may be assigned duties as station, unit or detachment commander and, when so assigned, they are vested with all powers normally exercised by a commissioned officer, except as indicated in AR 611-112.

Military Rank. Military rank is the relative position or degree of precedence bestowed on military persons which marks their station and confers eligibility to exercise command or authority in the military service within the limits prescribed by law.

Conferring honorary titles of military rank upon civilians is prohibited.

Chain of Command. The chain of command is the most fundamental and important organizational technique used by the Army. It is the succession of commanders, superior to subordinate, through which command is exercised. It extends from the President, as Commander-in-Chief, down through the various grades of rank to the enlisted persons leading the smallest Army elements and to their subordinates. Staff officers and administrative noncommissioned officers are not in the chain of command. A simple and direct command channel facilitates transmittal of orders from the highest to the lowest levels in a minimum of time and with the least chance of confusion.

No distinction is made between the terms commander and leader.

The command channel extends upward in the same manner for matters requiring official communication from subordinate to superior.

Each individual in the chain of command is delegated sufficient authority to accomplish assigned tasks and responsibilities.

Every commander has two basic responsibilities in the following priority: *Accomplishment of mission, and the care of personnel and property.* (Italics supplied.)

A superior in the chain of command holds subordinate commanders responsible for everything their command does, or fails to do. Thus, in relation to his or her superior, a commander cannot delegate any responsibilities. However, in relation to subordinates, an officer does subdivide assigned responsibility and authority and assigns portions of them to various commanders and staff members. In this way an appropriate degree of responsibility and authority becomes inherent in each command echelon. The necessity for a commander or staff officer observing proper channels in issuing instructions or orders to subordinates must be recognized. Constant and continuous utilization of the chain of command is vital to the combat effectiveness of any Army unit.

Temporary Command. In the event of the death, disability, or temporary absence of the commander of any element of the Army, the next senior regularly assigned commissioned officer, warrant officer, cadet, noncommissioned officer, specialist, or private present for duty and not ineligible for command will assume command until relieved by proper authority. A member in temporary command will not, except in urgent cases, alter or annul the standing orders of the permanent commander without authority of the next higher commander.

Emergency Command. In the event of emergency, the senior commissioned officer, warrant officer, cadet, noncommissioned officer, specialist, or private among troops at the scene of the emergency will exercise control or command of the military personnel present. These provisions are also applicable to troops separated from their parent units under battlefield conditions or in prisoner of war status. *(Caution by Officer's Guide: This is a matter which officers should understand and be prompt to apply when emergencies occur. A natural catastrophe, such as a fire, tornado, railroad wreck, or a riot or other unexpected, potentially dangerous situation requires the senior present to take charge of all troops present, and take prompt action as the situation demands.)*

Obedience to Orders. All persons in the military service are required to obey strictly and to execute promptly the lawful orders of their superiors.

MANAGEMENT PRINCIPLES

Management in Leadership. Expert execution of command responsibility is never an accident. It is always the result of clear purpose, earnest effort, intelligent direction, and skillful execution. It is thoughtfully directed hard work. The recurring problems of command are not complex. Quoting Mr. C. F. Kettering, a great industrial leader, "Any problem thoroughly understood is fairly simple."

Good management is an essential tool of the commander in the discharge of responsibilities. It is the judicious use of the available means to accomplish a mission.

Management often includes improvisation to make the best use of what you have to get what you want. Here "what you have" includes your available resources in personnel, equipment, funds and time. In the military it will be rare that you have all you want of anything; you must strive to succeed with what you have.

These steps have broad application to the approach of any problem.

First, Understand the Mission, Objective, or Job. Know exactly what is to be done.

The mission may be a continuing command responsibility, such as we discuss in this chapter. Or it may be a precise, detailed order. Or it may be a mission-type order which requires the officer to determine intermediate objectives.

Objectives of a commander are wisely regarded as of two categories. First, the long range objective which is to be attained in six months or a year, and which may involve accumulation of funds, or construction, or special training. Second, the short range objectives which can be undertaken at once and completed quickly.

Second, Develop a Detailed Plan. Now comes programming or scheduling which is a part of planning. After a decision of "what" is to be done there must follow "how it will be done" and "who will do it." A part of this step is the issuance of orders or instructions, with whatever incidental training, discussion, or explanation is advisable or necessary.

Subordinate leaders and technicians must know their own responsibilities as they must also know the soldiers and equipment available to them for the work directed. This requires also the decentralization to subordinates of a stated degree of authority and responsibility. When this is done subordinates need not stumble about in uncertainty because they can go ahead with confidence, as most people wish to do, and give their boss exactly what is wanted.

Third, Announce a Definite Time for Completion of Mission. Timing is essential to coordination. It is especially true when two or more commands or groups must mesh together in teamwork. There are some variants. "Task to be completed by 1500 hours today." Or, "Not later than 3 November." Or, "Without delay." The latter means to get at it at once and bring it to successful completion with effectiveness and dispatch. Time scheduling provides for coordination and more nearly insures completing the task at a projected time.

Let us now consider two necessary cautions. A good and necessary reason for time scheduling is to keep appropriate pressure upon subordinates. But this use may be abused and results harmed. Some officers demand speed to the point of absurdity. Unless an officer is willing to accept the half-done and slipshod, he or she must allow sufficient time for the capable, willing worker to do the job well. A Pentagon expression which applies to this situation is, "If you want it bad, you get it bad." Avoid becoming an officer who demands regularly that tasks be completed "yesterday."

But there is another caution, almost in conflict. Think of it well. In this military life there are rare occasions when the leader must ask the almost impossible in life-or-death, victory or defeat requirements. We differ from the humdrum vocations. Under some of these circumstances brave soldiers will try, even at the risk of death, and sometimes the finest among them will win. Here are the winners of the Medal of Honor; those who landed first in Normandy and pushed forward; those who drove on to the Yalu; the brave, superbly trained soldiers who executed "search and destroy" missions through the torrid, steamy jungles of Vietnam. In other days they were the soldiers who stuck it out at Valley Forge, and one such officer carried The Message to Garcia.

Complete Work—Clean as You Go. The phrase "clean—as you go" means that jobs started are finished. It means order and thoroughness as a matter of course. It means police of an area to keep it clean and tidy, in contrast to a periodic, hurried clean-up to make it momentarily fit to be seen. It means each soldier on top of his or her job, all the time, and proud of it. It means confidence and pride in doing a worthwhile job well. Beyond all this it means pride in organization, and pride in military service itself, not a grudging minimum of unwelcomed service. The wise commander will make it a command practice and advance the principle: *Go clean—as you go.*

Give Generously of Command Interest and Control. Issue of orders is prelude.

Management is not just planning; it is carefully supervising the execution phase to assure compliance with instructions and to adjust plans, if necessary. This includes minor on-the-spot adjustments, a word of praise or encouragement here, some prodding there. The commander must leave behind an improved and strengthened clarity of purpose and renewed determination to get on with the task and do it well.

Many a well-planned mission has failed because of the commander's failure to see that the execution phase is properly supervised.

Sizing Up the Task. The very first step for the officer is to evaluate or size up the assigned task as to the status of the organization and of the individuals who are its members. Is it an old unit partially or wholly trained? Or is it newly activated with an experienced cadre and untrained members?

Suppose It Is a New Unit. You must inform yourself as to the total mission; the time available to complete it; the capabilities of the officers, noncommissioned officers, and technicians available to assist you; the physical facilities available. Now you must gain knowledge about each member you are to train. Study the records to determine the education, civilian vocation or training, physical condition, aptitudes, age, former military training of each. Interview each member; talk about these things; learn individual interests and aspirations; seek the personal understanding of the task and the cooperation to attain it from each. (Reference: the later paragraph, *Exploiting of Acquired Skills.*) How much better is this approach to the task than the too common assumption that all soldiers to be trained are without usable knowledge, equally able to absorb knowledge, and equally interested in doing well? From this first contact the officer must be seeking the exceptional individual who can be raised quickly to become a leader or highly skilled technician; the officer must also identify the personnel who learn slowly or who may require patient handling and additional instruction to keep them abreast of the bulk of unit members; along with these slow learners are others who join late, or have missed instruction because of sickness, or who have been absent from a period of instruction. This is a summary of the way the good leader learns about subordinates and guides their individual and collective progress to attain the necessary results.

Suppose It Is an Old Unit. You must know of course the mission, and the time, personnel, and facilities available as for any other task. But you must determine quickly such things as the following: Is it a fine, well trained unit of high esprit? Or is it below standard in some specific way? Is it weak in discipline? Is it behind identical units in training or below their standards of training accomplishments? Has it failed in battle? Why? These are a few of the special situations which may face an officer in command of an established unit.

Once these matters have been identified and evaluated the course to follow is really quite similar to that described above. Study the records; study the individual; plan a course that fits them and fits the goal. But in the case of the old unit remove the cause for the unit's difficulties. Perhaps it is the replacement of ineffective officers or noncommissioned officers. It may include improvement in things which have caused discontent such as a poor mess, poor sanitation, poor policies regarding leaves and passes. These are only examples. You must determine all the reasons the organization has been considered substandard and then apply all measures within your control and power to correct them.

Exploiting Acquired Skills. The most important asset of any unit is the degree of usable skill possessed by each member of the command. This knowledge may have been acquired prior to entry into the Army, in school or college, or as a result of former employment and on-the-job training. The Army has an excellent classification system which identifies and makes of record the special skills or knowledge of new personnel. After this initial classification, men and women are assigned to units or to training centers where opportunities will occur to utilize this experience. When the skill possessed by an individual is one for which the Army has a need, the classification and assignment procedure operates smoothly. Personnel are placed where they can do the best work for the Army and the nation.

But there are some factors which need understanding. Civilian life has no specific counterpart for the Infantryman or the Artilleryman, as examples, and soldiers trained to meet these needs must be produced in very large numbers. More personnel may arrive with training in a civilian vocation than the Army needs on such duties; the surplus will be assigned to other duties. There are other civilian vocations, or individuals with specialized education, in which there is no Army requirement whatever. These readily understood truths are stated because of the frequent charge of misuse of civilian talents, usually objecting to assignment to the Infantry. They need understanding.

Acquired knowledge and acquired skills must be identified quickly and, to the extent such individuals are needed, they must be properly and promptly assigned. The Tables of Organization list most of the skills needed, each of which is identified as a Military Occupational Specialty (MOS). You must obtain explicit information as to the unit's needs for trained personnel. You must then consult the individual records to ascertain the resources in personnel trained in the missions required. Then by interview and testing, as well as by observation, you decide what you have and balance it against your known needs.

One way of evaluating the Army training requirement is the filling of the gap between the skills brought into the Army, or possessed by its members, and the training needed to meet the complete mission of the unit. If truck drivers are needed, the first place to search is the training and experience of your troops to determine whether you have them but they are on other duties. The examples can be infinite. The training load is magnified enormously unless the classification and assignment procedure is effective and properly used. Take for granted that every member desires to perform service of the maximum value to the Army and the nation. The Army leaders are determined to make the best possible use of each individual. Make your job easier, and your achievements greater, by making the best possible use of each individual, whether officer or soldier.

Our classification and assignment procedures are good. Observe and understand them. But in so doing, remember that assignment of individuals to specific duties is a command responsibility, and do your part as a responsible officer in placing your personnel wisely to meet Army needs.

Summary. This is an indication of the way you must apply your knowledge of leadership. You must size up your task and must learn all about any special situation which confronts you. You must learn as much as possible about each assistant and each subordinate to be trained. Then with your feet planted firmly on the ground, and a feeling of confidence in your mind, go ahead and from day to day apply the fundamentals of sound leadership to your specific task.

TRAINING OF JUNIOR LEADERS

One of the most important duties of a commander is the training of junior leaders, officer and noncommissioned officer alike. It is a duty "deferred" or ignored by some commanders who convince themselves it is easier and quicker to "do it themselves"; or resort continually to precise, detailed instructions to be followed by rote. There is work in preparing a well-planned, well-conducted instructional program to develop self-reliant, confident junior leaders who can proceed effectively under mission-type orders. Hesitant commanders may rationalize that it is better for their subordinates to do a job "right," that is—the way the senior would do it—than to chance a blunder. Such a course may seem to solve the requirements of the moment, but in the long run the performance of the entire unit will suffer. There must come a day when the commander is absent when an emergency arises; at that instant the lack of trained junior leaders to step in and do the job with confidence and skill, will be painfully apparent. If you really aspire to rise to positions of great responsibility in our Army, demonstrate it by good training of junior leaders.

Training includes more than studying and learning the contents of the applicable Field Manuals, Regulations and other publications. It must include also a chance to practice what has been learned from the books. This opportunity to practice is voided if you tell your subordinates not only what to do, but also how to do it.

It is natural that the senior officer often feels that he or she knows precisely how to tackle a particular problem so that it will be solved in the minimum amount of time, with the minimum of effort, and with the minimum expenditure of materials. That you do know the correct procedure is one of the reasons you are the senior officer. However, when you impart this knowledge to subordinates in the form of step-by-step instructions, you rob them of a chance to use their own initiative, to think a problem through, to try their hand at arriving at the correct procedure. In so doing, you will have ignored a vital requirement of the training process.

In the performance of your leadership duties, see to it that you do not rob your subordinates of a chance to display their own initiative and capabilities. Issue mission type orders—that is, define precisely what is to be accomplished and furnish information as to the equipment and materials available, the time by which the assignment is to be completed, and any other pertinent information which may help define the limiting boundaries of the problem. But then let your subordinates make their own plans as to the step-by-step accomplishment of the mission. They will make mistakes. Expect them—and be ready to deal with them. However, as time passes, the mistakes will be fewer and your own job will be made easier, for you truly will have trained your junior leaders. And who knows, in the process you may even learn better ways to accomplish a job for which you once knew the "right" procedure.

Special Note Regarding Noncommissioned Officers. The NCOs have been called "the backbone of the Army." This is no idle phrase. Good NCOs are tremendously important to the Army; with them, a unit functions like a smooth-running machine; without them, the best of unit officers will lead a hectic existence and probably will see poor unit performance besides. The NCO is a vital link in the chain of command.

Good NCOs are made in much the same way that good commissioned officers are made. The preceding paragraphs apply equally to both commissioned and noncommissioned officers. But there is more.

An NCO is truly an officer in a unit. That the NCO holds his or her position without a commission is indicative only of relative rank and perhaps also background and training. Each NCO should have specific duties and responsibilities assigned and should be delegated sufficient authority to enable accomplishment of these assigned tasks. NCOs spend most of their time among the troops in a unit. They are the ones who actually supervise the details involved in the accomplishment of the mission, but to do their jobs properly, they must have the respect of the troops. It is here that the attitudes of their seniors are very important. *In order to accomplish their duties properly, NCOs must have the respect and support of their seniors.*

Accord your NCOs the same respect that you feel your superior officers should give you. Support your NCOs as you would expect to be supported by your company commander or your battalion commander. Insure that your NCOs are properly trained, including the opportunities to exercise their own initiative and judgment. Expect and require that they carry their share of the inherent and assigned load of the unit. Do all these things, while not neglecting your own responsibilities regarding supervision and inspection, and you will be pleasantly surprised at how smoothly your unit functions. Your assigned tasks will be made lighter. You will have trained a true backbone for the unit—good NCOs.

It is true that the consolidation of many support activities has lifted much of the responsibility for food service out of the company and battery level, and with it the routine appointment of a company mess officer to act for the commander in mess supervision. Even so, there remains a definite command responsibility whether in garrison or in campaign conditions, because what soldiers are provided for food influences their morale, their willingness to serve, and their efficiency far beyond the power of any printed words. Officers assigned to duty with troops must be everlastingly mindful of the proper food service of their soldiers. The serving of a well-chosen menu, with well-prepared food items, in attractive surroundings, are all matters of the first magnitude.

The system of food service in Army use has been developed by experts of the highest standing and experience. It includes direction by the Chief of Support Services, with orders and publications for instruction and control, research and testing, development of equipment, the conduct of food-service schools, with the assignment of qualified food service supervisors and technicians as needed. The following list of official documents pertain to the food service.

TM 10–412-series. Army Recipes Book.
TM 10–405—Army Mess Operations.
DA Form 2970—Subsistence Report and Field Ration Request.
DA Form 3033—Mess Attendance Record.
DA Form 3034 series. Cook's Worksheet.
DD Form 1544—Cash Meal Payment Sheet.

Menus. *Master Menu.* A monthly publication of U.S. Army Subsistence Center. It is a standard menu for each meal for one month, with items required.

Revised Menu. This is a revision of the master menu which is prepared and published locally under direction of the food service supervisor. It takes into consideration local supplies and conditions. This is the menu to be followed by the mess unless there are very compelling reasons to depart from it.

The Mess. In garrison, with a consolidated mess, what should a company commander or a company officer supervise? Local policies will establish the actual responsibility of unit officers. But in any case, a considerable interest by unit officers should be displayed in the quality of the food service. You must assure yourself that your troops are satisfied, or that you make appropriate recommendations to the responsible officials. You should know about the choice of menu components; the quality of food preparation; the attractiveness of the food service and the surroundings; the orderliness and the sanitation of the kitchen and personnel; and the entire area as to sanitation.

In the field, or in active combat conditions, circumstances may arise where the mess responsibility is placed entirely under the control of the company or equivalent commander. Each company will have its TO/E kitchen equipment to maintain in garrison, including the passing of unit readiness tests and command inspections; in the field, this equipment is mounted in the back of a truck according to locally prescribed methods. The ingenuity of company officers in organizing the field kitchen truck, and preparing for its actual use, is a challenge.

But the real "challenge" is the effective operation of a satisfactory food service under combat or field conditions, when called upon to do so. The food may be prepared in the area of the battalion trains. Or the members of units in campaign or combat may dine on combat rations under the control of company officers. Clearly, there are important responsibilities for the company commander and his or her officers that require knowledge and leadership.

Suggested Points for Check and Correction. Under the assumption that a company or equivalent unit has a mess responsibility under field or combat conditions, the following items are listed to assist an officer who may be assigned the responsibility.*

Check the Mess Personnel and Be Certain of Their Qualifications. Go another step, and assure yourself of a workable division of duties and responsibilities as to working procedures. If the unit is to have good meals, served at the right place, at the right time, under suitable conditions of sanitation considering all the circumstances, it will require good personnel, hard work, and effective leadership.

Check the Food Supplies and the Storage. Be certain the food supply is adequate, stored properly to prevent spoilage, and secure from pilferage.

Check Your Kitchen Equipment. Assure yourself that the mess personnel have the needed or authorized tools and equipment, and that these are serviceable.

Recognize the Importance of the Kitchen Police. Never to be overlooked is the importance of the kitchen police. Few soldiers, if any, enjoy the task. But an appreciative word of instruction by an officer about the importance of the duty may help. It is better to regard KP as a military duty, and rotate the duty by roster; most experienced officers have learned that it is wrong to use the duty as punishment. Besides, it is a good way to identify personnel who have

---

*Some years ago a letter was received from an officer on his first assignment with troops, which read something like this: "Soon after joining my first troop unit, I was assigned as Mess Officer. All that stood between me and the abyss of ignorance was the brief information in *Officer's Guide* until I could obtain and study the official pamphlets. It was reassuring that someone had been there before me, and had left some pointers." Provision of a few "pointers," hoping they will be helpful, is the sole purpose of this very brief discussion of a very important subject.

an interest in cooking who may later be trained as cooks or the food service mission.

Field Inspections. In campaign or field conditions careful inspection of the food service is especially important. It is harder for the mess staff to maintain a high standard of cleanliness, and to operate at the needed high standard. Whenever a unit operates its own food service under field conditions, it becomes a first responsibility.

You must be certain of adequate food supplies.

Kitchen equipment must be checked frequently to be certain the required items are on hand and serviceable. In the field, an item broken, or lost through carelessness or pilferage, may cause real difficulties.

Sanitation is extremely important. It requires continual observation. Clean dishes used by the troops, or in food preparation, must be *free from grease.* Make a "spot check," as extensive as circumstances may require; feel the dish surface, don't just look at it. If any grease is found, the item is unclean and may result in serious illness. Have you ever been sick from food poisoning? It isn't pleasant, at all. You must make this check, when it lies within your responsibility, and be certain that adequate facilities are available to obtain cleanliness, which includes a generous supply of very hot water and soap or detergents.

Check the disposal of garbage and wastes. This can become a frightful nuisance and a threat to health. An ever-watchful eye is needed.

Food Service Checklist. There are official checklists, and good ones. This one has been used by thousands of officers until an official list is obtained or prescribed. It is included as a "help". Select the items which pertain to your situation, and add others as they may be needed.

1. *Bulletin board:* Check the food handlers' certificates.
2. *Mess accounts:* Check arithmetic of the forms utilized.
3. *Menu:*
    Posted near cook.
    Foods listed being served?
    Time of preparation—meals ready on time? Cooking completed too early?
4. *Serving of meals:*
    Hot foods hot; cold foods cold.
    Serving system carried out?
5. *Uniform and cleanliness of mess personnel.*
6. *Kitchen equipment and special points to observe:*
    a. Cooking ranges.
    b. Baking ovens.
    c. Fryolator; any grease on inside?
    d. Steam cookers; any food stains on inside?
    e. Coffee percolators; any coffee stains on inside?
    f. Mixer; any food particles on inside or on attachments?
    g. Meat block.
    h. Pots and pans; examine edges and corners carefully.
    i. Utensils; examine handles carefully and test cutting edges.
    j. Refrigerator room; temperature (40°—50° F.).
    k. Ice-cube freezer.
    l. Storeroom and bread box.
    m. G I cans for bulk foods; lids should fit tightly.

      n. Sinks and dish washers.

      o. Potato peeler; any potato fragments on inside?

  7. *Dining room equipment:*

      a. Steam table; examine corners and shelves carefully.

      b. Dishes and cafeteria trays; any grease film?

      c. Glasses; hold to light to observe any spots.

      d. Tables; any water streaks on top?

      e. Silverware; any food particles or food stains?

  8. *Floors:* Any grease spots?

  9. *Garbage stand:*

      Lids should fit tightly. Exteriors must be clean.

      Any refuse on cans, stand, or ground in vicinity of stand?

 10. *Weekly schedule of cleaning:*

      On Saturdays make complete inspection; on other days make list of items you will inspect, always including inspection of mess accounts.

UNIT READINESS

The Army's readiness objective is to provide units capable of performing their assigned missions in support of operational requirements. To conserve resources, only those units required early in support of contingency plans are normally maintained at the highest level of readiness. Other units are assigned readiness goals according to the resources provided. By resources, we mean personnel, equipment, funds, time and facilities for training and maintaining equipment. Each unit commander is responsible for maintaining the highest levels of unit training proficiency and equipment serviceability within the limitations of the resources provided. The unit commander is responsible for assuring that unit readiness ratings reflect actual unit conditions and that available resources are applied as necessary to prevent or correct degradation of unit readiness. Higher level commanders are charged with reviewing the status reports of subordinate units and taking such action as is within their capabilities to improve the readiness condition of these subordinate units.

The desired readiness condition of a unit is described by an Authorized Level of Organization (ALO). The ALO is the authorized level of manpower and equipment against which a unit may requisition personnel and equipment. The ALO may be expressed either numerically or by letter designations which represent percentages of full TOE/MTOE authorizations. For example, ALO 1 is 100 percent, ALO 2 is 90 percent, ALO 3 is 80 percent and ALO 4 is 70 percent or less. Units may be authorized different levels of personnel and equipment, in which case the lower of the two levels is considered to be the unit ALO.

Unit status reports, which are submitted both monthly and when a change of overall unit rating occurs, are designed to assist higher commanders in the allocation of resources and to assist in the assessment of total force readiness. Unit ratings for personnel, training and logistics are computed in accordance with the detailed instructions provided in AR 220–1. In addition, the unit commander determines an overall unit rating which he or she feels best describes the unit's ability to accomplish its mission. Ratings are computed against full wartime requirements and are indicated as numerical levels. A rating of 1 indicates the highest level of readiness. Ratings of 2 or 3 indicate a lesser degree of readiness. A numerical rating of 4 in any area indicates that the unit is incapable of performing its full MTOE mission, unless otherwise explained by the unit commander.

No unit is expected to achieve a readiness rating higher than the ALO for the unit. That is, if the unit is authorized to have on hand only 80 percent of its TOE personnel and equipment (ALO 3), it is not expected to have a unit readiness rating higher than 3. The goal is to achieve a readiness rating equal to the authorized ALO and to train to the highest level of proficiency possible with the resources provided to the unit. Since the reports are designed to inform higher levels of command, all the way up to Headquarters, Department of the Army, of the actual readiness condition of the unit, the reports must be accurate. Commanders at levels higher than the reporting unit are forbidden to change the rating provided by the subordinate unit commander.

Each level of command from Headquarters, Department of the Army to the unit is responsible to achieve the maximum state of readiness within the available resources and to accurately assess and report the actual status of unit readiness regardless of the resources allocated. Unit readiness is essentially the end product of managerial effort at all levels of the Army. Therefore the readiness condition of a unit should not be attributed solely to the leadership and managerial efforts of the reporting unit commander. To attempt to do so would ignore the limitations which exist within the system. *The report is not designed to provide an evaluation of unit commanders.* The unit status report is designed to indicate the actual status of unit readiness within these limitations and to serve as a management tool so that higher levels of command can determine where personnel and equipment resources can best be applied to achieve an optimum readiness level for all Army units.

Training of Personnel. As a unit commander, your first responsibility is to assign and use your assigned personnel in accordance with their prescribed military occupational specialty, MOS. Second, you should seek opportunity for your subordinates to attend service schools which provide training or advanced training in their specialties. Third, you must train them on-the-job, using the already trained and experienced personnel in your unit. Finally, you must be watchful that personnel trained for a definite position, or MOS, are not erroneously or carelessly assigned to duties of lesser importance. Correct assignment of personnel is a command responsibility and is an essential element in training.

"Train and Maintain." When a unit is not in combat, the mission is to "train and maintain." Follow the training schedules with precision, using all available lesson plans, field manuals and training aids. Inject realism. Use and test your equipment. Conduct the training with vigor and enthusiasm and it will rub off on your soldiers.

Logistics. The unit must have its authorized equipment on hand (including spares and repair parts). It should be stored in equipment store rooms or on the proper vehicles as prescribed, ready for inspection or for movement. The junior officer has a major responsibility for the maintenance of unit equipment. Maintenance procedures are prescribed in technical manuals and bulletins. The end-of-day maintenance periods should be organized and performed with the same seriousness as the training periods earlier in the day. Operational maintenance must be supervised by the officer and the NCOs; never leave the unit area until the equipment is combat-ready and, as the responsible officer, you are certain of it.

The Reward of Thoroughness. The Army's splendid units of this period have proven the value of the procedures over and over again. Many Army units have passed from training situations directly into combat without delay or confusion, confident of their own "combat readiness." The junior officer in a unit has a heavy responsibility. He or she must learn the standards of unit readiness and "adhere to the book." The "book" is the accumulation of experience. Lean upon the knowledge and the experience of the old hands. Be a tough inspector, fair and thorough, but never chicken. Require your soldiers to prove their own capabilities and the readiness of their equipment. These painstaking steps can mean the difference between combat success and combat failure, and for some of your soldiers the difference between life and death. The reward of thoroughness is confidence—and a clear conscience.

UNIT ADMINISTRATION

The company and battery are administrative units in the sense that their commanders are required to prepare and forward to battalion or similar headquarters prescribed records and essential data. Supervision of these administrative, or paper work tasks, is a continual responsibility of the commander. He or she may delegate to others the daily tasks of preparing reports, checking accounts and records, verifying inventories, and submission of whatever data is required. But it is the commander's responsibility.

There is great importance to this constant problem. Unless data are correctly supplied as to each individual's records, all manner of complications follow with respect to pay accounts, later claims for disability under veteran's benefits, and the like. Strength reports originating in the company form the basis for all personnel accounting and if they are incorrect all is wrong. Individual and unit property records must be accurate. Strive for the *Zero Error* objective of all administrative managers.

Some officers have a serious misconception of this matter. As they abhor "paperwork," they shun the responsibility, or content themselves with slipshod results. There are other officers who devote so much of their own time to the task, instead of a proper decentralization with supervision, that they have inadequate time for other responsibilities, such as training. Both concepts are wrong. Here are some tests: Are there complaints about reports being submitted after the date or hour due? Do they "bounce" because of inaccuracies? Have outside checks of mess records, supply records, individual records shown an abnormally high number of errors? Is it necessary for the commander to personally prepare detailed reports which should be done by others? Or in nearly all cases is it necessary only that he or she sign the reports? The point is this: Unit administration requires a sound leadership, just as there must be leadership in training, in mess management, supply management, and other responsibilities of command. The officer who neglects administrative tasks is riding for a hard fall; as is also the officer who devotes so much time to the task that other responsibilities are neglected.

Leadership in Administration. Unless you are a capable administrator you are unlikely to succeed as a commander. The first requirement is to learn, as to each responsibility within the organization, the records and reports which are required to be prepared; exactly what they include; how they are kept; and when recorded or submitted.

The next step in management is to assign to the appropriate leaders the specific missions of preparation and maintenance of records. This should be precise and include the what, how, when, who.

As in all other tasks, there is an important element of training. Very likely in the processes of personnel assignment there are precious few individuals with clerical, typing, bookkeeping, and such skills, who reach the small units.

Most of these trained individuals are screened out and assigned elsewhere.

More than likely, the company or battery commander must find and train soldiers to perform these tasks.

This is not so difficult. The records to be kept are not complex. It is only that there are many of them, and each must be correct. Select individuals for the tasks who are intelligent, thorough, reliable, who have some aptitude for such work. See that they have correct reference sources, or models, on which to base their work. Require the supervisory leaders to make careful checks, point out mistakes, conduct training periods, and report progress. As records must be legible, hold fast to the requirement for easily read, neat writing. Hammer on accuracy, completeness, timeliness.

It is a certainty that a small unit must train its own typists. Provide a standard typing manual and encourage or require practice (AR 340–15, *Correspondence*). Insist upon correct form from the start, however slowly it is executed. An alert person can develop into a fair typist in a short time, though perhaps establishing no speed records. Avoid selecting the mentally sluggish who are all thumbs, for they cannot progress.

Once the separate administrative tasks are identified and allotted to specific individuals for execution, with a supervisory system for checking plus time for developing individual proficiency, the situation should be in hand. Thereafter the commander should be able in most instances to read a proposed paper or report, accept as facts the statements therein made as facts, and sign, if he or she agrees, with minimum consumption of time. It is another form of leadership.

Military Letters and Indorsements. For the convenience of officers there is included herewith a standard form for a military letter and for an indorsement. For discussion and additional examples, see AR 340–15.

Official Signature. An official signature consists of the name, grade, branch of the Army, organization, and title.

RICHARD D. AMES	K. K. KELLY
MG, USA	MAJ, Inf
Commanding	Trans Officer

A signature that pertains to the signer personally, includes his or her social security account number (SSAN).

RODGER D. HILL	MARY L. SMITH
512-34-0849	363-28-6675
MAJ, Inf	CPT, QMC
3d Inf Regt	

The signed name will be written plainly and legibly and will be identical with the typewritten, stamped, or printed name when used. Use only black or blue-black ink.

IMPORTANT CAUTION: *An officer's signature on an official document means that he or she vouches for the accuracy of the facts stated, and that each recommendation represents his or her carefully considered, professional view. A false official statement, whether oral or written, is a grave offense. Your word, or your signature, is your bond. Be very certain of the correctness of the official papers you sign.*

LEADERSHIP AND ARTICLE 15

The relationship between a commander's leadership responsibility, the standard of discipline maintained within the unit, and the commander's use of the authority to punish under Article 15, are subjects so closely tied together as to constitute in some respects a single function of command. Certainly it is informative to analyze and consider them together.

We have always claimed that "The Army builds men," and it is true. But we have never been very convincing as to how it is accomplished. Perhaps it includes with other things the wise application of leadership, the right sort of discipline, encouragement, and the use of punishment as a corrective rather than a punitive measure. The subject is worthy of contemplation.

What is Leadership? Consider these definitions: *"A leader is a person fitted by force of ideas, character, or genius, or by strength of will or administrative ability to arouse, incite, and direct men in conduct and achievement." "Leadership is the art of imposing one's will upon others in such a manner as to command their respect, their confidence, and their whole-hearted co-operation."*

Many thoughtful observers who have enjoyed prolonged opportunity to study military leaders in the routine conduct of their duties, have reached a similar conclusion: "Officers who are proficient in leadership have a high standard of discipline in their units, and in their day-to-day experience they encounter few disciplinary problems; also, their need to invoke or to use their power to punish under Article 15, or other powers stated in the Manual for Courts Martial, is used with less frequency than in units with less capable leaders." Continuing this same line of thought, under similar conditions in combat, the quality of leadership and the standard of discipline in a unit has a direct and predictable bearing upon accomplishment of mission and the number of casualties. When there is good leadership and good discipline, achievement of mission with minimum casualties is a standard expectancy.

It is instructive to consider discipline and punishment as major parts of the duties and responsibilities of Army leaders.

The Importance of Discipline. One difference between a fine military unit and a mere rabble is the degree of obedience to the will of the leader. The combat value of units is determined by their training, experience, morale, and "will to fight." It may be explanatory to approach your conclusion through a negative: *"I say to this man GO, and he goeth,"* is not a proof or even a test of discipline; he may start briskly at the word GO, and later turn off into a green or alluring pasture, instead of plunging onward through the morass of jungle and marsh beyond which lies his mission. A continual responsibility of military leaders, especially of those officers in direct command of soldiers such as company and platoon commanders, is intelligent, willing, and cheerful achievement of assigned missions or compliance with orders. This is discipline. Fine discipline is the cement or cohesive force of a good organization. Where discipline is weak, leadership is faulty.

The way to obtain a disciplined command, as a habit of individual and group conduct, is to make certain of two things: (1) the leader must be careful that orders are militarily correct, and capable of execution by subordinates; and (2) the leader must insure by observation that orders are meticulously complied with by each individual. Don't be fooled by superficialities. Discipline goes deep, and is the result of many mission achievements, of complete tasks, of

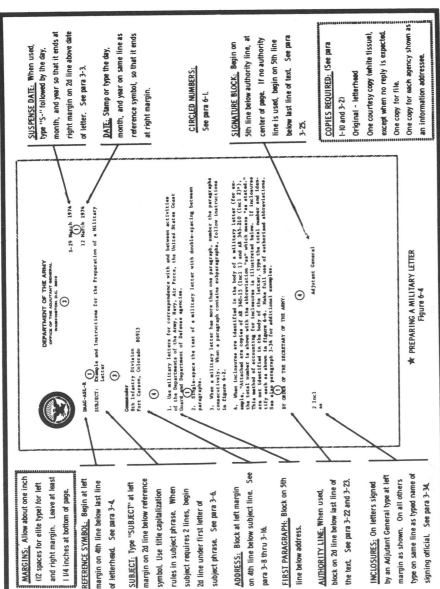

MARGINS: Allow about one inch (12 spaces for elite type) for left and right margin. Leave at least 1 1/4 inches at bottom of page.

REFERENCE SYMBOL: Begin at left margin on 4th line below last line of letterhead. See para 3-4.

SUBJECT: Type "SUBJECT" at left margin on 2d line below reference symbol. Use title capitalization rules in subject phrase. When subject requires 2 lines, begin 2d line under first letter of subject phrase. See para 3-6.

ADDRESS: Block at left margin on 4th line below subject line. See para 3-8 thru 3-16.

FIRST PARAGRAPH: Block on 5th line below address.

AUTHORITY LINE: When used, block on 2d line below last line of the text. See para 3-22 and 3-23.

INCLOSURES: On letters signed by an Adjutant General type at left margin as shown. On all others type on same line as typed name of signing official. See para 3-34.

SUSPENSE DATE: When used, type "S-" followed by the day, month, and year so that it ends at right margin on 2d line above date of letter. See para 3-3.

DATE: Stamp or type the day, month, and year on same line as reference symbol, so that it ends at right margin.

CIRCLED NUMBERS: See para 6-1.

SIGNATURE BLOCK: Begin on 5th line below authority line, at center of page. If no authority line is used, begin on 5th line below last line of text. See para 3-25.

COPIES REQUIRED: (See para 1-10 and 3-2)
Original - letterhead
One courtesy copy (white tissue), except when no reply is expected.
One copy for file.
One copy for each agency shown as an information addressee.

DEPARTMENT OF THE ARMY
OFFICE OF THE ADJUTANT GENERAL
WASHINGTON, D.C. 20315

S-29 March 1974
12 March 1974

DAAG-ASL-R
SUBJECT: Example and Instructions for the Preparation of a Military Letter

Commander
8th Infantry Division
Fort Carson, Colorado 80913

1. Use military letters for correspondence with and between activities of the Departments of the Army, Navy, Air Force, the United States Coast Guard, and Department of Defense agencies.

2. Single-space the text of a military letter with double-spacing between paragraphs.

3. When a military letter has more than one paragraph, number the paragraphs consecutively. When a paragraph contains subparagraphs, follow instructions in figure 6-2.

4. When inclosures are identified in the body of a military letter (for example, "Attached are copies of AR 340-15 (Incl 1) and AR 345-210 (Incl 2)"), the total number is shown with the abbreviation "as" which means "as stated." This method of accounting for inclosures is illustrated below. If inclosures are not identified in the body of the letter, type the total number and identify each as shown in figure 6-6. Make full use of authorized abbreviations. See also paragraph 3-3A for additional examples.

BY ORDER OF THE SECRETARY OF THE ARMY:

Adjutant General

2 Incl
as

★ PREPARING A MILITARY LETTER
Figure 6-4

FORM FOR MILITARY LETTER.

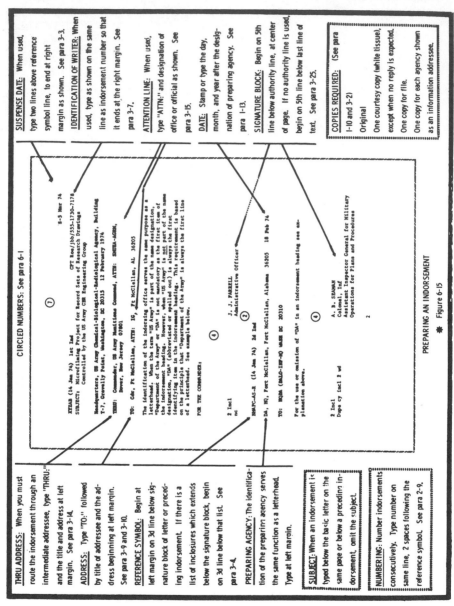

THRU ADDRESS: When you must route the indorsement through an intermediate addressee, type "THRU:" and the title and address at left margin. See para 3-14.

ADDRESS: Type "TO:" followed by title of addressee and the address beginning at left margin. See para 3-9 and 3-10.

REFERENCE SYMBOL: Begin at left margin on 3d line below signature block of letter or preceding indorsement. If there is a list of inclosures which extends below the signature block, begin on 3d line below that list. See para 3-4.

PREPARING AGENCY: The identification of the preparing agency serves the same function as a letterhead. Type at left margin.

SUBJECT: When an indorsement is typed below the basic letter on the same page or below a preceding indorsement, omit the subject.

NUMBERING: Number indorsements consecutively. Type number on same line, 2 spaces following the reference symbol. See para 2-9.

CIRCLED NUMBERS: See para 6-1

SUSPENSE DATE: When used, type two lines above reference symbol line, to end at right margin as shown. See para 3-3.

IDENTIFICATION OF WRITER: When used, type as shown on the same line as indorsement number so that it ends at the right margin. See para 3-7.

ATTENTION LINE: When used, type "ATTN:" and designation of office or official as shown. See para 3-15.

DATE: Stamp or type the day, month, and year after the designation of preparing agency. See para 1-13.

SIGNATURE BLOCK: Begin on 5th line below authority line, at center of page. If no authority line is used, begin on 5th line below last line of text. See para 3-25.

COPIES REQUIRED: (See para 1-10 and 3-2)
Original
One courtesy copy (white tissue), except when no reply is expected.
One copy for file.
One copy for each agency shown as an information addressee.

PREPARING AN INDORSEMENT.
* Figure 6-15

FORM FOR INDORSEMENT.

compliance with orders, of attaining little objectives as well as great ones.

Apply the reasoning to the continuing responsibilities, such as the kitchen staff to serve good meals, on time, under high conditions of sanitation; leaders charged with training to proceed from day to day bringing along their soldiers to meet the desired high standard; the maintenance of high standards of individual neatness of dress and personal appearance; the regular observance of military courtesies; of always being at the prescribed place at the stated time. Apply your doctrine of good discipline also to the new and specific tasks which occur daily, even in combat: In the attack, to seize an area starting from a prescribed place, at a definite time, following a planned route; to go on patrol to accomplish a definite mission; to repair a truck, or any other job to be done. The habit of obedience, or achievement of mission, is the proof of discipline. The leader obtains it by example in meeting the goals established by his or her own commander, and by requiring compliance with orders or mission.

The officer has strong powers to exact obedience. But their use should be graduated from mere statement of the shortcoming to show that it was observed, mild admonition, rebuke, denial of privilege, official reprimand, withdrawal of rating, and as last resort or for genuinely serious offenses, trial by court-martial. Consider always the soldier and his or her past record, the intent, the gravity of the offense or failure. Act objectively and calmly. Choose always the lesser punishment until convinced it will be ineffective. Never resort to scorn or ridicule. Get all the facts before action of any kind. Assume, as an example, failure of a group under an NCO to arrive at a distant point at the time prescribed. Quietly get from the NCO a statement of the reason. Assume these answers: "The bridge was out at Blankville and we were obliged to make a 30-mile detour." The lateness may be dropped. "I took a wrong road and lost the way." A check of the NCO's map reading ability, or instruction, or caution, or mild admonition should be the action because it was simple carelessness or ignorance. "The truck driver let the gas tank run dry and we had to send back 10 miles for gasoline." This is buck passing and unacceptable; the NCO must be instructed firmly as to his or her responsibilities. "I spent the night in town and no one told the troops to be ready to move out." This is lack of appreciation of an NCO's responsibilities and, if indicative of habit or unreliability generally, consideration should be given to extensive training, or reduction. The point is, the leader must detect transgressions, determine the cause, and apply sound corrective action. If the leader habitually overlooks transgressions, or lightly passes them by, he or she is lost; when the big test comes, the unit will fail to take the hill and soldiers will die who should have lived.

This we submit is true discipline and how to attain it.

How Should a Leader Use The Power To Punish Under Article 15? Discussed very briefly above is the importance of good military leadership, and its proven influence upon achievement of mission with the minimum of casualties; discussed also is the true meaning of discipline with the observation many individuals have noted that when leadership is of a high order few disciplinary problems are presented. Soldiers strive to please the leader they trust and admire, with avoidance of acts which would lower their personal standing in his or her eyes.

Even so, as long as most soldiers are young, and as long as people are people, which will be a very long period indeed, there will continue to be human transgressions which require the application of the military leader's power to punish. The leader is authorized to use a carefully regulated power to enforce obedience and discipline, according to the severity of the offense and the past record of the offender. Most such acts are taken in small units, such as the platoon, company, or battalion, under the provisions of Article 15, concerning which extensive instruction is provided at courses in service schools and in unit instruction. It is discussed below only as to its close relation to sound discipline and to good leadership.

There are three possible actions which a commander may take when an offense has been committed: *First,* a soldier may be given extra attention and certain prescribed duties without resort to a recorded action. This applies especially to trivial or minor offenses, and first offenders. Most young soldiers intend to do the right things. *Second,* a soldier or officer may be punished under Article 15. This punishment is minor, non-judicial, and may be administered by a company commander or a battalion commander for which procedure the reader should consult the Manual for Courts-Martial. After each such disciplinary action the individual should be counseled; not scolded, not threatened —but advised, counseled. Sometimes it is best to transfer the soldier to a different leader, or into different work. When a soldier leaves the unit his or her record of punishment under Article 15 is destroyed. (Not so as to the officer; for the officer, Article 15 action becomes a part of his or her permanent record.) *Third,* repeated offenders under Article 15, and those guilty of serious offenses, may be tried by a court-martial.

Leadership, Discipline and Punishment as Part of the Truth, "The Army Builds Men and Women." Most soldiers are young men and women in their late teens or their twenties. As to their habits of obedience, behavior, diligence at work, ambition for advancement, understanding of the obligations of the citizen to perform military service, they are the individuals who have been produced by our family life, our schools, our churches, our national environment. Don't sell them short, nor be deceived by the critic who belittles our modern young citizens; they will be equal to any test, as their predecessors have proven, and the great majority of them will have all that it takes, and more, to provide for the national security. In any case, you, as the commander, must take those assigned to your unit and work out your destiny with them. You must resolve to lift each soldier entrusted to your care to that individual's highest level of capability. You must provide a high standard of leadership, sound discipline, and when necessary you must resort to a proper measure of punishment.

We are talking of building men and women. Good leaders are careful to issue clear instructions, and make certain they are understood. They avoid trivial, irritating restrictions. They never show favoritism, nor threaten, nor belittle. They are careful to note good work by a soldier and comment about it. "Good work, Soldier" (but know and use his or her name), heads off many little disobediences. When a soldier does something wrong, skilled leaders tell or show the person how to do it right, and follow up to see that the lesson is learned. When necessary, they caution, or admonish, in private. When punishment is performed it is to be done impersonally, objectively, without rancor. The goal is to convince transgressors that they have everything to gain by doing their duty and being good soldiers.

Occasionally a soldier is encountered who is so determined to avoid military service, and obtain a discharge, that he or she chooses a most damaging course of action. The individual may commit deliberately a series of offenses in order to receive punishment under Article 15, or by court-martial, hoping to be separated from the service administratively under AR 635-206, for misconduct, or under AR 635–200 for incompatibility with service life or discipline. Here is a severe challenge to leadership. The temptation may be strong to "throw the book" at the offender. Such separations are a serious and permanent blot on an individual's life as well as his or her military record. The individual is thereafter considered to be unfit for further service and could not serve our country during war. There should be a sincere attempt at instruction and rehabilitation of the offender before permitting completion of such a disastrous course of action. As long as the leader feels there is something good in an offender which can be brought out and developed, the officer should be loathe to accept failure by having the soldier discharged.

Experienced officers know that many thousands of soldiers who have started off with the wrong concepts of military service, or sour on service in war or peace, have been brought into healthful understanding and have gone on to build commendable records of honorable service. Of course, there are others who cannot be influenced constructively, and whose discharge is necessary. But first a sincere effort for rehabilitation should be made.

Finally, to emphasize an axiom stated at the outset of this discussion, it is a fact that anyone may verify by observation, that few of our more effective Army commanders—starting at platoon level—encounter serious problems of discipline or of offenses requiring severe punishment. Such extremes occur, but they are rare. Most soldiers choose to serve their country with honor and with pride.

TAKING CARE OF YOUR SOLDIERS

Let us peer into the old truism that "a commander must take care of his or her soldiers" seeking to determine why he or she does this and precisely what is done to accomplish this goal.

Why has there always been such heavy emphasis upon the duty of commanding officers to take the best care of their soldiers? The commander provides as best he or she can for the physical, mental, and recreational welfare of the unit's personnel to make more certain that they are receptive to training, able and willing to perform their individual missions capably, proud of their own unit, and willing to perform military service in accordance with their enlistment contract.

The commander is provided with very strong authority, under federal law, by virtue of his or her commission and specific assignment to command a particular unit. Authority is power. The commander has far broader power than is extended to a civilian chief. Obedience to the commander's orders in battle may result in forfeiture of life under conditions where refusal to obey a proper order could result in trial with sentence to death. This is power, indeed. But with this great power goes at the same time a heavy responsibility. The unit personnel are responsible to the commander who, in turn, is responsible for them and all that they do in the performance of their duty. Authority and responsibility must go together.

The commander must train his or her soldiers and this is a part of the job of taking care of them. Unless they are thoroughly and properly trained the chance is increased that the unit will fall short of its mission. Individuals who are improperly or inadequately trained are far more likely than others to become battle casualties.

As an illustration, here are some of the things which are done as routine by a captain commanding a company upon completion of a long march before withdrawing to his or her own tent or quarters. Assigns unit bivouac areas or quarters. Designates locations for kitchen, vehicle park, latrines. Checks that arrangements are made at once for sick call or the medical attention of any soldiers who are injured or sick. Provides for foot inspection. Makes certain that arrangements are made for emergency issue of equipment. You must not look to your own personal comfort first, nor permit yourself to be entangled with some single facet of the task of getting the company settled. You must see to the whole job. Necessarily you must see that the subordinate leaders follow the same course. When these tasks are finished, with others which circumstances require, you may go to your own quarters. The needs of your troops come first. "Take care of your soldiers and they will take care of you," is an Old Army axiom to remember and to apply, for it is as true today as in earlier times.

The leader of a company or smaller unit must know a great deal about each individual. He or she must learn their names quickly, call them by name, and learn their specialties, their strengths, and their weaknesses. This creates a personal bond between the individual and the commander. "My captain knows me," the soldier will think, "and he knows of my hopes. He also knows the things I do wrong. My captain is a fair man and I am glad to serve in his company." The captain may think, "Jones is a lazy cuss. But if I am in a tight spot where I need someone I can depend on I would want him with me." A bond of mutual understanding born of knowing the soldier and the soldier knowing his or her officers is essential to success in a command. Soldiers cannot be fooled. They will not mistake a poor commander for a good one. The relationship is one of daily contacts and is too continuous, too varied, and too close to allow for this kind of deception. If they are satisfied that their commander is taking good care of them, there is no question that they will do their best to accomplish an assigned mission, however they may regard it, and look out for the commander's interests in doing it.

The Officer's Relationship with His or Her Troops. Command is a very personal relationship. The smaller the unit the more personal it becomes. How then should the officer conduct himself or herself with and before the unit personnel?

Some officers are always official, rather stern, unbending. Not arrogant, not heartless, not unjust. But official, stern, unbending. Others have a warm and friendly relationship to a point but are careful to maintain a dignity or reserve. They smile, make light of hardships, take hard things in stride. Still others carry this trait to extreme, seem to strive to shed responsibility, to be "one of the boys." Which is correct? Certainly not the latter example, for this is the path of weakness and failure. But of the first two, we can say only this: Each officer must follow the course which seems most natural and which gives the best results. For that officer, that way is best. Be yourself. Be natural.

This too can be said:* No officer can be on terms of personal intimacy with a few soldiers, while holding others at a distance, without developing the conviction among the less favored that he or she is "playing favorites." You must be objective, fair, impersonal, and do as to each soldier what duty requires. You are the commander. You cannot, and do your duty, display partiality, or favoritism, or preference.

---

*See also Chapter 1, *The Code of the Army Officer,* and its discussion, THE OFFICER'S RELATIONS WITH ENLISTED PERSONNEL, and Chapter 3, *The Officer Image.*

Never use ridicule. The worst violation of common sense and human decency a commander can adopt is to pour scorn or ridicule upon a soldier, or permit others to do so. Never refer to a soldier as an "8-ball," or a poor marksman on the range as a "bolo." To do so is to encourage others in the organization to use the same terms and apply them broadly. Pride is destroyed. Hatred may arise instead of tolerance.

Never talk down to your troops, as it will be resented even by the ones who are slow to learn. American young people have a high level of education and it will often be true that the enlisted ranks of a unit contain individuals of superior educational achievements. Such individuals are our greatest hope for leadership development and for technical assignments; talking down will first occasion resentment and then amusement among them. Never seem to be patronizing nor "Big I and Little You."

In any group of men or women there are variations in individual intelligence, mechanical aptitude, educational background, character, and all other human attributes. The military leader must take the individuals assigned to his or her unit, determine their potentials, assign them and train them for the most appropriate place in the organization, and do the best possible with them. The leader must get the most from each individual assigned to the unit, however far up or down the scale that "most" may be placed. Ridicule and scorn will reduce or destroy the capacity of any individual. Let it be clear that you recognize and value highly the talents of your soldiers, and that you expect each one to achieve highly.

Health and Physical Welfare. The line commander has a very definite responsibility for the health and physical welfare of his or her troops. Our splendid medical service will care for individuals who are sick, wounded, or injured; through checks, surveys, and examinations of all kinds our medical service will avoid or reduce all practicable hazards to the health of the command; they will inspect and advise commanders as to their health and sanitation situation. It is a joint job for the medical service and the organization commander.

What are some of the definite responsibilities if you are a line commander? You avoid unhealthy conditions in camp or in the field as conditions allow. You insist upon organization cleanliness through adequate clean-up and police measures. You insist upon individual cleanliness as to person and clothing; this will often require that you provide measures for bathing, individual washing of clothes, or provisions to get clothing to a laundry and back again for use. In the organization mess you must provide at all times for adequate refrigeration, a high standard of sanitation including facilities for washing mess gear and dishes, with cleanliness of all food handlers. There must be adequate lavatory and latrine facilities which are maintained in a sanitary, orderly condition. These are daily responsibilities of the line commander which have for their purpose the maintenance of health. They are illness-preventive measures in the eyes of the doctor.

There are the safety measures to avoid accidents. The military arts are especially hazardous. Great care must be used in the handling of guns and explosives. Power equipment in the hands of the poorly trained individual or the novice may be lethal. Accidents in the driving of motor vehicles of all kinds are a continual threat.

Receiving the New Soldier. The way a new soldier is received in an organization has a profound effect upon his or her immediate impressions. It may have lasting effect. Combat organizations of the Army have the ever-present problem of assimilating "replacements" (a poor word which some wise person should improve, and let it never be forgotten that the replacement of today is the veteran of tomorrow!). There is a place at once for the replacement's energy and skill, zeal in the cause, and the new soldier's determination to win.

Then we should take those steps which will enhance the new soldier's immediate value, and avoid those things which will delay or destroy it.

As the very first step, take care at once of the new soldier's creature necessities and comforts, while at the same time letting him or her know that all in the organization are glad he or she has arrived. See that the new arrival is fed, is given a place to stow personal gear, a place to sleep, and made to feel a member of an up and coming organization which knows how to care for its members and intends to do it.

At the very first opportunity the unit commander should meet and interview the new arrival. Who is he or she? Learn about the person's training, service, age, home community, education, family, service aspirations. Create the acceptance on the part of the new arrival that the commander wants to know his or her soldiers, is interested in them, and means to use them wisely.

Repeat the process by interviews held by junior officers and appropriate noncommissioned officers. Decide promptly upon the individual's squad assignment. Introduce the soldier to members of the squad who must be encouraged to extend the hand of comradeship.

If these measures are taken thoughtfully, newness will wear off very promptly; shyness, wishful thinking of former comrades, and other deterrents will disappear to be replaced by satisfaction of assignment, a feeling of "belonging," and determination to get on with the job whatever it may be.

A Look at "Coddling." Coddling is overlooking things soldiers do which are wrong. Avoiding night training, or long marches, or training in rain or cold, to spare physical discomfort are examples. It is to fail to send out a patrol, when there is grave need for information, because it is a dangerous mission, only to have many soldiers killed by surprise action of the enemy which might have been detected. Now is a good time to return to a definition of leadership in an earlier edition which starts, "The art of imposing one's will . . ." The leader must be a determined person, in matters concerning his or her duty and mission, holding subordinates squarely to the mark; but at the same time providing in every way for the training, mess and supply, administration, medical attention, recreation, and the human touch of welfare as it is needed. Coddling is weak and wrong. But full provision for the contentment of unit personnel is eternally right.

OFF-DUTY ACTIVITIES

While the training day or working day of a military organization is long, the commander has not discharged his or her responsibilities because recall has sounded. The average age of soldiers of a company may be under 25, or even under 20. Most will be single or will not have their families nearby. Because they are young most of them will have abundant energy to be employed when the official day has ended. Again the responsibilities of the military leader carry far beyond those of a civilian chief. This void in time must be filled by worthy opportunities, or soldiers through boredom may fill it otherwise.

It is Army policy to make the off-duty life of posts and stations so attractive and interesting that all personnel will find some one or more activities which consume their time and interest. People vary as to their interests. Most but not all like to take part in athletics; a portion will wish to read or study; the service club with its dances and activities will attract many. Others will prefer to remain in barracks with the activities immediately at hand. The point is this: There must be opportunities on a large scale for off-duty enjoyment, and there must be wide diversification in the things under way.

A sound off-duty program is a three-pronged affair. First, and possibly of highest importance, are the facilities at the barracks such as a suitable day room, and facilities for informal athletics. This is the primary responsibility of the company commander. Second, an extensive program for the garrison as a whole. Here we have the activities of Recreation Services in off-duty recreation; a broad athletic program; the religious program of the Chaplain; theaters; the educational programs of Information and Education. These are responsibilities of the station commander assisted by staff members. Third, are activities in adjacent civilian communities provided for personnel in uniform such as are provided by USO, civilian and civic organizations, churches, lodges, and the like. When the soldier leaves the post these facilities provide a place to go and things to do. These are responsibilities of the station commander, aided by his or her staff, in coordination with civilian leaders.

Recreational Program of a Company. Leadership is needed within a company if it is to have an attractive off-duty program. Many commanders assign an officer or noncommissioned officer to supervise this program in addition to other duties.

Two programs have direct application to the company in barracks. They are the day room, or recreation room, and the organization athletic program; this may consist of informal athletics of many kinds for wide participation, or the forming of company teams for scheduled games in a battalion, brigade, or station league.

The leader of the activity may proceed on this line of action. Make a careful check of facilities, both as to items issued and purchased from unit funds. Visit a number of organizations to see the general standard, and observe for especially popular ideas. Fix upon a standard of facilities and activities and go after it.

Apply first attention to the day room, or recreation room. Here is the place soldiers will assemble when off duty, in fair weather or foul, more regularly than elsewhere. A proper day room is equipped to be interesting; well lighted; clean and attractive in appearance. The equipment should include a number of comfortable lounge chairs; a larger number of straight chairs because they require less space; a large table; small tables as appropriate; floor or wall lamps. All must be strongly built. As to "things to do," all or most of the following should be provided: Basic supply of newspapers and magazines, remembering that the soldier has available the station library; radio; record player; television; pool table; table tennis.

Strive to arrange facilities so as to provide reading (and studying) and hobby rooms away from the vociferous day room activity. Many soldiers are taking study courses for various goals and should be assisted by access to a quiet area while off duty.

Part of the day room furnishings may be obtained by issue through the Morale Support officer of the station. The remainder may be purchased from the unit fund, with the approval of the company commander.

A good company athletic program is a matter of facilities, equipment, and guidance. The goal here is for everyone to participate—"athletics for all."

Again, the officer in charge of company off-duty activities should survey what equipment is on hand, what is unserviceable and can be repaired. By conference with NCOs he or she can determine what is wanted. Some athletic equipment may be obtained from the station Morale Support officer by issue. Anything additional must be provided by purchase from organization nonappropriated funds. A desired equipment list, with detailed costs, must be presented to the company commander for approval, or amendment.

The Morale Support Officer. The Morale Support Officer of posts and stations, and of large units, heads all recreational services including voluntary athletics. The closest coordination and support should be developed between commanders, especially small unit commanders, and the Morale Support Officer.

The Chaplain. Religious freedom is one of the basic foundations of the American form of government. Military chaplains are provided in the U.S. Army to ensure availability of a free choice in the exercise of religion. Ordained clergy perform as an extension of their denomination in conducting worship services, administering rites and sacraments, and providing an active religious education program. The chaplain is a technical expert serving on the personal staff of the commander and assists the commander in fulfilling command responsibility concerning matters of religion, morals, and morale as affected by religion.

The religious and spiritual welfare of the members of a command is an important factor in the development of individual pride, morale, and self-respect, essentials in a military organization. While Kipling may have over-emphasized the sordid side of the life led by some soldiers in saying that men in barracks do not grow into plaster saints, it is a fact the environment in some instances leaves a little to be desired. We are a religious people and our soldiers are subject to a wholesome, religious influence. There is a relation between morals and morale just as there is a relation between fair and just treatment and morale, or cleanliness and morale. The organization commander who is mindful of the religious and spiritual environment of his or her soldiers will be able to make a strong appeal to the better instincts of all, which may be impossible to attain for those who neglect it.

Unit Nonappropriated Funds. The earnings resulting from the operation of exchanges and motion picture theaters are paid monthly into unit nonappropriated funds. Each company receives the distribution, as does the central post fund, for an entire station, and the major command fund, such as an army in the CONUS. Expenditures from the funds are authorized for the good of an entire organization for things not supplied by the government, as stated in detail in AR 210–55. As to company funds, expenditures and accounts are a personal responsibility of the commander which may not be delegated to another officer.

AR 230–9 provides further regulations on fund management and the commander's responsibility. It is wise to consult with an experienced auditor, often the battalion executive officer, on the details and techniques of keeping the book, obtaining vouchers, and cautions concerning unit fund property. A council within the unit of officers and NCOs will advise the commander but the management of the fund is still his or her responsibility. Like all savings, they are hard to accumulate and easy to spend; but, unlike personal savings, the regulations are very specific on what can be purchased.

The United Service Organization, USO. The facilities provided by the USO for off-post recreation are of high value and deserve strong support from commanders. The Army itself has made notable progress in improving the recreation and athletic facilities within military stations through its strongly supported Morale Support program. The USO provides its assistance in nearby civilian communities through club and service facilities. A clean and attractive gathering place in cities visited by large numbers of service men and women is essential. Their activities of many kinds provide needed recreation. The USO also sends shows to overseas commands to entertain our service members.

Funds for support of the USO are raised through the annual Community Chest and United Givers Fund drives, all by volunteer giving.

Unit commanders can assist the USO program by knowing where their facilities are established, close acquaintance with the local leaders, cooperation by informing their personnel about USO, and a regular announcement of current activities. A frequent visit of the facilities by commanders of all grades is helpful to demonstrate a sustained interest in the work of the organization. They can assist in the fund-raising program by telling civilian leaders of the need for USO in cities and towns near Army stations.

SPECIAL PROBLEMS

There are other special problems which the leader will encounter in all categories of units whether infantry, artillery, armor, engineers, combat support, technical, or administrative. Several of these recurring problems, with suggestions as to their handling, are discussed below. There are others, of course, and some may have a "newness" which will startle the commander. In each such case, the officer must find the way to proceed quietly and objectively to determine the facts, weigh them, and decide what action, if any at all, should be taken for the benefit either of the individual concerned, the unit, or the broader good of the Army and the nation. The officer's commission is a public trust; he or she is expected to choose a wise course of action, and have the courage to follow it.

Absence Without Leave. Commanders of companies will certainly be faced with the problem of absence without leave. It is the military example of "cutting classes," or staying away from work which the civilian chief calls "absenteeism." But in a military command it is far more serious. Skulking in battle is an aggravated form of AWOL. Like other problems it can be reduced greatly, if not entirely eliminated, by a sound approach.

Many times soldiers are absent without leave when by asking they could as easily have received permission to be away. The first essential is that all personnel understand clearly how and when they may obtain passes for short absences, and leaves for longer ones. As duty permits there should be readiness to grant this authority within the scope of regulations. Then when duty requires all to be on duty continuously, individuals will be better prepared mentally to accept the situation.

Instruction will constitute the preventive for a large portion of the unit. Good soldiers cherish their standing in the eyes of their superiors and of their fellows. They must understand that such an absence is prejudicial to promotion or assignment to a responsible position. They should be made aware of the standing of the organization itself in this matter because senior commanders watch carefully the comparative standings of their units in AWOL and other transgressions. They must understand about loss of pay for the offense. That essential instruction is missed will influence some soldiers. The problem is reduced by being certain that sound, positive instruction is given about the gravity of the offense as to its individual effects, although it may not be eliminated by this method.

After an individual returns from an unauthorized absence there must be an interview with the commander. What was the true reason for the absence? Did the soldier understand the policy for leave or pass? Was he or she denied authority for absence? Was the absence an important one as to personal affairs, or trivial, or an example of character weakness? The commander must strive to learn the cause and having done so to apply such corrective action as is indicated.

A series of such interviews is almost certain to disclose that soldiers most prone to offend in this matter are those of lowest intelligence, or education, or ambition, or weakest in character. Patience in instruction of such individuals may be necessary.

Strong action must be taken as to repeated offenders who continue the practice despite instruction, sound appeals to pride, and milder punishments. Here will be found those most prone to skulking on the battlefield, or self-inflicted wounds. They are the ones most likely to be asleep when they should be alert to detect enemy action, or to turn back from a patrol. In such cases the only remaining action may be to let trials by court-martial run their course.

The commander must face this problem with wisdom and sound action.

Debt and the Commander's Responsibility. Debt beyond immediate capacity to pay is not a new problem of a soldier (or officer). Two old and trite savings must bear still another repetition: "I will gladly pay a dollar next week for a hamburger today," has been attributed to the American soldier. "All men are good soldiers—when they are broke," is also ancient, and has a vestige of truth.

There are merchants within the United States and abroad who go to extremes to get a soldier or an officer to place his or her name on an installment contract. It is one of our less admirable national traits that we want to have at once all the enjoyments of our contemporaries. It is the "Travel now—pay later" philosophy extended. The Legal Assistance counselors, who see the seamy and greedy side of it, say "Keep your pen in your pocket!"

What is the responsibility of the commander? He or she has a duty to instruct because some soldiers, even senior NCOs and officers, contract obligations beyond their capacity to pay. The commander can be certain that the majority of "temptations" are disclosed, such as car, appliance, china, travel, book, insurance, clothing, on and on. He or she can also prevent salesmen encroaching upon training time, or even the unit premises unless the salesman has an authorization in hand from appropriate authority.

When the damage is done, the commander may assist the person in financial difficulty to make a consolidated loan, save interest, and have repayment placed on an attainable basis. In some instances such loans may be obtained from the Red Cross, or Army Emergency Relief. This procedure includes opportunity to instruct in order to develop the "never again" attitude.

An associated administrative problem is the barrage of letters from creditors demanding collection assistance. There is a regulation which requires commanders to assist bona fide creditors in collecting amounts properly payable to them; and there is the accompanying duty of a commander to protect his or her soldiers against fraudulent or incorrect claims. Some creditors resort to threats against the commander as well as the debtor. What course should a commander follow? He or she should require the creditor to provide a copy of the contract, or a written agreement or record to substantiate the claim, with a statement of all payments to date; consult the soldier (or the officer) to determine whether there is an agreement between creditor and debtor; and determine the soldier's version of the indebtedness. Some cases may require guidance from the Legal Assistance Officer. When the commander is satisfied that there is an indebtedness, and payment is in arrears, it becomes his or her duty to require or try to arrange a suitable method of payment. A soldier (or officer) may be punished for failure to pay just debts.

This is an unpleasant duty which falls to commanders of companies, and even to battalion commanders. Expect to encounter the problem and regard it as a challenge to leadership.

About Those Who "Hate the Army." Regrettably, there are some soldiers and even some officers quite brazen in saying, "They don't like," or "that they hate the Army." Some few are so loud and insistent about it, and seemingly so proud of it, as to cause wonder about their loyalty to the nation that favors them with citizenship. For too many years we have overlooked such occurrences with a good natured tolerance, but the situation deserves consideration. What is the real meaning behind such assertions? What can be done to change the view of those who are antagonistic to the nation's defense forces? How can we change these individuals from poor and unreliable members into useful ones? Not by ignoring them, surely.

What these individuals are saying, perhaps without intent, is their hatred of the United States, their rejection of the duties of a citizen, or their fervent unwillingness to do anything whatever to protect their individual freedoms and opportunities, which they take for granted. Our country can endure a small portion of such individuals; but if the time should ever come that the majority of our people choose this philosophy, our nation will go the way of ancient Rome, and other vanished nations of the modern as well as the ancient eras. The correction of shallow beliefs and unpatriotic actions is worth a strong effort.

Some who do it are intentionally subversive, and let us not delude ourselves about it. Anything such individuals can do to weaken the determination of others to give their best in military service, or destroy confidence in the nation, its defense forces, its military or civil leadership, is beneficial to the secret cause of the subversive person.

It is entirely true that in the great majority of cases the service member or ex-member who makes hateful or derogatory remarks about the Army (Air Force or Navy as well) does so without intentional subversive intent. He or she is merely exercising an inalienable right to "blow off steam." Such persons may be stupid, uneducated, lazy, indifferent to the national needs in a troubled world. Also, they may be highly intelligent, well educated persons, and it is a tragedy for the Army to fail to gain the understanding support of its potentially most capable members. We can spare the stupid and lazy for their contributions will be of small value, at best. But we must seek to obtain the active support and best efforts of the true intellectuals for otherwise there is heavy damage to the cause of free people everywhere.

What can a commander do about it? How can this waste of potential high capability be saved and applied to constructive uses? Wisdom is needed here. If it is merely getting rid of a gripe, ignore it, certainly. Is the offender momentarily enraged as to one or more occurrences, or one or more individuals? Has the soldier been the recipient of an action which he or she believes unfair or unjust? Or is the offender lazy, stupid, indifferent to national needs? Finally, does the individual really have a deep-seated "Hate the Army" complex?

There are also the protestors, objectors, and the racists, who are a sign of our times, and present a special problem to be handled wisely. They require a patient, thoughtful leader whose emotions are circumscribed by common sense and the official regulations. The first step is to study the published regulations and ascertain the command policy. Important references are AR 600-50, *Standards of Conduct for Department of the Army Personnel;* AR 600–20, *Army Command Policy and Procedure;* the UCMJ. For specific situations the unit commander may also expect to receive local directives. Discussions with such individuals will be enhanced by a patient, thoughtful, well-informed leader who has the firm intention of making useful, willing, capable soldiers who are assigned under his or her jurisdiction, out of persons who might otherwise become a severe, undependable drag. Pitch the discussions to the intelligence and education level of the individual or individuals involved. A serious effort to reach minds with logic and reason is worth a major effort. Our nation needs citizens who are loyal and willing to perform the arduous duties of citizenship.

Not all will change their stated beliefs, or reveal their inner purposes. They must be apprised of their rights and limits in the presence of immediate commanders, officers and NCO's. It is wise to do this openly, calmly, objectively, in low key. This is not a new problem, and in our democracy it may never be old. Even so, the wisdom of Tom Paine continues to apply: *"Those who expect to reap the blessings of liberty, must, like men, undergo the fatigue of supporting it."*

The Curbing of Vulgar and Profane Language. In the spring of 1965, the Army's Chief of Staff, General Harold K. Johnson, issued instructions to curb the use of vulgarity and profanity in the conduct of instruction and official, oral conversation in the Army service. Officers experienced in command of United States soldiers, at all levels from platoon upward in size, must applaud the action as contributing to the pride in service of the vast majority of our armed forces personnel. In any case, as persons of education and responsibility, officers should never permit in their presence the use of foul, offensive language.

The Venereal Problem. A curse of mankind, shared by armies, is venereal infection resulting from unwise or foolish sexual contacts. It is a command responsibility to instruct soldiers on the broad subject of morality and clean living as well as measures to avoid infection.

The Complaint Problem. The commander must be accessible to members of the unit who wish to state a complaint. Some of the complaints will be petty. Others may be deliberate attempts to injure the reputation of another with a charge which is without foundation. There are other occasions, however, even in the best organizations, where genuine cause for dissatisfaction may occur. This is information which the commander must obtain lest the morale of the unit be seriously impaired. Members must know that they may state a cause for complaint to their commander with the knowledge that he or she will give them a hearing and correct the grievance if convinced of its truth. The Army has an "Open Door Policy" which calls for easy access to the commander through appropriate subordinate commanders unable to resolve the complaint. Good soldiers will seek to avoid making a complaint. But when ideas, or suggestions, or reports are stated to the commander which affect the welfare, the efficiency, or the morale of the unit, or any individual therein, it must be heard sympathetically. If the condition reported can be corrected, or deserves correction, the action should be taken at once. (See "Redress of Wrong," Chapter Twenty-Four.)

Delivery of Mail. Homesickness may well be said to be the "occupational disease" of the American soldier. Next in importance to food, the student of soldier psychology might place the prompt delivery of mail. Indeed, for the soldier with a wife or husband, a son or daughter, a sweetheart or a beloved father or mother, mail may be of far greater lasting importance than food. Commanders of units must pay particular attention to this necessary task. They must see to it that mail reaches the soldier quickly and safely. They must make very certain that none is lost and that chance of malicious opening and violation of privacy is reduced to the vanishing point. A letter from home is of the highest importance to the soldier as it serves to unite him or her for a moment with loved ones. For the most part, letters will quiet the soldier's apprehensions and dispel the worries which beset those who are far removed from their homes. Knowledge that all is well at home secures a peace of mind so strong that it justifies every effort a good mail service requires.

The commander is urged to check the method of receiving, guarding, and distributing the mail as it reaches the organization. Are the individuals charged with handling it completely trustworthy? Or are there unsolved complaints of rifled or stolen letters? Is the mail guarded scrupulously from the time of receipt until it is handed to the soldier? Or is it allowed to lie about, subject to scrutiny and mishandling? Is it tossed promiscuously into a milling throng with small regard to its actual delivery? Or is it handed to the individual to whom addressed? Is it held for long hours after receipt to be distributed at the whim of some individual? Or is the mail delivered as promptly as circumstances permit after receipt? Are registered and special delivery pieces handled with due regard to Postal regulations? Are your receipts for these classes of mail maintained exactly as prescribed? The soldier treasures packages from home. Are packages zealously guarded so that petty pilfering is surely prevented? These are all matters which are very important in the daily life of the soldier.

Personal Problems of Soldiers. All soldiers have left interests, or roots, or problems behind them which may require their attention or action while in the military service. At home the soldier would turn for advice to a parent, a friend, a lawyer, a minister or priest, or other person in whom he or she has trust and confidence. In the Army, the soldier will usually turn to the company commander.

These occasions provide a fine opportunity for the commander to show a deep interest in the welfare of his or her soldiers. The commander should adopt an impersonal and kindly attitude in hearing these problems. If the matter is confidential it must never be divulged improperly. When it is proper to do so, the commander should give the counsel he or she knows to be correct, or obtain the necessary information, or direct the soldier to an authority who can supply the information.

In many cases, after hearing the soldier's problems, the officer will need to refer the soldier to another authority. The legal assistance officer for legal matters; the American Red Cross field director for investigation and action about family conditions at home; the chaplain on many matters of religion, marriage, and human relationships; the surgeon if the problem is one of worry about health.

A good leader must have a genuine understanding of human relations. His or her tools are men and women, and therefore the leader must be able to deal with people. The necessary warmth of military leadership may be demonstrated when soldiers carry their baffling personal problems to their commander for advice or solution.

Importance of Letters to Parents. In a number of organizations, commanders make it a practice to write letters to parents of their soldiers when important personal events have occurred in which they may take pride. The people of the United States are tremendously and vitally concerned about the progress of the Army to which they have given the services of their sons and daughters. Their impressions are formed by the reports they receive from their children and their neighbors and friends. No amount of big-name announcements as to Army morale and conditions will offset the local effect of an unfavorable report from a personal acquaintance. The interest and satisfaction which can be developed by contact, even by letters, with the folks at home are worth the effort required.

Many company, battery, or platoon leaders write these letters. "Dear Mrs. Brown," they may write, "I am pleased to tell you that I have recommended your son for promotion to the grade of corporal. He has worked hard here and his record is splendid. He is quite a good soldier." Or this: "As you know, your son has been confined to the station hospital. I have visited him several times and have had frequent reports about his condition from his medical officer, the chaplain, and others. I can tell you now that he is well on the road to recovery, and his return to his organization will occur very soon. He is performing a service to his nation of which you and he, too, will always be proud." The American soldier is a young man or woman who is usually away from home for the first time. The soldier's parents are anxious that he or she perform creditably.

Have you been present when a letter is received from a young soldier? Do you know how it is discussed and passed around or read aloud to others? Can you not imagine the effect of a letter from a soldier's commander? Form the habit of writing personal letters to the parents of your soldiers on proper occasion. It places a human touch on a relationship which is impersonal and detached.

CONCLUSION

Now that you as an actual leader have progressed through the study of leadership as an academic subject, have received some practical application of principles as a cadet, ROTC student, or officer candidate, and have performed the responsibility of an actual assignment in command, you may recognize some consoling truths. There are no quick thumb rules or easily memorized axioms that will assure a junior leader of success. The superlative qualities which have been described are impossible for all leaders to have, and no leader has had all of them. The young leader will understand that diligence, patience, honor, integrity, devotion to a cause and to his or her soldiers, when combined with knowledge, are all included. After progressing for a time with your first responsibility in command you will have learned that it is results in the execution of command that count. You will develop acceptance of a further truth: *Army commanders must anticipate that someday they may lead troops in battle,* and set about the development of the qualities which they must possess to meet this responsibility successfully. Then the young leader has adopted a sound course.

There are visible rewards for success in leadership. It may lead to promotion with increased pay, decorations, the finest assignments. But the greatest reward is the trust and approval of your officers and soldiers, plus the invisible reward of satisfaction with being a leader who accomplishes the missions assigned. If you should aspire to become a Bradley, MacArthur, Eisenhower, Pershing, Lee, Grant, or Washington (and why not?) set your goal and proceed. The Army has vast opportunity for talent.

17

Staff Assignment

Any military organization has a commander who alone is responsible for all that the unit does or fails to do. All policies, basic decisions, and plans must be authorized by the commander before they are put into effect. All orders from a higher unit to a lower unit are given to the commander thereof and are issued by or for the commander of the larger unit. Each individual in the Army is accustomed to look to his or her immediate superior for orders and instructions. By this means, authority and responsibility are definitely fixed and the channels of command are definitely established.

WHY A STAFF?

It should be apparent, however, that there are a myriad of details involved with the day-to-day operation of any organization. As the size of the organization increases, the number and variety of the details increase. The commander cannot devote personal attention to all of them.

Therefore, a staff is provided as an aid to command. It serves to relieve the commander of details by providing basic information and technical advice by which he or she may arrive at decisions; by developing the basic decision into adequate plans, translating plans into orders, and transmitting them to subordinate leaders; by insuring compliance with these orders through constructive inspection and observation for the commander; by keeping the commander informed of everything he or she ought to know; by anticipating future needs and drafting tentative plans to meet them; by supplementing the commander's efforts to secure unity of action throughout the command; and by learning the commander's policies and working within them. In short, a properly functioning staff is an extension of the eyes, ears and will of the commander.

Value of a Staff Assignment. An assignment to staff duties provides an opportunity for increased knowledge and capability for an officer of any grade. The staff officer learns the detailed organization and missions of each component of the command and how the commanding officer and the subordinate commanders solve the problems which confront them. The staff officer works with each staff section and gains a knowledge of their responsibilities and methods. It is splendid training for a future assignment to command.

STAFF ORGANIZATION

The organization of the staff of any military unit is prescribed in the Tables of Organization, and is based upon the duties and responsibilities of the commander whom it serves. The battalion is the smallest unit which has a staff although even in the company there are officers and noncommissioned officers who have duties which parallel those of staff officers. These include such duties as Mess Officer, Supply Officer, and Motor Officer, and the Training NCO and Information and Education NCO. At the company level, such duties generally are assigned in addition to the primary duties of the company officers or noncommissioned officers.

Functional Areas. The staff assists the commander in the performance of *four functional areas* of responsibility, which are as follows: (1) Personnel, (2) Military Intelligence, (3) Operations and Training, and (4) Logistics. At the battalion level, the staff officers having general responsibility in these areas are designated the S1, S2, S3, and S4, respectively. At division level and higher, these staff officers are designated G1, G2, G3, and G4; while on joint and combined staffs, the designation J1, J2, J3, and J4 is used. In addition, on higher level staffs, additional numbers sometimes are used for staff officers having responsibility in specific areas of prime importance to the organization, for example, Civil Affairs or Communications.

General Staff. These four functional areas comprise the areas of responsibility of the general staff. The size of the staff section provided in each case is determined by the workload and complexity of operations encountered. The general staff operates under the supervision of the *chief of staff* who is the principal assistant to the commander. The chief of staff transmits the will of the commander to those who act in the commander's name, and is the principal coordinating agent to insure efficient functioning of the staff and of all troops in the command. At battalion level, the *executive officer* fills the function of the chief of staff, while the company executive officer serves in a similar capacity.

Special Staff. Within the overall framework of the four functional areas, there are certain specific functions which warrant the attention of a specialist. These specific functions vary with the size and the mission of the organization, but may include such matters as engineering, transportation, communications, ordnance, and medical support. To fill these specific needs, a *special staff* is provided, consisting of such staff officers as the Engineer, the Transportation Officer, the Signal Officer, the Ordnance Officer, or the Surgeon. These special staff officers operate under the direction of the general staff, reporting to such general staff officer as may be appropriate. For example, on matters pertaining to construction or maintenance of roads, cantonment areas, or similar facilities, the Engineer deals with the G4, while on matters pertaining to operations or training he or she deals with the G3. Similarly, the Engineer deals with the G2 on Engineer Technical Intelligence matters.

Personal Staff. In addition to the *general staff* and the *special staff,* commanding generals are authorized a *personal staff.* This personal staff consists of authorized aides, or *Aides-de-Camp,* and other assistants. The whole purpose of the personal staff is to relieve the general from time-consuming personal matters so that he or she may devote full attention to matters of command, and discharge heavy responsibilities with efficiency and continuity. Information on the duties of an aide to a general officer is the final discussion of this chapter.

FUNCTIONS OF A BATTALION STAFF

The staff of a battalion includes the Executive Officer, the S1, S2, S3, S4, and Special Staff Officers. The commander either may follow the TO/E and assign staff officers to duties consistent with AR 611–101 which details their job descriptions or may "tailor" the staff in accordance with his or her mission and their numbers, experience, capabilities, and grades.

The commander may divide the staff's functions into administration and operations; and, to reduce the span of control while enhancing supervision, assign the executive officer to monitor administration and the S-3, operations.

The Executive Officer. At battalion and brigade level, the Executive Officer may serve as the second-in-command and as the principal assistant to the commanding officer. He or she usually directs, coordinates, and supervises the activities of the staff sections. The ExO is often appointed the Materiel Readiness Officer. It is the best possible training to become a battalion commander.

The S1 (Adjutant). The S1 is charged with staff responsibility for personnel management, matters pertaining to unit strength, morale, discipline, and miscellaneous administrative tasks. He or she is usually charged with correspondence of the Executive Officer and the Commanding Officer, and with the Headquarters files requiring familiarity with AR 340–15, *Preparing Correspondence.*

The S2 (Military Intelligence). The S2 is responsible for the production and dissemination of combat intelligence and counterintelligence matters. He or she assists the commanding officer and other staff officers in security matters including safes, filing, clearances, intelligence training, and related duties. To fulfill the primary responsibility of producing combat intelligence, the S2 collects, collates, evaluates, and interprets information of the enemy, weather, and terrain, which may influence the accomplishment of the unit mission. Of equal importance is the duty of disseminating this information to the commanding officer, other staff officers, subordinate commanders and adjacent units.

The S3 (Operations). The S3 has staff responsibility for planning the successive combat operations, organization, and training as directed by the commanding officer. In his or her field are operational directives, plans, orders, command post exercises (CPXs), field training exercises (FTXs), training aids, ammunition requirements, school allocations and quotas, and a host of related duties. The S3 prepares estimates and recommends to the commander actions or decisions for the accomplishment of the mission. It is a vital mission in which he or she works in close coordination with the Executive Officer and the Commanding Officer.

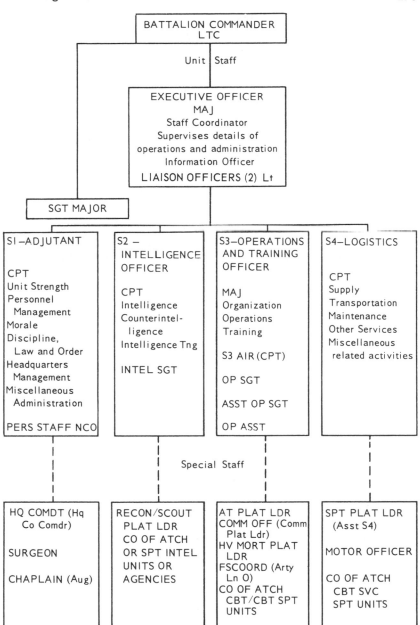

BATTALION COMMANDER
LTC

Unit Staff

EXECUTIVE OFFICER
MAJ
Staff Coordinator
Supervises details of
operations and administration
Information Officer
LIAISON OFFICERS (2) Lt

SGT MAJOR

S1—ADJUTANT	S2 — INTELLIGENCE OFFICER	S3—OPERATIONS AND TRAINING OFFICER	S4—LOGISTICS
CPT	CPT	MAJ	CPT
Unit Strength	Intelligence	Organization	Supply
Personnel	Counterintel-	Operations	Transportation
Management	ligence	Training	Maintenance
Morale	Intelligence Tng		Other Services
Discipline,		S3 AIR (CPT)	Miscellaneous
Law and Order	INTEL SGT		related activities
Headquarters		OP SGT	
Management			
Miscellaneous		ASST OP SGT	
Administration			
		OP ASST	
PERS STAFF NCO			

Special Staff

HQ COMDT (Hq Co Comdr)	RECON/SCOUT PLAT LDR	AT PLAT LDR	SPT PLAT LDR (Asst S4)
	CO OF ATCH	COMM OFF (Comm Plat Ldr)	
SURGEON	OR SPT INTEL	HV MORT PLAT LDR	MOTOR OFFICER
	UNITS OR	FSCOORD (Arty Ln O)	
CHAPLAIN (Aug)	AGENCIES	CO OF ATCH CBT/CBT SPT UNITS	CO OF ATCH CBT SVC SPT UNITS

— Unit Staff responsibility for staff supervision.

BATTALION STAFF ORGANIZATION.

The S3 has staff responsibility for the unit readiness of the command. Especially in this function, the S3 works closely with the Executive who is usually appointed the Materiel Readiness Officer.

The S4 (Logistics). The S4 is the battalion logistics officer and has staff responsibility for the logistic services and facilities available to the battalion. These are supply, transportation, maintenance, logistic plans and records, and other matters in the field of logistical support. The S4 prepares logistical plans and appropriate portions of published plans and orders. During operations, he or she is responsible for the location and operation of the battalion trains. The S4 is responsible for local security measures within the trains area and for coordination with higher units and adjacent units in this responsibility. In some battalions the S4 is also a commander of a service supporting unit.

The Special Staff. There are certain specific functions which warrant the assignment of a specialist. These special functions vary with the size, mission, and organization of a battalion or larger unit. The preceding chart of the Battalion Staff Organization illustrates the staff, including the Special Staff, of an infantry battalion. Special Staff activities are coordinated by some part of the unit staff. In some units the members of the Special Staff command the related support unit which increases their responsibilities.*

BASIC FUNCTIONS OF A STAFF OFFICER

The Army has standardized many of the basic staff techniques and procedures. The primary reference is Field Manual 101–5, *Staff Officer's Field Manual.* In addition, branch service schools have developed excellent texts and as a useful example the *Operations and Training Handbook,* U.S. Army Infantry School, Fort Benning, Georgia. Effective staff procedures are essential in the effective performance of mission by the entire unit; a fine staff accomplishes completed staff action with coordination and timeliness.

Informing. Exchange of information is the first key of good staff procedures. It is the first step in assuring a common basis of understanding by staff officers and their commander in making estimates and decisions. No staff officer can operate effectively as a "loner" or in a "vacuum." He or she must provide information to other staff officers, as well as receive information from them. This goal is attainable only by good working relationships within a staff, and with other staffs, with a talent for good human relationships leading to fine coordination and teamwork.

Estimating. An estimate of the situation is a procedure for the logical analysis of a problem by which one arrives at the workable choices of mission accomplishment, and the selection of the one to be adopted. It is continuous, systematic, and as complete a process of reasoning as time permits. The accompanying illustration shows the definite steps in the process.

The sequence established by the standard estimate of the situation is applicable to all staff problems, not alone the classic one of a combat decision. The staff uses the estimate procedure to recommend a course of action, while the commander uses it to choose or decide what he or she will order.

Recommending. Staff officers make recommendations upon their own initiative or when requested to do so. Such recommendations result from careful

---

*Because of their special technical skills, warrant officers often are assigned as special staff officers.

ESTIMATE OF THE SITUATION

   1. MISSION (Problem)

   2. THE SITUATION AND COURSES OF ACTION:

      a. Considerations affecting possible courses of action.

      b. Opposing conditions.

      c. Own courses of action.

   3. ANALYSIS OF OPPOSING COURSES OF ACTION.

   4. COMPARISON OF OWN COURSES OF ACTION.

   5. DECISION.

ESTIMATE OF THE SITUATION.

estimate of the situation and, when offered, must be clearly presented, neither with equivocation nor ambiguity. If another staff agency is involved, which is usually the case, the recommendation must be coordinated with that agency. Should a failure to agree develop, the divergent view must be presented fairly and objectively. The staff officer is not settling a debate, but is presenting facts and views, with a recommendation, on which the commander will make a decision which may be quite different than the one recommended.

Noteworthy Tradition. When the commander chooses a course of action different, or opposite to the staff officer's recommendation, as happens in all headquarters, the staff officer applies his or her maximum talents to make certain the commander's decision is executed precisely. No pique, no bruised feelings, no silent resolution that "next time she will get what I think she wants." The tradition is based in the discussion, *Foundation of the Code,* Chapter One, *The Code of the Army Officer,* and especially in General Ridgway's directive to the Army Staff. The staff is an arm or a tool of the commander to assist in the discharge of heavy responsibility involving many people, many problems, and many techniques. But the commander is the responsible official, and the one who decides. The staff officer shows an understanding of this essential principle of carrying out the commander's decision to his or her highest capability, never indicating that he or she had recommended a different course of action.

Preparing Plans and Orders. Once the commander has stated a decision, the staff prepares the detailed orders for the entire command, if the circumstances require written orders and if time permits their preparation. Routine matters coming under previously approved policy are handled by the staff without repeated visits to the commander; however, as to important matters or action which is unusual, the staff informs the commander at the first convenient opportunity. Orders involving missions for subordinate commanders, particularly tactical ones, are prepared with more consultation and approval by the commander.

Estimating the value of good plans and orders for achieving success in battle is hazardous at best; some authorities have stated they are 90 percent of the battle and implementation 10 percent. But it is certainly true that the commander must direct clearly *what* is to be done, *where* and *when* it is to be done, with a specific mission for each element involved, or the "who" factor, and in some instances a statement of the *why* is helpful. Good plans and good orders are clear and precise. The staff officer should have in mind the ancient truth that "any order which *can* be misunderstood, *will* be misunderstood."

The following both quotes and describes General Marshall: *"The order must be comprehensive, yet not involved. It must appear clear when read in poor light, in the mud and rain. That was Marshall's job, and he performed it 100 percent. The troops which maneuvered under his plans always won."* George C. Marshall, *Education of a General,* by Forrest Pogue, The Viking Press, 1963.

PLAN FOR AN OPERATIONS ORDER

An accompanying illustration shows the plan format for an operations order, or the standard five-paragraph field order form. It is more than a mere form —it is a logical process of thought which should be used as a matter of course in the issue of simple instructions as well as detailed, written, operations orders. It is helpful for staff officers as well as commanders to memorize the sequence and develop skill in its use.

Supervision. The execution or implementation of plans and resultant orders must have both command and staff supervision. The beginning staff procedure calls for being informed which involves seeing, visiting, and inspecting by direct contact. Desk or "mahogany bound" staff officers are unlikely to serve the commander ably. Going out to see and check is the better way to keep informed. On the part of the staff officer it requires tact, for he or she is not the commander. If erroneous action is discovered, and the time factor requires, the staff officer may issue corrective orders on the spot but only in the name of the commanding officer: "The Commanding Officer directs—." In the usual case the staff officer will inform the commander at the earliest opportunity of his or her action. In inspections and reports to the commander, the staff officer is not a talebearer; many successful staff officers inform the subordinate commanders of their finding; discuss it with them, and inform them of the exact nature of the report to be made to the commander.

A staff visit, which is discussed above as a part of supervision or follow-up, has the essential purpose of coordination, teamwork, and mutual understanding between the commander and subordinate commanders, between staff divisions, and the staff and subordinate commanders. Such visits may uncover misunderstandings and provide correction before becoming serious and requiring command action. The written word is not always clear, however carefully it is prepared, just as the oral word may also be misunderstood. Here is ever-present opportunity for the staff officer to serve the commander well, and help in an important manner the achievement of the mission.

LIMITATION OF STAFF AUTHORITY

A staff officer, as such, has no authority to command. He or she does not prescribe policies, basic decisions, or plans, for that responsibility rests with the commander.

When it becomes necessary for a staff officer to issue an order in the name of the commander, responsibility for such an order remains with the commander even though he or she may not have seen the order as actually written or heard it if given orally.

Staff officers who exercise supervision over any phase of operations must restrict their control to the sphere of the commander's announced decisions and orders. When circumstances arise which in their opinion may make advisable a deviation from established policy, even in the most minor degree, the situation should be presented to their commander for decision.

When a commander has given specific instructions to a staff officer, the actual issue of the necessary orders or instructions to members of the command are properly given in the name of the commander by the staff officer, thus: "The Commanding Officer directs" or "For the Commander." The orders may be given orally or over the signature of the staff officer.

Where a commander has decided upon a policy to be followed and has

OPERATION ORDER/PLAN FORMAT
(Based on STANAG 2014, 2d Edition)

(CLASSIFICATION)

(Changes from verbal orders)

H E A D I N G

Copy No._____
Issuing Headquarters
Location of CP (Coord)
Date/Time Group
Message Reference No.

OPORD/OPLAN**   (Serial Number/Code Name**)

References:

Time Zone: *

B O D Y

Task Organization:

1. SITUATION.
   a. Enemy forces:
   b. Friendly forces:
   c. Attachments and detachments:
   d. Assumptions:**

2. MISSION.

3. EXECUTION.
   a. Concept of operation:
   b. Coordinating instructions: (Last subparagraph).

4. ADMINISTRATION AND LOGISTICS.

5. COMMAND AND SIGNAL.
   a. Signal:
   b. Command:

E N D I N G

Acknowledgment Instructions:

               Commander's Last Name
               Commander's Grade

Annexes:

Distribution:

Authentication:*

(CLASSIFICATION)

OPERATION ORDER/PLAN FORMAT (BASED ON STANAG 2014, 2d ED.)

indicated that policy to a staff officer, all future questions that fall completely under that policy should be handled without further reference to the commander. Routine matters are handled according to written or uniformly observed SOPs—Standing Operating Procedures.

Some commands and staffs have a formal policy file for non-routine but special matters of concern to the commander. All experienced staff officers will establish an informal personal policy file if a formal one does not exist. An established policy provides the limits within which the staff can function without continual reference to the commander.

A staff officer must never usurp the prerogatives of command. In the event of an unforeseen emergency when immediate action is imperative and the commander cannot be consulted, the staff officer should be prepared to state to the senior line officer with whom he or she is able to get in touch the action he or she believes the commander would desire. The decision then becomes the responsibility of the senior officer consulted, and is not the responsibility of the staff officer.

Relation of the Staff to the Commander. No two commanders operate exactly the same with respect to the details of this relationship. Some commanders announce broad policies and desire members of the staff to proceed with confidence in the execution of tasks with little consultation on the details; others will wish to give personal approval to at least the more important phases which are encountered. The staff must adjust itself quickly to the method of operation desired by the commander.

COMPLETED STAFF WORK

Completed staff work is Army doctrine. The staff officer who is skilled will think through each problem assigned for staff action and then will plan courses of action. The staff officer must determine the information needed and where to seek it and must list the individuals who have an interest in the problem, or knowledge of the problem, and plan to see them. He or she will determine all the "angles" and consider the varying viewpoints on important matters. "Leg work" is the requirement. A staff officer who neglects these essentials is unlikely to succeed.

The "completed staff work" doctrine means more work for the staff officer, but it results in more freedom for the commander to do the things and see the things which are essential to the discharge of his or her own responsibilities. It also spares the commander from half-baked ideas, immature oral guesses, or voluminous memoranda which he or she has no time to study.

The final test of completed staff work is this: *If you were the chief would you be willing to sign the paper you have prepared, and stake your professional reputation on its being "right"?* If not, take it back, and do it over for it is not "completed staff work."

There is a special dividend about being a skilled staff officer. The "young" staff officer of today may be assigned to command much sooner than he or she has anticipated. The requirements of a fast-moving Army, on the vast missions of this period in our history, find the "best qualified" officers and lead them forward, as discussed in Chapter 12, *Professional Development. The officer who becomes an excellent staff officer, thoroughly trained in staff responsibilities, limitations, and procedures, will find on becoming commander that he or she knows what to expect from a staff and how to handle one.* It is a major attribute to success in command.

<table>
<tr><td colspan="1">HOW TO GET IT</td><td>HOW TO DO IT</td></tr>
</table>

HOW TO GET IT	HOW TO DO IT
Assignment of a problem and a request for a solution in such a way that completed staff work is readily possible.	Study of a problem and presentation of its solution in such form that only approval or disapproval of the completed action is required.
1. Know the problem.	
2. Make one individual responsible to you for the solution.	1. Work out all details completely.
	2. Consult other staff officers.
3. State the problem to him clearly, precisely; explain reasons, background; limit the area to be studied.	3. Study, write, restudy, and rewrite.
	4. Present a single, coordinated, proposed action. Do not equivocate.
4. Give the individual the advantage of your knowledge and experience in this problem.	5. Do not present long memorandums or explanations. Correct solutions are usually recognizable.
5. Set a time limit; or request assignee to estimate completion date.	6. Advise the chief what to do. Do not ask him.
6. Insure that you are available for discussion as work progresses.	If you were the chief, would you sign the paper you have prepared and thus stake your professional reputation on its being right?
Adequate guidance eliminates wasted effort and makes for completed staff work.	If not, take it back and work it over; it is not yet completed staff work.

COMPLETED STAFF WORK.

A sometimes baffling situation confronts the staff officer as to which problems or communications should be presented to the commanding officer, and which ones should be handled by the staff without reference to the commander. The commander must be informed of matters of importance, surely, and must be spared from trivia. But where to draw the line? There is no single answer, or policy, because commanding officers differ in their wishes, just as staff officers "differ." Indeed, the confidence of the commander in the individual members of the staff bears upon the problem and its solution.

Reproduced below is a memorandum for the staff, written many years ago, which was included in early editions of *The Officer's Guide*. The author was Major General Frank S. Cocheu, now deceased. It is far from universally applicable, of course. But it may point the way to the choice of a workable policy in the busy headquarters of today.

MEMORANDUM: For the Staff.

1. The following will be brought without delay to the attention of the Commanding General:

a. Subjects of importance which require prompt action and are not covered by existing policies and instructions.

b. Disapprovals from higher authority.

c. Errors, deficiencies or irregularities alleged by higher authority.

d. Communications that allege neglect or dereliction on the part of commissioned personnel.

e. Correspondence or proposed correspondence conveying even a suggestion of censure.

f. Appeals from subordinates from decisions made at this headquarters.

g. Subjects which affect the good name or reputation of an officer or organization.

h. Subjects involving financial or property irregularities.

i. Serious accidents involving personnel of the command.

2. The following will be presented to the Commanding General for final action:

a. Requests and recommendations to be made to higher authority.

b. Suggested disapprovals.

c. Communications that contain a suspicion of censure.

d. Communications that involve the good name of an officer or organization.

e. Reports of financial and property irregularities.

f. Letters to civil authorities in high positions.

g. Endorsements on efficiency reports.

h. Correspondence concerning war plans.

i. Communications of exceptional information.

3. A copy of these instructions will be kept exposed at all times upon the desk of each staff officer of this headquarters.

SELECTED STAFF PROCEDURES

The basic reference of staff officers in the understanding of command and staff relationships, responsibilities, functions, and procedures is Field Manual 101–5, *Staff Officer's Field Manual.* In addition, any well organized headquarters has a staff manual or administrative procedures manual which contains the organization chart of the headquarters and details the responsibilities of each staff section.

Obtaining Background on a Staff Assignment. After studying the headquarters staff manual, the newly assigned staff officer should then become familiar with all important staff actions of his or her particular section during some reasonable past period, such as the past six months or the last training cycle. Staff sections of tactical headquarters generally are obliged to keep journals wherein such staff actions are recorded. Individual staff officers maintain files or correspondence, "stay-backs," on which or together with which is a "Memorandum for Record" which summarizes the events leading up to the particular action in question, with a statement of concurrences, or other information which might be useful for future reference. From these sources, the newcomer can quickly get oriented. He or she will learn that the major problems confronting the staff section are few, although the details and ramifications may be myriad. All of the problems quite likely have roots; and after they have been identified, the handling of details or new developments of an old problem will be less difficult.

The Staff Officer's Records. The commander relies upon staff officers for the maintenance of required and useful charts, files, and records as well as for the initiation of routine reports. This is an important responsibility for the staff. In the field there are required records which are prescribed in Field Manuals. In garrison there are other records and correspondence which must be available when needed. A staff officer should become completely familiar with the administrative requirements of his or her office, train the personnel charged with preparation of records or filing, and frequently check to assure that they are maintained as desired.

However, the staff officer should not become "chart happy," covering office walls with multitudinous useless status charts that are impressive to see but require major efforts by staff assistants and submitting lower echelons to prepare and maintain.

Mission Analysis and Staff Studies. Although the use of formalized procedures for mission analysis and preparation of written staff studies pertains more to the headquarters of major commands and the Army Staff in Washington, the principles are generally applicable. In any case, the actual use of a staff study, and the analysis which leads to its preparation, depends upon the complexity of the problem, and the time available for its consideration. It is a good principle that formal, written staff studies should be avoided, unless they are truly needed; but a staff officer at any level of organization may need to make such an analysis, and write such a study.

The accompanying diagram, *The Sequence of Staff Actions,* provides the basis for mission analysis and the staff estimate. Noteworthy is the planning guidance which is often supplied by the commander; this guidance will not suggest the "answer," but may provide factors to consider, people to consult, the time to complete the study, or other matters which the commander considers to be essential for staff understanding.

The staff study is a logical analysis which leads through a consideration of the specific problem, the facts and assumptions which bear upon the problem, information to set forth the facts, the reaching of conclusions, and the action the staff officer recommends. It should be both "complete and brief." A way of describing a good staff study is the presentation of a problem so that the commander can reach an independent decision, as well as exercising the option of accepting the recommendation submitted by the staff officer. The accompanying illustration, *A Staff Study Format,* should be followed, whether the study is prepared in 12 months or 12 hours, for it is time-tested and generally used. The condensed essential points should be presented on a single page, although some commanders will accept two pages. If detail is needed, attach annexes and appendices, as required, but keep the basic paper brief. Busy commanders depend upon their staffs to save their time, and one way to do it is to prepare clear, concise, brief staff studies—when a staff study is needed.

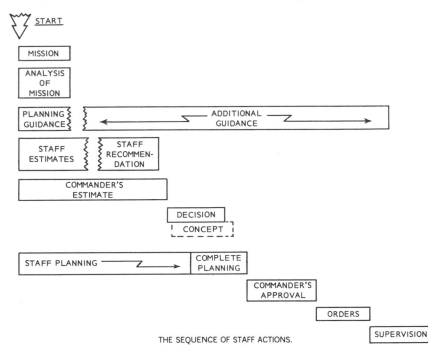

THE SEQUENCE OF STAFF ACTIONS.

Relations with Higher Headquarters. It is important to the commander that good relations are enjoyed with higher headquarters. His or her own standing and capacity for getting results will be enhanced when a favorable situation is created, and harmed seriously when bad relations exist. Therefore, each staff officer must become personally acquainted with his or her "opposite number" on the next senior staff, for the same reasons that he or she must know opposite numbers in subordinate staffs. It is all a matter of acquaintance, understanding, and teamwork.

Relations Between the Staff and the Troops. The staff serves the troops as well as the commander. It has been said that the staff which serves the troops best serves its commander best. Good staff work requires the staff to know and appreciate fully the situation of the troops, their morale, their state of training, the state of their equipment and supply, and all other conditions affecting their efficiency.

As a rule when a staff officer visits troop units he or she first calls upon the commander. It is desirable that the staff officer state at once the purpose, if any in particular, which the visit is to accomplish. A cordial relationship between staff officers and subordinate troop commanders must be developed. It is desirable that, before leaving, the result of his or her observations be disclosed to the unit commander, and disclosed exactly in the same way to the

A STAFF STUDY FORMAT

PROBLEM: Concise mission statement of what is to be accomplished by the study and/or the problem.

ASSUMPTION(S): Influencing factors which are assumed to be true. May be non-factual or incapable of being proved.

FACTS BEARING ON THE PROBLEM: Essential facts considered in the analysis and in arriving at the conclusions.

DISCUSSION: An analysis and evaluation of the facts as influenced by the assumptions and which present sufficient detail to support the conclusions.

CONCLUSION(S): Statement of the findings and the implications of an analysis and evaluation.

ACTION RECOMMENDED: Concise statement of what is to be done to solve the problem and who should do it.

ATTACHMENTS: (Supporting detail on each of the above sections).   A STAFF STUDY FORMAT.

commanding officer. Distrust is easily created and is difficult to dissipate. A mutual feeling of trust and confidence must be built up and confirmed by each recurring contact.

Coordination and Concurrences. Proper coordination among staff officers is absolutely essential. Without it, the commander easily could be placed in the position of issuing conflicting orders or directives.

During the course of preparation of any staff action, be sure to contact all other staff officers or staff sections who may have an interest in the problem or its solution. Obtain the views of other staff members as to the recommended solution and take these views into account when completing your action. When your action is completed, but before presentation to your chief, take the completed package back to the interested sections to obtain their concurrence.

The purpose of this coordination is not to share responsibility with others— it is to insure that your action has not compromised the position of other staff sections and that it is not in conflict with previous actions.

The concurrence of all interested staff sections is desirable before the completed action is submitted for the approval of the commander; however, it is not mandatory. It sometimes happens that different staff sections have conflicting viewpoints on the proper solution of a problem. In such a case, the views of the differing section should be so noted and considered in the action; however, if you are convinced that your solution is the correct one, stick to your guns. Just don't be bullheaded about it (and remember that you will have to continue working with the other section tomorrow and next week and next month). Usually the executive officer or the chief of staff will decide between conflicting points of view or recommendations. If he or she cannot, the commander must and will.

Maintaining Perspective. It is very easy for an officer immersed in details at a desk to lose perspective. He or she may become desk-tied in viewpoint and fail to understand the impact which his or her recommendations, if approved, may have in the field. Some call it an occupational disease. It is a good reason for limitation of length of assignment. When it happens the value of a staff officer shrinks swiftly. Never put aside your own appreciation of the impact of official communications which reach the field.

It is a wise course as opportunity offers to make field trips. Go and see for yourself how the projects of your interest are working. Talk with the officers concerned. Urge them to state their views. See if you can work out better ways to accomplish the ends sought with a higher standard, in swifter time, at reduced cost. Get the feel of the field with all its enthusiasms and zeal, its hardships, and human frailties. Then go back to your desk with perspective renewed. You will do a better job.

AIDES TO GENERAL OFFICERS

General officers commanding large units and other general officers occupying positions designated specifically by the Department of the Army are authorized aides, or *Aides-de-Camp,* as a personal staff. (AR 614–16.) *Duties of aides are not prescribed in training manuals but are such as the general officer may prescribe.*

Number and Grades Authorized. Aides-de-camp are authorized, in the numbers and grades stated below. *Exceptions:* General officers assigned as Chiefs of MAAGs, JUSMAGs, and Military Missions are authorized one aide-de-camp per general officer not to exceed the maximum grade appropriate for the rank of the general as stated in the table below.

General Officers	COL	LTC	MAJ	CPT	LT	Total
General of the Army .... (or Chief of Staff, USA)	1	1	1	..	..	3
General	..	1	1	1	..	3
Lieutenant general	..	..	1	1	..	2
Major general	..	..	..	1	1	2
Brigadier general	..	..	..	..	1	1

When a general officer is authorized two or more aides the senior in rank generally is designated unofficially as the Senior Aide and in this capacity coordinates the activities for which he or she may be charged. This may include the issue of instructions to the other aide or aides, the secretarial staff which serves the general, the orderlies, driver, and others. When a general officer uses two aides, one may be used to advantage as Operations Aide and one as Administrative Aide. Normally the maximum continuous tour of duty as an aide-de-camp will be 2 years, although there is no limitation on length of tour.

Duties of Aides. As stated earlier in this chapter, there is great need for a personal staff to free the general from time-consuming personal arrangements so that he or she may perform heavy responsibilities with efficiency and continuity. A good aide will see to it that the tools and facilities needed by the general are on hand when needed. Examples of duties which a general officer may wish an aide to perform are discussed below.

The establishment of a new command post may involve an aide. The aide will learn from the chief of staff the location of the area to be used by the general. Measures will be taken at once to move all equipment and personnel in the routine use or service of the general to the new site and resume operations.

While the general is in the office or at the command post, an aide often is assigned to keep the general's appointment schedule to facilitate the transaction of business. In the performance of this task the aide should consult the chief of staff and be guided always by his or her desires, for the aide is in no sense a link in the chain of command. It is likely that all generals will expect an aide to maintain a list of future appointments, including social engagements, and remind them in ample time so they may be kept. The general's spouse should be kept informed of the general's social engagements, especially those to which the spouse is invited, as well as those which will require the general's presence outside of office hours.

Many generals will wish their aides to assume charge of their personal and confidential files.

On change of station or other moves, the aide should take full charge of all arrangements as directed by the general so the general may work with full efficiency up to the time of departure and resume operations at once upon arrival.

Careful thought should be given by aides to arrangements for trips of whatever length or duration. The aide should make all arrangements for tickets, hotel reservations if needed upon arrival, movement of baggage, and all other matters. If appropriate, notification of expected time of arrival, security clearance (if required), and how many members in the general's party, should be sent to the proper officials.

The aide should keep the record of expenses incurred which are reimbursable by submission of the necessary voucher after completion of the journey. Many general officers provide the aide with a personal fund from which to make expenditures for the general for minor items, keeping an informal record as they are paid.

Welcoming committees or individuals meeting or receiving a general officer for some official or unofficial occasion may assume expenses on behalf of the visiting general from their own resources. This is a courtesy, of course, but general officers wish to avoid accepting the payment of expenses which are covered by their official travel allowances, or which should be borne from their own funds. In such instances, the aide should ascertain the expenses and provide reimbursement with expression of appreciation for the thoughtfulness and the courtesy.

Aides are often used to transmit highly personal, important, or secret messages.

It is common practice for general officers to assign aides as assistants to staff officers, particularly in general staff sections of the headquarters. This is particularly the case when the general is to be absent and unaccompanied by aides, or during times of stress when *additional* staff assistants are needed in the staff section. Accordingly, a good aide will become schooled in the duties and techniques of each staff section to become a useful member of the group even if the assignment is temporary. While so assigned, the aide is responsible to the chief of section in the same manner as other officers.

Visiting dignitaries may be accompanied by an officer to serve them temporarily as aide. Senior officers may be detailed to serve in this capacity for high officials, such as very senior officials of a friendly foreign power.

On social occasions the aides may assist in preparing the invitation list, or they may make the invitations orally for their general. When this is the case they must be very careful to provide the date, hour, place, nature of the event and other appropriate information. If spouses are to be present, the aides will save much time by including information about dress, and whether the general's spouse will wear formal or informal dress may as well be settled at the time the invitation is issued as later. The nature of the occasion must be made clear, too, and if it is to be a dinner, or cocktail gathering which does not include a dinner, the invitation should not be susceptible of misunderstanding. For a social event to be held at a club or hotel the aide may be charged with making all arrangements after being instructed by the general. At a formal reception the aide is often asked to introduce the guests; in this case the aide's position is near the head of the receiving line where he or she greets all guests, ascertains their names, and introduces them clearly to the individual heading the receiving line. This action and position may cause the aide some concern until familiar with the experience. The aide too is a guest. Certainly he or she must not behave like a butler or servant, nor for that matter, the host. Perhaps it is best described as the position of an elder son or daughter assisting parents in the pleasant task of entertaining friends.

On ceremonial occasions aides must familiarize themselves with the appropriate regulations and the exact arrangements in so far as they can be foreseen. Field Manual 22–5 and Army Regulations 600–25, with their most recent changes, will answer most questions.

Some aides prepare an SOP and a checklist for recurring activities such as trips by motor, air, rail, movement of the command post or headquarters, and other events.

A general officer is obliged to meet a very large number of people, military and civilian. The aides may render a most valuable service to their commander by maintaining a list of names of individuals with whom more than passing contact has been held or may be held. This file should contain, in addition to names, essential data about each individual such as position or business connection, former military status if any, address, telephone number, current activities of military interest, and a statement of occasions when the general has been in touch with the individual. Before any occasional visitor, military or civilian, is permitted to fill an appointment with the general the aide should brief the general on the visitor including "who he is" as well as "what he wants," if the latter is known. When the general is to attend any large gathering, it will be helpful for the aide to ascertain the more important personages who will be present and inform the general in advance.

Care must be exercised by aides to avoid transgressing upon the fields of other staff officers. In this connection, many general officers require that their secretary, chauffeurs, and orderlies work under personal control of the aides. Where a pilot is provided, the aide and the pilot must work closely together, the pilot generally receiving all information about proposed trips from the aide.

General officers will expect their aides to be models of military courtesy, tact, military appearance, and soldierly attitude and bearing. They will also wish them to be unobtrusive and quiet, as well as ladies or gentlemen. Aides are cautioned that they are not commanders or assistant commanders. It is an honored, responsible position. Most general officers choose their aides based on their fine records, experience in extended combat, decorations for valor, as well as their personality and appearance. An officer chosen as aide to an Army general has opportunity to acquire experience which will be extremely helpful as his or her responsibilities increase.

For lapel and other insignia worn by aides, see Chapter 21, *Uniforms of the Army.*

18

New Duty Assignment

It is a fact of Army life that the officer experiences periodic reassignments to new responsibilities and new positions, as well as station changes within the United States and oversea commands. Do you like variety? A change from staff to command, to a specialty, to duty as student? Or instructor? If so, the Army is surely the life for you with its great breadth of duty and experience. The normal career includes as a matter of course a series of assignments, each building upon the present for something bigger and more challenging as the years arrive. With each new assignment there is opportunity to make a fresh start, to apply the lessons learned so as to do a better job, to avoid the errors of the past, and build better because of experience gained. Chapter Twelve, *Professional Development,* explains the scope and makes clear the reasons for these periodic changes. The wise officer will seek to make the most of each change of duty assignment to increase his or her knowledge and professional capacity.

The Commander's Responsibility and Opportunity. The commander or chief who receives a newly assigned officer has a special responsibility which may have a most important effect upon the future success of the newcomer. Each officer should be carefully counseled on the scope of his or her work, standing operating procedures, objectives to be attained, job expectations, and standards of performance expected. (DA Pam 600–3, *Commissioned Officer Professional Development and Utilization* and DA Pam 600–11, *Warrant Officer Professional Development.*)

In the building of a proud organization, in which individuals have arrived one by one or in small groups, the way in which each person is received by the commander, or chief, and new associates, is extremely important. Each person must be made to feel welcome on arrival. It is important that the commander makes certain the mission is understood. The commander will start each newcomer with a clean slate and with his or her trust. Most officers will live up to it.

Many years ago, at the outset of a mobilization, a skilled commanding general assembled several hundred of his newly arrived officers on a high hill overlooking the area of the camp. He caused them to face so that they could look out over the area and identify the places where they were assigned. He then addressed them: *"Gentlemen, as your commander I bid you welcome. There before you are the training areas in which we will work, and the men we must train. Ours is a grave responsibility. Some among us will succeed greatly, win promotions, decorations, and victories against our enemies. Perhaps a few will fail. We expect and hope that all will succeed and be able when it is all over to return to your homes with pride and satisfaction that you served your country well.*

"That is all. Return to your men."

MAKING THE BEST POSSIBLE FIRST IMPRESSION

Whenever you assume a new duty assignment it follows that you will work under new superior officers and have new associates and new subordinates. While it is likely that all will extend a true welcome, and take for granted that you are competent, it is of the highest importance that you put your best foot forward at the outset in order to obtain initial good will and confidence of the official group which you join.

Let it be known at once that the assignment is welcomed; find things to comment upon favorably, avoiding all criticism; become acquainted promptly with associates, especially junior leaders; learn your responsibilities and discharge them fully from the start, seeking information and assistance as circumstances require. Solicit the support of your new organization. Try to stimulate a feeling of confidence and enthusiasm in the minds of associates as to your assignment.

Some Useful Don'ts. Strive to make a favorable first impression, of course. Use equal care to avoid those things which give a bad one.

Don't "overtalk," especially of yourself. Your standing among new associates will depend wholly upon what you accomplish in the future, not your prideful past. While you are sizing up the new command and its members, as you must, your new associates are also sizing up their new officer. Some will find occasion for critical comment, given a chance. Just weigh those words!

Go slow, too, with changes which affect the life and likes of your personnel. More than likely they prefer things the way you find them. Later, when you have complete information, improvements you may make will be satisfying and enhance your own standing. But bide your time until surmises can be replaced with reasoned conclusions fortified by discussions and recommendations of subordinates. Make improvements, make changes for the good, mold the organization to your special judgments—but don't do it all at the start.

Never make a statement which could possibly be considered as a reflection upon your predecessor. As he or she has departed, and cannot defend himself or herself, such acts are cowardly. More than likely the former commander has the respect and even the admiration of all or most of the troops, because that is the rewarding experience of most good officers; for you as the new commander to make harsh or belittling remarks about your predecessor is to injure greatly and perhaps permanently your own chances of gaining the trust and respect of these same individuals.

In a sense, the commander holds a lonely position. You must put your best foot forward, and keep it there. You must set the example. Thoughtless statements, careless attention to appearance, little violations, weigh heavily when done by the commander whereas by others they might be forgotten. The higher the command, the more they weigh.

First Actions. Whatever the nature of the new assignment, there are certain first actions which are necessary to gain knowledge of the missions, responsibilities, and personnel. They are keys to getting off to a good start.

What Is the Mission? Seek information from the departing predecessor whenever this is possible. Go to your new chief and listen most carefully. Study the policy file, if one is available. Discuss the job to be done with other officers, noncommissioned officers, or civilians concerned with the work of the organization.

What Are the Current Training or Work Projects? You need to know at once what is being done to execute the missions, and this means the principal immediate projects, who is working on them, their status, expected completion dates.

Who Are Your Officers and Soldiers? Meet them and talk candidly with them. Precede this discussion by study of each individual's personnel record. Determine their experience and special training. Establish as to key individuals the normal length of further service with the organization prior to reassignment or discharge. Provide an opportunity for each to state personal aspirations as to progress in the military service. Inquire about family problems.

What Reports are Required? Obtain a list of periodic reports required to be submitted, when they are due, and who is to prepare them.

Find Out, "Who Does What?" To the extent necessary, have each key individual write out his or her specific duties and responsibilities.

Check on Handling of Classified Material. Find out quickly what classified material is held by the unit and learn the local regulations for its physical security. If there are indications of carelessness, correct them at once. Many officers have been reprimanded (or worse) for inattention to the security of classified documents and for overlooking the procedures for their handling.

ASSUMPTION OF A STAFF POSITION

Staff officers are selected for assignment by the commander whom they serve. Upon reporting for duty on a staff assignment you should report to the chief of your section, branch, or division, and then as directed to the executive or chief of staff.

All well-administered headquarters have staff manuals or Standing Operating Procedures (SOP) which set forth the organization of each staff section and its specific responsibilities. This manual should show you the specific duties of your own particular segment of the staff. Your first effort must be to become thoroughly familiar with this manual for you have become a member of the staff team and the purpose of the manual is to provide for teamwork. (See Chapter Seventeen, "Staff Assignment," for helpful information of responsibilities and procedures.)

The next step should be to become acquainted with other members of the staff with special reference to those individuals of other staff sections with whom you will work. The chief or executive of the branch or division will provide this information. At the same time the acquaintance should be sought of the unit commanders and unit officers served by the staff. For example, as the new staff officer of a battalion, you should seek out and introduce yourself to the company commanders and company officers of the battalion. Each staff officer must work continually with officers having similar spheres of responsibility, in headquarters junior as well as senior to his or her own. Such individuals are referred to frequently as "opposite numbers." For example, the intelligence officer of a battalion will work regularly in coordination with the intelligence officers of other battalions and with one or several individuals of the intelligence staff of brigade or division headquarters. He or she must have close working liaison with intelligence officers of other units of the division. Personal acquaintance with commanders and staff officers with whom you work should be acquired as soon as practicable after assuming a staff position.

Each staff will have its own operating procedures and ways of getting things done. They will depend upon the desires of the commander, chief of staff, or executive. There may be special office forms and routines; prescribed ways of writing reports or staff studies; prescribed reports to be received and studied, and the like. In order to become a good member of the team these measures must be learned and followed.

A staff assignment is a splendid place to develop tact and diplomacy, the ability to coordinate, and the capacity to keep the work of the day within your own field running smoothly and harmoniously.

ASSUMPTION OF A COMMAND POSITION

The Opportunity. As an Army officer, you must anticipate that you may be assigned without warning to assume command of a unit larger than ordinarily associated with your grade.

Familiarity with problems of command of the next higher unit should be a part of individual training and planning. Be ready for such opportunities. In battle they are normal. Success of an engagement may depend upon the speed and efficiency with which losses of leaders are replaced. Command duty is the highest honor which can be given an officer.

Assumption of Command In Battle. During operations against an enemy, replacement of fallen leaders must be accomplished at once. In the absence of prior instructions to the contrary, seniority of the officers assigned to the unit will determine the line of succession. But this procedure may itself lead to defeat. Circumstances will govern but there will be no time for inquiry or the niceties of position. If you are the officer who discovers the situation assume prompt command and adjust as necessary as time permits. This will require you to notify at once your commander and leaders of subordinate and adjacent units of your assumption of command. Aggressiveness, promptness, and the need for control require the most available officer to take over the task of leadership. At once you must learn your predecessor's mission and, if available, his or her plan to meet it. Next, you must learn the position of your new units. Thereafter you must meet with positive action whatever situations may arise.

The leader who develops a knowledge of the officers and noncommissioned officers of adjacent units will find the information useful when suddenly becoming responsible for their command.

It should be clear that learning your own job is not enough. You must learn your captain's job and your major's job as well.

Assumption of Command Under Conditions Other Than in Battle. Whenever the commander is detached from command of an organization for any reason, the senior officer present for duty with it automatically assumes command, pending different orders from higher authority. If you are that officer who succeeds to any command or duty, you stand in regard to your duties in the same situation as your predecessor. Within the bounds of reason and common sense, you should avoid those actions which amount to permanent commitments.

Transfer of Command Responsibilities. An officer assuming command of an organization is required to take over the mission and all administrative, fiscal, logistical, training, and any other responsibilities of his or her predecessor. The changeover must be made so that the old commander is fully relieved and the successor fully informed. A period of three to five days (or three to five nights) is not unusual to complete the required steps and it is to be remembered that the work of the organization must continue during the transfer period.

Transfer of the responsibilities of a company will include the following steps: The mission of the command; organization records including classified documents; property supplied the unit as shown by the Company Property Book; property in hands of organization members; official funds or allowances; the unit fund and property purchased from the fund; and a clear understanding of training or work in progress.

Suggestions To an Outgoing Commander. Careful preparation in advance of the transfer will be required. Make certain that subordinates have all their records posted correctly and up to date, that the number of actions pending is reduced to a minimum, and that property to be checked and that funds to be transferred are all in correct order. Smooth transition of command requires the elimination of dangling, unfinished actions.

Transfer of property may be a time-consuming task. Supply personnel should make their own preliminary check. Are there missing articles? Broken or unserviceable articles? Take steps to clear the records at once. Never seek to conceal such matters or to deceive the incoming commander. Are there overages? They should be returned or picked up on property records. Never depart a unit with the property records not signed over to another officer.

The same principles apply to the unit fund. Pay the outstanding bills, and determine any further obligations. Check the property which has been purchased from the fund. If there are shortages, or items which are broken or unserviceable, take appropriate steps to clear the records or repair the articles. Be sure all is in balance, and all is clear.

The outgoing commander will wish to make a clean, complete severance. You must never try to cover-up or deceive the incoming commander as it must all be disclosed later to harass you. One inescapable test of your competence as a commander, and important because it will be the impression remembered, is the condition of your unit, disclosed upon your transfer from command.

Suggestions to the Incoming Commander. Simplify the problem by finding out at the start exactly what is to be done. The old and new commanders should make a joint inventory and check all of the matters involved. The transfer is often supervised by an officer designated by the appropriate higher commander. Still, the responsibility passes from the old commander to the new. Understand the requirements, and do it thoroughly.

The Unit Mission. Discuss with the commander being relieved, and with the next higher commander, the status and mission of the organization. Find out about the state of training, work or training in progress, and current problems. As soon as command has been assumed you will be expected to execute the new responsibility effectively.

Administrative Records. As the incoming commander, you must learn about the company files, personnel records, and organization records, where they are kept, by whom, and the extent of your responsibilities. If there are classified documents, you must inventory them and assure yourself that they are being correctly safeguarded.

Organization Property. All property in the organization (platoon, company, or battalion) is the responsibility of the commander; even though the Army system calls for records consolidation at battalion level with hand-receipts to individual officers and noncommissioned officers. They are responsible, too, but the commander is in no ways relieved. You must know what your soldiers are equipped with and its readiness for use. As soon as possible check all major items of equipment on a serial number basis. Have the battalion supply section assist you on nomenclature and proper maintenance. The first Saturday inspection have all the troops display their individual clothing and equipment; with supply personnel in assistance; again, the check can be one against records and for completeness and readiness. Other property responsibilities are discussed in Chapters 16 and 17 but the basic principle is simple; all are responsible that the property is available, always serviceable and ready for use.

A question which will arise is the disposition of overages. The supply system cannot function properly unless units requisition for items they need, and unless they are able to eliminate shortages of their authorized equipment. "Pack-rat" policies by a few units can be ruinous. They store up secret surpluses which may prevent another unit from obtaining supplies or equipment desperately needed. The best and the ordered action is to turn overages in to the battalion supply system as soon as they are found.

In general, if an article charged to the unit is there, see it, check it, and if reasonably serviceable check it off. Don't be picayunish, but do an accurate, swift, common sense job with which you can live after your predecessor has departed.

Organization Funds. Wise use of the unit fund and its monthly income is a tool of vast importance to the commander. Maladministration of these funds invites failure. Start by assuming the responsibility correctly.

Check fully the cash assets on hand or on deposit, the accounts receivable, the items of property purchased from the fund for the benefit of the organization. Check also the obligations and liabilities of the fund such as bills payable.

It is of the highest importance that the new commander assume responsibility for the unit fund in complete compliance with the ARs and the regulations of higher headquarters. Learn the local regulations about administering funds from an auditing officer or the inspector general.

Know Your Personnel. As the commander of a small unit, you must become intimately acquainted with your troops. In the small unit, such as the platoon or company, if you are a wise commander you will have your soldiers appear before you, one by one, and seat them; you should have their individual records at hand during the interview, and go over the salient service, skills, and achievements.

Prepare a card or a page of a notebook for each individual on whom basic personal data can be pre-recorded and on which you can make notes. Question each soldier about his or her duty assignment, hopes, specialization, promotion concerns, schools, and career thoughts. Try to obtain sincere recommendations about improving performance, enhancing morale, and other unit matters but don't make it a complaint session. The spirit of the interview is to get to know the soldiers, letting them meet you, and showing them you care about them individually and personally.

Brigade and division commanders meet members of their large commands at group meetings, in a theater or outdoor assembly, with as many individual meetings with senior officers and noncommissioned officers as is feasible and as time permits. The more of their subordinates who are interviewed personally, or have personal contact with their senior commanders, the better for the command and its commander.

The important thing is to establish a personal, face to face contact with members of the organization at the start. Skillfully done it will work wonders in securing a favorable reaction from the new subordinates and give you as the new commander personal knowledge on which to build.

Development of Your Own Policies. Command of a unit is a very personal responsibility. The methods followed successfully by one commander may be entirely unsuited to another. With the passage of time, adjustment of these matters will be advisable. Such changes, however, should be made only after mature consideration. Infrequently, a new commander will unwisely set forth the opinion that the organization was at a very low ebb of efficiency when he or she assumed command. Such statements are usually accompanied by the further observation that since his or her own unusual powers were applied the very highest standards have been achieved. This approach to the assumption of command is a cowardly assault on the previous commander. The inevitable result is resentment by those members of the unit who may have worked for its progress. Study the methods in use, and when an opportunity for improvement is seen, do not hesitate to adopt it. Face each new assignment as a challenge to do better work and improve results.

19

Pay and Allowances

Army personnel are assured that their services are appreciated by our government. There have been times in the past when military pay rates lagged far behind the pay scales in private industry, and indeed even far behind the pay scales of the Federal civilian employees. Pay raises during the 1960's and 1970's brought military pay up to a level more comparable to that of civilian counterparts in the Federal Government and private industry. Inflation during the late-1970's coupled with "caps" on pay raises caused the military pay to fall behind again. However, action taken during 1980 and 1981 restored comparability of military pay to that in the civilian sector.

How Pay is Established. Military pay rates are set in accordance with the provisions of the Federal Pay Comparability Act of 1970, which became law in January, 1971. This Act, of far reaching significance for all Federal workers, provides that each year the Federal civilian pay rates will be examined in relation to rates for comparable work in private industry. By 1 September of each year, the President will propose to the Congress adjusted pay rates based upon this comparison and, unless Congress disagrees, these new rates will become effective on 1 October.

While the comparability study applies strictly to Federal civilian employees, by separate law the military pay rate is tied to the civilian rate. Thus, an increase in Federal civilian pay automatically results in an equitable increase in military pay.

The increases initially were applied only to base pay. By 1974, this feature of the laws had resulted in disparities among the base pay rates and the subsistence and quarters allowances. Accordingly, Congress took action during 1974 to assure that future pay increases would be applied to the quarters and subsistence allowances as well as to the base pay. This change became effective with the pay raise of October 1974.

Military Pay. Rather than publish data probably obsolete by the time it might appear in print, pay table specifics are omitted from *The Army Officer's Guide.* For current pay specifics, consult your Finance office or check Service-oriented journals where the newest tables are usually prominently featured.

Allowances. In addition to pay, there are allowances for quarters (unless government quarters are supplied), subsistence, family separation, dislocation, uniform allowances for some officers, and others which are discussed briefly in this chapter or the chapter which follows, *Travel Allowances.* None of the allowances are included in the computation of retired pay.

Quarters and Subsistence Allowances. As indicated earlier, both quarters and subsistence allowances are adjusted with each adjustment in base pay. The adjusted pay rates, if any, recommended by the President by 1 September of each year for civilian employees, normally are applied on a percentage basis to both the base pay and to the quarters and subsistence allowances for officers. This has the effect of keeping the total pay and allowances of officers in line with civilian pay scales, but ultimately it will result in retired pay being less costly to the government (and less remunerative to the retirees) than if the entire pay adjustment had been applied to base pay alone, as was the case prior to 1974.

Service Creditable for Basic Pay. As seen in most tables, pay increases in each grade with length of service. In computing the years of service for pay purposes, credit is given for all periods of active service in any Regular or Reserve component of any of the uniformed services. Credit may also be granted for service other than active duty. Officers are advised to consult the Finance Officer servicing their pay accounts with a statement of all their military service for consideration of credit which may be given under the laws.

Definition of Dependent for Quarters Allowance. The law which authorizes the allowance for quarters for an officer with dependents provides that it includes at all times and in all places the lawful spouse and the legitimate unmarried children, under twenty-one years of age. There are important additional provisions for other dependent family members and for rulings in these instances the best course to follow is to consult the unit Personnel Officer or the Finance Officer.

OTHER PAY AND ALLOWANCES

In addition to basic pay and to allowances for subsistence and for quarters (for those officers not furnished government quarters), the following provisions for special pay or allowances are important.

Hazardous Duty Pay. Several types of duty assignment are classed as hazardous. Incentive pay is authorized for performance, under competent orders, of these types of duty: Aerial flight duty as a crew member, aerial flight duty as a noncrew member, parachute duty, demolition duty, experimental stress duty.

A member may receive hazardous duty pay for two types of such duty for the same period if qualified and required to perform multiple hazardous duties in order to carry out the mission of the unit. (An example would be to engage in regular and frequent aerial flights and also to perform demolition duty when required to accomplish the mission of the unit.)

Incentive Pay for Flight Duty. The monthly rates of additional incentive pay for flying as a crew member vary from $125 to $400 per month, depending upon grade and years of service.

Incentive Pay for Hazardous Duty Other Than Aerial Flight Duty. The monthly rate of additional incentive pay for hazardous duties other than aerial flight duty as a crew member (parachute, thermal stress or demolition duty, or aerial flights not as a crew member) is as follows:

Officer or warrant officer $110.00

Divers' Pay. An officer on diving duty may receive $200 special pay per month.

Hostile Fire Pay. The Military Pay Act of 1965 provided for payments of $65 per month to military members serving in areas where they are subject to injury or are injured as a result of enemy action. (See AR 37–104.)

Special Pay to Medical Officers. Medical officers are eligible for special pay of $100 per month for less than two years service. The rate is $350 monthly for two or more years of service. In addition, PL 96-284, effective July 1, 1980, established an annual payment of up to $10,000 to physicians based upon length of service, a $2,000–$5,000 bonus for board certified doctors, and an $8,000 incentive for doctors who are specialists in short-supply fields.

Special Pay to Dental Officers. Dental officers are entitled to special pay at the following rates:

$100 per month if they have completed less than two years services.

$150 per month if they have completed two but less than six years of service.

$250 per month if they have completed six but less than ten years of service.

$350 per month if they have completed ten or more years of service.

Special Pay to Veterinary Corps Officers and Optometry Officers. Veterinary Corps officers and Optometry officers are entitled to special pay at the rate of $100 per month.

Family Separation Allowance. This allowance is payable only to service members with dependents. The Family Separation Allowance is of two types, both of which are payable to the same individual if he or she meets the qualifications for both listed below. Each type of allowance may be paid to a member who qualifies therefor in addition to any other allowance or per diem to which the member may be entitled.

(1) One allowance, equal to the basic monthly allowance for quarters payable to a member in the same pay grade without dependents, is payable to a member with dependents who is on permanent duty in Alaska or anywhere else outside the continental United States, when:

(a) Movement of dependents to the member's permanent station or a place nearby is not authorized at government expense, and the member's dependents are not residing at or near the station; and

(b) No government quarters are available for assignment to the member.

(2) The other type of Family Separation Allowance, equal to $30 *per month,* is payable (except in war time or national emergency declared by Congress) to a member with dependents who is authorized a basic quarters allowance, when:

(a) The member is in pay grade E–4 (with more than 4 years of service) or a higher grade;

(b) Movement of dependents to the member's permanent station or a place nearby is not authorized at government expense and his or her dependents are not residing at or near the station; *and*

(c) The member is on duty aboard ship away from the ship's home port continuously for more than 30 days; or

(d) The member is on temporary duty away from his or her permanent station continuously for more than 30 days and the member's dependents do not reside at or near the temporary duty station.

Dislocation Allowance. Upon permanent change of station, when dependents are authorized to accompany the officer, a dislocation allowance is payable in the amount of one month's quarters allowance. There is a limitation of one such payment per year with two exceptions: Two allowances are paid under some conditions when officers are ordered to service schools, and a second exception when approved by the Secretary of the Army.

Uniform Allowance, Reserve Officers. *Upon initial appointment.* (Armed Forces Reserve Act of 1952.) A newly appointed Reserve officer or officer of the Army of the United States without component is entitled to $200 as reimbursement for the purchase of required uniforms. This accrues upon first reporting for active duty for a period in excess of 90 days; upon completion as a member of a Reserve component of not less than 14 days active duty or active duty for training; or completion of 14 periods of not less than two hours each in the Ready Reserve where wearing of the uniform is required. In addition to the $200 initial allowance, a Reserve officer upon first reporting is also entitled to a $100 active duty allowance. Warrant officers are entitled to the $200 initial allowance when first appointed and to the additional $100 if they had not previously been on active duty.

Uniform Allowance, ROTC Vitalization Act of 1964. This act provides a uniform allowance of $300 for all ROTC graduates on their initial appointment, whether commissioned in the Regular Army or the Army Reserve. It is not an allowance in addition to that stated above; but it extends to individuals commissioned into the Regular Army from the ROTC the uniform allowance of $300.00.

The Four-year Allowance. A Reserve officer is entitled to an additional $50 upon completion of each 4-year period of active status in a Reserve component which must include at least 28 days of active duty or active duty for training.

The Allowance for Re-entry upon Active Duty. A Reserve officer who has been on inactive duty for a period of two years, and is then recalled to active duty of more than 90 days duration, may qualify for $100 as reimbursement for additional uniforms and equipment required on such duty.

Station Allowances, Overseas. Station allowances to equalize the cost-of-living and housing are authorized for uniformed personnel stationed in a number of foreign countries. The allowances are planned to equalize the total of selected essential expenditures of the foreign station with those in the United States. It is to be noted that there must be an officially computed difference in the cost of living factors which are considered, as to the United States and oversea stations, and the cost greater in the oversea station, for the allowance to be authorized. It is known as the *Cost of Living Allowance or COLA.* Consult the Finance Officer as to the allowance, if any, at a station of interest.

PAYMENTS AND HOW OBTAINED

A Military Pay Voucher (DA Form 2349) is prepared by the unit personnel officer for each person entitled to pay. All items of entitlement or obligation are shown. The Voucher is forwarded to the most convenient Disbursing Officer who makes the payment, furnishing a copy of the voucher to the payee which shows in detail the total amount due, and how the pay was computed. Payment is made monthly, normally on the last duty day. *Caution:* Check the copy each month to be certain pay is correctly computed.

Advance and Partial Pay. Prior to starting travel an officer may draw an advance of pay. The approval of the commanding officer is often required but is granted liberally. This is meant to assist the officer in purchasing transportation tickets or in paying automobile expenses. Should an officer need funds at another time, he or she may draw up to the amount accrued for that month as a partial payment of that month's salary. Partial payments are not encouraged as a routine need; however; no officer is expected to borrow money at an interest rate when that officer's own salary can provide for an emergency.

Income Tax. Military base pay (not allowances) is subject to federal and state income tax. As in the civilian community, an amount is withheld from the pay each month, based upon the number of exemptions claimed and the estimated total pay for the year. The amount withheld is itemized on the monthly pay voucher, DA Form 2349. About 1 February of each year, the Finance Officer furnishes a Form W–2 showing total taxable pay, the total deducted for federal income tax, state income tax, and the total deducted for social security.

Dislocation allowances and incentive pay are taxable.

Deduction From Pay, Social Security Tax. The Finance Officer is required to deduct Social Security Tax (F.I.C.A.) from each pay account. See Chapter 7, *Financial Planning.*

SEVERANCE AND READJUSTMENT PAY

Regular and Reserve officers who are involuntarily separated with more than five but less than twenty years commissioned service are entitled to a lump sum separation payment equal to 10% of their annual base pay times the years of service, not to exceed $30,000. *Caution:* Retirement pay and VA compensation may be influenced by acceptance of this pay. The rules for computation are complex and require referral to the DoD *Military Pay and Allowances Manual* and a qualified finance clerk. An individual concerned with this situation should take his or her complete military record to the appropriate agency for complete information and computation.

20

Travel Allowances

This chapter provides information normally required by an officer performing travel under individual travel orders, moving dependents on permanent change of station, and shipping household goods. Excluded are unusual situations and special cases of travel not generally encountered by the majority of individuals performing routine travel. (See AR 37–106 and Joint Travel Regulations.)

TRAVEL OF OFFICERS

Travel Status Defined. Officers are entitled to travel and transportation allowances as authorized in accordance with existing regulations, only while actually in a "travel status." They are in travel status while performing travel away from their permanent duty station, upon public business, pursuant to competent travel orders, including necessary delays en route incident to mode of travel and periods of necessary temporary duty or temporary additional duty. "Travel status," whether travel is performed by land, air or sea (except as a member of ship's complement), will commence with departure from permanent duty station or ship, and will include any of the conditions shown below:

Temporary Duty or Temporary Additional Duty. Travel in connection with necessary temporary duty or temporary additional duty, including time spent at a temporary duty station or a temporary additional duty station, without regard to whether duty is required to be performed while traveling, and without regard to the length of time away from the permanent duty station. Temporary Duty (TDY) assignments will normally be limited to periods not in excess of six months.

Permanent Change of Station (PCS). Travel from one permanent duty station to another permanent duty station.

Delay. Delay incident to mode of travel, such as necessary delay while awaiting further transportation after travel status has commenced.

To and from Hospital. Travel to or from a hospital for observation or treatment.

Travel by Air. Travel performed by military or commercial aircraft when proceeding from one duty station to another under orders of competent authority. Air travel includes one or more landings away from the starting point and the necessary delays incident to this mode of travel. Aircraft flights for crew training purposes come under this category.

Aerial Training Flights. Aerial flights for training purposes made in the absence of travel orders when it is necessary to remain away overnight.

Special Circumstances or Conditions. Special circumstances or conditions not heretofore defined which may be determined jointly in advance, contemporaneously or subsequently, by the Secretaries of the uniformed services to constitute a travel status.

Traveling with Troops. An officer is "traveling with troops" when he or she is physically traveling as a member of, or on duty with, any body of troops which is subsisted en route from a kitchen car, rolling kitchen, field range, ship's galley, or other comparable facilities for preparing complete cooked meals en route.

Members traveling with troops will not be paid mileage or reimbursed on a per diem basis for expenses incurred. Under no circumstances will members obtain meals on meal tickets, or meal receipts. Transportation, and sleeping accommodations, if available and required, will be furnished in kind.

Group Travel. Group travel is a movement of three or more members traveling under one group order from the same point of origin to the same destination when a member is designated in the order as being in charge of the group.

Standard of Accommodations. When a member is entitled to transportation in kind and requests Government transportation requests, such member shall be issued first-class transportation, including sleeping accommodations or parlor-car seat when appropriate. When travel is by commercial aircraft, tourist class accommodations normally are furnished.

Type of Carrier on Which to Travel. Within the continental United States the individual may elect to travel by any mode of transportation at personal expense, subject to reimbursement upon completing the journey.

Termination of Travel Status. Travel status will terminate with return to the permanent duty station or upon reporting at a new permanent duty station ashore or afloat, except that travel status terminates when the member reaches the assigned port if the vessel to which he or she is reporting for duty is already in port.

Transportation in Kind and Transportation Requests. Transportation in kind includes travel by all modes of commercial transportation and military facilities, but does not include travel at personal expense. In all matters pertaining to transportation consult your transportation officer, *prior to commencing travel.*

TRAVEL ORDERS

No reimbursement for travel is authorized unless orders by competent authority have been issued therefor. Reimbursement for travel is not authorized when the travel is performed in anticipation of or prior to receipt of orders.

Travel orders issued under unusual conditions which are not originated by competent authority must be approved by competent authority to allow reimbursement for travel expenses.

Types of Travel Orders. *Permanent Change of Station.* The term "permanent change of station," unless otherwise qualified, means the transfer or assignment of a member of the uniformed services from one permanent station to another. This includes the change from home or from the place from which ordered to active duty, to first station upon appointment, call to active duty, enlistment, and from last duty station to home or to the place from which ordered to active duty upon separation from the service, placement upon the temporary disability retired list, release from active duty, or retirement.

Temporary Duty. The term "temporary duty" means duty at a location other than permanent station to which a member of the uniformed services is ordered to temporary duty under orders which provide for further assignment to a new permanent station or for return to the old permanent station.

Blanket or Repeated Travel. Blanket travel orders are issued to members who regularly and frequently make trips away from their permanent duty stations within certain geographical limits in performance of regular assigned duties. Travel must not be solely between place of duty and place of lodging.

REIMBURSEMENT FOR TRAVEL EXPENSES

Travel at Personal Expense. When authorized travel is performed at personal expense the member will be reimbursed a monetary allowance in lieu of transportation at the rate the government would have paid for a commercial ticket in addition to authorized per diem. It is wise to consult a Transportation Officer or Finance officer, prior to starting the journey, as to requirements for reimbursement.

Travel by Privately Owned Vehicle (POV). For travel actually performed by privately owned vehicle (POV) under orders authorizing such mode of transportation as more advantageous to the Government, an officer will be paid a monetary allowance in lieu of transportation at the rate of 22.5 cents per mile for the official distance in addition to authorized per diem. When the official travel by POV is for the convenience of the individual, the rate is 7 cents per mile.

Mileage. Mileage is an allowance applicable to permanent change of station under the following circumstances:

(1) When travel is by privately-owned conveyance.
(2) When travel is by rail and available transportation requests were not used.
(3) On relief from active duty.
(4) On separation from the Service.
(5) On transfer to the temporary disability retired list.
(6) On retirement.

Mileage is computed by finance officers from a table of official distances. These distances govern, regardless of the actual route followed by the traveler.

Per Diem. The per diem allowances are designed to cover room rentals, meals, tips, street car or taxi fares (other than to and from station, wharf, or landing field), laundry, and other similar incidental expenses. Rates of per diem for travel are specified in Joint Travel Regulations. For round trips of 10 hours or less within 1 calendar day no per diem is authorized.

The maximum per diem rate generally authorized within the United States is $50.00, computed on the basis of $21.00 for meals and miscellaneous expenses plus the actual cost for lodging up to $29.00. If lodging costs more than $29.00, only the $29.00 is payable, but if it costs less than $29.00, only the actual cost is payable. Thus, if an officer elects to stay with a friend while on a trip and incurs no charge for quarters, the allowable per diem for that day is limited to the $21.00 for meals and miscellaneous expenses. Certain metropolitan areas are considered as high cost areas and are authorized higher per diem rates ranging up to $75.00 per day. See your travel and per diem specialist at the Finance Office.

Trailer Allowance. Costs of transporting a mobile home during a permanent change of station move are reimbursable up to an amount equal to the estimated cost of transporting a member's baggage and household effects via commercial movers. Mobile homeowners also are entitled to a dislocation allowance for quarters and in-transit mobile home storage of up to 180 days.

Reimbursable Expenses. In the past many officers have paid travel expenses for which reimbursement might have been received. On a long trip that loss can be material. Don't miss them. The following are reimbursable:

Taxi Fares. Reimbursement is authorized for taxicab fares between places of abode or business and stations, wharves, airports, other carrier terminals or local terminus of the mode of transportation used, between carrier terminals while en route when free transfer is not included in the price of the ticket or when necessitated by change in mode of travel, and from carrier terminals to lodgings and return in connection with unavoidable delays en route incident to the mode of travel. Itemization is required.

Allowed Tips. Tips incident to transportation expenses are reimbursable as follows:

(1) Tips to Pullman porters, not to exceed $1.00 per day, or $0.35 for trips of less than 5 hours duration;

(2) Tips to baggage porters, red caps, etc., are not to exceed customary local rates, but not including tips for baggage handling at hotels; the number of pieces of baggage handled will be shown on the claim. Itemization is required.

Checking and Transfer of Baggage. Expenses incident to checking and transfer of baggage are reimbursable. The number of pieces of baggage checked will be shown on the claim. Itemization is required.

Excess Baggage. When excess baggage is authorized, actual costs for such excess baggage in addition to that carried free by the carrier are reimbursable. Receipt is required.

Registration Fees. Registration fees incident to attendance at meetings of technical, professional, scientific, or other non-federal organizations are reimbursable when attendance thereat is authorized or approved. Receipt is required. (See annual appropriation acts.)

Bachelor Officers' Quarters Fees. When government quarters are available and used, the cost of the lodging in the government quarters is reimbursable. A receipt from the billeting facility is required.

Government Auto. Cost of storage of government automobiles when necessary is reimbursable if government storage facilities are not available. Receipt is required.

Telephone, Telegraph, Cable, etc. Cost of official telephone, telegraph, cable, and similar communication services is reimbursable when incident to the duty enjoined or in connection with items of transportation. Such services when solely in connection with reserving hotel room, etc., are not considered official. Copies of messages sent are required for all mechanical transmissions unless the message is classified in which case a full explanation and a receipt will suffice. Local and long distance telephone calls are allowable when itemized.

Stenographic Services. Charges for necessary stenographic services or rental of typewriters or similar machines in connection with the preparation of reports or official correspondence are reimbursable when authorized or approved by the headquarters directing the travel. This provision does not apply when stenographic services are performed by military personnel or government employees. Receipts are required.

Local Public Carrier Fares. Expenses incident to travel on streetcar, bus, or other usual means of local transportation may be allowed in lieu of taxicab fares under the conditions and limitations stated. Itemization is required. Commercial or government (GSA) "Rent-a-Car" expenses are reimbursable; authorizations for such rentals are normally made in advance and indicated on travel orders.

Toll Fares. Ferry fares, and road, bridge, and tunnel tolls are reimbursable when travel is performed by government vehicle or by authorized hired conveyance; or when performed by privately owned conveyance within the surrounding area of a duty station.

Receipts. Receipts should be obtained for all reimbursable expenses greater than $15. Without a supporting receipt, your claim may be denied.

Advance Payment of Travel and Transportation Allowances. Travel and transportation allowances for an officer's travel are authorized to be paid in advance, except in connection with retirement and upon first entering active duty. See the post finance officer.

TRAVEL EXPENSES NOT PAYABLE BY THE GOVERNMENT

Travel expenses of the type listed in the examples below are not payable from government funds:

(1) Expenses incurred during period of travel which are incident to other duties (such as traveling aboard a vessel in performance of temporary duty on such vessel).

(2) Travel from leave to official station for duty. Individuals departing from their official duty station on leave do so at their own risk. If ordered to return from leave they must assume the expense involved.

(3) Travel under permissive orders to travel in contrast to orders directing travel requires the individual to pay the costs.

(4) Travel under orders but not on public business. Example: travel as a participant in an athletic contest. Such travel may be paid from unit or command welfare funds which are generated through operation of exchanges and motion picture theaters.

(5) Return from leave to duty abroad. Unless government transportation is available, such as space on a transport, the individual on leave in the United States from an oversea command must defray his or her own return expenses.

(6) Attendance at public ceremonies or demonstrations whose expenses are borne by the sponsoring agency.

TRAVEL OUTSIDE THE UNITED STATES

Travel expenses for travel outside the United States are furnished in advance or are reimbursable on essentially the same basis as temporary duty travel performed in the United States. That is to say, the traveler is entitled to the costs of transportation, per diem allowance, and costs of incidental necessary expenses.

Per diem rates for oversea travel also vary according to quarters and mess availability and charges for same. Consult your local finance officer for assistance prior to and after any oversea travel.

Certificates are required from the traveler and from the commanding officer or a designated representative of an installation at which a traveler performs temporary duty. Consult Finance Officer.

PASSPORTS

Passports issued by the Department of State are required for persons visiting foreign countries. Mexico and Canada do not normally require passports for entry from United States citizens. (AR 600–290.)

There are four classes of passports: Diplomatic, Special, Regular, and Dependent.

Diplomatic passports are issued to officers accredited to any embassy or legation of the United States abroad and to members of the household of such officers. Field grade officers and above assigned to military assistance program missions have been granted diplomatic passports.

Special passports are issued to officers proceeding abroad under orders in the discharge of their official duties. Dependents accompanying or traveling to join bearers of special passports who are stationed abroad may apply for special passports.

Regular passports are issued to persons who are traveling abroad for personal reasons.

Dependent passports are issued to dependents of military and civilian personnel who are authorized by the appropriate offices of the Department of Defense to reside with such personnel while on active duty outside the continental limits of the United States.

When the applicant for a passport is in Washington, D.C., application is made through the headquarters of the Department concerned. In New York, Boston, Chicago, New Orleans, or San Francisco apply in person to the passport agent of the Department of State. In other places apply to the clerk of a United States court or a state court authorized to naturalize aliens.

Two recently taken photographs must be submitted by each applicant. A group photograph should be used when more than one person is included in one application. Photographs must be full-face on thin unglazed paper with light background and not over three inches nor less than two and a half by two and a half inches in size. Each photograph will be signed in black ink in such manner as not to obscure the facial features.

Each passport application must be accompanied by documentary evidence of citizenship.

Visa. An indorsement made on a passport by the proper authorities (usually Embassy or Consular officials) of a country to be visited, showing that the passport has been examined and that the bearer may proceed to that country.

TRAVEL OF DEPENDENTS

Basic Entitlement. Members of the uniformed services are entitled to transportation of dependents upon a permanent change of station for travel performed from the old station to the new permanent station or between points otherwise authorized. As to officers there are some important exceptions as follows:

(1) An officer assigned to a school or installation as a student, if the course of instruction is to be of less than 20 weeks duration.

(2) Separation from the service or relief from active duty under conditions other than honorable.

(3) Call to active duty for training for less than one year.

(4) Call to active duty for other than training duty for less than 6 months.

(5) An officer who fails to receive revocation of permanent change of station orders because he or she took advantage of leave of absence and the notice of revocation was received at the officer's old permanent station sufficiently in advance of the time that would have been required to proceed under the original orders.

(6) When the dependent is a member of the uniformed service on active duty on the effective date of the orders.

(7) For any portion of travel performed by a foreign registered vessel or airplane, if American registered vessels or airplanes are available by the usually traveled route.

(8) Where the dependents departed old permanent station prior to the issuance of orders, and the voucher is not supported by a certificate of the commanding officer, or a designated representative, of the headquarters issuing the orders that the officer was advised prior to the issuance of change of station orders that such orders would be issued.

(9) When dependency does not exist on the effective date of the order directing permanent change of station.

(10) For dependents receiving any other type of travel allowances from the Government in their own right.

Reimbursement for Costs of Dependent Travel. An officer who transports lawful dependents at personal expense, from a location where transportation requests are not available, may elect to be reimbursed for the actual cost of the transportation authorized in lieu of the monetary allowances stated below.

An officer who elects to transport dependents at personal expense may obtain reimbursement. The amount is payable only after travel has been completed. The total entitlement is determined on the basis of $50 per day plus 13 cents per mile for the service member, seven cents per mile for each dependent over 12 years of age, and 3.5 cents per mile for each dependent under age 12.

Travel of Dependents Beyond the Continental Limits of the United States. Upon the permanent change of station of an officer to a station outside the continental United States to include Alaska, Hawaii, and possessions of the United States, he or she becomes entitled to transportation of dependents, when authorized, at government expense.

TRANSPORTATION OF HOUSEHOLD GOODS

Shipment of household goods consists of transportation, including packing, crating, drayage (at point of shipment and destination), temporary storage, uncrating, and unpacking at government expense. DA Pamphlet 55–2, *Personal Property Shipping Information,* should be used as a basic reference by all officers preparing to move, and a copy should be in each officer's library of important official documents.

These services are performed or expenses paid for an officer ordered to active duty at a permanent station, or assigned to a new permanent station, or relieved from active duty or retired. (See AR 55–70)

Local transportation officers should be consulted in connection with such movements as soon as orders are received. They will provide the best possible guidance in preparing for the shipment of household property so that it will proceed smoothly for the family making the shipment. Follow their guidance carefully. Special attention should be given to the necessity for temporary storage and the allowable period for such storage up to 90 days. An additional 90 days may be authorized under exceptional circumstances.

Household Goods Shipped at Government Expense. The term "household goods" includes clothing, baggage, all other personal effects of a similar character, professional books, papers and equipment, as well as the items normally required to equip a home with furniture, appliances and the like.

There are items which are excluded from government shipment and the recommendation is to consult the Transportation Officer. There are special requirements as to shipment of personal household property in a house trailer.

Authorized weight allowances are shown in the accompanying table.

Excess Costs. The cost of draying or hauling unauthorized articles or any weight in excess of weight allowances will be borne by the owner.

Insurance. A prudent officer who ships personal property of value should arrange for insurance. Strongly advised is the broad coverage which may be obtained at favorable rates from the Armed Forces Cooperative Insurance, Ft Leavenworth, Kansas, or the United Services Automobile Association, San Antonio, Texas. Insurance secured through the carrier is not recommended, since officers are eligible to obtain coverage from the associations named which are maintained to serve the needs of officers and their families. A claim against the government for damage or loss incident to a shipment may be relied upon to obtain a fair and just settlement. Always consult the JAG Claims Officer.

Very Important Caution. All reliable moving companies are in business to provide good service. These companies are doing all that is possible to insure speedy, efficient moves, with the avoidance of confusion and disappointment. Still, not all meet the standard. It is essential that Army officials be able to identify the superior companies, the average ones, and the poor ones. Keeping current on this information requires the cooperation of Army families.

Fill out with care and accuracy the *Carrier Performance Report.* Be accurate and be prompt. Be fair to the company, but be fair also to yourself, the Army, and Army families who will make future moves. This report indicates to the transportation officials and to the transfer firm just what kind of service you received.

A good way to start is to confer with the Transportation Officer well in advance of the move. Get his or her advice as to preparation. And learn precisely the service you are supposed to receive. In that way most misunderstandings are prevented. You are supposed to receive fine service. Do your full part to get it. Report on the proper form just what you did receive.

What You Should Do To Assist in the Move. (1) Contact your transportation officer as soon as possible after receipt of orders.

(2) Advise the transportation officer that you have professional books and papers to be shipped in order that they may be packed and weighed separately from your household goods.

(3) Have sufficient copies of your change of station orders (usually six to nine for each shipment).

(4) If you will proceed to your new duty station prior to the time you will want your household goods shipped, leave or send your dependent or agent sufficient copies of your change of station orders. Be sure that you or your duly authorized agent is on hand at the time of packing, loading, unpacking, and unloading of your household goods and has been furnished instructions regarding the signing of the packer's inventory, the "Accessorial Services Certificate," the carrier's shipping documents and the Government bill of lading.

(5) If you have silver, gold, or other valuables to be shipped, inform your transportation officer in order that special arrangements can be made for shipment of these items.

(6) Request storage at point of origin whenever you are in doubt as to the place you will want your goods shipped. Be sure to check the allowable time limits for storage to match your plans for leave, house hunting, and the like.

(7) If your household goods are moving by van, be sure to obtain a copy of the carrier's inventory from the driver; also, you will be requested to sign a DD Form 619, "Accessorial Services Certificate." The certificate contains an itemized list of the units of packing performed at your residence. Be sure to check the certificate carefully and never sign it in blank.

(8) Notify your transportation officer immediately if your orders are cancelled or modified or if a change in the destination of the shipment is desired.

(9) Appliances are serviced for transporting at government expense. The transportation officer makes arrangements for you with the packing or moving firm. Similarly, after delivery, the appliances are to be "de-serviced." Be certain that you check to see both operations are performed by trained and reliable servicemen—do not assume the moving van driver and helpers are qualified. *Insist upon this authorized service.*

(10) The refrigerator should be defrosted and well cleaned the day before

Table of Weight Allowances (Pounds) on Change of Station

	Temporary Change:	PCS Allowance:
General & General of the Army	2,000	13,500
Lieutenant General	1,500	13,500
Major General	1,000	13,500
Brigadier General	1,000	13,500
Colonel	800	13,500
Lieutenant Colonel	800	13,000
Major & Warrant Officer (W–4)	800	12,000
Captain & Warrant Officer (W–3)	600	11,000
First Lieutenant & Warrant Officer (W–2)	600	10,000
Second Lieutenant & Warrant Officer (W–1)	600	9,000

the move, so that its interior will be dry at time of loading. The shelves and trays will be removed by the packers and placed in suitable containers for safe movement.

(11) Obtain from your transportation officer the approximate time of arrival of your household goods at destination.

(12) Be sure you or your agent are at home on the day of expected move and make arrangements for receipt of the property at destination.

(13) Turn over all your household goods for the same destination at one time, except silver, gold, items of extraordinary value, or items to be shipped by express.

(14) Clean china and cooking utensils before packers arrive.

(15) Set aside and call to the attention of the movers extra fragile items such as chinaware and delicate glassware, and to professional books which must be packed and weighed separately.

(16) Keep groceries and food supplies together in one area for proper packing.

(17) Remove articles from drawers of the furniture intended for shipment. Let the packer determine which, if any, light, bulky articles may be shipped in the drawers.

(18) Be sure to inventory your household goods with the van driver. Do not allow an entry of "marred and scratched" on the inventory form unless such entry is correct. This broad language may cover extensive damage. Insist upon accurate descriptions of the condition of the furniture, such as, "1-inch scratch, left leg," or "rubbed, right front corner."

(19) Make arrangements to have telephone service and other utilities disconnected.

(20) Dispose of opened but unused foods that might spill or spoil enroute. They should never be stored or shipped.

(21) Don't include plants, fresh fruits, or flowers in shipment as this is prohibited in many states.

(22) It is advisable to arrange for disposition of contents of deep freeze units. Most deep freeze units are not constructed to withstand the strains of weight of a full load of frozen foods during the handling necessary to transportation and damage to the unit may occur.

(23) Separate and collect into one place all items that are not to be included in the shipment. Show the van operator the articles, if any, that have been set aside and are not to be included in the shipment.

Claims for Loss or Damage Incident to Shipment. Regardless of when your household goods are delivered, cause the carrier or local agent to unpack all boxes and to de-service all appliances. Carefully note all damaged and lost items on the carrier's forms; be as meticulous as the company was that packed you. Usually, the local agent will make immediate arrangements for repair or replacement. Once you have checked all your belongings including the operation of appliances, consult with your Transportation officer, the Claims officer, and the local agent. You may claim for the difference between what you believe fair and what the carrier or the insurance company will allow (See AR 27–29). All have deduction tables for depreciation in values according to how old the item is and all have time limits for presenting claims.

21
Uniforms
of the Army

This chapter contains essential information about the Army's uniforms which is of special interest to officers. Extracts and illustrations have been drawn from the following official publications:

AR 670-1, *Wear and Appearance of Army Uniforms and Insignia.*
CTA 50-900, *(Peace) Clothing and Equipment.*
AR 700-84, *Logistics, Issue and Sale of Personal Clothing.*

GENERAL

There are eight official uniforms for male officers of the Army and thirteen official uniforms for female army officers. Included are uniforms of appropriate weight and material for cold weather and warm weather; there are service uniforms, dress uniforms, and field uniforms to meet all contingencies. Some are required to be in the possession of all officers while others are optional.

In this chapter are condensed descriptions and illustrations of the several uniforms with occasions for their use and wear. Insignia, ornamentation, distinctive unit insignia and many other useful subjects are covered for the convenience of Army officers. Tables, *Composition of Uniforms,* will be found with the detailed description of the uniforms which gives each article pertaining to a particular uniform.

Wearing of the Uniform by Members of the Active Army. The uniform will be worn by all personnel when on duty unless an exception for wear of civilian clothes for mission reasons has been granted by a major Army commander or by the head of an agency at the Army Staff level or higher. Installation commanders may prescribe the uniforms to be worn in formations. The uniform will

315

not be worn when engaged in off-duty civilian employment, when specifically prohibited by Army regulations, or when wearing the uniform would bring discredit upon the Army. Uniforms will be properly fitted, clean, serviceable, and pressed as necessary. They will be worn buttoned, zippered or snapped as appropriate, metallic devices will be kept in proper luster and shoes will be cleaned and shined.

When an option to choose among various authorized fabrics for uniforms is exercised, individuals must assure that all outer garments are made of the same type material. Garrison caps of Army Green Shade 44 or 344 may be worn interchangeably with uniforms of either shade.

The wearing of combinations of various articles of the uniform other than combinations prescribed by regulations and tables of allowances is prohibited. *Suggestion:* Form the habit of checking the appropriate table, *Composition of Uniforms,* shown later in this chapter, as to the complete components of each uniform.

Wearing of Civilian Decorations, Jewelry, etc. The only civilian decorations or ribbons which may be worn with the uniform are as authorized in AR 672-5-1; see Chapter Twenty-Two, *Decorations, Service Medals and Badges.*

The wearing of a personal wrist watch, identification wrist bracelet, and not more than two rings is authorized so long as the style is conservative and in good taste. Wearing a purely religious medal on a chain around the neck is authorized provided neither the medal nor the chain is exposed. Earrings, earposts of any size or shape, fad devices, vogue medallions, personal talismans or amulets are not authorized for wear with the uniform or on duty.

No jewelry, watch chains or similar civilian items, to include pens and pencils, will appear exposed on the uniforms. Authorized exceptions are a conservative tie tack or tie clasp which may be worn with the black four-in-hand necktie and a pen and pencil may appear exposed on the Hospital Duty and Food Service Uniforms.

Wearing of Civilian Clothing. Civilian clothing may be worn by all Army personnel when off duty unless the wear is prohibited by the installation commander within CONUS or by the oversea commander outside CONUS. When civilian clothing is worn, such clothing will be in keeping with the standards of appearance and good taste inherent in the wearer's position as a representative of the Army.

SUGGESTED UNIFORMS

AR 670-1, states that commissioned and warrant officers are responsible for procuring and maintaining uniforms appropriate to their assigned duties. CTA 50-900 lists appropriate uniforms and personal equipment according to categories of climate. Usually the officer will receive a listing of appropriate uniforms when he or she is commissioned, called to active duty or transferred overseas. Hence, no regulation prescribes the number of each uniform nor will any requirement be given for personal items like underwear and socks. The regulation states: *It is mandatory that all officers dress in accordance with their position as an Officer of the United States Army, and in accordance with the traditions and customs of the service.* Sufficient quantities of other personal items necessary to meet acceptable standards of hygiene and appearance are to be purchased and maintained.

Military units and their members are provided with clothing and equipment depending upon the mission of the unit, and the climatic conditions to be expected in the area of employment. Items of equipment which pertain to the mission of the unit, such as weapons, are authorized in the Table of Organization of the unit. Individual items of general use, both clothing and equipment, are prescribed in the TA's. Further, as to clothing and some other items, the allowances are based upon seven categories of climate from *Zone I, Warm or Hot All Year, to Zone VII, Mild Summers, Very Cold Winters.*

The major items of uniform clothing which are normally prescribed with minimum quantities that should be in the possession of all officers, are as follows:

Item	Male	Female	Note
Raincoat, Army Black	1	1	1
Uniform, Army Tan	3	N/A	2
Uniform, AG-388 Skirt and Jackets	N/A	2	3
Uniform, Army Green Pantsuit	N/A	1	
Uniform, Army Green	1	1	
Uniform, Army White	Optional	Optional	4
Uniform, Army Blue	1	1	5,8
Uniform, Army Green Maternity	N/A	2	6
Uniform, Field/Utility	4	4	7
Coat, Cold weather (Field Jacket)	1	1	

Notes.
1. The AG-44 overcoat, AG-274 raincoat or the new Army black raincoat are all acceptable.
2. The Army tan shade 445 (Poly/Ctn) or AG shirt 415 grey/green shirt are acceptable.
3. This uniform replaces the Army green cord uniform which is also acceptable until 1 October 1981.
4. This uniform may be required by major commanders for all officers on active duty for 6 months or more, in clothing allowance zones I and II as defined in CTA 50-900.
5. This uniform is required for all officers on extended active duty for periods of 6 months or more.
6. As required by AR 635-100 and chapter 24.
7. The field uniforms may be either the cotton OG 107, durapress OG 507, or battledress.
8. Additional quantities required by officers for performance of official duties in units when the missions include Band formations, reviews, parades, ceremonial events, and the like, are authorized as organizational issue by CTA 50-900.

Accessories. Officers are also responsible for procuring and maintaining adequate quantities of appropriate accessories, insignia, footwear, undergarments, headgear and handgear for use with the above uniforms.

HOW TO DRESS WELL AND SAVE MONEY

The junior officer faces a dilemma of what to buy, how to dress well and yet not become impoverished. The above suggests what to buy; the following will provide recommendations on how to do it wisely.

The total expenditure for these uniform items is considerable. It is true that an initial uniform allowance is provided to Reserve officers, (and also to some newly appointed Regular Army officers); nevertheless the expense necessary for a career officer is a heavy one. (See Chapter Nineteen, *Pay and Allowances.*) The wise officer will exercise care and judgment in selections to make certain that the articles bought will meet service standards and inspections and that they fit well, all to the end that he or she may wear the uniform with pride and credit to the service. To be an Army officer, one should strive not only to be a good officer but also to look like a good officer.

Where to Purchase Uniforms. Army Clothing Sales Stores. Required items of uniform and equipment are for sale at these official outlets. The purchaser may be certain that each article conforms to the official specifications. Maximum economy in price will be obtained here, but it is to be noted that the optional items of uniform and equipment must be purchased elsewhere.

Officers find that the Army Clothing Sales Stores provide well-fitting serge uniforms at very favorable prices. Junior officers should fill the bulk of their requirements for uniforms at these stores.

Post Exchange Uniform Sales. All uniform items sold in post exchanges conform to the specifications for required and optional items. As to outer uniforms, exchanges generally carry a stock and, in addition, have facilities for special orders, alterations, and prompt, economical service.

Civilian Tailoring Companies and Individual Custom Tailor. Here are some words of praise and some words of caution.

First the words of praise. There are a number of quite large and reliable companies in the United States which specialize in uniforms for officers. There are many small custom tailoring establishments well known as uniform specialists, and some of these tailors have been in this field for years with very well established reputations. There is just one reason to choose a proven civilian source over the official outlets and that is quality of individual tailoring. Officers who can afford the cost, career officers and senior officers especially, are justified in purchasing some of their uniforms from carefully chosen custom tailors. The added cost should pay for the belief that they look their military best.

Now the words of caution. Let the buyer beware. It is a simple matter to sell for less any item which is manufactured of cheap components or by poor workmanship; a civilian outlet attempting to compete on a price basis should receive most careful examination before a purchase is made.

Summary. Officers of all components, all grades, of short service or long, are obliged to meet the high standards as to their uniforms. There is no variation in official requirements. Still, as a practical matter, the standard will be established at the top, by general officers and field officers of a command. A high standard will be expected of career officers. Whatever your grade or component, do your part. Be meticulous in procurement of uniforms which fit very well indeed, which are maintained always in a clean, well-pressed condition, so that you may wear them with pride.

The Commanding Officer's Responsibility. The commanding officer is required to make periodic inspections of the uniforms with which members of his or her command, including officers, have equipped themselves. Inspection will include check as to possession of the items required; that uniforms fit properly; that they are maintained in a neat and correct manner; and that only duly prescribed items of insignia and ornamentation are worn with the uniform.

Cautions in Purchasing Uniforms. There are cautions to be observed in buying uniforms. The first caution is to know what is required and what may soon change.

Various kinds of cloth are authorized for the Army Green uniform, with a choice of weights to meet varying climatic conditions. Uniforms may not be mixed, e.g., do not wear a serge coat with trousers or skirt of gabardine. Reserve officers on limited tours of active duty, who wish sensible economy, may choose the wool serge material, because these uniforms may be obtained through the Clothing Sales Store; at most stations within the United States two uniform weights will be needed for the calendar year—the lightest weight serge for the summer months, and a medium weight for the winter months. Regular Army officers and Reserve officers on long tours of active duty may prefer a wider choice.

Cautions: Officers buying uniforms from sources other than Army Clothing Sales Stores and Post Exchanges should check for the warranty labels certifying to the quality and meeting of Army standards. Uniforms and accessories bought at bargain stores may have been rejected by government purchasers.

Apply the same kind of reasoning to choice of material for the Army Blue and

Army Blue or Black Mess uniforms. These are all-year uniforms except in those areas where the Army White and Army White Mess uniforms may be in order. The officer will seek a fine appearance in these uniforms, and should be mindful of comfort in summer as well as winter. Should you buy a cape to wear with the blue uniforms? It is an optional item. But it is a good appearing, comfortable, distinctive garment. If your circumstances permit it, and the blue uniforms are worn frequently, you will be glad to own it. If you are a senior officer or a career officer the decision should be a simple one.

As to the white materials for the Army White and Army White Mess uniforms, the options provide materials which are normally laundered and others which are normally dry-cleaned. At your station, what is the nature of the laundry or dry-cleaning service, and what of its costs?

There are numerous items of ornamentation such as gold lace, gold bullion, or authorized substitutes of gold color nylon or rayon. Here are the rules:

Wherever gold lace or gold bullion ornamentation and stripes are prescribed for wear with uniforms, gold color nylon or rayon may be substituted subject to the following limitations—

> If trouser and sleeve ornamentation is gold bullion, cap decoration and shoulder strap insignia must be bullion.
> If trouser and sleeve ornamentation is of synthetic material, cap ornamentation and shoulder strap material may be of either bullion or synthetic material.

Ornamentation on visor or hatband of Army Green service cap will be of gold bullion.

Gold bullion presents the best appearance. With excellent care it will retain its good appearance and serviceability for a very long time indeed. The individual must make the choice with reason and judgment based upon his or her own situation and expectancy.

The Reserve officer on inactive duty status is required to provide himself or herself with service uniforms and insignia of branch in which commissioned for use when ordered to active duty. A proper minimum for such officers is suggested as a complete Army Green uniform with extra trousers or skirts and one or two extra shirts in winter, with an overcoat. This minimum will permit the officer to report for duty and perform duties in uniform until he or she can procure basic needs of his station and duty. The total cost of all the suggested items would approximate the initial allowance provided for the purchase of uniforms. The allowance is provided to permit newly appointed officers to procure the uniforms needed for their start, without financial sacrifice.

Care of Uniforms. Good uniforms and appropriate accessories deserve the treatment which will assure maximum durability and appearance to the owner who has paid good money to obtain them. An old uniform of good quality which fits well, is clean, neat, and unfaded, will look better than a new and costly one which is noticeably soiled or out of press. The care which should be given to uniforms and equipment need not be burdensome. But it must be done regularly and correctly. This discussion is an attempt to be helpful and includes points of common experience.

A modest amount of regular care of your uniforms is necessary. Upon removing uniform garments, brush them, inspect for spots or soil, and make prompt use of effective cleaning fluids, not forgetting soap and water; place them upon good wooden or plastic hangers, and hang the garments where they can air and dry. Trousers are best hung at full length. Such care will result in restoration of the press, removal of small wrinkles, and provide a uniform ready to wear when needed. It isn't necessary to have a uniform cleaned and pressed as frequently when these habits are followed as is the case where there is careless-ness.

Underarm sweating is destructive to uniforms, including shirts, causing rot as well as discoloration.

Have a number of regulation neckties. A soiled or badly wrinkled tie is as visible and objectionable as gravy on a vest. Ties soil quickly and require dry cleaning. Replace them before they approach the point of unattractiveness.

Moths and mildew from excess humidity, are the enemy of uniforms in storage. Be certain such uniforms are clean at the time of storage, and well brushed. Place them in a tight container with an adequate supply of moth preventive. Some dry cleaning establishments provide mothproofing service.

Care of Ribbons, Decorations, and Service Medals. Ribbons for decorations and service medals must always be worn fresh and bright. Never wear frayed or soiled ribbons. Never use ribbons covered with a transparent plastic, or impregnated with a substance to increase their life. Dry cleaning will not injure them. Keep the metallic parts clean; some of them require shining. Wear them with pride.

Care of Brass Items of Uniform. Items of solid brass, such as the belt buckle, must be brightly shined. The cloths impregnated with polish, as sold at ex-changes, are very good for the purpose. Avoid touching a freshly shined article with the bare hands, as it tarnishes at once.

Uniform buttons may be cleaned with ammonia and water; do not clean them with brass polish. Permanently shined, anodized aluminum buttons are author-ized.

Care of Gold Braid. Gold braid, now a part of several uniforms, is found on such items as the cap, shoulder knots, insignia of grade of dress uniforms, sleeve ornamentation, and trouser stripes. Gold braid items are costly. With correct care they will remain serviceable for a very long time, but incorrect handling can ruin them quickly. If cleaning is attempted at all it should be done only by someone who has proven skill in doing it.

Tarnish is the enemy of gold braid. When not in use these items should be stored where they will be dry, protected from light, and wrapped in tarnish-proof paper. Such paper may be obtained from jewelers. Ordinary paper con-tains sulphur and will cause tarnish. Rubber will also cause tarnish. Dry clean-ing will not injure trouser stripes or sleeve decorations.

Care of Shoes. The most important point in preserving and prolonging the useful life of good shoes is to place them on properly fitted trees as soon as removed. They will then dry in correct shape, without wrinkles, and be comfort-able when worn again.

Clean them as required. Saddle soap does well. Castile or other mild soap is a good cleaning agent for leather. The application of coat upon coat of polish, without intermediate cleaning, merely piles polish on dirt. Leather which becomes dry or lifeless may be restored with leather dressings, or by a light application of neat's-foot oil applied on the flesh side. Use good polishes; exchanges carry reliable brands.

Boots worn in field service must be strong, well-fitted, comfortable, and treated to resist penetration by water. The wise officer will keep one pair of such boots in top-notch condition ready for instant use.

Mighty few slovenly appearing individuals have ever become officers, or remained long as officers. But the Army has had its careless individuals. If you look like a fine officer it may aid you in gaining the reputation of being a fine officer. It is worth a try.

UNIFORMS FOR MALE OFFICERS

The names of the Army uniforms for male officers are as follows:

Army Green Uniform
Army Blue Uniform
Army Tan Uniform
Army White Uniform
Army White Mess Uniform
Army Blue Mess Uniform
Army Blue Evening Dress Uniform
Field and Work Uniforms

The composition of all uniforms as to what is worn with each one is shown in the accompanying table. The chapter and paragraph numbers therein refer to AR 670-1. Form the habit of checking against this tabulation to be certain your uniform is complete.

THE ARMY GREEN UNIFORM

The Army Green uniform is authorized for year-round wear by officers and enlisted men. It is the normal service (duty) uniform during the winter. The wearing of this uniform by officers during other than normal duty hours is also acceptable and for social functions after retreat. It is also worn as prescribed by local commanders and while in travel status.

Weight of Uniform Fabrics. A broad range of fabric weights is authorized for the Army Green uniform. Except in regions of low temperatures for extended periods, garments made of the lighter or medium weight fabrics may be worn comfortably during the major portion or all of the year.

Materials, Coat and Trousers, Uniforms for Officers. There are seven materials which may be chosen by officers for the uniform coat and trousers. *Caution:* Consistency is required; the coat and trousers are to be of the same material. The materials are:

Wool serge, 12 or 15 ounces, Army Green shade 44.
Wool elastique, 16 ounce, Army Green shade 44.
Wool gabardine, 11 ounce, Army Green shade 44.
Polyester/wool blended fabric, gabardine weave, 11 ounce, AG shade 344.
Polyester/wool blended fabric, tropical weight, plain weave, AG shade 344.
Polyester/wool blended fabric, double knit weave, 16 ounce, AG shade 444.
Polyester textured woven serge, 9.9 ounce, AG shade 434.
Polyester/wool, serge, 11 ounce, AG shade 344.

The wool serge and the polyester/wool tropical weave are the two materials furnished enlisted men and are two of the options available to officers.

Coat. The coat is single-breasted, four-button, of adopted design.
Ornamentation. General officers: A band of black mohair or mercerized cotton braid $1\frac{1}{2}$ inches wide on each sleeve, the lower edge 3 inches up from end of sleeve.
Other officers: Same as above except the braid width is $\frac{3}{4}$ of an inch.
Shoulder and Lapel Insignia. See the later discussion and illustrations.

COMPOSITION OF UNIFORMS
(MEN'S)

Item	Service and Dress Uniforms				Mess and Evening Dress Uniforms			Field and Work Uniforms				
	Army Tan/Khaki, chapter 3	Army Green, chapter 4	Army White, chapter 5	Army Blue, chapter 6	Army White Mess, chapter 7	Army Blue Mess, chapter 8	Army Blue Evening Dress, chapter 9	Cold Weather, chapter 10, section I	Hot Weather, chapter 10, section I	Utility, chapter 10, section I	Hospital Duty, chapter 10, section II	Food Service, chapter 10, section III
Aiguillette, Dress (26-24)			X	X	X	X	X					
Aiguillette, Service (26-23)	X	X	X	X								
Badges, Combat and Skill, Full Size and Miniature (27-20)	X	X	X	X								
Badges, Combat and Skill, Dress Miniature (27-20)			X	X	X	X	X					
Badges, Identification, full size (27-21)	X	X	X	X	X	X	X					
Belt, Web, Waist, and Buckles (11-1)	X	X	X	X				X	X	X	X	X
Beret (11-2)	X	X						X	X	X		
Boots, Combat, Black (11-3)	X	X						X		X		X
Boots, Hot Weather, Black (10-9b)									X			
Cap, Cold Weather, OG-107 (10-9a)								X		X		
Cap, Food Handler. White (10-23)												X
Cap, Garrison, Army Green (4-8a)	X	X									X	X
*Cap, Service, Army Blue (6-9)				X		X	X					
*Cap, Service, Army Green (4-8b)	X	X										
*Cap, Service, Army White (5-8)			X		X							
Cap, Utility, OG-507 (10-9a)								X	X	X		
*Cape, Army Blue (11-5)						X	X					
*Coat, Army Blue (6-5)				X								
Coat, Army Green (4-5)		X										
*Coat, Army White (5-5)			X									
Coat, Cold Weather (Field Jacket)(10-8)								X		X		
Coat, Cotton Poplin, OG-107 (10-6)									X			
Coat, Food Handler, White (10-20)												X
Cord, Shoulder, Infantryman (26-29)	X	X	X	X								
*Cuff Links and Studs, Gold (11-22)			X	X	X	X						
*Cuff Links and Studs, White (11-22)							X					
*Cumberbund, Black (11-9)					X	X						
Decoration Ribbons, Full Size (27-11)	X	X	X	X								
Decorations, Full Size (27-8). Note 1		X	X	X								
Decorations, Miniature (27-12)					X	X	X					
Distinctive Unit Insignia (26-21)	X	X						X	X	X		
Fourrageres and Lanyard (27-13)	X	X	X	X	X	X	X					
Gloves Black w/inserts Lt. Duty Wk (11-9b)								X	X	X		
Gloves, Black (11-9a)		X		X							X	X
*Gloves, White (11-9c)				X	X	X	X					
Hat, Drill Sergeant, Men (11-10)	X	X						X	X	X		
*Jacket, Army Blue (8-5)						X	X					
*Jacket, Army White (7-5)					X							
Medals, Service, Full Size (27-8). Note 1		X	X	X								
Medals, Service, Miniature (27-12)			X	X	X	X	X					
Medals, Service Ribbons, Full Size (27-11)	X	X	X	X								
*Neck tie, Bow, Black (11-14b)		X	X	X	X	X						
Neck tie, Bow, White (11-14c)					X		X					

COMPOSITION OF UNIFORMS
(MEN'S)—Continued

Item	Service and Dress Uniforms				Mess and Evening Dress Uniforms			Field and Work Uniforms				
	Army Tan/Khaki chapter 3	Army Green chapter 4	Army White chapter 5	Army Blue chapter 6	Army White Mess chapter 7	Army Blue Mess chapter 8	Army Blue Evening Dress, chapter 9	Cold Weather, chapter 10, section I	Hot Weather, chapter 10, section I	Utility, chapter 10, section I	Hospital Duty, chapter 10, section II	Food Service, chapter 10, section III
Neck tie, Four-In-Hand, Black (11-14a)		X	X	X								
Overcoat, Army Green (11-15)		X		X		X					X	X
Raincoat, Army Black (11-17a), Note 2	X	X	X	X	X	X	X		X	X	X	X
Raincoat, Army Green (11-17b), Note 2	X	X	X	X	X	X	X		X	X	X	X
Scarf, Army Black (11-18d)	X	X	X	X	X	X	X				X	X
Scarf, Army Green (11-18a)	X	X									X	X
Scarf, Olive Drab (11-18b)								X	X	X		
*Scarf, White (11-18c)			X	X	X	X	X					
Scarves, Branch of Service (26-19)	X	X						X	X	X		
Shirt, Army/Tan (chapter 3)	X											
Shirt, Army Grey/Green—415 (4-10)		X										
Shirt, Durapress, OG-507 (10-7)										X		
Shirt, Wool Flannel, OG 108 (10-5)								X				
*Shirt, White (11-20c)		X	X	X								
*Shirt, White, Semiformal (11-2d)					X	X						
*Shirt, White, Formal (11-19a)					X		X					
Shoes, Oxford, Black (11-20a)	X	X	X	X	X	X	X				X	X
Shoes, Oxford, White (11-20b)											X	
Smock, Food Inspector, White (10-21)												X
Smock, Medical Assistant, White (10-14)											X	X
Socks, Black (11-21a)	X	X	X	X	X	X	X				X	X
Socks, White (11-21b)											X	
*Sweater, Army Green or Black (11-23)		X									X	X
*Trousers, Army Black Mess (7-6)					X							
*Trousers, Army Blue (6-6)				X								
*Trousers, Army Blue Mess (8-6)				X		X	X					
Trousers, Army Green (4-6)		X										
Trousers, Army/tan (chapter 3)	X											
*Trousers, Army White (5-6)			X									
Trousers, Cotton Poplin, OG-107 (10-6)									X			
Trousers, Durapress, OG-507 (10-7)										X		
Trousers, Food Svc., White (10-22)											X	X
Trousers, Medical Assistant, White (10-15)											X	X
Trousers, Wool Serge, OG-108 (10-5)								X				
Undershirt, White (11-24a)	X	X	X	X	X	X	X	X	X	X	X	X
Undershirt, Olive Green (11-24b)								X	X	X		
*Vest, White (11-25)					X		X					
*Windbreaker, Army Green/Black (11-26), Note 3	X	X									X	X

Notes.　1. Items may be worn on Army green uniform only if worn for social functions.
　　　　2. Raincoat is authorized for wear with the field and work uniforms only in garrison environment.
　　　　3. Worn in lieu of Army green coat with green shirt.
　　* OPTIONAL ITEMS

Trousers. The same materials as authorized for the coat.

Ornamentation. General officers: Two ½-inch wide black mohair, polyester or mercerized cotton stripes spaced ½ inch apart.

Other officers: One 1½-inch black mohair, polyester or mercerized cotton stripe.

Caution: The bottom of the trousers must rest on top of the shoes without a break in front, and one inch above the top of the heel in the back. Both measurements to be taken when wearing low quarter shoes. The trouser crease must hang straight, not twisted.

Beret. A green beret is worn by all Special Forces units. It is worn with the Army Green and tan uniforms, and with utility uniforms when in a garrison environment. It is not worn with the Army Blue, White, White Mess, Blue Mess, or Blue Evening dress uniforms.

The material is knitted, wool, moth resistant and water repellant treated, rifle green, Army Shade 297.

Ranger personnel are authorized to wear a black beret and Airborne personnel are authorized to wear a maroon beret with the same uniforms and under the same conditions as Special Forces personnel wear the rifle green beret.

The beret is worn with the headband (edge binding) straight across the forehead, 1 inch above eyebrows. Top of beret draped over right ear; and stiffener for affixing insignia positioned over left eye. Ends of adjusting ribbon will be cut off and the ribbon knot secured inside the edge binding at rear of head.

Distinctive unit insignia for EM and grade insignia for officers will be centered on stiffener above left eye.

Caps. Two caps are provided, the garrison cap and the service cap, each of which is shown in an accompanying illustration.

Garrison Cap. This cap is worn with the Army tan uniform, with the Army Green uniform when in a travel status or assigned to airborne or air assault units, and with the Army green shade 415 shirt when worn as an outer garment with the Army green trousers. Braid is secured to the top edge of the curtain

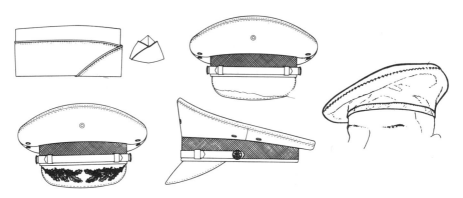

HEADGEAR WORN WITH ARMY GREEN AND ARMY TAN, UNIFORMS.

Upper left—Garrison cap, side and front view.
Lower left—Service cap with ornamented visor as worn by general and field grade officers.
Upper and lower center—Service cap.
Right—Beret.

of the garrison cap; general officers wear cord edge of gold bullion or synthetic metallic gold yarn, and other commissioned officers wear cord edge braid of gold bullion or synthetic metallic gold yarn with black rayon or black polyester intertwined. Warrant officers wear cord edge braid of silver bullion or synthetic metallic silver yarn or silver color rayon with black rayon or black polyester intertwined.

The garrison caps authorized for wear with various uniforms by male officers are worn only when the shirt or the shirt with the windbreaker is worn as an outer garment; or when the individual is in a travel status away from his home station.

There is a prescribed "wear" position for the garrison cap. Bottom of the front vertical crease of the cap at center of the forehead in straight line with the nose and at a point between 1 and $1\frac{1}{2}$ inches above eyebrow level. The cap will then be tilted slightly to the right, but in no case will the side of the cap rest on top of the ear. The cap will be placed on the head in such a manner that the front and rear vertical creases and the top edge of the crown form unbroken lines in silhouette. The crown will not be crushed or shaped so as to form peaks at the top front and top rear of the cap.

Service Cap. This (the visored cap) is of adopted standard as illustrated. Officers are authorized at their option to wear the cap frame with removable cover. This cap is worn with the Army Green and Army Tan uniforms and is mandatory for wear by officers with the Army green coat; it may be worn with the Army green shirt.

There is a prescribed "wear" position for the service cap. *Caution:* When you purchase a cap, be careful that your hair is trimmed just as you wish it to obtain a perfectly fitted cap and use care to obtain a cap that fits perfectly because an Army cap a little too large or a little too small looks bad and is uncomfortable. This is the way to wear the cap: Straight on the head so that the braid band establishes a straight line around the head parallel to the ground. Such positioning of the cap on the head automatically positions the leather visor correctly so that it does not interfere with vision, nor ride up on the forehead.

Headgear Insignia. See the later discussion and illustrations.

Insignia and Other Uniform Accessories. These subjects are discussed for the several uniforms at a later place in this chapter.

THE ARMY BLUE UNIFORM

The Army Blue uniform is authorized for wear by all male personnel. It normally is the prescribed uniform for officers for social functions after retreat. Its wearing may be prescribed by local commanders for specific occasions. On other appropriate occasions it may be worn as desired by the individual.

All officers are required to own the Army Blue uniform for wear on appropriate occasions, except Reserve Component officers in a Reserve status or on active duty for training for periods of 6 months or less. They may purchase the Army Blue uniform on an optional basis.

When this uniform is worn with the four-in-hand tie, the usual procedure, the Army Blue uniform is a semidress uniform. When worn with a bow tie, it constitutes a dress uniform and corresponds to a civilian tuxedo. Miniature decorations and medals may be worn with this uniform.

Choice of Materials. Many people believe that the better appearing Army Blue uniforms are tailored from the heavier weights of cloth. However, since it is an all-year uniform except in prescribed areas of the tropics or sub-tropics, the choice of lighter weight fabrics provides the best year-around comfort. A well fitted, carefully tailored uniform, clean and freshly pressed, will look well with any of the authorized weights of material. Advised: the light weight fabrics, for reasons of economy and comfort.

Blue Uniform Materials. There is a choice of barathea, 14 ounce; wool gabardine, 11 or 14.5 ounce; wool elastique, 16 ounce; or wool tropical, 10.5 ounce, each in dark blue, Army shade 150; or polyester/wool blend in twill weave, 9.5 ounce or polyester/wool blend in plain weave, 9.5 ounces, tropical weight each in dark blue, Army shade 450.

Trousers. General officers same as the coat. Other officers and enlisted men wear trousers of the same material as the coat, except the color is light blue, Army Shade Number 151 or 451.

Headgear, Cap. Of approved specification or pattern. Officers may wear the cap frame with a removable cover of the same material as the rest of the uniform.

Shoulder Ornamentation. Shoulder straps of adopted pattern are worn with the Army Blue uniform. For general officers, the background of the strap is blue-black velvet; for other commissioned officers it is of prescribed cloth in the color (or first named color) of the officer's basic branch; for warrant officers it is brown. The strap is bordered by a gold, or a gold color nylon, rayon or synthetic metallic gold strip $\frac{3}{8}$-in. in width, surrounded on inside and outside by a single line of gold Jaceron. Where the officers' basic branch has two colors, the second named color is used in place of the inside line of Jaceron.

Grade insignia, embroidered, are placed on the strap as prescribed.

ARMY GREEN UNIFORM.   ARMY BLUE UNIFORM.

Ornamentation of Trousers. General officers wear two $\frac{1}{2}$-inch stripes of two-vellum gold lace or of two-vellum synthetic mettalic gold, gold color nylon or rayon braid, spaced $\frac{1}{2}$-inch apart.

Other officers wear a strip of two-vellum gold lace or two-vellum synthetic gold, gold color nylon or rayon braid $1\frac{1}{2}$ inches in width.

Ornamentation of Cap Visor. The visor is black leather, or poromeric material with a leather finish. For general and field grade officers, the top of the visor is of black cloth with two arcs of oak leaves in groups of two, embroidered in gold bullion or synthetic metallic gold braid or manufactured from anodized aluminum in 24 karat gold color. General officers have similiar ornamentation on the cap band. For company grade officers and warrant officers, the top of the visor is of plain black shell cordovan finish leather.

Insignia Authorized for Wear with Army Blue Uniform. Officers wear only the following insignia:

Headgear Insignia
U.S. Insignia
Insignia of grade.

ARMY BLUE CAPS, OFFICERS AND WARRANT OFFICERS.

Top left, general officer
Top right, field grade

Bottom left, company grade
Bottom right, warrant officer

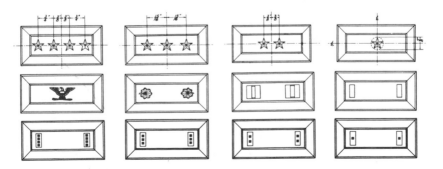

SHOULDER STRAPS, ARMY BLUE UNIFORM.

Insignia of branch to which assigned or detailed.

Authorized decorations and service medals (full size, ribbons or miniatures) and badges may be worn with this uniform.

Distinctive items authorized for Infantrymen.

The manner of attaching and wearing insignia is discussed and illustrated at a later place in this chapter.

ARMY TAN UNIFORM

The Army Tan uniform, comprised of shirt and trouser combination of the same material is authorized for wear by officers and enlisted men when on duty, off duty and during travel. Authorized materials are polyester/rayon blend in twill weave, 6.8 ounce; and polyester/cotton blend in tropical weave, 6.8 ounce. The Army Green shirt, shade 415, long or short sleeve, when worn as an outer garment with the Army Green trousers, will replace the Army Tan uniform, which is authorized for wear until 30 September 1985.

ARMY WHITE UNIFORM

The Army White uniform is authorized for optional year-round wear by officers and enlisted men. It may be a required uniform for some officers and the following is quoted from par. 5-1, AR 670-1: "Officers serving in Clothing Allowance Zones I and II, as defined in CTA 50-900, may be required by their major commander to own the Army White uniform and wear it on appropriate occasions. Excepted are non-Regular Army officers who have 2 years or less to serve on their current tour of active duty or category commitment."

Occasions for Wear. Officers wear the uniform on duty as prescribed by local commanders in areas where possession of the uniform is required, and off duty as appropriate. In other areas, on appropriate occasions as desired by the individual officer.

Materials—Coat, Trousers, Headgear. Coat, trousers, headgear, have these optional materials: white cotton twill, 8.2 ounce; polyester/wool blended fabric in tropical weave, 9 ounce; polyester/viscose blended fabric in gabardine weave, 8 ounce; and polyester textured woven serge, 6.5 ounce.

Coat. Ornamentation is a band of white cotton or mohair braid, appropriate to the uniform fabric, ½ inch in width, on each sleeve, the lower edge 3 inches from end of sleeve.

Headgear. Officers are authorized at their option to wear the cap frame with removable cover of the same material as the white coat.

Ornamentation of cap visor is the same as for the service cap for the Army Green and the Army Blue uniforms.

Insignia. Only the following insignia are authorized for wear with the Army White uniform:

Headgear Insignia

U.S. Insignia.

Insignia of grade.

Insignia of branch to which assigned or detailed.

Authorized decorations and service medals (full size or miniature), or ribbons, and badges may be worn with this uniform.

Distinctive items authorized for Infantrymen.

The manner of wearing insignia is discussed and illustrated at a later place in this chapter.

ARMY WHITE MESS UNIFORM

The Army White Mess uniform is authorized for optional year-round wear by male officers.

Occasions for Wear. It is worn after retreat at social functions of a general or official nature. It is worn also at private formal dinners and other private social functions after retreat. It is a formal uniform that corresponds to the civilian tuxedo.

Materials. *Jacket and Vest.* White cotton twill, 8.2 ounce; polyester/wool blended fabric in plain weave, tropical weight, 9 ounce; polyester/wool blended fabric in gabardine weave, 10.5 ounce; or polyester texturized woven serge, 6.5 ounce.

Trousers. Black lightweight material, commercial tuxedo type.

Jacket. The jacket is worn with shoulder knots of gold bullion or gold color nylon or rayon cord $\frac{1}{4}$ inch in diameter.

Sleeve Ornamentation. *General Officers.* A cuff of white mohair or mercerized cotton braid, 4 inches in width, $\frac{1}{8}$ inch from bottom of sleeve. Insignia of grade of synthetic metallic gold or embroidered white cloth, is placed 1 inch above upper edge of sleeve cuff. Stars are 1 inch in diameter.

All Other Officers. A $\frac{1}{2}$ inch band of white mohair or mercerized cotton braid with the lower edge 3 inches from end of sleeve, with a trefoil consisting of a knot composed of three loops of $\frac{1}{4}$ inch white soutache braid, interlaced at points of crossing, with the ends resting on the sleeve bands. Insignia of grade, metal or embroidery, is worn vertically in the center of the space formed by the lower curves of the knot and the upper edge of the sleeve band. Previously authorized sleeve ornamentation may be worn for the life of the jacket, but the number of trefoils must reflect the correct grade.

Trousers, Design. Cut on the lines of civilian dress trousers with a high waist and with black silk or stain stripe, without pleats, cuffs and hip pockets.

Vest. Single-breasted, cut low, with rolling collar; with pointed bottom and fastened with three detachable extra small white buttons; worn with a white formal dress shirt with wing collar.

Optional substitute: Black cummerbund, when worn with a white semiformal dress shirt with a turndown collar.

Headgear. The white cap as described for the Army White uniform.

Insignia. Only the following insignia are authorized for wear on the Army White Mess uniform:

Headgear Insignia.
Insignia of grade.
Aiguillette, dress.
Badges, miniature.
Decorations, miniature.
Service medals, miniature.
Badges, combat and skill, dress miniature.
Identification badges, full size.
Fourragere.
Aiguillette, dress.

Further information as to wearing insignia is discussed and illustrated at a later point in the chapter.

ARMY BLUE MESS UNIFORM

The Army Blue Mess uniform is authorized for optional year-round wear by all male personnel.

Occasions for Wear. It is appropriate for wear at social functions of a general or official nature, as well as for private formal dinners and other private formal affairs after retreat. It corresponds to the civilian tuxedo.

Composition. A table earlier in this chapter provides full information as to the composition of the uniform.

Materials. *Jacket.* Dark blue in 14 ounce wool barathea, 11 or 14.5 ounce wool gabardine, 15 ounce wool elastique, or 9 ounce wool tropical, all in Army shade 150; or 9.5 ounce polyester/wool in gabardine weave or 9.5 ounce polyester/wool in tropical weave, each in Army shade 450.

Trousers. General officers, same material as the jacket. Other officers, light blue, Army shade No. 151 or 451, with same types and weights of cloth as stated for the jacket.

Jacket, Partial Description. Illustrations accompany this abridged description.

Lapels. Color of facings: General officers except chaplains—dark blue; chaplains—black. All other officers—the first named color of their basic branch.

Shoulder Knots. Shoulder knots of gold bullion or synthetic metallic gold or

GENERAL OFFICERS   OTHER THAN GENERAL OFFICERS

ARMY BLUE MESS UNIFORM.

gold color nylon or rayon cord ¼ inch in diameter. (Same as for Army White Mess and Army Blue Evening Dress uniforms.)

Sleeve Decoration. On the Army Blue Mess uniforms for general officers a cuff of blue-black velvet 4 inches in width positioned ⅛ inch from the bottom of the sleeve, with a band of oak leaves in groups of two, about 1 inch in width, embroidered in gold or synthetic metallic gold or gold color nylon or rayon, placed 1 inch below the upper edge of sleeve cuff. Insignia of grade is placed one inch above the upper edge of the sleeve cuff. Whenever the insignia of branch is worn, it is placed 1 inch above the upper edge of cuff, and insignia of grade is 1 inch above insignia of branch.

Other officers, commissioned and warrant, wear on each sleeve a band of two ¼-inch two-vellum gold lace or synthetic metallic gold or gold color nylon or rayon stripes placed ¼-inch apart over a silk stripe of the first-named color of their basic branch, the bottom of the sleeve band to be 3 inches above the bottom of the sleeve. A trefoil consisting of a knot of three loops of ¼-inch gold or synthetic metallic gold or gold color nylon or rayon braid, interlaced at points of crossing, with the ends resting on the sleeve band. Insignia of grade, metal or embroidery, is worn vertically in the center of the space formed by the lower curves of the knot and the upper edge of the sleeve band. Previously authorized sleeve ornamentation may be worn for the life of the jacket, provided the number of trefoils reflects the correct grade.

Trousers. Cut on the lines of civilian dress trousers with a high waist, without pleats, cuffs or hip pockets. Ornamentation as described for the trousers of the Army Blue uniform.

Cummerbund. Only a black cummerbund is authorized for wear with this uniform.

Headgear. The blue cap as described for the Army Blue uniform.

Insignia. As described for the Army White Mess uniform.

ARMY BLUE EVENING DRESS UNIFORM

The Army Evening Dress uniform is authorized for optional year-round wear by all male personnel.

Occasions for Wear. Social functions of a general or official nature after retreat, as well as private formal dinners and other private social functions after retreat. This is the most formal uniform for male officers and corresponds to the civilian "white tie and tails".

Composition. The Army Blue Mess jacket and trousers are the basic components of the Blue Evening Dress uniform. When worn as evening dress, the Blue Mess jacket and trousers are worn with full dress shirt, wing collar, white vest, white bow tie, and white cuff links and studs.

Vest. The white vest worn with the Army White Mess uniform is the vest worn with the Army Blue Evening Dress uniform.

Shirt. A white long sleeve formal dress shirt with a stiff bosom, french cuffs, and a wing type collar.

Headgear. The cap as described for the Army Blue uniform.

Insignia. As described for the Army Blue Mess uniform.

ACCESSORY ITEMS OF UNIFORMS

There are a number of articles which are used with all or several of the Army uniforms. They are discussed here and further reference is made to the table, *Composition of Uniforms,* earlier in this chapter.

Combination Raincoat/Overcoat. A combination black raincoat of polyester/-cotton poplin, Army black shade 410, with three button fly front, slash front pockets, and a zip-out liner for conversion to an overcoat has been adopted by the Army. It replaces the previously authorized separate raincoat, shade 274, and overcoat, shade 44. The older coats are authorized for wear until 30 September 1985.

The black raincoat may be worn with or without the liner, buttoned except for the neck closure which may be worn open or closed, with or without a scarf. It is authorized for wear with the service, dress, mess, and evening dress uniforms and, without insignia, it may be worn with civilian clothes.

A raincap cover, transparent plastic, with or without visor protector, is authorized for wear with the service caps when wearing the raincoat or overcoat.

Cape, Blue. The blue cape is for wear with the evening dress uniform and for optional wear with the Army Blue, Army Blue Mess and Army Blue Evening Dress uniforms in lieu of the overcoat. The lining for general officers is of dark blue, and for all other officers the first named color of the officer's basic branch.

Materials are wool barathea, 14 or 18 ounce; wool gabardine, 14.5 ounce; wool elastique, 16 or 18 ounce. All Army Shade 150.

Belt, Waist. There are two types which may be worn by officers. The standard belt is a $1\frac{1}{4}$-inch web belt, black color, equipped with a plain-faced solid brass buckle, oval-shaped, $2\frac{1}{4}$ inches long and $1\frac{3}{4}$ inches wide. For optional wear a $1\frac{1}{4}$ inch woven elastic belt, black color, may be substituted.

Caution: Not more than two inches of the belt should be showing through the buckle.

Buttons. Buttons used on the uniforms are of prescribed design, gold plated or anodized aluminum. Officers other than those of the Corps of Engineers wear the button bearing the United States Coat of Arms. Engineer Officers wear the Essayons button. This is believed to have been designed by Colonel Jonathan Williams, first Chief Engineer of the present Corps of Engineers, who was also the first Superintendent of the United States Military Academy. The first authoritative reference to the device is contained in General Orders No. 7, AGO, Feb. 18, 1840.

Gloves. Black leather gloves of commercial type are authorized for general wear. They may be lined or unlined, snap-fastened or pull on. Gloves may be worn with the overcoat, raincoat, windbreaker or Army Green uniform as desired depending on temperature, and in formation when prescribed by the local commander.

White gloves of white kid, silk, cotton, or other suitable material are authorized for wear with the Blue, Blue Mess, White, White Mess, and Evening Dress uniforms. White gloves may be worn with the service uniform when prescribed by the commanding officer on occasions of ceremony.

Neckties. The black, four-in-hand necktie in a tropical worsted or similar woven fabric is worn with the Army Green, the Army Blue, and the Army White uniforms. Knitted fabric is authorized on an optional basis. This tie also is worn with long sleeve green shirt and may be worn with the green short sleeve shirt when worn as outer garments.

A commercial type black bow tie with square ends, of silk or satin without stripe or figure, is worn with the Army Blue Mess and the Army White Mess uniforms. It is authorized on an optional basis for wear with either the Army Blue or the Army White uniform to constitute a dress uniform.

For wear with the Army Blue Evening Dress uniform, and optionally with the Army White Mess uniform, a conventional, civilian, full dress type white bow tie is prescribed. Authorized is a plain, white bow tie of silk, satin, or material matching the shirt, without stripe or figure not more than $2\frac{1}{2}$ inches in width.

Shoes. The shoes worn by officers with all uniforms are of adopted design, black leather or of poromeric material with leather finish, plain toe, with non-contrasting sole, oxford; chukka boot or similar commercial design is also authorized. Patent leather finish is not authorized. White oxfords are worn with the hospital duty uniform.

Socks. Black socks are worn with all uniforms except for the hospital duty uniform which has white socks for wear with white shoes. Material is of cotton or other material suitable to climatic conditions.

Scarf. A scarf of adopted design may be worn by officers and enlisted men with field clothing. It is made of wool, olive drab, Army Shade 208.

When the overcoat is worn with the Army Green uniform, Army Green neckwear may be worn. It is of woven wool, Army Green shade No. 44, or of woven silk or rayon, Army shade 279. Commercial design, size about $12'' \times 52''$.

When the green raincoat, green overcoat, black all-weather coat or blue cape is worn with the Army White, Army White Mess, Army Blue Evening Dress, Army Blue, or Army Blue Mess uniforms, white neckwear (scarf) of commercial pattern, woven rayon, silk or wool, bleached white, is authorized to be worn.

A black scarf, of wool, silk, or rayon, and of commercial design, approximately 12 inches by 52 inches, is authorized for wear with the Army Black raincoat.

Shirts. The shirt worn with the Army Green uniform is long or short sleeve, Army Green, shade 415. It replaces the Army Tan shirt, shade 446, which is authorized for continued wear until 30 September 1985. The shade 415 shirt, long or short sleeve, worn with Army Green trousers replace the Army Tan uniform, which is also authorized for continued wear until 30 September 1985. A commercial design white dress shirt is worn with the Army Blue and Army White uniforms. A white, semi-formal civilian dress shirt is worn with the Army Blue Mess and the Army White Mess uniforms. A full dress white shirt of formal civilian design is worn with the Blue Evening Dress and may be worn with the Army White Mess uniforms.

Sweater. A black cardigan sweater, 100 per cent acrylic, is authorized for optional purchase and wear as an outer garment with green trousers and shirts in the immediate work area. A black pullover, V-neck, 100 per cent wool sweater is also authorized for optional purchase and wear as an outer garment. The sweater is worn with a name plate and shoulder marks indicating grade.

Windbreaker. The Army Black windbreaker, shade 385, may be worn with the Army Tan uniform, Army Green long or short sleeve shirt and Army Green trousers, Food Service uniform and the Hospital Duty uniform. When worn with a uniform, it will be worn zipped at least ¾ of the way up. Without insignia, it may be worn with civilian clothing.

Overshoes. Black rubber or synthetic overshoes of commercial design are authorized for optional wear with dress oxfords when not in formation.

Studs and Cuff Links. Commercial pattern. With Army Blue Evening Dress uniform, wear plain white studs and cuff links with or without rims of platinum or gold. White mother-of-pearl is the conventional material. With the white mess and the blue mess uniforms wear gold or gold color metal.

With the Army Blue and Army White uniform, cuff links when worn will be of plain gold or gold color metal.

Name Plates. Name plates are one by three inches, of black, nongloss laminated plastic with a white border, $\frac{1}{32}$" wide. Lettering is white, indented, block, $\frac{3}{8}$" high, with last name only. Worn on the flap of the right breast pocket centered between the top of the button and the top of the pocket.

Identification Tags. Identification Tags, "Dog Tags," will be worn at all times when in the field, when engaged in field training, when traveling in aircraft, and when outside CONUS.

Security Identification Badges. Security identification badges will be worn in restricted areas as prescribed by the commanding officer.

Name Tapes. A name tape is worn on each item of utility and field clothing on which the distinguishing "U.S. Army" tape is worn.

FIELD AND WORK UNIFORMS

Appropriate commanding officers will prescribe the field or work uniform from appropriate items in CTA 50-900 and Table 4-1 of AR 700-84. The field and work uniform is authorized for year-round wear on duty as prescribed by local commanders. The basic components of the field and work uniform are:

Cold Weather—shirt and trousers, olive green, Army shade 108.

Hot weather (tropical combat)—coat and trousers, cotton poplin, olive green, Army shade 107.

Utility—shirt and trousers, cotton sateen, olive green, Army shade 107.

Durapress Utility—shirt and trousers, cotton polyester, olive green, Army shade 507.

Field Jacket—Cotton and nylon sateen, olive green, Army Shade 107.

Combat camouflage—Shirt and trousers, 50/50 nylon and cotton blend, in a four-color woodland camouflage pattern with infra-red reflectance.

Ornamentation. Only the following ornamentation may be authorized for wear on the field or work uniform: (See AR 670–5 and AR 672–5–1.)

Brassards
Bib type scarfs (branch of service or camouflage).
Combat leaders identification.
Distinctive unit insignia.
Combat and special skill badges (subdued type).
Insignia of branch (officers only, subdued type).
Insignia, distinguishing, "U.S. Army."
Insignia of grade (subdued type).
Name tapes.

Special military police markings.

Organizational shoulder sleeve insignia (subdued type; none on cold weather uniform).

Ranger tab.

No insignia will be sewn on the one-piece Nomex flight suit. Instead, a black leather nameplate, 2" × 4", will be worn affixed to the velcro fastener on the suit. Embossed on the nameplate in silver are the crewmember badge on the first line and, in ¼-inch block style letters, the member's full name on the second line, and the abbreviated grade and the words "U.S. Army" on the third line. No other accouterments or shoulder sleeve insignia will be worn on the Nomex flight suit. Black leather combat boots and the fatigue cap are worn with Nomex flight clothing.

On other flight clothing, commanders may prescribe insignia to be worn, or they may prescribe name tapes which will include abbreviated grade and full name in ⅜-inch block letters. Local commanders may also authorize the wear of solid color baseball caps by aircraft and groundcrew members as a safety and identification measure.

HOSPITAL DUTY UNIFORM

The Hospital Duty uniform is authorized for year-round wear by male officers of the Army Nurse Corps and Army Medical Specialist Corps. The smock and trousers of white cotton twill are worn with black oxford shoes and black socks. White oxfords and white socks may be worn on an optional basis. The garrison cap completes the uniform when out-of-doors.

CHAPLAINS' APPAREL

Chaplains are authorized special articles of apparel for wear when appropriate in the discharge of their religious duties.

Scarf, Christian Faith. A scarf of standard Army ecclesiastical pattern, of black material 9 feet long. It bears prescribed decorations including the coat of arms of the United States and Chaplain's insignia, Christian.

Scarf, Jewish Faith. A scarf of standard Army ecclesiastical pattern, of suitable white or black material 9 feet long. It is decorated in a manner similar to the scarf of the Christian Faith except that it bears the Chaplain's insignia, Jewish Faith.

Vestments. When conducting religious services, the chaplain is authorized to wear vestments which are required or customary in the denomination which the chaplain represents. When they do not wear such vestments, chaplains will wear the uniform while conducting religious services.

JUDGES' APPAREL

Officers designated as military judges and appellate military judges, when participating in trials by court-martial, hearings by a court of military review and other judicial proceedings, wear judicial robes of the type customarily worn in the U.S. Court of Military Appeal.

INSIGNIA

Insignia worn on the Army's uniforms identifies the wearer as to status. Insignia denotes grade, branch, organization, duty assignment, and prior Army service.

Insignia are made of appropriate color metal or embroidery.

The "U.S." Insignia. Male Officers wear the "U.S." insignia on both collars of the coat, ⅝-inch above the cut of the lapel. See the accompanying illustration.

Branch Insignia. Except for most general officers, officers wear branch insignia on the coat lapels, as illustrated. The "U.S." and branch insignia will be of the same metal or embroidery.

Branch insignia is worn on the left collar of the shirt of the Army Tan uniform and the smock of the Hospital Duty uniform, as illustrated, except for general officers, who wear insignia of grade on both sides of the collar.

Except for chaplains, branch insignia is not worn on either the long or short sleeve Army green shirt. Chaplains wear their branch insignia centered over the left breast pocket for males, or in a comparable position for females.

In the usual case, officers wear the insignia of the branch to which assigned or in which detailed. In case of doubt, consult the unit personnel officer.

General Staff Corps Insignia. The General Staff Corps insignia will be worn by those commissioned officers, other than general officers, whose assignments meet the following exact conditions—

(1) Assigned to the offices of the Secretary of the Army, and the Assistant Secretaries of the Army who are authorized by the Secretary of the Army to wear this insignia during their tour of duty in these offices.

(2) Detailed to duty on the Army General Staff.

(3) Detailed in General Staff with troops. (See AR 614-100.)

(4) As directed by the Chief of Staff.

Inspector General Insignia. The Inspector General insignia will be worn by The Inspector General and those officers detailed as inspectors general under AR 614-100.

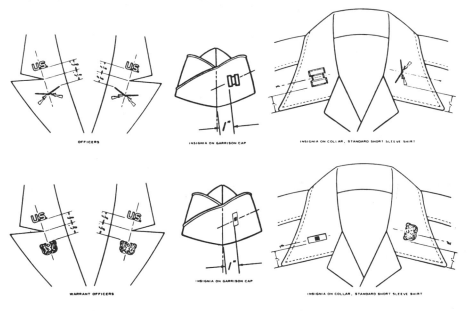

| INSIGNIA ON LAPELS AND COLLAR OF COAT | INSIGNIA, GARRISON CAP. | INSIGNIA WORN ON SHIRT AS OUTER GARMENT. |

Insignia of Grade. Officers' insignia of grade is shown on the following pages. On the Army Tan shirt, grade insignia is worn on the right collar as illustrated. On the Army green shirt, green shoulder mark with embroidered insignia of grade is worn with the gold stripe nearest the shoulder sleeve seam. Grade insignia worn with the Army White Mess, Army Blue Mess, and Army Evening Dress uniforms is positioned as directed in the discussion of those uniforms.

Grade insignia are worn on the shoulder loops of the windbreaker, overcoat, raincoat, and coats of the Army Green and Army White uniform. Note that on the Army Blue uniform, the grade insignia are of the shoulder board type.

Cautions Regarding Affixing Grade Insignia. Observe that there is an exact position for attaching each item of grade and other articles of insignia and ornamentation on the uniform. Here are some special ones easily overlooked.

A point of each of a general's stars points to the button of the shoulder loop, and is placed point upward on the shirt collar, garrison gap, helmet, helmet liner, and the sleeves of the blue mess, white mess, and evening dress uniforms. The beaks of each of the colonel's eagles are extended forward, never backward. The stem of the silver leaf and the oak leaf, of lieutenant colonel and major, are on the outside or on the bottom, as affixed to shoulder loop, garrison gap, or shirt collar.

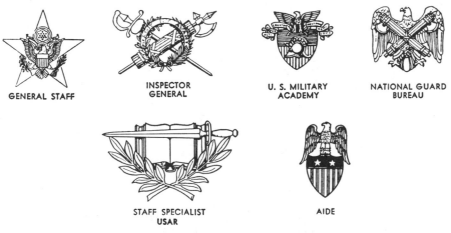

GENERAL STAFF   INSPECTOR   U. S. MILITARY   NATIONAL GUARD
                       GENERAL   ACADEMY   BUREAU

STAFF SPECIALIST   AIDE
     USAR

OFFICERS' INSIGNIA—OTHER THAN BASIC BRANCH.

Combat Leader's Identification. The combat leader's identification will be worn by leaders of Category I (organization TOE specifies category) Regular Army, Army National Guard, and Army Reserve organizations, plus Division and Corps commanders of Category II organizations, the majority of whose subordinate elements are Category I units. The specific leaders are: commanders, deputy corps and assistant division commanders, platoon leaders, command sergeants major, first sergeants, platoon sergeants, section leaders, squad leaders and rifle squad fire team leaders. This identification is a green cloth loop, $1\frac{5}{8}$ inches wide, worn in the middle of both shoulder loops of the service coat, jacket, overcoat, or shirt when worn as an outer garment. It will cease to be worn when an individual entitled thereto is reassigned from a command position or from a combat unit which had provided authority for its wear.

The commanders and units authorized to wear this insignia are listed in AR 670-5. *Caution:* Commanders of units and major organizations will issue instructions making it perfectly clear as to eligibility to wear this coveted device. Let no person assume the privilege of wearing it until he makes certain of his right.

Distinctive U ˙it Insignia and Trimmings. Subject to Departmental approval in each case, units as designated in AR 670-1 are authorized distinctive unit insignia for members as a part of the uniform as a means of promoting esprit de corps. These devices will be worn by individuals only while assigned to a unit having the authorization.*

"Airborne" insignia may be worn when prescribed by appropriate commanders. It consists of a white parachute and glider on a blue disk, with a red border, approximately $2\frac{1}{4}$ inches in diameter overall. Officers wear it on the garrison cap, centered on the right curtain, 1 inch from the front.

Aiguillettes, Service and Dress. Service and dress aiguillettes are provided to officers authorized or required to wear them as stated in Par. 26–23 and 26–24, AR 670-1.

Insignia, Distinguishing, "U.S. Army." A label, $4\frac{1}{2}$ inches in length and 1 inch in width, consisting of "U.S. Army" in black block letters $\frac{3}{4}$-inch in height on an olive green background.

It is worn centered, immediately above and parallel to the top edge of the left breast pocket (or comparable position) of all field and utility coats and shirts and on the OG-107 parka.

Organization Shoulder Sleeve Insignia. Approved designs of shoulder sleeve insignia are authorized for wear by personnel of units definitely assigned to an organization having Department of the Army authorization for its use. See par. 26–16 and 26–17, AR 670-1.

Individuals entitled to the privilege may wear the insignia of their current unit on the left sleeve of the Army green coat, and, in a subdued version, on all field and utility coats and shirts. It is NOT worn on the overcoat, raincoat or any dress uniform.

In the same manner, but on the right sleeve, former organization shoulder sleeve insignia approved by the Department of the Army may be worn by individuals entitled to do so. Such individuals must have World War II service between 7 December 1941 and 2 September 1946, inclusive; or service in Korea between 27 June 1950 and 27 July 1954, inclusive; or service in Vietnam between 1 July 1958 and 28 March 1973, inclusive; or service in the Dominican Republic subsequent to 29 April 1965; or service in Korea between 1 April 1968 and 31 August 1973, provided the individual received as a result

---

*The wearing of unit emblems originated in the American Civil War. General Kearney, Union general of the Civil War killed in the Battle of Chantilly as he rode in darkness into Confederate lines, originated the practice of wearing unit emblems. He observed a group of Union officers resting in the shade of a tree. Assuming they were officers of his brigade he administered a sharp rebuke, as others have done, before and since. But they were from another organization, to the embarrassment of the general who extended his apologies and rode on. Although this is not particularly unusual, General Kearney was the first officer who did anything constructive to ease identification. He ordered all officers of his command to wear a red patch on their forage caps. The enlisted men of the brigade liked the idea and while not required to wear them were proud of their brigade and adopted the patch. From this beginning descends the unit insignia of our modern Army. It is a symbol of pride in unit and a means of establishing identification.

INFANTRY

FIELD ARTILLERY

AIR DEFENSE ARTILLERY

ARMOR

CORPS OF ENGINEERS

SIGNAL CORPS

TRANSPORTATION CORPS

ORDNANCE CORPS

Chemical Corps

ADJUTANT GENERAL'S CORPS

QUARTERMASTER CORPS

MILITARY POLICE CORPS

JUDGE ADVOCATE GENERAL'S CORPS

CAVALRY

FINANCE CORPS

MILITARY INTELLIGENCE

CHAPLAINS (CHRISTIAN)

CHAPLAINS (JEWISH)

MEDICAL CORPS

DENTAL CORPS

ARMY NURSE CORPS

VETERINARY CORPS

MEDICAL SERVICE CORPS

ARMY MEDICAL SPECIALIST CORPS

WARRANT OFFICERS

CIVIL AFFAIRS USAR

OFFICERS' INSIGNIA OF BRANCH.

ENLISTED

SERGEANT MAJOR OF THE ARMY (SMA)

LAPEL INSIGNIA

SERGEANT MAJOR OF THE MARINE CORPS (SgtMaj)

MASTER CHIEF PETTY OFFICER OF THE NAVY (MCPON)

CHIEF MASTER SERGEANT OF THE AIR FORCE (CMSAF)

COLLAR INSIGNIA

CAP INSIGNIA

COMMAND SERGEANT MAJOR (CSM)

STAFF SERGEANT MAJOR (SSM)

(SgtMaj) (MGySgt)
SERGEANT MAJOR   MASTER GUNNERY SERGEANT

MASTER CHIEF PETTY OFFICER (MCPO)

CHIEF MASTER SERGEANT (CMSgt)

FIRST SERGEANT (1SG)   MASTER SERGEANT (MSG)

FIRST SERGEANT (1stSgt)   MASTER SERGEANT (MSgt)

SENIOR CHIEF PETTY OFFICER (SCPO)

SENIOR MASTER SERGEANT (SMSgt)

PLATOON SERGEANT (PSG) or SERGEANT FIRST CLASS (SFC)

GUNNERY SERGEANT (GySgt)

CHIEF PETTY OFFICER (CPO)

MASTER SERGEANT (MSgt)

STAFF SERGEANT (SSG)

SPECIALIST 6 (SP6)

STAFF SERGEANT (SSgt)

PETTY OFFICER FIRST CLASS (PO1)

TECHNICAL SERGEANT (TSgt)

SERGEANT (SGT)

SPECIALIST 5 (SP5)

SERGEANT (Sgt)

PETTY OFFICER SECOND CLASS (PO2)

STAFF SERGEANT (SSgt)

CORPORAL (CPL)

SPECIALIST 4 (SP4)

CORPORAL (Cpl)

PETTY OFFICER THIRD CLASS (PO3)

SERGEANT (Sgt)

PRIVATE FIRST CLASS (PFC)

LANCE CORPORAL (LCpl)

SEAMAN (Seaman)

AIRMAN FIRST CLASS (A1C)

PRIVATE, E-2 (PVT)

PRIVATE FIRST CLASS (PFC)

SEAMAN APPRENTICE (SA)

AIRMAN (Amn)

PRIVATE, E-1 (PV1) (No Insignia)

PRIVATE (Pvt)

SEAMAN RECRUIT (SR)

AIRMAN BASIC (AB)

* A speciality mark in the center of the rating badge will indicate the wearer's particular rating.

ENLISTED INSIGNIA OF GRADE.

SERVICE			
Army	**Air Force**	**Navy**	**Marine Corps**
SILVER SILVER BLACK BLACK W-1 W-2 CHIEF WARRANT WARRANT OFFICER OFFICER	GOLD SKY BLUE GOLD SKY BLUE W-1 W-2 CHIEF WARRANT WARRANT OFFICER OFFICER	W-1 W-2 CHIEF WARRANT WARRANT OFFICER OFFICER	GOLD GOLD SCARLET SCARLET W-1 W-2 CHIEF WARRANT WARRANT OFFICER OFFICER
SILVER SILVER BLACK BLACK W-3 W-4 CHIEF CHIEF WARRANT WARRANT OFFICER OFFICER	SILVER SILVER SKY BLUE SKY BLUE W-3 W-4 CHIEF CHIEF WARRANT WARRANT OFFICER OFFICER	W-3 W-4 CHIEF CHIEF WARRANT WARRANT OFFICER OFFICER	SILVER SILVER SCARLET SCARLET W-3 W-4 CHIEF CHIEF WARRANT WARRANT OFFICER OFFICER
SECOND LIEUTENANT	SECOND LIEUTENANT	ENSIGN	SECOND LIEUTENANT
FIRST LIEUTENANT	FIRST LIEUTENANT	LIEUTENANT JUNIOR GRADE	FIRST LIEUTENANT
CAPTAIN	CAPTAIN	LIEUTENANT	CAPTAIN
MAJOR	MAJOR	LIEUTENANT COMMANDER	MAJOR
LIEUTENANT COLONEL	LIEUTENANT COLONEL	COMMANDER	LIEUTENANT COLONEL

GRADE INSIGNIA, OFFICERS.

Note: Grade insignia of 2d Lieutenant and Major are gold; of other officer grades in Army, Air Force, and Marine Corps, silver. Naval insignia is gold color. The Navy pin-on (collar) insignia is the same as for the other services except that the devices are smaller, and the enamel bands on the warrant officers' bars are Navy blue.

SERVICE			
Army	**Air Force**	**Navy**	**Marine Corps**
COLONEL	COLONEL	CAPTAIN	COLONEL
BRIGADIER GENERAL	BRIGADIER GENERAL	COMMODORE	BRIGADIER GENERAL
MAJOR GENERAL	MAJOR GENERAL	REAR ADMIRAL	MAJOR GENERAL
LIEUTENANT GENERAL	LIEUTENANT GENERAL	VICE ADMIRAL	LIEUTENANT GENERAL
GENERAL	GENERAL	ADMIRAL	GENERAL
GENERAL OF THE ARMY	GENERAL OF THE AIR FORCE	FLEET ADMIRAL	(NONE)

GRADE INSIGNIA, OFFICERS, (Continued).

Note: All insignia above is silver color except Navy, which is gold. The rank of Commodore is not used in the Regular Navy. The temporary Commandore rank was revived during World War II for certain individuals in certain staff or administrative positions. It is an autthorized grade for temporary use, but the Navy of today has no commodores.

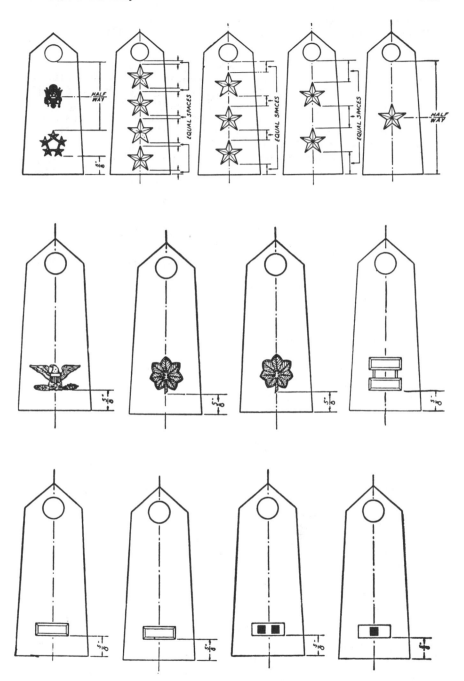

ATTACHMENT OF SHOULDER LOOP INSIGNIA.

of this service the Purple Heart, Combat Infantryman Badge, Combat Medical Badge, or credit for at least one oversea service bar for duty in the Korean hostile fire zone.

Oversea Service Bars. This device is a gold color rayon bar 1-$\frac{5}{16}$ inches in length, $\frac{3}{16}$ inches in width, within an Army Green schragg stitch border $\frac{3}{32}$ -inch around the bar, on a cloth background of Army Green shade No. 159. As an optional item the bar may be of lace or bullion.

One oversea bar is authorized for wear for each period of 6 months' active Federal service as a member of the Army during periods of hostilities as designated in AR 670-1, when serving in hostile fire areas. Service of less than 6 months' duration which otherwise meets the requirements may be combined with additional service to determine the total number of oversea bars authorized.

Worn centered on the outside half of the right sleeve with the lower edge of the bar $\frac{1}{4}$ inch above the braid. Additional bars will be worn parallel to and above the first bar with $\frac{1}{16}$ inch space between bars, the space being formed of the background.

Colors of Branches. There are official colors of branches and corps of the Army. These colors appear as piping on uniform components, in facings, and elsewhere in the blue and white dress uniforms. They are as follows:

Adjutant General's Corps. Dark blue piped with scarlet.
Air Defense Artillery, Scarlet.
Armor, Yellow.
Army Medical Department. Maroon piped with white.
Cavalry, Yellow.
Chaplains. Black.
Chemical Corps. Cobalt blue piped with golden yellow.
Civil Affairs, USAR. Purple piped with white.
Corps of Engineers. Scarlet piped with white.
Field Artillery, Scarlet.
Finance Corps. Silver gray piped with golden yellow.
Infantry. Light blue.
Inspector General. Dark blue piped with light blue.
Judge Advocate General's Corps. Dark blue piped with white.
Military Intelligence. Oriental blue piped with silver gray.
Military Police Corps. Green piped with yellow.
National Guard Bureau. Dark blue.
Ordnance Corps. Crimson piped with yellow.
Quartermaster Corps. Buff.
Signal Corps. Orange piped with white.
Staff Specialist, USAR. Green.
Transportation Corps. Brick-red piped with golden yellow.
Warrant Officers. Brown.
Unassigned to Branch. Teal-blue piped with white.

Distinctive Items Authorized for Infantry. Officers and enlisted personnel of the Infantry who have been awarded the Combat Infantryman Badge, the Expert Infantryman Badge, or who have, as members of assigned infantry units, successfully completed an appropriate unit Army training program or the equivalent thereof, wear the Infantry Shoulder Cord of Infantry Blue.

Officers and enlisted men of the Infantry may wear a rayon bib-type scarf of Infantry Blue. It is an article of optional wear at the discretion of local commanders. Occasions for wear are with service uniforms only for ceremonial type formations, and with the field or fatigue uniforms.

An individual joining an Infantry unit which wears these items, or is being reassigned from such a unit, should consult the personnel officer as to his right to wear the articles.

Distinctive Items for Branches Other Than Infantry. Personnel of branches other than Infantry are authorized to wear bib-type scarves at the option of local commanders. When prescribed, the scarf will be provided without cost to each individual in the unit. Manner and occasion for wear are the same as for the Infantry scarf. Colors are as indicated below:

Silver Gray—Finance
Maroon—Medical
Scarlet—Artillery, Engineers and Permanent Professors, USMA
Green—Military Police and Staff Specialist
Crimson—Ordnance and Maintenance
Buff—Supply, Quartermaster, Supply and Service, Supply and Transportation, and Support
Orange—Signal
Brick Red—Transportation
Oriental Blue—Intelligence and Army Security
Ultramarine Blue—Aviation
Teal Blue—Branch unassigned
Bottle Green—Special Forces and Psychological Operations
Yellow—Armor and Cavalry
Purple—Civil Affairs
Dark Blue—National Guard Bureau, Judge Advocate General, Inspector General and Adjutant General
Black—Chaplain
Camouflage—Determined by local commander
Note: Warrant officers will wear the scarf of the branch by which controlled.

UNIFORMS FOR FEMALE OFFICERS

The names of the Army uniforms for female officers are as follows:

Army Green Classic Uniform
Army Green Skirt and Jacket Uniform
Army Green Dress and Jacket Uniform
Army Green Pantsuit Uniform
Army Green Uniform
Army White Uniform
Army Blue Uniform
Army Black Mess Uniform
Army White Mess Uniform
Army All-White Mess Uniform
Army Black Evening Dress Uniform
Army White Evening Dress Uniform
Field and Work Uniforms

The composition of all uniforms as to what is worn with each one is shown in the accompanying table, *Composition of Uniforms.* The chapter and paragraph numbers therein refer to AR 670-1. Form the habit of checking against this tabulation to be certain your uniform is complete.

The uniform generates trust and respect in the minds of citizens because of their confidence in those who wear it. An officer who wears the correct uniform for the occasion, confident of its fit and condition, and that it is worn in the manner prescribed, is justified in a feeling of pride in having the right to wear the Army's uniform.

Personal Appearance. Officers wear their uniforms with pride and maintain them in clean, neat, serviceable condition. Local orders govern the specific uniform to be worn on duty and the uniforms considered appropriate for various occasions. The policy for wearing civilian clothing will be included in local orders. Upon arrival at a first station, or a new station, learn and adjust to the local policies at once.

Hair is to be neat, well groomed, and must not extend below the bottom edge of the collar, not to be cut so short as to present an unfeminine appearance. Makeup and nail polish are to be used with good taste.

Wrist watches, wrist identification bracelets, and rings are the only jewelry and ornaments worn with the uniform. Earrings of whatever type are forbidden.

Fitting the Coat and Skirt. The coat front will overlap to form a straight line from bottom of the lapel to the bottom of the coat. It will be fitted to produce a military effect, but with ease over the hips. It will not be buttoned so closely at the waist as to cause folds or wrinkles. The skirt will fit smoothly, so it does not drape in folds under the coat. It will form a continuation of the lines of the coat and will not flare at the sides; nor will it be pegged.

Choice of Uniform Materials. Considerable choice is provided in the selection of materials for the uniform as to the weave of fabric, its material, and its weight. This is a pleasing privilege, and at the same time it can lead to extravagance. As to the type of fabric for a uniform, there is a considerable advantage in choosing the preferred fabric and sticking with it. By this means a degree of interchange potential is established. In addition to the choice of fabric, such as serge, there is the important choice of its weight. Members of the Army must anticipate changes of station with service under varying climatic conditions. *Suggestion:* Satisfaction, comfort, as well as economy may be obtained by choosing medium weight fabrics, or even from the lighter weight fabrics. The uniform includes a raincoat/overcoat with removable liner for wear when needed.

Hats and Caps. A hat or cap will be worn outdoors when not under cover except when the Army Mess or Evening Dress uniforms are worn. Headgear is not required if the Army White or Army Blue uniform is being worn to an evening social event. Headgear will not be worn indoors unless under arms or directed by the commander.

There is a prescribed way to wear the headgear (see AR 670-1). The cap is worn with the center front placed slightly to the right of center approximately 1 inch above the right eyebrow, and opened to cover the crown of the head. The hat is worn straight on the head with the insignia centered on the front. Hair will not be visible on the forehead and there should be a $\frac{1}{2}$ to 1 inch distance between the eyebrow and the hat-forward position. A black, fur felt beret is authorized for optional wear on or off duty with the Army Green, Army Green Pantsuit, Army Green Dress and Jacket, Army Green Skirt and Jacket, Army Green Classic, Army Blue, Army White, Hospital Duty, and Training Duty uniforms. See AR 670-1 for manner of wear.

COMPOSITION OF UNIFORMS
(WOMEN'S)

Item	Service and Dress Uniforms							Mess and Evening Dress Uniforms					Field and Work Uniforms					
	Army Green Cord, chapter 12	AG-388 Skirt and Jackets chapter 13, section I	AG-388 Dress and Jacket chapter 14, section II	Army Green Pantsuit chapter 14, 15	Army Green chapter 14, 16	Army White chapter 17	Army Blue chapter 18	Army White Mess chapter 19	Army All-White Mess chapter 20	Army Black Mess chapter 21	Army White Evening Dress chapter 22	Army Black Evening Dress chapter 23	Cold Weather chapter 24, section I	Hot Weather chapter 24, section I	Utility chapter 24, section II	Hospital Duty chapter 24, section II	Food Service chapter 24, section III	Maternity Uniform chapter 24, section IV
Aiguillette, Dress (26-24)						X	X	X	X	X	X	X						
Aiguillette, Service (26-23)	X	X	X	X	X	X	X											
Apron, Food Handler, White (24-22)																	X	
Badges, Marksmanship and Skill, Full Size and Miniature (27-19, 20)	X	X	X	X	X	X	X											
Badges, Marksmanship and Skill, Dress Miniature (27-19, 20)						X	X	X	X	X	X	X						
Badges, Identification, Full Size (27-21)	X	X	X	X	X	X	X	X	X	X	X	X						
Belt, Web, waist w/Buckle (25-1)														X	X			
Beret, Black (25-2)	X	X	X	X	X	X	X									X	X	X
*Blouse, White, Formal (25-5)								X	X	X	X	X						
Boots, Combat, Black (25-3)													X		X			
Boots, Hot Weather, Black (24-10b)														X				
Cap, Cold Weather, OG-107 (24-10a)													X		X			
Cap, Food Handler, White (24-24a)																	X	
Cap, Garrison, Army Green Cord (12-7a)	X																	
Cap, Garrison, OG-108 (24-10a)													X					
Cap, Hospital Duty, White (24-17a)																X		
Cap, Utility, OG-507 (24-10a)													X	X	X		X	
*Capes, Army Blue or Army Black (25-6)							X	X	X	X	X	X						
*Coat, Army Blue (18-5)							X											
Coat, Army Green (16-5)					X													
Coat, Army Green Cord (12-5)	X																	
*Coat, Army White (17-5)						X												
Coat, Cold Weather (Field Jacket) (24-9)													X		X			
Coat, Cotton Poplin, OG-107 (24-7)														X				
Coat, Wool Serge, OG-108 (24-6)													X					
*Cummerbund, Black (25-7a)								X		X	X	X						
*Cummerbund, White (25-7b)									X									
Decoration Ribbons, Full Size (27-11)	X	X	X	X	X	X	X											
Decorations, Full Size (27-8). Note 1					X	X	X											
Decorations, Miniature (27-12)					X	X	X	X	X	X	X	X						
Distinctive Unit Insignia (26-21)	X	X	X	X	X										X	X	X	
*Dress, AG-388 (14-6)			X															
*Dress, Hospital Duty, White (24-15)																X		
Fourrageres and Lanyard (27-13)	X	X	X	X	X	X	X	X	X	X	X	X						
Gloves, Black (25-8a)	X	X	X	X	X											X	X	X
Gloves, w/liner Lt duty wk (25-8d)													X	X	X			
*Gloves, White, Dress (25-8c)						X	X	X	X	X	X	X						
*Handbag, Black, Dress, Leather (25-9a)							X											
*Handbag, Black, Dress, Fabric (25-9a)							X	X		X	X	X						
Handbag, Black, Service (25-9b)	X	X	X	X	X		X								X	X	X	X
Handbag, Black, Clutch type (25-9c)													X	X	X			
*Handbag, White, Dress, Leather (25-9c)						X												

COMPOSITION OF UNIFORMS
(WOMEN'S)—Continued

Item	Service and Dress Uniforms							Mess and Evening Dress Uniforms					Field and Work Uniforms					
	Army Green Cord, chapter 12	AG-388 Skirt and Jackets, chapter 13, section I	AG-388 Dress and Jacket, chapter 14, section II	Army Green Pantsuit, chapter 14, 15	Army Green, chapter 14, 16	Army White, chapter 17	Army Blue, chapter 18	Army White Mess, chapter 19	Army All-White Mess, chapter 20	Army Black Mess, chapter 21	Army White Evening Dress, chapter 22	Army Black Evening Dress, chapter 23	Cold Weather, chapter 24, section I	Hot Weather, chapter 24, section I	Utility, chapter 24, section I	Hospital Duty, chapter 24, section II	Food Service, chapter 24, section III	Maternity Uniform, chapter 24, section IV
*Handbag, White, Dress, Fabric (25-9c)						X		X										
*Hat, Service, Army Blue (18-9a)							X											X
*Hat, Service, Army Green (16-8b)	X	X	X	X	X													
*Hat, Service, Army White (17-8a)						X												
Hat, Drill Sergeant (25-10)	X	X	X	X	X								X	X	X			
*Jacket, Army Black (21-5)										X		X						
Jacket, Army Green Pantsuit (15-5)				X														
*Jacket, Army White (19-5)								X	X		X							
*Jacket, Cardigan, AG-388 (14-5)			X															
Jacket, Long Sleeve, AG-388 (13-5)		X																
Jacket, Short Sleeve, AG-388 (13-6)		X																
Medals, Service, Full Size (27-8). Note 1					X	X	X											
Medals, Service, Miniature (27-12)								X	X	X	X	X						
Medals, Service, Ribbons, Full Size (27-11)	X	X	X	X	X	X	X											
Necktab, Black, Service (25-13a)					X	X							X					X
*Necktab, Black, Dress (25-13b)								X		X	X	X						
Overcoat, Army Green (25-14)					X	X		X			X					X	X	X
Pantsuit, Food Service, White (24-22)																	X	
Pantsuit, Hospital Duty, White (24-16)																X		
Raincoat, Army Black (25-16a). Note 2	X	X	X	X	X	X	X	X	X	X	X	X		X	X	X	X	X
Raincoat, Army Green (25-16b). Note 2	X	X	X	X	X	X	X	X	X	X	X	X		X	X	X	X	X
Scarf, Black (25-17c)	X	X	X	X	X	X	X	X	X	X	X	X				X	X	X
*Scarf, White (25-17a)	X	X	X	X	X	X	X	X	X	X	X	X				X	X	X
Scarf, Olive Drab (25-17b)													X	X	X			
Scarves, Branch of Service (26-19)	X	X	X	X	X								X	X	X			
Shirt, Grey/Green-415 (25-18)					X	X												X
Shirt, Cotton Poplin, OG-107 (24-8)															X			
Shirt, Durapress OG 507 (24-8)															X			
Shirt, White (25-18)					X	X	X	X					X					
Shirt, Wool Flannel, OG-108 (24-5)													X					
Shoes, Oxford, Black (25-19a)	X	X	X	X	X								X			X	X	X
*Shoes, Oxford, White (25-19b)																X		
Shoes, Pumps, Service, Black (25-19c)	X	X	X	X	X		X						X					X
*Shoes, Pumps, Service, White (25-19c)						X												
*Shoes, Pumps, Dress, Black (25-19d)								X		X	X	X						
*Shoes, Pumps, Dress, White (25-19d)						X			X									
Skirt, Maternity (24-25)																		X
*Skirt, Army Black, Evening (22-6)											X	X						
*Skirt, Army Black, Mess (19-6)								X		X								
*Skirt, Army Blue (18-6)							X											
Skirt, Army Green (16-6)					X													
Skirt, Army Green Cord (12-6)	X																	
Skirt, Army Green AG-388 (13-7)		X																
*Skirt, Army White (17-6)						X												

COMPOSITION OF UNIFORMS
(WOMEN'S)—Continued

Item	Service and Dress Uniforms							Mess and Evening Dress Uniforms					Field and Work Uniforms					
	Army Green Cord, chapter 12	AG-388 Skirt and Jackets chapter 13, section I	AG-388 Dress and Jacket chapter 14, section II	Army Green Pantsuit chapter 14, 15	Army Green chapter 14, 16	Army White chapter 17	Army Blue chapter 18	Army White Mess chapter 19	Army All-White Mess chapter 20	Army Black Mess chapter 21	Army White Evening Dress chapter 22	Army Black Evening Dress chapter 23	Cold Weather chapter 24, section I	Hot Weather chapter 24, section I	Utility chapter 24, section I	Hospital Duty chapter 24, section II	Food Service chapter 24, section III	Maternity Uniform chapter 24, section IV
*Skirt, Army White Mess (20-6)									X									
Skirt, Wool Serge, OG-108 (24-6)													X					
Slacks, Army Green Pantsuit (15-6)				X														
Slacks, Cotton Poplin, OG-107 (24-8)															X			
Slacks, Durapress, OG-507 (24-8)															X			
Slacks, Maternity (24-25)																		X
Slacks, Wool Serge, OG-108 (24-5)													X					
Stockings, Sheer (25-20)	X	X	X	X	X	X	X	X	X	X	X	X	X			X	X	X
Stockings, White (25-20)																X		
Sweater, Army Green or Black (25-2)	X			X	X											X	X	X
Trousers, Cotton Poplin, OG-107 (24-7)														X				
*Tunic, Army Green (15-7)				X														
Tunic, Maternity (24-25)																		X
Umbrella, Black (25-22)	X	X	X	X	X	X	X	X	X	X	X	X				X	X	X
Undergarments (Brassieres and Panties)	X	X	X	X	X	X	X	X	X	X	X	X	X	X	X	X	X	X
Undergarments (slips)	X	X	X		X	X	X	X	X	X	X	X						X
Undershirts, Green or White (25-23)															X	X	X	
*Windbreaker, Black (25-24). Note 3	X	X		X	X											X	X	X

Notes.   1. Items may be worn on the Army green uniform only if worn for social functions.
   2. Raincoat is authorized for wear with the field and work uniforms only in garrison environment.
   3. Worn in lieu of the Army green coat with grey-green shirt.
   * OPTIONAL ITEMS

Army Green Classic Uniform. This uniform will replace all other female service uniforms: Army Green Skirt and Jacket, Army Green Dress and Jacket, Army Green Pantsuit and Army Green. Changeover dates are not yet published. The Army Green Classic uniform is authorized for year-round wear by all female personnel on duty, off duty and during travel. It is acceptable for social functions after retreat.

It consists of an Army green coat, skirt and slacks and green, shade 415, long- and short-sleeve shirts. The coat, skirt and slacks are of the same fabric, either polyester/wool blend, serge weave, 7 ounce, Army green shade 344; or 100% polyester, 6.5 ounce, Army green shade 44. The skirt and slacks may be worn interchangeably. An Army green tunic, shade 413, is authorized for optional wear with the coat and slacks. Either the green service hat or the black beret is worn with this uniform.

Ornamentation on the coat and slacks is the same as on the male Army Green uniform except for braid widths. Females, other than general officers, wear a ½-inch wide band of black mohair or mercerized cotton braid on the coat sleeve and a 1-inch stripe on the legs of the slacks.

The long- or short-sleeve green shirt with the black service necktab will be worn with the coat. Either shirt may be worn as an outer garment with the slacks or the skirt, in which case the black necktab must be worn with the long-sleeve shirt, but is not required with the short-sleeve shirt. The shirts may be worn either tucked inside or outside the skirt and slacks. A white shirt may be worn with the coat and skirt for formal social functions.

Army Green Skirt and Jacket Uniform. The Army Green Skirt and Jacket uniform is authorized for wear on duty, off duty and during travel by all Army women. The uniform consists of a skirt and short and long sleeved jackets of polyester warp knit, 6.9 ounce, Army green shade 388. It is worn with the Army green service hat or the black beret.

Army Green Dress and Jacket Uniform. The Army Green Dress and Jacket uniform is authorized for optional wear by all Army women when on duty unless otherwise prescribed by the local commander and when off duty and during travel. It consists of a dress and cardigan jacket, both Army green shade 388, of polyester warp knit, 6.9 ounces. The dress may be worn with or without the jacket, but the jacket may be worn only with the dress. The green service hat or the black beret are worn with this uniform.

Army Green Pantsuit Uniform. The Army Green Pantsuit uniform is authorized for year-round wear by all Army women when on duty, off duty or during travel. It consists of a jacket and slacks of polyester/wool blended fabric in twill weave, 10.6 ounces, Army green shade 344, or polyester warp knit, 6.9 ounces, Army green shade 444. It is worn with a green tunic of polyester rib knit, 5.5 ounces, Army green shade 413, or with the white short sleeve or green long or short sleeve shirts. The white or green shirts may be worn as outer garments. The tunic is worn outside the slacks. The green shirts with black service necktabs are worn with the jacket, tucked inside or out of the slacks. When the short sleeve green shirt is worn as an outer garment, wear of the necktab is optional. The green service hat and the black beret are authorized for wear with this uniform.

Army Green Uniform. The Army Green uniform is authorized for year-round wear on duty and off duty for all Army women. It includes the uniform coat and skirt and a hat or garrison cap of Army Green, or black beret, plus accessories.

Choice of Materials. There is a wide choice of materials for this uniform to meet service and climatic conditions: wool serge, 12 ounces, Army Green Shade 44; wool gabardine, 11 ounces, Army Green shade 44; polyester/wool, tropical, 10.5 ounces, Army Green Shade 344; polyester/wool twill weave, 9.5 ounces, Army Green Shade 344; polyester/wool, double knit, 8.2 ounces, Army Green shade 444, and polyester textured, 6.5 ounce, Army Green shade 434.

Army White Uniform. The Army White uniform is authorized for year-round wear by women of the Army, except that it may be required for certain officers (See AR 670-1). The uniform includes the coat, skirt, white shirt with necktab, hat and hatband.

Choice of Materials. The materials authorized for the coat and skirt are polyester/rayon, gabardine, 6 or 8 ounces, white; cotton uniform twill, 8.2 ounces, white; or polyester stretch woven serge, 6.5 ounces, white.

Army Blue Uniform. The Army Blue uniform is mandatory for wear by officers and is authorized for year-round wear. It is worn for social functions after retreat, as prescribed by the local commander, and on appropriate occasions as desired by the individual. The uniform includes the coat, skirt, and Army

Blue hat plus appropriate accessories. (See the table, *Composition of Uniforms.*) Shoulder straps are worn with this uniform. They are identical to the straps described for male officers except they are 3½ inches instead of 4 inches in length.

Army Black Mess Uniform. The Army Black Mess uniform is authorized for optional year-round wear by officers, at social functions of an official or private nature after retreat. The uniform includes a jacket, skirt (street length) and cummerbund. A hat is not worn with this uniform.

Choice of Materials. Jacket, skirt and cummerbund—Wool tropical, 8.5 ounces, Army Black shade 149; or Polyester/wool tropical 10 ounces, Army Black shade 332.

Army White Mess Uniform. The Army White Mess Uniform is authorized for optional wear by officers under the same conditions and with the same composition as for the Army Black Mess Uniform except that the jacket is white.

Choice of Materials. Jacket—Polyester/rayon gabardine, 6 or 8 ounces, white or texturized polyester serge, 6.5 ounce, white. Skirt and cummerbund —as for Army Black Mess uniform.

Army All-White Mess Uniform. Same as for Army White Mess uniform except that skirt and cummberbund are also of polyester/rayon gabardine, 6 or 8 ounces, white.

Army Black Evening Dress Uniform. This uniform is the same as the Army Black Mess uniform except that the skirt is full length. It is worn optionally by officers at social functions of an official or private nature and when the Blue Evening Dress uniform is prescribed for male officers.

Army White Evening Dress Uniform. This uniform is the same as the Army White Mess uniform except that the skirt is full length. It is worn by officers as prescribed for the Black Evening Dress uniform.

Hospital Duty Uniform. The Hospital Duty uniform is authorized for wear by female officers in the Army, Medical Department, and enlisted women with a medical or dental or veterinary MOS. The Hospital Duty uniform consists of a white dress and, on an optional basis, a white pantsuit. It is worn outdoors with the black beret. The Hospital Duty Cap is authorized for wear only by the the the Army Nurse Corps and Army Medical Specialist Corps officers. The uniform is worn when on duty as prescribed by the hospital commander.

The hospital duty cap is of cotton broadcloth, 3.5 ounces, fused, white; the dress is of polyester/cotton (80/20) bengaline, 4.5 ounces (wash and wear finish); the pantsuit is polyester, double knit, white.

Field Uniforms. The utility uniform and the hot and cold weather field uniforms are authorized for year-round wear by women in the Army. They are worn on duty as prescribed by the local commander.

Utility Uniform. The utility uniform is the male OG 507 durable press cotton polyester shirt and trousers with standard black webbed belt and open face buckle. It is designed for a loose fit and may not be altered for form fit. It may not be starched. Note: A camouflage uniform replaced the utility uniform starting on 1 October 1982. The utility uniform may be worn until 1 October 1985.

Hot Weather Field Uniform. The coat and slacks are intended to fit loosely for ease of movement. Alterations to make them form-fitting are not author-

ARMY GREEN UNIFORM

ARMY BLUE UNIFORM

ARMY WHITE UNIFORM

ARMY WHITE MESS UNIFORM

ARMY ALL-WHITE MESS UNIFORM

ARMY WHITE EVENING DRESS UNIFORM

WOMEN'S ARMY MESS AND EVENING DRESS UNIFORMS.

ized. The coat is worn outside the slacks. The sleeves may be rolled. Slacks are bloused when the service boot is worn.

Cold Weather Field Uniform. The wool shirt is worn as an outer garment and only with the wool serge slacks. The collar may be worn open or closed. The shirt and slacks are intended to fit loosely and alterations to make them form-fitting are not authorized. The sleeves may not be rolled up. Slacks are bloused when the service boot is worn.

A wool serge coat is also authorized for wear with the wool serge slacks or a wool serge skirt, all olive green shade 108. The white shirt with black necktab is worn with the skirt or slacks, under the coat, and tucked into the skirt or slacks. Nylon stockings and pumps or black oxfords are worn with this uniform.

Maternity Uniform. The Maternity uniform is authorized for year-round wear by pregnant women as prescribed by local commanders (see AR 670-1 for details). It consists of an Army green, shade 434 tunic, skirt and slacks with expanded front panels, with either a white short-sleeve or a green long- or short-sleeve shirt. It is worn with either the green service hat or the black beret.

Accessories. Accessories to the several uniforms include articles which are a part of all uniforms, such as shoes, and other items required for convenience, appearance or climatic conditions. (See the table, *Composition of Uniforms.*)

Cape, Army Blue. A fingertip-length cape with fitted shoulders, a high rounded soft collar and lined with 4.2 ounce rayon twill or 4.5 ounce satin of the first-named color of the officer's basic branch. The capes of general officers are lined in dark blue. The authorized cape materials are the same as for the Army Blue uniform. Authorized wear with the Army Blue uniform and with the Army Mess uniforms and Army Evening Dress uniforms.

Cape, Army Black. A knee-length cape, approximately one inch below the skirt hem, lined with 4.5 ounce white rayon satin. The cape is of wool gabardine, 11 ounces, Army Black shade 149. An agraffe is worn across the front center neck closure of the cape. The cape may be worn with the Army Blue uniform, Army Mess uniforms, and Army Evening Dress uniform.

Gloves. Three types of gloves are authorized. Black leather of adopted or similar commercial design for wear with the Army green coat, jacket, windbreaker, overcoat, raincoat and all-weather coat; white dress of nylon, cotton, kid, doeskin, or leather of appropriate commercial design for year-round wear with the Army Blue, Army White and all of the Mess and Dress uniforms; and light-duty black leather gloves for wear with the field and utility uniforms.

Handbags. There are four types of handbags.

Black, dress, of leather or fabric, commercial design, untrimmed, envelope or clutch style, with or without chain. The leather bag may be worn with the Army Blue uniform during or after duty hours. The fabric bag will be worn with the Black Mess and Black Evening Dress uniforms, and may be worn with the Army Blue uniform after duty hours. The handbag and shoes must be of the same material.

Black, service, leather or polyurethane of adopted design which may be worn with all service, field and utility uniforms, the Army Blue uniform and with civilian clothes.

White, dress, of leather or fabric, commercial design, untrimmed, envelope or clutch style, with or without chain. The leather bag may be worn with the Army White uniform during or after duty hours. The fabric bag will be worn with the Army All-White Mess uniform and may be worn after duty hours with the Army White uniform. The handbag and shoes must be of the same material.

Black, clutch type, of coarse grain leather, for optional wear with field and utility uniforms.

Raincoat/Overcoat. The black raincoat/overcoat with removable liner and removable havelock serves as either a raincoat or overcoat. It is of 50/50 polyester/cotton, poplin, 6 ounce, of adopted design. It replaces the older green raincoat and green overcoat, which may still be worn. The coat is worn buttoned, except for the neck closure, which may be open or closed with or without a scarf. The coat will cover uniform sleeves by $\frac{1}{2}$ inch at the cuff and 1 inch at the skirt hem. Without insignia, it may be worn with civilian clothing.

Shoes. A wide choice of shoes is provided for service needs and for the several uniforms, as shown by the items described below.

Boot. This is the black, combat boot for women, to be worn with the field uniforms.

Boot, inclement weather. Of leather, rubber or synthetic material. Plain style, not more than knee-high with inconspicuous zipper or snap type closing. Optional for wear with service uniforms when going to or from duty. Must be exchanged for standard footgear indoors.

Oxfords, Black. This shoe is of leather or poromeric material with closed toe and heel; with black heels no more than 2 inches in height. Authorized for wear with all uniforms except the Army White, Army Blue, Army Mess, Army Evening Dress, Hot Weather and utility uniforms.

Oxford, White. This shoe is of leather or poromeric-type material with leather finish. It is of commercial design, closed toe and heel with a minimum of three eyelets and a white heel no higher than 2 inches. It is worn with the hospital duty uniform.

Pumps, Black/White. These shoes are of calfskin, fine grain, or of poromeric-type material with leather finish. They are plain, untrimmed, of current commercial design with closed toe and heel; black/white heel from 1 to 3 inches. The black pumps are worn with all service uniforms except the Army White uniform, with which the white pumps are worn.

Pumps, Dress, Black/White. These shoes are of fabric; plain, untrimmed, of current commercial design, with closed toe and heel; with black/white heels from 1 to 3 inches. These shoes are worn with the Army Blue, Army White and the various Mess and Evening uniforms as appropriate, with matching handbag of the same material.

Overshoes. Authorized are black rubber or synthetic overshoes of commercial design.

Shirts. The white, short sleeve shirt is of polyester/cotton broadcloth, durable press, with attached necktab. The collar is worn closed and the shirt is worn with the Army Green, Army Green Pantsuit, Army White, and Army Blue uniforms.

The green shade 415, long or short sleeve with black necktab may be worn with the Army Green, Army green classic and Army Green Pantsuit uniforms, as an outer garment with the green skirt, and with the Maternity uniform.

Necktab. The necktab is of polyester/cotton broadcloth, black shade 305. It is worn with the long or short sleeve green shirt when worn with the Army Green coat and the Army Green Pantsuit jacket, or when the long sleeve shirt is worn as an outer garment. The necktab may be worn with the short sleeve shirt when worn as an outer garment. A dress necktab of commercial design is worn with the white formal blouse of all Army Mess and Evening Dress uniforms.

Scarves. A white scarf of 100% acrylic woven fiber is authorized for wear with all service, dress, mess and evening dress uniforms when the overcoat, all-weather coat or raincoat is worn. The scarf is worn folded in half, lengthwise, and crossed right over left at the neck, with the ends tucked neatly into the neckline of the coat.

A black scarf of wool, silk or rayon, of commercial design, approximately 12 inches by 52 inches, is authorized for optional wear with the black raincoat/overcoat.

A wool, olive drab scarf, shade 30 A, is authorized for wear with the field jacket or other field clothing.

Stockings. Stockings are of commercial design, sheer or semi-sheer, with or without seams, and in a shade complementary to the uniform. White stockings are worn with the Hospital Duty uniform when white shoes are worn. Plain black cotton or cotton/nylon socks may be worn with the black oxford shoes when wearing the Army Green Pantsuit. Olive green socks, 20 per cent cotton, 30 per cent nylon, 50 per cent wool with ribbed top and cushion sole must be worn with combat boots.

Sweaters. A black cardigan sweater, 100% acrylic, shade 435, is authorized for optional wear as an outer garment with the Army green skirt, green pantsuit slacks and the long- and short-sleeve green shirts within the immediate confines of the working area. It may also be worn as a subgarment under the Army green coat and green pantsuit jacket. This sweater replaces the Army green cardigan sweater, which may be worn until 30 September 1983. A black, pullover, V-neck sweater of 100% wool, shade 458, is also authorized for optional wear as an outer garment with the green shirt and the green skirt or slacks. When worn with the short-sleeve shirt without necktab, the shirt collar will be worn outside the sweater. It may also be worn as a subgarment under the overcoat/raincoat and the windbreaker. Shoulder marks indicating the officer's grade are worn on this sweater.

Umbrella. All Army women may purchase, and use when in uniform, a plain black umbrella of commercial design. It is not used with field or utility uniforms.

Windbreaker. A black windbreaker of polyester/cotton poplin, shade 385, is authorized for optional purchase and wear with the white shirt when worn as an outer garment, with the Army Green Pantsuit slacks, the Army Green Dress and Jacket uniform, the Hospital Duty uniform and the long- and short-sleeve green shirts when worn as outer garments. It may not be worn in formation unless authorized by the local commander. Without insignia, it may be worn with civilian clothes. When worn with the uniform, it must be zipped up at least ¾ of the way.

Insignia. The insignia worn by members of the Army, officer or enlisted men or women, include devices which show their grade, branch of service, and in some cases their capacity or duty assignment and prior Army service.

Insignia other than items specifically authorized in AR 670-1 will not be worn on the uniform, except that the Department of the Army may grant specific authorization otherwise.

Hat and Cap Insignia Worn by Women Officers. See the illustrations and the discussion of these items of the uniforms.

U.S. Insignia. Worn on the right collar of the Army Blue, Army Green, Army green classic, Army Green Pantsuit, and Army White coats; worn 1 inch above the notch, with the center line of the insignia bisecting the notch and parallel to the inside edge of the collar.

Insignia of Branch. Worn on the left collar of the Army Blue, Army Green,

Wear of Insignia

WEARING INSIGNIA

Army green classic, Army Green Pantsuit, and Army White coats, centered 1 inch above the notch and parallel to the inside edge of of the collar. Also worn on the left collar of the Army Green Dress and Jacket, Army Green Skirt and Jacket, Hospital Duty uniform, all field work and utility uniforms, and on the white shirt when worn as an outer garment with the Army Green Pantsuit slacks, centered on the collar, 1 inch from the lower edge of the collar, with the center line parallel to the lower edge of the collar. Note that on the Army green classic uniform, the U.S. and branch insignia are positioned equidistant from each edge of the collar and parallel to the inside edge of the collar.

Insignia of Grade. Worn on the shoulder loops ⅝ inch from the shoulder seam, on the uniform coats, jackets, raincoat, overcoat, and windbreaker. Worn centered on the right collar, 1 inch from the lower edge of the collar, with the center line of the insignia parallel to the lower edge of the collar on the Army Green Dress and Jacket, Army Green Skirt and Jacket, Hospital Duty uniform, all field, work and utility uniforms, and on the white shirt when worn as an outer garment with the Army Green Pantsuit slacks. Shoulder marks with insignia of grade are worn with the long or short sleeve green shirt and the wool, pullover sweater.

On the garrison cap, left side, centered 1 inch from the front.

On the utility caps, OG 106 (hot weather) and OG 107 (cold weather), centered on the front.

On the helmet and helmet liner, 2½ inches from the front bottom, painted in prescribed color and size.

Distinctive Branch Scarves. Branch scarves are authorized and may be worn at the discretion of the local commander: colors are as prescribed earlier in this chapter. The scarf is worn fastened around the neck to cover the throat.

Insignia of Branch. Illustrations of all branch insignia are shown earlier in the chapter.

Insignia of Grade. The devices showing insignia of grade for officers and warrant officers are illustrated earlier in this chapter. Note the smaller sizes of shoulder boards and shoulder marks for female officers.

WEAR OF THE UNIFORM BY PERSONNEL OTHER THAN MEMBERS OF THE ACTIVE ARMY

Individuals who possess a current military status other than as a member of the Active Army are restricted as to the occasions when they may wear the uniform. Part V, AR 670-1 establishes detailed regulations under which the categories of personnel listed below may wear the uniform.

Army National Guard officers while not serving with the Active Army.
Army Reserve officers while not serving with the Active Army.
Retired officers and enlisted men.
Persons who have been awarded the Medal of Honor.
Separated personnel who have served honorably during war.

Occasions of Ceremony. Authority to wear the uniform on "occasions of ceremony" requires definition. It means an occasion essentially military in character at which the uniform is more appropriate than civilian clothing, e.g., military balls, military parades, military weddings, military funerals, memorial services, and meetings or functions of associations formed for military purposes, the membership of which is composed largely or entirely of honorably discharged veterans of the Armed Forces or of Reserve personnel. This authorization includes authority to wear the uniform while traveling to and from the ceremony, provided such travel can be completed on the day of the ceremony.

Army National Guard and Army Reserve Officers, Inactive Status. Officers of the National Guard and of the Army Reserve while on inactive status are authorized to wear the uniform during periods of military instruction. They may also wear it on occasions of ceremony, as stated above. Consult the Unit Instructor or the commanding officer for authority to wear the uniform on other occasions.

Retired Officers and Enlisted Personnel. The uniform of retired personnel which may be worn on occasions of ceremony, as discussed above, will be at their option—either that for persons of corresponding grade and branch of service on date of retirement or that of persons on the active list, but the two uniforms will not be mixed.

Persons Who Have Been Awarded the Medal of Honor. Persons who have been awarded the Medal of Honor are authorized to wear the uniform at any time except:

In connection with the promotion of any political or commercial interests or when engaged in civilian employment;

When participating in public speeches, interviews, picket lines, marches, rallies, or public demonstrations except as authorized by competent authority;

When wearing the uniform would bring discredit on the Army; and

When specifically prohibited by regulation.

22

Decorations, Service Medals, and Badges

Decorations awarded to members of the Armed Services are a symbol of acknowledgment by the Government of our nation for a job well done. They consist of awards for heroism, the highest of which is the Medal of Honor, and awards for achievement, the highest of which is the Distinguished Service Medal. Just as there is a variation in degree of heroism or achievement above and beyond the call of duty, so is there also a variation in the rank of the several awards given for these two purposes.

The granting of awards by governments stems at least as far back into history as the Roman era. It was during that period that Roman rulers took the laurel wreath unto themselves. The Greeks crowned citizens who were outstanding in war, athletics, literature, and oratory with the laurel wreath and therefore it is natural that it forms a part of our nation's highest award for valor. During the Age of Feudalism there grew up a system of "rewards" in the form of titles and prerogatives. The "strong men," or barons, would honor the "knights" who performed valiant feats of arms not only by giving them increased titles, lands, and pensions, but also by encouraging them in the growing habit of decorating their shields and other armor with insignia which were, in effect, a pictorial history of their deeds. As the deeds increased in numbers and complexity of insignia, there developed the whole field of heraldry and heraldic art, and the production of "coats of arms" for the families which had evolved them.

The several subjects discussed in this chapter have been placed in the following sequence:

Decorations and Awards (a general overview)
United States Army Decorations (Illustrated)

United States Military Service Medals (Illustrated)
United States Army Badges and Tabs (Illustrated)
Appurtenances to Decorations and Service Medals (Illustrated)
Foreign Decorations
Certificates and Letters for Service
Unit Awards (Illustrated)
Guide for Wearing Awards (Illustrated).

DECORATIONS AND AWARDS

Purpose and Categories of Awards. The purpose of the awards program of the Army, with similar programs in the other services, is to provide tangible recognition for acts of valor, exceptional service or achievement, special skills or qualifications, and acts of heroism not involving actual combat. Medals constitute a principal form for such evidence but other methods are provided and all are discussed within this chapter. Most awards are made to individuals. There are also unit awards and citations. Most awards may be given only to a member of the military service; a few may be awarded to either a member of the service or a civilian; and there are awards which may be granted to civilians only.

This chapter is based on official publications and is intended to be sufficiently comprehensive for the personal needs of the officer. For the administration of the program, or for official action regarding the program, reference should be made to the official publications, with their changes. The basic publication is AR 672-5-1. AR 672-5-2 provides color illustrations of high awards. Wearing of decorations, medals and badges is discussed in AR 670-1. Other documents of reference are cited as they apply in the discussions within the chapter.

The broad categories of awards include the following:

Individual Awards—
Decorations for valor or achievement.
Good Conduct Medal (for enlisted men only).
Service medals.
Combat and special skill badges and tabs.
Foreign individual awards.
Certificates and letters.

Unit Awards—
Unit decorations.
Infantry and Medical streamers.
Campaign streamers, war service streamers, and Campaign Silver bands.
Foreign unit decorations.

Important Definitions. Definitions of words or terms which are in common use in recommending individuals for awards, or in making awards, must be understood. The following are important.

Active Federal Military Service. The term means all periods of active duty and excludes periods of active duty for training. Service as a cadet at the USMA is considered to be active duty. For the award of the Armed Forces Reserve Medal, active duty for training counts in determining eligibility.

Above and Beyond the Call of Duty. This is exercise of a voluntary course of action the omission of which would not justly subject the individual to censure for failure in the performance of duty. It usually includes the acceptance of existing danger or extraordinary responsibilities with praiseworthy fortitude and exemplary courage. In its highest degree it involves the voluntary acceptance of additional danger and risk of life. (This is the most important definition.)

Citation. A citation is a written, narrative statement of an act, deed, or meritorious performance of duty or service for which an award is made.

Combat Heroism. This covers an act or acts of heroism by an individual engaged in actual conflict with an armed enemy, or in military operations which involve exposure to personal hazards due to direct enemy action or the imminence of such action.

Combat Zone. The region where fighting is going on; the forward area of the theater of operations where combat troops are actively engaged. It extends from the front line to the front of the communications zone.

Distinguished Himself by. A person to have distinguished himself must, by praiseworthy accomplishment, be set apart from other persons in the same or similar circumstances. Determination of this distinction requires careful consideration of exactly what is or was expected as the ordinary, routine, or customary behavior and accomplishment for individuals of like rank and experience for the circumstances involved.

Duty of Great Responsibility. Duty which, by virtue of the position held, carries the ultimate responsibility for the successful operation of a major command, activity, agency, installation, or project. The discharge of such duty must involve the acceptance and fulfillment of the obligation so as to greatly benefit the interests of the United States.

Duty of Responsibility. Duty which, by virtue of the position held, carries a high degree of the responsibility for the successful operation of a major command, activity, agency, installation, or project, or which requires the exercise of judgment and decision affecting plans, policies, operations, or the lives and well-being of others.

Heroism. Heroism is defined as specific acts of bravery or outstanding courage, or a closely related series of acts performed within a short period of time.

In Connection with Military Operations against an Armed Enemy. This phrase covers all military operations including combat, support, and supply which have a direct bearing on the outcome of an engagement or engagements against armed opposition. To perform duty or to accomplish an act of achievement in connection with military operations against an armed enemy the individual must have been subjected to either personal hazard as a result of direct enemy action, or the imminence of such action, or must have had the conditions under which his duty or accomplishment took place complicated by enemy action or the imminence of enemy action.

Key Individual. A person who is occupying a position that is indispensable to an organization, activity, or project.

Meritorious Achievement. An act which is well above the expected performance of duty. The act should be an exceptional accomplishment with a definite beginning and ending date. The length of time involved is not a primary consideration but speed of accomplishment may be a factor in determining the value of an act.

Meritorious Service. Service which is distinguished by a succession of outstanding acts of achievement over a sustained period of time.

Officer. Except where stated otherwise, the word "officer" means commissioned or warrant officer. And "he," "his," "him," includes "she" and "her" as appropriate.

Army Personal Decorations. A decoration is awarded in recognition of performance of duty involving heroism, or high achievement. There are degrees of heroism and of achievement, and for that reason there are awards to recognize these varying standards. All soldiers are expected to do their duty, and to accept the normal hazards of duty, for which there is no special individual award. Return for a moment to consider the definition of "above and beyond the call of duty." This is the key to understanding. In the field of combat heroism, the Medal of Honor is our highest award; other awards for heroism in descending scale are the Distinguished Service Cross, Silver Star, Distinguished Flying Cross, Bronze Star Medal, Air Medal, Joint Service Commendation Medal, and the Army Commendation Medal. In the area of achievement, the Defense Distinguished Service Medal is the highest award. Those which follow are the Distinguished Service Medal, Legion of Merit, Distinguished Flying Cross, Bronze Star Medal, Defense Meritorious Service Medal, Meritorious Service Medal, Air Medal, Joint Service Commendation Medal, Army Commendation Medal. Some awards, it is to be noted, may be awarded both for heroism and for achievement. The Purple Heart, the oldest decoration in our service, is awarded only for wounds.

The table following, from AR 672–5–1, lists the awards to Army individuals in the order of their precedence, and the order in which worn on the uniform.

Approval Authority for Decorations. The regulations are specific and detailed as to the approval authority for award of the various decorations. The criteria vary depending on whether the award is made during peacetime or wartime. Consult the regulations, AR 672–5–1, for details.

UNITED STATES ARMY DECORATIONS

Interesting information about decorations is provided in the following pages.

Medal of Honor. The Medal of Honor, established by Act of Congress in 1862, is the highest and most rarely awarded deocration conferred by the United States. The deed for which the Medal of Honor is awarded must have been one of personal bravery or self-sacrifice so conspicuous as to clearly distinguish the individual for gallantry and intrepidity above his comrades and must have involved risk of life. Incontestable proof of the performance of the service will be exacted and each recommendation for the award of this decoration will be considered on the standard of extraordinary merit.

Presentation of the Medal of Honor is made only by the President.

No special personal privileges or exemptions from military obligations accompany the award. However, Medal of Honor winners may receive free air transportation (MAC) on a space-available basis. Sons of winners of the Medal of Honor, otherwise qualified for admission to the United States Military Academy, will not be subject to quota requirements.

Army personnel holding the Medal of Honor may apply to The Adjutant General, Attn: AGPB-AC, to have their names entered upon the Medal of Honor Roll. Persons on the roll and otherwise eligible may, upon application, qualify for a special lifetime pension of $200 per month.

Distinguished Service Cross. Established by Act of Congress on 9 July 1918 and amended by act of 25 July 1963, this medal is awarded to a person who while serving in any capacity with the Army, distinguishes himself by extraordi-

Decorations (In order of precedence)	Established By	Awarded for		Awarded to				
				United States Personnel			Foreign Personnel	
		Heroism	Achievement or Service	Military	Reserve Components	Civilian	Military	Civilian
Medal of Honor	Joint Resolution of Congress, 12 July 1862 (amended by acts 9 July 1918 and 25 July 1963)	Combat		War[1]				
Distinguished Service Cross	Act of Congress 9 July 1918 (amended by act of 25 July 1963)	Combat		War		War[2]	War	War[2]
Defense Distinguished Service Medal	Executive Order 11545 9 July 1970		War Peace	War Peace				
Distinguished Service Medal	Act of Congress 9 July 1918		War Peace	War Peace	Peace	War[2]	War[2]	War[2]
Silver Star	Act of Congress 9 July 1918 (amended by act of 25 July 1963)	Combat		War		War[2]	War	War[2]
Defense Superior Service Medal	Executive Order 11904, 6 February 1976		War Peace	War Peace				
Legion of Merit	Act of Congress 20 July 1942		War Peace	War Peace	Peace		War Peace[4]	
Distinguished Flying Cross	Act of Congress 2 July 1926	Combat Noncombat	War Peace	War Peace	Peace		War	
Soldier's Medal	Act of Congress 2 July 1926	Noncombat		War Peace	Peace		War Peace	
Bronze Star Medal	Executive Order 9419, 4 February 1944 (superseded by Executive Order 11046, 24 August 1962)	Combat[3]	War Peace	War Peace		War Peace	War Peace	War Peace[2]
Defense Meritorious Service Medal	Executive Order 12019, 3 November 1977		Peace	Peace	Peace			
Meritorious Service Medal	Executive Order 11448, 16 January 1969		Peace	Peace	Peace			
Air Medal	Executive Order 9242-A, 11 September 1942	Combat[3] Noncombat	War Peace	War Peace	Peace	War	War	War
Joint Service Commendation Medal	DOD Directive 1348.14, 17 May 1967	Combat[3] Noncombat	War Peace	War				
Army Commendation Medal	War Department Circular 377, 18 December 1945 (amended in DA General Orders 10, 1960)	Combat[3] Noncombat	War Peace	War Peace[5]	Peace		War Peace[5]	
Purple Heart	General George Washington, 7 August 1782, revived by War Department General Orders 3, 1932 as amended by Executive Order 11016, 25 April 1962	Wounds received in combat		War Peace		War		

Footnotes:

*1—The Army Medal of Honor is only awarded to United States Army military personnel.

2—Not usually awarded to these personnel.

3—Awarded with Bronze V device for valor in combat.

4—Awarded to foreign military personnel in one of four degrees.

5—Not awarded to general officers.

nary heroism not justifying the Medal of Honor while engaged in an action against an enemy of the United States, while engaged in military operations involving conflict with opposing forces, or while serving with friendly forces engaged in an armed conflict against an opposing armed force in which the United States is not a belligerent party.

Defense Distinguished Service Medal. Established by Executive Order 11545 of 9 July 1970, this medal is awarded by the Secretary of Defense to any military service officer who, while assigned to joint staffs and other joint activities of the Department of Defense, distinguished himself by exceptionally meritorious service while in a position of unique and great responsibility. It ranks between the Distinguished Service Cross and the Distinguished Service Medal in order of precedence. It will not be awarded to any individual for a period of service for which a Distinguished Service Medal or similar decoration is awarded.

Distinguished Service Medal. Established by Congress on 9 July 1918, this medal is awarded to any person who, while serving in any capacity with the Army, shall have distinguished himself by exceptionally meritorious service to the Government in a duty of great responsibility. For service not related to actual war the term "duty of great responsibility" applies to a narrower range of positions than in wartime, and requires evidence of conspicuously significant achievement. Awards may be made to persons other than members of the

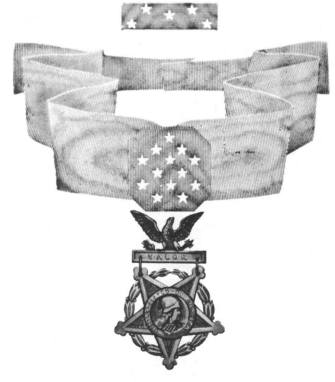

MEDAL OF HONOR.

Armed Forces of the United States for wartime service only, under exceptional circumstances, and with the approval of the President.

Silver Star. Established by act of Congress 9 July 1918 as amended by act of 25 July 1963, the Silver Star is awarded to a person under the same circumstances as described above for the Distinguished Service Cross but where the gallantry is of a lesser degree but performed with marked distinction.

Defense Superior Service Medal. Established by Executive Order 11904 of 6 February 1976, this medal is awarded by the Secretary of Defense to any member of the Armed Forces of the United States who, while assigned to joint staffs and other joint activities of the Department of Defense, has rendered superior meritorious service while in a position of significant responsibility. It ranks between the Silver Star and the Legion of Merit in order of precedence. It will not be awarded to any individual for a period of service for which a Legion of Merit or similar decoration is awarded.

Legion of Merit. Established by Congress 20 July 1942, this medal is awarded to any member (usually key individuals) of the Armed Forces of the United States or of a friendly foreign nation who has distinguished himself by exceptionally meritorious conduct in the performance of outstanding services. For service not related to war the term "key individuals" applies to a narrower range than in wartime. Awards are made to US nationals without reference to degree and, for each award, the Legion of Merit (Legionnaire) will be issued. The award may be made to foreigners, under conditions prescribed in AR 672–5–1, in one of four degrees—Chief Commander, Commander, Officer, or Legionnaire.

Distinguished Flying Cross. Established by Congress 2 July 1926, this medal is awarded to any member of the Armed Forces of the United States and of friendly foreign nations who, while serving in any capacity with the Army, shall have distinguished himself by heroism or extraordinary achievement while participating in aerial flight.

Soldier's Medal. Established by Congress 2 July 1926, this medal is awarded to any person who, while serving with the Army, shall have distinguished himself by heroism not involving actual conflict with an armed enemy. The same degree of heroism is required as for a Distinguished Flying Cross. The award will not be made solely on the basis of having saved a life.

Bronze Star Medal. The Bronze Star Medal was established by Executive Order in 1944, which was superseded by Executive Order 11046, 1962. It is awarded to any person who, while serving in any capacity in or with the Army of the United States after 6 December 1941, shall have distinguished himself by heroic or meritorious achievement or service, not involving participation in aerial flight, in connection with military operations against an armed enemy; while engaged in military operations with an opposing foreign force; or while serving with friendly foreign forces engaged in an armed conflict against an opposing armed force in which the United States is not a belligerent party.

Awards may be made for acts of heroism which are of lesser degree than required for award of the Silver Star.

Awards may be made for achievement or meritorious service which, while of lesser degree than that required for the award of the Legion of Merit, must nevertheless have been meritorious and accomplished with distinction.

Defense Meritorious Service Medal. Established by Executive Order 12019, 3 November 1977. It is awarded in the name of the Secretary of Defense to any active duty member of the Armed Forces of the United States who distinguishes himself/herself by noncombat meritorious achievement or service

DISTINGUISHED SERVICE
CROSS.

DISTINGUISHED SERVICE
MEDAL.

DEFENSE DISTINGUISHED
SERVICE MEDAL.

DEFENSE
SUPERIOR
SERVICE MEDAL.

SILVER STAR.

LEGION OF MERIT.

while assigned, or on temporary duty for at least 60 days, to joint staffs and other joint activities of the Department of Defense. It ranks between the Bronze Star Medal and the Meritorious Service Medal. It will not be awarded to any individual for a period of service for which any similar decoration has been awarded.

DISTINGUISHED FLYING CROSS.

SOLDIER'S MEDAL.

BRONZE STAR MEDAL.

MERITORIOUS SERVICE MEDAL.

AIR MEDAL.

JOINT SERVICE COMMENDATION MEDAL.

Meritorious Service Medal. Established by Executive Order 11448, 16 January 1969. It is awarded to a member of the Armed Forces who, after 16 January 1969, has distinguished himself by outstanding meritorious achievement or service in a non-combat situation. It ranks between the Bronze Star Medal and the Army Commendation Medal as a non-combat award.

Air Medal. Established by Executive Order on 11 May 1942, this medal was awarded to any person who, while serving in any capacity in or with the Army, distinguished himself by meritorious achievement while participating in aerial flight. Effective in 1974, revised criteria provide that the medal will be awarded for heroism in combat, for single acts of meritorious service involving superior airmanship, and for meritorious service involving sustained distinction in the performance of duties which require regular and frequent participation in aerial flight for a period of at least 6 months in combat.

Joint Service Commendation Medal. Department of Defense Directive 1348.-14, 19 July 1965, established this medal. This decoration is awarded in the name of the Secretary of Defense and takes precedence with, but before the Army Commendation Medal. It is awarded to any member of the Armed Forces who distinguishes himself by meritorious achievement or service while serving with offices and agencies of the Secretary of Defense and the Joint Chiefs of Staff as described in AR 672-5-1. Awards may include the "V" device if the citation is approved for valor in a designated combat area.

Army Commendation Medal. The Army Commendation Medal established by the Secretary of War on 18 December 1945, and amended in Department of the Army General Orders 10, 1960, is awarded to any member of the Armed Forces of the United States who, while serving in any capacity with the Army after 6 December 1941, shall have distinguished himself by heroism, meritorious achievement or meritorious service. Award may also be made to a member of the Armed forces of a friendly foreign nation for acts of heroism, extraordinary achievement or meritorious service which has been of mutual benefit to a friendly foreign nation and the United States.

ARMY
COMMENDATION
MEDAL.

PURPLE HEART.

Awards may be made for acts of valor performed under circumstances described above which are of lesser degree than required for award of the Bronze Star Medal. These acts may involve aerial flight.

An award may be made for acts of non-combatant related heroism which do not meet the requirements for an award of the Soldier's Medal.

The Army Commendation Medal will not be awarded to general officers.

Purple Heart. The Purple Heart, established by General George Washington at Newburgh, N.Y., on 7 August 1782 and revived by the President as announced in War Department General Orders 3, 22 February 1932, as amended by Executive Order 11016, 25 April 1962, is awarded, in the name of the President of the United States, to any member of an Armed Force or any civilian national of the United States, who, while serving under competent authority in any capacity with one of the United States Armed Services after 5 April 1917 has been wounded, killed, or who has died or may hereafter die after being wounded

> In any action against an enemy of the United States;
>
> In any action with an opposing armed force of a foreign country in which the Armed Forces of the United States are or have been engaged;
>
> While serving with friendly foreign forces engaged in an armed conflict against an opposing armed force in which the United States is not a belligerent party;
>
> As the result of an act of any such enemy or opposing armed force; or
>
> As the result of an act of any hostile foreign force.

A Purple Heart is authorized for the first wound suffered under conditions indicated above, but for each subsequent award an oak-leaf cluster shall be awarded to be worn on the medal or ribbon.

A Purple Heart will be issued to the next of kin of each person entitled to a posthumous award. Issue will be made automatically by the Commanding General, MILPERCEN upon receiving a report of death indicating entitlement.

Presidential Medal of Freedom. By Executive Order on 22 February 1963, the Medal of Freedom was reestablished as the Presidential Medal of Freedom. This decoration can only be awarded by the President to any person who has made an especially meritorious contribution to the security or national interests of the United States, to world peace or to cultural or other significant public or private endeavors. Announcement of awards will be made on or about the 4th of July each year.

UNITED STATES MILITARY SERVICE MEDALS

Service (campaign) medals denote the honorable performance of military duty within specified limiting dates in specified geographical areas. Or they may also denote military duty anywhere within specified time periods.

They are worn as described later in this chapter.

United States service medals are those awarded by the Army, Navy, and Air Force. Other service medals of the Federal Government or awarded by a State or other inferior jurisdiction are regarded as being civilian service medals and will not be worn on the uniform.

Service Medals Authorized Prior to World War II. The medals which pertain to wars or campaigns prior to World War II are shown below.

AMERICAN DEFENSE
SERVICE MEDAL.

WOMEN'S ARMY CORPS
SERVICE MEDAL.

AMERICAN
CAMPAIGN MEDAL.

ASIATIC-PACIFIC
CAMPAIGN MEDAL.

EUROPEAN—AFRICAN—
MIDDLE EASTERN
CAMPAIGN MEDAL.

WORLD WAR II
VICTORY MEDAL.

Service Medal:	Date of Service:	Date Authorized:
Civil War Campaign Medal	15 April 1861—9 April 1865; or in Texas until 20 August 1866	1907
Indian Campaign Medal	Thirteen specific campaigns, 1865–1891	1907
Spanish Campaign Medal	Cuba, 11 May—17 July 1898. Puerto Rico, 24 July—13 August 1898. Philippine Islands, 30 June—16 August 1898	1905
Spanish War Service Medal	Service other than above 20 April 1898—11 April 1899	1918
Army of Cuban Occupation Medal	Cuba service, 18 July 1898—20 May 1902	1915
Army of Puerto Rico Occupation Medal	Puerto Rico service, 14 August—10 December 1898	1919
Philippine Campaign Medal	Specified service in the Philippines, 1899—1913	1905
Philippine Congressional Medal	Specified service 1898, and 1899–1902	1906
China Campaign Medal	China, 20 June 1900—27 May 1901	1905
Army of Cuban Pacification Medal	Cuba, 6 October 1906—1 April 1909	1909
Mexican Service Medal	Specified campaigns 1911—1917	1917

Mexican Border Service Medal	Mexican border, 9 May 1916–6 April 1917 .	1918
World War I Victory Medal	6 April 1917—11 November 1918; or with American Expeditionary Force in Russia, 12 November 1918—5 August 1919; or in Siberia, 23 November 1918—1 April 1920.	1919
Army of Occupation of Germany Service Medal, World War I	Service in Germany or Austria-Hungary, 12 Nov. 1918–11 July 1923	1941

Service Medals for the World War II Period. The following list shows the service medals pertaining to the WW II period, with the dates of required service. See AR 672–5–1 for description of the medals and the areas of required service.

Service Medal:	Date of Service:
American Defense	8 Sept 1939–7 Dec 1941
Women's Army Corps	20 July 1942—31 Aug 1943 for WAAC and 1 Sept 1943–2 Sept 1945 for WAC
American Campaign	7 Dec 1941–2 March 1946
Asiatic—Pacific Campaign	7 Dec 1941–2 March 1946
European—African—Middle Eastern Campaign	7 Dec 1941—8 Nov 1945
World War II Victory Medal	7 Dec 1941—31 Dec 1946

Army of Occupation Medal. After World War II, occupation forces were established in countries which had been in possession of the enemy, pending establishment of peace or permanent agreements. Service with these occupation forces, as prescribed by AR 672–5–1, entitles an individual to award of the Army of Occupation Medal. Clasps inscribed "Germany" or "Japan" are issued with the medal to denote occupation duty rendered in Europe and/or the Far East.

The Berlin Airlift Device, awarded for service in the Berlin airlift during the period 26 June 1948—30 September 1949, is worn on the Army of Occupation Medal.

ARMY OF OCCUPATION
MEDAL AND CLASPS.

MEDAL FOR
HUMANE ACTION.

NATIONAL DEFENSE
SERVICE MEDAL.

Medal for Humane Action. Required is service for at least 120 days during the period 26 June 1948—30 September 1949 within the boundaries of the Berlin airlift operations while participating in, or in direct support of, the Berlin airlift.

National Defense Service Medal. This medal has been authorized for honorable active service for any period between 27 June 1950 and 27 July 1954, and between 1 January 1961 and August 14, 1974. A second award of this medal is designated by an Oak Leaf Cluster. Persons on active duty for purposes other than extended active duty are not eligible for this award.

Korean Service Medal. This medal is awarded for service in or in direct support of Korea during the period 27 June 1950 through 27 July 1954.

Antarctica Service Medal. The Antarctica Service Medal is awarded to persons serving with U.S. expeditions to the Antarctic from 1 January 1946 to a date to be determined by the Secretary of Defense.

Armed Forces Expeditionary Medal. This medal, established by Executive Order on 4 December 1961, is authorized for specified US military operations, US operations in direct support of the United Nations, and US operations of assistance for friendly foreign nations. Generally 30 days in the following areas of operations are required:
Berlin—From 14 August 1961 to 1 June 1963.
Lebanon—From 1 July 1958 to 1 November 1958.
Quemoy and Matsu Islands—From 23 August 1958 to 1 June 1963.
Taiwan Straits—From 23 August 1958 to 1 January 1959.
Cuba—24 October 1962 to 1 June 1963.
Congo—From 14 July 1960 to 1 September 1962, and 23–27 November 1964.
Laos—From 19 April 1961 to 7 October 1962.
Vietnam—From 1 July 1958 to 3 July 1965 and 29–30 April 1975.
Dominican Republic—From 28 April 1965 to 21 September 1966.
Korea—From 1 October 1966 to 30 June 1974.

KOREAN
SERVICE MEDAL.

ANTARCTICA
SERVICE MEDAL.

ARMED FORCES
EXPEDITIONARY
MEDAL.

Cambodia—From 29 March 1973 to 15 August 1973 and 11–13 April 1975.
Mayaguez Operation—15 May 1975
Thailand—29 March 1973 to 15 August 1973.

Vietnam Service Medal. The Vietnam Service Medal was established in Executive Order, 1 October 1965. It was awarded to servicemen serving in Vietnam or contiguous waters or air space from 3 July 1965 through 28 March 1973.

Servicemen who served in Vietnam and are qualified to wear the Armed Forces Expeditionary Medal, discussed above, are qualified to receive the newer award in lieu of the Expeditionary Medal. However, no person may be awarded both medals for Vietnam service.

Humanitarian Service Medal. Established by Executive Order 11965, 19 January 1977. It is awarded by the Secretary of Defense or by the Secretary of Transportation to members of the Coast Guard when that service is not operating as a military service in the Navy. It is awarded to members of the Armed Forces of the United States, including Reserve Components, who meritoriously participate in a military act or operation of a humanitarian nature. Award of this medal does not preclude or conflict with other medals awarded on the basis of valor, achievement, or meritorious service. However, only one medal for service may be awarded for participation in a given military act or operation. Meritorious participation in subsequent acts or operations will be recognized by award of a numeral.

Armed Forces Reserve Medal. Required is honorable and satisfactory service in one or more of the Reserve components of the Armed Forces for a period of 10 years, not necessarily consecutive, provided such service was performed within a period of 12 consecutive years. Periods of service as a member of a Regular component are excluded from consideration. Required also is the earning of a minimum of 50 retirement points per year. (AR 135–80.) Individuals are advised to consult the unit instructor of their organization as to individual eligibility.

10-year Device. One 10-year device is authorized to be worn on the suspension and service ribbon to denote service for each 10-year period in addition to and under the same conditions as prescribed for the award of the medal. It is an hour glass, bronze, with a Roman numeral "X" superimposed thereon, $\frac{5}{16}$ inch in height.

Army Reserve Components Achievement Medal. Established by DA General Orders 30, 1971, this medal may be awarded upon recommendation of the unit commander for four years of honest and faithful service on or after 3 March 1972. Service must have been consecutive, in the grade of colonel or below, and in accordance with the standards of conduct, courage and duty required by law and customs of the service of an active duty member of the same grade. The reverse of this medal is struck in two designs for award to personnel whose service has been primarily in the Army Reserve or primarily in the National Guard.

United Nations Service Medal, DOD Directive of 27 November 1951, authorized the wearing by eligible personnel of the United Nations Service Medal. It is given for service in defense of the principles of the charter of the United Nations to those who participated in the Korean campaign from 27 June 1950 to 27 July 1954.

United Nations Medal. Established by the United Nations Secretary-General, 30 July 1959, and DOD Instruction 1348.10, 11 March 1964. It is awarded

VIETNAM SERVICE
MEDAL.

HUMANITARIAN SERVICE
MEDAL.

ARMED FORCES
RESERVE MEDAL.

HOUR GLASS
DEVICE.

UNITED NATIONS
SERVICE MEDAL.

UNITED NATIONS
MEDAL.

GOOD CONDUCT
MEDAL.

for service of not less than six months with United Nations teams and forces which are in or have been in Lebanon, Palestine, India and Pakistan, and Hollandia.

Philippine Ribbons. There are three: Philippine Defense Ribbon, Philippine Liberation Ribbon, and Philippine Independence Ribbon. See AR 672-5-1.

Republic of Vietnam Campaign Medal. Authorized for award to individuals by DOD Instruction 1348.17, 31 January 1974, for 6 months service in Vietnam or in direct combat support of operations in Vietnam during the period 1 March 1961 to 28 March 1973; during this period, the recipient must have met the criteria established for the Vietnam Service Medal or the Armed Forces Expeditionary Medal (Vietnam).

Good Conduct Medal. This is a medal awarded only to enlisted personnel in recognition of exemplary behavior, efficiency, and fidelity, under prescribed conditions as to time and ratings. A distinctive clasp is awarded for each successive period of three years' service which meets the requirements.

UNITED STATES ARMY BADGES AND TABS

Badges and tabs are appurtenances of the uniform. In the eyes of their wearers several badges have a significance equal to or greater than all but the highest decorations. There is no established precedence between badges as there is with decorations and service medals, or ribbons. They are of three types: combat and special skill badges, marksmanship badges and tabs, and identification badges. Major commanders are also authorized to approve subdued cloth badges and patches for *local* adoption and *temporary* wear on the field and work uniforms in the interest of improved morale, training and esprit. Badges are awarded as recognition of attaining a high standard of proficiency in certain military skills. Subdued combat and special badges and the Ranger tab are now authorized on field uniforms.

Combat and Special Skill Badges. These include: The combat infantryman badge; combat medical badge; expert infantryman badge; expert field medical badge; parachutist badges; air assault badge; aviator and aircraft crewman badges; glider badge; diver badges; explosive ordnance disposal badges, pathfinder badge; nuclear reactor operator badges, ranger tab and the driver and mechanic badge.

Marksmanship Badges and Tabs. These include basic marksmanship qualification badges, excellence in competition badges, distinguished designation badges, the United States distinguished international shooter badge, and the President's Hundred tab.

Identification Badges. These include Presidential service badge; Vice Presidential service badge; office of the Secretary of Defense identification badge; Joint Chiefs of Staff identification badge; Army General Staff identification badge; Guard, Tomb of the Unknown Soldier identification badge; Army Student Nurse Program identification badge; Drill Sergeant identification badge; U.S. Army Recruiter badge; Career Counselor badge; the US Army Reserve Recruiter badge; and the Army National Guard Recruiter badge.

Eligibility Requirements for Combat and Special Skill Badges. These badges are awarded to denote excellence in performance of duties under hazardous conditions and circumstances of extraordinary hardship as well as special qualifications and successful completion of prescribed courses of training. (See AR 672–5–1 for details.)

Combat Infantryman Badge. Awarded to infantry personnel in the grade of colonel or below who, subsequent to 6 December 1941, satisfactorily perform duty while assigned or attached in a permanent status as a member of an infantry brigade, regiment, or smaller unit during any period such unit was engaged in active ground combat. Members of attached ranger companies are also eligible, as well as officers of other branches who command similar size infantry units under similar circumstances for 30 consecutive days. This badge is authorized for otherwise qualified Army members for service in Vietnam subsequent to 1 March 1961, in Laos from 19 April 1961 to 6 October 1962, and in Korea subsequent to 4 January 1969.

Expert Infantryman Badge. Awarded to infantry personnel who satisfactorily complete prescribed proficiency tests.

COMBAT INFANTRY BADGE.*

Combat Medical Badge. Awarded to members of the Army Medical Department, the Naval Medical Department or the Air Force Medical Service in the grade of colonel (Navy captain) or below who have satisfactorily performed medical duties while assigned or attached in a permanent status to a medical detachment of an infantry unit meeting the requirements for the Combat Infantryman Badge.

Expert Field Medical Badge. Awarded to Army Medical Service personnel who satisfactorily complete prescribed proficiency tests.

Stars for Combat Infantryman and Combat Medical Badges. The second and succeeding awards of these badges, made to recognize participation and qualification in additional wars, are indicated by the addition of stars to the basic badges.

Note that either the combat infantryman or the combat medical badge may be awarded for the same period of service in Vietnam or Laos, but not both.

Parachutist Badges. *Master Parachutist Badge.* An individual must have participated in 65 jumps, 25 with combat equipment, 4 at night; and 5 mass tactical jumps; have graduated as jumpmaster or served as jumpmaster on one or more combat jumps or on 33 non-combat jumps. He must have been rated excellent in character and efficiency and have served on jump status for not less than 36 months.

Senior Parachutist Badge. An individual must have been rated excellent in character and efficiency with participation in 30 jumps, to include 15 jumps made with combat equipment, 2 night jumps, and 2 mass tactical jumps; must have graduated from a jumpmaster course or served as jumpmaster on one or more combat jumps or 15 non-combat jumps; and must have served on jump status for not less than 24 months.

Parachutist Badge. Awarded for satisfactory completion of the course given by the Airborne Department of the Infantry School, or for participation in at least one combat jump.

Army Aviator Badges. There are nine Army Aviator Badges. Individuals who seek information on the subject are referred to the following publications:

*The Expert Infantry Badge does not have the wreath.

Glider badge

Master Parachutist

Air Assault badge

MASTER ARMY AVIATOR

FLIGHT SURGEON BADGE

EXPERT FIELD MEDICAL BADGE

EXPLOSIVE ORDNANCE DISPOSAL BADGE
(SUPERVISOR)

PATHFINDER BADGE

NUCLEAR REACTOR OPERATOR FIRST CLASS BADGE

MASTER DIVER

DRIVER AND
MECHANIC BADGE

EXPERT

SHARPSHOOTER

MARKSMAN

QUALIFICATION BADGES

AR 672–5–1, *Awards.*

AR 600–106, *Aeronautical Designation and Flying Status for Army Personnel.*

AR 600–107, *Suspension, Flying Evaluation Boards and Flight Status Selection System.*

The *Master Army Aviator Badge,* the *Senior Army Aviator Badge,* and the *Army Aviator Badge* are awarded upon satisfactory completion of prescribed training and proficiency tests as outlined in AR 600–106.

The *Master Flight Surgeon Badge,* the *Senior Flight Surgeon Badge,* and the *Flight Surgeon Badge* are awarded to Army Medical Corps officers who complete the training and other requirements prescribed by AR 600–106.

The *Master Aircraft Crewman Badge,* the *Senior Aircraft Crewman Badge,* and the *Aircraft Crewman Badge* are authorized for award to enlisted men who meet the prescribed requirements. (AR 672–5–1.)

Glider Badge. No longer awarded, but still authorized for wear by individuals who were previously awarded the badge.

Air Assault Badge. Awarded to personnel who have satisfactorily completed the prescribed proficiency tests and the standard air assault course while assigned or attached to the 101st Air Assault Division since 1 April 1974.

Divers Badges. Awarded after satisfactory completion of prescribed proficiency tests (AR 611–75).

Explosive Ordnance Disposal Badges. There are three badges under this heading, any of which may be awarded to officers: *Master Explosive Ordnance Disposal badge, Senior Explosive Ordnance Disposal badge,* and *Explosive Ordnance Disposal badge.* They are awarded to individuals assigned to duties involving the removal and disposition of explosive ammunition under hazardous conditions.

Pathfinder Badge. Awarded upon successful completion of the Pathfinder course conducted at The Infantry School.

Nuclear Reactor Operator Badges. The *Shift Supervisor Badge,* the *Operator First Class Badge,* the *Operator Second Class Badge,* and the *Operator Basic Badge* are awarded upon completing the Nuclear Power Plant Operators Course or equivalent training and after operating nuclear power plants for specific periods. The *Reactor Commander Badge* (Same as the *Shift Supervisor Badge*) is authorized for award to officers.

Ranger Tab. Awarded to any person who successfully completes a Ranger course conducted by The Infantry School.

Driver and Mechanic Badges. Awarded only to enlisted men to denote a high degree of skill in the operation and maintenance of motor vehicles.

Eligibility Requirements for Marksmanship Badges and Tabs. *Marksmanship Badges.* Only members of the Armed Forces of the United States and civilian citizens of the United States are eligible for these qualification badges. Qualification badges for marksmanship are of three types; basic qualification, excellence in competition, and distinguished designation. *"Basic qualification"* badges (including expert, sharpshooter, and marksman badges) are awarded to those individuals who attain the qualification score prescribed in the appropriate field manual for the weapon concerned. *"Excellence in competition"* badges are awarded to individuals in recognition of an eminent degree of achievement in firing the rifle or pistol. *"Distinguished designation"* badges are awarded to individuals in recognition of a preeminent degree of achievement in target practice firing with the military service rifle or pistol.

Distinguished International Shooter Badge. Awarded to military or civilian personnel in recognition of an outstanding degree of achievement in international competition.

President's Hundred. A President's Hundred Tab is awarded each person who qualifies among the top 100 contestants in the President's Match held annually at the National Rifle Matches.

Identification Badges. *Presidential Service Badge.* The Presidential Service Certificate and the Presidential Service Badge were established by Executive Order 11174, 1 September 1964.

The Presidential Service Certificate is awarded in the name of the President of the United States, as public evidence of deserved honor and distinction, to members of the Armed Forces who have been assigned to duty in the White House for at least one year subsequent to 20 January 1961. It is awarded to Army members by the Secretary of the Army upon recommendation of the Military Aide to the President.

The Presidential Service Badge is issued to members of the Armed Forces who have been awarded the Presidential Service Certificate. Once this badge is awarded, it may be worn as a permanent part of the uniform.

Vice Presidential Service Badge. The Vice Presidential Service Badge was established by Executive Order 11544, 8 July 1970. It may be awarded upon recommendation of the Military Assistant to the Vice President and may be worn as a permanent part of the uniform.

PRESIDENTIAL SERVICE BADGE   OFFICE OF THE SECRETARY OF DEFENSE IDENTIFICATION BADGE

Office of the Secretary of Defense Identification Badge. Military personnel who have been assigned to duty and have served not less than one year after 13 January 1961 in the Office of the Secretary of Defense are eligible for this badge. Once awarded, it may be worn as a permanent part of the uniform. It also is authorized for temporary wear by personnel assigned to specified offices of the Secretary of Defense.

Joint Chiefs of Staff Identification Badge. To recognize important and loyal service in positions of responsibility by members of the Armed Forces while assigned to the Organization of the Joint Chiefs of Staff for a period of at least one year after 14 January 1961, a certificate of eligibility for the JCS Identification Badge may be awarded, in the name of the Chairman of the Joint Chiefs of Staff. Once awarded, this badge may be worn as a permanent part of the uniform.

JOINT CHIEFS OF STAFF
IDENTIFICATION BADGE

DEPARTMENT OF THE ARMY
GENERAL STAFF IDENTIFICATION BADGE.

Army General Staff Identification Badge. This badge has been awarded by the Army since 1920, and is the oldest of the five types of identification badges now authorized for officers. It was instituted to give a permanent means of identification to those commissioned officers who had been selected for duty on the War Department General Staff, with recommendation for award based upon performance of duty. It has been continued under the present departmental organization.

The present requirements for award of this badge include service of not less than one year as a commissioned officer while detailed to duty on the Army General Staff and assigned to permanent duty in a designated TDA position on the Army General Staff, to the Office of the Secretary of the Army, to the National Guard Bureau, or to the Office, Chief Army Reserve. Since 30 September 1979, the badge also may be awarded to the Sergeant Major of the Army or to another Senior Staff NCO (SGM E9) position on the same staff units. Once awarded, this badge may be worn as a permanent part of the uniform.

Guard, Tomb of the Unknown Soldier Identification Badge. (See AR 672–5–1.)

Army Student Nurse Program Identification Badge. (See AR 672–5–1.)

Drill Sergeant Identification Badge. (See AR 672–5–1.)

U. S. Army Recruiter Badge. (See AR 672–5–1.)

Career Counselor Badge. (See AR 672–5–1.)

Army National Guard Recruiter Badge. (See AR 672–5–1.)

U. S. Army Reserve Recruiter Badge. (See AR 672–5–1.)

APPURTENANCES TO DECORATIONS AND SERVICE MEDALS

Appurtenances are authorized as indicated in the following paragraphs.

Oak-Leaf Cluster. A bronze (or silver) twig of four oak leaves with three acorns on the stem, is issued in lieu of a decoration for the second or succeeding awards of United States military decorations (other than the Air Medal), the National Defense Service Medal and unit awards. A silver Oak-Leaf Cluster may be worn in lieu of five bronze Oak-Leaf Clusters for the same decoration. Oak-Leaf Clusters are worn attached to the ribbons of the decorations to which they pertain with the stem of the oak leaves toward the wearer's right.

Numerals. Arabic numerals $\frac{3}{16}$ inch in height are issued in lieu of a decoration for second and succeeding awards of the Air Medal and the Humanitarian Service Medal. The numerals are centered on the ribbon of the medal and on the ribbon bar.

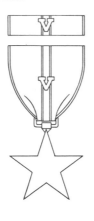

BRONZE STAR
WITH V DEVICE.

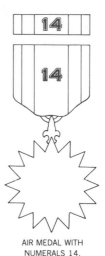

AIR MEDAL WITH
NUMERALS 14.

SERVICE RIBBON
WITH V DEVICE
AND OAK LEAF
CLUSTER.

WEARING
ARROWHEAD AND
SERVICE STARS ON
SERVICE RIBBON.

BERLIN AIRLIFT DEVICE.

Letter "V" Device. A bronze block letter "V" is worn on the suspension and service ribbons of the Bronze Star Medal, the Air Medal, the Joint Service Commendation Medal, and the Army Commendation Medal to denote an award made for valor. Not more than one "V" will be worn; when one or more clusters are on the same ribbon, the "V" is to the wearer's right.

Arrowhead Device. A bronze Arrowhead Device is awarded for wear on the appropriate service medal ribbon to signify that the wearer participated in a parachute jump, a glider landing, or an amphibious assault against enemy-held territory. The device is worn with the point upward. It is placed to the right of all service stars.

Berlin Airlift Device. A gold colored metal miniature of a C–54 type aircraft, worn on the Army of Occupation Medal to denote participation in the Berlin airlift. It is worn with the nose pointed upward toward a 30-degree angle to the wearer's right.

Service Stars. Service stars, signifying participation in a combat campaign, are worn on service medal ribbons, point of star upward. A silver star is worn in lieu of five bronze stars.

Miniatures. Miniature decorations and appurtenances are replicas of the corresponding decorations and appurtenances on the scale of one-half. Miniatures are not presented or sold by the Army but may be purchased from civilian dealers. There is no miniature of the Medal of Honor or the Legion of Merit, degree of Chief Commander and Commander.

FOREIGN DECORATIONS

The Constitution requires the consent of Congress for an individual holding a Federal office or position of trust to accept a foreign decoration. However, individuals may participate in ceremonies and receive the tender of a foreign award or gift. Foreign awards may be accepted and worn after receiving approval of Headquarters, DA (DAPC-POS-A). The foreign award with accompanying documents will be retained by the individual until the individual is informed of the final DA action. Gifts of minimal value (retail value of less than $100) may be accepted and retained by the individual. However, the burden of proof as to the value is the responsibility of the individual accepting the gift. For gifts of more than minimal value, receipt of the gift will be immediately reported through command channels to HQDA (DAPC-POS-A) and within 60 days the gift must be forwarded to the same address.

CERTIFICATES AND LETTERS FOR SERVICE

Several types of certificates may be awarded to individuals, as follows:

Certificates for Decorations. Each individual who has been awarded a decoration is entitled to a certificate, on a standard Department of the Army form, bearing a reproduction of the decoration.

Certificate of Honorable Service. The certificate (DA Form 1563) is issued to the next of kin of those who die in line of duty while on active service in time of peace. In time of war an accolade with facsimile signature of the President has been used.

Certificate of Achievement. Commanding officers may issue such a certificate in recognition of faithful service, acts, or achievements. There is no standard form, and no distinguishing device.

Letters of Commendation and Appreciation. Acts or services which do not meet the criteria for decorations or the various certificates may be recognized by letters of commendation or appreciation. Such letters, typed on letterhead stationery, may be issued to military personnel and, as specified in AR 672–20, to civilians or civilian groups.

UNIT AWARDS

Unit awards are authorized in recognition of group heroism or meritorious service, usually during a war, as a means of promoting esprit de corps. They are of the following categories: Unit decorations, Infantry and medical streamers, Campaign streamers, Campaign silver bands, and War service streamers.

United States Unit Decorations. United States unit decorations, in order of precedence shown below, have been established to recognize outstanding heroism or exceptionally meritorious conduct in the performance of outstanding services:

> Presidential Unit Citation (Army)
> Presidential Unit Citation (Navy)
> Valorous Unit Award
> Meritorious Unit Commendation
> Navy Unit Commendation
> Air Force Outstanding Unit Award

These unit awards may be worn permanently by those who served with the unit during the cited period and temporarily by those now serving in that unit.

Presidential Unit Citation (Army). The Presidential Unit Citation (Army), formerly the Distinguished Unit Citation, is awarded to units of the Armed Forces of the United States and cobelligerent nations for extraordinary heroism in action against the armed enemy occurring on or after 7 December 1941. The unit must display such gallantry, determination, and esprit de corps in accomplishing its mission under extremely difficult and hazardous conditions as to set it apart and above other units participating in the same campaign. The degree of heroism required is the same as that which would warrant award of a Distinguished Service Cross to an individual. Extended periods of combat duty or participation in a large number of operational missions, either ground or air, is not sufficient. Only on rare occasions will a unit larger than a battalion qualify for award of the decoration.

The Presidential Unit Emblem (Army) is a blue ribbon set in gold colored metal frame of laurel leaves. It is authorized for purchase and wear as a permanent part of the uniform by those individuals who served with the unit during the cited period. It may be worn temporarily by those persons now serving in that unit.

Valorous Unit Award. Criteria are the same as those for the Presidential Unit Citation except that the degree of valor required is that which would merit

PRESIDENTIAL
UNIT EMBLEM.

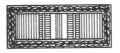

VALOROUS UNIT
EMBLEM.

MERITORIOUS
UNIT EMBLEM.

award of the Silver Star to an individual. The initial eligibility date is 3 August 1963. The emblem is a scarlet ribbon with the Silver Star color design superimposed in the center, set in a gold colored metal frame with laurel leaves.

Meritorious Unit Commendation. Awarded for at least 6 months of exceptionally meritorious conduct in support of military operations to service and support units of the Armed Forces of the United States and co-belligerent nations during the period 1 January 1944–15 September 1945, during the Korean War, and after 1 March 1961. The degree of achievement is that which would merit the award of the Legion of Merit to an individual. The emblem is a scarlet ribbon set in a gold colored metal frame with laurel leaves.

Infantry Streamers. Infantry streamers are awarded to United States infantry units which have participated in combat or which have been designated as Expert Infantry units. When 65% or more of the TOE strength of an infantry unit, brigade or smaller, has been awarded the Combat Infantryman Badge, the unit is awarded the *Combat Infantry Streamer*. It consists of a white streamer with the words "Combat Infantry (Brigade) (Battalion) (Company)" embroidered thereon in blue. The *Expert Infantry Streamer* is awarded when 65% of the TOE strength has been awarded either the Combat Infantryman Badge or the Expert Infantryman Badge. It consists of a white streamer with the words "Expert Infantry (Brigade) (Battalion) (Company)" embroidered thereon.

Combat Medical Streamer. The Combat Medical Streamer is awarded when 65% of the TOE strength of a medical unit authorized a guidon has been awarded the Combat Medical Badge. It is a maroon streamer with a $\frac{1}{16}$ inch white stripe on each edge and the words "Combat Medical Unit" embroidered in white.

Campaign Silver Bands. Campaign Silver Bands are awarded for active federal military service to units authorized a guidon to recognize award of combat credits which cannot otherwise be commemorated. They are awarded only if the company or comparable unit is not a table of organization component part of an organization which is authorized an organizational color or standard and has been awarded a campaign streamer.

Campaign Streamers and War Service Streamers. Campaign Streamers are awarded for active federal military service to organizations which are authorized an organizational color or standard, to recognize award of campaign participation credit. War Service Streamers are awarded to organizations which are authorized a color or standards to recognize active federal military service in a theater of operations.

GUIDE FOR WEARING AWARDS

The discussion which follows gathers into one place all the necessary information about wearing decorations, service medals, badges, and other devices.

When an officer wears decorations, service medals, badges, and other uniform accoutrements, he or she must be certain to wear them correctly. This means wearing them on proper occasions, on the correct garments, and in prescribed order or arrangement. There is a prescribed place and position for each item authorized in relation to others which may be worn at the same time. Metallic portions must be clean and bright, ribbons clean. Wear them correctly —or don't wear them at all!

Military tailors assemble the ribbons of decorations and service medals in rows, when a wearer is entitled to several or many, and attach them to the garments in correct position. The wearer must indicate the order of arrangement, and be certain of its accuracy upon completion. This is the simplest and best practice. They can also be assembled on pins for use on any appropriate garment.

Occasions for Wearing Decorations, Service Medals, or their Ribbons. Commanding officers may prescribe the wearing of these items at parades, reviews, inspections, funerals and on ceremonial and social occasions.

They may be worn at the option of the wearer on the service and dress uniforms on normal duty (when not prohibited) and when off duty.

Prohibited Wearing. The items are not worn when equipped for combat or simulated combat; by officers while suspended from either rank or command; by enlisted men while serving sentence of confinement; or when wearing civilian clothing. The wearing of a lapel button in the form of a miniature service ribbon may be worn.

Penalty for Unauthorized Wearing. It is a violation of law to wear decorations other than those to which an individual is entitled, or to wear their ribbons or other decoration substitutes. Serious penalties may be invoked. See AR 672–5–1.

Order of Precedence—Categories of Medals. The listing below indicates the order of precedence by category, when medals of two or more categories are worn simultaneously. The same order of precedence applies when service ribbons are worn in lieu of decorations, Good Conduct Medal, and service medals.

> United States military decorations
> United States unit awards
> United States nonmilitary decorations
> Good Conduct Medal
> United States campaign and service medals (in order earned)
> Armed Forces Reserve Medal
> Army Reserve Components Achievement Medal
> United States Merchant Marine Decorations.
> Foreign military decorations
> Foreign unit awards
> Non-US service awards
> Foreign service awards

Order of Precedence—United States Military Decorations. The listing above gives the order of precedence of different categories of medals with the United States military decorations at the top, or most honored position. United States military decorations of the Army, Navy, and Air Force are worn by Army personnel in the following order:

> Medal of Honor (Army, Navy, Air Force)
> Distinguished Service Cross
> Navy Cross
> Air Force Cross
> Defense Distinguished Service Medal
> Distinguished Service Medal (Army, Navy, Air Force, Coast Guard)
> Silver Star
> Defense Superior Service Medal

Legion of Merit
Distinguished Flying Cross
Soldier's Medal
Navy and Marine Corps Medal
Airman's Medal
Coast Guard Medal
Bronze Star Medal
Defense Meritorious Service Medal
Meritorious Service Medal
Air Medal
Joint Service Commendation Medal
Army Commendation Medal
Navy Commendation Medal
Air Force Commendation Medal
Coast Guard Commendation Medal
Army Achievement Medal
Navy Achievement Medal
Purple Heart
Combat Action Ribbon

Order of Precedence—United States Nonmilitary Decorations. These decorations may be worn on the uniform only with one or more military decorations or service medals. They are worn after the Purple Heart and before service medals. They are listed in order of precedence.

Presidential Medal of Freedom
Gold Lifesaving Medal
Medal of Merit
Silver Lifesaving Medal
National Security Medal
Medal of Freedom
Distinguished Civilian Service Medal
Outstanding Civilian Service Medal

Foreign Decorations. The wearing of foreign decorations on the uniform is governed by both law and regulations. The reader is referred to AR 672-5-1, for check of complete information as to authorized wearing of foreign decorations.

The Good Conduct Medal Worn with Other Decorations. The Good Conduct Medal takes precedence immediately after all authorized United States military and nonmilitary decorations, and immediately preceding all authorized United States Service Medals.

Order of Precedence of Service Medals. All United States service medals are worn in the order in which earned—the date upon which the person became eligible for the award. This general statement must be considered with other requirements:

The World War II Victory Medal is worn following other World War II service medals.

The following are listed in their own order of precedence:

National Defense Service Medal
Korean Service Medal
Antarctica Service Medal

Armed Forces Expeditionary Medal
Vietnam Service Medal
Humanitarian Service Medal

The Armed Forces Reserve Medal follows all United States service medals regardless of when earned.

Service medals of the United States Navy, Marine Corps, Air Force and Merchant Marine may be worn on the uniform. Others issued by state and local governments, fraternal societies, United States Maritime Service, professional groups and organizations are prohibited for wear on the uniform.

Order of Precedence, Non-US Service Medals and Ribbons.

Philippine Defense Ribbon
Philippine Liberation Ribbon
Philippine Independence Ribbon
United Nations Service Medal
United Nations Medal
Republic of Vietnam Campaign Medal

Manner of Wearing Decorations, Service Medals, Ribbons, and Badges. Full size decorations and service medals may be worn only on the Army Blue and Army White uniforms, and on the Army Green uniform when worn for social functions.

The accompanying illustrations will answer most questions about the placing of decorations and other devices upon the uniform.

The Medal of Honor is worn around the neck outside the shirt collar and inside the coat collar, the medal proper hanging over the necktie near the collar.

Other United States decorations are worn in order of precedence from wearer's right to left, and in one or more lines, $\frac{1}{8}$ inch between lines. No line will contain fewer medals than the line above it. Medals may be overlapped between lines, but not within lines; and the method is illustrated.

On men's uniforms, they will be worn immediately above the left breast pocket.

On women's uniforms, they will be worn centered on the left side of the uniform, not more than three medals in a line, and with the bottom line positioned opposite the top edge of the top button of the coat. They may be adjusted slightly to conform to individual figure differences.

Wearing of Miniatures. Only miniature decorations and service medals may be worn on the mess and evening dress uniforms. They may be overlapped, so that each medal partially covers the medal at its left, the right medal showing in full. Overlapping must be equal, and not more than a 50% overlap. See illustrations. Miniatures may also be worn on the Army White and Army Blue uniforms.

Wearing of Ribbons. Service ribbons representing decorations will be worn in the same order of precedence as the decoration, not more than four ribbons to a line, either without a space or with $\frac{1}{8}$ inch between lines, and the bottom edge of the lowest line $\frac{1}{8}$ inch above the top edge of the pocket flap for males and parallel to the top of the top coat button for females. Service ribbons will not be impregnated with unnatural preservatives nor worn with protective coverings. Purchases at Post Exchanges and Army Clothing Sales Stores are recommended.

Wearing of Badges and Tabs. There is no order of precedence for badges. The following badges may be worn on the uniform:

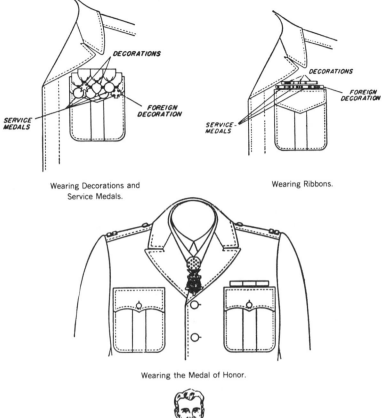

Wearing Decorations and
Service Medals.

Wearing Ribbons.

Wearing the Medal of Honor.

Wearing Miniature Decorations on Evening Dress Uniform.

WEARING DECORATIONS, SERVICE MEDALS AND RIBBONS.

(1) Military badges awarded by the Department of the Army, the Navy, and Air Force, including qualification badges issued by the Director of Civilian Marksmanship.

(2) Badges of the Regular Army and Navy Union and the Army and Navy Union of the United States.

(3) Badges pertaining to the national matches.

(4) Badges awarded by friendly foreign nations. But see AR 672–5–1. May be worn only within nation which awarded the badge.

Badges of civic and quasi-military societies may be worn while the service member is attending meetings, ceremonies and functions of such societies, but not on any other occasion—not even while proceeding to or returning from the gathering.

Limitations on Wearing Combat and Special Skill Badges and Qualification Badges. Only one badge from each of the below listed groups will be worn, except that any two badges from group four may be worn simultaneously. The total will not exceed four.

(1) Combat Infantryman Badge and Expert Infantryman Badge.

(2) Combat Medical Badge and Expert Field Medical Badge.

(3) Aviation Badges and Aircraft Crewman Badges.

(4) Parachutist Badges, Pathfinder Badge, Air Assault Badge and Glider Badge.

(5) Explosive Ordnance Disposal Badges, Divers Badges, Nuclear Reactor Operator Badges, and Driver and Mechanic Badge.

Not more than three marksmanship badges will be worn at one time. Order of precedence for wear is Distinguished International Shooter Badge, Distinguished Rifleman Badge, Distinguished Pistol Shot Badge, National Trophy Match badges, Interservice Competition badges, Excellence-in-Competion Badges, and Marksmanship Qualification Badges.

Manner of Wearing Badges. (See illustrations.) When worn with ribbons or decorations and service medals, any badge listed in (1) above will be worn centered above the top line of ribbons; any badge listed in (2) above will be worn centered above the top line of ribbons, but below any badge listed in (1) above; any badge listed in (3) above will be worn centered above the top line of ribbons, but below any badges from (1) and (2) above; if only one badge from (4) and (5) is worn, it will be centered on the pocket flap above the button —if one badge from each of (4) and (5) is worn, they will be worn on the pocket flap side by side, spaced approximately 1 inch apart; badges from (4) and (5), when worn without badges from (1), (2), or (3), will be worn above the top line of ribbons. When badges are worn without ribbons, the above applies, substituting the top of the pocket for the top line of ribbons.

Marksmanship badges and Driver and Mechanic badges are worn only on the flap of the left breast pocket or on the lower portion of the pocket when also wearing combat and special skill badges on the pocket flap.

Manner of Wearing Identification Badges. (See illustrations.) No more than two identification badges may be worn on one pocket at one time.

The Presidential Service Badge is worn as follows. *Men.* The badge will be worn centered between the bottom of the flap and the bottom of the right breast pocket. On the mess and evening uniforms it will be worn centered between the upper two buttons on the right side of the jacket. *Women.* The badge will be worn centered on the right side opposite the third button of the uniform coats. It will be worn on the Evening Dress uniform in a position comparable to that prescribed for the service uniform.

The General Staff Identification Badge is worn on the right side by both men

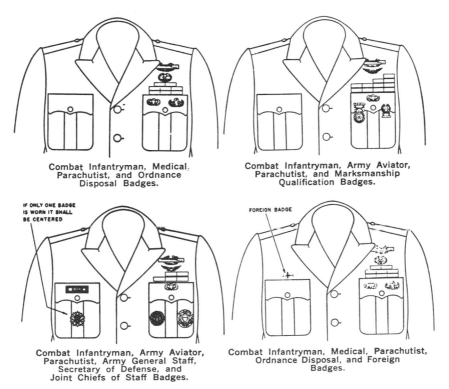

Combat Infantryman, Medical, Parachutist, and Ordnance Disposal Badges.

Combat Infantryman, Army Aviator, Parachutist, and Marksmanship Qualification Badges.

Combat Infantryman, Army Aviator, Parachutist, Army General Staff, Secretary of Defense, and Joint Chiefs of Staff Badges.

Combat Infantryman, Medical, Parachutist, Ordnance Disposal, and Foreign Badges.

Wearing Badges, Appurtenances, and Unit Emblems.

and women in the manner prescribed for the Presidential Service Badge. If both the Presidential Service Badge and the General Staff Identification Badge are authorized, they may be worn simultaneously side by side, with the Presidential Service Badge placed to the wearer's right.

The Office of the Secretary of Defense Identification Badge is worn by both men and women on the left side, but otherwise as described for the Presidential Service Badge.

The Joint Chiefs of Staff Identification Badge is worn by both men and women on the left side, but otherwise as prescribed for the Presidential Badge. If both the Joint Chiefs of Staff Identification Badge and the Office of the Secretary of Defense Identification Badge are authorized, they may be worn simultaneously side by side, with the office of the Secretary of Defense Identification Badge placed to the wearer's right.

Wearing of Other Badges and Tabs.

Foreign badges will be worn on the right side above the line of unit award emblems (see below) *only* when at least one United States medal or service ribbon is worn simultaneously, and only in nation which awarded the badge.

The Ranger Tab is worn ½ inch below the shoulder seam on the left shoulder. Organization sleeve insignia, when authorized, is worn ¼ inch below the Ranger Tab.

Wearing of Unit Award Emblems. Unit award emblems are worn on a line, centered over the right breast pocket, in the following order of precedence beginning on the wearer's right: (1) Presidential Unit Emblem (Army); (2) Presidential Unit Emblem (Navy); (3) Valorous Unit Emblem; (4) Meritorious Unit Emblem; (5) Navy Unit Commendation Emblem; (6) Air Force Outstanding Unit Emblem, with not more than three emblems per line.

Wearing of Foreign Unit Awards.

The French Fourragere is worn on the left shoulder, the cord passing under the armpit.

The Belgian Fourragere is worn on the left shoulder, the cord passing under the armpit.

The Philippine Presidential Unit Citation Badge is worn with the blue of the badge to the wearer's right over the right pocket, immediately to the left of any United States unit citation emblems.

The Republic of Korea Presidential Unit Citation Badge is worn, with the red portion of the central figure uppermost, over the right pocket to the wearer's left of the Philippine Presidential Unit Citation Badge.

The Vietnam Presidential Unit Citation Badge, the Republic of Vietnam Gallantry Cross Unit Citation Badge and the Republic of Vietnam Civil Actions Unit Citation Badge may be worn in that order, starting immediately to the left of the Republic of Korea Presidential Unit Citation Badge. No more than one Gallantry Cross and one Civil Actions Medal will be worn by any individual. This precludes wear of the Vietnamese fourrageres which represent additional awards.

Announced, but not yet described in the regulations: Outstanding Unit Commendation. Awarded for exceptionally meritorious service or achievement during peace time.

23
Authorized Absences

The Army recognizes that all personnel require periods of respite from routine duty and to permit personal attention to matters not related to the military service. The types of authorized absences from duty include leave, passes and administrative absences. It is Army policy that all personnel be encouraged to utilize their authorized leave to the maximum extent possible. Frequent utilization of leave is beneficial to health and morale which are essential to the maintenance of maximum efficiency. The judicious application of leave policies of the Army is an important command responsibility. (This chapter is based upon AR 630–5.)

DEFINITIONS AND TYPES OF LEAVE

Leave. Leave is authorized absence from place of duty, generally chargeable against the service member's leave account, for the purpose of providing the member a rest from the working environment or for other specific reasons.

Accrued Leave. Accrued leave is earned by active service performed. Leave accrues at the rate of $2\frac{1}{2}$ calendar days for each month of active service and is credited to the member's leave account. In general, the service member must be in normal performance of duties to accumulate leave credits; absence without leave and other improper acts void leave credit accumulation.

Annual Leave. Annual leave, also called ordinary leave, is absence granted at the request of a service member within the limits of accrued leave and/or that leave which may be advanced. Annual leave programs are established to provide maximum opportunity for all personnel to take leave.

Advance Leave. This is leave granted a service member, with pay and allowances, prior to its accrual based on the reasonable expectation that the amount advanced will be earned prior to the member's separation. The maximum will not exceed 45 days or $2\frac{1}{2}$ days for each month remaining in active service, whichever is lesser.

Excess Leave. Leave in excess of that which is accrued and that which may be advanced is designated as excess leave. It may be granted upon application of a service member under emergency or unusual circumstances. Excess leave when authorized will be without pay and allowances.

Leave en Route. Leave en route, formerly called delay en route, is leave granted upon request of the service member when traveling to a new station in connection with temporary duty and/or permanent change of station orders. It is charged to the member's leave account and is in addition to authorized travel time. Leave en route is authorized only by use of a leave request, DA Form 31.

Emergency Leave. Emergency leave is granted upon request of a service member when it is established that a family emergency exists requiring the member's presence. It normally is granted for a 30-day period, is chargeable to the member's leave account, and is the basis for priority travel at government expense from, to, and between oversea areas, as specified in AR 630–5. Leave within the continental United States, even though prompted by emergency circumstances, is annual leave.

Convalescent Leave. Convalescent leave for the purpose of recuperation from wounds or illness is granted by the hospital commander or by the organization commander upon recommendation of the attending physician. It normally is granted for a period not to exceed 30 days and is not charged to the member's leave account. Personnel who have incurred illness or injury in line of duty while eligible to receive hostile fire pay (Chapter 19, *Pay and Allowances*) are entitled to travel and transportation allowances for a round trip from place of hospitalization in the United States (including Hawaii and Alaska) to a selected place that is approved by the Secretary of the Army or his designee.

Prenatal and Postpartum Leave. An individual who becomes pregnant while on active duty will continue to perform duty during the prenatal period until such time as duty is no longer considered feasible by the attending physician. Time spent in the hospital for delivery is duty time. Following completion of inpatient care, the member will be granted convalescent leave until her medical condition permits her to return to duty, normally not to exceed 6 weeks after her release from the hospital.

Rest and Recuperation Leave. Rest and recuperation (R&R) leave is granted in conjunction with R&R programs established in those areas designated for hostile fire pay, when military considerations preclude full execution of annual leave programs. One R&R leave is permitted each 12-month period. Military transportation to and from R&R areas is provided on a space-required basis, with time spent in travel status considered duty time. The leave period in the R&R area is charged to the member's leave account.

Environmental and Morale Leave. Environmental and morale leave is granted in conjunction with an environmental and morale leave program established at oversea installations where adverse environmental conditions exist which offset the full benefit of annual leave programs. It differs from R&R leave in that military transportation is on a space-available rather than a space-required basis and the entire period of absence, including travel time, is chargeable to the member's leave account.

Graduation Leave, USMA. This is leave granted at the time of graduation from the United States Military Academy and is not chargeable to accrued leave, or to leave to be accrued in the future. It is limited to 30 days. Leave taken in excess of 30 days is chargeable to advance leave.

Leave Awaiting Orders. Leave which may be granted to a service member while awaiting orders pending final action on disability retirement proceedings and which is chargeable as ordinary leave, to the maximum extent possible.

LEAVE COMPUTATION AND LEAVE REQUEST

Computation. The day of departure on and the day of return from leave will not be counted as days of leave if the member is at his or her place of work and performs duty for at least three-fourths of the normal workday. Otherwise, these days will be charged to leave. If the day of departure is a non-duty day, that day will be charged to leave regardless of the hour of departure. If the day of return from leave is a non-duty day, that day will not be charged to leave regardless of the hour of return.

Requests for Leave. Leave may be granted only upon request by the individual concerned. DA Form 31 is used as request for leave and as the document authorizing leave. See illustration.

Extension of Leave. A request for extension of leave may be submitted by any convenient means. It must include specific reasons for justification of the extension, the period of extension desired, and current leave address. Normally, such requests are submitted to the authority granting the original leave. However, a Personnel Assistance Office has been established at MILPERCEN with authority to extend leaves. Call Autovon 221–0170 or write Commander, U.S. Army MILPERCEN, ATTN: DAPC-MSF-M, 200 Stovall Street, Alexandria, VA 22332. For unusual cases see AR 630–5.

Limitations on Cash Settlements and Leave Accruals. Personnel may accumulate up to 60 days of accrued leave. Accrued leave in excess of 60 days is lost at the end of the fiscal year. It is Army policy to have its members make full use of the leave time to which they are entitled. At the time of separation or retirement, unused leave up to 60 days will be compensated by a final payment.

Individual Record of Leave Accruals and Leaves Taken. The commander having custody of the individual personnel record is responsible for the accurate maintenance of leave records.

Leave taken and leave credited will be accounted for on a fiscal year basis. When only a part of the fiscal year is considered, leave will be credited at the rate of $2\frac{1}{2}$ days for each month of active service.

Leave of absence which commences in one and is completed in another fiscal year will be apportioned to the fiscal year in which each portion falls and charged accordingly.

PASSES

A pass, as differentiated from leave, is an authorized absence from post or place of duty for a relatively short time. A pass is a privilege when granted by a commander, but is not a right to which one is entitled.

REQUEST AND AUTHORITY FOR LEAVE

For use of this form, see AR 630-5; the proponent agency is US Army Military Personnel Center.
(See Instructions on Reverse)

PART - I

1. NAME (Last, First, Middle)	2. SOCIAL SECURITY NO.	3. PAY GRADE	4. DATE	5. CONTROL NO.

6. ORGANIZATION AND STATION	7. TYPE OF ABSENCE	8. DATES

7. TYPE OF ABSENCE
a. ☐ ORDINARY LEAVE
b. ☐ OTHER (Specify) _____

8. DATES
a. FROM   b. TO

9. NO. OF DAYS LEAVE	10. NO. OF DAYS ACCRUED LEAVE	11. NO. OF DAYS ADVANCED LEAVE	12. NO. OF DAYS EXCESS LEAVE

13. LEAVE ADDRESS (Include ZIP Code and Telephone No.)	14. SIGNATURE OF REQUESTOR	15. SUPERVISOR RECOMMENDATION

15. SUPERVISOR RECOMMENDATION
☐ APPROVAL   ☐ DISAPPROVAL
SIGNATURE

16. NAME, TITLE, ORGANIZATION OF APPROVING AUTHORITY	17. SIGNATURE OF APPROVING AUTHORITY

18. DATE/TIME OF DEPARTURE	19. NAME/TITLE OF AUTHENTICATING AUTHORITY	20. SIGNATURE OF AUTHENTICATING AUTHORITY

21. EXTENSION (No. of days and date approved) APPROVING AUTHORITY

22. DATE/TIME OF RETURN	23. NAME/TITLE OF AUTHENTICATING AUTHORITY	24. SIGNATURE OF AUTHENTICATING AUTHORITY

PART - II

APPLICABLE TO AUTHORIZED TRAVEL ONLY

25. SO, LO, DA FORM 662 OR AUTHORITY FOR TRAVEL

26.

INSTRUCTIONS FOR SERVICING STATION/ORGANIZATION
(APOE, APOD, TDY Station, Others)
DATE/TIME STAMP WHEN SERVICE MEMBER ARRIVES/DEPARTS YOUR STATION/ORGANIZATION

a. ARRIVE STATION 1	b. DEPART STATION 1	c. ARRIVE STATION 2	d. DEPART STATION 2
e. ARRIVE STATION 3	f. DEPART STATION 3	g. ARRIVE STATION 4	h. DEPART STATION 4

27. DATE/TIME OF ARRIVAL	28. NAME OF GAINING/PARENT ORGANIZATION	29. SIGNATURE OF AUTHENTICATING AUTHORITY

30. REMARKS:

DA FORM 31, 1 OCT 73   EDITION OF 1 AUG 65 IS OBSOLETE.

Regular. Regular passes may be granted to deserving individuals for those periods when they are not required to be physically present with their unit. Normally, regular passes are valid only during specified off-duty hours.

Special. Special passes may be of 3-day (72-hour) or 4-day (96-hour) duration. The 3-day special pass period may include non-duty days, but must include at least one duty day. The 4-day special pass period must include at least two consecutive non-duty days. Special passes may be granted to deserving individuals on special occasions or in special circumstances as specified in AR 630–5.

Pass forms are not required by any military personnel.

Limitations. A pass will not be issued to an individual so that two or more passes are effective in succession, or used in series through reissue immediately after return to duty. They will not be granted in conjunction with leave. They will not be combined with a public holiday or with a nonduty weekend when the combined period of continuous absence will exceed 72 hours for the 3-day pass or 96 hours for the 4-day pass.

Such absences in compliance with all of the above are not chargeable against accrued leave.

When it is desired to extend a period of absence granted as a pass beyond 72 hours for a regular or 3-day special pass or 96 hours for a 4-day special pass, the entire period of continuous absence is converted to leave, except that portion, if any, which, at the beginning of the absence, was during an off-duty or regular pass period.

OTHER ABSENCES

An individual may be away from post or place of duty without being considered as in a leave status or on pass.

Administrative Absence. Examples are activities of a semi-official nature such as medical, ecclesiastical, professional or scientific, or participation in competitive sports events such as those sponsored by the Army. These absences are without expense to the government.

Proceed Time. Proceed time, not to exceed 4 days, may be granted for the purpose of allowing the military member to accomplish necessary processing prior to departing the old duty station and after arrival at the new duty station. It is designed to provide the individual an adequate period of absence from duty to attend to the details of changing and arranging a residence, auto licensing, voting registration, tax and similar personal matters. It is not intended as time to process on or off post, which are to be accomplished during normal working hours. Proceed time is duty time for record purposes and is granted consistent with the needs of the individual and military operational requirements. When granted, it will immediately precede the date the individual officially departs the old duty station and will commence immediately subsequent to signing in at the new duty station. It may not be granted as a substitute for leave or pass, nor to personnel being reassigned at the same station, between two stations in CONUS, between two stations in an oversea command in proximity to one another, nor incident to assignment to the member's first duty station, or separation, release from active duty or retirement.

HOLIDAYS

Public holidays, established by law and listed below, will be observed except when military operations prevent. When such holidays fall on a Saturday, the preceding Friday will also be considered a holiday, and when such holidays fall on Sunday, the succeeding Monday will also be considered a holiday.

Holiday	Date Observed
New Year's Day	1 January
Washington's Birthday	3rd Monday in February
Memorial Day	Last Monday in May
Independence Day	4 July
Labor Day	1st Monday in September
Columbus Day	2nd Monday in October
Veterans Day	11 November
Thanksgiving Day	4th Thursday in November
Christmas Day	25 December

While not classified as public holidays, the following have special significance to the Army and are observed as directed by local commanders or the Department of Defense.

Army Birthday, 14 June.
Armed Forces Day, third Saturday in May.
Flag Day, 14 June.

VISITING AREAS OUTSIDE THE UNITED STATES

Specific permission must be obtained by active duty personnel to visit foreign countries and to visit territories or possessions of the United States unless assigned to duty therein.

Reporting requirements, authorized clothing which may be worn, and documents which must be in the member's possession vary from country to country. Readers are advised to consult AR 630–5 and to initiate action to obtain permission for the visit well in advance of the intended leave date.

24

Rights,
Privileges,
and Restrictions

A citizen who enters the military service undergoes at once a change in legal status. He or she assumes additional hazards, obligations, and responsibilities. They are balanced by the grant of additional benefits. Think about it. The military service cannot be "democratic" in operation. It cannot be managed, led, or directed efficiently if the whim of each individual is to be honored. Members must go as directed to the station assigned and perform their duties as their orders require. Military efficiency requires the imposition of restrictions and, in return, there is the grant of rights and privileges. They pertain to military status during and after military service. Thus former members enjoy "veterans benefits," while retired members enjoy benefits but are restricted from dealings which might impair the functioning of those still active. The laws bestowing rights, privileges, and restrictions must be in a reasonable balance in our Republic.

This chapter seeks to illuminate this important subject which is so widely misunderstood. The chapter is not all inclusive, nor could it be. But it establishes sound principles for reasoning, and it provides a large number of examples of importance to Army officers. These examples should enable the reader to fit other benefits or requirements into the pattern established.

MILITARY STATUS

The sum of these factors constitutes a definite part of the military way of life. When a citizen assumes the office of an officer, or becomes a soldier, that individual must become informed on these matters and continue to keep his or her understanding current because laws, regulations, local orders and customs change with the passage of time.

Justification for Benefits. There are strong reasons for the granting of military rights and privileges, which herein are called benefits. Those citizens who are members of the Army, Navy, Marines, or Air Force have the primary mission of protecting and preserving the Constitution including our free institutions and way of life; the prosecution of wars with the incident hazard; and the service of the Federal Government wherever duty is directed. They give up many freedoms of choice which the civilian takes for granted and which, if denied, would be considered unreasonable.

The development of an efficient military system depends upon the volunteers who are the Regulars. They are backed up by the several categories of Reserves, also volunteers, many of whom serve extended tours with the active Army. Volunteers will not be obtained in the numbers required or the quality necessary unless the conditions of their life and lot are acceptable. If unacceptable it must be presumed they would choose another vocation or avocation. Beset as we are by international strains and recurrent wars, our country needs as its first essential the armed force necessary to protect itself; and this armed force must be strong enough, brave enough, and proud enough to do its job. The expansion of the Army officer corps during emergencies must continue into the greater numbers a moral fiber which is tough and resilient.

A phase of this subject invariably overlooked by the critic of things military is that even in wartime officers of the Regular and Reserve components are volunteers. *As long as the nation has the need of the best military leadership of all grades and ages, it will be pleased to recognize this condition by granting appropriate benefits, first to attract them to service, and then to hold them.*

There is an inescapable difference between the individual in civilian employment and the member of the service. The civilian may quit or refuse a task with no greater penalty than loss of employment, being thereafter free to choose another job, even to be sustained on relief funds. But the wearer of the uniform can do so only at the peril of punishment by action of court-martial which, if refusal or cowardice before an enemy is involved, may result in a death penalty.

We may hope that the voices raised periodically against military benefits, always louder when danger is remote, will grow dim through a proper understanding.

Justification for Restrictions. There is a sufficient case also for the imposing of restrictions upon military people, especially officers, which are not borne by civilians.

The Government must have a clearly defined power to deploy its forces and require individuals to perform specific missions, however unpleasant or hazardous such locations or duties may become.

The Government must insist upon full service of its officers and thus is justified in defining and prohibiting improper outside activities of individuals.

Since procurement officers and others in the business end of government have many prerogatives incident to the letting of contracts, the Government must require high standards of ethics as well as clearly codified methods of conducting these affairs.

In order to assure fair treatment for all, and prevention of abuses in the exercise of federal power, limitations must be placed on authority especially in the field of punishments, sentences of courts-martial, and the like.

Let no one rebel inwardly over these restrictions in principle. Whenever circumstances change so as to make them unnecessary they are removed.

RIGHTS

You cannot possibly have a broader basis for any government than that which includes all the people, with their rights in their hands, and with an equal power to maintain their rights.—William Lloyd Garrison.

Let us be sure in this military way of life of our meaning in this matter of rights. To do so, if followed by consideration of some examples, will identify many benefits in their true perspective. It will be seen that while there are many obligations of service there are not many actual rights.

Definition. The dictionary helps only a little. We must contrive our own definition. A right in the sense of this discussion is a benefit established for military people by federal law. Unless a benefit is established by law, in contrast to a department regulation which is subject to administrative change or withdrawal, it is something less than a right.

Acquisition of Military Rights. A citizen who has subscribed to the oath of office as an officer, or oath of enlistment if an enlisted person, becomes entitled at once to certain rights of military service; for example, the right to wear the uniform. Other rights accrue only by completing specified requirements; example, the right to retire after completing a stipulated period of service.

The Right to Wear the Uniform. Members of the military service have the right to wear the uniform of their service. That the department may require the wearing of the uniform off duty as well as on duty is beside the point. First of all, it is a right.

Members of the Reserve components on inactive status, retired personnel, and former members of the services who have been honorably separated have the right to wear the uniform only at stipulated times or circumstances and unless these conditions exist the right is denied. Chapter Twenty-One describes these conditions fully.

The Right of Officers to Command. In the commission granted an officer by the President will be found these words: *". . . And I do strictly charge and require those Officers and other personnel of lesser rank to render such obedience as is due an officer of this grade and position."* The commission itself may be regarded as the basic document which gives military officers the right to exercise command and to exact obedience to proper orders.

Army Regulation 600–20, as to the Army, establishes this right in further detail, along with definite restrictions on this right.

Warrant officers, when assigned duties as station, unit or detachment commander, are vested with all powers usually exercised by commissioned officers except as indicated in AR 600–20.

The Right to Draw Pay and Allowances. Pay scales for grade and length of service are established by law. See Chapter Nineteen, *Pay and Allowances,* and Chapter Twenty, *Travel Allowances.*

The rights as to pay and allowances may be suspended, in part, by action of a court-martial or forfeited in part by absence without leave.

The Right to Receive Medical Attention. Members of the military service are entitled to receive appropriate medical or dental care for the treatment of their wounds, injuries, or disease. In fact, refusal to accept treatment ruled to be necessary may be punishable by courts-martial.

The Right to Individual Protection Afforded by The Uniform Code of Military Justice. All members of the military service are under the jurisdiction established by the Articles of the Uniform Code of Military Justice. Many persons regard the Manual for Courts-Martial, United States, which contains these articles, merely as the authorization of courts-martial and the implementation of their procedures as a means of maintaining discipline or awarding punishment for crime. This is a shallow view. Except for the punitive articles, Nos. 77 to 134, incl., UCMJ, they pertain in considerable measure to the protection of individual rights. Here are samples:

No person may be compelled to incriminate himself/herself before a military court.
No person shall without his/her consent be tried a second time for the same offense.
Cruel and unusual punishments of every kind are prohibited.
While the punishment for a crime or offense is left to the discretion of the court, it shall not exceed such limits as the President may from time to time prescribe.

The Right to Administer Oaths. Article 136 of the Uniform Code of Military Justice establishes the right of designated persons on active military duty to administer oaths. (See AR 600–11.)

The Soldiers' and Sailors' Relief Act. The Soldiers' and Sailors' Relief Act, passed in 1940 and still in effect, has for its purposes the relief of draftees, enlistees, and reservists on active duty of some of the pressure of heavy financial obligations they may have assumed in civil life. Of importance to officers on active duty, the Act protects military personnel from double taxation in such cases as state income taxes, automobile licenses, etc.

The Right to Obtain a Home Loan. The Federal Housing Authority (FHA) can guarantee to a mortgage company that an in-Service loan will be paid by an officer on active duty or the government will pay it. This home loan program applies principally to officers who do not have a Veteran's Administration (VA) loan entitlement and who have 2 or more years on active duty. Those who have served in wars or conflicts (Korea, Vietnam), recognized by Congressional act, may receive a home loan guaranteed by the VA. An officer is a good credit risk because of his or her high principles and stabilized income. See Chapter 7, *Financial Planning*.

The Right of Equal Opportunity. It is a policy of the Army to conduct all of its activities in a manner which is free from racial discrimination, and which provides equal opportunity and treatment of all uniformed members irrespective of their race, color, religion, or national origin. This applies to on-duty matters and off-duty situations including on-post housing, transportation, facilities, and schooling. AR 600–21 prescribes the regulations which carry out the principles of Title II of The Civil Rights Act, 1964. Strict compliance with these regulations is more than a matter of law, it is a matter of good leadership resulting in the willing service of each service member.

Redress of Wrong. Each of the armed services provides a procedure by which any member of the military service may seek redress of wrong. Each officer should become fully acquainted with this matter. An officer may have occasion to register an official objection, or complaint, with respect to personal treatment although such occasions should be rare since most officers complete their entire service without finding it necessary to use this privilege. But he or she should certainly know that juniors also enjoy this right and if the officer takes action which is grossly injurious to an individual, or so considered, he or she may be obliged to endure the process as the injuring party rather than the injured. (Article 138, Uniform Code of Military Justice).

The Right to File Claims for Losses Incident to Service. The Military Personnel Claims Act (AR 27–20) establishes the right of military personnel on active duty to file claims for losses to personal property incident to military service.

A claim for loss may be submitted for consideration and in proper cases will be approved for payment. Examples of claims which are covered are as follows:

(1) Damage to property located at quarters or other authorized place from fire, flood, hurricane or other serious occurrence;

(2) Transportation losses (see Chapter Twenty);

(3) Marine or aircraft disaster;

(4) Enemy action or public service;

(5) Money held in trust for others, and personal funds, under some conditions; and

(6) Motor vehicles lost when used in mandatory performance of military duty and during authorized shipment overseas.

Caution: In order to secure reimbursement for losses it is necessary to establish the facts and immediately upon an occurrence which may justify a claim the interested individual should set about the task of collecting essential documents, statements of witnesses, or other matters which will be of assistance in supporting the claim.

The Right to Vote. Legislation enacted by the Congress in 1955 establishes the right of voting by members of the armed forces and commanding officers are required to establish facilities for absentee voting for members of their commands. See AR 608–20.

The Right to Retire. After satisfying specific requirements of honorable service, or having endured physical disability beyond a fixed degree, officers of the armed forces have the right to retire.

The Right to be Buried in a National Cemetery. The rights of a deceased serviceman or woman to be buried in a National Military Cemetery are discussed in Chapter Seven, *Financial Planning.*

PRIVILEGES

In the discussion of rights of military people, it was argued that unless a benefit were established by federal law it was something less than a right. There are other benefits of importance. For the most part they are granted or authorized by departmental regulations. Some have been established through custom and with respect to such privileges reference is made to Chapter Five, *Customs of the Service.* Some important privileges are granted by civilian communities, churches, clubs, and fraternal organizations.

Now let us examine some examples. The list is illustrative only and could not be complete. But its analysis will enable the reader to identify others and classify them as genuine or assumed accordingly.

Post Exchange, Commissary, Theater, and Medical Privileges. Authorized patrons and their family members, must qualify themselves as to eligibility for the receipt of certain benefits such as obtaining medical service by family members, patronage of post exchange or commissary, attendance at theaters of the Army and Air Force Exchange Service, and others. Possession and display of the correct Personnel Identification Card is necessary. (AR 606–5).

The Privileges of Rank and Position. That "rank has its privileges" (RHIP) is a saying as old as armies. It is the deference extended in all walks of life to one's elders or seniors. It is no more nor less pronounced, although it may be more codified, than among faculty members, or in a business establishment, a legislative body, or among doctors, lawyers, ministers. Throughout Chapter Four,

Military Courtesy, and Chapter Five, *Customs of the Service,* will be found numerous examples.

Leave of Absence. Under current laws and regulations military people become entitled to accumulate leave and to take it when their duties permit. This is merely the civilian vacation. See Chapter Twenty-Three, *Authorized Absences.* But people in uniform must apply for permission to take leave from their stations and duties regardless of its accumulation to their credit. Application may be denied. The training or tactical situation will govern the decision. If service members absent themselves without this permission they are subject to forfeiture of pay and to disciplinary action. Hence it is a privilege.

Political Activities and Election to Public Office. An officer who considers entering political activity of any kind whatever should study most carefully AR 600–20 in its latest change or issue. See also Article 88, Uniform Code of Military Justice.

Members of the Army while on active duty will not use their official authority or influence for the purpose of interfering with an election or affecting the course or outcome thereof. They are not permitted to participate in any way in political management or political campaigns. This includes the making of political speeches, activity at political conventions or on political committees, the publication of articles, or any other activity looking to the influencing of an election or the solicitation of votes for themselves or others.

Membership in Officers' Clubs and Messes. All officers assigned at a station have the privilege of membership in the open mess (club and mess). They must follow the rules of the mess as to payment of dues, bills, and other matters and unless they do so this privilege may be curtailed or denied.

The Privilege of Writing for Publication. The professional Army officer who has ideas or experience of great importance to the nation, or a high degree of interest to our citizens, should grasp the opportunity to write for service magazines or journals, magazines of general circulation, or in books. It is the only means of making known the point of view of the military professional; just as it is also the only means for expanding sources of information and reference on military subjects. An active duty or a retired officer may with complete propriety write for publication. Official regulations are not especially restrictive. It is the only way we can continue to develop a military literature. There is ample precedent for it. Articles of military interest are sought by service journals. Stackpole Books, publishers of *The Army Officer's Guide,* has produced a large number of books written by military authors.

Nor need the field be restricted to military subjects. The entire field from history to almanacs is available.*

When will the military author write for publication? He or she will regard writing as a hobby and devote such time to it as others will utilize for their hobbies such as gardening, woodworking, photography, golf, bridge, the movies, just sitting around, and so on. If time does not permit, an officer does not write. Certainly it must not interfere with the performance of duty.

Here is the departmental policy, as announced in AR 600–20: The policy of the Department of Defense, is that military personnel who desire to engage in public writing for personal profit are on an exact parity with civilian profes-

---

*See also Sec. II, AR 360—5 which details Army policies and cautions members of the Army to "exercise good judgment."

sional writers so far as accessibility to classified current technical or operational military information is concerned. This policy covers military personnel on active duty, retired persons, and members of the Reserve components. Further, an officer may use his or her military title as author, as authorized specifically in AR 600–50.

Officers desiring to write on military subjects must obtain the approval of the Chief of Public Information, Department of the Army prior to furnishing a manuscript to the publisher except for articles for service journals and official Army publications. Material prepared for service journals may be prepared as an official duty utilizing military facilities and clerical help. Manuscripts will be submitted for review and clearance as to security of safeguarded information to the Chief of Public Information at least 15 days in advance of the proposed release. It is wise to allow even more time. The officer should work with the local information officer in processing the manuscript. There is no charge for this review.

Retired Officers and Military Writing. There is no requirement that retired Army personnel submit writings and public statements for official review. If material they prepare may violate security regulations, they may submit it for review to the Chief of Public Information, Department of the Army, Washington D.C., 20310. Retired officers who write on military subjects are advised to consult DA Pam 600–5.

Authorized Use of Military Titles After Retirement. Retired Army members not on active duty are permitted to use their military titles socially, and in connection with commercial enterprises subject to precise restrictions. Retired officers who wish to use their military titles in connection with their employment or a commercial enterprise are advised to consult DA Pam 600–5. Of course, they must never be used in any manner which would bring discredit upon the Army.

See also Chapter 4, *Military Courtesy,* under "The Correct Use of Titles."

Authors of material for publication may use their military titles while on either extended active duty or in inactive status. Clearance by the Department of Defense is required prior to publication. (AR 600–50.)

See the discussion under *Restrictions,* below, wherein the authority to use military titles in connection with a commercial enterprise is prohibited for personnel on extended active duty.

Inventions and Incentive Awards. Active duty personnel may seek to supplement their income through inventions and suggestions. In the case of inventions, AR 27–60 prescribes the techniques of obtaining a patent while in service and a pamphlet is available from the Commissioner of Patents, Washington, D. C., pertaining to all citizens.

The Army Incentive Awards Program is detailed in AR 672–20 which provides for cash awards for adopted suggestions which result in tangible monetary savings. These can be ideas for improving procedures as well as inventions pertaining to materiel. This privilege is infrequently used by officers whose ideas and inventions are eagerly sought by the Army. Scientific achievements are also awarded but most officers could take advantage of the idea category without any specialized or technical background.

Concessions and Scholarships at Civilian Educational Institutions. Several civilian educational institutions offer concessions to Army children and grant scholarships to discharged enlisted personnel of the Regular Army whose record and educational qualifications warrant the action. Consult the unit personnel officer, and see DA Pam 352–2.

For scholarships or loans to college-bound Army children, see the discussion in Chapter Seven, *Financial Planning.*

RESTRICTIONS

There are many *Thou Shalt Nots* in the military life. They consist for the most part of restrictions or standards of conduct inapplicable to the civilian. Some are contained in federal laws. Others are in departmental regulations. A few are included only in observed customs. See also Chapter Five, *Customs of the Service,* and Chapter Fourteen, *Evaluation Reports.*

They need not be regarded as onerous. They have come about through experience and necessity. In any event they are well balanced by the military benefits which have been discussed. Since their violation would be regarded as a serious matter, at the worst resulting in trial by a court martial, officers should know of them. The list herein is not represented to be complete. There are certainly many more. For example, local commands often find it necessary to prescribe restrictive orders. But they serve as examples and establish a pattern.

Effect of Conduct Unbecoming an Officer and a Gentleman, or Lady. The 133d Article, Uniform Code of Military Justice, reads as follows: *Any officer, cadet, or midshipman who is convicted of conduct unbecoming an officer and a gentleman shall be punished as a court-martial may direct.*

There are certain moral attributes which belong to the ideal officer and the gentleman or lady, a lack of which is indicated by acts of dishonesty or unfair dealing, of indecency or indecorum, or of lawlessness, injustice, or cruelty. Not every one can be expected to meet ideal standards or to possess the attributes in the exact degree demanded by the standards of the time; but there is a limit of tolerance below which the individual standards in these respects of an officer or cadet cannot fall without his or her being morally unfit to be an officer or cadet or to be considered a gentleman or lady. This article contemplates such conduct by an officer or cadet which, taking all the circumstances into consideration, satisfactorily shows such moral unfitness.

This article includes acts made punishable by any other articles of the UCMJ, provided such acts amount to conduct unbecoming an officer and a gentleman or lady; thus, an officer who embezzles military property violates both this and the preceding article.

Instances of violation of this article are: Knowingly making a false official statement; dishonorable neglect to pay debts; opening and reading another's letters without authority; giving a check on a bank where the officer knows or reasonably should know there are no funds to meet it, and without intending that there should be; using insulting or defamatory language to another officer in his or her presence, or about the officer to other military persons; being grossly drunk and conspicuously disorderly in a public place; public association with notorious prostitutes; failing without a good cause to support one's family.

Liability Regarding Classified Documents. By the very nature of their duties, officers are required to have possession of and to utilize secret, confidential, and other classified or specially restricted documents. Officers must be mindful of the restrictions placed upon such documents and the punitive action which may be taken against them for their improper handling or use.

AR 380–5, *Department of the Army Information Security Program,* is the principal source of instructions. The inclusion of classified military information in any article, speech or discussion by a member of the Army of the United States is prohibited unless specifically authorized by the Department of the Army. Additional information may be found in AR 600–20.

The statute which governs the subject is quoted below.

"Whoever, being entrusted with or having lawful possession or control of any document, writing code book, signal book, sketch, photograph, photographic negative, blueprint, plan, map, model, note, or information, relating to the national defense, through gross negligence permits the same to be removed from its proper place of custody or delivered to anyone in violation of his trust, or to be lost, stolen, abstracted, or destroyed, shall be punished by imprisonment for not more than ten years and may, in the discretion of the court, be fined not more than $10,000. (June 5, 1917, c. 30, Title I, Sec. 1; 40 Stat. 217. Act of March 28, 1940; Public No. 443, 76th Congress. 3d Session.)"

Keeping of Personal Diary Containing Classified Information Restricted. An officer who keeps a personal diary in which he or she records classified information is in violation of departmental orders.

Participation in Public Demonstrations. Participation by members of the Army in public demonstrations, not sanctioned by competent authority, including those pertaining to civil rights, is prohibited:

(1) During the hours they are required to be present for duty.
(2) When they are in uniform.
(3) When they are on a military reservation.
(4) When they are in a foreign country.
(5) When their activities constitute a breach of law and order.
(6) When violence is reasonably likely to result.

Clearly the principles are twofold: the demonstration is not to receive an official Army sanction nor is the Army to be discredited by the presence of a member. (See AR 600–20)

Officers Subject to Fine by Action of Commanding Officer. Non-judicial punishment is exercised by authority of Article 15, UCMJ, using *The Manual for Courts-Martial, United States,* as amended, paragraph 131b (1) (b) of which prescribes the authorized punishment upon officers, if imposed by a general officer or officer exercising general courts martial jurisdiction, as forfeiture of half pay for two months, or detention of half pay for 3 months.

Restrictions of an Officer Under Arrest. An officer in arrest (AR 633–30)—

Cannot exercise command of any kind.
Will restrict himself/herself as directed.
Will not bear arms.
Will not visit his/her commanding officer or other superior officer, unless directed to do so.
Will make requests of every nature in writing, unless otherwise directed.
Will, unless otherwise directed, fall in and follow in the rear of his/her organization at formations and on the march.

Effect of Disrespectful Language Concerning Certain Government Officials. The 88th Article, UCMJ, reads as follows: *Any officer who uses contemptuous words against the President, Vice President, Congress, Secretary of Defense, or a Secretary of a Department, a Governor or a legislature of any State, Territory, or other possession of the United States in which he is on duty or present shall be punished as a court-martial may direct.*

It is an act of wisdom to refrain from critical comments publicly expressed about former civilian officials. The officer must support with equal zeal leaders of either major political party when they are in positions of responsibility and power. Criticism of a former official may be interpreted as a statement with political intent.

Officers on active duty retain the right to vote, to express their opinions privately and informally on all political subjects and candidates, and, in certain cases, to become candidates for public office. See AR 600–20. Active participation in other political activities is strictly limited.

Restrictions on Use of Military Titles, Active Duty Personnel. Military titles may not be used in connection with a commercial enterprise by individuals on active duty. This applies specifically to Regular personnel of the active list, and Retired and Reserve component personnel on extended active duty. *Exception:* Authorship of material for publication is exempted from this provision, but such material is subject to review and clearance by the Department of Defense. See AR 600–50 and the preceding discussion, *Privileges.*

Restrictions on Outside Activities. Officers of the Army will not engage in or permit their names to be connected with any activity, participation in which is incompatible with the status of an officer of the Army. (AR 600–20 and 600–50.)

Acting as Attorney or Agent. No member of the Military Establishment on the active list or on active duty, or a civilian employee of the Army or of the Department of the Army, whose official duties are concerned with patent activities shall act as agent or attorney in connection with the inventions or patent rights of others, except when such action is a part of the official duties of the person so acting. (AR 27–60.)

Restrictions on Representing Clients. An officer previously assigned to military duty is disqualified for life after the time such service has ceased from representing in any manner or capacity any interest opposed to the United States with which he or she was directly connected during government service. There is also a 2-year ban on representing anyone on a matter which was previously under the officer's official responsibility.

Acting as Consultant for Private Enterprise Prohibited. No member of the Military Establishment on the active list or on active duty, or a civilian employee of the Army or of the Department of the Army, shall act as a consultant for a private enterprise with regard to any matter in which the Government is interested. (AR 600–50.)

Stoppages of Pay. The pay of officers may be withheld under section 1766 of the Revised Statutes on account of indebtedness to the United States.

Contributions or Presents to Superiors Prohibited. Military and civilian personnel of the Department of the Army will not solicit a contribution from other government employees, military or civilian, for a gift to an official superior; will not make a donation as a gift to an official superior; and will not accept a gift from other government personnel subordinate to themselves. However, voluntary gifts or contributions of nominal value are permitted on special occasions such as marriage, transfer, illness or retirement, provided any gifts acquired with such contributions shall not exceed a nominal value.

Acceptance of Gratuities Prohibited. The acceptance of gratuities by either military or civilian personnel of the Department of the Army, or members of their families, from those who have or seek business with the Department of Defense or from those whose business interests are affected by Department functions is forbidden. Such acceptance, no matter how innocently tendered or received may be a source of embarrassment to the Army, may affect the objective judgment of the personnel involved, and may impair the public confidence in the integrity of the government. With certain limited exceptions, DA personnel will not solicit, accept, or agree to accept any gratuity for themselves, members of their families, or others, either directly or indirectly from any source with business interests of the type noted above. The exceptions are detailed in AR 600–50. Officers are urged to study the regulation so as to be fully aware of both the details and the philosophy involved. In case of doubt, consult your superior or the Legal Assistance Officer.

General Prohibition. All Department of the Army personnel, military and civilian, will avoid any action, whether or not specifically prohibited by the regulations, which might result in or reasonably be expected to create the appearance of:

Using public office for private gain.
Giving preferential treatment to any person or entity.
Impeding government efficiency or economy.
Losing independence or impartiality.
Making a government decision outside official channels.
Affecting adversely the confidence of the public in the integrity of the government.

Conferring Honorary Titles Prohibited. Conferring honorary titles of military rank upon civilians is prohibited. Honorary titles heretofore conferred will not be withdrawn. (AR 600–20.)

Effect of Refusal of Medical Treatment. An officer or enlisted person may be investigated by a board of medical officers and subsequently be separated from the Army or be brought to trial by court-martial for refusing to submit to a surgical or dental operation or to medical or dental treatment, at the hands of the military authorities, if it is designed to restore or increase his or her fitness for service.

Attempts to Influence Legislation Prohibited. Except as authorized by the Department of the Army, efforts by any person in the active military service of the United States or by any retired member of the Regular Army to procure or oppose or in any manner influence legislation affecting the Army or to procure personal favor through legislation except to procure the enactment of private relief legislation are forbidden. (AR 600–50.) However, any member of the Army may communicate directly with any member of Congress concerning any subject unless such communication is in violation of law or in violation of regulations necessary to the security of the United States.

Abuse of Privilege. A few people have the idea that authority is always right no matter how it may choose to exercise itself. A throwback, perhaps, to the ancient but discredited doctrine, "The King can do no wrong." The thought is a grave mistake. The possession of authority does not make the possessor any less the hired servant of the society in which his or her authority is exercised. The evil which has been practiced by the few and which has discredited many of the officer corps is abuse of privilege. It consists of taking advantage of position or rank to secure pleasures or facilities to which they are not entitled by law, regulation, or custom. It is the "getting away with something."

Here is a simple way to determine whether an alleged benefit or privilege is genuine or spurious. Find the answer to these two questions. If it is affirmative for either you are quite secure in its enjoyment.

(1) Is there authorization in any current Army or major command document?
(2) Observe the five or ten best officers of experience known to you whom you observe frequently. They must have high standing as good officers among their fellows. Is the questioned privilege practiced by half or more of them?

Standards of Conduct, AR 600–50. The code of the Army and of Army officers is for a high standard of action and conduct in all matters, official and personal.

This applies with special emphasis upon avoiding all possible conflict between private interests and official duties (AR 600–50).

This regulation is very inclusive and very precise. Except when your activities are entirely official, or entirely personal—as in the routine investment of personal funds—you should be mindful of the possibility of conflict of interest. One need not jump behind trees in the matter, or live in fear of unintentional involvement. But in case of any slight doubt you should consult your commanding officer, or the Legal Assistance Officer, for guidance.

25

Resignation and Elimination

The Army must have ways of removing from active duty, or terminating appointments within the corps of officers, those individuals who do not measure up to its standards of conduct or efficiency. This is protection of the essential interests of the Government and of the Army. Since these matters are of grave importance to the individual officer, the laws and regulations require thorough examination by boards of officers following judicial processes, and the review of their recommended action. This is protection of the individual. This chapter is based for the most part upon AR 635–100, *Officer Personnel,* and AR 635–120. *Officer Resignations and Discharges.* However, they are not all inclusive on this subject. Officers may be dismissed or reduced in grade by sentence of a general court-martial. Regular Army officers twice passed over for permanent promotion may be removed from the active list as discussed in Chapter Twenty-Six, *Retirement.* Officers may be separated from active duty for reasons of age or physical incapacity. During any period of reduction of military strength, such as is necessary to meet reduced budgetary authorization, separation of non-Regular officers may be made by routine administration action.

Character and Integrity Standard Identical for All Officers. Officers must meet high standards of personal honor and integrity because otherwise they could not continue to be useful members of the corps of officers. In this respect all officers must meet identical standards, without regard to their grade, length of service, component, or other consideration. Failure to measure up will result in elimination by action of a board of officers or trial by court martial.

An interesting and helpful discussion of the importance of integrity in establishing a favorable impression on others is contained in Chapter Three, *The Officer Image.*

Standards for Performance of Duty. The situation as to standard of duty performance is quite different, for in this quality there is an acceptable variation. See Chapter Fourteen, *Evaluation Reports,* with special reference to the parts of the report form which compare the rated officer with others of the same grade, military schooling, and time in grade.

ELIMINATION AND THE CAREER PLANNING PROGRAM

It is not a pleasant subject to discuss, or to include in *The Army Officer's Guide.* But elimination of officers after a period of service is a necessary part of personnel administration and should be understood by all. This is an appropriate place to emphasize the fair, carefully governed process used by the Army in applying this essential power.

The Army's concept of career planning and individual development of each officer continues to broaden, and its purposes continue to be more clearly defined. Just as promotion of those best qualified is a part of the planning process, so also is elimination of those officers who for adequate reasons have not attained or maintained the standard required.

Each officer deserves a fair chance to demonstrate individual capabilities. The Army system requires and insures it. Special counseling and training must be given to newly commissioned officers and newly appointed warrant officers who encounter initial difficulties from inexperience. The officer who fails to achieve or maintain minimum standards must be identified promptly and positive action taken to improve his or her performance. If the officer fails to respond to reasonable standards of performance or conduct, elimination action must be taken. (See also the discussion of counseling, Chapter Fourteen, *Evaluation Reports.*)

FRIENDLY ADVICE TO OFFICERS ASKED TO "SHOW CAUSE"

The receipt of a letter about elimination action proposed under AR 635–100, as discussed in the remainder of this chapter, will be a disconcerting experience. Thoughtless actions at this time may prejudice the outcome. The wise officer who wishes to salvage the most from the situation may be assisted by following these well-intended suggestions.

Upon receipt of the letter, keep your own counsel. Don't spout. Don't start hunting for a fight. Don't rush to the originator of the letter with recriminations and countercharges. If liquor is at the root of the trouble, as will be the case in some instances, don't choose this occasion to go off on a bender. Don't discuss the matter with associates. Study the letter most carefully. Study this chapter. Obtain official regulations cited in your letter of notification and study them. Continue to perform your duties and be sure to do them well.

If a selection board decides you should show cause for retention, a commanding officer with General Court Martial (GCM) jurisdiction will notify you and give you five days to select an option to resign, request discharge, apply for retirement, if eligible, or appear before a board of inquiry. Should the case originate in another manner, the commander with GCM jurisdiction will give you 7 days to submit a statement in regards to the allegations and recommendation for elimination. You may secure counsel including civilian counsel at your own expense or one will be provided you who is legally qualified. The commander upon forwarding your statement will offer you the same options as in the first case.

Assuming you take one day to settle down and to seek counsel, your perspective should have adjusted somewhat. Although the time limits seem short for reaction, you may be assured the administrative process will be careful, deliberate, judicial, and unhurried. You will have full opportunity to present your case, be represented by a counsel of your choice, and be protected under both law and regulation from such matters that could constitute self-incrimination and double jeopardy.

The next step is to consult others. Go first to your immediate commander even though he or she may in some way be responsible for the action. Regardless of your commander's position in your case, an expression of regret on your part along with a positive declaration that you had aspired to be a good officer will be beneficial. Your commander will grant you the time to prepare your case, and may offer assistance and provide advice. Your next step is to seek additional counsel from a more senior officer whom you consider capable and objective enough to give you impartial and wise advice.

The remaining days are spent in preparing your case with the accumulation of refutations, mitigating circumstances, and other supporting evidence to establish why you should remain on duty. An honest, but difficult, appraisal on your part along with counsel from others could be to elect one of the other options. If you elect to appear before the board, the intervening time should be spent in proving the desirability of your retention. Work with your counsel, accepting his or her advice and providing factual evidence based on candor and truth.

If the outcome is favorable, as will be the case in a fair percentage of hearings, start anew with determination to be a fine officer, casting out weaknesses which led to the action. The history of these hearings has many examples where officers retained in service have gone on to make exemplary records. If given the opportunity you will wish to do the same.

ELIMINATION PROCEDURES

Detailed procedures for elimination proceedings are spelled out in AR 635–100. Officers who may be concerned with such action are advised to consult this regulation, the provisions of which are summarized briefly in the following paragraphs.

Elimination Policy. Retention of officers substandard in performance of duty or conduct, deficient in character, or otherwise unsuited for military service, cannot be justified in peace or war. There is no room for such individuals in any part of the Army. Elimination action, however, is not used in lieu of disciplinary action under the Uniform Code of Military Justice.

Elimination, Officers with More Than 3 Years' Service. Elimination proceedings are judicial in nature with the officer concerned entitled to legal counsel. Elimination actions progress from the immediate commander through the commander exercising general courts-martial jurisdiction, through a Selection Board at Headquarters, Department of the Army, through a Board of Inquiry, through a Board of Review, to the Secretary of the Army. At each point, in accordance with the procedures established by law and detailed in AR 635–100, a determination must be made that there is cause for elimination before the case progresses to the next step. At any point in the chain, a determination that there is not cause for elimination is enough to cause the case to be closed.

The decision of the Secretary of the Army is final in those cases reaching that level.

Within five days of official notification to show cause for retention, the officer concerned must acknowledge receipt of the notification and state his or her election:

To tender a resignation; or

To request discharge (applicable only to Regular Army commissioned officers); or

To apply for retirement in lieu of elimination, if otherwise eligible for voluntary retirement; or

To appear before a Board of Inquiry to show cause for retention.

Elimination, Officers with Less Than 3 Years' Service. In addition to the causes for elimination listed earlier, which are applicable to all officers, the following additional reasons are applicable to Regular Army commissioned officers and Regular Army warrant officers having less than 3 years' service in their present component and to all officers having less than 3 years' service in the AUS without component:

Failure by a Regular Army officer of a basic service school course.

Failure to be considered fully qualified for promotion to first lieutenant or to chief warrant officer, CW–2.

The discovery of medical conditions or other conditions which, if they had been known at the time of appointment, would have precluded appointment.

The discovery of any other condition which evidences that the officer's retention in the Army would not be in the best interests of the United States.

Elimination Procedure. Processing of officers with less than 3 years service will not normally include reference to a Board of Inquiry and a Board of Review. Cases are referred to a Selection Board which will recommend for retention or elimination of the officer. The Selection Board may, however, determine that the officer should be required to show cause for retention before a Board of Inquiry in the same manner as for the officer of longer service.

Special Action When a Student Officer of Less Than 3 Years' Service Fails a Service School Course.

Failure by a Regular Officer is handled as stated above.

An Army Reserve officer who fails a Branch Orientation or Branch Familiarization Course is subject to relief from active duty and discharge by the school commandant. Under like circumstances, a National Guard officer's name is forwarded to The Adjutant General for appropriate action.

Refusal of Regular Army Appointment. In accordance with the Defense Officer Personnel Management Act (DOPMA), commissioned officers who do not already hold Regular Army appointments are offered such appointments at the time they are selected for promotion to major. Failure to accept such an appointment will result in termination of the officer's active service.

Conclusion. There are several truths here worth noting. Action to separate an officer from his or her commission or warrant is a serious matter, and is taken seriously by the Army. Such recommendations must never be submitted lightly and to do so will bring discredit upon the recommending officer. On the other hand, to fail to put them in when justified is to hold in the service an unfit officer, a serious weakness in itself. The elimination procedure should be understood as thorough, unhurried, and objective so as to eliminate hasty or ill-considered actions.

RESIGNATION

If mature consideration indicates a true preference for a different vocation, a person with but one life to live is entitled to make his or her own choices. An officer in good standing who decides to change to a different vocation must base the decision on facts. The tender of a resignation is a very serious act for upon acceptance military status is terminated and, although it is possible to be reappointed, the time lost in terms of grade and rank cannot be recouped. Should reappointment be denied, the resignation is permanent.

It appears to be quite true that the resignation of a commission or warrant by an officer must be an act completely voluntary. However, there are several categories of resignation which are now provided, from that of an officer in highest standing who has completed all service obligations and merely wishes to terminate his or her military status, to the officer who resigns in the face of certain conviction by court martial. Because of this broad situation, officers are advised to consult AR 635–120, with all changes, when they seek information as to any category of resignation.

The following information is supplied as first reference.

Service Requirements for Unqualified Resignation Eligibility. Although an officer may be in good standing in every way, his or her right to resign the commission or warrant as an "unqualified resignation" is subject to a number of requirements. During periods of emergency when Reserve component units have been called into active Federal service, resignations are not accepted by the Secretary of the Army unless reasons considered to be in justification for the action are stated and accepted. During periods of emergency, Department of the Army may announce restrictions on the approval of applications for resignation for individuals who possess critical skills or who hold assignments in key positions. Officers contemplating voluntary resignation should see their unit personnel officer.

A Regular Army officer must meet the following requirements to be eligible for acceptance of unqualified resignation: (AR 601–100, and AR 635–120.)

Have served at least 3 years of active service, commissioned or warrant, subsequent to date of acceptance of appointment in the Regular Army except individuals whose source of commission is the United States Military, Naval or Air Force Academy, who have a service obligation of 5 years active duty.

Resignation in Lieu of Elimination. An officer who has been selected or recommended for elimination or removal from the active list under any provision of law may tender a resignation at any time prior to final action on the proceedings. (AR 635–120.) Such action saves time and paperwork for the Army, and may save embarrassment for the officer. The type of discharge to be furnished will be determined on the basis of facts and will be discretionary with the Secretary of the Army.

Resignation for the Good of the Service. A resignation for the good of the service generally involves a violation of honor or commission of offenses for which trial by court martial would follow. When the nature of the offense is such that punishment more severe than dismissal would be warranted, such a resignation is denied so that trial may follow. There must be no element of coercion in a tender of such a resignation. However, an appointed counsel will advise the officer of the implications of such resignation. The officer should be allowed a reasonable time to decide on a course of action.

A resignation for the good of the service, if accepted by the Department of the Army, normally will be accepted as under other than honorable conditions, in which case the officer will be furnished a Discharge Certificate (Under Other Than Honorable Conditions). (DD Form 794A). If it is determined by the Department of the Army that the resignation should be accepted under honorable conditions, the officer will be furnished an Honorable Discharge Certificate (DD Form 256A), or a General Discharge Certificate (DD Form 257A), as appropriate. In addition to these types of certificates, a warrant officer may be awarded a Dishonorable Discharge Certificate (DD Form 260A) if such is deemed appropriate.

Benefits Cancelled by Discharge Other Than Honorable. Military service is rewarded by many benefits available to veterans upon separation from the service, always assuming that the separation is under honorable conditions. The list which follows comprises the important losses an officer would endure whose service is terminated under other than honorable conditions and for which Discharge Certificate DD Form 794A or Dishonorable Discharge Certificate DD Form 260A is supplied:

Severance, or Readjustment Pay.

Compensation for unused leave credit.

Transportation of dependents and household goods.

Physical disability retirement benefits, or severance pay.

In addition, it may be a bar from all rights, based upon the period of service from which separated, under laws administered by the Veterans Administration.

Resignation of Women Officers for Reason of Marriage, Pregnancy, or Parenthood. Women officers of the Army have broad options as to resignation in event of marriage, pregnancy, or parenthood, for which see Ch. 6, 7, 8, AR 635–120.

Withdrawal of Resignation. An officer may request that his or her tender of resignation be withdrawn at any time prior to commencing travel pursuant to orders issued for the purpose of separation. Such requests are forwarded through channels with each indorsement recommending approval or disapproval.

Acceptance of Resignation. Until the acceptance of a resignation becomes effective, the officer tendering it continues to be an officer of the Army. The effective date of resignation is the date specified in the Department of the Army orders which announce the separation of the officer.

Resignation may be declined by the Department for a number of reasons: In time of war, when war is imminent, or in a period of emergency declared by the President; or when the officer is under investigation, under charges, awaiting result of trial, absent without leave, absent in hands of civil authorities, insane, or in default with respect to public property or funds.

26
Retirement

The laws governing retirement from the armed forces are important to the Government in order to maintain capably led armed
forces, and they are important to the individual who elects to follow
a military career. The purpose of retirement, voluntary and involuntary, is to assure that the Army has an officer corps of the highest
caliber. To achieve this standard, officers are retired by statutory
provisions involving physical limitations, age, time in grade, and by
board action when performance of duty or conduct is below standard. The officer who serves well need not fear early retirement.
The officer who desires a second career may retire with full and
deserved honor (but with $\frac{1}{2}$ pay) at 20 years, creating a promotion
vacancy and stimulus for those who choose to serve to complete
the full 30-year career. Retirement laws which are fair and equitable, both to the government and to the individual officer, are essential to governmental military personnel administration.

This chapter will serve to orient the officer on this important
subject; however, serious study of retirement should include the
following references:

(1) AR 635–100 *Officer Personnel.*

(2) AR 635–40 *Physical Evaluation for Retention, Retirement,
or Separation.*

(3) DA Pamphlet 600–5, *Handbook on Retirement Services.*

(4) AR 608–25, *Retirement Services Program for Army Personnel and Their Families.*

STATUS OF RETIRED OFFICER

It is noteworthy that an officer who is retired retains status as
an officer with many of its rights and privileges. He or she may be

returned to active duty under laws and departmental regulations applicable to a particular individual and remains on the official rolls of the Army. By tradition and law, retired Army personnel are considered to be in a real sense members of the Army. Therefore, close affinity does exist between the active Army and its retired personnel. The Retired List is not a roster of former officers; it is a designation of personnel, who by age, length of service, or disability should be regarded as having been transferred from one Army category to another.

Upon retirement from the Army, members are placed on one of the following retired lists: *U.S. Army Retired List,* for Regular Army commissioned officers, warrant officers, and enlisted personnel retired for any reason, who are granted retired pay. *Army of the United States Retired List,* for officers other than Regular Army officers, who are members and former members of the Reserve Components, and personnel who served in the Army of the United States without component, who are granted retired pay, and retired warrant officers and enlisted personnel of the Regular Army who by reason of service in temporary commissioned grade are entitled to receive retired pay of the commissioned grade. *Temporary Disability Retired List,* is for officers and enlisted personnel placed on the list in accordance with law for physical disability which may be of a permanent nature. Emergency Officers' Retired List is a list of officers, other than Regular Army, who incurred physical disability in line of duty while in the service of the United States during WWI and who are entitled to pay from the Veterans Administration.

Use of Military Title After Retirement. See Chapter Four, *Military Courtesy,* under "The Correct Use of Titles," and the cross references therein.

Retirement Services Offices. Retirement Services Offices have been established at Headquarters, Department of the Army, in Army areas throughout the United States, and in some oversea commands. These are the offices from which retired individuals may obtain guidance and assistance regarding their rights, benefits and privileges. Retired members are invited to write or visit these units whenever assistance is needed in their personal affairs.

Correspondence directed to the Department of the Army should be addressed to The Adjutant General, ATTN: AGPO-AA, Department of the Army, Washington, D.C. 20315. DA Pamphlet 600–5, *Handbook on Retirement Services* provides information about Retirement Services Offices; it is issued to each retiring officer.

Computation of Retired Pay. Retired pay once increased in the same ratio as active duty pay. However, the Military Pay Act of 1963 established the principle that retired pay would be subject to cost-of-living adjustments without regard to active duty pay scales. For recent and current retirees, this procedure has worked well, but it has resulted in great inequities for those officers who retired prior to about 1960. The Retired Officers Association, the National Association for Uniformed Services, and others have urged Congress to rectify this problem.*

AFTER ARMY RETIREMENT—WHAT NEXT?

It is prudent for Army officers to anticipate the life they wish to lead after military retirement, and to plan with long-range foresight the vocation they may

---

*As this is written, there is an Administration proposal to cap retired pay increases for several years until the resulting retired pay is about the same as would be the case for an officer retiring now based on the same grade and years of service.

choose to follow as a second career. The present retirement laws are sound. They are subject to change, but if changed, the options are more likely to be broadened than curtailed. Under our current laws, officers who begin their Army careers at the normal ages of 21—24 will retire for length of service in their early fifties; or if they elect to retire after 20 years' service, in their early forties. Unless disability is a factor, many officers will wish to enter a new vocation. They may require additional income to meet family obligations, or to realize special desires. They may follow a new vocation to achieve results in a different field. All the "reasons" will be personal, but for everyone a thorough consideration of the possibilities, starting long before retirement, is a prudent course to adopt.

RETIREMENT: AFTER 20 OR AFTER 30 YEARS' SERVICE?

An officer may apply for retirement after completing 20 years of active service. Such retirements retain the right to retired pay and other benefits which are discussed in Chapter Seven, *Financial Planning.* The law and its current implementing policy are stated later in this chapter under the headings, *Voluntary Retirement* and *After Twenty Years' Service.*

This law was enacted by the Congress after thorough consideration. At the time of its enactment, vacancies in the higher grades of the Army had been so limited as to create a history of severe promotion stagnation. It was recognized that to provide attractive Army careers there must be sufficient vacancies to permit capable individuals to reach grades above lieutenant colonel at ages permitting adequate utilization by the government. Retirement of officers who wished to terminate their active service at 20 years permitted other officers who wished to remain to be promoted, and to hold the positions of high responsibility to which their grades pertained. Liberalization of the retirement laws was considered a valuable inducement to enter the service by individuals of special training and talents. These are some of the advantages to the government in developing better careers and a better corps of officers.

The law also provided advantages to the individual officer. While many officers wish to remain in active service until the date of compulsory retirement, it is not the case of all officers. Situations develop during long years of service, which could not possibly have been foreseen at appointment, which make it necessary or desirable for an officer to terminate a military career, often with great regret. Such reasons are usually very personal. They may be caused by a cruel health situation of a family member which precludes the change of station situation of the Army officer. They may result from financial requirements, coupled with opportunity to secure a higher income. The officer may contemplate his or her military record, conclude that it offers little chance of high success during the remaining years, and prefer to leave the Army to start an entirely new career. There are other personal reasons, all understandable, but not necessarily overriding those for not retiring.

The Wisdom in Thorough Analysis. The officer should approach this decision with care. There is need for thorough analysis of his or her present and future prospects in the Army, the forces suggesting retirement, and the civilian expectancy for employment and living. Retirement is extremely "final." There have been tragic mistakes by some officers who found upon retirement that their decision was unwise. Others have been highly successful and entered rewarding lives. It is because of these diverse developments that this discussion is included. It is not intended to advise officers to retire or not to retire, as they attain eligibility to choose. The purpose is to assist in understanding and evaluating.

The Change in Living Conditions. The officer who loves the service life, and his or her family who find it equally attractive, will undergo a serious adjustment if the tie is severed. Some of the customs and benefits officers and their families take for granted have very real values. These intangibles merit thought.

The Rewards of the Final Ten Years. During the final ten years of service, your assignments will be among those of heaviest responsibility and the greatest interest. You will have the opportunity for selection to high position. You will receive some of the benefits of seniority such as assignment of more desirable quarters. The officer with an outstanding record who terminates active service forfeits prospects of great value and of high rewards.

Consider the Pay Shrinkage. The need for prudent analysis is illustrated by comparing the retirement pay of a lieutenant colonel with twenty years' service who might have retired as a colonel with 30 years' service. Other examples may be computed from the pay tables.

In the case at hand, however, the colonel's monthly retired pay will be nearly twice that of the lieutenant colonel, the lieutenant colonel's retired pay being computed at only 50% of basic active duty pay, but the colonel's based on 75%.

In candor, there is another side to this coin. Let us look at it. Fewer than half the lieutenant colonels can attain the grade of colonel under present law, because of the lack of vacancies. A similar situation obtains for warrant officers contemplating promotion from CW3 to CW4. Lieutenant colonels may anticipate retirement upon completing 28 years' service. Suppose a commissioned officer approaching the end of his or her 20th year contemplates the future, and estimates chances of reaching the grade of colonel as low, an "estimate" perhaps gained by consulting the specialty manager at OPMD, in Washington. Now the concern involves the difference in retired pay computed at 50% (20 years' service) vs. 70% (28 years' service).

This comparison discloses a different (and difficult) situation. The officer who wishes to make the most of remaining employable years may find these facts to be convincing reasons for 20-year retirement to start a new career. He or she may have financial obligations which cannot be satisfied by the prospective retired income in the grade of lieutenant colonel. This discussion states the factual comparison. It is neither to advocate retirement at the earliest opportunity, nor to remain on active duty without regard to the probabilities. The decision is wholly personal and should be based on personal preferences, financial considerations, opportunities in another vocation, and the many likes and dislikes of the individuals concerned.

Consider the Reduction in Security. As discussed in Chapter Seven, *Financial Security,* important benefits provided active duty personnel are terminated or curtailed upon retirement. These are subjects to be identified and evaluated. They must be faced by officers who retire after 30 years' service, too; but the officer retiring at an earlier year accepts them at a younger age.

In Your Own Case What About Civilian Employment? It is certainly true that many officers of long service who have resigned or retired have obtained civilian employment with above average earnings, and a large number hold positions of the highest importance in civilian fields. We may be proud of our fellow officers who have won such outstanding recognition. One might assume it to be a "group expectancy" but it isn't universal and no certainty exists in changing times and in nongovernmental, highly competitive, and variable occupations. It is an individual matter entirely, worth most careful examination before forwarding the retirement application.

What was your education as to beckoning civilian employment? What has been your service training and experience fitting you for specific civilian employment? Or, have you planned to undertake training to fit you for a profession or employment?

Do you have a definite, responsible offer from a company or a responsible person who has such a decision in his or her power?

Summary. Early retirement may be wise for some officers, heartbreakingly unwise for others. Decision as to this problem should be reached only on an evaluation such as you have been trained to make in military service: Get all the facts, analyze them carefully, then decide which is best for you and for your family.

RETIREMENT SITUATION IN SUMMARY

It is true that the beginning of military retirement calls for a major readjustment in the lives of most officers and their families. It is a new and different period of life which most people find very rewarding. There is a real need for the career officer to gain a clear understanding of his or her own post-retirement situation and the probable wishes of family members as they can be foreseen. A reasonable degree of planning for the period of retirement is advisable. The planning should start long before retirement is requested or ordered.

Medical Service for Retired Individuals and Their Family Members. Retired personnel and their dependents are authorized to receive medical care and hospitalization at facilities of the uniformed services, when available, and at civilian facilities, if military facilities are unavailable. See Chapter Seven, *Financial Planning.*

Use of Post and Station Facilities. Retired members, their dependents, and unremarried widowed spouses are authorized the use of various facilities on military installations when facilities are available. This privilege includes authority to use and patronize the following: (DA Pamphlet 600–5.)

Commissaries.

Post Exchanges.

Clothing Sales Stores.

Laundry and Dry Cleaning Plants.

Military Theatres.

Army Special Service Facilities.

Officers messes, which includes club facilities (upon application to and approval of the club concerned).

Hospital and out-patient care.

Identification will be required.

As inter-service custom, retired members are usually welcomed into club and other facilities of the sister services.

Travel to Home. An officer of the Army may select and proceed to a home, at government expense, so far as authorized, at any place in the world at which he or she desires and intends to establish a bona fide home at any time within one year after retirement. For details, consult a Post Transportation Officer.

RETIREMENT FOR PHYSICAL DISABILITY

The Career Compensation Act of 1949 established a very important departure in remuneration following separation from active service as a result of physical disability. The rescinded laws provided 75 percent of active duty base and longevity pay without regard to the degree of disability or length of military service. Thus the officer retired with minimum incapacity and the officer with a most serious disability received the same percentage of active duty pay, as did the officer of long service in comparison with the officer of the shortest possible service. The current law gives consideration to the degree of incapacity as well as to the length of service. Indeed, certain officers with less than 8 years' service (those whose disability was NOT the proximate result of the performance of active duty) receive severance pay only whereas under the old law they might have received retirement pay for life. All officers should become thoroughly informed about this provision because it may be of the highest importance to them in the event of any physical shortcoming.

First stage in any proceeding for separation for physical reasons is a finding by the Service that the person, by reason of a disability, is not qualified to perform his or her duties. If a person is kept on duty, there are, of course, no separation proceedings.

But if a finding is made that the person *cannot* be retained in service, the proceedings enter a second stage. If the disability was due to "intentional misconduct" or "willful neglect" or incurred during unauthorized absence, the Government gives the member nothing, merely separates him or her.

Third, if the disability was not due to misconduct or neglect, the next question is: Is the disability 30 percent or more under the Veterans Administration standard rating? (Loss of an eye or loss of use of a limb, and chronic, severe, high blood pressure are disabilities of 30 percent or more; loss of one or two fingers or one or two toes, loss of hearing in one ear, or defects or scars which do not seriously interfere with functions, are not.)

If the disability is less than 30 percent, no retirement is given (except for some persons of long service). Instead, the person is given *severance pay,* which is 2 months' basic active duty pay for each year of active service, to a maximum of 2 full years' active pay. Half or more of a year counts as a full year.

VOLUNTARY RETIREMENT

Voluntary retirement includes all types of retirement which the officer initiates by his or her own application. Approval of an officer's voluntary retirement may be mandatory, or discretionary, dependent upon specific provisions of the law under which retirement is sought.

After Twenty Years' Service. A commissioned officer of the Army who has at least 20 years of active Federal service at least 10 years of which have been as a commissioned officer, may upon personal application and in the discretion of the Secretary of the Army, be retired. A warrant officer must have at least 20 years of active Federal service.

After Thirty Years' Service. An officer of the Army who has at least 30 years of service may upon his or her own application and in the discretion of the President be retired. After 40 years of service an officer shall be retired upon personal request without need of approval.

Policy on Acceptance of Retirement Applications. When an officer has completed all service obligations prescribed in AR 635–100, his or her retirement application normally is approved. During periods of emergency, Department of the Army may announce restrictions on the approval of retirement applications. Individuals who possess critical skills or hold assignments in key positions, may be denied retirement (or resignation). Officers should consult their unit personnel officer for information which may influence their action.

MANDATORY RETIREMENT

Mandatory retirements are those retirements required by law and must be effected regardless of the desire of the individual, or of the preferences of the Department of the Army. Computation of service is based on AR 635–100.

Retirement for Age. Unless retired or separated at an earlier date, each commissioned officer whose grade is below Major General, other than a professor or the Registrar of the USMA, shall be retired on becoming 60 years of age. Unless retired or separated earlier, each commissioned officer whose grade is Major General, and whose retirement has been deferred, shall be retired at age 60, or if not deferred or retained, will be retired at age 62.

Retirement for Length of Service. Unless retired or separated at an earlier date, officers shall be retired for length of service as follows:

Major Generals. Each officer in the grade of Major General shall be retired on the 5th anniversary of the date of appointment in that grade or on the 30th day after completion of 35 years of service, whichever is later.

Brigadier Generals. Each officer in the grade of Brigadier General, other than a professor of the USMA shall be retired on the 5th anniversary of the date of his or her appointment in that grade or on the 30th day after completion of 30 years service, whichever is later.

Colonels. Each officer in the grade of Colonel shall be retired on the 5th anniversary of the date of his or her appointment in that grade or on the 30th day after completion of 30 years of service, whichever is later. Also, upon the determination of the Secretary of the Army that there are too many Colonels on the active list the Secretary may convene a board of 5 general officers to recommend officers for early retirement.

Lieutenant Colonels. Each officer in the grade of Lieutenant Colonel shall be retired on the 30th day after completion of 28 years of service. In each of the above cases, retirement takes place on the 1st day of the month following the month in which service requirements are met. If the officer is on a recommended list for promotion to the next higher grade, the officer will be retained and fall under the criteria for the next grade when promoted.

Selective Retirement. In accordance with the Defense Officer Personnel Management Act (DOPMA), lieutenant colonels and colonels may be selected for early retirement by board action, where rapid reduction of the numbers of officers in these grades is necessary.

Retirement of Warrant Officers. Regular Army Warrant Officers, unless retired earlier under provisions of law, may remain on active duty until age 62. Regular Army Warrant Officers are mandatorily retired when they complete 30 years of active service.*

---

*Warrant officers who hold shortage MOS's may, under current regulations, volunteer to remain on active duty beyond 30 years.

Deferred Officers Not Recommended for Promotion—Majors, Captains, and First Lieutenants.
Under the provisions of the Defense Officer Personnel Management Act (DOPMA), officers in the grades of first lieutenant, captain, and major who twice fail to be selected for promotion will be involuntarily separated from the Army. However, DOPMA also contains provisions that allow the Secretary of the Army to selectively continue in grade certain of the captains and majors to fill Army specialty needs. In such cases, captains may be continued in grade to a maximum of 20 years service and majors may be continued in grade to a maximum of 24 years service.

Regular Army Warrant Officers. A Regular Army warrant officer who has twice failed of selection to the next higher permanent grade will be retired 60 days after the second failure of selection, if he or she has at least 20 years of active service. If the warrant officer has at least 18 years of active service, retirement will be on the last day of the month in which he or she completes 20 years and 60 days of service.

Retirement of Female Officers. The retirement laws are generally applicable to both male and female officers. However, there are exceptions for female officers of the Army Nurse Corps and the Army Medical Specialist Corps.
The Secretary of the Army may defer the retirement of a lieutenant colonel in either of the corps named above until the last day of the month in which she completes 30 years and 30 days of service as computed officially.

Removal From Active List. If an officer is removed from the active list of the Regular Army under the provisions of Title 10, U.S.C., Chapter 359, and, if on the date of removal he or she is eligible for voluntary retirement under any provision of law then in effect, then the officer shall be retired in the grade and with the retired pay to which entitled had the retirement been upon his or her own application.

RETIRED GRADE, RANK, AND STATUS

Retired Grade. In accordance with the provisions of DOPMA, officers promoted to lieutenant colonel and above after 15 September 1981 must serve in the new grade for at least three years to be eligible to retire in that grade. Unless specifically exempted by the President, officers who elect to retire prior to completion of three years service in grade will be retired at the next lower grade in which they have served for a minimum of six months.

Retirement of Warrant Officers in Highest Grade. Any warrant officer of the Army who is retired is entitled, when his or her active service plus service on the retired lists totals 30 years, to be advanced on the retired list to the highest commissioned grade in which he or she served on active duty satisfactorily for 185 days or more as determined by the Secretary of the Army. (AR 635–100.)

Physical Disability. An officer of the Regular Army retired for physical disability incurred while serving under a temporary appointment in a higher grade shall have the rank and receive retired pay computed as otherwise provided by law for officers of such higher grade.
It is noteworthy that a retired officer continues his or her status as an officer of the Army, subject to return to active duty under provisions of our laws. In time of war or emergency many officers are recalled, although few (if any) are restored to active duty without their consent.

The laws are quite favorable as to the protection afforded officers recalled from retirement in the event of incurring physical disability, or additional physical disability. Officers on the retired list who have return to active service under consideration are urged to inform themselves as to the specific basis their own return would include.

Retired Status. A Regular Army officer placed on the retired list is still an officer of the United States (31 Ct. Cl. 35).

Certificate of Retirement. Each member of the Army, upon retirement, will be furnished a Certificate of Retirement (DD Form 363–A) by the Adjutant General.

RETIREMENT OF NATIONAL GUARD AND RESERVE OFFICERS

Retirement for Physical Disability. The laws governing retirement for physical disability apply equally to all officers on active duty whether of the Regular Army or the Reserve components. This principle was first established by enactment of the Act of 3 April 1939 and is affirmed in the Career Compensation Act of 1949 and codified in Chapter 61, Title 10, USC.

Retirement for Age and Length of Service. Title III, The Army and Air Force Vitalization and Retirement Act of 1948 (JAAF Bulletin No. 29, 1948), codified in Chapter 67, Title 10, USC, establishes retirement opportunities for Reserve and National Guard officers who meet the following requirements: (AR 135–180.) (See also AR 635–100.)

Have attained age 60.
Have a minimum of 20 years of satisfactory federal service.
Have served at least eight years of qualifying service as a member of a Reserve component. Simultaneous service as a member of a Reserve component and as a member of the Regular Army, Navy, Air Force, Marine Corps, or Coast Guard shall not be deemed to be service in a Reserve component.
If a member of a Reserve component prior to 15 August 1945, have performed active federal service during some portion of either of the two periods from 6 April 1917 to 11 November 1918 and 9 September 1940 to 31 December 1946, all dates inclusive.

RETIRED OFFICERS ASSOCIATION

The Retired Officers' Association has for its purpose the aid of retired personnel in every proper and legitimate manner. Included are the presentation of subjects important to Retired officers before the appropriate members of Congress. It provides assistance in securing employment, and many other services which are helpful. It is located at 201 North Washington Street, Alexandria, Virginia 22314.

UNITED STATES ARMY WARRANT OFFICER ASSOCIATION

The United States Army Warrant Officer Association is a professional association of Army warrant officers of all components, both active and retired, dedicated to recommending programs for the improvement of the Army and the Warrant Officer Corps, and to disseminating professional information to warrant officers in the field. Services include a bi-monthly newspaper to members, liaison with the Department of the Army, Department of Defense, Veterans Administration and Congress. Membership is open to any Army warrant officer who holds or has held a warrant issued by the Secretary of the Army. The address of the Association is P.O. Box 2040, Reston, Virginia 22090.

NATIONAL ASSOCIATION OF UNIFORMED SERVICES

The National Association of Uniformed Services (NAUS) has for its purpose the promotion of legislation which will uphold the security of the nation, sustain morale of the Armed Forces, and provide equitable consideration for all members of the uniformed services—active and retired. NAUS is non-profit and non-social. Membership is open to all servicemen and women. It is located at 5535 Hempstead Way, P.O. Box 1406, Springfield, Virginia 22151. Telephone (703) 750-1342.

Heaven: the place where at last you can do all the things you never had time to do before.—Anonymous.

27

Organization and Missions

"The fact is that armies have always existed for one ultimate purpose: to go to war. For the U.S. Army, fulfillment of our major mission—deterrence—depends on our possession of real military power capable of effective employment. If our interest is to dissuade an aggressor of the utility of war, he must be convinced that we are prepared to respond under circumstances of his choosing. Hence, the U.S. Army must be ready to go to war, today, tomorrow, whenever challenged. And in that mission statement we have the crux of what you and I must prepare for.
* * * * * * These are exciting times to be a soldier. No profession was ever founded on easy tasks and today is no exception. While I intend to make the case for our needs, we must not entrench ourselves behind our deficiencies. Rather, we must recognize our imperfections, focus our efforts and mold our soldiers into units prepared to go to war. It is in that task that we are honored to be called professionals." General Edward C. Meyer, Chief of Staff, U.S. Army, October 1979, for the Army *Greenbook*, October 1979.

This statement by the Army's Chief of Staff expressed his views as to the Army's mission during a time of peace. This mission is for the Army, and its sister services, to preserve their wills and their capabilities such that they can continue to preserve the freedom of our great country.

The Army must be ready to fight today, with the weapons and equipment on hand today, anywhere in the world as directed by our nation's civil leaders. The mission continues to provide for the security of the nation, and of our people, and to its assigned tasks in upholding the commitments made by our government. Prevention of war is the primary goal. But if war—or combat short of war

LESSON RELEARNED.

(Reproduced by permission of the Allentown (Pa.) *Morning Call*. The first use in
The Officer's Guide of this significant cartoon was in the 16th edition in 1950.

—cannot be prevented, the mission of the Army and its sister services is to end
the conflict as quickly as possible under conditions acceptable to our government. *The Army must be ready to fight at once with the personnel and with the
equipment we have ready for immediate deployment.*

At the same time that we are fighting with personnel and equipment on hand,
we also rush into an era with new developments as to weapons and other
equipment, with the need for personnel especially trained in their effective
employment. There is a certainty that versatile and powerful weapons will be
developed to become available for employment where needed. *Just as the
Army must be ready and able to fight effectively and promptly, wherever
ordered, with personnel and weapons available, it must also prepare itself to
fight the battles of the future, with the weapons it will then have on hand.
Members of the armed forces expect that weapons and equipment provided
for their use will be the very best our national capabilities can develop and
produce.*

This chapter is provided as a source of authentic, interesting, current information about the Army. It includes discussions of the following subjects:

OBJECTIVE OF THE ARMY

The objective, or purpose of the Army should be understood clearly by all members of the Army, and by each of our nation's citizens. It is firmly established in title 10, US Code, as follows:

It is the intent of Congress to provide an Army that is capable, in conjunction with the other armed forces, of—

(1) preserving the peace and security and providing for the defense of the United States, the Territories, Commonwealths, and possessions and any areas occupied by the United States;

(2) supporting the national policies;

(3) implementing the national objectives; and

(4) overcoming any nations responsible for aggressive acts that imperil the peace and security of the United States.

In general, the Army, within the Department of the Army, includes land combat and service forces and such aviation and water transport as may be organic therein. It shall be organized, trained, and equipped primarily for prompt and sustained combat incident to operations on land. It is responsible for the preparation of land forces necessary for the effective prosecution of war except as otherwise assigned and, in accordance with integrated joint mobilization plans, for the expansion of the peacetime components of the Army to meet the needs of war.

ARMY CHANGE AND PROGRESS

While the objectives or missions of the Army remain unchanged through the years, the Army itself undergoes continuing change in order to be able to best meet these objectives. The Army is trained and equipped to wage many forms of war: general, limited, nuclear, conventional, counterinsurgent. It must be ready to meet a crisis with whatever the situation requires and as our government directs. The Army is doing this job, as directed by the civil leaders of our government, around the world. There is a flexibility of organization and equipment to provide a measured and effective response to any form of aggression.

To attain and retain this flexibility requires that the Army be in a continual state of change, adapting its thinking and organization to new doctrine and equipment as they are developed. Failure to make these adjustments would result in a loss of the capability and flexibility so necessary to meet the exacting tasks assigned.

The strength of the active Army is established by our Nation's leaders to meet the estimated need for Army forces in support of national goals. Current policy is to maintain an active Army of about three-quarters of a million soldiers organized into divisions, separate brigades and regiments, and support units as necessary to provide adequate defense for our Nation and to back up and give support to our foreign policy decisions.

These divisions and smaller supporting units are using the best weapons and equipment our country has to offer, and which are very good indeed. Even better weapons and equipment are under development. As newer weapons and equipment and doctrine become available, the Army will change as necessary to make the best use of what is furnished, always with the view of performing in a superb manner the tasks assigned to it by the civil leaders of our government.

It takes trained and determined personnel to do these vital jobs. This is a fact to be remembered always by our civil leaders, by industrial and educational leaders, members of vocations who mold public opinions, and our citizens generally. Understanding of the requirements to provide for our nation's security, or in the keeping of its solemn commitments is enhanced when a person thinks of the soldier behind the rifle who aims it and fires it, or the crew of a tank or helicopter who drive and guide, aim, and fire. The emphasis must remain upon equipping the soldier, not merely manning the equipment. Army power means power applied by soldiers in person, at close range, as the nation's mission demands. The heart of the Army is the officer and the soldier. The soldier's training, pride in service, confidence in the excellence of equipment, and conviction as to the worthwhileness of the national cause, are all matters which must concern our government, our leaders, and our citizens.

ORGANIZATION—HEADQUARTERS, DEPARTMENT OF THE ARMY

The Headquarters, Department of the Army, in the Pentagon, Washington, D.C. is the place of final decision as to Army affairs, and the nerve center for control of execution of the military missions pertaining to the Army. It is an organizational component of the Department of Defense. Located together are the command and control elements of the Department of Defense, and the Departments of Army, Navy, and Air Force, so they may work together in easy teamwork, and operate together in jointly planned and executed combined operations. (AR 10–5).

The Secretary of the Army. The Secretary of the Army, a civilian, is the head of the Army, the "boss," and it is he or she who has the primary responsibility for all affairs of the Army establishment. The position illustrates the application of civilian control under our constitution. The Secretary is assisted by other civilian officials, as follows:

The Under Secretary of the Army. This official acts as deputy to the Secretary and is his or her principal assistant.

The Assistant Secretaries of the Army, A/SA. Four Assistant Secretaries of the Army are for, Installations, Logistics, and Financial Management; Manpower and Reserve Affairs; Research, Development and Acquisition; and Civil Works.

Other Assistants to the Secretary. The following officials are also responsible directly to the Secretary: Administrative Assistant, General Counsel, Deputy Under Secretary for Operations Research, Chief of Public Affairs, Chief of Legislative Liaison, and Director, Office of Small and Disadvantaged Business Utilization.

The Army Staff. The Secretary of the Army is assisted by the Army Staff, which is the professional military staff at the Headquarters, Department of the Army.

It consists of the Chief of Staff, the Army General Staff, the Special Staff and the Personal Staff.

The Chief of Staff. The Chief of Staff is the highest military assistant or advisor to the Secretary of the Army. He or she occupies the pinnacle position within the Army. He or she is a member of the Joint Chiefs of Staff and as a member thereof is advisor to the President, the National Security Council and the Secretary of Defense. As Army Chief of Staff, his or her responsiblility is to the Secretary of the Army and includes the worldwide Army mission as well as its administration, training, and supply.

Office of the Chief of Staff. The Office of the Chief of Staff includes the Vice Chief of Staff, Director of the Army Staff, and other staff members as may be required.

The Army General Staff. The Chief of Staff is assisted by other staff officers, each heading a general staff agency charged with a particular function. These functions pertain to the people, dollars, planning, materiel acquisition, logistics, and intelligence aspects of the Army. The general staff officers are: the Deputy Chief of Staff for Operations and Plans (DCSOPS), the Deputy Chief of Staff for Personnel (DCSPER), the Deputy Chief of Staff for Logistics (DCSLOG), the Deputy Chief of Staff for Research, Development, and Acquisition (DCSRDA), the Comptroller of the Army (COA), the Assistant Chief of Staff for Intelligence (ACSI), and the Assistant Chief of Staff for Automation and Communications.

The Special Staff. The Chief of Staff also is assisted by staff officers heading special staff agencies, each of which is charged with exercising responsibility for specialized activities.

The Special Staff consists of the following officers:

The Adjutant General	
Chief of Engineers	Chief, National Guard Bureau
The Surgeon General	
Chief of Chaplains	Chief, Army Reserve

The Personal Staff. The personal staff assists the Chief of Staff in specifically designated areas. It consists of the aides to the Chief, other individual staff officers whose advice and assistance he or she desires to receive directly, and those staff agencies whose functions and activities he or she desires to coordinate and administer directly.

The personal staff officers include:

The Inspector General	The Judge Advocate General
The Chief of Chaplains	The Auditor General

The heads of the following Special Staff agencies command personnel, facilities, and organizations in addition to their staff duties. These are separate and distinct functions:

The Adjutant General	The Judge Advocate General
The Chief of Engineers	The Inspector General
The Surgeon General	The Auditor General

MAJOR ARMY FIELD COMMANDS

The missions of the Army are carried out through ten major Army field commands, whose missions are described below.

DEPARTMENT OF THE ARMY

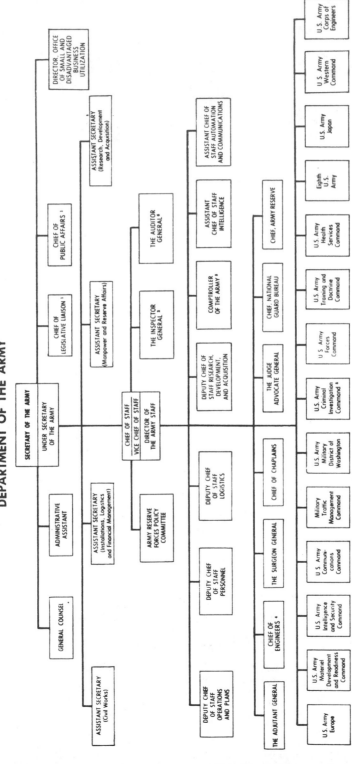

THE ARMY FLAG.

The Army Flag is made up of the national colors with a yellow fringe. It is of standard size. The flag of white silk bears an embroidered blue replica of the official seal of the War Office over a broad scarlet scroll on which "United States Army" is inscribed in white letters. Beneath the scroll are the numerals "1775" denoting the year of the Army's founding by action of the Continental Congress on 14 June 1775. The flag was unfurled officially on 14 June 1956.

U.S. Army Forces Command (FORSCOM). The Forces Command, with headquarters at Fort McPherson, Georgia, is responsible for the operations and readiness of active Army and Army Reserve units and the unit training of the Army National Guard. The Commanding General of FORSCOM serves as the Commander-in-Chief, U.S. Army Forces, Readiness Command, and for planning purposes as the Commander-in-Chief, U.S. Army Forces, Atlantic. Also, the Army elements of the Rapid Deployment Force (RDF) are FORSCOM units which will deploy with the RDF when authorized by National Command Authority.

Continental Armies.
   The Commanding Generals of the three continental armies command the U.S. Army Reserve, plan for mobilization, coordinate domestic emergencies, and supervise training of the Army National Guard. Subordinate to FORSCOM, these armies operate through nine Army Readiness and Mobilization Regions. The geographical boundaries of the armies, First, Fifth, and Sixth, as well as the headquarters locations of the associated Readiness and Mobilization Regions are shown on the included map. Each Readiness and Mobilization Region has a small staff to control Readiness Groups which assist and advise Army Reserve and National Guard units on a day-to-day basis. The continental armies also are responsible for civil defense planning, defense of the Army areas, support of forces engaged in civil disturbances, and planning for and support of relief operations for wide-spread natural disasters.

U.S. Army Training and Doctrine Command (TRADOC).
   With headquarters at historic Fort Monroe, Virginia, the Training and Doc-

trine Command (TRADOC) is responsible for determining how the Total Army will train and fight and how it will be organized and equipped. In fulfilling these responsibilities, TRADOC manages all institutional training for officers from the basic officer courses through the Command and General Staff College, and for enlisted personnel from basic training through the Sergeants Major Academy. TRADOC commands the Army's service schools and manages officer procurement through the Reserve Officer Training Corps (ROTC) and the Officer Candidate School (OCS). Doctrinal and materiel requirements are developed by the service schools and are coordinated through three integrating centers—the Combined Arms Center at Fort Leavenworth, Kansas; the Soldier Support Center at Fort Benjamin Harrison, Indiana; and the Logistics Center at Fort Lee, Virginia, all under the command of TRADOC. Additionally, TRADOC supports Total Army training by developing, producing, and distributing training support materials to commanders in the field. In accomplishing these missions, TRADOC conducts extensive coordination with DARCOM, FORSCOM, our sister services of the Navy, Air Force, and Marine Corps, and representatives of allied armies. TRADOC also operates a world-wide network of liaison officers to maintain effective communication with Army operational forces as well as those of our sister services and our allies.

Installations. Major installation commanders have designated geographical areas of responsibility within which they are responsible for budgeting, funding, and logistical support of Army, Army Reserve, and ROTC elements, as well as special functions such as public relations and disaster control. The installation commander may be responsible to FORSCOM or TRADOC, or both, in carrying out assigned functions, depending upon the activities and units assigned within his or her area.

U.S. Army Materiel Development and Readiness Command (DARCOM). The U.S. Army Materiel Development and Readiness Command, with headquarters

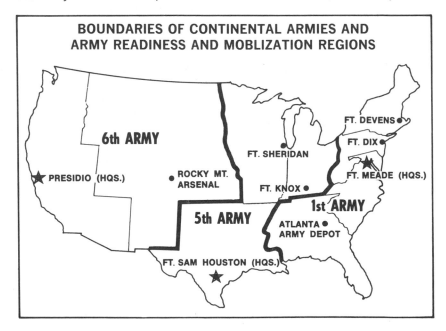

BOUNDARIES OF CONTINENTAL ARMIES AND ARMY READINESS AND MOBLIZATION REGIONS

in Washington, D.C., directs the development, test and evaluation, procurement, distribution, maintenance and disposal of nearly all Army equipment. It deals with the Army's "hardware." DARCOM controls various research and development and material readiness subordinate commands.

The subordinate elements of DARCOM are the Army Missile R&D Command, the Mobility Equipment R&D Command, the Natick, Massachusetts R&D Command, the Tank-Automotive R&D Command, the Armament R&D Command, the Army Missile Material Readiness Command, the Tank-Automotive Material Readiness Command, the Armament Material Readiness Command, the Aviation R&D Command, the Communications & Electronics Materiel Readiness Command, the Communications R&D Command, the Electronics R&D Command, the Depot System Command, the Test & Evaluation Command, the Troop Support & Aviation Materiel Readiness Command, and the Security Assistance Center.

U.S. Army Intelligence and Security Command (INSCOM). The U.S. Army Intelligence and Security Command, with headquarters at Arlington Hall Station, Virginia, near Washington, D.C., has world-wide responsibilities for intelligence collection and production, counterintelligence and security.

U.S. Army Communications Command (USACC). The U.S. Army Communications Command, with headquarters at Fort Huachuca, Arizona, manages the Army's portion of the world-wide Defense Communications System (DCS), including the planning, engineering, installation, and operation of the Army's portion of this system. It also provides engineering, installation, and technical support services, as required, for assigned Army communications; and for Army air traffic control facilities.

Military Traffic Management Command (MTMC). The Military Traffic Management Command, with headquarters in Washington, D.C., executes the Army's function as Single Manager for the Department of Defense of all military traffic management, land transportation, and common-user ocean terminals within CONUS, and for worldwide movement and storage of household goods for the Department of Defense.

U.S. Army Criminal Investigation Command. The U.S. Army Criminal Investigation Command has its headquarters in Falls Church, Virginia, near Washington, D.C. It exercises centralized command and control of Army criminal investigative activities worldwide.

U.S. Army Military District of Washington (MDW). The Military District of Washington commands Army units, activities, and installations and is responsible for designated Army functions in the metropolitan area of Washington, D.C. Its headquarters are located at Fort Leslie J. McNair in Washington. D.C.

U.S. Army Health Services Command. The U.S. Army Health Services Command, with headquarters at Fort Sam Houston, Texas, is the Army's single manager for health care delivery and supportive services within CONUS and in Alaska and Hawaii. It supervises all medical training for the Army.

U.S. Army Corps of Engineers (USACE). The U.S. Army Corps of Engineers, with headquarters in Washington, D.C., manages Army real property; manages and executes engineering, construction, and real estate programs for the Army and the Air Force; and manages and executes the civil works program for the Army.

ARMY COMPONENTS OF UNIFIED COMMANDS

The Army furnishes components of unified joint service commands operating under the operational direction of the Secretary of Defense through the Joint Chiefs of Staff. The Secretary of the Army is responsible for administrative and logistical support of these component commands and elements.

There are now four Army components of unified commands:

U.S. Army, Europe. The U.S. Army, Europe, with headquarters in Heidelberg, Germany, is the Army component of the unified U.S. European Command.

Eighth U.S. Army. The Eighth U.S. Army is the Army component of the unified U.S. Forces Korea.

U.S. Army, Japan. The U.S. Army, Japan, is the Army component of the unified U.S. Forces Japan.

U.S. Army, Western Command. The U.S. Army, Western Command, with headquarters at Fort Shafter, Hawaii, is the Army component of the unified U.S. Pacific Command.

Other unified commands, such as the U.S. Readiness Command, U.S. Alaskan Command, and U.S. Southern Command have Army elements which receive their administrative and logistical support from the U.S. Forces Command (FORSCOM).

ORGANIZATION BY COMPONENT

The Army of the United States consists of the Regular Army, the Army National Guard, and the Army Reserve. The terms of service differ as to each of the three components, but the purposes for which each is formed and maintained are identical: The security of the United States, its Constitution, its Government and people, and its commitments with allies.

The Regular Army. Members of the Regular Army, both officer and enlisted members, are on active, full-time military duty, as volunteers. It is the permanent, professional force. The station and duty of members is as directed by military authority. In war or peace, in good times or bad, the Regular Army must be ready to undertake whatever mission is directed by proper governmental authority. Members of the Regular Army are the "United States Army."

The Reserve Components. The Reserve Components are The Army National Guard of the United States and The Army Reserve. Members of these components may be on inactive military status, at their homes or locations of their own choice, while receiving military instruction at times of minimum interference with their civilian vocations. They may be called into active federal military service in time of war or other national emergency, when so determined by the President in accordance with law. That is to say, a member of the Reserve forces may be "inactive" and perform part-time military service, or may be "active" and be as fully engaged in military affairs as a member of the Regular service, with the same hazards and the same rewards.

The Active Army. That part of the Army of the United States which is on full-time service is called the Active Army. It includes under all conditions the United States Army (the Regular Army) as our full-time professional force, plus those individuals or complete units drawn from the Army National Guard or Army Reserve to serve on a full-time basis to meet conditions of war or overall strength requirements determined by the President and the Congress. Specified units of the reserve components are designated to roundout or augment active Army units in an emergency.

ORGANIZATION BY BRANCH

Officers of the Army are appointed into a basic or special branch, wear the branch insignia as a part of their uniforms, and are known, for example, as Infantry officers, Engineer officers, Quartermaster officers, etc. In a broad sense, branch assignment designates the general field of interest to the officer. Certain branches are associated closely with particular specialties as discussed in Chapter 12, *Professional Development.* An introductory description of the branches appears in Chapter 28, *Branches of the Army,* and each branch is described in detail in Chapters 29 through 32.

ORGANIZATION BY UNITS

There follows a short discussion of Army units, from the smallest to the largest. The system and the terminology are fairly uniform throughout the different arms and services, and once identified the various terms fit readily into the total pattern.

Tables of Organization and Equipment (TOE), issued by the Department of the Army, establish as to each category of Army unit its title, the number and grades of its officers and enlisted personnel, its organic equipment, and its interior organization. Tables of Distribution (TD) and Tables of Allowances (TA) prescribe the organization and equipment for special purpose temporary units. A newly assigned officer should study his or her unit's TOE or TD as soon as possible.

Units of Separate Arms and Services. The *rifle fire team* is the smallest tactical unit under a noncommissioned officer as leader. It is a team which can be controlled by one person, generally by use of voice.

The *squad* is the smallest and basic military unit. The number of soldiers assigned to a squad varies but may be visualized as from 8 to 11 persons.

The *platoon* consists of the platoon leader, an officer in the grade of lieutenant, and two or more squads.

The *company* has been the appropriate command for a captain. It includes its headquarters, two or more platoons, and is an administrative as well as a tactical unit. That is, it has supply and mess personnel, maintains organization records, and can function for short periods as a separate command. In the artillery, the term "battery" is used instead of company, and the "section" corresponds to the squad. In cavalry units, the term "troop" is used instead of company.

Battalion. Traditionally, the battalion included its commander, his or her staff and headquarters element, with two, three, or four companies (Infantry, Armor), batteries (Field Artillery), or troops (Cavalry). The cavalry unit corresponding to the battalion is designated squadron. In the ROAD division, a highly flexible type of organization, there are from six to fifteen combat battalions (infantry, airborne infantry, mechanized, or tank), the number and type of battalions depending on the type of division and its mission.

There are also, in the division "base," battalions of artillery, engineers, signal, air cavalry, aviation, and those in the support command providing maintenance, supply, and other administrative and logistical support.

Brigade. In the ROAD division there are three brigade headquarters each capable of controlling from two to five combat battalions. The necessary combat support and administrative elements are furnished the brigade by the division base.

Division. Except for the Armored Cavalry Regiment, which contains a mix of units, the division is the smallest unit of the combined arms and services. There are currently five types of combat divisions: armored, mechanized, infantry, airborne and air assault. The division is the appropriate command of a major general. The typical division has a strength of approximately 16,000 officers and enlisted personnel. It is a self-sustaining force capable of independent operations over extended periods of time.

Each type of division has command and control, combat, combat support, and combat service support elements. The command and control element includes division headquarters and three to four brigade headquarters. The combat element includes varying proportions of six to fifteen combat battalions of the different types (armor, infantry, mechanized, air assault and airborne infantry) to make up divisions ("armored"—6 tank and 5 mechanized battalions; "mechanized"—7 mechanized and 3 tank battalions; "infantry"—8 infantry and 2 tank battalions; "airborne"—9 airborne infantry and 1 tank battalion; and "air assault"—9 infantry and 3 air assault infantry battalions). The "mix" of units can be further tailored to accomplish a specific task. The armored division combines fast maneuver with tremendous firepower. The mechanized division resembles the infantry division but has greater mobility and shock power. The airborne division is for vertical envelopment by airborne assault, using parachutes and Air Force troop carrier and assault landing aircraft. The air assault division with its helicopters demonstrated in Vietnam its ability to deliver firepower quickly anywhere. The combat support and combat service support elements are included in the division base.

The Army last reorganized in the mid-1960s as a result of the ROAD study.

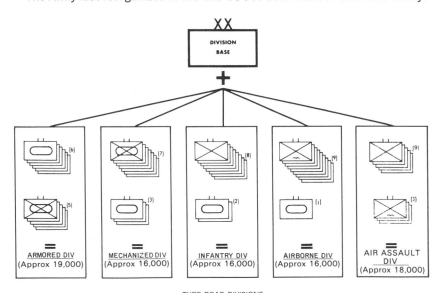

TYPE ROAD DIVISIONS.
(The numbers in parentheses show how many battalions in each)

In structuring for the Vietnam conflict, with its infantry-airmobile emphasis, the Army had, in fact, missed a modernization cycle. In 1976, the Army began a restructuring study to develop the optimum size, mix, and organization of Army divisions for the 1980–1985 timeframe. This effort was designated Division 86—the modernized heavy division of the future. The objective of Division 86 is to develop the most effective organization for the Army's heavy division (armor and mechanized infantry) by developing advanced battlefield concepts and harnessing the combat power of the new generation of weapons and systems to enter the force by the mid-1980s.

Significant changes in the future heavy division include the division cavalry squadron, three brigades, six tank battalions, and four mechanized battalions for the armored divisions; five tank and five mechanized battalions for the mechanized infantry divisions; a remodeled division support command; and the consolidation of all aviation assets into a cavalry brigade (air attack).

Army Corps. An army corps consists of its headquarters, two or more divisions, and such other organizations as its mission may require. The additional units may consist, for example, of artillery, armor, Army aviation, engineer units, medical units.

Field Army. A field army consists of its headquarters, two or more army corps, armor and perhaps an armored division, and other organizations of all kinds needed for sustained field operations.

Army Group. An army group consists of its headquarters, two or more field armies, plus supporting combat and logistical units of many categories as supplied for sustained operations against an enemy.

Regiments and Groups. It is necessary to discuss regiments and groups as a special case to avoid confusion. There are numbered groups of two or more battalions and in some cases four or more companies or batteries. These are tactical assignments for such units as field artillery, engineers, special forces, and air defense artillery. Such groups are constituted for units that are not organic to divisions. *Regiments* applies to the few armored cavalry regiments which have three cavalry reconnaissance squadrons. The historical and heraldic term, *regiment,* is just that. For example, the 1st Battalion of the 9th Infantry Regiment, is no longer physically a part of the 9th Infantry Regiment but carries on its traditions of insignia, colors, battle and campaign streamers. Although there may be more than three battalions in a given heraldic regiment, the first generally preserves its trophies, silver, memorabilia and records. The other battalions share in all the traditions.

ARMY AVIATION

Army Aviation exists to augment the capability of the Army to conduct prompt and sustained operations on land. By definition, it is aviation which is organic to the Army and is employed to enhance the mobility, flexibility, firepower, and efficiency of ground forces. This aviation stems from a War Department General Order of 6 June 1942 which assigned organic light aircraft to certain artillery units. The Cubs of World War II provided an important capability for observation, adjustment of fire, reconnaissance, command, control, and liaison. During the Korean conflict these light planes were augmented by the helicopter which found additional important uses for swift evacuation of battlefield casualties, patrolling, transport of commanders, delivery of critical supplies and many other uses. The helicopter served as the best and sometimes the only means of transportation of men and supplies in Vietnam. It was also used extensively as a weapon platform to deliver suppressive fires against the Viet Cong during the conflict in Vietnam.

Army aviation makes a major contribution to land combat and fights as a member of the combined arms team in a high threat environment. The objectives of Army aviation are to augment the capability of the Army to conduct prompt and sustained land combat, to provide the commander with the mobility, firepower, and staying power needed to win the first battle, and to help forces win while outnumbered.

Army Aviation is not a separate branch or corps within the Army. It is an integrated effort by personnel of many branches. Those which are authorized aviation are: Infantry, Armor, Engineer, Signal, Transportation, and Medical Services. Some officers may elect aviation as their accession career field specialty (see Chapter 12, *Professional Development*).

ARMY SPECIAL FORCES

The mission of Army Special Forces is to train personnel and to form units for the conduct of counterinsurgency operations, psychological operations, and unconventional warfare; and for employment as directed by constitutional authority in cold, limited, or general war. Members of these forces are selected individuals who must be airborne-qualified before beginning the training. With rare exceptions, and then only for officers, all Special Forces personnel are volunteers. The officer volunteer must have at least two years service remaining at the time of entering Special Forces. Training includes amphibious, swamp, jungle, and arctic environments; training time ranges from 24 weeks to as much as 58 weeks, according to the specialty in which trained. Members are authorized to wear the distinctive beret.

The Army initiated psychological warfare training in 1950 when it established the Psychological Warfare Division, Army General School at Fort Riley, Kansas. In 1952, it was transferred to Fort Bragg, North Carolina, and given the name of the Psychological Warfare Center. At the same time, the 10th Special Forces Group (Airborne) was activated at Fort Bragg. While closely allied in interests, the Center was a training organization, while the 10th Special Forces Group (Abn) was an operational force of the Army. Today, the Psychological Warfare Center has become the U.S. Army Institute of Military Assistance, while the 10th Special Forces Group (Abn) has become the John F. Kennedy Center for Military Assistance, in recognition of the interest of then President Kennedy in Special Warfare activities.

The U.S. Army Institute for Military Assistance is a command under the U.S. Army Training and Doctrine Command (TRADOC). It provides training to officers and enlisted personnel in Civil Affairs, Psychological Operations, and Special Forces. The John F. Kennedy Center for Military Assistance is part of the Army's combat forces and is controlled by the U.S. Army Forces Command (FORSCOM). Subordinate units include the 4th Psychological Operations Group, the 5th Special Forces Group (Airborne), the 7th Special Forces Group (Airborne) (two battalions), and the 96th Civil Affairs Battalion.

The Special Forces performed perilous and highly creditable work in southeast Asia during the conflict in Vietnam. Many members voluntarily served consecutive or repetitive tours to aid the beleaguered natives of that region. With the ending of that war, however, the strength of the Special Forces dropped from a high of about 12,500 to a current strength of about 4,000.

RANGERS

Announced in 1974 was formation of three Ranger battalions, the first of which, the 1st Battalion (Ranger), 75th Infantry, was activated on January 31, 1974. The Ranger name goes back to an irregular force used during the 18th century in the French and Indian War. During World War II, inspired by the British Commandos, the first Army Ranger battalions were formed, and they trained in Northern Ireland during 1942. During World War II, except for one battalion used in the Pacific area (Merrill's Marauders), to which the newly formed 1st Battalion (Ranger) traces its lineage, the Rangers saw service only in Europe. With the Rangers now reactivated, the Army continues another proud tradition.

All personnel assigned to Ranger units must be volunteers and must be airborne-qualified. All key leaders, including all officers, must also be Ranger-qualified.

ASSOCIATION OF THE UNITED STATES ARMY

Members of the Association of the United States Army believe that a strong Army, well led, of high morale, and provided with an adequate supply of weapons and equipment as good or better than can be thrown against it, is essential to protect the United States during these times of danger. The Association's membership includes officers and soldiers of the Regular and Reserve components of the Army, leaders of government, leaders in industry, science, and education, and interested civilians generally. The essential characteristic of members is belief in our Army, its mission, and its capability of providing the necessary security for our nation and our people. Their convictions are sound. The organization is necessary. It corresponds to the Navy League and the United States Air Force Association.

A monthly magazine, *ARMY,* is published which is essential reading for the active Army officer of Regular or Reserve component. Army officers and others interested in the Army should be members of the Association. Headquarters of the Association are at 1529 Eighteenth St., Washington, D.C. 20036.

ALWAYS READY—THE U.S. ARMY SOLDIER.

28

Branches of the Army

The classification of military personnel according to "branch of service," symbolized by means of distinctive devices of metal and enamel worn on the uniform, represents no recent development in military history nor even a tradition that is peculiar to the United State Army. The existence of at least two separate species of fighting men—mounted (cavalry) as well as unmounted (infantry)—can reasonably be assumed to trace back to the domestication of the horse. The Old Testament recounts (I Chronicles 18) of an ancient battle that "David slew of the Syrians seven thousand men which fought in chariots, and forty thousand footmen." Further refining this rudimentary division of labor, Alexander the Great (356–323 B.C.), whose invincible field armies conquered much of Asia, was obliged to create a massive combat service support corps to maintain supply lines extending from his kingdom in Macedon to northern India. And the famous Roman legions are known to have been organized into light and heavy infantry, cavalry, and siege trains; this third category, roughly comparable to the modern FASCOM, contained ordnance, quartermaster, and transportation elements, together with Caesar's celebrated corps of engineers, whose durable roads, aqueducts, and fortifications can still be found in parts of Europe.

The branch of service concept persists, in the Army as in civilian life, because it has repeatedly been proved to provide a highly workable management device for any large organization with a variety of missions and a considerable technological capability. Thus every modern corporation is structured along functional lines, with a separate department and specially trained personnel for each major activity, such as production, sales, advertising, research and development, accounting, and so on. The same is true of other large enterprises—governmental agencies, schools and colleges, and professional societies. The Army's branch system resembles those developed for civilian institutions in that it is designed to insure the most efficient and economical deployment of skilled manpower and, at the same time, to assist the individual in realizing full potential.

In actual practice, however, there are subtle differences between the branches of the Army and those of most civilian endeavors. The most conspicuous of these is the strong tradition that a person commissioned in any arm or service should be an officer first, and only then a specialist. In the past, this unwritten rule was observed quite literally, to the effect that the basic function of every officer (other than those with specified graduate degrees, such as chaplains and medical officers) was to command troops. In an era of ever-increasing reliance upon technology and specialization, this ideal has lost much of its previous relevance. In fact, the Army's professional development program (see Chapter 12) assures that each officer will be qualified initially in an initial or accession specialty and, after about 8 years service, in an additional specialty. Today, however, the "officer-first" tradition is interpreted as meaning that an officer, irrespective of branch or specialty or assignment, is above all things a leader, rather than a super-technician; and, that in the exercise of professional duties he or she is still required to exhibit the qualities of honor, integrity, and responsibility. The warrant officer, of course, is expected to be a super-technician and normally can expect to remain in and become most proficient in his or her primary MOS.

There are indicators of the importance the Army attaches to professionalism among its officer corps. Perhaps the most important of these is the fact that officers tend to remain within the arm or service in which they were originally commissioned. Army Regulations provide opportunities for both permanent branch transfer and temporary (usually for two years or less) branch details, but such mobility is the exception, rather than the rule. The branch of service with which an enlisted soldier is identified varies with the unit of assignment; that is, the enlisted soldier will normally wear infantry insignia while serving with an infantry brigade, Transportation Corps insignia when assigned to a transportation company, and so on. On the other hand, an officer's branch of service will rarely be changed as the result of transfer from one assignment to another.

Finally, the sense of professional esprit kindled by association with a particular branch of service is sustained by the relative stability of the branches themselves. With the gradual evolution of the Army's mission and its techniques for achieving that mission, the need for a given branch sometimes disappears; World War II saw the last days of both the historic cavalry and the somewhat youthful Coast Artillery Corps. Similarly, new challenges occasionally produce new branches such as Civil Affairs (USAR) and Air Defense Artillery, both of them created since World War II. By and large, however, the arms and services have responded to new weapons and new requirements, and not a few of them existing today may be traced back to the very beginnings of the United States Army. The advent of OPMS as described in Chapter 12 has tended, particularly for the support branches, to emphasize specialties rather than branches, but as can be seen from the specialty listings in Chapter 12, many specialties are closely related to particular branches, so the branch ties still continue.

The operative principle governing one's initial appointment in a given arm or service and assignment of accession specialty is "convenience of the Government"; that is, the manpower needs of the Army at a particular time. This immutable fact is not always understood by newly commissioned officers who feel they could serve more effectively in a branch and/or specialty other than that to which they have been appointed. More than one ROTC student majoring in business administration, for example, has been disappointed to be commissioned a second lieutenant of Infantry after having expressed a preference for the Finance Corps, the Quartermaster Corps, or the Adjutant General's Corps. In such a situation, the likelihood is that, perhaps because of casualties or a shortage of replacements, infantry units throughout the Army are understrength while the technical services have achieved or surpassed their authorized manning levels; under these circumstances, the infantry assignment is inevitable. At the same time, it is the policy of the Department of the Army to assign officers in accordance with their specific desires and abilities. Not infrequently, therefore, an officer who can present a reasonable case for transfer to another branch is given ample opportunity to do so. Army Regulation 614–100 outlines the procedures for requesting such an action. Similarly, procedures are available to change specialties. See DA Pam 600–3 for details.

One of the fringe benefits of permanent affiliation with a particular branch of the service is the feeling of camaraderie that develops among its members, particularly seasoned officers with a multitude of assignments behind them. This family spirit, the almost inevitable result of common interests and shared experiences, is pleasant in itself and for younger officers has the additional advantage of providing a dependable, first-hand source of professional counsel and supervision. On a more formal, but scarcely less valuable, basis, the junior officer has always at his or her disposal the services of the career branch chief, who maintains individual files and a guidance facility in the Officer Personnel Management Directorate of the Military Personnel Center. Officers are authorized and encouraged to communicate directly with this service and to make arrangements, from time to time, for personal visits to the branch chief for such purposes as examining evaluation reports, reviewing their professional progress, and obtaining timely and informed advice on future schooling, assignments, and the like. Few private corporations offer so helpful and comprehensive a system of career management for their personnel, but much of the responsibility for exploiting this unique service is left to the initiative of the individual officer. (See Chapter 12).

At this time, there are a total of 22 branches of the Army authorized for active service. They are:

Infantry	Medical Corps
Air Defense Artillery	Dental Corps
Field Artillery	Veterinary Corps
Armor	Medical Service Corps
Corps of Engineers	Army Nurse Corps
Signal Corps	Army Medical Specialist Corps
Military Police Corps	Chaplain Corps
Chemical Corps	Judge Advocate General's Corps
Military Intelligence	Ordnance
Adjutant General's Corps	Transportation
Finance Corps	
Quartermaster	

The Army has a number of ways of classifying these branches (e.g., arms and services, basic and special), but perhaps the most convenient and readily understood categories would be combat, combat support, and combat service support. Combat arms are those directly involved in the conduct of actual fighting; these are Infantry, Air Defense Artillery, Field Artillery, Armor and Corps of Engineers. Combat support arms are those which provide operational assistance to the combat arms, including engagement in combat when necessary, but who have additional responsibilities in providing logistical and administrative support to the Army as a whole; these include the Signal Corps, Military Police Corps, Chemical Corps, and Military Intelligence. Finally, the combat service support branches are those whose chief mission is to provide logistical and administrative support and whose personnel are not usually directly engaged in combat operations; these are the 13 at the end of the listing. In addition, there are two branches which exist only in the Reserve components: the Staff Specialist (Corps) and Civil Affairs. In the event of mobilization of the USAR, the former would be absorbed by existing branches, while the latter would probably retain branch integrity. Finally, there exist a small number of officers who wear distinctive insignia, such as Inspector General or General Staff insignia, while temporarily detailed to duties apart from the established branches.

Each of the active duty branches of the Army is explained in the next four chapters, with a brief history of each, a general discussion of its purpose and functions, and an outline of the various kinds of duty assignments one might expect to receive if assigned to that branch. All the duties that could conceivably be assigned to an officer of a given branch cannot, of course, be described in detail. Certain types of assignments are appropriate to all branches and, moreover, junior officers are usually called upon to perform duties unrelated to branch or specialty when "additional duty" assignments are made. (See Appendix.) The typical jobs referenced within each branch description have been chosen to represent types of assignments which are peculiar to that branch only or would be more likely assigned to officers of that branch than any other. Chapter 12 on *Professional Development* provides information on usual educational assignments. Chapter 8, *Army Posts and Stations* specifically indicates the major activities of each installation, and for most branches will serve as a guide to the places personnel of a particular branch might be assigned. Because of the extensive treatment of both subjects in these chapters, the branch material following does not attempt to cover them in detail. Rather, it has been written specifically to present the young junior officer with an objective "image" of the Army's branch organization, and especially to aid the ROTC cadet in finding and requesting that branch assignment and initial or accession specialty which will most fully utilize his or her talents and training in a way that will best serve both the individual's and the Army's needs.

BRANCH COLORS AND INSIGNIA

Contrary to beliefs held by many officers through the years, branch insignia and colors are basically in existence only for the purpose of identification. Selection of insignia in most cases was completely arbitrary although the evolution of logical symbolism can be found in every design. The choice and assignment of a branch color or colors is purely for providing immediate recognition when worn as a significant part of the uniform. According to the Institute of Heraldry, US Army, there is no basis for widespread assumption that a particular branch color has a specific symbolism (i.e. blue was not chosen to indicate courage; red, bravery; and so on). That fact, however, should not make the designation and use of branch colors any less influential in the development of *esprit de corps,* nor discourage inclusion and reference to the branch color in traditional ceremonies and morale-building activities.

Although illustrative and descriptive detail on branch insignia appears in Chapter 21, each of the branch descriptions includes a short historical narrative of the insignia to help set the "image" of that branch.

29

The Combat Arms

Air Defense Artillery (ADA), a combat arms branch of the Army, has the primary mission of destroying, nullifying, or reducing the enemy air threat. Considerations for land warfare require the provision of protective air defense over the battlefield which has truly become tridimensional. Air defense is now provided by various theater level guided missile systems, and the Chaparral (missile)/-Vulcan (20-mm gun) systems which are organic to every division. In the future, the newly developed 40-mm DIVAD gun system will replace Vulcan in providing air defense coverage for the division.

Guided missiles, in the sense that they can be controlled and guided to specific targets, are a recent phenomenon in warfare, although military use of self-propelled projectiles dates back at least to the 13th century in China. Following the recorded uses of rocket propulsion techniques by the Chinese, India was next to recognize the potential of such a weapon. Prince Hyder Ali, during the latter part of the 18th century, organized a rocket corps of 1,200 men who used an iron tube about 8 inches long and $1\frac{1}{2}$ inches in diameter to launch missiles that reached distances up to $1\frac{1}{2}$ miles. British use of rockets during the War of 1812 is immortalized in our own national anthem. Experimentation with rockets by US forces is known to have occurred in 1846–1848 during the war with Mexico and then was abandoned for lack of efficiency compared to the rifled cannon in use at the time.

Serious military thought about missiles as weapons lay dormant until the German "buzz" bomb attacks on Britain caused a new look at this possibility. By the end of World War II the United States had developed a missile comparable to the German V–1, but the missile development program became, for a time, a victim of postwar reductions in priorities. The idea for the first US air defense artillery missile, the Nike Ajax, was conceived in the fall of 1944 at Fort Bliss, Texas.

Officers assigned to Air Defense Artillery consider themselves members of one of the oldest and most demanding combat arms of the Army. Indeed, the ability to lead troops having control of such highly technical equipment requires a unique leadership ability. The US Army Air Defense School at Fort Bliss, Texas, which plays an important role in developing this leadership, traces its lineage directly to the Coast Artillery School, which was organized at Fort Monroe, Virginia, in April 1824. This school, the oldest service school in the Army, laid the foundation for the present system of military education in the Army. On 18 May 1858, the name was changed to the Artillery School, which was eventually split into the Field Artillery and the Coast Artillery Schools on 1 August 1907. The Coast Artillery School had responsibility for antiaircraft artillery which was developed during and after World War I. By 1940, antiaircraft artillery subjects predominated the courses at the Coast Artillery School, and in March 1942, the antiaircraft responsibility was transferred to the newly established Antiaircraft Artillery School at Camp Davis, North Carolina. In October 1944, the School was moved to Fort Bliss, Texas, its present home. On 1 July 1957, after several name changes, the School was officially designated the US Army Air Defense School.

Officers commissioned in ADA start their career with attendance at the ADA Officer Basic Course at the Air Defense School. During this 10-week course, they are prepared for their first duty assignment, and become familiar with the family of air defense weapons and their tactical employment. Based on assignment, graduates of the course immediately attend a particular weapon system course which follows the 10-week basic course.

After this basic schooling, new officers are normally assigned as platoon leaders in a Nike Hercules, Hawk, or Chaparral/Vulcan battery, or as Redeye/Stinger section/platoon leaders. Assignments will also be available in the near future with new ADA weapons such as the Patriot missile and the DIVAD gun, which will replace Nike Hercules and Vulcan. The officers' responsibilities will include the operational training and tactical employment of their units, maintenance of equipment, and the welfare and morale of unit personnel.

Officers assigned to platoons in Hawk or Nike Hercules units will have the responsibility of initiating and controlling the engagement sequence which includes launching missiles to destroy hostile aircraft. In the near future, with the Patriot system, officers will have similar responsibilities. With Chaparral/-Vulcan units or the newly-developed 40-mm DIVAD gun system, the platoons will often operate independently from parent batteries to provide area air defense support for infantry and armor elements. As Redeye/Stinger section

Design of the Air Defense Artillery insignia was first approved in 1957 for the then single Artillery branch. The crossed field guns indicate branch ties to the Field Artillery, the superimposed missile symbolizing modern developments. This insignia became the identification of ADA when it was authorized as a separate branch in 1968.

leaders, their teams will be deployed to protect elements of the maneuver battalions and supporting field artillery.

Through this training and experience, the ADA officer normally qualifies for positions of increasing responsibility as Air Defense Artillery Unit Commander, ADA Command and Control Officer, and ADA Staff and Missile Systems Officer in the various Air Defense organizations deployed. These positions provide for both new challenges and professional development opportunities in a branch with a vital mission for preserving peace.

Troop unit duty might be with any one of the current authorized TOE organizations: Hawk, Chapparal/Vulcan, Nike Hercules, or Redeye/Stinger, deployed overseas and throughout CONUS. The Patriot missile and DIVAD gun systems will provide additional duty assignments in the near future for ADA officers.

The next phase of formal training—the 26-week Air Defense Artillery Officer Advanced Course—follows at the US Army Air Defense School after several years of troop duty. This course is very important to the career of every air defense artillery officer because it is in many respects the pinnacle as far as career education is concerned. The course offers the officer the experience of self-expression among the officer's peers based on knowledge accumulated in pursuing an air defense profession. The course covers all the existing air defense artillery weapon systems, along with such related topics as computers, command and control, combined arms, and nuclear weapon employment.

A quick reacting air defense, provided by a family of complementary weapon systems, is required for security today. This requirement is justified by the destructive power of the aircraft and the nuclear weapon threat. Air defense artillery provides many deterrent weapons, not only for the support of land warfare operations, but also for the defense of CONUS. Research into ballistic missile defense technology for the defense of CONUS is also an ADA responsibility. The burden of these vital responsibilities rests with the dedicated and capable officers of the Air Defense Artillery.

Air Defense Artillery continues to be one of the major combat activities of the Army and its proper utilization could spell the difference in a given combat situation. As technology advances, the future of this branch will be filled with changes and the necessity for dedicated, technically qualified officers.

Approved in 1950, the current Armor insignia blends the past and present. Its base is formed by the traditional crossed sabers adopted for the Cavalry in 1851, on which a front view of the M26 tank is superimposed. It symbolizes Armor's heritage in the first "mounted" troops and today's role as a mechanized force.

ARMOR

The responsibility for the development and conduct of mobile warfare, originally the province of the horse Cavalry, rests with the United States Army's Armor Branch. Although modern technology has produced weaponry and transportation systems that are far more efficient than the horse, the incomparable spirit of the Old Cavalry and the impetuous character of its leaders are instantly recognizable in its modern counterpart. The impulse to devastating attack that has governed the tactics of mounted warfare from antiquity continues to dominate the doctrines and combat operations of Armor Branch. Its three subcomponents of Armored Cavalry, Air Cavalry, and Armor provide the Army with its most powerful reconnaissance and striking forces, all of which are trained to maneuver and fight under the most stringent of conditions.

The concept of combative systems augmented by armor protection and increased mobility is not a new one. Military leaders of man's most ancient cultures constantly sought means through which to increase the individual's destructive force on the battlefield while rendering him impervious to harm.

The introduction of the horse to combat brought an entirely new dimension to warfare, as conflicts could now be fought swiftly—and won even by numerically-inferior forces who used their agile mounts to maximum advantage. Imperial Egypt and Assyria—as well as Asia's Huns and Mongols—all achieved their greatest conquests through the concentrated application of cavalry, and all exploited its psychological impact to the fullest.

The distinguished history of the United States Cavalry dates from the Revolutionary War. One outstanding cavalry unit of that war was the Light Horse of the City of Philadelphia, a troop organized in 1774 and still active today in the Pennsylvania Army National Guard. It served as General Washington's personal escort through the bitter days of Trenton and Princeton, displaying, in Washington's words, ". . . a Spirit of Bravery which will ever do Honor to them and will ever be gratefully remembered by me." Although the Army maintained no Regular Cavalry units for the better part of the next fifty years, volunteer units existed in all of the states. Mounted Kentucky militia played a crucial role in General Anthony Wayne's victory at Fallen Timbers in 1794, driving the Indian warriors from their covered positions to the open prairie.

Union cavalry was employed largely as an escort and security element in the early part of the Civil War, and hence was of no strategic and only limited tactical value. However, Union cavalry commanders, impressed by the accomplishments of massed Confederate cavalry under Generals Turner Ashby, Stuart, and Forrest, were employing their forces much more efficiently by the end of the war. Grant's use of Grierson's cavalry during the Vicksburg campaign was instrumental to Union success in the West.

From 1868 until the turn of the century, those cavalry units retained on an active status were sent to the western frontier to meet the growing threat of the Plains Indians. Conventional infantry proved to be ineffective against the mounted raiding parties of the Sioux and the Comanches, and ten cavalry regiments dispersed among fifty-five posts throughout the West finally brought peace to the new territories. In every major ground action until the first world war—from Colonel Theodore Roosevelt's Rough Riders in Cuba (who, however, fought on foot during the entire war,) to General Adna Chaffee's Sixth Cavalry, the first force to take the "Forbidden City" during China's Boxer Rebellion—the United States Cavalry led the way. General Pershing's pursuit of the Mexican bandit, Pancho Villa, in 1916 was the last major action of the horse cavalry. From that point on, cavalry was to undergo an all too gradual mechanization that was to lead to its present incorporation into Armor Branch's combined arms team.

World War I heralded the birth of the team's second component, the tank. First developed by the British Royal Navy, and disguised for intelligence purposes as "tanks for water in Russia" or "tanks for water in Mesopotamia", tanks saw their first engagement in September of 1916, when they participated in the Battle of the Somme. The American Tank Corps, initially a part of the Infantry Branch, fought its first battle in 1918, using French tanks due to the non-availability of American-built machines. During the Meuse-Argonne attack General Pershing offered ". . . anything in the A.E.F." for five hundred additional tanks, but they were simply not available. By the end of the war, tanks had been employed by the British, French, Germans, and Americans in over ninety engagements.

Although the value of tanks in modern warfare had proved substantial, few major military leaders were prepared to recognize this. The United States Army —together with the principal European armies—believed that tanks should be relegated to an infantry-support role. Consequently, through the National Defense Act of 1920, the Tank Corps was assigned to the Chief of Infantry. The first Tank School was organized at Fort Meade, Maryland, but the program was subsequently moved to Fort Benning, Georgia and renamed the Tank Section of the Infantry School. During this same period the Chief of Cavalry was authorized to develop mechanized weapons, and Fort Knox, Kentucky was designated as the new home of the mechanized cavalry.

The spectacular successes of German armor in the early days of World War II helped speed the creation of a United States armor-based military branch. A War Department order of July 10, 1940 created the Armored Force, and the U.S. Army Armor School was instituted a few days later. Although there had been little involvement in tank-to-tank fighting in the early stages of the war, the North African campaign soon changed the concept of armored warfare. In those tremendous expanses of open terrain, tanks—often as many as five hundred on each side—clashed in massive engagements. In Europe, General George S. Patton, Jr. commanded the armored elements of his Third Army so aggressively that they sometimes advanced more than one hundred miles in one day, outdistancing their own lines of supply. Supplementing the sixteen American Armored divisions deployed to Europe were several Armored Cavalry units employed in the classic reconnaissance-security role.

When the Korean conflict erupted in June of 1950, North Korean-manned Soviet T-34 tanks accompanied the Communists in their southward drive. The United States Army, which had not originally considered the terrain in that part of the world "tankable," fought without them until mid-July, when the first American tanks reached the peninsula. By August there were over five hundred tanks in action within the Pusan Perimeter, outnumbering the enemy's by over five to one. For the remainder of the war, tank units of battalion size and smaller participated in most combat actions.

After the Korean truce the Army launched a serious investigation relating to the possibilities of the rotary wing aircraft for use in combat operations. The first "Sky Cavalry" unit, equipped with unarmed helicopters for reconnaissance purposes only, underwent testing during exercise "Sagebrush" in 1955. Shortly after the "Sagebrush" exercise The Continental Army Command directed the Army Aviation School to establish a project entitled "Armed Helicopter Mobile Task Force." In 1958 the Armor School was first charged with the responsibility of preparing the doctrine for tactical employment of Air Cavalry. By 1962 three Air Cavalry troops had been organized, one at Fort Knox, Kentucky, one at Fort Carson, Colorado, and another at Fort Hood, Texas. Also in 1962 the Defense Department directed General Hamilton Howze to establish an "Air Mobility Requirement Review Board." The Howze Board established the requirement for organizing the Air Assault Division and the Air Cavalry Squadron.

In 1965 the First Cavalry Division (Airmobile) was deployed to South Vietnam. Its Air Cavalry squadron proved so successful that additional Air Cavalry units were organized and deployed to Vietnam. The earliest helicopter "gunships" were the UH–1 "Hueys"—originally designed as troop carriers. A later arrival was the AH–1G "HueyCobra"—the first aircraft in the Army inventory designed specifically as a weapons platform. Although the terrain in South Vietnam initially was considered unsuitable for armored vehicles, as had been the case earlier in Korea, the air cavalry soon was complemented on the ground by the employment, between 1965 and 1973, of three medium tank battalions and seventeen armored cavalry squadrons and separate troops. These units utilized the M48A2 and M48A3 tanks, the M551 General Sheridan Armored Reconnaissance/Airborne Assault Vehicle, and the versatile M113 Armored Personnel Carrier. These three dimensions of Armor, working in conjunction with both mechanized and dismounted infantry forces, achieved substantial combat success in the counterinsurgency environment of the Republic of Vietnam. Near the end of U.S. troop participation in Vietnam, armored units, both ground and air, comprised over 54% of the total combat maneuver forces and were the last units to redeploy to the United States. Air Cavalry, particularly when teamed with ground units of Armor and Armored Cavalry, proved its worth as one of the Army's most versatile combat weapons systems.

Contemporary Armor and Cavalry tactics incorporate cohesive and aggressive emphasis upon mobility, firepower, and shock action to overcome an enemy force. The combined arms team concept includes tanks, armored and air cavalry, mechanized infantry/artillery/engineers, and Army aviation, all supported by a flexible and swift communications network and a highly-mobile and responsive combat service support system. While the tank continues to be the principal armor-defeating weapon in the combined arms team, it is primarily intended for general application against the entire enemy force. Armor is continually evolving to meet worldwide challenges and potential threats. Two of its newest additions, the Attack Helicopter Squadron and the Air Cavalry Combat Brigade, significantly extend the reach and the lethality of Armor's third dimension.

Armor officers have educational patterns and career programs similar to those found in other branches, including selection of and subsequent assignments in an additional specialty after about 8 years of service. The Armor School at Fort Knox offers the Armor Officer Basic and Advanced Courses, as well as specialized instructional programs for noncommissioned officers and senior-grade commissioned officers. Notable among the special courses for officers is the Motor Officer Course. In the eight weeks of the Motor Officer Course, students receive meticulous instruction on maintenance management, supervision and inspection of vehicular maintenance and repair procedures, and the complex material requirements of Armor/Calvalry field operations.

Upon completion of the Advanced Course, Armor officers will usually gain experience in plans and operations through assignment to command or staff positions in battalions, squadrons, brigades, or divisions. Armor officers are also in demand as planners, directors, and special staff officers at major Army headquarters, on joint staffs, at the Department of the Army, and in research and development projects related to combined arms concepts.

Armor is rich in tradition and exciting in potential. Officers who apply and are selected for assignment to Armor Branch are assured of an unusually dynamic and rewarding career.

1875 was the year a design of crossed muskets was authorized for wear by Infantry officers. Several subsequent changes reflecting newer models ended in 1924 when the present design, based on the first type of musket used by US Army troops, was approved.

INFANTRY

The Infantry is the oldest of the combat arms. From the dawn of time, wars have been predominantly fought by men on foot. Long before men domesticated the horse, or invented any kind of boat, the Infantry was represented in the intertribal wars of prehistory.

At first, Infantry battles were really hand-to-hand encounters of pairs of warriors, or simple mob actions. Rude tactical plans were sometimes carried out, but more often than not, tactical plans miscarried due to the lack of discipline and cohesiveness of the "Armies" of prehistory.

The Greeks overcame this problem with one of the great military innovations of all times—discipline. Under the Greek system, Infantrymen were drawn up in a solid block of men, sixteen ranks deep. Armed with spears nearly twenty feet long, trained to a high degree of physical fitness, and held in their ranks by discipline, the Greek Infantrymen were almost invincible. They changed the course of history when they formed their *Phalanx* on the Plain of Marathon and defeated the Medes and Persians who threatened to overwhelm the entire civilized world.

The Greek *Phalanx* dominated warfare for centuries, until the Romans developed a superior organization. The Roman Legion combined the discipline of the *Phalanx* with a flexible battle formation called the *Maniple*. Maniples were small "handfuls" of men who fought under the leadership of junior officers. Because of their small size, they could be easily manuevered over rough ground. The Roman armies were trained so that the individual members of the maniples worked as a team, and the maniples in turn worked together to bring about victory. One advantage that the maniple had was that it placed a premium on the intelligence and initiative of the junior leader. Since Roman times, four factors have characterized all successful Infantry: discipline, teamwork, initiative, and resourceful junior leadership.

In the years after the fall of the Roman Empire, the Roman Infantry organization fell out of use, and for almost a thousand years, the wars of Europe were fought by knights on horseback. Infantry was represented on the medieval battlefield by footmen and pages who cared for the knights' horses and equipment.

Near the end of the Middle Ages, the Swiss mountaineers rediscovered the military organizations of the Greeks and Romans. Armed with pikes reminiscent of the spears of the *Phalanx* and drawn up into squares called "hedgehogs" the Swiss were able to stop the charge of the armored knights. At about the same time, the English bowmen were demonstrating the havoc they could wreak on cavalry with their yard-long arrows; with the adoption of gunpowder and firearms, the Infantry fully regained its former role as the first and foremost combat arm—a role which it retains to this day.

The Infantry is the basic ground-gaining arm of the Army. Its mission is "to close with the enemy by fire and maneuver in order to destroy or capture him, or to repel his attack by fire, close combat, or counter-attack."

Modern Infantry is much more complex than the Infantry of the Greeks, Romans, or Swiss. Today's Infantryman can move by land, sea or air. The modern Infantryman may fight on foot, or go into action by parachute, helicopter, armored personnel carrier, assault boat, or the Bradley fighting vehicle. The Infantry can operate at night, or under any climatic conditions, and can overcome natural and man-made obstacles which would stop other forces.

The Infantry has been variously described as "the Queen of Battle" and "the ultimate weapon". Both of these descriptions are fully justified in terms of the role of the Infantry in warfare. The foot soldier has picked up some less elegant titles. "Doughboy" is a nickname that dates back to the Mexican War, and refers to the mixture of flour and water that the Infantry ate as their first meal in 48 hours after storming Molino del Rey. "Dog Soldier" is a nickname the Infantry picked up fighting Indians on the plains. The Indians likened the Infantry to the most respected and feared of the "war societies" of the Plains tribes, the Cheyenne Dog Soldiers.

The oldest Infantry regiment still on active duty is the Third Infantry, "the Old Guard", authorized by Act of Congress on June 3, 1784. The First Infantry was authorized on 3 March 1791, and the Second Infantry on 12 April 1808. Many other units have been authorized since then, and many reorganizations have been made, but the purpose of the Infantry remains the same.

Perhaps two keywords in describing an Infantry officer's role are *diversity* and *accomplishment.* The satisfaction and personal development the officer experiences from the leadership of soldiers and the management of challenging staff assignments proves invaluable both within the military and in later civilian pursuits. Normally, all Infantry officers have the opportunity to lead a platoon during their initial two years of duty. A few command companies during the same period.

The involvement of infantry officers with personnel of their commands is total. It will tax the depth of their backgrounds and develop them in all areas. They serve as instructors, counselors, and focal points bearing total responsibility for their assigned personnel. The soldier's problems become their problems, the soldier's needs their needs. To be successful, they must know their soldiers.

The command of an Infantry platoon or company is the opportunity to lead and practice leadership in a demanding, complex job. It is the managing of priorities among training (collective as well as individual), maintenance, communications, messhalls, supply, athletics, marksmanship, discipline, and public relations. It is the opportunity to make tough decisions and to accept responsibility in combat and peacetime roles. This opportunity to command in no way reflects the entire range of a junior officer's duties. A large percentage of all Infantry lieutenants completing their first two years' of service have experienced at least one staff assignment. To a large degree, such assignments are at the troop level, filling positions in battalion- and brigade-size units. Positions such as assistant adjutant, supply officer, and motor officer are but a few such positions normally held by lieutenants.

A second major area in which Infantry officers can expect to serve in staff roles is the Army's special commands where training, administration, and management are the principal functions of the organization. For example, Infantry lieutenants presently serve at Ft. Benning at the training center. Duty positions include company training officer and instructor. Newly commissioned infantry officers receive training in basic military techniques in order to enable them to serve competently and confidently in any initial assignments they might face. Infantry officers must first receive a solid background at the small unit level. Later in their careers they may be eligible for additional schooling opportunities, both military and civilian.

The first assignment for all newly-commissioned Infantry officers is attendance at the Officer Basic Course at Fort Benning, Georgia. The course is designed to prepare each newly-commissioned Infantry officer to train and lead an infantry platoon and to serve as a training officer of a training company. The officers study techniques of tactics, leadership, management, and administration that each must know to be effective.

The learning environment at Fort Benning rivals that of any university in the nation; a professional and experienced faculty, constantly revising the course curriculum to reflect only the most current concepts, presents classes that are interesting as well as informative. The Officer Basic Course is of sixteen weeks' duration and is composed of approximately one-third classroom work and two-thirds field practical exercises.

In order to enhance an officer's background between major schooling periods some temporary duty (TDY) courses of instruction are offered. The Ranger Course was established in order to provide training in the techniques of small-unit tactics. Emphasis is placed on tactical realism, patrolling, and exposure to various terrain and climatic environments while further developing individual leadership qualities such as prompt obedience, self-discipline, self-confidence, resourcefulness and determination. The Airborne Course is a three-week program designed to qualify volunteers in military parachuting. The course is divided into three phases (ground week, tower week, and jump week), during which an individual progresses from physical conditioning and mastery of parachute landing falls, to control of an opened parachute, and the proper exiting from an aircraft.

The Advanced Course is normally given to Infantry officers between their third and eighth years of commissioned service. It prepares officers to command companies and to serve on battalion and brigade staffs. Successful completion of the course is essential for the career officer and is required before an officer can proceed into specialization or into post-graduate civil schooling programs. All officers will also attend the Combined Arms and Services Staff School between their seventh and ninth years of commissioned service. This school, which is sometimes called the Army Staff Course, prepares the officer for brigade, division, and installation staff assignments. During the eighth through fifteenth years of service, the officer progresses through the intermediate stage of professional development, gaining proficiency in a designated additional specialty. During this period the officer may be selected for higher level civilian and military schooling. Each officer is engaged in command and staff duties designed to develop a broad understanding of the overall role of the Army.

An Infantry officer's chances of pursuing graduate study at leading universities are good. Selection is made on a voluntary, though competitive basis by Infantry branch. Present policy in selecting officers for the graduate program is that an officer is not selected until after completion of the Infantry Officer Advance Course. Factors bearing on selection include an officer's undergraduate record, the degree of competitiveness as reflected by the officer's evaluation report scores, and whether the officer has had a good branch background in terms of proficiency in positions held.

Also during the seventh through thirteenth years, an officer may be considered for attendance at the Command and General Staff College located at Fort Leavenworth, Kansas. The nine-month course is designed to provide an officer with an understanding of the procedures and tactics involved in the higher level command and staff positions. Specially selected officers will attend one of the other service staff colleges with an equivalent program of instruction, in lieu of the Command and General Staff College. Following this phase and between the fifteenth and twenty-third years of service, the officer is considered for attendance at one of the senior service colleges; this will further enhance the officer's background and capability to assume responsibility of the highest level.

In the near future, officers' careers will be guided by the Military Qualifications Standards (MQS). This is a comprehensive set of manuals consisting of training tasks and standards. It is envisioned that there will be one manual for each rank and one for precommissioning training. Tasks will include not only resident instruction, but also considerable non-resident study and reading.

The advanced portion of an officer's career pattern, consisting of performing high-level staff and command duties, ranging from the command of an Infantry brigade to the management of a critical Department of the Army staff agency, is reached at some time between the officer's sixteenth and twenty-third years of service. Outstanding officers may qualify for senior service schooling to enable them to perform at the highest Army levels.

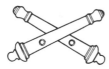

Field Artillery officers have been identified by the insignia of crossed field guns since 1834 and, although the design went through several variations with the establishment of the Coast Artillery and the advent of missiles, the current design is basically that of the original.

FIELD ARTILLERY

The idea of artillery as a facet of warfare is as old as the written word. The Bible mentions the use of ingenious machines, comparable to artillery, on the walls of Jerusalem over 2,700 years ago. Archimedes, with his oversized slingshot capable of hurling a 300-pound stone 300 yards, terrorized the Roman Legions of Marcellus at the siege of Syracuse in 211 B.C. Caesar's ballista, a huge crossbow apparatus, supported his landing on the shores of Britain.

The first use of rockets as a weapon of war was recorded in 1232, when they were used by the Chinese against the Tartars. The first rocket was an arrow with a propelling device tied to it. The development of artillery as we know it, however, began in a serious way during the Hundred Years' War in the fourteenth century. Cannon were used extensively during sieges; but the cannon of that age had no carriage; they were placed on the ground and elevated only by building dirt piles under the muzzle. By the year 1600, the gun had developed firepower which was not surpassed by the weapons of the mid-19th century. One tremendous weapon of the 1600's was the Mons Meg of Edinburgh Castle, which threw a 19½-inch iron ball 1,400 yards or a stone ball twice that far.

Gustavus Adolphus, the great Swedish warrior-king of the seventeenth century, is credited with putting artillery in its rightful place on the battlefield. He limited his Artillery to weapons no heavier than 12-pound cannon; he increased the rapidity of the fire by combining the powder charge and projectile into a single cartridge; he frequently assembled guns into strong batteries which could neutralize enemy fire with concentrated firepower. His cavalry neutralized immovable enemy guns. Thus he developed the three primary facets of victory: firepower, mass, and mobility, and his plan of the use of artillery remains valid today.

Artillery has been "American" since *before* the Revolution. The Ancient and Honorable Artillery Company of Boston (founded in 1637), served with the British Royal Artillery at the fall of the French bastion, Louisberg, during the French and Indian Wars, in 1745.

During the Revolutionary War, the Colonies' artillery, under the command of Alexander Hamilton, performed greatly at the Battle of Trenton, and the skill of American gunners forced the British into siege trenches at Yorktown.

Throughout the early years of the country, artillerymen were considered the Army's elite. Their pay was above the rate for infantrymen and even the cavalry. In 1784, when all of the Army was abolished except for a single detachment of 80 men to guard government stores, those men were artillerymen. Thus the Artillery is the only part of the Army which has been in continuous service since the Revolution. In 1824, the Artillery School was established at Fort Monroe, Virginia beginning the comprehensive system of service schools which is important today. The many uses and value of artillery through the 19th century military campaigns, including the Civil War is far too comprehensive to detail here.

It wasn't until 1907 that two separate artillery corps were established. The Field Artillery and the Coast Artillery were organized with specific missions obvious from the names and during World War I the Coast Artillery was given the additional job of developing railroad-mounted and antiaircraft artillery pieces.

Development of bigger and better guns and vastly improved Field Artillery tactics and techniques for using them was rapid with the onset of World War II. By the end of the war, artillery firepower had grown beyond all dimensions previously known to man. During this war, new weapons were developed which were to revolutionize our concept of war—nuclear weapons, guided missiles, and radar.

The modern field artillery officer is trained to know all of the Artillery weapons, fire direction operations, and target acquisition systems and how to employ them in support of combined arms operations. This training includes the study and practices of both non-nuclear and nuclear ammunition. Once commissioned, the Field Artillery officer is trained to be a technical expert as well as troop leader and attends Basic and Advanced Courses at the Field Artillery School, Fort Sill, Oklahoma at appropriate career points. Between the Basic and Advanced Courses, assignments are varied as much as possible to allow overall development of the officer's potential.

Some of the units in the Field Artillery to which most officers will be assigned early in their tour of duty include the 155mm self-propelled battery; 105mm towed battery; 8-inch self-propelled battery; Pershing, and Lance missile units, warhead support units; Target Acquisition batteries; and, of course, the applicable headquarters and service batteries of the weapons unit.

Although the number and type of field artillery units and organizations is one of the most extensive in the TOE structure, the actual MOS's required for field artillery officers are few, which indicates the interchangeability expected of those assigned to this Branch. These MOS's are basic to the branch: Cannon Field Artillery Officer, Light Missile Officer, Heavy Missile Officer and Target Acquisition Survey Officer.

Further evidence of the versatility of the Field Artillery Officer is contained in the official job descriptions. The Field Artillery Unit Commander, for instance, is also qualified to serve as an Artillery Aerial Observer, Forward Observer, and Fire Support Officer. As commander, the officer is trained to control and direct the tactical employment of either a cannon or missile unit in combat. This includes related combat necessities such as intelligence evaluation, situation estimates, and battle-plan formulation. The officer is called upon to advise higher commanders, staffs, and supported units on the capabilities of artillery. In combat or otherwise, the Field Artillery Unit Commander is solely responsible for the unit's administration, training, supply, transportation, communications, organizational maintenance, and security.

In order for the field artillery officer to accomplish these duties, training at the Field Artillery School centers on developing the qualifications needed. In the Basic Course, the newly commissioned lieutenants are provided with knowledge of the Field Artillery systems, with skills and in-depth knowledge in the areas of observed fire, fire direction, and management of individual training that prepares them to become fire support team (FIST) chiefs, to serve as cannon battery executive officers and to manage maintenance and training at the battery level. This training qualifies the officer to be a cannon field artillery officer. Depending upon the officer's initial assignment, training may continue in either the Lance Officer Course or the Pershing Officer Course to qualify the individual as a light or heavy missile officer.

The Advanced Course develops the knowledge and skills required to perform as a battery commander, fire support officer, or battalion fire direction officer. This course includes maneuver force, target acquisition, survey, and counterfire training. Also included are the Field Artillery gunnery problems, to include fire direction, observed fire, and firing battery operations. Leadership, training management, maintenance and supply procedures, and communications/electronics complete the Advanced Course. Based on future assignments, approximately 20% of the Advanced Course students also attend the Nuclear and Chemical Target Analysis Course.

Each field artillery officer is expected to have this basic knowledge. To qualify for some assignments, however, some special training is required. For instance, the Field Illumination Unit Commander needs experience in electrical illumination phenomena and the Nuclear Weapons Officer must be able to meet stringent security tests and know all of the complicated details of storage, transportation, logistical management staff procedures, policies, directives, and procedures for interservice cooperation, and of course, the special tactical applications.

As with each of the other combat arms, the Field Artillery officer is trained to be a diverse individual, providing accurate, effective and responsive fire support when required. As with officers of all branches, Field Artillery officers select an additional specialty after about seven years of service. Qualified officers request and are selected for Atomic Energy or Research and Development as specialties where the officer's interest and talents can assure the improvement of equipment in a way that can be easily utilized for the success of combat operations.

As the Field Artillery Officer advances in grade and experience, there is every opportunity for staff level assignment and selection for attendance at top-level Army schools.

CORPS OF ENGINEERS

This branch, one of the most widely diversified in responsibility, has a history of developments and activities which have benefited the Nation as a whole. Engineer officers such as Lewis and Clark have figured prominently in the history of the expansion and development of the Nation from the Atlantic States to the Pacific Ocean and beyond. The Corps activities encompass, today, both military engineering and civil works, and all related planning, organization, training, operation, supply, and maintenance.

As an integral part of the U.S. Army, the Corps of Engineers traces its beginning to 16 June 1775, when the Continental Congress provided for a Chief Engineer with two assistants ". . . at The Grand Army". On 3 July 1775, General Washington appointed Richard Gridley to this post, and one of his first efforts was to lay out the defenses of Breed's Hill. He later directed the fortifications which forced the British to evacuate Boston in March, 1776. Further development came in 1778, when the Congress authorized three companies of sappers (British slang for construction worker in an Engineering unit) and miners (engineering troops). These first three companies of engineers built the siege works and fortifications which brought a final victory for the Colonies at Yorktown. In 1779, Congress formally established the first Commandant of the "Corps of Engineers". In 1783, the Corps was dissolved along with most of the Army but re-established in 1802, when Congress provided for the present Corps and "constituted" it a military academy at West Point, N.Y. Thus, in the beginning and for nearly 64 years, the United States Military Academy was almost exclusively an engineering school.

Combat engineers—engineer units which accompany the forward elements of the Army in the field to assist the advance of combat arms and, when necessary, fight as infantrymen—became a reality in 1846 with service during the Mexican War. Some of the combat engineers in that conflict who were later to distinguish themselves were (then) Captain Robert E. Lee and Lieutenants George B. McClellan and P.G.T. Beauregard. Military engineering became more complex during the Civil War, with the successful building of the first pontoon bridge being only one of an extensive list of engineering achievements.

The first World War was a conflict full of accomplishments for the Corps of Engineers. The Corps acquired and developed many of the military functions

The triple-turreted castle identifying members of the Corps of Engineers was adopted in 1840 and symbolizes two major functions: construction and fortifications.

which it has today: construction of ports, docks, roads, bridges, transportation facilities, camps, hospitals, and depots; and responsibility for mapmaking, camouflage, mine warfare, water supply, obstacle emplacement and reduction, and terrain analysis.

Engineer battalions became organic to all types of divisions by the time World War II was on the horizon and, in 1941, the construction, maintenance, and repair of all Army facilities, as well as acquisition and disposal of all real estate were added to the responsibilities assigned to the Corps. Among the many notable accomplishments during the war were the Alcan Highway, Burma Road and the Manhattan Project—the development of the atomic bomb. Some have said that the Pacific Island operations in general were "an engineer's war."

In the United States, the Corps of Engineers has undertaken all navigational and harbor improvements since the first Rivers and Harbors Bill, passed by Congress in 1824. Many public structures, such as the Washington Monument, the Library of Congress, the Pentagon and the St. Lawrence Seaway project have been built by the Corps. One foreign achievement known to all was the construction of the Panama Canal. In the more recent past, the construction support of our highly successful space program, such as NASA Headquarters in Houston and the J. F. Kennedy Space Center launching facilities at Cape Canaveral, was accomplished by the Corps. Support has not been limited to this planet. Prior to the consolidation of the mapping, charting and geodesy functions of all the services in a single DOD agency—the Defense Mapping Agency—in 1972, the U.S. Army Topographic Command, which had responsibility for the Corps' geodesy and mapping mission, had begun mapping the moon. This imaginative and aggressive thinking is also being applied on earth as the Corps works hand-in-glove with the Environmental Protection Agency to prevent further pollution of our streams and waterways and to restore them to their former purity and beauty. The increased amount of leisure time now available to all strata of American society has only heightened the importance of the Corps' role in providing for recreational facilities, major factors in the decision to construct inland lakes and waterways.

Engineer officers are responsible for training and leading troops in combat and construction operations essential to the Army in the field. They direct the operation and maintenance of Army facilities world-wide. They also develop and manage the Army's extensive Military Construction and Civil Works Programs.

Engineers participate in combat operations as members of the combined arms team. They assault fortifications as well as construct them; they breach mine fields as well as emplace them; they reduce obstacles as well as create them; and they participate in assault river crossings and amphibious operations in addition to other combat engineering tasks.

Officers serve as engineer staff officers at all levels, coordinating, planning, and providing staff supervision of engineer operations, to include support of the Air Force.

Fort Belvoir, Virginia, is the "home" of the Corps of Engineers and the U.S. Army Engineer School, which is the center of Army Engineer activities, including combat and training developments, training and doctrine, and proponency and evaluation of engineer equipment. Most engineer officers begin their careers there and return periodically to become qualified to handle one or more of the many assignments open to engineer officers. Such assignments for which they are trained at the Engineer School include: supervising the design, construction, and contract administration of military construction and government civil works projects; developing, producing, and reproducing maps; surveying and mapping projects; bridge classification and construction; terrain studies; natural resource and environmental studies; and, of course, combat engineer assignments. Engineer officers are also trained to process and exploit captured engineer equipment; plan, supervise, and participate in research and development activities; test and evaluate all military engineering hardware and software; plan, construct; repair, and rehabilitate posts, camps, stations, airfields, structures, ports, harbors, roads, inland waterways, railways, pipelines, and utility plants and systems. These, and a myriad of related responsibilities involving real estate are reflected in extensive and diversified engineer units and duty positions.

Types of engineer organizations to which an officer will likely be assigned include the various combat engineer units attached or organic to infantry or armored elements; medium girder bridge companies; float bridge companies; mobile assault bridge companies; port construction companies; engineer equipment companies; topographic companies; terrain analysis detachments; and utilities maintenance units.

In addition to the diversified unit commander positions, engineer officer assignments include special jobs such as Division Engineer, District Engineer, Facilities Engineer, Topographic Engineer, Project Engineer, Staff Engineer and Civil Engineer.

Branch schooling includes basic, advanced, and special courses. Many engineer officers have the opportunity to return to graduate school to participate in such highly sophisticated fields of study as Civil Engineering, Nuclear Engineering, Geodetic Science, Engineer Administration, and Operations Research/ Systems Analysis.

Officers selected for the Corps of Engineers can look forward to professional opportunities which are limited only by their own abilities and ambitions.

30

Combat Support Branches

 First adopted in 1917, the Chemical Corps insignia alludes to the chemistry-related functions of the branch.

CHEMICAL CORPS

As a combat support arm, the Chemical Corps provides the Army with expertise concerning all aspects of Nuclear, Biological, and Chemical (NBC) warfare. Typical areas of operational responsibility include chemical and nuclear weapons employment, NBC technical intelligence, defensive procedures and equipment, decontamination, surveying and monitoring techniques, and NBC hazard predictions. Approximately 80 percent of the positions within the branch are oriented toward these operational, training, and staff duties.

The Chemical Specialty also has a wide variety of research, development, and logistical functions relating to NBC systems and combat development. These responsibilities, which make up the remaining 20 percent of available positions, involve the management of weapon systems and defensive equipment, including their conception, development, and employment. Some disciplines which are often utilized in these areas are Chemical Engineering, Nuclear Engineering, Chemistry, Physics, and Systems Management.

Chemical Officers, if they are to be effective, must ultimately grasp how their expertise can best support the "Combined Arms" effort. As a result, the majority of newly commissioned lieutenants in the Chemical Specialty will begin their careers in operations/training assignments at company, battalion, or brigade level. Because of the unique nature of the branch, these assignments offer many diverse and challenging experiences in direct support of front-line combat units. Specifically aimed at providing the lieutenant with basic tactical experience, these positions serve as preparation for higher level command and staff or service school instructor jobs.

There is one common misconception about the Chemical Corps which unnecessarily discourages many future officers from even considering the branch. Specifically, being a Chemical Officer *does not* require an academic background in the basic sciences or engineering. Although the branch is technically oriented, specific assignment to jobs requiring these disciplines is a matter of choice. If an officer desires such an assignment, he/she may be sent to graduate school to obtain a masters degree in the required field.

Modern gas warfare began in 1915 at Ypres, Belgium, two years before the United States entered World War I. During the war, a Gas Service was established overseas to coordinate all uses of gas as an offensive weapon by the American Expeditionary Force. As a result, the Chemical Warfare Service (CWS) was established in 1918 as an integral part of the temporary wartime army and became a permanent part of the Regular Army in 1920. CWS units distinguished themselves in battle during both world wars by providing a variety of combat and combat support functions, such as the Chemical Mortar Battalions which gave close-in fire support (smoke, flame, high explosive) to the Infantry from their 4.2 inch heavy mortars.

The advent of the nuclear age brought two new missions to the Chemical Corps (renamed from the CWS)—radiological weaponry and the responsibility for nuclear and biological defense. Particularly during the 1950's and early 60's, advances in NBC warfare necessitated the further development of highly skilled officers trained in the complexities of this three-fold responsibility.

The changing political climate and declining interest in NBC warfare during the late 1960's and early 1970's resulted in a move to disestablish the Chemical Corps as a branch of the Army. In July 1976, this movement was dramatically reversed by the Secretary of the Army as a result of a heightened awareness of the Soviet Union's capability to wage NBC warfare on a massive and deadly scale. With its reestablishment, the Chemical Corps was given the mission of improving NBC readiness throughout the Army to meet the Soviet threat.

Since this time, significant changes have been made to expand the role of the Chemical Corps as reflected in its redesignation from a Service Support to a Combat Support Branch. As a part of this revitalization effort, the size of the Corps is expected to almost triple by 1985, making it the Army's *fastest growing branch.* Additionally, many new NBC defense units are being assigned as divisional and corps assets to improve the Army's ability to operate in an NBC environment.

MILITARY INTELLIGENCE

Although the Military Intelligence Branch is the newest branch of the active United States Army, military intelligence has a history which dates back to the beginning of human conflict.

It is evident that foreknowledge of the capabilities and probable courses of action on the part of the enemy, or a potential enemy, is of the greatest value to a government and its military commanders in making sound decisions for the conduct of state affairs and military operations.

A symbolic Sun, patterned after that of the mythical Helios, God of the Sun, who could see and hear everything, provides the base for the Military Intelligence design. The sun's rays indicate the world-wide mission of the branch, the superimposed Rose revives the ancient symbol of secrecy, and the partially concealed dagger reminds of the aggressiveness, protection, and element of physical danger inherent to branch operations.

Military Intelligence is a basic branch and a combat support arm of the Army. Military Intelligence officers are primarily concerned with the intelligence aspects of the Army's mission. This field of activity encompasses intelligence, counterintelligence, cryptologic and signal intelligence, security, order of battle, interrogation, aerial surveillance, imagery interpretation and all related planning, organization, training and operations. Intelligence officers are assigned to both branch material and branch immaterial positions within all Army, joint and combined commands and staffs.

The United States up to and including World War I found its Army ill-prepared in all fields of military intelligence, due to the lack of a consistent policy of planning and coordination in this field.

Out of expediency, and from a small information division under the Adjutant General, which was actually the first so-called departmental military intelligence agency, there eventually evolved in June 1918 a more realistic agency, called the Military Intelligence Division under the then reorganized War Department General Staff.

In this same period official recognition was given to the counterintelligence aspect by defining and organizing intelligence into two classes: positive and negative. Subsequently, with the signing of the Armistice, certain peacetime events took place such as reorganization of the General Staff, government economies and pressures from pacifist and isolationist groups, all of which adversely affected the prestige of intelligence and severely curtailed training. The Corps of Intelligence Police which had been organized and trained in France in 1917 was reduced to a mere handful, and counterintelligence training was discontinued completely.

It was not until World War II then, that military intelligence, due to excellent staff planning and coordination, began to take on the broad range and professional nature which characterizes this field today.

The Military Intelligence Service was organized in this early period of the war, and began to gather specialists in intelligence and intelligence-related areas. Among these were linguists and language and area students, professional investigators, geographers, economic and technological experts, world travelers, and editors. Counterintelligence training was reconstituted in February 1941, and the official designation of the organization became Counter Intelligence Corps in 1942.

The Signal Security Agency was created in 1943 under the Chief Signal

Officer, and assumed the responsibilities and performed the functions formerly carried on by the Signal Intelligence Service.

In September 1945, the US Army Security Agency (USASA) was created and placed under the direction of the Assistant Chief of Staff, G2, intelligence, Department of the Army. It was redesignated as a major field command of the Department of the Army in 1964, and is now known as the U.S. Army Intelligence and Security Command (INSCOM).

In June 1962, the Military Intelligence Branch, composed of ASA, Intelligence Corps, and strategic and combat intelligence officers, was formalized to meet the growing requirements for control and career guidance of the increasing numbers of officers in the intelligence field. It was designated as Army Intelligence and Security Branch.

In July 1967, the Army Intelligence and Security Branch was redesignated the Military Intelligence Branch and its mission was changed from combat service support to combat support.

The primary function of Military Intelligence officers is the collection, analysis, production and dissemination of Intelligence. To accomplish this function, it is essential that they possess comprehensive knowledge of military strategy and tactics.

Military Intelligence Officers are especially qualified through education, training and experience for the following:

Command of intelligence organizations or elements thereof which provide intelligence capabilities and support to major commanders;

Serving as intelligence staff officers at all levels providing advice and assistance to commanders and their staff; coordinating assigned aspects of planning and providing staff supervision of intelligence operations; participating in the planning, coordination and execution of National intelligence and counterintelligence efforts;

Developing communications and electronic intelligence;

Providing communications and electronic security;

Developing and managing programs for safeguarding defense information;

Developing order of battle information;

Interrogating prisoners of war, defectors, and other personnel as appropriate;

Providing information on all ground sensor systems and aerial surveillance and reconnaissance sensors and platforms, preparing aerial reconnaissance plans, employing Army Aerial surveillance assets, coordinating requests for USAF tactical Aerial Reconnaissance, and participating in aerial surveillance missions;

Analyzing and interpreting photographic and electronically produced images;

Conducting the Army personnel security program;

Conducting the Army industrial security program;

Managing the Army censorship program, less press censorship;

Providing linguistic and analytical support to all levels of command;

Developing organization and operational concepts, planning and coordinating highly specialized worldwide intelligence and counterintelligence operations;

Participating in the design, research and development and testing of intelligence material and equipment and development of Intelligence doctrine;

Serving as Defense and Army representative with military attache offices in all nations of the world maintaining diplomatic relations with the United States;

Performing highly classified duties within the broad field of signal intelligence;

Performing specialized duties in the electronic warfare field;

Serving as Commandant, Staff and Faculty members of service schools primarily engaged in presenting intelligence instruction and as faculty members at other schools conducting related instruction;

Participating in the Army Aviation Program and other special career programs;

Performing tasks associated with the career planning, development, management and assignment of Military Intelligence officers.

All newly commissioned Military Intelligence officers attend the Military Intelligence Officer Basic Course conducted at the U.S. Army Intelligence Center and School. This training is followed by training in the officer's accession specialty, followed by an assignment in this specialty in a troop environment.

Officers are programmed to attend the Military Intelligence Officer Advanced Course or the Defense Intelligence Course as soon as practicable after being promoted to captain. Following completion of this training and a utilization tour, selected officers can expect consideration for additional special intelligence training and possible assignment in another intelligence functional area. Selected officers will also complete language training and other special courses to broaden their knowledge and perspective and increase their value to the Army. Selected officers will receive the opportunity to participate in civilian educational programs, and specialty programs, particularly the Foreign Area Specialty program during the latter portion of this period.

The crossed pistols insignia of the Military Police Corps was officially adopted in 1922. The model for the insignia was the 1806 Harper's Ferry pistol—the first official U.S. Army handgun.

MILITARY POLICE CORPS

The Military Police Corps is a basic branch of the Army. It is both an arm and a service whose personnel perform combat, combat support, and combat service support missions. Military police contribute to battlefield success by conducting combat operations against threat forces in the rear areas, combat support by expediting the forward movement of critical combat resources, and combat service support by evacuating enemy prisoners of war from the battle areas. Additionally, military police provide security in war and peace to critical Army facilities and resources, such as command posts and nuclear ammunition. Military police also support the Army in peacetime by providing varied law enforcement services that insure a secure environment for the Army community. Military police units provide support on a flexible mission basis, keyed to the commander's priorities, ranging from the aggressive execution of combat operations against rear area threat forces, to the application of law enforcement measures in peacetime crisis situations.

Military police activity dates back as far as the Norman conquest of England. In those days, the provost marshal was personally appointed by the King to maintain the peace, safeguard royal interests, and handle disciplinary matters. By the time of King Henry VIII, the provost marshal's assignments were carried out by "provost companies" and by 1611 a provost marshal was serving in the Colony of Virginia under a "Martial Code" drawn up by the Deputy Governor.

A Provost Marshal was appointed to General Washington's Army of the United Colonies in January, 1776, and two years later Congress passed a resolution establishing a "Provost Corps, to be . . . mounted on horseback and armed and accoutered as Light Dragoons." At the same time, General Washington directed the Corps to apprehend ". . . deserters, marauders, drunkards, rioters and stragglers" and to perform other military police duties.

For nearly 80 years, little was recorded about military police matters. It is known that in September 1862, a "Provost Marshal General of the War Department" was appointed with a primary function generally similar to today's Director of Selective Service; that is, enforcement of the draft laws. He was also responsible for apprehending deserters, arresting disloyal persons, recovering stolen government property, and detecting spies.

An Invalid Corps, later called the Veteran Reserve Corps, was established in 1862 to perform military police duties and was composed of personnel unfit for other duties. The disadvantages of such a policy were apparent, but the manpower shortage was so serious that there was no other workable alternative. By 1866, both the Veteran Reserve Corps and the Office of the Provost Marshal General had been abolished, and from then until World War I, military police work was the responsibility of individual commanders using personnel at their disposal.

Organization of a military police corps was attempted again in World War I, but time did not permit it to become fully established by the war's end. World War II was to be different, however, and on 23 September 1942 the Secretary of War ordered the establishment of the Corps of Military Police. During World War II, the Corps reached a peak strength of 8,000 officers and 200,000 enlisted men. During the Korean War, military police were responsible for controlling large numbers of refugees in addition to their normal police functions. It was here that the helicopter was first used by military police for battlefield circulation control and area security.

The Military Police Corps won widespread praise for its performance of duty during operations in the Republic of Vietnam. In 1965, the 18th Military Police Brigade became the first of its kind to be deployed in combat. Brigade missions were expanded to include port and harbor security, and infantry-type tactical operations. During the Tet Offensive of 1968, military police distinguished themselves in the defense of the US Embassy and other critical installations in Saigon, while keeping vital roads and waterways open throughout the Republic of Vietnam. The activities of the Military Police Corps in its combat support role led to the designation of the Corps as an arm as well as a service on 14 October 1968. This designation reflects formal recognition by the Department of the Army of the combat role which the Military Police Corps has always performed.

Today, military police personnel and units perform a wide range of combat, combat support, and combat service support operations. To accomplish battlefield support functions, Military Police Corps officers must possess a comprehensive knowledge of combat operations and tactics. Specifically, MP officers must be qualified through education, training, and experience to plan and execute military police combat, combat support, and combat service support operations. These include Battlefield Circulation Control, Area Security, Rear Area Combat Operations, Enemy Prisoner of War and Civilian Internee Operations, and Law and Order Operations. In the garrison environment, military police are responsible for law enforcement, physical security, criminal investigations, and the confinement and correctional treatment of US military prisoners. The fundamental objective for the Military Police Corps in all of these garrison-related functions is to protect and assist fellow soldiers and their families.

A career in the Military Police Corps is one of wide variety, many different assignments, and educational opportunities. While most officers in the Corps are commissioned through the ROTC program, opportunities are also available for OCS graduates to request this branch. In addition, during each year since 1968, graduates from the US Military Academy have been commissioned in the Corps. The Military Police Corps continually provides opportunities for additional education for its officers. From the beginning, when they receive their first comprehensive training in military police operations, until shortly before they retire, officers of the Military Police Corps receive formal professional training at progressively advancing levels. At the Military Police School at Fort McClellan, new officers are taught the principles and techniques of small unit leadership; tactical operations; management; and military police operations. Emphasis is placed on developing platoon leaders who are equally at home in both the tactical and garrison environments. Subsequent military schooling will include the MP Officer Advanced Course at Fort McClellan, the Combined Arms and Services Staff School at Fort Leavenworth and, in all likelihood, other functional specialty courses as the opportunities arise. Then, as their careers progress, MP officers may be selected for attendance at the US Army Command and General Staff College and senior service schools. In past years, Military Police Officers have taken part in graduate study programs in the fields of education, personnel management, area studies, comptrollership, organizational behavior, operations research, ADP systems, criminology, correctional administration, and police science and administration.

The Military Police Corps' combination of battlefield and peacetime functions provides its officers with real opportunities, not only to achieve a unique blend of skills, but also to serve in a variety of challenging assignments. Since the Military Police Corps serves the entire Army, an officer may be assigned to almost any type of organization stationed wherever our troops are throughout the world. The initial assignment of a junior officer will probably be to an MP company or battalion, but may also be to a specific functional law enforcement position on any Army installation. Later, an officer could be selected for company command, for duty as a Staff MP Officer, or as a member of the staff and faculty at the US Army Military Police School, an ROTC element or the US Military Academy. Other possible assignments include duty as a correctional treatment officer, as a reserve component advisor, as a member of the Department of the Army Staff, with the US Army Criminal Investigation Command, or any other of a variety of branch related and branch unrelated positions. Officers naturally take on more and more responsibility in their assignments as they progress in rank and experience.

The latest and most exciting chapter in the history of the MP Corps is even now taking shape. A greatly expanded role on the battlefield has brought with it significant increases in firepower and combat effectiveness. At the same time, the motto "Of the Troops and for the Troops" is taking on renewed meaning for military police serving Army communities throughout the world.

The pace is fast and the esprit is high as the Military Police Corps continues to welcome all professional challenges that the future may hold.

The present design of crossed flags and torch was adopted in 1884 although enlisted men of the acting signal corps wore crossed flags since 1868. The insignia represents the signalling system invented by the first signal officer which used flags during the day and torches at night.

SIGNAL CORPS

In the entire history of the U.S. Army since the invention of semaphore, it would be difficult to find a commander who would not agree with the statement ". . . the secret of command lies in the secret of communications". Signalling was, of course, the first effective means of fast communication between elements in the field, hence the name of this branch . . . although a much more apt and descriptive term for today's activities is "electronic communications."

Within the classifications of combat, combat support, and combat service support, the Signal Corps is a combat support branch with the overall mission of planning, installing, operating, and maintaining the Army's worldwide communication systems.

Historically, the Signal Corps traces its beginning from 21 June 1860 when Major Albert J. Myer, who had developed the signalling system we know as semaphore as a result of his work with the deaf, was appointed Signal Officer of the Army. As a branch it was officially established in March 1863. Its value to the Army is a proven fact.

Subsequently, signal officers and enlisted men were deeply involved in every aspect of the Nation's growth and explorations. The use of the telegraph became a tactical necessity during the Civil War.

Later, signalmen played important roles in developing the national weather service, linking the West to the East as the country expanded, exploring the Arctic, and opening Alaska to the Gold Rush. Thousands of miles of telegraph wire were installed and maintained during this period.

War with Spain in 1898 found only eight officers and 52 enlisted men assigned to the Corps. Authorizations were received quickly to expand this group to a total of 138 officers and 1,115 enlisted men. It was during this conflict that the combat photographer became an integral part of the Corps.

Ballooning became a Signal responsibility in 1885; this led to the development and control of aviation by the Corps during World War I. The Corps had been busily engaged in the development of military aircraft since the successful flight of the Wright Brothers and an aviation section had been authorized in 1914. By 1918 there were 16,000 officers and 147,000 enlisted men engaged in air operations and in May of that year they became the branch known as the Air Corps.

During the same period, many innovations in sound-producing communications systems were developed and the first permanent Signal Corps post and training center was activated at Fort Monmouth, New Jersey. Among the new kinds of equipment designed by Corps personnel were vacuum-tube radios and detection gear to indicate approaching aircraft. In the field, the Signal Corps provided the required meteorological service for artillery and aviation, and photography operations were expanded to include motion pictures.

World War II saw the next major contribution of communications and sound to military operations. Radio had been perfected to then unbelievable levels of performance, and the development of radar, sonar, and radio-controlled weapons systems was only the beginning of technological advances undreamed of only a few years before.

Today, the responsibilities of the Signal Corps are as varied as ever. Establishing, maintaining, operating, and refining communications networks for tactical operations; operating the Army portion of the global strategic communication network; training signal specialists, officer and enlisted; carrying out research and development projects; handling the logistics of storage, distribution and repair of communications-electronics materiel; staffing the Army photographic and pictorial services; experimenting in the atmospheric sciences and training meteorological specialists; developing highly specialized electronic equipment for use in the space satellite program; and special research in the fields of avionics and combat surveillance offer unsurpassed technological opportunities for junior officers.

The complexities of today's Army require a flexible Signal Corps organization. While many types of TOE Signal organizations are authorized, if not in actual existence, Signal personnel are employed in practically every organizational structure throughout the Army. Major roles for Signal Corps personnel are found within the Training and Doctrine Command, Army Communications Command, and Forces Command.

The Army's training facility is the U.S. Army Signal Center and Fort Gordon, Fort Gordon, Georgia. The Signal Center at Fort Gordon provides military education and practical training for officers to prepare them for positions concerned with C-E activities in tactical or strategic operations. This school also provides enlisted personnel with the specialist training required to support tactical, and some strategic operations.

After completing the Signal Officer Basic Course at Fort Gordon, a most challenging career lies ahead. The graduate of the Signal Officer Basic Course will receive further training in one of the Signal Corps accession specialties: Combat Communications-Electronics, Communications-Electronics Engineering, Communications-Electronics Materiel Management, or Teleprocessing Operations. In addition, depending upon the officer's duty assignment, functional courses such as the Radio Systems Officers Course, Communications Center Officers Course, and the Communications-Electronics Staff Officers Course are provided. The Army depends upon the Signal Corps to provide the communications required by the operational needs of the Army's commanders. The Signal Corps provides command communications systems superimposed upon area communications systems to meet this requirement. The organizations supporting the system are organized in a "building block" concept, thus allowing for the highly flexible organization needed to support the immediate tactical requirements.

The U.S. Army Communications Command (USACC) at Fort Huachuca, Arizona, is the Army's communications-electronics organization employed to provide voice and data communications for the interconnection of the theater armies with activities of the Department of Defense, whether locally or over intercontinental distances.

A Corps Signal Brigade is the communications-electronics organization expressly formed to provide the command and area communications systems for the corps. This brigade is responsible for providing communications systems planning, supervision, and control of the command and area communications systems within the corps area. The Corps Signal Brigade consists typically of a Headquarters and Headquarters Company, a Command Operations Battalion, a Command Radio Relay and Cable Battalion, and four Area Signal Battalions. The brigade assigns its various organic Signal battalions (i.e., communications and construction) to plan, install, maintain, and operate the integrated network of the command communications systems serving corps headquarters down to each division and separate combat brigade. Each division has its own organic Signal Battalion. In addition, at each combat brigade within the division, there is a Signal Corps officer who serves as the combat brigade Communications-Electronics staff officers, and (for instance) every maneuver battalion assigned to the combat brigade—whether an infantry battalion, an armored battalion, or a mechanized battalion—also has its own Communications-Electronics staff officer in charge of organic communications.

A career in the Signal Corps, therefore, offers a wide range of assignment possibilities punctuated at appropriate intervals with schooling which parallels other Branch career programs. During the first eight years, the officer gets to the Basic and Advanced courses, with in-between assignments designed to provide opportunities for the development of leadership skills while working within the accession specialty area.

At about the end of the 8th year of service, the officer's additional specialty will be designated and, in the years following, assignments will be aimed toward developing proficiency in this additional specialty. By about the 15th year of service, that specialty area in which the majority of the officer's future assignments may be expected is determined and the pattern for the remainder of the officer's career is set.

From this point on, the Signal Corps officer concentrates on broadening and deepening professional qualifications, and developing higher level management capability and increased managerial capacity for handling the most complex communications activities of the Army and Department of Defense.

In summary, the Signal Corps provides the expertise and facilities that support communications activities at every level of the Army. It continually researches, develops, and improves the materiel required to provide that support and it trains its officers and enlisted personnel to use and care for the materiel the right way. Because of the impressive capabilities of the Signal Corps, the Army's readiness to respond quickly to any situation is assured.

31

Service Support Branches

ADJUTANT GENERAL'S CORPS

Historically, the "adjutant" always has occupied a strong position on the commander's staff. This dates from the Roman legions, the word "adjutant" being derived from the Latin verb "adjutare", meaning to assist or help. The term "adjutant general" was first used by the French, recognized as great military organizers during the 16th and 17th centuries, the term interpreted as "aid to general". The original function and the continuing mission of the AG has been to assist the commander. The entire staff structure as we know it today developed from this beginning. By the time of the English Civil War the British had adopted the title for officers who, in the modern American Army, would be adjutants general, chiefs of staff, and executive officers.

On June 16, 1775, the Continental Congress passed a resolution creating the Continental Army. The following day, it named Horatio Gates as Adjutant General. General Gates thus became the first officer after George Washington to be named to the Continental Army. In line with English precedent, the new Adjutant General assumed responsibility for a wide range of functions, all designed to unburden his commander. This included security, intelligence, and coordination, as well as purely administrative and clerical tasks for the commander—even to keeping correct time so watches could be kept synchronized in all units of the Army.

For a long time after the Revolutionary War nobody seemed to know what the Adjutant General should do, which is reflected in the fact that at one time or another the "Adjutant General" post was held by every rank from lieutenant through major general! While the office has been in existence since 1775, the present Corps has its main roots in the Adjutant General's Department as organized in 1813, which included Inspector General responsibility. The IG was split off in 1821, and from then until the Army General Staff was created in 1903, the job of the Corps consisted largely of administration, recruiting, and detention facility management.

After the Spanish-American War, Secretary of War Elihu Root made major changes in the military organization, including creation of a General Staff Corps. In 1904 the Adjutant General's Department was re-named the Military Secretary's Department, but in 1907 it regained its traditional designation.

World War I finally brought a significant designation of duties for the Adjutant General's Department. This included the procurement, assignment, promotion, transfer, and discharge of all officers and enlisted men and the record keeping that went with it. All these functions expanded enormously during World War II when The Adjutant General had a dual role—Adjutant General of the Services of Supply and Adjutant General of the Army—which ended in 1946 when the branch became an administrative service and Headquarters. In 1950, The Adjutant General's Department was redesignated as the Adjutant General's Corps, thus becoming a basic branch of the Army.

The 1960s brought some sweeping changes to The Adjutant General's Office (TAGO). The responsibility for data processing came to TAGO with the Army Data Services and Administrative Systems Command in 1962. In that same year, certain functions relating to military personnel management were transferred from TAGO to a newly created Office of Personnel Operations (OPO). Concurrent with this change, The Institute of Heraldry was created and administrative responsibility for the Standby and Retired Reserves was assigned to TAGO. Responsibility for Ready Reserve Mobilization was transferred to TAGO in 1965. This involved consolidation of almost 500,000 personnel records in a center at St. Louis, Missouri. The center later became the Reserve Components Personnel and Administration Center (RCPAC).

While OPO was formed in 1962, it did not represent total Army personnel consolidation under a single manager. A decade later, in 1972, the Military Personnel Center (MILPERCEN) was established in Alexandria, Virginia. All active Army personnel matters came under the cognizance of MILPERCEN, including activities concerned with separations, personnel records, promotions and awards, which previously had been the responsibility of TAGO.

The Adjutant General Center (TAGCEN) was formed in 1973 to meet the demands for initiative and response in the fields of administrative management and personal environmental support. It operates under the command of The Adjutant General to fulfill some of the Adjutant General's many responsibilities.

The shield identifying officers of the Adjutant General's Corps was first approved in 1872. However, it was not until 1924 that the colors of red, white (now silver) and blue were authorized. Differing slightly from, but nevertheless based on the shield portion of the Coat of Arms of the United States, it symbolizes the support of this Branch to the Army and nation.

Today, The Adjutant General continues the role as a Special Staff Officer on the Department of the Army staff, while commanding The Adjutant General Center and directing the operations of the Army Reserve Components Personnel and Administration Center. The Adjutant General's Office (TAGO) assures a smooth flow of correspondence, orders and directives at Headquarters, Department of the Army. The Adjutant General Center (TAGCEN) provides the Army with a single manager responsible for policy, program improvement, and management control of such diverse areas as publications; field printing; postal services; records management; administrative systems relating to microfilm, word processing and office environment applications; heraldic activities; courier service; dependent's education; casualty reporting; memorial affairs; nonappropriated funds management; recreation; and general education development. The Reserve Components Personnel and Administration Center (RCPAC), located in St. Louis, Missouri, provides and maintains the capability to mobilize members of the Individual Ready Reserve, the Standby Reserve, and the Retired Reserve.

The RCPAC begins its managerial and administrative support of a soldier's affairs at the time the soldier completes active Army service, if he or she reverts to the Reserve forces. The Center serves as the hub of Reserve affairs and is the central point of control for all non-unit U.S. Army Reserve personnel, regardless of where they reside. The principal task of RCPAC is to insure that non-unit Reserve personnel can be mobilized to augment both active Army and Reserve component units in the event of a national emergency. The Center provides to the Reservists those personalized services that are so necessary for high morale and esprit de corps. In addition, the RCPAC furnishes information from its records upon request of various Federal and State agencies, veterans, next of kin, and the public.

The Adjutant General Center (TAGCEN) is divided into fifteen directorates and offices, each responsible for a functional area of The Adjutant General's responsibility. The Adjutant General is assisted by two Deputies to The Adjutant General (DTAGs) and a third general officer who commands RCPAC. One DTAG, in addition to TAGCEN duties, also serves as the Executive Director of the Military Postal Service Agency, which discharges the Army's responsibility as the DOD Single Manager of the Military Postal Service.

The *Plans and Management Support Directorate* handles internal administration, planning, and staff coordination. It advises on management matters, is the focal point for officer personnel management matters, and it coordinates the TAGO Study Program. The Directorate provides a variety of administrative support and oversight services, such as property accountability, information security, physical security, personnel security, and safeguarding of classified information, as well as exercising staff supervision over all automation activities in TAGO.

The *Resource Management Directorate* is responsible for resource programming and budgeting of all TAG functional areas, including control of TAG manpower and funding requirements.

The *Reserve Personnel Coordination Office* supports TAG on all matters relating to the management of Reserve officers and enlisted personnel, veterans affairs, and mobilization.

The *Quality of Life Office* deals with matters that affect the welfare of active duty and Reserve personnel, and DA civilians. The Quality of Life program addresses both the duty environment of soldiers and civilians, and the living conditions of soldiers and their families. Major components of the program involve pay, housing, health care, education, and community and morale support facilities and services.

The *Administrative Management Directorate* develops Army methodology for managing information, spanning the process from creation of the information through the organization, maintenance, and ultimate disposition of the information. Its responsibilities include correspondence, reports, forms, directives, files equipment, copiers, word processing equipment, and vital records preservation.

The *Publications Directorate* deals in matters relating to printing, storing, and issuing all Army publications and blank forms, including the design, control, and standardization of forms. The Directorate supervises the operation of more than 80 printing plants, and two major, and hundreds of secondary publications distribution points throughout the United States and overseas. It does not control map printing, which is a function of the Corps of Engineers.

TAGCEN also provides the Army support for the *Armed Forces Courier Service,* which is a joint departmental agency operating worldwide, providing services to the DOD and other agencies of the Federal government in moving highly classified material requiring protective handling.

The *Headquarters Administrative Systems Directorate* is the administrative systems manager for DA Headquarters and also provides administrative support services to the Office of the Secretary of Defense and the Joint Chiefs of Staff. This Directorate is responsible for planning, developing, testing, and implementing fully automated administrative systems.

The *Institute of Heraldry* is responsible for the development and quality control of heraldric items from the design concept to the introduction into the supply system. Heraldric items include decorations, medals, badges, all types of insignia, lapel devices, flags, streamers, and other items of a symbolic nature that are worn or displayed.

The *Army Library Management Office* is responsible for policy that affects all Army libraries. It provides a central management structure to avoid wasteful duplication and fragmented library management, and it provides information about the total Army library program, including its services and resources.

The *Morale Support Directorate* is responsible for assuring the best possible leisure activities for soldiers and their families. Its activities fall into the general groupings of physical activities, library activities, and community and skill development.

The *Education Directorate* provides the opportunity for soldiers to participate in quality education and development programs worldwide, in support of the Army's belief that continued education is a key to personal and professional development.

The *Community Support Directorate* develops programs and policy guidance, and is the DA proponent for numerous "people programs" for the Army. These include the Army Community Service, the Army Child Advocacy Program, and child support services. It provides policy direction and guidance for the Retired Services Program, the Retiree Councils Program, the Survivor Benefit Plan, and installation support functions worldwide.

The *Casualty and Memorial Affairs Directorate* is responsible for the Army casualty reporting and notification system worldwide, the Army survivor and next-of-kin assistance program, administration of Servicemen's Group Life Insurance, and line-of-duty determinations for Army members killed or injured while on active duty. The Directorate also has Army staff supervision for the worldwide care and disposition of remains and effects of deceased Army personnel, operation and maintenance of Arlington and Soldiers Home National Cemeteries and more than 25 post cemeteries.

The *Club and Community Activities Management Directorate* is charged with the efficient management of nonappropriated funds and activities. The funds are those generated through the nominal fees and charges for the use of certain morale, welfare, and recreational facilities as well as those funds generated by resale activities such as the post exchanges, theaters, and clubs.

Essential both to administration and morale is the efficient collection, processing, and distribution of mail. Few things mean more to men and women away from home than their mail. The *Military Postal Service Agency* was established as a TAG operating agency in 1980 to fulfill the Army's mission as Single Manager of the Military Postal Service for the Department of Defense. Each military service continues to operate its own internal postal facilities, but MPSA has the mission of providing overall mail services worldwide.

Officer assignments within the Corps are as varied as in any other service support branch. Professional development of the Adjutant General's Corps officer parallels that of other branches in offering both the Basic and Advanced Courses along with many special courses at the Adjutant General's School, Fort Benjamin Harrison, Indiana. The expected accession specialty for AGC officers is Personnel Administration or Community Activities Management. All AGC officers are expected to have a thorough knowledge of the duties and activities of an Adjutant or Adjutant General. Examples of other military jobs primarily assigned to AGC officers are Postal Officer, Administrative Officer, Personnel Officer, Personnel Management Officer, Manpower Control Officer, Recruiting and Induction Officer, Archivist, Military Historian, Morale Support Officer, Army Band Officer, Publications Officer, Public Education Officer, Public Affairs Officer, Automatic Data Processing Officer, and Director of Personnel and Community Activities.

Major activities within the United States which offer a variety of challenging staff assignments are The Adjutant General's Office and TAGCEN, Headquarters, Department of the Army; the U.S. Army Reserve Component Personnel and Administration Center, St. Louis; The Adjutant General's School, Fort Benjamin Harrison, Indiana, and the Military Personnel Center, Alexandria, Virginia. Presently many branch immaterial staff assignments throughout Headquarters, DA; the Joint Chiefs of Staff; and the combined staffs in the Department of Defense are open to and filled by highly qualified AGC officers.

The next decade and beyond promises to bring forth many new concepts in all of the areas of Adjutant General's Corps responsibility, all of which will require a contingent of knowledgeable, imaginative, and dedicated officers—as much, if not more so, than any other technical service in the U. S. Army.

CHAPLAIN CORPS

Clergy serving in the U.S. Army are called chaplains. The English word chaplain derives from a legend: It is said that St. Martin of Tours divided his military cloak, giving a large piece to a beggar, and wearing the rest as a cape. This *capella* became a religious article and was taken on military campaigns for its supernatural value, just as the Ark of Covenant was carried by the Israelites. The place where the relic was safeguarded was known as the chapel, a term still used to designate houses of worship on military installations. The bearer of the religious article was the *capellanus,* or chaplain.

As a member of the clergy, the military chaplain is a representative of a particular religious faith. The primary mission of a chaplain is to perform

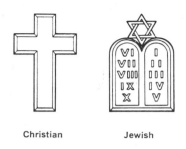

Christian   Jewish

The Chaplain Corps is authorized two distinctive insignia, the Cross and Tablets. The Cross is a symbol of Christianity and is worn by all Christian Chaplains, with no distinction between Protestant and Catholic. The Cross was approved as an insignia in 1898. Jewish Chaplains wear the insignia symbolizing the Tablets of Moses which have numerals representing the Ten Commandments inscribed on them. Above the Tablets of Moses is the six-pointed Star of David. The Jewish insignia was approved in 1918.

ministry by conducting religious services and by providing a complete program of religious education for the American soldier, the dependent family, and authorized civilians. Chaplains conduct sacraments, rites, and ordinances consistent with their endorsing faith group. Counseling is one of the primary religious functions of the Army chaplain. Chaplains counsel on religious and quasi-religious subjects in chapels, hospitals, quarters, and in combat, training and recreational areas.

Chaplains are distributed throughout the Army by assignment to units or installations in an approximate ratio of one chaplain per seven hundred soldiers.

The chaplain is also a staff officer, and serves on the personal staff of the commander. In this capacity, the chaplain advises the commander on matters of religion, morals, and morale as affected by religion. The chaplain maintains liaison with civilian religious groups and welfare agencies to facilitate cooperative programs. The chaplain has responsibility for participating in civic action projects and for advising the commander on matters of religion in the culture of the local inhabitants in oversea areas of operations.

In combat, the chaplain performs the functions of religious ministry, including the spiritual care of the wounded and dying as well as for prisoners of war. When captured and imprisoned, special status is accorded under the Geneva Convention which permits the chaplain to continue ministry among fellow prisoners of war.

Army chaplains receive their training at the U.S. Army Chaplain Center and School, Fort Monmouth, New Jersey. Early in the career pattern, there is a nine-week basic course; sometime between the fifth and seventh year of service, there is a twenty-one week advanced course.

In addition to specialized military schooling, the Army chaplain is considered for special civil schooling in one or more disciplines, including religious education, clinical pastoral education, drug and alcohol abuse, and preaching. Other continuing education programs, some available from the Chaplain Center and School, supplement these educational opportunities.

The Army chaplain is responsible for providing religious coverage to all members of the unit of assignment and to a designated area of responsibility. Religious coverage is provided as permitted by the chaplain's endorsing faith group, and by other military or civilian clergy according to the religious needs of the command and/or area.

The organized chaplaincy in the American Army was established prior to the Declaration of Independence. The Second Continental Congress created the position of chaplain on 29 July 1775 on the recommendation of General George Washington. Since that time, Army chaplains have served in all areas of the world, from the battlefields of the Civil War to the Bataan "Death March" and in the jungles of South Vietnam. Since the founding of the Corps, over two hundred and seventy chaplains have died as a result of hostilities.

In recognizing the professional character of the chaplains, the Department of the Army provides chaplains with enlisted assistants. These enlisted volunteers, known as Chapel Activities Specialists, provide administrative support, perform as vehicle drivers, and guard the chaplain's life in combat. (Chaplains are defined as noncombatants by the Geneva Convention of 1949.) The enlisted assistant is a very important link between chaplains and service personnel in the religious program within the U.S. Army.

To qualify for commissioning as an Army chaplain, the clergy person (male or female) must have satisfactorily completed college and theological or equivalent graduate training acceptable to the Department of the Army. The chaplain must be endorsed by a particular faith/denomination for ministry to Army personnel. A direct commission as an Army officer is the usual procedure for appointment of a chaplain. Theological students may be commissioned as chaplain candidates and begin training before graduation and ordination.

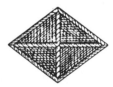

The diamond insignia worn by members of the Finance Corps is not without historical significance. Prior to the minting of coins, goldsmiths utilized the orle (diamond) as a mark of identification and to stamp the weight on gold bullion used in trade. Originally chosen by General Washington for his Paymaster General, it was approved by the Secretary of War in 1896 to be the insignia of the Pay Department, and later the Finance Corps. The Finance diamond represents the four basic functions of the Finance Corps (accounting, disbursing, administration and auditing) with the inner lines representing the coordination between the pay and procurement agencies of the Army.

FINANCE CORPS

There has not been an army in history that was not influenced in one way or another by its "pay", whether loot and plunder or legal tender. As the transition from occasional pillage to regular payment progressed, the need for a service to administer pay and account for monies, with a corps of officers to supervise, became inevitable.

The Finance Corps was born amid the tumult of the Revolutionary War. In June 1775, one year before the Declaration of Independence, the second Continental Congress created the office of Paymaster General to manage and disburse the wages of General Washington's army. Even though the war ended and the army disbanded, thePaymaster General's office continued in order to service the small force that remained on active duty. In 1816 with increasing financial demands, the Paymaster General's office gave way to the separate, enlarged, and renamed Pay Department. The Pay Department remained active through two wars until 1912 when, in a major reorganization, it was merged with the Quartermaster Department. This quickly proved to be impractical, and in 1920 Congressional action made the Finance Department a separate branch of the War Department. The office of the Chief of Finance remained a separate entity until World War II, when it was integrated with the office of the Fiscal Director, Army Service Forces and given additional duties such as the sale of War Bonds and promotion of the National Service Life Insurance Program. After the war, the office of the Fiscal Director was dissolved and the Finance Department again became an independent Army Staff Agency.

The Army Organizational Act of 1950 changed the Finance Department to the Finance Corps with no changes in its primary mission. There were changes, however. Since 1949, with the designation of the position of Comptroller of the Army and the placement of comptrollers at every level of command, the Finance Corps has taken on wider responsibilities in budgeting and financial planning.

Today's Finance Corps has advanced immeasurably over the first Paymaster General's office, not only in size but in quality. Since 1950, the Corps has felt the impact of automation in the form of a mechanized pay system, and, in the early 1970s, the computerized Joint Uniform Military Pay System (JUMPS) which centralized the entire Army payroll at the U.S. Army Finance and Accounting Center at Fort Benjamin Harrison. This pervasive implementation of computers relieves the Finance officer from mundane routine matters and frees his or her time for the intensification of comptrollership functions. Increasingly the Finance Officer serves as the management consultant of the command, assisting with the overall management of personnel, money, and material resources. His or her new responsibilities do not end with the obligation of funds but continue to the point where resources are actually used. In this era of constant evolution, the Finance Corps, although it is the smallest branch by comparison, has been characterized by progressive accomplishments.

The official home of the Finance Corps is the Army Finance School at the Soldier Support Center, Fort Benjamin Harrison, Indiana, which is part of the U.S. Army Institute of Personnel and Resource Management. The Finance School was founded in 1920 to standardize and develop instruction for all members of the Finance Corps, to include Civil Service Personnel. Today the School annually trains several thousand individuals in subjects ranging from cashier duties to comptroller functions.

Newly-commissioned officers can expect to attend the Finance Officer Basic Course shortly after entrance on active duty. Upon completion, some officers will attend the Military Accounting Course. The Finance Officer Advanced Course is attended by career officers normally between their third and eighth year of service.

The Finance officer will find varied, yet interrelated duties such as assignment to any of the broad occupational specialties fields of Finance Disbursing Officer, Accounting Officer, Cost Analyst, Finance and Accounting Officer, Finance Staff Officer, Program and Budget Officer, Public Finance Officer, or Comptroller. Each is an interesting and challenging experience which contributes to the officer's personal potential for leadership and management.

JUDGE ADVOCATE GENERAL'S CORPS
(The World's Largest Law Firm)

The legal affairs—military and civil—of the Army and the personnel in it are entrusted to this special group of officers, all of whom are graduates of accred-

The Army's legal arm traces its insignia to the year 1890. The crossed pen and sword symbolize the recording of testimony and the military character of the branch. The wreath is the traditional symbol for achievement.

ited law schools, members of their state's bar, and commissioned in the Judge Advocate General's Corps. This Corps traces its beginning from July, 1775, when William Tudor—a leading Boston lawyer—became the first "Judge Advocate of the Army." A year later the designation of "Judge Advocate General" and the rank of lieutenant colonel were prescribed for this office.

Until 1802 other individuals were designated as Judge Advocate of the Army, but after that date and until the Corps was officially established, the term "Judge Advocate" was used rather freely in designating officers whose primary function was the prosecution of courts-martial and advising military commanders on matters pertaining to military justice and enforcing discipline in the Army.

By an act of Congress in 1849, the office of "Judge Advocate of the Army" was established on a permanent basis, but a corps of officers was not authorized until 1862, when the Judge Advocate was granted the rank and pay of a brigadier general. The "Bureau of Military Justice" was created a few years later and the Judge Advocate General was placed in charge of that agency. A merger of the Bureau and the corps of Judge Advocates in the field took place in 1884 and resulted in the creation of the Judge Advocate General's Department, by which it was known until 1948, when "Corps" was substituted for "Department."

Military law grew in scope and intensity from the time of the Civil War so that today the Judge Advocate General's Corps performs many duties and services not envisioned by those who created it. From The Judge Advocate General, who acts as legal advisor to the Secretary of the Army and all other agencies within Headquarters, Department of the Army, to a legal officer in a small installation, the day-to-day situations are more diversified than in most general civilian law practices. Today's Judge Advocate is skilled in the law of nations, the environment, labor relations and contracts as much as in the traditional law of the Army and its criminal justice system. He or she also advises the commander on installation problems, personnel administration, patent and tax law, and a variety of claims by and against the Government.

A primary responsibility of the Judge Advocate General's Corps is the complete administration of the Uniform Code of Military Justice in the Army. In order to fulfill its ever increasing military justice responsibility, the strength of the Corps has been greatly increased in the past few years to provide competent legal advice and counsel for the accused in areas where previously no such right was guaranteed. Moreover, constant refinements in the Uniform Code and the implementing regulations foster an atmosphere of professionalism, free from the command restraints and influence of the past. For example, the Judge Advocates who act as military judges in courts-martial are organized in a separate command, the United States Army Legal Services Agency, and are assigned and rated in that channel.

Other services to and protections for the individual soldier have been introduced by recent regulations. Like the military judge, the military defense counsel has been placed in a separate organization, the U.S. Army Trial Defense Service; counsel is provided to the soldier in the many administrative and non-judicial proceedings which can affect his or her career; and Judge Advocates are now authorized to take an active role in assisting soldiers with personal legal problems under the Expanded Legal Assistance Program.

The Judge Advocate General's School, located on the grounds of the University of Virginia at Charlottesville adjacent to the prestigious University of Virginia Law School, is where all new Judge Advocate officers receive initial orientation into the Army, and where other members of the Corps return for advanced and specialized courses. The Judge Advocate General's School is the Home of the Army Lawyer; its students include other uniformed Judge Advocates and civilian United States Government attorneys from many agencies, and some legal officers from the armed forces of friendly foreign nations. The School's program of Continuing Legal Education supplements and hones the general skills of the practicing attorney with graduate-level instruction in more than 20 fields of law necessary to fulfill the Corps' complex mission. In addition to the Basic and Advanced Courses, the School offers "short courses" to military judges, contracting officers, commanders, counsel, international law specialists and others concerned with Army administration.

The Corps is a special branch and its services are required throughout every level of command. Therefore the opportunities for assignment anywhere the U.S. Army has troops are plentiful and diversified. Early in his or her career, a Judge Advocate is likely to be involved in legal assistance, claims or courts-martial. They are basic missions of the Corps, provide valuable trial experience, and are essentials to the development of the well-rounded legal officer. Experienced Judge Advocates can look forward to challenging assignments at levels within the Army's structure where policy and decisions of general importance are made.

The "shell and flame" insignia of the Ordnance Corps is patterned after a similar design used by British troops and became official in 1832. Considered the oldest of branch insignia it represents the early explosive devices and properly symbolizes that particular branch function today.

ORDNANCE

"Service to the line, on the line, on time" is the motto of the Ordnance Corps. The Ordnance mission is to insure that the maximum number of combat weapon systems are ready and available to combat commanders.

The explosive growth of science and technology in the years since World War II has contributed significantly to the development of military materiel. The major developments of World War II—nuclear weapons, missiles, and electronics—have been exploited, refined, and applied in a variety of ways. As the pace and complexity of technological advancements have grown, the interaction between military materiel and operations has become increasingly important and has also had a significant impact on the manner of accomplishing the support mission. Ordnance officers can be found worldwide, performing the enormous task of maintaining Ordnance type equipment used by both our armed forces and those of our allies.

Ordnance officers may pursue a career in three challenging areas (accession specialties): Missile Materiel Management (guided missiles and free flight rockets); Munitions Materiel Management (nuclear and conventional); and Maintenance Management (conventional tank and ground mobility equipment).

Officers assigned in the Missile Materiel Management specialty can expect to play a vital role in the development, fielding, support, and final disposition of the Army's surface-to-surface and surface-to-air missile systems. Their sophisticated guidance systems, complex target acquisition radars, and other related ground support systems are ready made for officers with good scientific or managerial skills.

Munitions Materiel Management officers are assigned to management positions around the world concerned with conventional and nuclear munitions and their associated production, maintenance, testing and handling equipment. The overall technical sophistication of the myriad of munition items in the Army's inventory requires officers who have developed expertise in a broad spectrum of management techniques and engineering technologies. The munitions system is unique in that virtually the entire ammunition industry in the United States is owned and managed by the Army. Opportunities are available for Ordnance officers to participate at all levels in managing this multi-billion dollar industry.

A sub-specialty within Munitions Materiel Management is Explosive Ordnance Disposal (EOD), the "bomb disposal" service of the Army. Locating, deactivating, removing, and disposing or salvaging unexploded conventional or special explosive ordnance, including chemical and nuclear munitions, are typical EOD functions.

Maintenance Management officers are responsible for maintenance of armament, wheel and track vehicles, engineer construction and earthmoving equipment, power generation equipment, and office equipment, as well as metalworking, welding, and equipment recovery. The role of every officer in Maintenance Management is to efficiently and effectively insure that the maximum number of weapon systems are operational, ready, and available to combat commanders. Non-operational equipment cannot contribute to victory. Management of the Army's maintenance, in concert with actual maintenance operations in support units, is becoming an increasingly sophisticated challenge. Twice the acquisition cost of most Army equipment is spent on maintaining it during its life cycle. Skilled and dedicated maintenance managers are required to insure that these billions of dollars are spent so as to maximize equipment operational readiness at minimum cost.

The organization of ordnance support today still follows the concept and philosophy upon which it was founded—direct support to the combat arms. The Ordnance Corps had its beginning with an Act of the Continental Congress on 27 May 1775 which established a committee to study and plan for the supply of weapons and other war materiel to the Continental Army. Soon after the Act was passed, General Washington appointed Ezekiel Cheever to be the Commissary General of Artillery Stores. Cheever became, in essence, the first Chief of Ordnance of the Army. From this beginning up to the present, the Ordnance Corps has changed as the Army changed. Early in the Revolutionary War, design of weapons was not considered an Ordnance function, primarily because U.S. Army weapons were either purchased abroad or captured from the enemy. Individual weapons were usually the property of the individual soldier. However, in 1777 the first arsenal for the manufacture of weapons was established at Springfield, Massachusetts. During the same year a storage facility was set up at Carlisle, Pennsylvania.

In 1801, Eli Whitney demonstrated to the War Department that mass production of weapons was practical. This process revolutionized the manufacture of weapons and was quickly adopted by our military armories, leading to formal authorization of the Ordnance Department on 14 May 1812. The first formally designated Chief was Colonel Decius Wadsworth.

Ordnance personnel received their baptism of fire in the War of 1812. When the British approached the Washington Arsenal, the installation was evacuated. Departing ordnance storage personnel dumped the remaining stores of powder in a near-by well. A British detachment investigating the premises lowered a lantern into the well. The resulting explosion killed several officers and about 30 enlisted men.

After the War of 1812, the Chief of Ordnance was responsible for contracting for arms and ammunition, for supervising the Government armories and storage depots, and for recruiting and training artificers to be attached to regiments, corps, and garrisons. By 1816, five Federal arsenals were in operation. These were Springfield and Harper's Ferry, making small arms; Watervliet producing artillery equipment and ammunition; Watertown producing small arms ammunition and gun carriages; and Frankford making ammunition. Two others, Rock Island and Picatinny, were added before or during the Civil War. Early in the Civil War, Harper's Ferry was destroyed.

As a result of the large-scale, widely dispersed operations during the Civil War, ordnance concepts and activities were greatly improved.

The war with Spain brought new and difficult problems to the Ordnance Corps. Procurement methods had to be revamped, and methods of supply expanded to meet the requirements of our first "overseas" conflict. Most war supplies had been stored at established arsenals and depots and in most cases were delivered directly to military units in field locations. When forces were being prepared for shipment by sea, a large depot was set up in Tampa, Florida, to complete the equipping of units moving through the port. This port depot and those field depots set up in Cuba were the beginning of Ordnance field service. From this experience came the realization that this job, now called logistics, must be performed by separate agencies so that combat troops could concentrate on fighting. World Wars I and II and the Korean Conflict did not change the mission of the Ordnance Corps, but the amounts of items procured, distributed, and maintained stagger the imagination. During this period, small arms procurement mounted into the millions, rounds of ammunition into the billions and other items produced increased proportionally. Ordnance field service was expanded along with the training of personnel and development of techniques in order to be responsive to the needs of the fighting forces.

The Atomic Age began an entirely new era of weapons and weapons systems and the continuing improvement of more conventional equipment. To meet these changes and the more complex requirements of a modern army, and to plan for the future, a new agency was created. The new Army Materiel Command (now the Development and Readiness Command) was given the responsibility for procurement and distribution of materiel which had formerly been divided among the various technical services. The Ordnance Corps, which in the past had been represented in organizational structures by name and was somewhat restricted in areas of employment, now furnishes Ordnance trained personnel to staff all logistic elements of the Army.

In the field of research and development, Ordnance Corps personnel have always had a major role. During the greater part of its history this role was restricted in research but had almost complete freedom in development. From its beginning in 1814 until the late 1930's, the Ordnance Corps was given requirements by the various chiefs of branch for equipment that would perform as each chief of branch desired. From these requirements, Ordnance engineers would produce the needed item. In 1942 the Ordnance Board was organized. The board was to be the research and development arm of the Chief of Ordnance, with a mission to design equipment, develop training procedures, study improvements in operational techniques, and develop TOE's for Ordnance units.

The test and evaluation mission of the Ordnance Corps had no established facility during its early history. At the turn of the century its first designated proving ground was established at Sandy Hook, New Jersey. Sandy Hook served its purpose until the beginning of World War I, at which time it became apparent that it was no longer suitable. Located on the seacoast, it was vulnerable to attack and sabotage; in addition, it had no direct rail connections. Despite the urgency, it took nearly two years before negotiations were completed for the purchase of a 35,000 acre tract along the Chesapeake Bay near Aberdeen, Maryland. Sandy Hook was eventually phased out and all its Ordnance activities transferred to the new location at Aberdeen. At first, Aberdeen Proving Ground was utilized for testing field artillery weapons, trench mortars, anti-aircraft guns, ammunition and railway artillery. Observation towers, small arms ranges, a hard surface area for testing bombs and other facilities were added later. On 10 November 1918, Dr. Robert H. Goddard, the "Father of American Rocketry" successfully demonstrated test rockets of his own design at Aberdeen.

From the beginning, the Ordnance Corps trained its personnel on an informal basis. Then, in 1902, the Ordnance School of Application was established at Sandy Hook. This school was replaced by the Ordnance School of Technology, activated at Watertown Arsenal in 1906. Later, in 1917, there were 12 supply schools established in various universities throughout the country. All of these schools, plus several others, graduated over 50,000 personnel, both commissioned and enlisted, during World War I. In 1936, all Ordnance training was centralized at Aberdeen Proving Ground. As a result, the ordnance field school for enlisted men was moved from Raritan Arsenal in July 1940 and combined with the officer school to form the Ordnance School. This consolidated school for a time handled most of the school training for the Corps. In January 1942, the Bomb Disposal School was activated at Aberdeen and remained active until 1955. In October 1956, Bomb Disposal/EOD training was transferred to the Naval School at Indianhead, Maryland.

After rockets, missiles, and ammunition became almost an entity of its own, a second ordnance-oriented school was established at Redstone Arsenal, Alabama. The U. S. Army Missile and Munitions Center and School and the U. S. Army Ordnance Center and School remain as the principal training centers for Ordnance personnel.

In July 1973, the U.S. Army Chemical School was merged with the Ordnance School, giving that school the added mission of providing the defense establishment with trained CBR specialists and continuously updated doctrine in the chemical field. In 1979, the Chemical School was moved to Fort McClellan, Alabama.

In addition to these Army training establishments, use is made of civilian universities and technical training establishments for selected officers and enlisted personnel.

The Ordnance officer of today's Army is a materiel-oriented manager. He or she functions and operates in an atmosphere of electronics, mobility, and high-technology weaponry—rifles, machine guns, artillery, trucks, tanks, rockets, missiles, and nuclear and conventional fire power. The Ordnance officer must have a basic qualification in military organization, operation and tactics in addition to technical and managerial expertise to function in a variety of duties.

In staff positions, Ordnance officers provide advice and assistance to all commanders and other staff officers at all levels on ordnance matters. They are also assigned to instruct and train military and civilian personnel in maintenance, repair parts, ammunitiion, missile and general logistical support doctrine and procedures.

In assignments to planning staffs, the Ordnance officer helps to develop concepts, doctrines, policies and procedures for furnishing ammunition and maintenance support to the Army.

Performing integrated commodlty (life cycle) management of ground vehicles, missile systems, weapons systems and ammunition, duties related to EOD, formulating plans, programs and policies for industrial mobilization and providing technical supervision and inspection for designated commodities are some of the fascinating assignments awaiting those who qualify, choose, and are selected for the Ordnance Corps.

Because of its widely diversified field mission, numerous TOE units are authorized Ordnance officers. From the Ammunition, Missile, and Maintenance Companies, Nuclear Weapons Support Detachments and EOD Detachments, to the Depots, Arsenals, and Ordnance Plants, assignments are varied and diversified. Ordnance jobs for company grade officers include Platoon Leader, Missile Maintenance Officer, Technical Supply Officer, Production Control Officer, Ammunition Stock Control Officer, EOD Officer, EOD Detachment Commander, Company Commander, Service School Instructor, Maintenance Test Officer, Product/Procurement Manager, Research Officer, and Range Officer.

Further schooling at both the Ordnance School, the Missile and Munitions School, and selected civilian institutions is usually in the future of many career officers in the grade of captain and above. After appropriate field experience with battalion- and higher-level field organizations, and/or logistics staffs, selection for top level Army schools is a possibility.

Changes in weaponry and the need to maintain weapons in fighting condition will be a primary activity so long as armies exist. Therefore, the young officer selecting Ordnance will quickly encounter exciting challenges and responsibilities in the Ordnance arena. Initial assignments are usually as maintenance or missile/munitions platoon leaders. Such assignments involve management of supply and maintenance personnel and maintenance of sophisticated Army equipment, such as the new M-1 Abrams tank or high technology missile systems.

The current range of Ordnance career possibilities is extensive. With weapon systems and equiment ranging from conventional to laser (computer and space age technology), the Ordnance Corps of today and the future presents a tremendous opportunity for those who qualify.

QUARTERMASTER

Advanced data processing equipment, sophisticated communications networks, and modern transportation techniques are the tools of the Quartermas-

One of the more complex branch insignias is that of the Quartermaster Corps. A key, symbolic of storekeeping, is crossed with a sword indicating "military" and superimposed on a wagon wheel, pertaining to the delivery of supplies. The stars and spokes of the wheel represent the original 13 colonies and the origin of the Corps during the American Revolution. The eagle is used as a national symbol.

ter Corps officers in performing their logistical support missions around the world.

It's a far cry from the beginnings of the Corps in 1775, when the first Quartermaster General was appointed to provide some items of camp equipment and the transportation for the Army. Having virtually no money and no authority and dependent upon the several states for supplies, it seems incredible that the early Quartermaster Department could accomplish its mission. Yet the Quartermaster played an important role in the successful defense of liberty made by the young nation. The most effective early Quartermaster General was Major General Nathaniel Greene. He established the Army's first depot system, which in those days was used to supply forage for Army animals.

Military supply was largely under civilian control in the post-Revolutionary War period. At the outbreak of the war with England in 1812, Congress appointed a brigadier general to supply the Army. In 1814, quartermaster sergeants first appeared and were assigned to each of the three regiments of riflemen.

From 1818 to 1860, the Quartermaster General was Brigadier General Thomas S. Jesup, a remarkably able administrator. During his tenure the Quartermaster Department made great strides, emerging as the integrated, permanent supply agency of the Army. In this period the Department took over the procurement and distribution of clothing and other items of supply.

The Civil War brought the development of an effective depot system and railroads were used extensively in establishing supply lines. The supply system and procedures developed during this period formed the basis for supply doctrine until World War I. In 1862, the Department assumed responsibility for the burial of the war dead and the maintenance of national cemeteries.

Congress, in 1912, consolidated the former subsistence, pay, and Quartermaster departments to create the Quartermaster Corps with its own officers and troops. The First World War showed the increasing importance of supply. The United States participated long enough to give the Quartermaster Corps its first set of huge figures: nearly four billion pounds of food valued at 727 million dollars, a billion dollars spent for clothing, and 3,606,000 tons of supplies.

To fill an increasing need for specialists in Army supply problems, the Quartermaster School was begun in a small way in 1910 at the Philadelphia Quartermaster Depot. The school remained in Philadelphia, except for a short period at Camp Johnston, Florida, in World War I, until it moved to Fort Lee in 1941. The School continues today to train the officers and enlisted specialists assigned to the Army's sophisticated logistical system.

During World War II, the Quartermaster Corps sent more and a greater variety of supplies to more men in more places in the world than any other Quartermaster activity had done in the history of the world. Also, the Quartermaster soldier often worked in the combat zone, and if the need arose, he took his turn fighting. It was during this conflict that transportation and construction were transferred to the Transportation Corps and the Corps of Engineers, respectively. With the loss of these two original functions, the Quartermaster concentrated entirely on its supply and service missions.

The Corps pioneered in the field of air supply of ground troops, using both free fall and parachute delivery extensively in Korea as a regular means of supply for the first time in military history.

When the Department of the Army was reorganized in 1961–1962, the Office of the Quartermaster General was abolished and its functions and responsibilities reassigned to the Department of the Army staff agencies and commands established under the functional concept. The Quartermaster Corps, however, remained as one of the Army's important technical branches and Quartermaster personnel are still performing the logistical functions within the new functional framework. The Commandant of the Quartermaster School is now the principal Quartermaster adviser and the School is the "Home of the Quartermaster Corps." '

Officers assigned to the Quartermaster Corps, while they function as members of a team within the current complex of logistical concepts, are still identified with the basics of supply—supply management, procurement, cataloging, inventory, management, storage, distribution, salvage, disposal, and the supervision of troop testing of all material except medical and cryptological items. A host of supply specialties and service support responsibilities include graves registration, laundries, bakeries, dry cleaning plants, issue points at reception centers, food service, open mess management, commissary management, and petroleum product testing.

Quartermaster officers are part of numerous TD organizations to provide staff advice and counsel on supply and service operations. Within the TOE authorizations, officers can expect assignments to units like the Supply and Transport Battalion, Combat Support Battalion, Supply and Service Battalion, Supply and Service Company, Petroleum Operating and Supply Companies, Air Equipment Support Company, Air Delivery Company, Air Equipment Repair and Depot Company, Airdrop Equipment Repair and Supply Company, and Supply Depot Company.

Among the jobs offered by this branch are Supply Management Officer, Supply Staff Officer, Food Advisor, Bakery Officer, Subsistence Officer, Supply and Service Officer, Commissary Officer, Materiel Project Officer, Procurement Control and Production Officer, and Storage Officer . . . all of which provide unusual career opportunities for the individual with a supply-related background and interests.

Formal schooling, including the basic and advanced Quartermaster officer courses at Fort Lee, is in the future of all Quartermaster officers. Each junior officer may expect training and early duty assignment in one of the accession specialty areas of POL Management, Food Management, or General Troop Support Materiel Management. During career development, many special educational opportunities at the Quartermaster School and selected civilian institutions are open to Quartermaster officers. Officers also compete equally with officers from other branches for selection to attend top-level Army schools such as the Command and General Staff College, the Army War College, and the Industrial College of the Armed Forces.

Today's highly mobile Army requires professionalism in all stages of combat service support. Whether it's computing requirements for missile repair parts or operating a petroleum pipeline to keep the helicopters in the air, the Quartermaster officer provides the technical knowledge to get the job done right, and now. For the dedicated officer, the Quartermaster Corps offers unlimited opportunities for personal and professional development.

Transportation by rail (represented by a flanged, winged wheel on a rail), land (symbolized by the shield used as standard US highway markers), and water (indicated by the ship's steering wheel) make up the Transportation Corps insignia. The current design was approved in 1942 and is based on a similar one in use since 1919.

TRANSPORTATION CORPS

Firepower and mobility are the two fundamental, inseparable capabilities that insure success in tactical operations, and the basic ingredient of mobility is transportation—equipment to do the job in the best, fastest way, and people who know how to use it properly. That's the Transportation Corps.

The Transportation Corps grew out of the increased necessity for centralized control and operations as a result of the Army's expansion during the mobilization and war years of 1940–1942. Prior to that, transportation responsibilities were split between Quartermaster and Engineers. The establishment of the Transportation Corps came at a critical time. The problems of moving millions of men and uncountable tons of supplies to virtually every corner of the world had no precedent in the history of man. Fledgling officers, many drafted from civilian counterpart jobs, became the nucleus of the new branch and admirably accomplished many of the most successful transport operations ever recorded. Every type of carrier was used. Ships of all sizes and description (the Army still has a navy of its own), aircraft, railroads, trucks, busses, military vehicles—everything that could be used was put to work to get the job done. Volumes have been published on the statistics and accomplishments of the Transportation Corps during World War II, which cannot even be capsuled here. Suffice to say that the Corps earned a place in the heart of every fighting man who reached for ammunition and found it or who walked into a rest area and discovered a full course hot meal waiting. At the same time, it earned a permanent place in the technical support elements of an ever-mobile Army.

Transportation Corps officers are engaged in activities within all three of the Army's major field commands. Those assigned to the development and improvement of tactical vehicles work under the Development and Readiness Command (DARCOM). Transportation specialists concerned with the plans, doctrine and methods of getting people and equipment to far places for specific combat missions labor within the Training and Doctrine Command (TRADOC). And those Transportation Corps officers providing the day-to-day support to Army units maintaining their readiness status while standing prepared for deployment anywhere in the world as may be necessary are working for the Forces Command (FORSCOM).

The tremendous expansion of Army Aviation in response to the Army's need for improved tactical and logistical mobility on the modern battlefield has absorbed much of TC's interest and activity in recent years. Transportation Corps personnel are indeed prominent among the pilots, copilots and flight crews who fly and maintain the Army's aircraft. Approximately one-fourth of the commissioned officers within the Transportation Corps are qualified aviators.

The Transportation Corps mission of aviation logistics is clearly of paramount importance in keeping Army aircraft flying. Transportation Corps units perform direct and general support maintenance and provide repair parts for all Army aircraft. The significance and challenge of keeping the Army's aircraft flying can be expected to increase with greater emphasis on airmobility and technology improvements in the coming years.

In addition to the glamour of Army aviation, TC officers are trained and involved in every conceivable transportation operation. As the Transportation officer of a post, camp, or station, he or she may control the use and movement of all kinds of vehicles from helicopters and fixed-wing aircraft to operating the intra-post bus schedule. The organizational structure of the Army includes highway transport, units like the light truck, medium truck, heavy truck, motor transport, aircraft maintenance, terminal service, medium boat, light amphibian, floating craft support maintenance, railway equipment, train operating and medium- and heavy-lift helicopter companies, as well as service teams for railway, watercraft, and aircraft—all of which provide the Transportation Corps officer with a huge diversity of assignment and professional possibilities.

Under the Officer Personnel Management System (OPMS), Transportation Corps officers will begin their careers in one of the accession specialties assigned the Transportation Corps: Aviation Logistics, or Transportation Management. Numerous additional specialties such as ADP, Supply Management, and Procurement are available for selection by the officer. The selection of an additional specialty is based on the needs of the Army and the officer's desires. The officer's career pattern will normally be in assignments requiring his or her accession or additional specialty.

Fort Eustis, Virginia, located near historic Williamsburg, Jamestown, and Yorktown, is the home of the U.S. Army Transportation School and center of TC activities. While attending the basic, advance, or specialty training courses here, the Transportation Corps officer is well grounded in the fundamentals of doctrine and operations. He or she sees the full range of Transportation Corps responsibilities from the systems operating within the continental United States—air, rail, highway, and inland waterways—to the many foreign ports used to funnel supplies and equipment to Army troops wherever they may be; learns where and how transportation fits into overall logistical planning for the fighting force; reviews the need for research and development; and may, at some time after completion of the advance branch course, be selected for graduate training at a college or university in a special field such as industrial management, transportation engineering, or management. College graduates with degrees majoring in these areas are prime prospects for the Transportation Corps.

Of course there are a wide variety of staff positions at all levels of Army organization open to TC officers and selection for attendance at a top-level Army or Armed Forces college is a real possibility.

The helmeted profile of the goddess "Pallas Athene" was first authorized for the Women's Army Auxiliary Corps in 1942. Pallas Athene was associated in mythology with an impressive variety of womanly virtues; with handicrafts, wisdom, peace, storms, battle, victory, and prosperity.

WOMEN'S ARMY CORPS

The Women's Army Corps was abolished by Congress in 1978. Prior to that time, women in the Army, excluding female members of the six medical corps and the Chaplain Corps, had been assigned to the WAC and then detailed to one of the Army's various branches. However, with passage of the FY 1979 Defense Authorization Bill, female officers were assigned directly to the branches, were integrated on the same promotion lists, and began competing directly with their male counterparts. The history of women in the Army, however, is deserving of special mention in the following brief summary.

The Women's Army Corps, as an official component of the Army, was a twentieth century phenomenon although women have in one way or another supported their fighting men in conflicts since time began. From our own Revolution the stories of "Molly Pitcher," who substituted for her wounded artilleryman husband, and Deborah Gannett, who masqueraded as a soldier for several years, are well known. Women's value to the Army, however, is a natural outgrowth of their increased participation in all social, political, and economic areas of modern life.

As the emancipation of the woman worker during the 20's and 30's began to take hold, increasing numbers went to work in offices and factories developing skills that ultimately, with the onset of World War II, provided a talent pool that was quickly recognized for the potential it held in doing jobs within the previously all-male military structure.

Women in the Army (excluding the medical service) became an official reality on 14 May 1942 when long-established precedents of military tradition gave way to urgent need. Congress authorized the Women's Army Auxiliary Corps (WAAC) as the way to bring these skills, abilities, and talents into the military establishment. It proved so workable that a year later "Auxiliary" was dropped and the Women's Army Corps became a temporary component of the Army.

Oveta Culp Hobby was appointed Director, with the rank of colonel, the first training center was established at Fort Des Moines, Iowa, and the helmeted profile of Minerva (Pallas Athene), the ancient goddess of wisdom, was adopted as the Corps insignia. By October, 1942, the first WAAC administrative companies and aircraft warning service units were sent into the field, and in January 1943 the first WAAC unit was sent overseas to North Africa.

During World War II, more than 150,000 women served in the WAC, performing over 300 different Army jobs, but the corps did not attain permanent status in the Army until 12 June 1948 when the Women's Armed Services Integration Act became effective. This made the Corps a component of the Regular Army and a part of the Army Reserve.

The Corps expanded again during the Korean War but was still without a permanent home. Finally, the redesignated United States Women's Army Corps was headquartered at Fort McClellan, Alabama, and in September, 1952, the Center was designated as an Army Service School.

Members of the WAC assumed increasingly important roles during the decades of the 1950's and 1960's. By the early 1970's, women officers were being detailed permanently to one of the various branches, although they still were carried on a separate promotion list and were assigned to the WAC.

The abolition of the Women's Army Corps in 1978 marked the beginning of a new era where female officers take their places as full equals with the male officers of the Army.

An eagle rising, with wings displayed standing on a bundle of two arrows, all enclosed in a wreath. This insignia is worn by all warrant officers regardless of branch assignment.

WARRANT OFFICER CORPS

The warrant officer designation has long been recognized by various navies of the world. In the navies, the warrant officer traditionally has been a technical specialist whose skills and knowledge were essential for proper operation of the ships, but who did not hold a commission to command. That is, he was "warranted" as an officer rather than "commissioned" as an officer. The warrant officer grade in one form or another has been in continuous use in the U.S. Navy since that service was established. In the U.S. Army, the warrant officer lineage can be traced back only to the Headquarters Clerks of 1896, later designated Army Field Clerks. However, the recognized birth date of the Army's Warrant Officer Corps is 7 July 1918.

On that date, an Act of Congress established the Army Mine Planter Service as a part of the Coast Artillery Corps and appointed in it "warrant officers" to serve as masters, mates, chief engineers and assistant engineers of each vessel. An Act of 1920 expanded the use of warrant officers, authorizing their appointment in clerical, administrative and band-leading activities. In effect, the Act of 1920 designated the warrant officer grade as a reward for enlisted personnel of long servvice and as a haven for former commissioned officers of World War I who lacked either the education or other eligibility requirements to retain their commissions after that war.

Between 1922 and 1935, no warrant officer appointments were made except for a few Band Leaders and Army Mine Planter Service personnel. In 1936, competitive examinations were held to replenish lists of eligible personnel and some appointments began being made again. Warrant officers who were qualified pilots were declared eligible for appointments as lieutenants in the Air Corps in 1939. By 1940, warrant officer appointments began to occur in significant numbers for the first time since 1922, although the total strength of the Warrant Officer Corps decreased until 1942 because of the large numbers of warrant officers who were being transferred to commissioned status during that period.

The second truly important piece of legislation affecting Army warrant officers was passed in 1941. An Act of August 1941, amplified by an Executive Order in November of that year, provided that warrant officers could be assigned duties as prescribed by the Secretary of the Army and that when such duties necessarily included those normally performed by a commissioned officer, the warrant officer would be vested with all the powers usually exercised by commissioned officers in the performance of such duties. The Act of 1941 also established two warrant officer grades, Chief Warrant Officer and Warrant Officer Junior Grade, and authorized flight pay for those whose duties involved aerial flight.

Warrant officer appointments were made by major commanders during World War II and warrant officers served in some 40 occupational areas during that war. In January of 1944, the appointment of women as warrant officers was authorized and by the end of the war there were 42 women warrant officers on active duty.

After World War II, the concept of using the warrant rank as an incentive rather than a reward was instituted. It was to be a capstone rank into which enlisted personnel could advance. This use of the warrant officer grade combined with the earlier concept of using the grade as a reward for long and faithful service resulted in mixed utilization such that, in practice, warrant officers became largely interchangeable with junior commissioned officers or senior enlisted personnel.

The Career Compensation Act of 1949 provided two new pay rates for warrant officers. The designations of Warrant Officer Junior Grade and Chief Warrant Officer were retained, but the grade of Chief Warrant Officer was provided with pay rates W-2, W-3, and W-4. In the Warrant Officer Personnel Act of 1954, these three pay rates became grades and the Warrant Officer Junior Grade became Warrant Officer, providing the four warrant officer grades we have today.

Warrant officers were used extensively during the Korean War, but by 1953 it had become apparent that use of the warrant officer grade as either a reward or an incentive was inadequate. Needed as a basis for continuation of the Warrant Officer Corps was a new concept consistent with functional Army requirements. From 1953 until 1957, the Department of the Army conducted an analysis to determine whether or not the warrant officer program should be continued and if so in what form and for what purpose.

In January of 1957, as a result of the Department of the Army study, a completely new warrant officer concept was announced which affirmed the need for the warrant officer and the continuation of the Warrant Officer Corps. It stipulated that the warrant officer grade would not be considered as either a reward or an incentive for enlisted men or former commissioned officers, and it defined a warrant officer as ". . . a highly skilled technician who is provided to fill those positions above the enlisted level which are too specialized in scope to permit the effective development and continued utilization of broadly-trained, branch-qualified, commissioned officers." The new concept was formally announced in DA Circular 611–7 of 12 April 1960. It remains the basis for the warrant officer program of today, although much progress has been made since then in the areas of pay, promotion, utilization and education for warrant officers, as can be seen by reference to other chapters of *The Army Officer's Guide.*

In today's Army, warrant officers comprise about 14% of the total officer corps. They are skilled specialists who are essential to the proper operation of the Army and its increasingly complex equipment. Warrant officers serve in some 90 specialty areas (MOS) in 13 career fields:

Administration	Marine Operations
Aviation	Mechanical Maintenance
Communications-Electronics	Services
Criminal Investigation	Supply
Graphics	Weapons Maintenance
Health Care Delivery	Utilities Maintenance
Intelligence	

The career patterns of warrant officers differ from those of commissioned officers since the warrant officers can expect repetitive assignments within their specialty which is essential to sustain and to increase their technical expertise. (See Chapter 12, *Professional Development,* for details.) The Warrant Officer Corps fills a vital need in today's Army in that warrant officers provide a continuity that is not available from commissioned officers and a high degree of technical skill that is not available from enlisted specialists.

DA Pam 600–11, *Warrant Officer Professional Development,* is highly recommended reading for all who would learn more about the past history, the present workings and the bright future of the Warrant Officer Corps.

32

The Army Medical Department

Of particular significance to the capability of all of the other arms and services to perform assigned missions are the six Corps of the Army Medical Department. Under various names, the medical services have been a part of the military establishment since appointment of the first Director General and Chief Physician, on 27 July 1775. Mankind has benefited ever since through the discoveries and techniques of military medical personnel working to assure improved treatment of casualties, or fitness for duty through preventive medicine. The Army Medical Department continues, as ever, to provide for every soldier and the soldier's family, medical care of the highest standards of the profession.

The basic insignia for the Corps of the Army Medical Department is the Caduceus, a two-serpent adaption of the Staff of Aesculapius —one serpent each signifying preventive and corrective medicine —gold in color except for the Medical Service Corps which is silver. The Caduceus alone serves as the insignia for the Medical Corps. Each other Corps is identified by a letter or letters superimposed on the Caduceus . . . "D" for Dental Corps, "N" for Nurse Corps, "V" for Veterinary, "MS" for Medical Service Corps and "S" for Medical Specialists Corps.

Army medical facilities and units are located throughout the world. Almost every permanent Army post has a modern hospital of recent construction, its size depending upon the assigned mission and the population served. These permanent hospitals are staffed and equipped in accordance with their approved Table of Distribution and Allowances (TDA). This authorization document provides considerable flexibility for adjusting personnel and equipment authorizations to meet changes in workload.

The Army Medical Department also includes a large variety of "field" medical units. These units are established on the basis of approved Tables of Organization and Equipment (TO&E). Currently there are in excess of 50 different types of these units. Some of these, such as the Division Medical Battalion, are organic to an Infantry, Airborne, or Armor Division. Other medical units which are usually under a medical group, brigade, or medical command, also furnish direct support to combat troops and include the Combat Support Hospital, Field Hospital, Mobile Army Surgical Hospital, Evacuation Hospital and General Hospital. Also within the "field" medical unit inventory are the Medical Depot, Preventive Medicine Teams, Medical Laboratory, and the Convalescent Center; currently, General Hospitals and the Convalescent Center are not operational in the active Army, but are included in the Reserve forces and are in contingency plans for quick mobilization should the requirement arise.

The Army reorganization of 1973 established the U.S. Army Health Services Command with Headquarters at Fort Sam Houston, Texas. This Command acts as a single manager for health care delivery and supportive services within the United States, Panama, Alaska and Hawaii, and supervises all medical training for the Army. The Surgeon General, with the rank of Lieutenant General, is a physician commissioned in the Medical Corps who is nominated by the President and confirmed by the Congress to hold that office. As such, he or she serves as advisor directly to the Chief of Staff on all matters affecting the health of the Army. Each of the Chiefs of the other five Corps (Dental, Veterinary, Medical Service, Nurse, and Medical Specialist) and a Special Assistant for Medical Corps affairs are consultants to The Surgeon General; each has certain staff responsibilities for activities of the Corps he or she heads. The six Corps of the Medical Department have many things in common and these commonalities have been included only in the material which follows about the Medical Corps and not in each of the individual Corps descriptions.

First used as a cloth insignia in 1851, the Caduceus in its present form was approved in 1902. Except for the Medical Corps, the Caduceus worn by officers of the other Medical Department branches is superimposed with a letter or letters indicative of the specific Corps. Rooted in mythology, the Caduceus has historically been the emblem of physicians, symbolizing knowledge, wisdom, promptness, and skill.

THE MEDICAL CORPS

After the Continental Congress appointed General George Washington as Commander-in-Chief of the Continental Army, he requested medical support for his troops and on 27 July 1775 a Hospital Department was authorized; the forerunner of the original Army Medical Department.

From the end of the Revolutionary War until 1818, when the title of Surgeon General was authorized, the Chief of the Medical Department had little control over those physicians on duty with Army units, since they took their orders from the officers who commanded the units.

The Army Medical Department has kept pace with the times. When the early settlers were moving into the West, Army doctors went with them to dress their wounds and deliver their babies. The very first Medal of Honor was awarded to 1st Lt. Assistant Surgeon Bernard J. D. Irwin for an act of heroism during an attack against Cochise and his Apache band of Chiricahua, on 14 February 1861, in the area that later became the State of Arizona. The Army Medal of Honor was not authorized until 3 March 1863, and the award to Dr. Irwin was not made until 21 January 1894. Another pioneer medical officer, Dr. Leonard Wood, also received the Medal of Honor for service in the Indian campaigns in the Southwest. He later became the only physician ever to serve as Chief of Staff of the Army.

The busts of two Army physicians are included in New York University's Hall of Fame—Dr. Walter Reed, for conquering yellow fever, and Dr. William Crawford Gorgas, for using Reed's discovery to improve health conditions in Panama to make the building of that canal possible. As an added honor, the very first Distinguished Service Medal ever issued went to Dr. Gorgas when he retired as Surgeon General of the Army in 1918.

One of the Army's finest contributions to medical knowledge began in 1836, when Dr. Joseph Lovell started collecting medical books for the Surgeon General's Library. After the Civil War, Dr. John Shaw Billings was appointed Librarian, and before he retired in 1895, the collection had expanded to several thousand volumes, and he was publishing the *Index Medicus* to make it possible for a physician to find a reference to everything ever published on any given medical subject. In 1956, the Library was turned over to the Department of Health, Education and Welfare (now the Department of Health and Human Services) to become the National Library of Medicine. It is the most complete collection of medical literature in the world.

During the Civil War, Dr. William A. Hammond started a collection of morbid specimens for pathologic study. This was the beginning of the Army Medical Museum, which expanded to the Armed Forces Institute of Pathology, one of the foremost diagnostic, teaching and research institutions in this country.

The Army Medical Corps has contributed to civilian health and medicine in many other ways: Army doctors established the first American school of medicine; they published the first American textbooks on surgery, psychiatry and bacteriology, and the first pharmacopoeia (encyclopedia on drugs and their uses); introduced smallpox vaccination in this country; started the first systematic weather reporting; published the first summary on vital statistics; began the chlorination of water, and developed numerous vaccines against diseases of man and animals.

Today the Army maintains some of the finest medical treatment facilities in existence. Medical Centers, like Walter Reed Army Medical Center in Washington, D.C., are accredited teaching institutions where internship and residency training are given, and medical and dental research are of world renown.

With centralized control vested in The Surgeon General, the Medical Department initiated many far reaching projects that affected the medical profession in general, and brought prestige and status to the Medical Corps. Military physicians held such titles as "Surgeon," "Assistant Surgeon," or "Medical Inspector,' and were not given military rank until 1847, when military rank was assigned to members of the Medical Corps then on active duty. An Act of Congress in 1908 established the Medical Corps Reserve, the first such Army Reserve group in this country, and the forerunner of the Officers Reserve Corps in 1916.

The all-physician Medical Corps is responsible for setting the physical standards for all individuals entering military service; maintaining their health while in service; and processing them for discharge or retirement. The clinical care of dependents and retired personnel give the Army doctor a well-rounded practice, but essentially military medicine is aimed at the care of troops, whose average age at induction is 18. Hence prevention of disease and injury is as important as rehabilitation. The control of the environment is becoming increasingly vital in the Army's relations with its civilian neighbors.

Since 1969, the Special Assistant to The Surgeon General for Medical Corps Affairs has served as the equivalent of the Chief of the Medical Corps. This position is currently authorized in the grade of Brigadier General and entitled Chief, Medical Corps Affairs. He shares responsibility for the professional guidance, assignment, education, training and career development of Medical Corps officers with the Commander, U.S. Army Medical Department Personnel Support Agency. In addition, the Chief, Medical Corps Affairs is currently responsible for all Professional Services to include professional standards, preventive medicine, patient administration, and professional policies and practices for the delivery of health care in the Army.

Beginning in 1971, a program was established to train enlisted personnel to be physician assistants. Graduates of this two-year program are appointed as warrant officers. They serve in combat units and in troop health clinics under the supervision of a physician.

DENTAL CORPS

All specialties of dentistry are represented in the Army Dental Corps. The mission of the Corps is one of providing all levels of dental care necessary to preserve the oral health of the Army in support of its fighting strength.

The Chief of the Dental Corps, who is also designated as the Assistant Surgeon General for Dental Services, holds the grade of Major General. He or she serves as the principal advisor to The Surgeon General and Chief of Staff of the Army on all matters concerning the Dental Corps and dental services, establishes professional standards and policies for dental practice, and initiates and reviews recommendations relating to dental doctrine and organizations.

Prior to 3 March 1911, when it was established as a branch, dental support of the military was performed by civilians under contract. The first Dental Corps consisted of 60 dental surgeons. In 1916, along with most of the Medical Department, the Dental Corps was reorganized, expanded, and became fully established as a needed and valuable contributor to the health and welfare of the entire Army. Since 1978, dental personnel have been organized into Dental Activities (DENTACs) and Area Dental Laboratories (ADLs), which are commanded by Dental Corps officers. The U.S. Army Institute of Dental Research, which has provided significant contributions to health care delivery, conducts research and assists in the development of materials and techniques related to combat dentistry.

Officers are appointed to the Dental Corps upon graduation from an accredited school of dentistry and after being awarded either a degree of Doctor of Dental Surgery (DDS) or Doctor of Dental Medicine (DMD). During his or her Army career, a dental officer can expect a variety of assignments throughout the world. Early in their career, officers are normally assigned to dental clinics in direct patient care. Opportunities for advanced education and accredited residency training in a dental specialty are offered, on a competitive basis, usually after four to five years of active service. Other positions which may be available later in one's career are clinician, residency mentor or director, dental researcher, clinic chief, dental staff officer, or dental activity commander.

THE VETERINARY CORPS

Veteinarians have been associated with the nation's military services since the mid-1800's when veterinary surgeons were authorized for each cavalry regiment. The Veterinary Corps was made a part of the Medical Department on 3 June 1916, to centralize control of the veterinary personnel caring for the Army's animals, and inspecting food supplies.

With the evolution of the mechanized cavalry and technological changes in food processing, the Veternary Corps officer assumed new roles. By virtue of education and training, the veterinarian is eminently prepared to function not only in animal medicine, but in matters of public health and comparative medicine as an integral member of the military community health team. His or her professional services encompass food hygiene, veterinary public health and preventive medicine, and veterinary medical care of military animals. The veterinarians' services are vital to the management and care of the extensive laboratory animal resources and to military research and development. The Corps' primary mission is to protect and preserve the health of people in the Armed Forces.

The Chief of the Veterinary Corps, who is also designated as the Assistant Surgeon General for Veterinary Services, holds the grade of brigadier general. He or she participates in assignment and career planning of Veterinary Corps officers.

All members of the Corps are veterinarians who have graduated from an accredited college of veterinary medicine after being awarded either a Doctor of Veterinary Medicine (DVM) or Veterinary Medical Doctor (VMD) degree. Many positions in the Army now require postgraduate specialized training and the Veterinary Corps takes this into account in matching talents and interest in career planning. Veterinary officers are assigned wherever food hygiene and nutritional quality control, preventive medicine, animal medicine, or research are conducted. Veterinary Corps specialties include veterinary services, laboratory animal medicine, veterinary pathologist, veterinary microbiologist, and veterinary comparative medicine.

In 1980, the Air Force Veterinary Service was disestablished and the Army Veterinary Corps became the executive agent for Department of Defense Veterinary Services. In 1981, a program was established to train enlisted personnel to be veterinary food inspection technicians. Graduates are appointed as warrant officers. They will assist the Army Veterinary Corps in the greatly expanded mission of providing veterinary services support throughout the Department of Defense.

MEDICAL SERVICE CORPS

There are two distinct purposes for the existence of this Corps. One is to provide scientists and specialists in the specialties allied to medicine, and the other is to provide officers technically qualified to make the Medical Department selfsustaining in the areas of administration, supply, environmental sciences, and engineering activities. The Medical Service Corps is the one Corps within the Medical Department which relies heavily on the ROTC as a source of officers.

The Chief of the Corps, who has the grade of Brigidier General, serves as an advisor and consultant to the Surgeon General and participates in the assignment and career planning for MSC officers and Medical Department Warrant Officers. Within the allied sciences, pharmacists, optometrists, biochemists, physiologists, podiatrists, audiologists, and many other specialists are commissioned to support the full range of health care services available to all members of the Army, their dependents and other beneficiaries.

As it is now constituted, the Medical Service Corps was established in 1947 to replace the Medical Administrative Corps, Sanitary Corps, and Pharmacy Corps. It is presently organized into four sections: Pharmacy, Supply, and Administration (PS&A); Medical Allied Sciences; Sanitary Engineering; and Optometry. The four sections are further divided into twenty distinct career fields or areas of specialization. The PS&A section includes positions related to personnel management, financial management, pharmacy operations, supply management, and patient administration. MSC officers are also assigned to units equipped for medical evacuation by helicopter or fixed wing aircraft. The specialties included in the Sanitary Engineering section are: environmental engineering, environmental science, medical enomology, and nuclear medical science. Except for the PS&A Section, where changes do occur, officers commissioned in the Medical Service Corps usually remain within their specialty for their entire career. The specialties which are included in the Medical Allied Sciences section are: audiology, medical laboratory sciences, (physiology, microbiology, biochemistry, immunology, parasitology, and related laboratory sciences) psychology, sociology, and podiatry.

Along with those in other Medical Department Corps, officers commissioned in the Medical Service Corps can expect to attend an orientation course at the Academy of Health Sciences, U.S. Army, located at Fort Sam Houston, Texas. Upon completion of this course they are assigned to a medical facility or activity or other Army unit requiring their particular skill.

At higher levels of operation, MSC officers are assigned to duties as a comptroller, plans and operations officer, personnel manager, materiel officer, in research and development, as an Executive Officer in medical centers and community hospitals or medical units, and as key staff advisors in major headquarters, Department of the Army, and Department of Defense.

A Medical Service Corps officer may perform as a faculty member at the Academy of Health Sciences, U.S. Army, or as an instructor or advisor to Army Reserve or Army National Guard medical units. The Medical Service Corps provides an excellent opportunity for the ROTC cadet. Those who have been awarded at least a bachelor's degree with a major in accounting, business administration, chemistry, education, health care administration, management engineering, personnel administration, or statistics are eligible for direct appointment to the PS&A section; and those receiving special degrees in the allied sciences of optometry, environmental engineering, entomology, environmental sciences, health physics, or other health care related disciplines are, of course, also encouraged to apply for appointment in the Medical Service Corps.

THE ARMY NURSE CORPS

The Army Nurse Corps, established in 1901 as a result of the devoted efforts of civilian nurses employed by the Army to care for the sick and wounded during the Spanish-American War, is the oldest Military Nurse Corps in the United States and the first women's component of the United States Armed Forces. Since 1955 both women and men have been eligible for commissions in the Army Nurse Corps. An all-officer Corps, its mission is to provide the best possible nursing care to the American soldier and his or her family.

The Chief of the Corps, who is a Brigadier General, serves as an advisor and consultant to The Surgeon General on staff policies, procedures, activities, and other matters pertaining to nursing, nursing personnel and the Army Nurse Corps.

Army nurses serve in seven clinical specialties—Community Health, Psychiatric-Mental Health, Pediatrics, Obstetrics, Operating Room, Anesthesia, and Medical-Surgical Nursing—and three functional areas—education, administration, and research—and in nurse staff positions in the major Army commands, the Office of the Surgeon General, and TOE units.

Army Medical Department short courses and civilian education programs prepare the Army nurse for practice in traditional as well as the expanded nursing roles such as Nurse Midwifery, Nurse Practitioner, and Nurse Specialist.

In the summer of 1981, the Army Nurse Corps and the U.S. Army Training and Doctrine Command (TRADOC) began a joint effort to increase nursing student participation in ROTC. To this end, 50 scholarships were dedicated specifically for nursing students. As an additional incentive, a hospital-based, preceptorship-type summer camp was offered as an alternative to the regular ROTC summer camp. Response was highly enthusiastic and as a result, it will be offered as an approved option for the ROTC Nursing Cadet.

THE ARMY MEDICAL SPECIALIST CORPS

The Army Medical Specialist Corps, formulated by the enactment of Public Law 36 on 16 April 1947, is composed of three unique medical specialties— dietitians, occupational therapists, and physical therapists. Although one of the youngest Corps of the Army Medical Department, the individual specialties of the Army Medical Specialist Corps have been contributing far longer; as early as the Spanish-American War, dietitians were serving as civilian practitioners, and all three specialties played a large role in the rehabilitation of World War I and II casualties.

The minimum educational qualification is a bachelor's degree within the particular specialty and the appropriate professional licensures, certification, or registration. However, the Army does provide specialty post-baccalaureate training for those qualified accessions who must complete a dietetic internship or occupational therapy affiliation to become eligible for registration or certification. Additionally, a master of physical therapy degree program, affiliated with Baylor University, is conducted to provide basic, entry-level professional education. In addition to the provision of specialty training of qualified individuals or the direct accession of fully qualified practitioners, ROTC graduates, when professionally qualified, are also eligible for commission within the Army Medical Specialist Corps.

The Chief, Army Medical Specialist Corps holds the rank of colonel and serves as an advisor and consultant to The Surgeon General on all matters pertaining to the Corps. By statute, there are three Assistant Chiefs who serve as consultants in their professional specialty areas, and make recommendations on career management and professional development within their specialty.

In October 1981, the Army Medical Specialist Corps implemented clinical specialization paralleling current practice in civilian health care programs to enhance the provision of patient care, to support graduate medical education, and to increase career opportunities and job satisfaction.

Army Medical Specialist Corps officers play a vitally important role in not only the comprehensive treatment and rehabilitation of patients, but also the promotion of health and prevention of injury.

Since 1955, both men and women have been eligible for commission in the Army Medical Specialist Corps and are assigned to all Army Medical Centers and Army Community Hospitals in the United States and the major oversea commands; to the Academy of Health Sciences, teaching both officers and enlisted personnel; to data processing agencies; research units; the Office of The Surgeon General; and to major command headquarters.

Appendix—Additional Duty Guide

The additional duty is the Army's way of assigning mission, administrative, housekeeping, and personnel-related responsibilities outside of primary military occupations. This appendix brings together the practical and detailed counsel necessary to get started right and to develop a program to meet the needs of a particular assignment. It doesn't, of course, tell exactly how to do any particular job, but is rather a guide to the things that will get the job started and much easier.

A few of the mission-related duties like motor officer, mess officer, supply officer, training officer, etc., require more time and effort than others. Many additional duties formerly assigned at company level are now assigned at battalion or higher level. Some duties formerly assigned to officers at company level may now be assigned to noncommissioned officers.

The twenty-one jobs described herein were selected as comprising the hard core of a seemingly unlimited number of additional duties. They are typical of those additional duties to be found, with minor variations, at almost every organizational level. What is said about each of them focuses somewhat on small unit operations, and shares experience about the most practical ways of carrying out the instructions, the intent, and the programs or procedures prescribed in the related host of official directives.

Readers will find here a valuable auxiliary guide giving an introduction, references and new emphasis to many areas and details often overlooked. This information can speed the acquaintance with new additional duties and will serve as a long-term reference for young officers. It will also serve as a concise and handy reference for commanders at all levels.

The thing to get acquainted with early in any additional duty assignment is the officially published material about that particular job.

Unit reference libraries should have at least one copy of whatever is needed. But how does one know what is needed? In addition to the references recommended for each additional duty described here, these DA Pamphlets will tell the story:

108–1: Index of Army Motion Pictures and Related Audio-Visual Aids

310–1: Index of Administrative Publications (Regulations, Circulars, Pamphlets, etc.)

310–2: Index of Blank Forms

310–3: Index of Doctrinal, Training, and Organizational Publications

310–4: Index of Technical Manuals, Technical Bulletins, some Supply Manuals and Bulletins, Lubrication Orders

310–6: Index of Supply Catalogs and Supply Manuals

310–7: Index of Modification Work Orders

Sometimes reference copies of publications are kept in more than one library. The appropriate ones may be in the training office, maintenance shop, supply room, mess hall, etc. Be sure to check this possibility before deciding a publication isn't available.

If the unit library doesn't have the needed references, don't hesitate to order them; DA Pamphlet 310–10 should be your guide.

The material in this chapter originally was prepared by Theodore J. Crackle and published in book form as *The Army Additional Duty Guide.* It has been updated as necessary and the format has been changed for inclusion in *The Army Officer's Guide,* but it retains the flavor of the author and is incorporated here with his permission. The additional duties discussed, in order of their appearance, are:

Ammunition Officer
Army Emergency Relief Officer
NBC Officer
Claims Officer
Class A Agent (Pay) Officer
Courts-Martial Member
Income Tax Officer
Line of Duty (LOD) Investigation Officer
Mess Officer
Motor Officer/Maintenance Officer
Postal Officer
Range Safety Officer
Records Management Officer
Reenlistment Officer
Safety Officer
Savings Officer
Supply Officer
Training Officer
Unit Fund, Custodian/Recorder
Unit Fund Council, President/Member
Voting Officer

AMMUNITION OFFICER

Like most jobs, the effort and time that duty as ammunition officer takes depends on the type of unit to which one is assigned. Combat service support units may have little more than small arms ammunition, which may be stored in the arms room. A combat unit, on the other hand, may have a quantity and variety that at first makes the job seem almost impossible. Regardless of the type of unit, the ammo officer's responsibilities (and problems) will fall in three areas; storage, maintenance, and accounting.

No matter where or what type the ammo is, it needs protection. Proper storage will eliminate most ammo troubles.

First of all, be sure any storage area is well-policed of flammable materials of any kind. Pile ammo in neat stacks, separated by type, caliber and lot number. Within the limitations imposed by the size of the storage area, locate the stacks far enough apart so that if one blows, others won't immediately go up, too. In any case, keep the ammo off the ground. Have wooden strips laid between the tiers of cases to keep air circulating around the boxes to help keep them dry. Cover the stacks with a tarp or waterproof cover, but be sure to let the air circulate freely. Otherwise moisture will be trapped and eventually cause damage. If there is no covering material available, stack the boxes in such a way that water will drain off.

Repair and re-stencil damaged boxes immediately. (Unidentifiable ammo is automatically classified Grade 3 and is not fired.)

White phosphorous (WP or PWP) rounds need special attention. Segregate them to a clear area and store them with projectiles nose-up (except 3.5-inch rockets, which should be stored nose-down). The white phosphorous filler can soften or melt in hot weather and could dislocate within the projectile if not properly stored. Segregate rockets of all types and point them all one way— either nose-down or toward a revetment or barricade.

When storing ammo in vehicles, check the TM and SOPs for proper storage locations and procedures. Be sure that the primers of large-caliber rounds are properly protected both in handling and in storage. Break the seal on small arms ammo boxes only when absolutely necessary. Once the seal has been broken, however, remember to inspect and clean it periodically.

In many units a portion of the basic ammo load is carried in trucks or trailers that belong to the ammo section of the support platoon. Local SOP establishes the degree of responsibility that you as the ammo officer will have for these vehicles, but from a practical—and tactical—point of view, you'll be very interested since you depend on them to get needed ammo forward.

Check preventive maintenance (PM) on the truck. Even if ammo has been well cared for, it won't be of any use if the truck carrying it breaks down. This may take tact on your part since vehicle maintenance is usually someone else's responsibility.

Here are some hints to help keep this vehicle-loaded ammo in good shape:

—place it on wooden floor racks and insure that all drain plugs in the bed of the vehicle are open

—distribute the weight evenly over the entire bed of the vehicle

—brace the load to prevent shifting during movement

—place ridgepoles under the paulin to prevent water pockets

—raise the paulin periodically to air the load

If part of the basic load must be stacked off of the vehicle, stack it by vehicle load so that it won't have to be sorted when it's needed.

Ammunition stored in bunkers or other inside areas should also be on dunnage with stripping between layers. As usual, stack it by lot number with its nomenclature markings facing outward and readable. To allow for circulation, stack it at least six inches from walls and 18 inches from the ceiling.

There are special problems with ammo stored in tanks, APCs, and other combat vehicles. Keeping it dry is one. Open the ramp or hatches whenever possible and keep the air circulating. If ammo does get wet, wipe it off or, if possible, lay it out and let the air dry it. Any ammo that's unpacked will need a lot of care. Take care of the dirt on small arms ammo by wiping it off with a clean rag. Tank and artillery ammo is a wholly different problem, but it, too, has to be cleaned and, if it's painted, touched up frequently. Like most things, there's a right and wrong way to go about this. The vehicle or weapon TM will give the lowdown of that particular ammo and will outline any special problems.

Here are some general cleaning tips. Cartridges are usually either uncoated brass or steel with a varnish coat. Projectiles are generally either covered with enamel or a laquer paint.

Brass Cartridges   Use a clean rag to wipe off the dirt, and copper wool (not steel) to clean off corrosion. When it's clean, wipe it off with a rag dampened with solvent and let it dry.

Coated Cartridge Cases   Use steel wool to get the paint and foreign matter off corroded or rusty spots on cartridges and projectiles. Don't use steel wool on the rotating bands or fuses—for these USE ONLY COPPER WOOL. Clean the coated cartridge with solvent. Caution: Don't soak the cartridge in solvent. Unless one does a thorough job, it will have to be done over again in a short time. Finally, touch up the spots that are bare of varnish with the special epoxy varnish authorized for the job (never use any other type). If the unit doesn't have or can't get this varnish, turn the ammo in to someone who can. It's important that all of the exposed surface get proper protection from the atmosphere.

Projectiles   Clean corroded spots with steel wool, except the fuses. After that, use thinner to wipe it down. Again be sure that it's wiped thoroughly. Touch up bare spots with the correct enamel to match the area concerned. Don't get the paint on too thick, especially over the bourrelet. If stenciled markings are painted over, they should be restored immediately. (PS Magazine, Issue 153, has information concerning this.)

While the ammo is being cleaned, you will have an excellent opportunity to inspect and inventory it and to check it for dents, bulges or scratches. If a round seems badly damaged, turn it in to the ammunition support facility and let the experts make the final decision as to whether it is safe to fire or not. Not all dented or scratched rounds are bad. If dents and scratches are the only problems and if the rounds will seat properly in weapons, they are OK to fire. Try to wobble the projectile to see if it is loose. Check the eyebolt lifting plugs of separate-loading projectiles to see that they are not cracked. While inspecting small arms ammo look for short rounds (where the bullet has been pushed back into the case), loose bullets or long rounds, dents, burrs and cracks in cases, and corrosion or dirt on the cartridge. On finding a bad round, turn it in. If you feel that you need technical assistance in matters of serviceability, routine maintenance or supply, you should contact your ammunition support unit for a liason or technical assistance team.

There are two aspects of ammunition supply—training and combat. Combat resupply is requested from the S-4 in accordance with the unit SOP and moved forward on battalion ammunition trucks. Generally, the smaller unit ammunition officer isn't involved at all. With training ammunition, however, it's a different story. Then the ammo officer will be responsible for requesting it. Requests for issue and turn-in of ammunition are made on a DA Form 581. Common-type ammunition allowances for training, including qualification/- familiarization, are contained in TA 23–100–6. Special one-time allowances and allowances for special training or schools are contained in other publications of the TA 23–100 series. Regardless of the allowances, however, don't allow surplus ammunition to accumulate.

Requirements should be realistically determined and requisitions should be only for that needed—not necessarily for the total quantities authorized. After training is finished, turn in the excess ammunition and the spent cartridge cases. Inspect small arms brass thoroughly to insure that no live rounds are included. Check with the S-4 or the ammunition supply point for the turn-in procedure.

You must work closely with the training officer to be sure that you have adequate ammunition for scheduled training. In addition, you can assist others by procuring special training ammunition or demolitions for instructional use.

Ammunition malfunctions (except NBC) are reported in accordance with AR 75–1. You must make sure that both you and your personnel are familiar with the information in this regulation. Accidents or incidents involving NBC ammunition are reported in accordance with AR 395–40.

Record and file inventories and inspection reports. Use the ammunition inspection and lot number report (DA Form 3127 or 3128). The reports are prepared as prescribed by local instructions.

Safety is always a concern around ammunition. All types merit special attention and careful handling. The FM and TM for each weapon will spell out precautions. Conduct training in the safe handling and maintenance of ammunition often enough to instruct new personnel in the unit and to refresh the old hands.

The storage and maintenance of special munitions is spelled out in appropriate TM's and local regulations or SOP's. Study these carefully.

REFERENCES
AR 350–4 Qualification and Familiarization with Weapons and Weapon Systems
AR 385–63 Regulations for Firing Ammunition for Training, Target Practice and Combat
AR 385–64 Ammunition and Explosive Safety Standards
AR 710–2 Materiel Management for Using Units, Support Units and Installations
AR 742–9 Ammunition Advisors and Specialists
FM 9–6 Ammunition Services in the Theater of Operations
TM 9–1370–200 Military Pyrotechnics
TM 9–1901–1 Ammunition for Aircraft Guns
TM 9–1300–206 Care, Handling, Preservation and Destruction of Ammunition
TM 9–1300–250 Ammunition Maintenance
TM 9–1300–200 Ammunition, General
TM 9–1305–200 Small Arms Ammunition
TM 9–1330–200 Grenades, Hand and Rifle
TM 9–1345–200 Land Mines
A Subj Scd 6–1 Care and Handling of Ammunition
Training Film 9–2120 Ammunition Storage and Handling

ARMY EMERGENCY RELIEF OFFICER

Army Emergency Relief (AER) came into being in 1942 to provide assistance to members of the rapidly expanding Army and their dependents who were faced with financial problems with which they were unable to cope, and for which no appropriated funds were available. The Army Relief Society (ARS), now assimilated into AER, was established in 1900 to assist needy widows and orphans of Regular Army personnel. One of the big jobs in representing Army Emergency Relief is to see to it that all members of the command and their dependents know that they may receive financial assistance when emergencies arise that are beyond their ability to handle.

Generally AER officers are appointed only at posts or installations with AER branches or sections; however, they could be appointed by a commander of an isolated unit to aid local personnel in seeking AER assistance, and to coordinate the annual Army-wide fund drive.

As AER officer you must familiarize yourself with the policies and procedures governing emergency financial assistance contained in appropriate regulations. You should confer with local American Red Cross representatives to understand the operating relationships of these two organizations.

As the custodian of the AER Fund you are responsible for receiving, safeguarding, disbursing, and accounting for all of the funds and the initiation of requests for needed replenishment of these funds. You also prepare and maintain the required financial records and reports. You interview applicants for assistance, make necessary investigations, furnish counsel, and help them as necessary in accordance with AR 930–4. You may also make loan collections, although these are usually accomplished through Class E allotments. AR 930–4 contains the details of section operation including financial, accounting, and reporting requirements.

All members of the Army, active and retired, their dependents, and dependents of Army personnel missing in action, are eligible to receive emergency financial assistance from AER. Assistance is generally extended in the form of a loan (without interest) since military personnel usually want and are able to repay. Repayment (by Class E allotment) is usually in small monthly installments so as not to cause hardship. Occasionally, a combination of a loan and grant or an outright grant may be the best solution. Assistance to dependents of deceased personnel is almost invariably a grant.

Government funds are not appropriated to provide emergency financial assistance to military personnel and their dependents. AER therefore relies on voluntary contributions from members of the Army, repayments of loans, and income from investments to finance current operations. AER makes no appeal for funds outside the Army. Unsolicited gifts and legacies are accepted provided the donor does not use the name of AER for the purpose of gain or advantage.

AER is authorized to conduct an annual fund campaign to raise, with the least possible burden to the Army, sufficient funds to cover the anticipated requirements.

Campaign material is furnished by the headquarters of AER. As an overall guide a dollar goal is established, but neither units nor individuals should be assigned a dollar quota (see AR 600–29). Funds raised are merged with funds of the local AER section.

AER is organized to be an important and effective instrument of morale. The governing policies are intentionally broad to allow flexible utilization of AER. As the AER officer you will be most effective if you are aware of the view and policies of your commander and if you keep him or her regularly informed of the type and amount of assistance being rendered.

REFERENCES
AR 600–29 Fund Raising Within Department of the Army
AR 930–4 Army Emergency Relief: Authorization, Organization, Operations
       and Procedures
DA Pam 608–2 Your Personal Affairs

NBC OFFICER

As an additional duty this assignment presents a critical challenge. It is the NBC officer's responsibility to become proficient in ways to survive, exist, and function after a nuclear, biological, or chemical attack—and train the officer's unit to do the same.

First, it should be relatively easy for both the NBC officer and NCO to receive training at one of the Army's NBC schools. Find out from the unit training section what's available and apply right away. NBC training is a recurring subject and repeated classroom hours are a drudgery for instructor and instructed alike. Practical hands on training is without a doubt the best way, but it takes more planning, more material, and more instructors. Nevertheless, it's well worth the effort. The NBC officer must *plan ahead.* Plan for the time you'll need to prepare the instruction, get the supplies and training aids, and rehearse with assistant instructors. There are a number of training aids available for making training more realistic. TA 20–2 lists training equipment available for NBC training; training ammunition and miscellaneous ammunition and explosives are listed in TA 23–100 and TA 23–101; chemical supply data is given in FM 3–8; allowances of Chemical Corps expendable supplies is in TA 3–104; allowances of protective clothing are included in TA 50–901, TA 50–902 and TA 50–914. Each of these references can be used to advantage in planning the course. Appendix II of FM 21–48 discusses these training materials and practical ways to procure, fabricate and use them.

Proficiency tests and exercises are among the most effective training vehicles. FM 21–48 will give you valuable help in setting them up. Integrate NBC training whenever possible with unit tactical training. After all, the object is to train the unit to continue its mission in an NBC environment. The necessity of continuing the mission applies to all units, combat and support. Appendix III, FM 21–48 gives examples of this integrated training. Through experience and knowledge, you can devise other training situations to meet your unit needs.

You should seek professional advice and assistance from the staff chemical officer at brigade, division or other higher headquarters. He or she will advise in planning unit exercises and can give technical assistance when necessary.

One of the most vital aspects of NBC defense is the accurate and timely reporting of enemy attacks. You will have to use your imagination and experience to devise effective training mediums in this area—it has to be done. Merely writing the data on a slip of paper and handing it to a soldier to be put into the proper format and transmitted doesn't really accomplish much.

Once you have devised an effective training aid or system, you shouldn't keep it a secret. If you have set up a training course and trained assistant instructors to operate it, you can use it to train 500 people almost as easily as fifty or a hundred. You should expect to share your facilities with other units in the area. It's a two-way street and can be advantageous to all. Many units find it profitable (even necessary) to pool people and talents for NBC training.

The NBC officer's unit is required to have both survey and monitoring teams whose members are specially trained. You will have to set up these teams and train them. You will have to learn about area damage control. In rear areas this is directed primarily toward minimizing the impairment of combat service support after mass destruction or mass casualty attack. In forward areas this is directed toward minimizing interference with tactical operations and loss of combat power. The mission and organization of the particular unit determines to a large degree the mission of these teams, but in any case their make-up and procedures should be covered in the unit SOP. Since these teams are sent into hazard areas to assist individuals and units who have been subjected to an NBC attack, they need additional training on first aid, evacuation and decontamination techniques. Special effort here would pay large dividends.

In addition to Department of the Army NBC literature, almost every level of command publishes regulations, directives, pamphlets, or SOP's on the subject. These should be studied for pertinent information about local problems and special requirements.

Remember that, as the NBC officer, your effort should be aimed at keeping your unit operationally effective within an NCB environment. Also remember that although soldiers can learn the principles of NBC from lectures, films, and demonstrations, they can learn best by direct, first hand experience with toxic and simulated agents.

REFERENCES
AR 220–58 Organization and Training for Chemical, Biological, and Radiological Operations
AR 385–32 Protective Clothing and Equipment
FM 3–10 Employment of Chemical and Biological Agents
FM 3–12 Operational Aspects of Radiological Defense
FM 21–40 Chemical, Biological and Nuclear Defense
FM 21–41 Soldier's Handbook for Chemical and Biological Operations and Nuclear Warfare
FM 21–48 Chemical, Biological, and Radiological (CBR) and Nuclear Defense Training Exercises
FM 101–40 Armed Forces Doctrine for Chemical and Biological Weapons Employment and Defense
TM 3–210 Fallout Prediction
TM 3–215 Military Chemistry and Chemical Agents
TM 3–216 Technical Aspects of Biological Defense
TM 3–220 Chemical, Biological, and Radiological (CBR) Decontamination
TM 3–221 Field CBR Collective Protection
TM 3–240 Field Behavior of Chemical, Biological, and Radiological Agents
TM 3–303 Impregnating Set, Clothing, Field . . .
TM 3–4240–202–14 Mask Chemical-Biological; Field, ABC-M17
TM 3–6665–225–12 Maintenance Manual: Alarm Chemical Agent, Automatic . . .
TM 3–6665–253–12 Detector Kit Chemical Agent VGH, AN-M15A2A and AN-M15A2N
TM 3-6665-254-12 Detector Kit Chemical Agent ABC-M18A2
TM 8-285 Treatment of Chemical Agent Casualties
TM 10-277 Protective Clothing, Chemical Operations
TM 11-6665-209-15 Radiac Set AN/PDR-27J

TM 11-6665-213-12 Radiacmeter IM-174/PD
TM 11-6665-214-10 Radiac Meters IM-93/UD, IM-93A/UD, and IM-147/PD
TB SIG 276-8 Chargers, Radiac Detector PP-1578/PD and PP-1578A/PD
TB 3-4230-207-1 Decontaminating and Reimpregnating Kit, Individual M13
TC 3-15 Prediction of Fallout from Atomic Demolition Munitions (ADM)

CLAIMS OFFICER

The duties of a claims officer are primarily investigative. The gathering and accurate reporting of basic facts surrounding an incident are prerequisite to and most necessary steps toward claims settlement. Investigations fall into two categories: those to determine the facts in a situation where a claim has been made, and those which report facts about any incident that *may later* give rise to a claim. The latter is usually referred to as a "potential claim" investigation.

Claims also are divided into two categories, small claims, those which may be settled for $500 or less, and large—more substantial—claims. Officers investigating small claims should remember:

—That it's impractical to spend more on the investigation than the claim.

—That evidence about small claims may be gathered by telephone, personal interview, from incident reports and other heresay reports. Written statements of witnesses, estimates of repairs, etc., are not required.

—To use DA Form 1668 (Small Claim Certificate) for recording their investigations with brief summaries of the evidence attached.

—To be objective and fair during all phases of investigation, protecting the rights of both the claimant and the government.

—That evidence must establish that the amount claimed or agreed to is reasonable, that the claimant is the proper person, and that the government is liable for the damage or injury.

The objective in handling any claim is to gather all possible evidence in the shortest practicable time, and stressing facts and events which help to answer when, where, who, what, and how? In the full investigation required for large claims, this evidence should include statements of all available witnesses, accident reports including those in civilian police files, photographs, maps, sketches, etc. The investigator should visit the scene of the incident and make a physical inspection of any damage. If the claim involves injury, determine with the help of the claims judge advocate whether a medical examination is required, and if so, make the necessary arrangements. AR 27-20 provides some detailed guidance on investigations of specific incidents and the evidence required for dealing with any claim.

In completing the large-claim investigation, use DA Form 1208 (Report of Claims Officer) or DA Form 1089 (Claim for Personal Property) for the report. Make specific judgments about what the evidence says and recommendations as to the extent of the liability and the amount of compensation. Submit the report to the appointing authority, who comments if he or she desires, and forwards it to the appropriate approving or settlement authority.

As the claims officer you should assist persons who indicate a desire to file a claim. They should be given general instructions concerning the procedure to follow, necessary forms, and assistance in completing them. You may also assist them in assembling evidence; however, you may not disclose information which may be made the basis of a claim or any evidence that you may have collected unless you have the permission of the claims judge advocate. Your opinions and recommendations will not be disclosed to a claimant. In addition, you may not represent them in any way and must not accept any gratuity for your assistance. These claims should be presented to the Commanding Officer of the unit involved, or to the nearest Army post or other military establishment convenient to the claimant. Evidence to substantiate the claim should also be submitted with the claim.

One special situation worthy of mention is maneuver damage resulting from field exercises. In this instance anything that can be done on the spot for both the government and claimant in the way of collecting evidence and advising the claimant how to proceed will save much work later. Most such on-the-spot investigations come under the "potential claims" possibility, but they should be accomplished as fully as possible while all individuals and property involved are available. Reports are marked "potential claim" and submitted like regular claims.

Apart from more routine investigation and report preparation, you may find it helpful to have an idea how compensation is determined. In cases of property damage that can be economically repaired, the allowable compensation is the actual or estimated cost of restoring it to the same condition it was in immediately before the damage. Allowances may be made for the depreciation or appreciation after repairs. When property is destroyed or cannot be repaired economically, the measure of the damage is the value of the property immediately before the incident less any salvaged value. Lost property is compensated for on the basis of value immediately before the loss.

In claims involving personal injury and death, allowable compensation may include reasonable medical, hospital, or burial expenses actually incurred; future medical expenses, loss of earnings and services, diminution of earning capacity, pain and suffering, physical disfigurement, and any other factor which local law recognizes as injury or damage for compensation purposes. No allowances are made in any claim for attorney fees, court costs, bail, interest, travel, inconvenience, or any other miscellaneous expense incurred in connection with submission of a claim.

REFERENCES
AR 27-20 Claims
AR 27-40 Litigation
DA Pam 27-162 Claims
FM 105-5 Maneuver Control

CLASS A AGENT (PAY) OFFICER

Though most of the Army's payrolls have been automated it may still, under some circumstances, be necessary for an agent (of an accountable disbursing officer) to either pay troops, exchange foreign currency for military payment certificates (MPC) or U.S. currency, or make payments for specified purchases or rentals. Appointing orders specify what payments the agent may make.

If you are appointed Class A Agent, you are personally responsible for the funds entrusted to you and for the vouchers which account for that money. At your request, the unit commander should provide adequate armed guards to protect these funds and vouchers. If you have to keep funds overnight they should be secured in an adequate safe. Field safes and combination-lock file cabinets are not normally considered adequate. If these are all that are available, an armed guard should be kept posted. In addition, provision should be made for frequent checks of the secured area by a CQ or duty officer.

Here are a list of things which you should *NOT* do while a class A agent:
—Insure entrusted funds.
—Use funds except as stated in the appointing orders.
—Gamble while entrusted with funds—even with only personal money.
—Loan, use or deposit in any bank any portion of the funds, except as specifically instructed by the finance officer.
—Mix the funds with personal monies or attempt to balance the funds by adding to or deducting from them.
—Entrust the funds or paid vouchers to any other person for any purpose, even for the purpose of returning them to the Finance office. Unless otherwise directed, you must return the funds or vouchers personally to the finance officer. (Other possible means could be: through a class B agent, by courier, or by registered mail.)

Generally, class A agent duties will involve only the payment of troops. Here is a typical sequence of pay-day actions that such an agent might take:
—After receiving your orders, watch the daily bulletin or other local medium of notification for the time and place to pick up the funds and vouchers.
—Arrange for transportation (POV's should be avoided), guards, and a suitable place for payment (such as a dayroom or dining room).
—On the day of cash pick-up, inspect vehicle condition in advance. (It is also a good idea to periodically vary the route and timing of trips.)
—Upon arrival at the Finance office, you will need a copy of your appointing orders and your Armed Forces identification.
—Before you leave the office, you should verify the cash count given you. The currency is generally $1, $5, $10, and $20 bills, packed in bundles of $100. This eases the task of counting, but you should count the bills in each bundle to insure they contain the proper amount. You will receive a change list showing the number and denomination of bills making up the payroll. For example, it may show that you should have 280-$20 bills, 120-$10 bills, 100-$5 bills, 203-$1 bills. You should check your count of various denominations against this list. *This is the time for you to bring any discrepancy to the attention of the disbursing officer, not later.*
—Before departure, you must sign a receipt for payroll money received. You then proceed directly to the unit or activity to be paid.
—Before starting to pay, it is best to break the payroll down into individual payments. Errors are easiest to correct while you still have the money and vouchers. You should have the exact number and denomination of bills necessary to make up all of the different payments. So that everything will come out right, each payment is made up with the largest denomination of bills possible. (For example, if the amount is $237.00, use eleven $20 bills, and one $10 bill, one $5 bill, and two $1 bills.) Each individual payment can be placed in a plain mailing envelope or paper-clipped to the payee's copy of the voucher.

Your pay team should be made up of two or three individuals. You *will personally pass the money* to the person being paid. A responsible NCO should assist by obtaining signatures on the original (white) vouchers. You may have a clerk pass to the payee a copy of his or her voucher after payment has been made.
—The pay table should be set up in an area where troops cannot congregate. Payments should begin promptly at the designated time.
—At the proper time, a team NCO should call the name of the first individual to be paid.
—The payee moves to the table, salutes, and signs the receipt for payment.

As pay agent, you do not return the salute. The payee's signature, as part of the pay process, is checked with his or her identification card and the name on the voucher.

—If the signature is correct, the voucher is passed to you for payment. You then count out the payment and ask the payee to verify the amount. If a correction has been made by the Finance office to the amount-paid entry on the voucher (lined out and a new amount entered) the payee is required to initial the corrected amount when signing his or her name or receiving the cash.

—After verifying the amount paid, the payee receives his or her copy of the pay voucher.

—This procedure is repeated until all persons present are paid. Soldiers not present for the regular pay call may be paid as soon as possible thereafter. Hospitalized personnel on the payroll should be paid next if you can reasonably travel to their location. When considering the reasonableness of traveling to pay a soldier away from home station, you should keep in mind the hardship that not being paid on time may cause the payee. The mere fact that you must arrange special transportation or stay overnight does not in itself make the travel unreasonable. The payroll shouldn't include persons AWOL or in confinement, but if it does, they will *not* be paid, but rather their pay is returned with other funds remaining and paid vouchers upon completion of the unit payment.

—Regulations allow the class A agent 24 hours after payment for the return of paid vouchers and cash; however, you should return the funds as soon as possible.

—When returned, a clerk will verify the vouchers and furnish a receipt for both the return of funds and the paid vouchers.

—The amount indicated on the receipt should agree with the amount of cash returned.

—You deliver the vouchers and receipt to the cashier and turn in all cash not paid to individuals. After verification, the receipt will be signed by the finance officer and a copy returned to you. You are then properly relieved of responsibility for the funds that were entrusted to you. Such receipts, of course, should be retained at least a year in case any question should arise.

When you are paying troops that you don't know on sight, or when you pay commercial vendors, your biggest problem is establishing positive identification. In the case of paying troops, the problem is fairly simple. Since the vouchers are prepared from official records, the name on the voucher should correspond exactly to the name of the individual's Armed Forces identification card. The signature obtained must also match the signature on the identification card.

Occasionally a payee will sign his or her name in an incorrect form, i.e., not the "payroll" signature. If the signature is not in the same form as the name shown on the voucher, the incorrect signature must be lined out and the payee required to sign it again so that it does agree with the voucher.

If for some reason the payee can't sign his or her name (i.e., a man with a broken arm), the payee may authorize some other individual to sign for him or her and that signature will be regarded the same as if signed by the payee. This signing, however, must be certified to by two witnesses and the certificate attached to the voucher. The mark (X) of an individual unable to write must be witnessed by a disinterested person whose signature and address are placed adjacent to the mark (X).

Receipts for payment to commercial firms must be signed by a duly authorized officer or agent of the company. The receipt must be signed with the company name, followed by the autograph signature of the officer or agent together with his or her title. In addition to insuring positive identification of the company representative, you must assure yourself that the representative is authorized by the company to receive payment.

More detailed information on this subject is to be found in paragraph 6–41c, AR 37–103, Units may want to show the film *The Class A Agent Finance Officer* (TF 14–3420) which, though somewhat dated, will be useful for all officers who will assume this duty.

REFERENCES
AR 37–103 Finance and Accounting for Installations—Disbursing Operations
AR 37–104–3 Military Pay and Allowances Procedures, Joint Uniform Military
      Pay System (JUMPS)
AR 37–106 Finance and Accounting for Installations—Travel and Transporta-
      tion Allowances
FM 14–8 Class A Agent Officers
U.S. Treasury Pamphlet *Know your Money*

COURTS-MARTIAL MEMBER

The member of a military court is essentially a member of a jury. The president is, in the same context, the foreman. Member duties, as prescribed in the Manual for Courts-Martial, 1969, are like those of a juror in that each member will hear the evidence and arrive at his or her own determination of the guilt or innocence of the accused. In addition, if the accused is found guilty, courts-martial members act as "judge" to fix the penalty. Each member, regardless of rank or position, has an equal voice and vote with the other members in deliberating and determining a decision on all questions indicated by the specifications and charges.

In the absence of a military judge, the president of a special court instructs all members of the court generally on their duties. The instructions are important and worth repeating here.

"It is our duty as members of this court, and our duty alone, to determine the guilt or innocence of the accused as to the charges upon which he (or she) will be arraigned and, if the accused is found guilty, to determine an appropriate sentence. Neither the fact that charges have been preferred against the accused nor the fact that such charges have been referred to this court is any evidence of his (or her) guilt. With respect to any offenses to which there is a plea of not guilty, the determination of the court as to guilt or innocence must be based upon the entire evidence in the case and can only be arrived at after resolving all material issues of fact and applying the rules of law to those facts. Thus as to any such offense, it is important to keep an open mind until all the evidence and applicable law . . . have been presented . . . In particular, no member must ever depart from an impartial, judicial rule in asking questions of a witness. The examination of witnesses is primarily the duty and function of counsel, and any member desiring to question a witness must first obtain my permission. I may, if I so desire, require a member to submit his (or her) question to me either orally or in writing so that a ruling may be made as to the propriety of the question or course of questioning."

For any one of several reasons, an individual may be ineligible to sit as a member of a courts-martial in certain cases. Whatever the reasons, they are referred to usually as "grounds for challenge." A number of grounds for challenge are listed in paragraph 62f MCM, 1969. If you don't believe that you should sit on the court in a particular case, you should bring this to the attention of the convening authority before the court is formally opened. Usually, you will thereupon be relieved. If the grounds for challenge first come to your attention at the trial, the trial counsel will ask that you relate to them the "ultimate" ground for the challenge. You must thereupon be careful not to relate facts which, if heard by other members, might also prejudice or disqualify them.

Unlawful influence on any court member's decisions by a senior officer should never become a problem; however, members should bear in mind that neither the commanding officer, convening authority nor senior member of the court may lawfully attempt to influence their independent judgment. This doesn't mean that members should ignore the opinion of their seniors in court deliberations, but rather that they should not let position or rank sway their own judgment.

In order to reduce the influence which ranking members of the court might have, discussion and oral voting (when required) usually begins with the junior in rank. Votes by members of a general or special courts-martial on the findings and on the sentence, and by members of a special courts-martial without a military judge upon questions of challenge, are by secret written ballot. The junior member of the court usually collects and counts the ballots. This count is checked and announced by the court president.

A court has no power to punish its members. Nevertheless, members are expected to conduct themselves in a dignified and attentive manner and misconduct as a member of a court may be a military offense. No member should ever become a "champion" of either the prosecution or the defense. Such partisan behavior would cast substantial doubt upon the fairness of a trial. You must be particularly careful in your contact with counsel or other members of the court when the court is not in session. You may, however, without referring to any case pending or then being tried, carry on a normal official and social relationship with other prospective or appointed members of the court. It is proper to ask such administrative questions as the scheduled date for the court to meet, location of the trial, physical arrangements for the trial and other matters which have no bearing on the issues of a case.

Generally, there is no objection to making notes during the trial and these can also be taken into closed session so long as they are purely for the court member's individual use.

The guiding principle to follow at all times is that you should perform your duties without being subjected to any out-of-court influence, direct, indirect, or covert. The legal rights of an accused demand no less.

You should be well acquainted with the Manual for Courts-Martial, 1969. Reading it will allow a good orientation for court duty, even without having had the experience of before participating in a trial. A prospective but inexperienced court appointee may also take advantage of opportunities to watch actual trials, particularly those conducted by general courts-martial. When appointed to serve on a court you should resolve to do your best, as conscientiously as you can.

REFERENCES
AR 27–10 Military Justice
AR 350–212 Military Justice

DA Pam 27–2 Analysis of Contents Manual for Courts-Martial United States, 1969, Revised Edition
DA Pam 27–7 Guide for Summary Court-Martial
DA Pam 27–10 Military Justice Handbook: The Counsel and the Defense Counsel
DA Pam 27–12 Manual for Courts-Martial Annotation
DA Pam 27–15 Military Justice Handbook, Trial Guide for the Special Court-Martial
DA Pam 27–18 Desk Book for the Special Court-Martial Convening Authorities
DA Pam 27–173 Trial Procedure
DA Pam 27–174 Jurisdiction of Court-Martial

INCOME TAX OFFICER

This additional duty assignment is made so that members of a command will have the opportunity to get counsel and answers to questions about income tax. As the Income Tax Officer, you are not expected to be a full-fledged tax expert, but you are expected to know how the law applies to soldiers. The staff judge advocate, if available, is the place to send persons for assistance in complicated situations and that office may even offer some periodic formal training for all tax officers. Unit income tax officers should be sure to take advantage of it.

The questions which income tax officers are most often asked deal with filling out returns and with what expenditures are legitimate deductibles. In addition to the instructions received with each tax form, it behooves the income tax officer to get a copy of *Your Federal Income Tax.* It's revised each year to reflect changes and interpretations of the laws and provides easy-to-understand examples of how they are applied in specific cases. Many items of interest to the military person are indexed under Armed Forces. The nearest IRS office should be able to supply a copy. Another excellent source of tax information is *Federal Income Tax Information for Armed Forces Personnel.* This Department of the Navy pamphlet (NAVSO P–1983) is published annually and is available through normal publication supply channels.

These annual references are a good bet for helping the income tax officer stay up-to-date. However, here are some general guides:

—Military personnel should always include Service number and permanent home address on their return to help establish that they are in the Armed Forces.

—Military personnel have an automatic extension when in a combat zone. They must file within 180 days after leaving the area or after being discharged from a hospital outside CONUS. This rule applies to a joint return but not to the taxpayer's spouse if filing separately. If a soldier decides to take advantage of the extension, he or she indicates COMBAT ZONE on the return when it is finally filed. If his or her spouse files their joint return while the military member is still in a combat zone, the spouse also marks the form COMBAT ZONE (it is then unnecessary for the military member to sign the return).

—Military personnel who are prisoners of war or who have been detained in a foreign country against their will have 90 days after release to file a tax return.

—All military on duty outside the US and Puerto Rico are allowed until June 15 to file. However, anyone using the extension must pay 20% interest on the amount of tax from the due date and explain the reason for the delay.

Here's a guide to some of the taxable and non-taxable pay and allowances.
Taxable income is:
  Basic pay
  Reserve training basic pay
  Dislocation allowance
  Lump sum payments such as separation pay
    Non-taxable income is:
  Forfeited pay (but not fines)
  Trailer-moving allowances (actual expense)
  Subsistence, or the value of subsistence
  Uniform allowances
  Quarters allowances or the value of quarters furnished
  Housing and cost-of-living allowances received to defray the cost of quarters and subsistence at a permanent duty station outside the U.S.
  Payments made to beneficiaries of soldiers who died in active service.
  Pay received by enlisted personnel or warrant officers for any month or part served in combat zone. For officers, the first $500 of such monthly compensation is non-taxable.
  That part of a dependency allotment contributed by the government.
  Sick pay is non-taxable when one is in the hospital or not duty-assigned for 30 days or longer.
Reservists not on active duty may deduct the cost and maintenance of uniforms over and above allowances received and, if Reserve drills are in location away from the Reservist's *place of business,* he or she may deduct the cost of the round-trip transportation.
  A quick trial set of calculations will usually indicate that service personnel should take the standard deduction. Exceptions might be those buying a house or other property, or with substantial loans who pay a significant amount of interest.
  Military personnel are also required to file state income tax returns. Since the requirements vary from state to state, it may be necessary to advise the individuals to contact their states for copies of any material available.

REFERENCES
DA Pam 608–2 Your Personal Affairs
Your Federal Income Tax (Internal Revenue Service Pub 17)
Instructions for Preparing Your Federal Income Tax Return (IRS)
If Your Return is Examined (IRS Docu No 5202)
Federal Income Tax Information for Armed Forces Personnel
(NAVSO P–1983), published annually by Department of the Navy

LINE OF DUTY (LOD) INVESTIGATING OFFICER

  "Line-of-Duty" and "misconduct determinations" are phrases descriptive of the findings made to determine whether an individual's disease or injury was incurred while the person was conducting himself or herself properly *in his or her role as a member of the Army.* Those assigned to investigate and make these determinations must do so carefully since they will have a great effect upon the concerned individuals and their dependents. Investigations are made primarily to provide data for the administration of Federal statutes affecting the rights, benefits, and obligations of members of the Armed Forces.
  Under specific circumstances, a finding could cause a person to be sepa-

rated from the Service without entitlement to severance pay. In the case of death, these investigations could lead to findings which would make some person's dependents ineligible for many or all normal benefits. On the other hand, an LOD investigating officer could confirm that those concerned are indeed entitled to all benefits under the law. The importance of conducting a thorough and impartial investigation in accordance with the requirements of applicable regulations cannot be overemphasized.

The job of the line-of-duty investigating officer is generally to investigate, record, evaluate, make findings, and report these findings. The details of how to accomplish this are found in Chapter 5, AR 600–10 (Personnel-General: the Army Casualty System), and AR 15–6 (Boards, Commissions, Committees; Procedure for Investigating Officers and Board of Officers in Conducting Investigations). Here is a brief rundown of what you, as the LOD investigating officer, should be doing and some guides you may follow.

The Investigation   You must notify the individual concerned of the impending investigation. If practicable, he or she should be permitted to be present at the examination of witnesses if the investigation is to be continued beyond the examination of documentary evidence. If not present, the individual will be permitted to respond to adverse allegations.

You should visit the scene of the incident as early as possible. You should record all the relevant evidence such as statements of witnesses, photographs, diagrams, letters, results of laboratory tests, observations and reports of local officials, extracts of local laws and regulations, descriptions, weather reports, the date and exact time of the incident, etc. This documentation should reflect every fact and circumstance that you will consider in making your findings and report. Before the testimony of witnesses is taken, they must be advised of their rights under Article 31 of the Uniform Code of Military Justice, or the Fifth Amendment to the Constitution.

The subject of the line-of-duty investigation is permitted to submit evidence or statements, sworn or unsworn. Before his or her statement is taken, the subject must be advised of legal rights under Article 31, Uniform Code of Military Justice, and of the purpose of the investigation. If a statement from the individual is not obtained, you must state the reason in your report.

After you have acquired the evidence, you must *evaluate* it and *determine,* in your judgment, the *exact circumstances* under which the injury, disease, or death occurred. You make a summary of your findings in the "Remarks" section of the report of investigation. Findings as to line of duty and misconduct must be arrived at by the investigating officer in all actions except death, in which case Headquarters, Department of the Army makes the final determination.

Here is a set of general and special rules for commonly-recurring circumstances. A particular case may require application of two or more of the rules, while others may not clearly fall within any of them. In the latter case, you will have to apply the rule most analogous to the circumstances.

Rule 1   Injury or disease is presumed to have been incurred in line of duty and not due to the member's own misconduct.

Rule 2   Injury or disease proximately caused by the intentional misconduct or gross neglect of a member is incurred not in line of duty and due to misconduct.

Rule 3   Mere violation of military regulations, orders, or instructions, or of civil or criminal laws, in the absence of further showing of misconduct therewith, establishes no more than simple negligence.

Rule 4 Injury or disease incurred as the result of the intemperate use of habit-forming drugs, or the intentional consumption of poisons, is incurred not in line of duty and due to misconduct.

Rule 5 Injury or disease incurred as a result of the intemperate use of intoxicating liquor is incurred not in the line of duty and due to misconduct.

Rule 6 Injury incurred while knowingly resisting a lawful arrest, or while attempting to escape from a guard or other lawful custody, is incurred not in the line of duty and due to misconduct.

Rule 7 Injury incurred while tampering with, attempting to ignite, or otherwise handling an explosive, firearm, or highly-inflammable liquid in disregard of its dangerous qualities, is incurred not in the line of duty and due to misconduct.

Rule 8 Injury incurred as the result of an act of wrongful aggression, or of voluntary participation in a fight or similar encounter, where one is at least equally at fault with the adversary in starting or continuing the altercation, is incurred not in line of duty and due to misconduct.

Rule 9 Injury incurred as the result of driving a vehicle when in an unfit condition to drive, with which unfit condition the member has or is charged with knowledge, is incurred not in the line of duty and due to misconduct.

Rule 10 Injury incurred as the result of erratic or reckless conduct, or other deliberate course of conduct without regard for the personal safety of others, is incurred not in line of duty and due to misconduct.

Rule 11 A wound or other injury deliberately self-inflicted by a member who is mentally sound is incurred not in the line of duty and due to misconduct.

Rule 12 Intentional misconduct or gross neglect of another individual is imputed to a member if the latter exercises control over and is thus responsible for the former's conduct, or if the misconduct or neglect established concerted action sufficient to establish a joint enterprise.

Rule 13 Injury or disease incurred while not in a duty status (i.e., while neither on active duty nor engaged in authorized training in an active duty or inactive duty status) and which is not aggravated by military service, is incurred not in the line of duty.

Rule 14 Injury or disease incurred during a period of unauthorized absence is not in line of duty.

Rule 15 The line of duty and misconduct status of a member injured or incurring disease while participating in outside activities, such as business ventures, hobbies, contests, professional or amateur athletic contests, is determinable as in any other case under the applicable rules and facts presented in the case.

After you have completed your investigations, evaluation, and have arrived at your findings, you are ready to complete the report. These reports are submitted on Report of Investigation—Line of Duty and Misconduct Status (DD Form 261). You must be sure that all of your conclusions are based solely on the evidence reflected in and attached to your report, and that the source of all the evidence is properly reflected. Then the finished report is forwarded to the appointing authority.

REFERENCES
AR 15–6 Procedure for Investigating Officers and Boards of Officers Conducting Investigations
AR 600–10 The Army Casualty System
AR 635–40 Physical Evaluation for Retention, Retirement, or Separation

MESS OFFICER

There is little doubt that the quality of food, both preparation and serving, contributes to morale. It is one of the main—and could be the chief—motivating factors contributing to overall unit performance. The Mess Officer's job, therefore, is one that has to be taken seriously. Not only from a point of view of unit effectiveness, but personally because in most instances it offers a challenge to leadership capabilities.

In garrison, the easiest responsibility involves a consolidated mess. Proper coordination with the consolidated mess officer will solve most problems. A little "good will" here goes a long way toward seeing that your unit is well taken care of.

When a unit operates its own mess the responsibilities of the mess officer multiply, but are easily manageable. You'll need a broader working knowledge of regulations governing mess operations, food requisitioning, and food preparation.

Getting off on the right foot with the mess steward is an important first step. An early interview will be valuable in determining his or her attitude and degree of professional skill. It will assure the steward, without question, that you will be fulfilling your responsibility while at the same time recognizing that the mess steward must retain the professional authority to handle the day-to-day details. During this initial discussion, the mess steward should be able to present a complete rundown on:

—methods of securing and storing rations

—how he or she insures that food is being prepared and served promptly

—routine for insuring that the mess equipment is properly maintained and used

—what steps are taken to maintain a high standard of sanitary conditions and practice

—the forms that require your signature and why they are used

—the procedures for keeping mess supply and equipment records and mess accounts

—the mess steward's staff, with brief evaluations of the professional skill of each

—how he or she insures that only authorized personnel are being fed.

At the same time you should tell your mess steward that:

—you will periodically and without notice inspect the food preparation, cleanliness of the mess equipment and personnel, and the cook's worksheet as it relates to the master menu.

—you and the mess steward must expect to meet periodically to discuss any problems you may find concerning the mess and improvements that may be desirable through the use of the unit fund.

—you will be available at any time.

How successful you are as a mess officer depends on how well you follow through with what you have established as a working relationship. And, let's face it, most mess stewards will probably wish to see as little of the mess officer as possible. It's only natural, since they view the mess as their own private domain. This is where a talent for leadership will meet its greatest challenge.

How you conduct inspections of the mess influences greatly your success or failure as the mess officer. As a rule, ordinary daily activity will have to go on in the mess during such inspections. Make allowances for this, but don't let this be an excuse or cover-up for a poor mess operation. If some item, such as the coffee urn, is in use but there is concern about how well it is cleaned arrange to return later to see it and/or inspect it after it is cleaned.

Here are just a few tips about what to look for:

The Dining Hall   Clean tables, chairs, floor, condiment containers clean and contents fresh. Coffee urn is clean and coffee is fresh. China and silverware are free of grease and food particles. No broken china or glassware. Ice chest is clean, covered, used for ice only. Water fountain works and is clean. Milk dispenser works and is clean. Bread-box clean, well-ventilated, insect-proof. Day's menu is posted at troop entrance. Ashtrays and/or butt cans are clean, suitable, adequate, and strategically placed.

The Kitchen Ranges   That they are clean, free of grease, food, and rust. No undue accumulation of grease in range hoods. Meat block and work tables are clean and are not cracked or broken in any way. No garbage present anywhere. Refrigerators have no odor. Odor-imparting foods are not stored with odor-absorbing foods such as milk, butter. Nothing is stored on the floor. Storeroom locked when not in use. Dishwashing machines function properly and rules for preparing dishes and utensils for washing are followed. Manual dishwashing procedures are followed. Utensils, pots, and pans are stored properly.

The Serving Line   Food attractively displayed. Served in proper portions. The attitude of the mess and KP personnel in the serving line contributes to an appealing mealtime atmosphere. Serving line operates smoothly.

Food Preparation   Meat is not tainted. Cook's worksheet is followed. Cook's worksheet corresponds to master menu. Proper portions are prepared. Waste is properly controlled.

Outside Area   Adequately policed. Mop and broom rack properly constructed and used. Garbage-can lids are tight-fitting. Garbage cans adequate for maximum accumulation.

On Mess Administration   For an easy-check reference, here are some notes to help get familiar faster and started right.

Of the forms used in the mess operation, here's a rundown on those most commonly used.

Cash Collection Sheet (DD Form 715)   Any individual drawing subsistence allowance must reimburse the government for meals eaten in the mess. This includes all officers and certain enlisted personnel (the unit finance section can identify the ones). The mess sergeant should have a continually updated roster of all such individuals. The cash collection sheets are serially-numbered and closely controlled by the installation cash collection officer. Their issue, use, and turn-in is fully detailed in AR 30–41 and every mess officer should be familiar with the requirements even though the details may be handled by the mess steward.

The Cook's Worksheet (DA Form 10–104)   This is probably the most important all-around document in the mess operation. It has several purposes. It shows the plan for preparing and serving food in a particular 24-hour period; it also reminds the steward and staff to keep leftovers at a minimum; it assigns duties within the mess team; and serves as a management guide in the absence of the mess steward. The mess officer should be sufficiently familiar with it to assure periodically that it is serving the intended purpose.

The Subsistence Report and Food Ration Request (DA Form 10–163)   This is prepared by the mess steward to indicate the expected number of meals to be consumed on a particular day or date. He or she naturally needs to coordinate these facts with the unit headquarters, generally the First Sergeant. The mess officer should become involved periodically to assure that rations are not being overdrawn. AR 30–46 provides the details on this.

Ration issue procedures are almost wholly determined by the local installation. It won't be difficult to find out what these procedures are and the mess officer must be familiar with them. A visit to the OIC of the Class I issue point should provide this information.

The Field Ration Issue Slip (DA Form 10–260)   This is used to record all field-ration issues. Vendors may deliver local-purchase items directly to the unit mess. When this procedure is used, the mess officer or a representative signs for the supplies when they are delivered on a notice of delegation of authority—receipt for supplies (DA Form 1687). The completed DA Form 1687 is then submitted to the installation subsistence office.

How the mess section works in the field is just as important. The mess officer probably will have little or no time to control or inspect it there. About the only way to insure good performance in the field is to have excellent performance in garrison, and through a scheduled program of inspection and maintenance that keeps field ranges, immersion heaters and other equipment ready to go. Make sure all concerned are up on what the ration issue and distribution will be.

A general discussion of field messing is contained in TM 10–405, Chapters 6 and 7. As a mess officer, study it and discuss ideas that could improve mess operation with the mess steward and First Sergeant, since they will have the most direct supervision over this in the field.

The references below contain valuable information on the following:

—duties and responsibilities of the mess steward, cooks, bakers, and kitchen police

—requirements for the food handler's certification and daily inspection for communicable diseases

—sanitary standards for personnel, equipment, and dining area

—treatment of leftovers—when and if usable

—details of cash collection and handling

—ration requisitioning

—food conservation programs and goals.

The ultimate responsibility for efficient operation of the unit mess belongs to the commander, who delegates the mess officer to act for him or her. The latter will want to be aware, too, that many food service personnel have a strong professional pride. Using this to the benefit of all is important.

REFERENCES
AR 30–1 Army Food Service Program
AR 30–7 Operational Rations and Authorized and Net Feeding Strengths
AR 30–10 Central Food Facilities
AR 30–11 Army Food Program
AR 30–46 Subsistence Report and Field Ration Report
TM 5–634 Refuse Collection; Repairs and Utility
TM 5–636 Kitchen Equipment; Repairs and Utility
TM 5–637 Inspection and Preventive Maintenance for Kitchen Equipment
TM 10–401 The Army Food Advisor
TM 10–405 Army Mess Operations
TM 10–410 Bread Baking
TM 10–411 Pastry Baking
TM 10–412 Armed Forces Recipe Service

TM 10–415 Operation of Garrison Mess Equipment
TM 10–419 Preparation and Serving of Food in the Garrison Mess
TM 10–4500–200–13 Operation and Maintenance Manual, Heater, Immersion
TM 10–701 Range Outfit, Field Gasoline/M-1937
TM 10–7310–201–25P Repair Parts List: Accessory Outfit, Gasoline Field Range
TM 10–7360–204–12 Range Outfit, Field, Gasoline: Model 59
DA Pam 350–52 Company Administration Programed Text for Mess Management

MOTOR OFFICER/MAINTENANCE OFFICER

As the new Motor Officer your first questions are usually about the type and quantity of equipment you'll be responsible for. This will vary from a few wheeled vehicles to more than a hundred, and from wheeled vehicles alone to a variety of wheel and track vehicles like those found in a tank or mech-infantry company.

One of the keys to success of the maintenance mission is the motor sergeant, who most likely was selected for technical knowledge, mechanical ability and, most important, aptitude for organization and supervision. He or she is responsible to you for the implementation of your policies and the enforcement of SOP and regulations governing the operation of the maintenance section. It's important that you work through and with him or her.

If you just joined the unit, you should get acquainted with the maintenance area right away and make some mental notes about the general conditions of the shop and the appearance of the mechanics.

—Is the shop adequately lighted?
—Are safety precautions such as fire regulations followed?
—Is the shop floor free of grease, oil and dirt?
—Are blocks used under jacked-up vehicles and are the wheels chocked?
—Are vehicles which are not being worked on removed from the shop?
—Do mechanics seem adequately supervised?
—Are mechanics using the TMs to perform or check their maintenance properly?
—Are mechanics using the equipment inspection and maintenance worksheet (DA Form 2404) in their work?
—Are mechanics or supervisors making proper entries in the equipment log books?

The answers to those basic questions will help you get the feel for the adequacy of your maintenance organization. If the answers are YES to all of these questions, then indications are that the organization is a real gem! If, on the other hand, you've had to answer NO to one or more questions, then you need to take a closer more critical look at the operation.

Next, you should study the unit maintenance SOP. You should find out what the policy has been and not be in too big a hurry to change things. Check higher headquarters maintenance SOP and directives to see what can be expected in the way of support and what is required to receive it. Usually when unit workload exceeds the capabilities of a section, help can be obtained from battalion maintenance. (The same is often true of direct support maintenance assistance to separate companies.) One shouldn't ask for help unless it's needed, but when it is, neither foolish pride nor independence should be allowed to get in the way of insuring that a unit's vehicles are ready to move.

Repair parts supply support is normally handled by the battalion maintenance shop. The repair parts stocked locally are determined by consolidated authorized organizational stockage lists (AOSL), organizational maintenance technical manuals and parts manuals on individual items of equipment, and by documented demand experience of the unit. A list of the repair parts to be stocked locally is known as the prescribed load list (PLL). Necessary parts or assemblies other than those stocked will be ordered by the battalion parts section from the direct support maintenance unit servicing it. Arrange to follow the paperwork on some repair parts supply actions to see how the system works. You will probably find that you spend a lot of time checking on parts that have been ordered and not received. *Proper "follow-up" is necessary.* After designated periods (dependent on the priority of parts requests) the parts clerk should initiate tracers to check the state of requisitions. You should be sure that he or she does and that you are informed of the answers received. DA Pam 700–2 contains a detailed discussion of the repair parts supply system.

When you become a maintenance officer, you usually must sign for some or all of the tools, equipment, and vehicles assigned to your section. Here, as everywhere else, there should be a complete joint inventory with the old hand-receipt holder or property book officer. Don't sign for anything that can't be seen or found. Somewhere, sometime, there has to be an accounting, so don't get stuck with the responsibility (and pecuniary liability) for something that was never there.

One of the big bugaboos in an automotive maintenance account are the tool sets. The new maintenance officer cannot be expected to know what is in these sets or even what all of the items look like. PS Magazine, however, has come to the rescue and published complete lists of the tools with drawings to assist in their identification. Get these issues or reprints of them:

—Automotive Mechanics Tool Kit   Issue 156
—No. 1 Common   Issue 160
—No. 2 Common   Issue 176

Some separate units responsible for their own semi-annual PM service may also get a No. 1 Supplemental Set. If that is the case, see PS Issue 172.

Reprints of these PS magazine articles are often available in text or in the form of supplementary material for service schools. All of these tool sets are also described in applicable supply publications.

In addition to these "common" tool sets, Tool Kit, Special Set A, consists of special tools peculiar to each different vehicle and not included in the organizational maintenance or general mechanic's tools. These special sets are described in the organizational maintenance parts manual (−20P) for the applicable vehicle.

On-equipment material (OEM) that should accompany each vehicle is described and listed in the back of the applicable operator's technical manual (−10).

In touring the maintenance area, you undoubtedly will see a variety of miscellaneous equipment such as generators, portable heating units, air compressors, etc. Most of these require special operator training and licensing. You should find out who is responsible for the operation and operator's maintenance of this equipment. One soldier and an alternate should be appointed by the motor sergeant to operate each item. It's also a good idea that you know who supports you with organizational and higher maintenance for this equipment. Operator manuals or instructions and applicable log book forms (see FM 38–750) should be available for inspection and daily use. Certain safety requirements apply particularly to these pieces; for example, gasoline must not be stored in these items when they're kept in the shop.

Not all maintenance jobs can be accomplished at the organizational maintenance level. To find out exactly what one can and cannot do, see the maintenance allocation chart in Appendix II of each −20 manual.

It's easy to see how important publications are to the maintenance effort. There's no substitute for the proper manuals. You should have the −10, −20, and −20P (Parts Manual) for each item of equipment in your unit. Check DA Pam 310–4 for the latest changes to technical manuals, supply manuals and lubrication orders. DA Pam 310–7 is an index to modification work orders (MWO) that will be needed. (DA Pam 310–6 is the index of supply catalogs which describe the common tool sets.)

Today's Army requires more and more reliable information to plan replacement and procurement of the equipment needed to keep its operational readiness at the highest possible level. Data which provides DA with information about equipment age, reliability, and potential is recorded in the Army equipment record forms. TM 38–750 is the guide and authority to this system. It contains a list of the necessary reportable equipment forms and instructions for completing and maintaining them.

Training organizational-maintenance personnel is always a problem. In the average unit, the ideal solution is to requisition school-trained replacements, or to utilize available schools by sending the unit's own untrained "replacements." The only disadvantage to the latter course is shortened retainability, but it does offer the advantage that you can personally select your maintenance people. The least acceptable, but probably most often used method is on-the-job-training (OJT). The most can be accomplished in OJT by pairing off the new individual with a knowledgeable "old hand." This apprenticeship arrangement can be doubly rewarding since the senior individual gets an opportunity to develop leadership abilities. Personal interest on the part of both the motor officer and the motor sergeant is necessary to the success of the OJT program. Individuals work harder and better when they know their supervisors are interested in *and* appreciate their efforts. The lack of formal training can be offset somewhat by local instruction. The DA Pam 350–25 series offers a few complete courses, including instructor materials. (By the way, DA Pams 350–23 and 350–24 are courses for motor officers and NCO's.)

If, after observing the operation for a while, you are not satisfied with the performance of your maintenance section, you should get together with the motor sergeant and work out a new arrangement. Support units may find that a job-by-job assignment of mechanics is best, while in a tactical unit, one mechanic may be assigned the responsibility for providing a single platoon with organizational-maintenance support. This will allow the mechanic to become intimately familiar with the equipment he or she is responsible for. These are but two of many possible solutions. Adopt the one that's best for the unit.

Being a motor officer is one job that requires some time—time to learn what it's all about, time to learn the mechanic's capabilities, time to supervise. The commander depends directly on the motor officer and maintenance section to provide vehicles and equipment for training or combat. If you learn your job well, train your people, and apply your knowledge and experience, you'll provide timely and efficient support.

A word about command maintenance inspections. These inspections are scheduled to check on the status of vehicles and equipment. These are usually scheduled and announced in advance so extra effort can be exerted to have everything in the best possible shape. They are designed to help motor officers tighten up on their maintenance procedures. Properly viewed, they are a valuable aid in the maintenance effort.

REFERENCES

AR 710–2 Material Management for Using Units, Support Units and Installations

AR 750–1 Army Material Maintenance Concepts and Policies

TM 9–243 Use and Care of Handtools and Measuring Tools

TM 9–8000 Principles of Automotive Vehicles

TM 21–300 Driver Selection and Training (Wheeled Vehicles)

TM 21–301 Driver Selection, Training, and Supervision, Tracked Vehicles

TM 21–305 Manual for the Wheeled Vehicle Driver

TM 21–306 Manual for the Tracked Combat Vehicle Driver

TM 38–750 The Army Maintenance Management System

DA Pam 310–4 Index of Technical Manuals, Technical Bulletins, Supply Manuals, Supply Bulletins, and Lubrication Orders

DA Pam 310–6 Index of Supply Catalogs and Supply Manuals

DA Pam 310–7 U.S. Army Equipment Index of Modification Work Orders

DA Pam 350–23 Commander's Maintenance Management Course

DA Pam 350–24 Maintenance Supervisor's Course

DA Pam 350–25–series Mechanic and Repairman Courses

DA Pam 350–26–series Mechanic and Repairman Courses

DA Pam 351–4 U.S. Army Formal Schools Catalog

DA Pam 700–2 Commander's Supply and Maintenance Handbook

DA Pam 750–1 Commanders Guide of Preventive Maintenance Indicators

DA PAM 750–38 TAMMS—Equipment Historical Records with Selected Maintenance Forms

PS Magazine—All Issues

POSTAL OFFICER

The Postal Officer has responsibility for the overall operation of unit mail service including active supervision of the mail clerk and daily checks and inspections of the mail room.

The mail room should be a separate and secure room, utilized for no other purpose. If registered or certified mail is handled, have a field safe or as a minimum, a locked container that can be physically secured to prevent its removal. Secure official registered or official certified mail that is held overnight in accordance with AR 380–5.

Only one mail clerk may have the keys or combinations to the mailroom and locked containers. The unit postal officer has the second key (there must be only two) or the only other copy of combinations. This second set of keys and/or combinations should be sealed in separate envelopes marked to identify the contents, signed across the flap (the postal officer and clerk) to protect against tampering. The envelopes should be kept in a safe place such as a company safe.

Mail clerks are appointed on DD Form 285 (appointment of unit mail clerk or mail orderly). Enough copies should be made to allow distribution to the individual, the unit file, the serving APO or post office, and the battalion or consolidated mail room, if one is used. The forms must be validated by the serving postal facility.

Mailboxes or receptacles for outgoing mail must be strong enough to make deposited mail reasonably safe and must be physically secured to prevent removal.

Establish hours for collection and distribution of mail, based on the schedule of the serving postal unit. Record mail collection hours on a DD Form 1116 and post on all mail receptacles. Insure that mail is picked up promptly as posted. Incoming mail must be delivered personally to addressees and *not,* for example, left on bunks or footlockers. Hold mail for soldiers temporarily absent or enroute for later delivery. Forward or return to the sender immediately mail for personnel no longer with your unit.

The mail room must maintain a unit directory of all personnel (other than dependents) who receive mail through the unit. Individuals joining or departing prepare a DD Form 1175, which is used in making or updating the directory. These forms are maintained in alphabetical order in one file, regardless of grade or status. Upon departure, locator cards are retained as prescribed in AR 65–75.

Undeliverable mail can be a problem. This is the type of mail that tends to pile up since it takes extra time to process. You should watch for this in your checks and inspections. AR 65–75 discusses the procedures and proper endorsements for returning undeliverable mail. A copy of this regulation and applicable changes must be kept in each mail room.

You should check daily that all registered, numbered insured, and certified mail is properly accounted for. You should verify the registers each day and retain them on file. Subordinate units, such as companies serviced by a battalion mail room, give a receipt for this; the original of this receipt remains at the battalion mail room. The duplicate is your record and you can use it to check accountability and delivery of these pieces. Each addressee signs the duplicate upon delivery of his or her mail. If a piece is undeliverable, the mail clerk should make a notation of the DD Form 4343 showing the reason. All of the undeliverable mail is returned to the source from which it was received. A chain of receipts must be maintained on all accountable mail.

Here are things to watch out for—first, the obstruction of correspondence and the theft or receipt of stolen mail (18 U.S.C. 1701, 1702, 1708); second, mailing obscene or indecent matter (18 U.S.C. 1461); and third, removal of postage stamps from mail (18 U.S.C. 1720).

The unit postal officer should report promptly any known or suspected postal offenses, including the loss, theft, destruction, or other mistreatment of mail to the installation postal officer, the postal officer at the serving APO, or the local military investigative agency. Unit mail clerks suspected of mistreatment of mail should not be relieved of postal duties while under suspicion or investigation.

Free mailing privileges have been granted military personnel serving in specifically designated combat areas. Personal letters, postcards, and taperecorded correspondence qualifies for this service when it has: complete return address in upper left corner; the word "Free" handwritten in the upper right corner. Envelopes should be no larger than 5" x 11½" and should not be endorsed "Air Mail."

Even in areas or times when the free mailing privilege is not in force, any member of the Armed Forces may send letters without a stamp. Postage is collected from the addressee. This service is extended to handle emergency correspondence when stamps are not available, and shouldn't be overused. The envelope is marked "Soldier's Mail" and signed by the unit commander.

Mail service is particularly important in the field as a morale factor, so unit postal officers should try to insure that everyone receives his or her mail as quickly as possible, especially those individuals in units that are cross-attached. Make arrangements also for proper handling of mail for dependents overseas who remain at "home station" during field exercises.

There are times in the field, usually around payday, when the troops need money orders, stamps, etc. The unit postal officer authorizes the mail clerk to purchase them for these individuals, using unit mail clerk's receipt for funds and purchase record (DD Form 1118) which the mail clerk and the purchaser complete in duplicate. The original is kept by the unit and the duplicate given to the purchaser. The purchaser acknowledges receipt of the item by signing the original. The original copies are retained in the unit files.

Courses of instruction for postal clerks are generally given periodically by the serving postal facility. Every unit postal officer should take advantage of this training to refresh abilities of mail clerks and to train necessary replacements.

REFERENCES
AR 65–1 Army Postal Operating Instructions
AR 65–10 Use of the Army Postal Service
AR 65–75 Unit Mail Service
AR 340–3 Official Mail
AR 340–5 Correspondence and Mail Management
AR 341–2 Mail Service

RANGE SAFETY OFFICER

The designation of Range Safety Officer conveys a special responsibility and obligation to see that conditions and procedures which are normally safe do not become unsafe, resulting in injury to personnel and damage to equipment. Specific safety requirements for each different weapon and category of ammunition are spelled out in the applicable technical and training publications. Before going to the range, the safety officer should become familiar with these requirements. The range safety officer works for the range officer-in-charge (OIC), who has overall responsibility for the conduct of firing. The latter should be contacted for instructions or considerations about:
    —maintenance and policing of range
    —selection of competent and qualified range safety personnel assistants
    —preparation of necessary maps
    —posting range guards, barriers, and signals
    —prescribing the wearing of steel helmets under certain conditions
    —stationing of ambulances, emergency-type medical vehicles, and medical personnel
    —arrangement for alternate means of medical evacuation, such as by air, and the applicable notification procedures, frequencies, signals, etc.
    —measures to protect down-range personnel
    —taking suitable precautions to prevent unauthorized trespass or presence on ranges
    —any other duty or activities to insure safe operation of the ranges.

As the range safety officer, you should contact your safety team as soon as its members are designated and brief them on what their job will be. It is important that they understand what is expected of them. The specific safety requirements that apply to the weapons and ammunition that will be on the range should be reviewed with them. Remember, however, that while you can delegate part of your authority in regard to safety, you cannot likewise delegate your responsibilities.

One of your first duties at the range is to conduct a safety orientation for all personnel. You should do this prior to the opening of the range. You should also supervise the safe handling of ammunition. Both before and during firing, all ammunition and explosives or hazardous components must be handled and assembled in the manner prescribed by applicable safety regulations and appropriate technical manuals and field manuals.

—Place all ammunition at firing sites out of range of any weapon back-blast and store it so as to minimize the possibility of ignition, explosion, or detonation.

—Issue ammunition to troops only on the "ready" or firing line.

—Cover all ammunition to protect it from the elements and against direct rays of the sun. Provide enough air circulation around the ammunition to maintain uniform temperature.

—Transport and store boosters, rockets, fuses, detonators, chemical munitions, etc. separate from other ammunition and as specifically prescribed.

—Fuse ammunition only on the firing line and only as needed.

—Do not allow any round of ammunition, including practice and blank ammunition, to be *forced* into the chamber of any type weapon.

See that weapons are handled safely. Be personally aware of all of the special requirements of each weapon, such as the danger areas behind weapons like rockets and recoilless rifles.

Are necessary warning signals and signs in place? Display range and danger flags and, when necessary, warning signs or flashing red lights at appropriate points. Proper warning devices are available from the office responsible for range maintenance and supervision.

Restrict all firing to designated firing points. No person should leave the firing line or remove material from it without permission from the range safety officer or the officer in charge of the range.

Individuals assigned as range safety officers will supervise the handling of misfires, hangfires, and cookoffs. It's important that all personnel understand the nature of these malfunctions as well as their proper preventive and corrective procedures.

You must make the final determination *before firing* that settings placed on weapons and ammunition will impact the rounds within safety limits. This includes settings on fire-control equipment, fuse setting, and correct ammunition and charge. After firing, you require all weapons to be clear and safe before they are removed from the firing line.

You position yourself where you can exercise maximum supervision over the safe conduct of firing. You should have no other assigned duties on the range while acting as safety officer. Your job is to minimize the possibility of accidents. At the same time, you keep your assistants organized so that you can accomplish your mission without unduly interfering with the smooth progress of training.

REFERENCES
AR 75–15 Responsibilities and Procedures for Explosive Ordnance Disposal
AR 385–26 Use of Explosives and Pyrotechnics in Public Demonstrations,
    Exhibitions and Celebrations

AR 385–62 Firing Guided Missiles and Heavy Rockets for Training, Target
   Practice, and Combat
AR 385–63 Regulations for Firing Ammunition for Training, Target Practice,
   and Combat
AR 385–64 Ammunition and Explosive Safety Standards
AR 385–65 Identification of Inert Ammunition and Ammunition Components
FM 5–25 Explosives and Demolitions
TM 9–1300–200 Ammunition, General
TM 9–1300–206 Care, Handling, Preservation, and Destruction of Ammuni-
   tion

RECORDS MANAGEMENT OFFICER

One of the things inspectors dig into first is a unit's records. A large part of
what goes on in every unit is reflected in its files of actions, transactions, and
training. A job as Records Management Officer involves inspecting and supervising unit record-keeping to insure compliance with regulations and established procedures. In most units files are everywhere—the orderly room, supply room, training office, maintenance shops, mess hall. The records
management officer must find them.

The Army has established a functional files system, a method for keeping
records and reference material, and a guide to its disposition when no longer
needed. Since your role as unit records management officer is mostly advisory,
you need to know the system thoroughly. You should study the references
listed below. Unit files, wherever they are, are the direct responsibility of those
who maintain them. Nevertheless, as records management officer, you have
the responsibility to correct any misuse of the system. This takes a real diplo-
mat and leader.

The records management officer's job is one of constant inspection which
should concentrate in two areas—proper *categorization* and proper *labeling*.

Many papers are difficult to classify for filing. However, there is always one
major subject which serves as a basis for filing. For most units these major
subjects—or functions—are spelled out in AR 340–2.

Because of the nature of the particular unit, there may be a need for special
files not described in AR 340–2, but provided for in AR 340–1. For example,
an engineer unit may have a need for mapping and geodetic files. Special files
are authorized, as needed, below division level.

As you dig into the mechanics of the system you'll see why labeling of file
folders and the position of the label is important. The label tells what is in the
folder, how long it will be kept in the active file, and what to do with it at the
end of the active period. Even the position of the label is important as a further
indicator of future disposition.

You have an indirect responsibility for all the files maintained by your unit.
It's your job to help those with direct responsibility by detecting errors and
helping correct them. Therefore, the more you know about the system, the
better you can manage the attendant records.

REFERENCES
AR 340–1 Records Management—Program, Policies, and Procedures
AR 340–2 Maintenance and Disposition of Records in TOE Units of the Active
   Army and the Army Reserve

AR 340–6 Maintenance and Disposition of Records in Organic Companies and Batteries of the Active Army

AR 340–18–series The Army Functional Files System

REENLISTMENT OFFICER

Officers with this primary duty are found in all major commands and in other commands or installations where the enlisted strength exceeds 5,000. Installations and organizations not authorized to have career-counseling personnel on a primary-duty basis appoint an officer and a noncommissioned officer to carry out the reenlistment functions on an additional duty basis. The Reinlistment Officer's job, hence, is to aid the commander in the reenlistment effort, and to provide guidance and assistance to NCO career counselors.

It is a cardinal rule that every reenlistment officer keep his or her commander informed on all matters pertaining to the reenlistment program. This includes changes in the qualifications or procedures used in processing applicants for reenlistment. These are outlined in AR 601–210.

As the reenlistment officer, you should be alert for changes in this and other pertinent documents by maintaining contact with reenlistment and personnel sections of higher headquarters. You should keep up to date on the availability and requirements for reenlistment options and other specialized career options.

The reenlistment officer should make sure that orientations are conducted for newly assigned officers and enlisted personnel in grades E-5 and above, informing them of the policies, procedures, responsibilities and objectives of the reenlistment program. The program needs to be a continuing thing but in the long run its effectiveness is a reflection of the prevalent attitude of the unit.

There are two films for use as a part of the orientation of new officers and NCOs. The first, THE COMPANY WE KEEP, offers suggestions and presents a philosophy for effective reenlistment programs. The second, THE ONE THAT GOT AWAY (MF 12–9323), may be shown to officers and NCOs at the discretion of the commander. If used, it should precede THE COMPANY WE KEEP. These films are available through the Audio-Visual Communication Center serving the unit.

New commanders want to be apprised of their responsibilities in relation to the reenlistment program. They are:

—Counseling and interviewing eligible individuals (see AR 601–210) 8 to 10 months prior to the expiration of term of service (ETS) and forwarding the name and mailing address of each individual recommended for reenlistment to the career counselor who includes him or her in a direct-mail reenlistment campaign. This campaign consists of five reenlistment information folders, mailed one per month by DA.

—Requiring all personnel completing their first tour (or with 4 years or less for pay purposes at ETS) to attend a showing of the film SOMETHING TO BUILD ON approximately 4 months before ETS.

—Informing recommended individuals of the reenlistment opportunities that will be available to them at the time of separation or within 3 months thereafter.

—Reenlisting individuals desiring unbroken service the day following the date of discharge, even when that day is a nonduty day.

—Establishing procedures to bar untrainable or unsuitable individuals from reenlisting (see para 8c, AR 635–200).

The REENLISTMENT HANDBOOK FOR UNIT COMMANDERS is a guide designed to give support and information needed to formulate and conduct an effective unit reenlistment program. You should be sure that your unit commander has one and you should get one for yourself. Occasionally a person is encountered who is felt to be exceptionally worthy of retention in the active Army, but who for some reason is not qualified for reenlistment. (The reason could be lost time, over-age, conviction of a minor offense, medical, etc.) In this case, you may request a waiver of reenlistment disqualification in accordance with AR 601–210. Waivers are also possible for personnel who want to attend an Army Service school, but who do not meet the minimum prerequisites for the desired course. These waiver requests are submitted as directed in paragraph 4–26, AR 600–200.

If the unit has room for a separate reenlistment office, it will do the most good if it is located where it is conspicuous enough to draw attention, yet private enough to allow an informal, friendly atmosphere for interviews. In any case each unit should have an effective display of reenlistment literature. In the unit area this should be a self-service display stocked with current reenlistment information.

You ought to use originality in the conduct of reenlistment ceremonies. The national flag should always be in the immediate vicinity, but this doesn't mean that reenlistments need to take place in an office. You can use the PIO facilities available to publicize enlistments and give your program a boost.

There is one important clerical area in the field of reenlistment—the reenlistment data card (DA Form 1315). It is designed as an aid to the reenlistment program. The form is initially completed at the Army Reception Station and forwarded with the individual's 201 file. If not, the unit personnel officer prepared one. When a person is transferred or reassigned prior to ETS, the losing unit commander makes an appropriate entry in the enlistment status section of the form. Review of the facts on the card will help prepare the officer for the interview. From it one can learn: age, dependency status, level of civilian education, civilian occupation, GT score, the top scores in the individual's qualifications battery, and whether the soldier is qualified for a reenlistment option. Prior interviews and viewing of a reenlistment film are recorded on the DA Form 1315. Stereotype remarks, e.g., "will not reenlist," "does not like Army," are *not* to be used. Chances are that you or someone else will have to interview the individual again and some pertinent information from the record about the previous interviews will help jog thinking or serve as a guide to the new interviewer.

The reenlistment officer is required to maintain sufficient statistics to indicate the reenlistment efforts of each company-size unit. Local regulations usually spell out the nature and form of the required statistics.

In talking to a soldier about reenlistment it's not surprising to hear gripes, etc., about KP, guard, bed-check or the billets. You should remember, however, that you are not reenlisting the soldier for a career of these things. What the Army wants are skilled technicians and leaders. You may point to these in your unit as an example that any young soldier should strive to emulate. You must try to make reenlistment the "in" thing to do, and gear your program to the individual.

In terms of broad objects, the most important goal of any reenlistment effort is to select and retain those qualified soldiers who have shown the potential for greater service to themselves and the Army. You assist in evaluating the capabilities and attitudes of every person in the command. You must remember that the soldiers you reenlist will serve as trained replacements under you or some other commander. So you should never shortchange anyone for the sake of good-looking reenlistment statistics.

REFERENCES
AR 600–200 Enlisted Personnel Management System
AR 601–208 Recruiting/Reenlistment Publicity Program
AR 601–210 Regular Army Enlistment Program
AR 601–280 Army Reenlistment Program
AR 635–200 Enlisted Personnel
DA Pam 601–1 The OCS Story
DA Pam 608–2 Your Personal Affairs
Reenlistment Handbook for Unit Commanders

SAFETY OFFICER

Briefly, the Safety Officer's job is to develop a sustained safety education and accident-prevention program. Normally much of this effort is necessarily directed toward creating an interest in safety on the part of all personnel in the command.

Here are some guidelines for the newly-appointed safety officer:

—Become familiar with the Army and subordinate command safety regulations (385-series), DA Pamphlet 385–1 (Unit Safety Management), and local SOPs.

—Hold periodic briefings to keep supervisors, platoon leaders, and NCOs alert to safety requirements and programs.

—Promote original campaigns to keep individuals constantly aware of their responsibilities for accident-prevention, both on and off the job.

—Be sure that directives, policies, plans and procedures on safety are realistic in terms of primary unit mission.

—Review accident statistics or reports to identify trouble areas and apply practical corrective measures.

—Investigate and report each accident accurately and promptly, irrespective of its severity, degree of injury or damage cost.

—Organize a unit safety council to make recommendations and suggestions to improve the accident-prevention program.

—Conduct safety inspections, recommend action to remove or control hazards and determine the need for safety training. Inspections help identify unsafe conditions or persons *before* accidents occur. This fact should be used to advantage.

Design safety programs to reduce or eliminate accidents, in essence to reduce hazards and to develop safe behavior among unit personnel. DA Pamphlet 385–1 (Unit Safety Management) is an excellent guide and reference for planning a unit safety program. Here is a simple program checklist based on the requirements of AR 385–10, AR 385–40 and AR 385–55. This can be modified to meet any specific unit situation.

—Do SOP's include provisions for safe practices and procedures?

—Does the commander personally review the accident experience of the command periodically?

—Does the commander include safety as a topic in staff meetings?

—Has the safety officer been appointed on orders?

—Does the command receive and display safety publications, posters, and material?

—Does the safety officer conduct training and prepare safety material for presentation by others?

—Does he or she conduct safety inspections and surveys?

—Are summaries of accident data periodically assembled and reviewed?

—Are reports, records and other accident information safeguarded as prescribed by current regulations (AR 385–40)?

—Do all unit SOPs contain clear and concise instructions on reporting of accidents?

—Are accident investigations thorough and timely?

—Are all accident reports being reviewed carefully for completeness and accuracy?

—Is remedial training for drivers involved in traffic violations required?

—Is disciplinary action initiated where traffic violations are the primary cause of an accident?

—Are the safe-driving rules for winter driving brought to the attention of the entire command?

—Is private-motor-vehicle accident-prevention emphasized?

—Does the command participate in local safe-driving campaigns?

—Are off-duty pass or leave personnel required to comply with directives regarding safe operation of private motor vehicles?

—Does the command have an adequate safety awards program?

—Is the program effective in stimulating interest in the reduction of accidental injury and/or property damage?

—Are individual safety awards being used and presented properly?

The best accident is one that has just been prevented. The time-proven methods which help keep accidents to a minimum are the "Three E's of Safety": Engineering, Education, and Enforcement, *Engineering* is identifying and locating hazards, eliminating hazards, compensating for those that cannot be removed, and avoiding the creation of hazards in new designs or operations.

Education and training have three aspects: the development of positive safety attitudes; the knowledge necessary for safe performance; and the skill level necessary for safe performance.

Engineering and education can prevent most accidents; however, there are some people who just won't be careful. For them, strict *enforcement* of safety practices, backed by prompt corrective action, is necessary. Punishment should not be for having an accident, but rather for violation of an order or procedure in effect to prevent such an accident.

Keep in mind the objectives of the program; to reduce hazards and develop safe behavior. Engineering and inspections help achieve the former, while education and enforcement contribute to the latter.

Safety inspections will generally be of the "continuing" type, conducted to discover accident-causing conditions or procedures throughout a unit area. As a part of this program, the safety officer should invite periodic inspections of specific areas by specialized teams. The installation safety director can help arrange these. Every unit safety inspection should cover all the activities of the unit in as much detail as possible.

Accident records and reports from previous inspections will indicate areas that may need particular attention. For each such inspection a check list should be used and a record of deficiencies kept. Appendix G, DA Pamphlet 385–1, contains a suggested safety inspection list. Additional safety criteria and information may be obtained from publications (ARs, TMs, FMs, TBs, PS Magazine) appropriate to the unit and equipment.

The safety officer should serve as recorder for the safety council (not as its chairman). The recorder prepares a detailed agenda before each council meeting, including enough detail to show the extent of problems to be discussed and the need for doing something about them. The ideas and suggestions that come out of the meeting are also recorded. They can be used as a basis for developing safety promotion campaigns. To add emphasis, council members should be selected by the unit commander. The deciding factors when selecting individuals should be their interest in safety problems and leadership ability. Here are some items which could be considered by the council:

—accident experience and trends
—accident reports, including cause-analysis and corrective action
—review of new equipment or procedures to determine any potential hazards and appropriate corrective action or SOP changes
—safety programs and recommended solutions
—evaluation of safety suggestions
—implementation of Army safety policy regulations and programs
—planning and implementation of safety contests, demonstrations, and orientation of personnel.

The safety officer, by virtue of his or her interest in safety and the experience gained, will normally be the best qualified person to act as accident investigator. A detailed discussion of accident investigation, reporting, and analysis is contained in DA Pamphlet 385-1. This material should be studied in depth before attempting to investigate an accident.

Remember that one major purpose of accident investigation is to provide information which will be useful in preventing further similar occurrences. It is essential that the investigator go beyond the superficial causes and determine the WHY of the accident, seeking reasons, not alibis.

A good safety officer will take advantage of the safety management extension courses and subcourses presented by the U.S. Army Adjutant General School. Information on these and other nonresident courses can be obtained by writing:

Commandant
US Army Adjutant General School
ATTN: Chief, Ext Crs Div, ODTL
Fort Benjamin Harrison, Indiana 46216

In planning unit safety programs, remember that in the end safety is a result of each individual's interest. Once this is developed sufficiently, accident statistics will begin to improve.

REFERENCES
AR 95-1 Army Aviation—General Provisions
AR 95-5 Aircraft Accident Prevention, Investigation, and Reporting
AR 340-18-6 Maintenance and Disposition of . . . Safety Functional Files
AR 385-10 Army Safety Program
AR 385-15 Water Safety
AR 385-30 Safety Code Color Marking and Signs
AR 385-40 Accident Reporting and Records
AR 385-55 Prevention of Motor Vehicle Accidents
AR 600-55 Motor Vehicle Driver—Selection, Testing, and Licensing
DA Pam 108-1 Index of Army Motion Pictures and Related Audio-Visual Aids
DA Pam 385-1 Unit Safety Management
DA Pam 385-2 You're Headed Home Stateside

DA Pam 385–3 Protective Clothing and Equipment
DA Pam 385–4 Army Safety Program
DA Pam 385–5 Fundamentals of Safety in Army Sports and Recreation
FM 105–5 Maneuver Control
TM 5–682 Repairs and Utilities; Safety Electrical Facilities
TM 21–300 Driver Selection and Training (Wheeled Vehicles)
TM 21–301 Driver Selection, Training and Supervision, Tracked Vehicles

SAVINGS OFFICER

The Savings Officer is primarily a "General Sales and Promotion Manager," whose objective is to plan and conduct a continuous educational program that will encourage regular and systematic savings. He or she is responsible for the Savings Bond Program. The whole idea is to encourage voluntary savings. It is accomplished through the payroll savings plan for the purchase of savings bonds.

Savings bonds have been sold continuously by the Treasury since 1935. The Payroll Savings Plan, initiated in 1941, has proved to be an easy and safe way for the average soldier to accumulate capital. The Department of the Army goal for this savings plan is 75 percent participation, with a long-range objective of 90 percent. These are Army-wide goals, and must not be interpreted as "quotas." The decision to participate in the program is entirely up to the individual. Savings officers must never use coercion, reprisals, or threats of reprisal to induce personnel to enroll in the program. Instead, the case for bonds should be presented on its own merits, together with information on how to enroll in the payroll savings plan—nothing more. The Army is very explicit that *this is all the savings officer can do.* How to best go about doing this much is the problem.

Each year the savings officer should conduct a person-to-person canvass to explain the advantages of the savings program and to solicit participants. This covers explaining the benefits to both the government and to the individual. If the soldier is already buying bonds, increasing his or her present deduction can be suggested. During the canvass, each soldier should be provided with a DA Form 2098-R (Prospect for Purchase of US Savings Bonds). The forms returned marked "YES" are sent to the finance section serving the unit or to some other designated office. Forms marked "NO" are kept for future reference. The savings officer may follow up on these periodically, but cannot harass or coerce. A good time to follow up any prospect—even those already taking a bond—is at the time of a pay raise or promotion when a payroll deduction would be most painless.

A canvasser's handbook and chairman's guide are usually available from the Treasury Department. A DA Circular announces the drive annually and provides overall guidance for conducting the canvass. It also lists promotional material that will be available. For stateside units, contact the nearest Treasury Savings Bond Division (addresses are contained in Appendix A to AR 608–15) for promotional films and other material. Whether stateside or overseas, a Savings Bond Features monthly promotional packet is available—by request for distribution from U.S. Savings Bonds Division, Treasury Department, ATTN: Advertising and Promotional Branch, Washington, D.C. 20220. Locally reproducible material for canvassers is suggested and illustrated in Appendix B of AR 608–15.

In view of the many benefits, the savings officer should try to make the presentation of the program continuous and dynamic. Explain the program, sell its merits and advantages, make enrollment as easy and painless as possible —and *that is all.* Nothing else is required; nothing else is expected; nothing else is wanted; nothing else is allowed!

REFERENCES
AR 37–104–3 Military Pay and Allowances Procedures, Joint Uniform Military
    Pay System (JUMPS)
AR 608–15 Army Savings Program
DA Pam 608–2 Your Personal Affairs

SUPPLY OFFICER

Duties of the unit Supply Officer will vary from unit to unit. It may simply require responsibility for the operation of a small unit supply room which does little more than dispense expendable items and provide storage for the unit equipment. On the other hand, it may involve a large supply operation complete with requisitioning and accounting responsibilities.

In most company-size units a supply sergeant (under the supply officer's supervision) runs the supply room. As a new supply officer, your first move should be to meet the supply sergeant and visit the supply room. There you should determine what property the unit is authorized. There should be an up-to-date file of TOE's, TA's, SM's, AR's, etc., that apply to the supply activities of the unit.

Organizational property such as weapons, vehicles, etc., are included in tables of organization and equipment. Certain other items such as helmets, canteens, ponchos, etc., are authorized by CTA 50–900.

Installation property, such as beds, mattresses, footlockers, chairs, filing cabinets, dishwashers, refrigerators, etc., are authorized by TA's of the 20 series. (This equipment does not usually accompany a unit on a change of station.)

Personal clothing is authorized by AR 700-84. This clothing is repaired and replaced with the cash maintenance allowance paid monthly to each enlisted soldier. AR 700-84 also outlines certain conditions for gratuitous issue and repair of personal clothing and describes the handling and disposition of clothing upon discharge or absence of the owner. The marking of the clothing is described in AR 746–10.

Morale Support property, such as athletic, welfare, and recreation supplies, has no basic publication. Its expendability is established by the Army SM's of the QM 5 series.

All non-expendable unit property, except components of kits and sets, is listed on hand receipts in the unit supply files. These files are a logical next step in the new supply officer's introduction to the supply room.

Unit supply files are established for supply control within the organization and are not records of accountability. Every unit has them. They should include as a minimum the following:

Hospital and Absence Without Leave File   Personal clothing of individuals in each of these categories is inventoried and a record of the inventory kept in this file.

Gratuitous Issue File   This file contains documents initiated in connection with gratuitous issue or repair of personal clothing.

Work Order File   This file contains work order requests for the repair of unit property. Responsibility for the items submitted for repair is temporarily transferred to the repairing agency. These work requests and job orders assist in supply control.

Laundry Files   These assist in the control and supervision of individual and organizational clothing sent to the post laundry. Most posts offer three laundry services: 1) Monthly payroll deduction rates, 2) Cash-per-bundle rates, and 3) Piece rates. The monthly payroll deduction rate plan has a maximum bundle limitation and a piece authorization though the fixed rate is charged whether or not the maximum authorization is used. The deduction is made by means of a roster. The per-bundle rates are collected when the laundry is turned in. The cash and signed voucher (DA Form 3136) accompany the bundles. Individual piece rate is handled as determined by the officials responsible for the local laundry service (DA Form 2741).

Two accountability records may at the discretion of the property book officer be maintained in the unit supply files. They are: The Organizational Clothing and Equipment Record (DA Form 10–102) which records individual draw and turn-in of CTA 50–900 property; and personal clothing records which are initially prepared upon entry into the service and forwarded to each new unit. Posting is accomplished by the supply sergeant (for example, as when uniform authorizations change).

You are now ready to take a critical look around. Is the supply room secure? Are "No Smoking" signs posted (AR 700–15) and are fire extinguishers present, filled, clean and in operating order? Are the last inspections of the fire fighting equipment entered on the inspection tags in accordance with local fire regulations? The general appearance and organization of the supply room is a clue to the quality of supply management one can expect to find.

Next check the storage of equipment. Metal tools should be clean, free of rust and oiled. Cutting edges should be protected. Wooden handles should be free of paint and treated with linseed oil (handles fitted to hammers, axes, etc., should be wedged to insure secure mounting). Blankets and wool items should be clean and adequately mothproofed. Mattresses should be stored off the floor in mattress covers. They should be stored flat, no more than three high and shouldn't have anything piled on top of them. Excess supplies, salvage and unserviceable items should be turned in promptly. Don't be afraid to dig around in the bottoms of bins to locate excess salvage items. Every supply room has them and they should be gotten back into the system—someone else may need them.

Canvas items should be dried and cleaned before storage. Canvas should always be stored off the floor on dry, clean dunnage. This allows air to circulate freely around it. Poles and stakes should never be rolled with tents for storage. Tents should be pitched periodically and inspected. They should be clean and dry before storing. They should be tagged when stored with nomenclature, FSN, date of storage and date last aired. Canvas repair kits (authorized at battalion and like level) can be used to repair small holes and rips and to replace missing grommets. Tips on canvas care are found in PS Magazine Issue 175, TM 10–269, TM 10–663 and FM 20–15.

Equipment which uses flammable fuels is stored in accordance with fire regulations. A mop string partially inserted into the fuel tank will act as a wick and insure that tanks are dry and safe.

Sometimes material for unit projects is unavailable through normal supply channels. On occasion it can be found in the salvage yard of the supply installation serving the unit. As a rule the items can be issued as long as the items are not used for their originally intended purposes. See AR 755–2 for details.

Supply control in most unit supply rooms is a pretty simple thing. Items that are lost, damaged, or no longer needed are reported or turned in to the property book officer. The loss, destruction, damage without fault or neglect of minor items of non-expendable property (value of $10 or less) is informally reported to the property book officer (usually on a DF or inter-office memo). He or she lists them quarterly on DD Form 22 and submits the list through channels with a request for relief of accountability. If granted, the items are removed from the hand receipts and property book.

When fault or neglect are involved and pecuniary liability for the loss is admitted, collection is made in cash on a cash collection voucher (DD Form 1131) listing the property, value and including the statement "Used in lieu of a report of survey, Para 13, AR 735–11", or is made in the form of payroll deductions by issuing a statement of charges (DD Form 362.) Receipted copies of either act as relief from responsibility. When pecuniary liability for the loss of other than low value items is not admitted, a report of survey must be initiated by the hand receipt holder on a DD Form 200.

Nonexpendable components of a kit or set, such as hand tools, which are worn out through fair wear and tear, are turned in and replacement requested. The chain of accountability is maintained by using a turn-in tag (shoe tag) DA Form 1115. The lower portion of the tag is a receipt for the item and is later exchanged for the new replacement item.

Study in detail the discussion of accountability and supply procedures contained in AR 735–5.

Check the qualifications of supply personnel next. Even if they are experts in garrison supply procedures (which is rare) there is a lot that can be done to insure adequate support in the field. For example, the supply section usually operates in rear areas, making daily trips between its unit and supply base. Map reading is an often neglected, but necessary subject. The same is true of NBC training, vehicle maintenance, and all other basic military skills. The supply section is often overlooked or allowed to miss unit training on these subjects. Guard against this. The training (or lack of it) that the supply section receives could someday be the deciding factor in some critical combat decision. Chances are that most local supply personnel could use some training so you may be able to arrange larger classes and assistance in presenting them.

Responsibilities for supply and property are serious. Laxness in this area can be expensive in a personal way, not to mention its impact on the unit mission. It's wise for a new supply officer to immediately become very familiar with the regulations, orders, instructions and SOP's that apply to supply and property accountability.

REFERENCES
FM 21–15 Care and Use of Individual Clothing and Equipment
AR 340–18–14 Maintenance and Disposition of Logistics Functional Files
AR 638–1 Disposition of Personal Effects of Deceased and Missing Personnel
AR 700–15 Preservation Packaging, and Packing and Marking of Items of Supply
AR 700–84 Issue and Sale of Personal Clothing
AR 710–2 Material Management for Using Units, Support Units and Installations
AR 735–11 Accounting for Lost, Damaged, and Destroyed Property
AR 735–110 Supply Operations Manual, Vol I: Distribution System Procedures

DA Pam 310–4 Index of Technical Manuals, Technical Bulletins, Supply Manuals, Supply Bulletins, and Lubrication Orders
DA Pam 310–6 Index of Supply Catalogs and Supply Manuals
DA Pam 700–1 DOD Supply Management Reference Book
DA Pam 350–55–1 Company Administration Programmed Text for Supply Management
TM 10–227 Fitting of Men's Uniforms
TM 10–228 Fitting of Footwear
TM 10–229 Fitting of Uniforms for Army Women
TM 10–255 Unit and Organizational Supply
TM 10–267 General Repair of Clothing and Textiles
TM 10–268 General Repair of Footwear and Leather Goods
TM 10–269 General Repair of Canvas and Webbing
TM 10–275 Cold Weather Clothing and Sleeping Equipment
TM 10–276 Hot Weather Clothing and Equipment
TM 10–280 Field Laundry, Bath and Clothing Exchange Operations

TRAINING OFFICER

Your duties as a Training Officer can vary considerably from unit to unit. In one, you might have a fairly free hand in planning and conducting your unit's training. In another, training may be directed almost completely from above. In either case, your responsibilities are considerable.

In all units, depending on what portion of the Army training program (ATP) is being conducted, certain training is mandatory. Whether your unit is undergoing individual or unit training, you should study FM 21–5 to get a good overall picture of training as the Army conducts it. For most combat-ready units, the Army subject schedules that pertain to the particular unit contain a detailed plan and program of training. You should be sure you have an applicable copy and have studied the requirements outlined in it. There are also training notes, sequence charts, and lesson outlines included which will help you. Next you should check the training directive of higher headquarters for a definition of training policies and particular requirements or objectives to be accomplished.

One of the first steps for you to take is to find out who actually plans the day to day training. You may be expected to do it, it may be done by the commander, by the training NCO, or it may be directed by higher headquarters. In any case, you will want to know how far ahead it is necessary to plan. This will depend to a great extent upon the availability of training areas, facilities and training aids. It takes a certain amount of time to procure training aids, but this shouldn't be much of a problem. Training areas, however, are another matter. Unless you are at a most unusual post, they must be requested far ahead at periodic range conferences. These conferences are usually held semiannually or quarterly, with more frequent updating sessions. Planning should therefore be done far enough ahead to register unit requirements at the "3" shop before these main meetings. If all the needed facilities are not available at first, they may become available at the interim meetings. This, however, requires that you remain flexible and alert to short-notice opportunities. Major activities such as armor-unit tank gunnery programs may be scheduled by Division. Other activities such as brigade or battalion field exercises will be scheduled by those headquarters. You must fit your unit training into the schedule to complement the plans of higher headquarters. For example, you should have platoon and company tactical training before a battalion field exercise rather than after it.

Combat service support units have special problems when it comes to field training. The supported units don't just vanish when the servicing unit needs field training. A solution is to send one element of the supporting company to the field at a time to operate during field exercises of the maneuver units that depend on its service. Even this may not work for all organizations. You have to apply your imagination. Regardless of the organization, there is never enough time, facilities or money to do all the training desirable. You will have to plan ahead and in detail, using knowledge, experience and ingenuity to get the job done right.

Time is an important element in training. Obviously time must be included in the unit's schedule for training, but it is not so obvious in the planning phase that sufficient time be made available to instructors to study, prepare, and rehearse their classes. No class should be given without a rehearsal, preferably several. Someone should critique each lesson sufficiently in advance to allow time for instructors to rewrite or revise weak or unsatisfactory parts. The time required is well spent.

Stick to the essentials in training. When writing or reviewing a lesson, always ask "What does the soldier NEED to know to accomplish the mission?" Be sure that soldiers get all they need to know and that they learn it. Don't waste training time—the instructors' or the students'—on unnecessary or irrelevant information.

As much training as possible should be "hands-on" practical work. Even simple tasks are learned best when done rather than described. Next best is a demonstration with actual equipment. For example, camouflage training, basic to every unit, is sometimes difficult to accomplish since there are few places which allow the tree cutting necessary to do a really effective job. Here is where a demonstration of one vehicle or position properly camouflaged can do the trick. At the position, a soldier can see what's expected and by moving to an enemy viewpoint, both proper and improper examples can be illustrated. Night-light discipline is another example. One can talk about it for hours, but a simple nighttime demonstration of a few typical sources of light is quite easy and effective. Don't forget to include a demonstration of how to solve the problems brought up in discussion, in this case how to shield necessary light.

For specialized training and training beyond the scope of unit capabilities there are Service schools in almost all theaters. DA Pam 351-4 with its current changes lists these schools. School quotas are requested through battalion or post S-3 (G-3) office.

Training paperwork generally falls in two areas, training schedules and individual training records. Both are important. Local training directives usually spell out the requirements and the form of both.

Training schedules must be timely, i.e., they must be prepared early enough to allow the instructors reaction time to prepare their classes, to schedule classrooms or training facilities, and to obtain necessary training materials.

Individual training records, when properly maintained, are important to the unit program. See that they are kept up-to-date. In addition to revealing how much each soldier is progressing toward fulfilling the training requirements, they also tell which classes need to be rescheduled, or alternatively which individuals need to be sent to another unit's class for make-up work. Here is an area where close cooperation and coordination between training officers can pay dividends. One make-up class could suffice for an entire battalion (or more). If training is staggered among units, some soldiers that need make-up work may often be sent to another unit giving the same instruction as a part of their regular program. To do this, you have to stay on top of your own requirements and the training being conducted by other units around you. You should be prepared to offer the same help to other units that you may want for your own.

The standards of training your unit will largely reflect the attitude, interest, and ingenuity that you bring to your job. You should seek help and ideas from your subordinates as well as your superiors. There is always more than one solution to a problem and you must always be prepared to pick or recommend the best.

REFERENCES
AR 71–7 Military Training Aids and Army Training Aid Center System
AR 380–18–10 Maintenance and Disposition of Training . . . Functional Files
AR 350–1 Army Training
AR 350–4 Qualification and Familiarization with Weapons and Weapon-Systems
AR 350–13 Material Readiness
AR 350–30 Code of Conduct
AR 350–225 Survival, Evasion, and Escape Training
AR 351–1 Military Education and Training
AR 351–20 Army Correspondence Course Program
AR 385–26 Use of Explosives and Pyrotechnics in Public Demonstrations, Exhibitions, and Celebrations
CTA 20–2 Equipment for Training Purposes
DA Pam 108–1 Index of Army Motion Pictures and Related Audio-Visual Aids
DA Pam 310–12 Index and Description of Army Training Devices
DA Pam 350–15-series Operations—Lessons Learned
DA Pam 351–4 U.S. Army Formal Schools Catalog
DA Pam 672–2 Conduct of Ceremonies Handbook
FM 21–5 Military Training Management
FM 21–6 Techniques of Military Instruction
FM 21–75 Combat Training of the Individual Soldier and Patrolling

UNIT FUND, CUSTODIAN/RECORDER

Each unit commander appoints himself or herself or, if a field grade officer, another commissioned officer as Unit Fund Custodian; the custodian shall also be the Recorder for the unit fund council (Para 3–6 c, AR 230–1).

The recorder is responsible for making and distributing the agenda prior to a scheduled meeting. (In small units this is a very informal—even word-of-mouth process.) During the meeting, the proceedings of the council must be recorded showing:
—members present and absent
—actions taken
—a copy of the new financial statement of the fund.

The minutes are signed by the president and the recorder. Excerpts from the minutes or a copy of the minutes are made available for the council and members of the unit. Generally this is done by posting a copy on the unit bulletin board.

The custodian is responsible to the council for fund administration and will:
—Receive, safeguard, disburse, and account for funds and property in ac-

cordance with AR 230–1 and AR 230–21 and other applicable regulations, policies and procedures prescribed by the council or local directive.

—Be financially liable for losses of funds and property when dishonesty, fraud, or culpable negligence on his or her part is established.

—Insure that the accounting system conforms with AR 230–21 and local regulations.

—Prepare periodic financial statements and reports, and attest to their accuracy.

—Serve as the fund purchasing and contracting officer in accordance with AR 230–1.

When "equitable benefits accrue to the military personnel of the unit as a whole", the unit fund is authorized to purchase or contract for:

—Supplies, equipment, or services which contribute to the entertainment, recreation, comfort, or education of the personnel of the unit, and enhancement of the unit mess. (The purchase of alcoholic beverages with an alcoholic content greater than 3.2 percent by weight is prohibited. See AR 210–65.)

—Supplies, materials, or services required for the maintenance of unit fund property and for emergency maintenance of government-owned welfare and recreational property issued to the organization.

—Labor-saving devices and articles that are not available through military supply services. If considering something of this nature, it is a good idea to get a Certificate of Nonavailability from the supply agency or section serving the unit.

—Authorized distinctive insignia or uniform trimmings for use, without reimbursement, by all eligible personnel of the unit.

Unit histories and related materials for presentation to all members of the unit, and to new members as they join the unit.

—Awards of property, cash, or the equivalent, as individual prizes for proficiency in military pursuits, such as Soldier-of-the-Month, and for recreational and educational contests conducted by the fund in which all members of the unit have equal opportunity to participate. Individual awards are not to exceed $25.

Become completely familiar with the accounting and audit requirements and procedures outlined in AR 230–21 and local regulations. It's important to keep the accounting work of the fund up to date day-by-day. If a fund is behind, or if it has been poorly handled, the new custodian will be wise to contact the adjutant or other members of the command who have had experience with such funds, and get the fund records straightened out as soon as possible.

REFERENCES
AR 210–65 Alcoholic Beverages
AR 230–1 The Nonappropriated Fund System
AR 230–21 Accounting Procedures for Nonappropriated Unit Funds, Inmates' Welfare Funds, Stockade Welfare Funds, and Commandants' Welfare Funds

UNIT FUND COUNCIL, PRESIDENT/MEMBER

Unit fund councils are composed of at least one commissioned officer, and two noncommissioned officers and/or Specialist E-4 and above. The number of members should be limited, but must include at least these three individuals. At company level, the commissioned officer is usually the unit commander. At higher headquarters, the commissioned officer is the unit commander or one of his or her staff. The enlisted representatives are members of the unit. The council president and members of the council are designated by the unit commander.

The council must meet at least once each quarter (more frequently when necessary) at the call of its president.

Every council member has a duty to:

—Ascertain and insure that the fund is being properly administered and safeguarded as provided in AR 230–21 and local 230-series regulations.

—Determine that all income has been received in full, been properly recorded in the book of accounts, and accurately reflected in the financial statements.

—Approve the amounts and purposes of all expenditures of the fund. Such approvals may be of a general nature such as total expenditures authorized for running a contest, fund administration, or recurring type program expenses or they may be of a specific nature (such as expenditures for a particular purchase of supplies, equipment or awards).

—Review the fund financial statements and other fund records as required to insure that all expenditures are made in accordance with approved council actions and within the purpose for which the fund was established.

—Assure the accountability of all fund-owned property, the conduct of physical inventories of such property, and recommend disposition of that which is surplus to requirements.

—Assure that audits are scheduled and conducted as prescribed, and review reports of audits and inspections and take appropriate action thereon.

—After the council has examined monthly accounts, found them correct, and approved the expenditures, both the recorder/custodian and the president sign the unit fund receipts and expenditures record (DA Form 3259–2).

REFERENCES

AR 230–1 The Nonappropriated Fund System
AR 230–21 Accounting Procedures for Nonappropriated Unit Funds, Inmates' Welfare Funds, Stockade Welfare Funds, and Commandants' Welfare Funds

VOTING OFFICER

The Voting Officer's job is to provide general voting information and to assist in the procedures of registering and requesting absentee ballots. He or she must also provide election information about respective states to include election date, officials to be elected, constitutional amendments and other proposals to be voted on.

DA Pam 360–503 is published each election year to help voting officers. It contains current election dates and summaries of the voting laws of all States, District of Columbia, and territories. Supplements are issued periodically throughout the year. Other informational aids, such as posters, are made available well in advance of general election dates.

While much of the information given in this pamphlet is applicable to any absentee voter, it is particularly directed to members of the Armed Forces and executive agencies of the Federal government and their spouses and dependents whose duty or service requires them to be away from their legal voting places at election time.

As specified in the Voting Assistance Act, these persons are:

—Members of the Armed Forces while in active service, and their spouses and dependents.

—Members of the Merchant Marine of the United States, and their spouses and dependents.

—Civilian employees of the United States, in all categories, serving outside the territorial limits of the several states and the United States and the District of Columbia, and their spouses and dependents when residing with or accompanying them, whether or not the employee is subject to the Civil Service laws and the Classification Act of 1949, and whether or not paid from funds appropriated by Congress.

—Members of religious groups or welfare agencies assisting members of the Armed Forces who are officially attached to and serving with the Armed Forces, and their spouses and dependents. These include American Red Cross, United Service Organization, Society of Friends, and similar organizations specified by the individual states.

The Federal Voting Assistance Act sets up recommended procedures for absentee voting by specified categories of people as guidance for the states. But, each state makes its own voting laws. It's important, therefore, that voting officers consult the summaries of the state laws in question, as given in DA Pam 360–503, before attempting to counsel persons on how to apply for registration or absentee ballot.

A special application form is printed and distributed for persons covered under the Act, called the Federal Post Card Application for Absentee Ballot (Standard Form 76, revised 1955), commonly referred to as the FPCA.

The Department of Defense has directed the Services to issue Federal Post Card Applications directly to all eligible personnel for general elections taking place at 2-year intervals (see AR 608–20).

The FPCA is used to apply for an absentee ballot and registration if the state or territory so authorizes. Standards of acceptance and procedures vary from state to state. Filling out an FPCA and sending it to the proper officials of a person's home state does not always entitle that person to absentee registration or voting privileges. In some states it does; in others, the FPCA serves as a request for the state's own forms which must be filled out and returned before final action is taken on the request.

In a few states, one FPCA serves for all elections in that calendar year. But one FPCA may never be used for more than one person. For instance, a spouse who is authorized by a state to use the FPCA must submit a separate form with his or her own signature.

In addition to abiding by the state's individual requirements for using the FPCA, voting officers should advise their personnel to follow these general rules:

—Print by hand or use a typewriter to fill in the form.

—Be sure all requested information is supplied and be sure that it is written clearly and legibly.

—Show the name of the applicant twice—once printed or typed and once in the applicant's own handwriting. Anyone may fill out the card, but only the person who is to receive the ballot may write his or her name on line 9 (signature of person requesting ballot), unless the state specifies otherwise.

—Street and number, rural route, or place of residence are called for on the FPCA. It is also essential that an applicant include the name of his or her home county. This helps state officials speed action on the application when the form is not sent directly to the home county.

—Military addresses, particularly in abbreviated forms, are often confusing to civilians. The addresses should be clearly printed or typed so that no letter or number will be misread.

—Applicant's legal voting residence must be in a place where he or she actually lived—not just-a residence of record. But no more than one such address may be given. If the applicant has had more than one such address in a state, give only the last, most current address.

—Members of the Armed Forces should have the FPCA certified by a commissioned officer unless the state specifies that a noncommissioned or warrant officer's attestation will also be accepted. Civilians not attached to the military should have the FPCA certified by a notary public or other person authorized to make attestations.

—Before addressing the FPCA, check the state's mailing instructions. In some cases, the card is to be addressed to the Secretary of State (who then sends it to the proper local official); in other cases it is to be addressed to a local official, such as the county clerk or auditor, or to an election board.

—Mail the FPCA as early as the state permits. No postage is required.

If the Federal Post Card Applications are not available, use a letter as an application for a State absentee ballot or registration. Provide the same information as the FPCA and mail in the same way you would the FPCA.

The state, city, county (township) in which a person lived before entering military or Federal service usually is considered a legal residence for voting purposes unless he or she establishes residence elsewhere.

All states will permit persons in the Armed Forces to acquire a new voting residence within their jurisdictions. When this is accomplished, voting rights in the old state of residence are lost.

Service personnel desiring to acquire a new voting residence must meet the new state's legal requirements. They must have lived within the state for the required length of time, normally must not have resided exclusively on military property, and presently must intend to make the new state their permanent home when they retire from active duty or are released from active service.

Time spent in military or Federal service counts in meeting the total residence requirements. For example, if a state requires a minimum residence of two years and a person lived in a state for one year and served in the Armed Forces or overseas as a foreign service officer for one year, he or she will have fulfilled the state's two years' residence requirement.

The law usually holds that the voting residence of the wife is the same as that of her husband. Where there is any question pertaining to voting residence, seek an answer through the legal affairs officer.

Many states permit registration by absentee process and some will register a qualified voter when they accept a voted absentee ballot. In others, a voter must be registered before applying for a ballot. Procedures vary from state to state and must be understood and followed exactly on a state-by-state basis.

In two states, Alabama and Louisiana, one must appear in person to register. Personnel who are not already registered will have to travel to their home to register. When possible, they should be both allowed and encouraged to do so.

Application for registration should always be made as early as the state permits, especially in cases where registration must be completed before applications may be made for absentee ballot.

In some states, registration is permanent. Where such permanent registration laws are in effect, a person is not required to re-register for each election so long as certain requirements are met. In general, the requirements are that the applicant vote regularly and does not legally change his or her name or move away from the area (such as precinct or district), where registered.

Most states permit minors to apply for registration if they will be of legal voting age by the date of the election.

When a ballot is received from a state, the envelope containing the ballot should not be opened until instructions on the envelope have been read. This is important because some states require that the envelope be opened in the presence of a commissioned officer, notary public, or other authorized person. If there are no instructions on the outside of the envelope, it may be opened as any other mail.

States usually include full instructions inside the ballot envelope with the ballot form as a guide for persons voting by absentee process. Voting officers should help personnel follow these instructions, or advise them whenever no instructions have been sent by the state.

Polls or straw votes are prohibited in relation to elections or voting choices. In addition, no commissioned, warrant, or noncommissioned officer may attempt in any way to influence any person's choice of candidate. The actual marking of the ballot—the voting—must be done secretly. It's required by law.

Where possible, the voting officer should provide a place where ballots may be marked in secret. A fabricated voting booth, however crude, will not only meet the requirement but offers an opportunity to publicize the voting effort.

Voting officers who need more information should not contact state officials, but should write:

> The Adjutant General
> ATTN: AGMZ-P
> Department of the Army
> Washington, D. C. 20315

REFERENCES
AR 608–20 Voting by Personnel of the Armed Forces of the United States
DA Pam 360–503 Voting Assistance Guide (Published at each General Election)
DA Cir 608–( ) Implements Voting Program at Each General Election
Film AFIF 128 The Vote—(see DA Pam 108–1)
Film AFIF 129 Ballots That Fly
Film AFIF 171 The First Tuesday After the First Monday

INDEX

FOR FREE INFORMATION ON FUTURE EDITIONS
OF **THE ARMY OFFICER'S GUIDE**, AND OTHER
STACKPOLE MILITARY TITLES, PLEASE SEND YOUR
NAME AND ADDRESS TO:

Armed Services Publications Dept.
STACKPOLE BOOKS, INC.
Cameron & Kelker Streets
P.O. Box 1831
Harrisburg, PA 17105